MW01140051

David L. Shultz and Scott L. Mingus Sr.

The Second Day at
Gettysburg

The Attack and Defense of
Cemetery Ridge, July 2, 1863

Savas Beatie
California

Library of Congress Cataloging-in-Publication Data

The Second Day at Gettysburg: The Attack and Defense of Cemetery Ridge on July 2, 1863 / David L. Shultz and Scott L. Mingus, Sr.
pages cm
Includes bibliographical references and index.
ISBN 978-1-61121-074-3 alk. paper—ISBN 978-1-61121-075-0 (ebk.)
1. Gettysburg, Battle of, Gettysburg, Pa., 1863. 2. Command of troops—Case studies. I. Mingus, Scott L., author. II. Title.
E475.53.S556 2015
973.7'349—dc23
2015034297

Second edition, first printing

Published by
Savas Beatie LLC
989 Governor Drive, Suite 102
El Dorado Hills, CA 95762

Phone: 916-941-6896
(E-mail) sales@savasbeatie.com

Savas Beatie titles are available at special discounts for bulk purchases in the United States by corporations, institutions, and other organizations. For more details, please contact Special Sales, P.O. Box 4527, El Dorado Hills, CA 95762, or you may e-mail us at sales@savasbeatie.com, or visit our website at www.savasbeatie.com for additional information.

Proudly published, printed, and warehoused in the United States of America.

MIX
Paper from responsible sources
FSC
www.fsc.org FSC® C011935

For Ed Bearss and Dean Shultz, with admiration.

Photo courtesy of George Evans of the "Joe Hooker Society"

The view north by northeast toward the Union center from Longstreet's tower. The Confederates attacked left to right over this ground. Barksdale's Mississippi brigade was divided by the Millerstown Road (middle), with the brigades of Wilcox, Lang, Wright, and part of Posey's extending the line north. The Sherfy farm is on the right and the Codori barn in the center distance. *David L. Shultz*

Looking west toward the thicket-lined ravine carrying Plum Run (middle-distance). The ground in the immediate front is the position held by Lt. Evan Thomas's 4th U.S. Artillery, Battery C. Lt. John Turnbull's 3rd U.S. Consolidated batteries F and K was overrun on the opposite side of the brush-choked creek. This is also the ground over which the 1st Minnesota and 111th New York charged into Cadmus Wilcox's Alabamians, and where the 19th Maine battled Lang's Florida Brigade. *Scott L. Mingus Sr.*

Table of Contents

Table of Contents (continued)

List of Maps and Photographs

Photos and maps have been distributed
throughout the book for the convenience of the reader.

Introduction

Students of the battle of Gettysburg range in experience from wide-eyed beginners, overwhelmed by the massive body of literature, to seasoned veterans who intensely debate every detail of the campaign from the relative comfort of their bar stools or on the Internet.

As a member of Gettysburg's Licensed Battlefield Guides and the author of *Sickles at Gettysburg* (Savas Beatie, 2009), a biography of the colorful Union Maj. Gen. Daniel E. Sickles, I have had the (usually) good fortune to interact with Gettysburg enthusiasts of all knowledge levels. I can say with certainty that anyone who argues "there is nothing new to be learned about Gettysburg" is simply wrong. Many aspects of the Gettysburg campaign are still imperfectly understood or open for debate. For example, when many readers and even historians think about the second day of battle, fought on July 2, 1863, their focus tends to center upon the attack and defense of Little Round Top, which they consider to be one of the conflict's defining moments. While that hill was indeed the scene of heroic fighting on both sides—and justifiably retains its status as an iconic battlefield landmark—it initially did not even figure into the Confederates' offensive strategy, and was certainly not the Union Army's only threatened position.

Generations of amateur and professional historians have analyzed and debated the many "what ifs" and "should haves" that resulted in a victory for Maj. Gen. George G. Meade's Army of the Potomac, but nearly everyone agrees that July 2 was the bloodiest of the battle's three days. A case can also be made that the second day was the battle's turning point. It was on this day that the momentum of General Robert E. Lee's July 1 victory was stopped by the Northern army's successful defense of Cemetery Ridge. Much of the second day's flow of battle was driven by two factors.

The first was General Lee's determination to launch his main attack against the Union army's left flank, a decision based upon a faulty understanding of the actual location of that flank. The reported results of an early morning reconnaissance undertaken by engineering staff officer Capt. Samuel R. Johnston and others misled Lee into believing that Meade's left flank did not extend to Little Round Top. General Lee's report of January 1864 described his plans:

> The enemy occupied a strong position, with his right upon two commanding elevations adjacent to each other, one southeast and the other, known as Cemetery Hill, immediately south of the town, which lay at its base. His line extended thence upon the high ground along the Emmitsburg road, with a steep ridge in rear, which was also occupied. . . . It was determined to make the principal attack upon the enemy's left, and endeavor to gain a position from which it was thought that our artillery could be brought to bear with effect. Longstreet was directed to place the divisions of McLaws and Hood on the right of Hill, partially enveloping the enemy's left, which he was to drive in. General Hill was ordered to threaten the enemy's center, to prevent re-enforcements being drawn to either wing, and co-operate with his right division in Longstreet's attack.

Although an increasing number of Gettysburg commentators have argued that Lt. Gen. James Longstreet's orders were to attack "up the Emmitsburg Road," Lee intended to gain a foothold there in order to leverage its value as an artillery platform for assaulting Cemetery Ridge. Unfortunately for the Confederates, when General Longstreet's two divisions moved into position to the attack that afternoon, they were stunned to discover that the Emmitsburg Road in their immediate front (an area since referred to as the Peach Orchard) was more strongly occupied than expected, and that the Union's left stretched from there toward the Round Tops. An attack "up the Emmitsburg Road" only made sense if Meade's left ended at or near the Peach Orchard—as Longstreet had been erroneously led to believe. Once the true state of affairs was discovered, Longstreet and his subordinates were forced to modify their plans.

The second major factor that influenced the day's fighting was the still-controversial decision by Union General Sickles to advance his Third Corps off Cemetery Ridge and place his divisions in the Peach Orchard and along the Emmitsburg Road. Sickles has since been criticized for nearly every aspect of his deployment, including a failure to occupy the higher ground at Little Round Top and for lacking the manpower to adequately defend his extended position. The wisdom of Dan Sickles, or lack thereof, has been hotly debated since the hour of his movement on July 2, 1863. I will mercifully not repeat that debate here. Suffice it to say that General Meade responded by shifting reinforcements from other parts of his battle line toward his threatened left flank. These reinforcements eventually stopped Longstreet's powerful attack, but it also weakened other parts of the Union position.

All of this brings us to the great value of David Shultz's and Scott Mingus's new study, *The Second Day at Gettysburg: The Attack and Defense of Cemetery Ridge, July 2, 1863*. Longstreet's and Sickles' actions have been meticulously scrutinized by historians, so Shultz and Mingus have taken a different approach by focusing most of their efforts on an aspect that is often short-changed in the Gettysburg literature: the attack against the Union's center on Cemetery Ridge, and the Union efforts to defeat it. While doing so, they explain the complications of the terrain, who could see what and when, and how the various elevations, fences, ravines, streams, farms, and roads effected the unfolding combat. Their micro-level discussion of these physical elements, supported by more than two-dozen invaluable original maps by Phil Laino (the author of *Gettysburg Campaign Atlas* and long-time contributor to *Gettysburg Magazine*), make this a wholly original and useful work.

As General Lee noted, Longstreet's offensive operations were supported by a portion of Lt. Gen. A. P. Hill's Third Corps. Hill had orders "to threaten the enemy's center, to prevent re-enforcements being drawn to either wing, and co-operate with his right division in Longstreet's attack." Hill's "cooperation" consisted of five brigades in Maj. Gen. Richard H. Anderson's division.

General Longstreet's performance was heavily criticized in the postwar years, for political reasons as much as military ones. Although criticism of Longstreet has subsided considerably in recent decades, General A. P. Hill has received essentially a free pass in comparison. Historians who want to understand the causes of Lee's defeat need to examine more closely what General Hill and his subordinates did, and did not, do on the afternoon and evening of July 2. Did Hill exercise appropriate command and control of his men? Did all of Anderson's brigades fulfill their objectives, and if not, why not? Shultz and Mingus shine a welcome light on the role played by Anderson's division, whose brigadiers turned in both heroic and flawed performances.

Union-held Cemetery Ridge was occupied by Maj. Gen. Winfield S. Hancock's Second Corps. Hancock is no stranger to Gettysburg scholars, although many forget that he was new to corps command and generally untested at this level. During the course of the fighting, Hancock showcased his abilities by masterfully shifting troops to support Sickles (such as moving Brig. Gen. John Caldwell's division into the Wheatfield) and by shifting about his own regiments, brigades, and artillery to plug holes he had created to reinforce Sickles. Commanding generals like Meade and Lee delivered their armies to the battlefield, but the tactical decisions were largely left to subordinates like Hancock and Longstreet. On all three days, Hancock owned this battlefield.

Neither author is a stranger to Gettysburg readers. David L. Shultz is a recognized preservationist and the author of several books, pamphlets, and articles including the short but highly acclaimed *Double Canister at Ten Yards: The Federal Artillery and the Repulse of Pickett's Charge* (revised and reprinted by Savas Beatie, 2016). The current book you are reading had its genesis in a earlier and much shorter work David co-authored entitled *The Battle Between the Farm Lanes: Hancock Saves the Union Center.*

Co-author Scott L. Mingus is the author of a dozen or so Civil War books as well as several articles for *Gettysburg Magazine.* His most recent full-length work, *Confederate General William 'Extra Billy' Smith: From Virginia's Statehouse to Gettysburg Scapegoat* (Savas Beatie, 2013) won the 2013 Nathan Bedford Forrest Southern History Award and was nominated for the Virginia Literary Award for Non-Fiction. Scott also maintains a popular blog on Civil War history (www.yorkblog.com/cannonball), is widely known in the wargaming community, and is a tour guide for the York (Pennsylvania) County Heritage Trust.

When one considers the extensive maneuvering of large bodies of troops in both armies, the endlessly unique personalities involved, and stakes of the outcome, and the enormous casualties incurred in only about three hours of combat, it is no wonder the second day at Gettysburg continues to fascinate readers.

But what was it all for? Would the battle have turned out differently if there had been no fighting on the Bliss Farm, or if Hancock had not dispatched Caldwell's division when he did, or if all of Anderson's divisions had joined the attack? Would the Confederates have attacked at all if they knew there was a second Union line behind what was visible? Of course we will never know (or agree upon) the answers to these and so many other questions, but Shultz and Mingus have provided plenty of information and insight, along with many personal human interest stories, to give Gettysburg's students ammunition to continue the debates.

James A. Hessler
Gettysburg, Pennsylvania
July 2015

Acknowledgments

So many books and articles have been written about the Gettysburg Campaign that it is nearly impossible keep track of them all. And yet, many aspects of the fighting remain either untold or deserve a second look from different perspectives.

This new study examines why and how the attack and defense of the Union center on July 2, 1863, came about. We begin by marching the respective armies to the battlefield and offering an overview of the fighting on July 1. Thereafter, our study digs deeper into the details about how the combatants who would fight the next afternoon and early evening ended up where they did. We explore how the attack and defense of Sickles's Third Corps salient directly affected the combat farther north on Cemetery Ridge, with our prime focus being the attack by Richard Anderson's division (A. P. Hill's Corps) against the Union center there held primarily by Winfield Scott Hancock's Second Corps. Our analysis examines the overall cause and effect of the command decisions made that day, with special attention paid to the routes taken by the troops involved, and how the varying terrain and ubiquitous physical impediments like fences, farms, and roads affected the fighting. Battles are not always decided by superior firepower, positioning, or morale, although these can (and usually do) prove decisive. Other human elements, such as how orders are interpreted, inadequate or inaccurate reconnaissance reports, the poor coordination of troops movements, a lack of clarity regarding objectives, and spur-of-the-moment tactical decisions made in the vacuum of an overall understanding of the general plan, influence, and sometimes dictate, the outcome. Our hope is that readers enjoy our work, and readily admit that any errors of fact or otherwise are solely our own.

To this end, we are thankful to many people and institutions both public and private. Although there are too many to individually cite, we sincerely appreciate the valuable insight and support from all our colleagues and friends, and apologize if your name does not appear here. Please know that we know of your contribution and are thankful.

For the past five years Edwin C. Bearss and Dean Shultz have provided valuable insight, support, and encouragement. Touring the Gettysburg battlefield with these revered gentlemen is one of life's great pleasures.

We would like to thank historians Bill Spoehr, James Hessler, J. David Petruzzi, and Eric J. Wittenberg who spent hours proofreading various parts of the narrative and offering many useful suggestions and comments that strengthened the manuscript. Bill in particular helped by fact-checking much of the minutiae. Phil Laino's many excellent original maps help illustrate this book. Without these maps it would be impossible for readers to follow the often-confusing movements of troop formations large and small, and keep track of the many farms, roads, lanes, wood lots, and other physical features mentioned throughout the text. Phil's keen sense of direction and vast knowledge of the fields and woodlots below Gettysburg is insurmountable. Some of the maps are derivatives of those that appear in his superb *Gettysburg Campaign Atlas*, while many others were created specifically for this book.

Many librarians and archivists over the years in institutions across the country helped us track down particular documents or books, and we appreciate their help.

Sal Prezioso offered the hospitality of his home, the venerable "Red Patch." There is not one Gettysburg aficionado who Sal has not helped in one way or another, including us. Sal contributed many of the fine photographs that grace this book. His larger-than-life personality and unselfishness when it comes to sharing his home, a dark cup of espresso, and his battlefield knowledge is deeply appreciated.

We also wish to thank Todd Wiley and Daniel R. Weinfeld for graciously contributing their photographic artwork and perspective. To our friends Don Ernsberger, Andrea Richard, Chuck Teague, Cliff Bream, and the late Richard Rollins and his widow, Ann, we owe a grateful, and yet humble, thank you. To our beloved families who supported us through it all and how we deeply regret the long periods of time away even though we were often home.

From 1915 to the present, the Gettysburg Association of Licensed Battlefield Guides has served to help us all discover what really happened on that hallowed ground. We are especially grateful to all the Civil War Round Tables across America that have not only helped keep the study of the Civil War alive and meaningful, but have also raised hundreds of thousands of dollars to help preserve battlefields for future generations. Many of these non-profit organizations opened their archives and helped this study, including the Daniel E. Sickles CWRT, in association with The White Plains Historical Society, and the Scottsdale (Arizona) CWRT. There are many others, and you know who you are.

We are also very grateful for the constant help from publisher Theodore P. Savas, the managing director and owner of Savas Beatie, and his talented staff, including marketing director Sarah Keeney and media specialist / author liaison Michele Sams. Ted has long believed in this project and championed it from the outset. It was his idea for Scott Mingus to work with Dave. We thank you, Ted, for your persistence in pushing this project forward to completion after several aborted starts.

David L. Shultz
Scott L. Mingus Sr.

The Second Day at
Gettysburg

The Attack and Defense of
Cemetery Ridge, July 2, 1863

Chapter One

"I am going straight at them and will settle this thing one way or the other."

— *Maj. Gen. George G. Meade, commander, Army of the Potomac*[1]

Up From Virginia

Great thick clouds of acrid, white sulfurous smoke belched from thousands of guns, filling the shallow Pennsylvania valley on this humid second day of July 1863. The deafening roar of exploding artillery shells echoing off the surrounding hills contrasted with the rattle of musketry across the verdant fields and gently rolling pastures south of the crossroads town of Gettysburg. Uniformed officers boldly shouted orders, bugles and drums echoed the martial commands, and supply wagons and heavily laden ammunition limbers and caissons creaked as they rumbled into position. The unnerving cacophony overshadowed the pitiful low moans and pain-filled shrieks of the wounded. Beginning at the southern end of the battlefield, one Confederate infantry division, followed a short time later by a second, had stepped off to begin what would be hailed as one of the most famous attacks of the war. A third division in a different Southern corps was tasked to follow up the attack. Names the nation had never heard would soon be immortalized—Devil's Den, Little Round Top, the Rose Woods, the Wheatfield, the Peach Orchard, and finally, Cemetery Ridge.

The hard-pressed Union troops defending the low smoke-shrouded ridge and nearby fields had marched for more than a week to intercept the Southerners. Lee's Rebels had been in the Keystone State for several days before the Army of the Potomac arrived. Elements of the two powerful armies met the previous day north and west of Gettysburg. The fighting shattered two Federal corps that retreated through town to reassemble on the heights below, while the rest of the army feverishly headed north in an effort to reach the field. The charismatic leader of the

---

1 George G. Meade to Wife, June 29, 1863, George G. Meade Collection #0410, Historical Society of Pennsylvania (HSP), Philadelphia.

Maj. Gen. Joseph Hooker,
commander of the Army of the
Potomac until June 28, 1863.
LOC

Union soldiers in the center of the defensive line on Cemetery Ridge on July 2 was Maj. Gen. Winfield Scott Hancock, a 39-year-old career army officer and West Point alumnus who had just recently taken command of the 11,350-man Second Corps. Gettysburg would be his first battle leading more than a division. The passionate native of Pennsylvania would more than reinforce his colorful nickname "Hancock the Superb." He would also effectively take command of the remnants of the badly shattered Third Corps on July 2, patching bits and pieces together with some of his own men to form a semblance of a defensive front to hold back the oncoming Rebels.[2]

The majority of the Confederates charging Hancock's center on Cemetery Ridge that early evening belonged to Maj. Gen. Richard H. ("Fighting Dick") Anderson's division of Lt. Gen. Ambrose Powell Hill's Third Corps, Army of Northern Virginia. Anderson, another career military officer, resigned from the U.S. Army in 1861 after his home state of South Carolina seceded from the Union, and rose through the ranks to lead a division. His advance that fateful early summer evening was in support of two divisions from Lt. Gen. James Longstreet's First Corps tasked with driving northward up the Emmitsburg Road to flank and crush the "exposed" Union left, and then help A. P. Hill sever and hold the Union center.[3]

Four weeks before the battle, Hill's corps, including Anderson's division, had been entrenched near Fredericksburg defending the Rappahannock River line, a position held by the Southern army since the battle of Chancellorsville in early May.

---

2 For more on Hancock, see Glenn Tucker, *Hancock the Superb* (Indianapolis, IN, 1960) and David M. Jordan, *Winfield Scott Hancock: A Soldier's Life* (Bloomfield, IN, 1988).

3 *The War of the Rebellion: A Compilation of the Official Records of the Union and Confederate Armies,* 128 vols. (Washington, DC, 1880-1901), Series 1, vol. 27, pt. 2, 283-91. Hereafter cited as *OR*. All references are to Series 1 unless otherwise noted. See also Lafayette McLaws, "Gettysburg," in *Southern Historical Society Papers* (hereafter *SHSP*), vol. 7, 1879, 64-90.

Hill's mission was to convince Maj. Gen. Joseph Hooker, commanding the Union Army of the Potomac across the river at Falmouth, that he still faced the entire Army of Northern Virginia. In reality, Gen. Robert E. Lee and his two other corps under James Longstreet and Richard S. Ewell had slipped around the Federal right and headed northwest, with the ultimate goal of invading Pennsylvania and taking the war to the Yankee heartland. Along the way Lee planned to collect supplies, horses, forage, and materiél of value to his army, thus sparing beleaguered Virginia farmers the burden of supporting his army in the field. In addition, Lee hoped a movement in force across the Mason-Dixon Line would force the Yankees to withdraw troops from around Vicksburg, Mississippi, the last significant Rebel-controlled city and bastion on the Mississippi River. Some Southern politicians also hoped a significant battlefield victory on Northern soil would bring the administration of President Abraham Lincoln to the negotiating table.[4]

For two days in early June, Hill's men screened Lee's withdrawal west toward Culpeper Court House. Longstreet's First Corps was the first to depart after dark on June 3, followed the next day by most of Ewell's Second Corps. Despite the presence of Union observation balloons and other lookouts, these initial movements passed undetected. Hooker heard early on June 4 that something was stirring below the river. His friend and chief of staff, Maj. Gen. Daniel A. Butterfield, sent a terse note at 9:45 a.m. to Brig. Gen. John Buford, commanding the First Cavalry Division: "Reports and appearances here indicate the disappearance of a portion of the enemy's forces from opposite our left. The general desires you to keep

Gen. Robert E. Lee, commander of the Confederate Army of Northern Virginia. *NA*

---

4 For more on the reasons why Lee invaded Pennsylvania, see Wilbur S. Nye, *Here Come the Rebels* (Baton Rouge, 1965). Although an older study, it is still outstanding.

a sharp lookout, country well scouted, and advise us as soon as possible of anything in your front or vicinity indicating a movement."[5]

At 10:00 a.m., Butterfield followed with another message to Maj. Gen. George G. Meade, who at that time commanded the Fifth Corps: "Balloon reports from Banks' Ford two camps disappeared and several batteries in motion. Balloon near Reynolds reports line of dust near Salem Church, and 20 wagons moving northerly on the Telegraph road."[6] By midday on June 5, Union intelligence officers surmised most of Lee's army was moving and that Hill's was likely the only corps still directly confronting the Army of the Potomac. Hooker remained unconvinced. Perhaps fearing another debacle as Chancellorsville, "Fighting Joe" opted to keep the broad, swift-flowing Rappahannock River between the bulk of his army and the enemy until he could obtain more definitive information. "The enemy appears to have moved the greater part of his forces from our front," Butterfield wrote to Meade. "By way of demonstration, [a] bridge is being laid at Franklin's. We cannot tell where they have moved to."[7]

Hooker's attention remained divided. He was focused on rebuilding his depleted army's manpower for tens of thousands had departed when their terms of enlistment expired in May and early June. Hooker set about obtaining more materiél, supplies, and ordnance and reorganizing his artillery corps to improve its effectiveness on the battlefield. Unwilling to challenge Hill's 23,000 entrenched veterans directly, Hooker remained cautious. Previous efforts to dislodge the Rebels near Fredericksburg by combat or maneuver had failed miserably in December and January (and resulted in the dismissal of his predecessor, Maj. Gen. Ambrose Burnside) and again in May. Hooker ordered Brig. Gen. Albion P. Howe's 4,000-man division of the Sixth Corps, now on the southern riverbank after crossing on a recently finished pontoon bridge, to do nothing more than observe. Although Hill quickly redeployed some of his force to meet the threat, he was satisfied to watch and not engage Hooker. Other than periodic artillery shelling, the situation along the Rappahannock remained relatively stable.[8]

---

5   OR 27, pt. 3, 5.

6   Ibid. Maj. Gen. John F. Reynolds, a native of Lancaster, Pennsylvania, commanded the First Corps and, for part of the campaign, led a three-corps wing of the army during the march to Maryland and into Pennsylvania.

7   Ibid., 8. Hooker's colorful nickname stemmed from the newspaper headline "Fighting— Joe Hooker Attacks Rebels," which with a clerical error became "Fighting Joe Hooker Attacks Rebels." General Lee derisively referred to him as "Mr. F. J. Hooker."

8   Ibid., 10-13. See Special Order No. 17 & 153, "Summer allowances and changes in the artillery corps"; pt. 2, 305.

Hooker's headquarters was at a virtual standstill as the uncertainty increased when occasional conflicting intelligence reports arrived. Beginning June 6, Butterfield's messages to the Union commanders confronting A. P. Hill south of the river warned against bringing on a general engagement. Although reports along the riverfront mentioned fewer enemy pickets, other messages suggested heavy skirmishing. Hooker's staff argued over their meaning. Countless hours slipped past while Federal troops marched and countermarched to different sectors where a Rebel buildup had been reported, only to learn it was a feint. On several evenings, orders were sent to every corps commander to pack three days of rations and have wagons loaded and ready: "Pickets not to be withdrawn, but to be supplied. Orders may possibly be given to move early to-morrow." However, nothing transpired for several days, which only served to further frustrate the Federals.[9]

Meanwhile, Longstreet's hard-marching lead elements reached Culpeper on June 6 and camped west and east of town. The next day Ewell's corps tramped through Culpeper and camped four miles beyond town. Ewell would lead the planned advance toward Pennsylvania. While Ewell and Longstreet rested their men for six days, Hill's corps, supported by some cavalry, maintained the ruse at Fredericksburg.[10]

Even though Hooker suspected large bodies of Rebels had disappeared to the west, he failed to act even after the War Department confirmed that two of Lee's corps were indeed marching toward the strategically important Shenandoah Valley. Persistent reports of lesser enemy numbers along the Rappahannock front also poured in, to no avail. On June 8, intelligence from Washington stated that enemy infantry and cavalry, with artillery support, had camped around Culpeper and scouts spotted a large force moving toward the Blue Ridge Mountains. This news finally ignited Hooker into action after a week of inactivity.[11]

Responding to reports of Rebels massing near Culpeper, Hooker ordered Maj. Gen. Alfred Pleasonton's cavalry to cross the Rappahannock River and engage and destroy Maj. Gen. J. E. B. (Jeb) Stuart's Confederate cavalry. The Federal troopers surprised Stuart's horsemen on the morning of June 9 at Brandy Station, six miles northeast of Ewell's infantry camps. A significant day-long battle ensued, though the mounted charges and countercharges failed to produce a clear victor.[12]

---

9 Ibid., 17.

10 Ibid., pt. 2, 546.

11 Jeffrey C. Hall, *The Stand of the U. S. Army at Gettysburg* (Bloomington & Indianapolis, IN, 2003), 11-13.

12 *OR* 27, pt. 2, 357-58, 439.

Pleasonton's thrust did not destroy Stuart's cavalry, but the fighting provided the Yankee troopers with a fresh confidence that they could now fight their counterparts and give a good account of themselves doing so. The swirling bloody action also provided Hooker with valuable information. The Union commander now knew A. P. Hill's Third Corps was the only antagonist facing him along the Fredericksburg-Falmouth front. Still, he did nothing aggressive south of the river except to telegraph Washington that his intention was to cross the Rappahannock in force and take Fredericksburg. That same day (June 10), Ewell's Second Corps began moving toward the Blue Ridge Mountains and the Shenandoah Valley. Confederate control of the vital Front Royal, Chester, and Manassas gaps would block Hooker from subsequently following Lee's Virginia army directly into the strategically vital Valley.[13]

Meanwhile, speculation mounted in Washington and in the Northern press that Lee's ultimate intention was to invade the North once again, just as he had in September 1862 during the short-lived Maryland Campaign. In response to the earlier thrust, the War Department formed the military Department of the Susquehanna, which covered much of south-central Pennsylvania. Major General Darius N. Couch, who had recently resigned from the Second Corps over his utter disgust with Hooker's performance at Chancellorsville, hastened to Harrisburg to take command of this department, although he lacked the trained troops to do much. On June 11, while Couch began preparing to defend the Keystone State in the event of a Rebel incursion, the War Department summarily dismissed Hooker's plans to advance against Hill at Fredericksburg. Pleasonton had sent word that deserters claimed Lee was at Culpeper with 60,000 infantry, including Pickett's, Anderson's, Hood's, and McLaws' divisions. Pleasonton added that Ewell was still at Fredericksburg at the head of Stonewall Jackson's former corps, and that Hill still held the heights there. Although none of this was accurate, the message forced Hooker into action.[14]

The following morning, Hooker issued General Order No. 62. In a carefully worded first paragraph, he blamed the army's inactivity along the Rappahannock and the enemy's disappearance on everyone except himself and his headquarters staff: "The lax of enforcement within this army of certain orders deemed absolutely necessary to keep it in the proper state of efficiency, and their consequent non-observance, has been brought to the notice of the general commanding."[15]

---

13 Ibid., 357, 440-41; United States Geological Survey Satellite Images, dated 1970 & 1990, map numbers 12346 and 22714. Hereafter cited as USGS MRC (for Map Reference Code).

14 *OR* 27, pt. 3, 62. Longstreet and Hill received orders on June 11 to move north.

15 Ibid., 78.

This verbiage did not sit well with some of Hooker's corps commanders or with many in Washington—all of whom knew better. Several senior officials clamored to replace Hooker, whose position was only weakened by three days of inactivity after Brandy Station. Pennsylvania's energetic Republican governor, Andrew Gregg Curtin, alarmed his citizens on June 12 when he proclaimed that "information has been obtained by the War Department that a large rebel force, composed of cavalry, artillery, and mounted infantry, has been prepared for the purpose of making a raid into Pennsylvania." Many Northern newspapers repeated his warning and, without any clear indication Hooker would soon march to the rescue, Curtin and other nearby governors sprang into action. They began repositioning existing state militia forces and, in the case of the Keystone State, raising short-term emergency troops to contest an invasion.[16]

On June 13 Hill received orders to abandon the Fredericksburg line and march to join Lee. Richard Anderson's five brigades led the way northwest on the afternoon of June 14 along the same general route of march the First Corps and Second Corps had taken toward Culpeper. The divisions under Maj. Gens. Henry Heth and William Dorsey Pender followed. Anderson made outstanding time and reached the old Chancellorsville battlefield that night. It was the first of many long marches over the next few days, some of which would cover up to 25 miles per day. Anderson's vanguard reached Culpeper on June 16.[17]

General Ewell's thrust down the Lower Shenandoah Valley toward Maryland and Pennsylvania was not without incident—or stunning success. On June 13, the day Hill received his orders to march, Ewell's corps approached Winchester and Berryville, where Maj. Gen. Robert H. Milroy's isolated division of the Union Eighth Corps guarded the northward passages to the Potomac River and beyond. Milroy's outnumbered command held out for three days, but in the end was overwhelmed and lost thousands of prisoners, an impediment Ewell needed to deal with before resuming his march to the Potomac River.[18]

---

16 Ibid., 79-80.

17 Ibid., pt. 2, 613, 635. Anderson's five brigade commanders were Brig. Gens. Cadmus M. Wilcox, William Mahone, Ambrose Wright, and Carnot Posey. The fifth, Col. David Lang, was temporarily in command of the small Florida Brigade for the ill Brig. Gen. Edward A. Perry. Major John Lane led Anderson's divisional artillery battalion.

18 For more details on Second Winchester, see Eric J. Wittenberg and Scott L. Mingus Sr., *The Second Battle of Winchester: The Confederate Victory That Opened the Door to Gettysburg* (El Dorado Hills, CA, 2016) and J. David Petruzzi and Steven Stanley, *The Gettysburg Campaign in Numbers and Losses* (El Dorado Hills, CA, 2013), 12-21. Ewell detached three regiments from Jubal Early's division to police Winchester and escort thousands of prisoners 96 miles south to the railhead at Staunton. From there, the captives were hauled to Richmond, where the officers were incarcerated in Libby Prison and the enlisted men in the Belle Isle camp.

After their respite at Culpeper, the leading elements of James Longstreet's miles-long column took to the road again on June 15 after learning that Hooker's army had finally broken camp at Falmouth. "All went well," one of Lee's staff officers crowed. "Hooker made no attempt to follow." Concerned with the War Department's directives to protect the roads to Washington and Baltimore in case Lee turned east, Hooker proceeded cautiously northward and made no effort to follow Hill's men, who by then were well on their way to Culpeper. Two days later, when Hill departed Culpeper, the Blue Ridge passes remained firmly under Confederate control. Hill's corps passed into the Shenandoah Valley without incident, overtaking and then passing Longstreet's First Corps, whose job it was to hold the gaps and cover the rear of the army. Longstreet's rear guard, Maj. Gen. George E. Pickett's division and some cavalry, was instrumental in helping keep the Army of the Potomac east of the mountains. Longstreet's infantry reassembled west of the Shenandoah River on June 22.[19]

Meanwhile, the Army of the Potomac's initial movement northward proved short-lived when Hooker halted to concentrate his scattered forces around Centreville. It took his combined columns four days to move just 42 miles, though the roads were crowded and several corps had to use longer routes that added eight to ten additional miles to their march. Hundreds of men dropped out because of the grueling pace, which was intensified by high heat, smothering humidity, and a lack of potable water in some of the regions. To the consternation of President Lincoln and the War Department, Hooker decided to rest his men for an additional six days.

While Hooker marked time, the Army of Northern Virginia continued to move. The bulk of Ewell's corps forded the Potomac River on June 22 and triumphantly entered Maryland. His men did not rest until after reaching Chambersburg, Pennsylvania, on June 23. The next day, Ewell sent Maj. Gen. Robert E. Rodes' division northeast toward Carlisle. Two days later Ewell ordered Maj. Gen. Jubal A. Early's division to march east toward York, the largest town between Harrisburg and Baltimore. Hill crossed the Potomac River at Shepherdstown, Maryland, on June 25 and continued through Chambersburg, reaching Fayetteville on the turnpike to Gettysburg and York on June 27. Longstreet would follow Hill across the river on June 26 and arrive with his men at Chambersburg two days later.[20]

---

19 G. Moxley Sorrell, *Recollections of a Confederate Staff Officer* (New York, NY, 1905), 159-62; *OR* 27, pt. 2, 366, 371, 613.

20 James Longstreet, "General Longstreet's Account of Gettysburg," *Philadelphia Weekly Times*, Nov. 3, 1876. See also *SHSP*, vol. 5, 46-58.

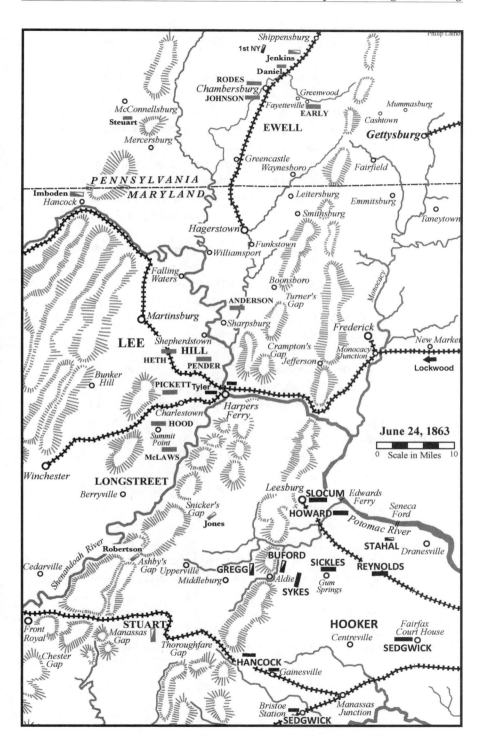

Philip Laino

Shippensburg

1st NY

Jenkins

Daniel

RODES
Chambersburg
JOHNSON

McConnellsburg

Steuart

Mercersburg

Greenwood

Fayetteville   EARLY

Mummasburg

Cashtown

EWELL

Gettysburg

PENNSYLVANIA
MARYLAND

Greencastle
Waynesboro

Fairfield

Imboden
Hancock

Leitersburg

Smithsburg

Emmitsburg

Taneytown

Hagerstown

Funkstown

Williamsport

Boonsboro

Turner's
Gap

ANDERSON

Martinsburg

*Falling
Waters*

LEE   *Shepherdstown*
HILL
HETH
PENDER

Sharpsburg

*Crampton's
Gap*   *Jefferson*

Frederick

New Market

Monocacy
Junction

Lockwood

*Bunker
Hill*

PICKETT Tyler

Charlestown   HOOD

*Summit
Point*

McLAWS

*Harpers
Ferry*

June 24, 1863

0   Scale in Miles   10

Winchester

LONGSTREET

Berryville

*Snicker's
Gap*

Jones

Leesburg   SLOCUM
HOWARD

*Edwards
Ferry*

*Seneca
Ford*

Potomac River

STAHAL
Dranesville

Robertson

Cedarville

*Ashby's
Gap*   *Upperville*

Middleburg

BUFORD

GREGG

Aldie

SICKLES
*Gum
Springs*

REYNOLDS

SYKES

Shenandoah River

*Front
Royal*

STUART

*Manassas
Gap*

*Chester
Gap*

*Thoroughfare
Gap*

HANCOCK
Gainesville

HOOKER

Centreville

*Fairfax
Court House*

SEDGWICK

*Bristoe
Station*

*Manassas
Junction*

SEDGWICK

The flower of the Confederate cavalry was also in transit. With Lee's permission, on June 23 Jeb Stuart and three brigades passed through gaps in Hooker's lines and headed east with the ultimate goal of reconnecting with Ewell's right-flank units in Pennsylvania. When Yankees blocked his planned path, Stuart swung farther south and then east. A series of minor skirmishes with elements of Hancock's Second Corps seems to have caused but little concern at Hooker's headquarters. By the following day, Stuart's saddle soldiers were closer to Washington than to the Army of Northern Virginia. This did not sit well with the U.S. War Department, which ordered Hooker to move. On June 25, he finally resumed marching north toward central Maryland. An unplanned side effect of this was that the move cut off of Stuart's direct path to rendezvous with the Army of Northern Virginia.[21]

Reports circulated on the 25th in Washington that Hooker had been spotted visiting the capital city instead of tending to his troops and keeping a watchful eye on Lee's movements. When newspapers picked up the story the next day, Hooker refuted the allegations in a telegram to Lincoln. The president responded, with a touch of sarcasm, that the tale "did not come from a newspaper, nor did I believe it, but I wished to be entirely sure it was falsehood."[22]

While Hooker spent valuable time defending his reputation, Rebel cavalry attached to Early's division approached the Adams County seat of Gettysburg on the afternoon of Friday, June 26, while his four brigades of infantry plodded in a driving rainstorm along hilly roads to the west and northwest. Ewell, meanwhile, received Lee's orders to advance on Harrisburg if it came within his means to do so. While Early headed east Ewell entered Shippensburg on the main road to Carlisle and Harrisburg, following Brig. Gen. Albert G. Jenkins' brigade of mounted infantry and cavalry.

Although ten thoroughfares radiated from Gettysburg, neither Early nor Ewell deemed the town strategically important enough to secure it for any length of time. Early's advance Virginia cavalry under Lt. Col. Elijah V. White dislodged inexperienced Pennsylvania emergency militia before raiding the region for horses, food, and rye whiskey. Early ordered all but one of his infantry brigades to bypass Gettysburg, and he camped the bulk of his forces near Mummasburg to the northwest. His objective was York, a significant railroad and manufacturing center along the turnpike 30 miles east of Gettysburg. By 10:00 p.m. that Friday night, Early's cavalry and Brig. Gen. John B. Gordon's veteran Georgia brigade had vacated Gettysburg and marched on the pike a few miles out of town, leaving

21 Sorrell, *Recollections*, 162-63.

22 *OR* 27, pt. 1, 58.

behind a strong provost guard. Except for the provisions and horses Early had demanded, Gettysburg had thus far escaped relatively unscathed.[23]

Farther south, the Army of the Potomac slowly closed on the Potomac River. Hooker instructed the Federal garrison at Harpers Ferry to be ready to move against Lee's crossings upstream. The War Department rescinded that order and dispatched Maj. Gen. William H. French to assume command at Harpers Ferry. General-in-chief Henry W. Halleck initiated the changes to ensure Hooker would not evacuate the garrison nor undermine its command and structure. The unexpected news elicited Hooker's full fury. Instead of leading his army across the Potomac, he rode to Harpers Ferry and telegraphed his resignation to Lincoln and Halleck, who after some deliberation accepted it that evening.[24]

Dissatisfaction with Hooker's performance had been brewing for some time. His inactivity along the Rappahannock had frustrated Halleck and Lincoln, as had his unnecessarily slow movement to Centreville, his subsequent stalling there for six more days, and Stuart's relatively uncontested passage through the Union army. Hooker's often pompous attitude toward his superiors and fellow generals disquieted Washington. Mentally fatigued, perhaps still suffering from the effects of a concussion suffered in the fighting at Chancellorsville, or both, Hooker seemed unable to grasp the full scope of the strategic situation as did Lincoln, Halleck, and Pennsylvania's Governor Curtin. Hooker had also questioned the president's assignment of Maj. Gen. Julius Stahel to his force because it would "much embarrass me and retard my movements." Rather than debate Hooker, Lincoln had agreed to transfer Stahel to General Couch's department in Harrisburg. This politically charged incident and the fact that Lincoln offered General Hancock formal command of the Second Corps to replace Couch further infuriated Hooker. Lincoln had finally had enough, and was willing to start anew with a fresh commander at the head of the army.[25]

A staff officer in the War Department penned a terse message to Hooker's headquarters three miles south of Frederick, Maryland, on the night two of Ewell's divisions camped at Carlisle on their way up to Harrisburg: "By direction of the President, Maj. Gen. Joseph Hooker is relieved from command of the Army of the Potomac, and Maj. Gen. George G. Meade is appointed to the command of that army, and of the troops temporarily assigned to duty with it. By order of the

---

23 Ibid., pt. 2, 443, 465. See USGS MRC 39077G2, 39077GH, 49077B2, and 49077B4.

24 Ibid., pt. 3, 339-45.

25 Ibid., pt. 1, 58-59. Unwilling to serve further under Hooker, Maj. Gen. Darius N. Couch resigned as Second Corps commander on May 22, 1863 and Hancock assumed temporary command.

Maj. Gen. George G. Meade, commander of the Union Army of the Potomac.
NA

Secretary of War." By 7:00 p.m. Lt. Col. James A. Hardie was en route via train to the Army of the Potomac's headquarters at Frederick to relieve Hooker.[26]

Hardie arrived in the Fifth Corps' camp at 3:00 a.m. on Sunday, June 28, and informed the hastily awakened Meade of his new responsibilities. Thereafter, both men rode into Frederick to inform Hooker, who greeted them in his full dress uniform. Word of the unexpected change in leadership raced through the army. Most of the senior commanders, except Hooker allies such as Maj. Gen. Daniel E. Sickles of the Third Corps, were ecstatic that the misnamed "Fighting Joe" and his timid ways were gone. His initial reorganization of the army after the battle of Fredericksburg the past winter was understandable and beneficial. However, his most recent shake-up—after openly blaming others for the army's defeat at Chancellorsville—was another matter. Hooker had blundered not only on the battlefield in front of Lee back in early May, but again in the weeks afterward with the Rappahannock River separating their armies. Opportunistic as he was, Lee had taken full advantage of Hooker's mistakes. While the Army of the Potomac sat idle north of the river, he reorganized his own army following Thomas J. "Stonewall" Jackson's death, resupplied it with fresh troops from Richmond, the Carolinas, and the coast, drilled his men repeatedly to increase their proficiency, built up stores of ammunition and ordnance, and most importantly, reinforced his army's high morale after thrashing the Yankees at Chancellorsville but losing Jackson to a mortal wound.[27]

---

26 Ibid., pt. 2, 443; pt. 3, 369, 370.

27 Hooker's resignation did not end his military career. He regained some of his reputation as a competent corps commander in the Western Theater under Gens. U. S. Grant and William Sherman. However, Hooker resigned from the army after Maj. Gen. Oliver O. Howard was

Despite that embarrassing defeat, Hooker had not tried to keep his name out of the Northern papers, so the enemy knew almost daily the locations of his army. In fact, the press was welcome at his headquarters during morning briefings. Hooker allowed the reporters to travel freely with the army and then camp near his staff at night. A lively group of correspondents followed Hooker's every move, enjoying free access to their employers via military telegraph. For all of the good Hooker had done rebuilding and replenishing the army and increasing its morale, his failure at Chancellorsville, followed by his dismal recent performance along the Rappahannock, justified his dismissal. The Harpers Ferry incident was simply the final straw.

Hooker took his removal with unaccustomed aplomb. When told that his resignation had been accepted, he wired Washington on June 28: "In conformity with orders of the War department, dated June 27, 1863, I relinquish the command of the Army of the Potomac. It is transferred to Maj. Gen. George G. Meade, a brave and accomplished officer, who has nobly earned the confidence and esteem of this army on many a well-fought field."[28]

Within hours of receiving command, Meade issued his first Special Order, No. 174, accepting Stahel's reappointment to the Department of the Susquehanna. A companion order reorganized the three brigades of cavalry previously under Stahel and dismissed several officers. It also promoted three young and aggressive junior officers—Wesley Merritt, George Armstrong Custer, and Elon J. Farnsworth—for duty with General Pleasonton as newly minted brigadiers. Having purged his army of the cavalry leaders (mostly foreign-born) Pleasonton deemed inefficient, Meade released Order No. 67, formally acknowledging his new role as commander of the Army of the Potomac.[29]

Rumors spread among the soldiers that popular former army commander Maj. Gen. George B. McClellan was returning, but the cheering stopped with the formal news that the relatively unknown Meade of the Fifth Corps was now in charge. Other than some of his own corps' men, few knew Meade other than by his reputation or "Old Goggle Eyes," or "Old Snapping Turtle."

Knowing that some of Lee's men had reached Carlisle and York north and northeast of Gettysburg, respectively, Meade ordered Pleasonton to send John

---

promoted to head the Army of the Tennessee (one of Sherman's three armies he led during his Georgia campaign) after its commander, Maj. Gen. James McPherson, was killed outside Atlanta.

28 *OR* 27, pt. 1, 373.

29 Ibid., pt. 3, 373-74. Unlike Joe Hooker, General Meade was given complete authority by General Halleck to replace, dismiss, or promote officers as he saw fit, which demonstrates the faith Halleck and Lincoln had in Meade—at least initially.

Buford's First Cavalry Division to Gettysburg in the hope of securing the crossroads and gathering intelligence on recent enemy movements. Uncertain where he might intercept Lee and give battle, Meade prepared for what he knew was unavoidable. "We are marching as fast as we can to relieve Harrisburg," he informed his wife on June 29, "but have to keep a sharp lookout that the Rebels don't turn around us and get at Washington and Baltimore in our rear. They have a cavalry force in our rear, destroying railroads, etc., with the view of getting me to turn back. I am going straight at them and will settle this thing one way or the other," he continued. "The men are in good spirits; we have been reinforced as to have equal numbers with the enemy, and with God's blessing, I hope to be successful. Good-by!"[30]

The same day he accepted command, Meade wired Halleck in Washington and asked permission to reduce the Harpers Ferry garrison by 7,000 men. Hooker had been denied a similar request, but Halleck immediately agreed to Meade's request. Accordingly, on June 29 Meade ordered General French to leave behind a portion of his garrison and march with the balance to Frederick. When French replied that Meade's order would not leave a sufficient force to hold Harpers Ferry, the army leader—without seeking Halleck's permission to do so—ordered French to evacuate the post. French was to ensure that his men took as much materiél, munitions, and ordnance as they could carry to Washington and destroy the remainder. Butterfield, whom Meade retained as chief of staff to ease the difficult transition, ended the communiqué to French with: "The commanding general expects to engage the enemy within a few days, and looks anxiously for your command to join."[31]

While the Federal army adjusted to yet another change in top leadership, General Lee continued his dual-pronged march to the Susquehanna River. He and his staff arrived in Chambersburg on Friday, June 26—the same day Jubal Early seized Gettysburg—and established headquarters in Messersmith's Woods just outside of town. For several days Lee oversaw his invasion from this bucolic setting, issuing orders and directives as each hour brought changing news. It was in this well-groomed grove about 52 miles northwest of Union headquarters at Frederick where, on the night of June 28, guards guided a travel-worn visitor into Lee's presence.

---

30 Meade to Wife, June 29, 1863, HSP. Several Confederate stragglers and deserters were captured in and around Gettysburg by Union forces after General Early vacated the crossroads town.

31 *OR* 27, pt. 3, 401-402.

"At night I was roused by a detail of the provost guard bringing up a suspicious prisoner," recalled Lt. Col. G. Moxley Sorrell, Longstreet's chief of staff. "I knew him instantly; it was [Henry T.] Harrison, the scout, filthy and ragged, showing some rough work and exposure. He had come to 'Report to the General, who was sure to be with the army,' and truly his report was long and valuable." Sorrell went on to say, "He brought his report down to a day or two, and described how they were even then marching in the direction of Gettysburg, with intention apparently of concentrating there. He also informed us of the removal of Hooker and the appointment of Meade to command the Army of the Potomac."[32] Sorrell roused Longstreet, who after listening to Harrison forwarded him to Messersmith's Woods to repeat his story to General Lee. Longstreet later stated that Lee treated Harrison with respect, listening intently to every word. "The general [Lee] heard him with great composure and minuteness," confirmed Sorrell. Longstreet suggested that because of the lack of cavalry and corroborating information regarding the enemy's movements, Lee had little choice but to react to the paid scout's troubling information.[33]

Shortly after sunrise on June 29, Lee sent mounted couriers dashing on the turnpike toward Carlisle to locate Ewell and rescind the previous discretionary orders to move on Harrisburg. "It was on this," Moxley Sorrell marveled, "the report of a single scout, in the absence of cavalry, that the army moved. Important as was the change, Lee was not long in deciding. He sent orders to bring Ewell immediately back from the North about Harrisburg and join his left. Then, Lee started A. P. Hill off at sunrise for Gettysburg, followed by Longstreet."[34]

It is likely that at some point during Lee's briefing the following morning in Messersmith's Woods the officers broached the subject of Meade succeeding Hooker. "General Meade will commit no mistakes on my front," Lee is alleged to have replied, "and should I make one, will be quick to seize upon it." In another version, a bit more dramatic, Lee supposedly stated, "General Meade will not blunder in my front, and if I make one will seize upon it."[35]

---

32 Sorrell, *Recollections*, 164.

33 Ibid. See also *SHSP*, vol. 5, 54-86, Longstreet paper datelined Columbia, Georgia. Harrison was a paid scout and an actor to boot, neither of which was much respected in the Civil War era. This is part of the reason Lee was initially skeptical of his claims.

34 Ibid.

35 There is no contemporary source for Lee's words. See Henry J. Hunt to James Longstreet, August 14, 1885, A. L. Long Papers, Wilson Special Collection Library, University of North Carolina, Chapel Hill. No one present at the meeting mentioned the conversation.

Sorrell suggested that Lee was planning an engagement at Gettysburg, but his opponent Meade was not laboring to concentrate his entire army there. Instead, Meade had sent a large reconnaissance force consisting of three army corps (John Reynolds' Left Wing) screened by General Buford's cavalry. By June 29, Meade was aware Ewell's corps had not only passed through Gettysburg but was spread out between Carlisle and York. With the rest of Lee's army known to be operating west of South Mountain, it made sense to secure the vital crossroads community. Gettysburg's proximity to Lee's army, combined with the converging roads, made it an ideal place for the Confederates to concentrate as well.

"I wrote you last night," Lee informed Ewell, "stating that General Hooker was reported to have crossed the Potomac, and is advancing by way of Middletown, the head of his column being at that point in Frederick County. I directed you in that letter to move your forces to this point." He continued, "If you have not already progressed on the road, and you have no good reason against it, I desire you to move in the direction of Gettysburg, via Heidlersburg . . . and you can thus join your other divisions to Early's, which is east of the mountains. When you come to Heidlersburg," Lee concluded, "you can either move directly on Gettysburg or turn to Cashtown."[36] With Harrison's verification of the Army of the Potomac's position, combined with the news that Meade had replaced Hooker, Lee changed his plans. "Preparations were now made to advance upon Harrisburg," the general later reported, "but, on the night of the 28th, information received from a scout that the Federal Army, having crossed the Potomac, was advancing northward, and that the head of the column north of Frederick, Maryland."[37]

Without Jeb Stuart's presence and his detailed information on the enemy positions, Lee decided to send Maj. Gens. Henry Heth's and William Dorsey Pender's divisions of A. P. Hill's corps on a reconnaissance-in-force to secure Cashtown with the idea of concentrating his army near there rather than have it scattered about the countryside. This also changed the previous order sent to Ewell. Located at the eastern entrance to South Mountain's Cashtown Gap, the tiny hamlet was not only strategically situated, but like Meade's suggested Pipe Creek

---

36 *OR* 27, pt. 3, 943. Meade issued non-discretionary orders to corps commanders ("you will proceed"), while Lee suggested ("if you desire"). The latter was at least partially the result of Lee's command style, and also because he had insufficient information in hand and so left some necessary discretion up to his chief subordinates. Lee didn't know Ewell all that well, but the handling of his corps thus far, and especially at Second Winchester, had satisfied Lee.

37 Ibid., pt. 2, 307, 443; "Jubal Early's response to Longstreet," *SHSP*, vol. 4, 283-302. For some reason General Lee reported on July 31, 1863, that his June 29 destination was Gettysburg. Dated orders dispute that assertion, including written instructions for Hill to move eastward to York.

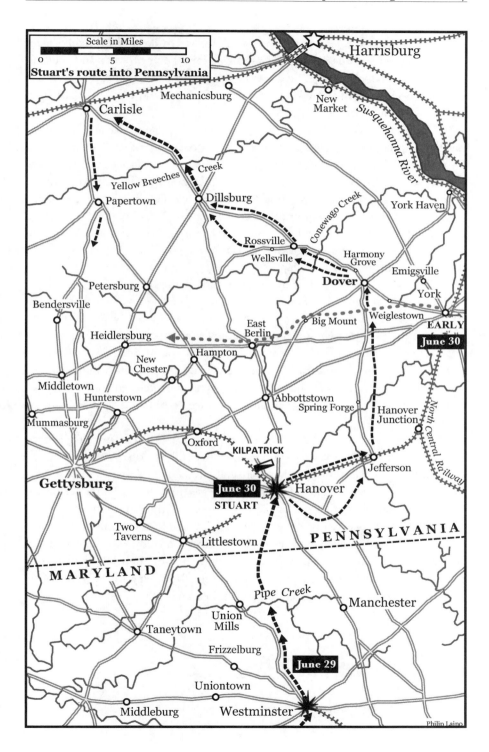

Scale in Miles

0   5   10

Stuart's route into Pennsylvania

defensive line in Maryland, would be an ideal place to defend. Lee could place troops along three roads leading to Cashtown from the north, east, and south to impede Meade's movement if he chose to advance to battle. Time, however, was short—especially considering that Jeb Stuart, "his eyes and ears," had last been reported on June 27 camped near Occoquan, Virginia.[38]

"I think Hooker's defeat [at Chancellorsville] was due to the absence of his cavalry on just such a useless raid as this," Confederate artillery officer Edward Porter Alexander argued in his memoirs. Although Lee had given Stuart some discretion in the matter, it is doubtful either of them anticipated the Army of the Potomac's march would prevent the Confederate cavalry from returning to the army once north of the Potomac. "Yet it is my humble opinion," continued Colonel Alexander, "it was bad play to let our cavalry get out of touch & reach of our infantry. The axiom of war is to mass one's strength. Then & then only can its fullest power be brought into play."[39]

"The movements of the army preceding the battle of Gettysburg had been embarrassed by the absence of cavalry," was how General Lee would later phrase it. Although other brigades of cavalry moving with Lee's army were sufficient to reconnoiter locally, they lacked enough manpower and the leadership and training necessary to range widely and provide the accurate and timely information to sustain such a large operation. Instead, Lee depended upon short-term scouting forays, often unreliable news obtained from citizens, and intelligence gathered from members of his army who had spent time in this region of Pennsylvania before the war.[40]

Lee had issued General Order No. 73 on June 27: "The commanding general has observed with marked satisfaction the conduct of the troops on the march, and confidently anticipates results commensurate with the high spirit they have manifested. No troops could have displayed greater fortitude or better performed the arduous marches of the past ten days." His men mostly enjoyed the trek, which took on a picnic-like atmosphere. "Our line of march into Pennsylvania was attended with many amusing incidence [sic]," remembered the 9th Alabama's Pvt. William C. McClellan. "The people seem to think that the Rebel army would eat them up without salt or bread, many of them actually begging for their lives." He went on to say that "the people in this part of Penn have the finest Barnes, largest

---

38 Ibid.

39 Edward P. Alexander, Gary W. Gallagher, ed., *Fighting for the Confederacy* (Chapel Hill, NC, 1989), 228.

40 *OR* 27, pt. 2, 321. In this context, "embarrassed" means "hindered" or "hampered."

Horses, fattest Cattle, finest grass and more whiskey than any people in the world, it is the same case in West Maryland."[41]

For most infantrymen, the goal was a fresh pair of shoes or perhaps a new coat, hat, shirt, or trousers. "We are daily getting large supplies," one soldier wrote home. "All these little Dutch Yankee towns are full of things we require, and we have clothing, shoes, provisions, letter paper even in great quantities—less clothing & shoes in proportion however, than anything else. Genl Lee's orders prescribe that requisitions be made on the towns . . . for any articles needed." He added, "If they fail to furnish it, then the town is to be searched & anything needed to be taken. We got a good deal by these two means in Chambersburg."[42] The bounty was indeed plentiful, but with word now of the approaching Yankees it was time to set aside foraging and gather the army together. By the time the sun set on Tuesday, June 30, every division scattered around the countryside east and west of Cashtown Gap (including General Pickett's, which was serving as Longstreet's rear guard) was within a day's marching distance of that planned rendezvous point.

Meade had sufficient information from his intelligence agents to realize Lee would probably consolidate his army somewhere between South Mountain and the Susquehanna River south of Carlisle. Whether Lee advanced upon Harrisburg or offered battle, as hoped, Meade knew he could do neither with his own army widely separated. Meade also knew, as did the War Department, that the amount of time the Army of Northern Virginia could spend in Pennsylvania was limited. Information that Couch's scouts passed on to the War Department was so accurate that it even suggested as early as June 28 that Lee's army contained 162 pieces of artillery, a number closer to reality than not. Telegraphers forwarded Couch's continued updates to Secretary of War Edwin Stanton and Meade's headquarters.[43]

As the Federal army approached the Mason-Dixon Line, Meade and Reynolds agreed on a contingency plan. Lacking definite knowledge on Longstreet's and Hill's whereabouts, Meade ordered Brig. Gen. Henry J. Hunt, his chief of artillery, to reconnoiter the hills paralleling Big Pipe Creek. Located in Carroll County in north-central Maryland, the shallow creek meanders from its source north of Manchester and flows southwest before angling past Union Mills, Westminster, and Taneytown before flowing toward Middleburg. An open and elongated ridge

41 bid., 942-43; William Cowan McClellan to his sister, July 9, 1863, Hagerstown, MD, in John C. Carter, ed., *Welcome the Hour of Conflict: William Cowan McClellan and the 9th Alabama* (Tuscaloosa, AL, 2007), 238.

42 C. Brown to family, June 25, 1863, as cited in *The Valley of the Shadow, The War Years*, Virginia Historical Society, Richmond.

43 *OR* 27, pt. 3, 407.

on the south side of the creek provided an ideal potential defensive position. Meade's logic was that if Lee consolidated his scattered forces before him, Big Pipe Creek was a secondary line to fall back upon. The ridge would also conceal offensive movements along its 20-mile length. This line also protected Westminster, a huge staging area in its immediate rear where reinforcements could arrive by rail, as well as Baltimore and Washington farther south.[44]

The contingency plan was just that—a contingency plan. Meade's principal plan on the 29th was to continue straight at Lee with Reynolds' Left Wing, which constituted almost one-third of the army's infantry strength. Reynolds would move toward Ewell's scattered forces, known to be threatening Harrisburg and York. Major General Henry W. Slocum's Right Wing (the Fifth Corps and his own Twelfth Corps) would follow within supporting distance. These two wings would close as opportunity presented itself, with the rest of the army in reserve. Meade apparently had no intention of fortifying the Pipe Creek line unless necessary. Verification of this comes from the fact that on the same day General Hunt began to reconnoiter the area, Meade ordered Pleasonton to send Buford's division to "Emmitsburg then thence to Gettysburg" with explicit orders to "not bring on a general engagement." Pleasonton dispatched another cavalry division to Littlestown, roughly 10 miles southeast of Gettysburg, while the last of the army's three cavalry divisions was broken apart across northern Maryland within supporting distance of both the infantry and the rest of the scattered cavalry corps, all hoping to locate the Army of Northern Virginia and Stuart's cavalry.[45]

Stuart, meanwhile, was still out of communication with Lee's army. Although his capture of a large Union supply train and more than 400 prisoners on June 28 near Rockville, Maryland, normally would have gained him praise, the ponderous wagons became a hindrance and, to him personally, a headache. Stretching for nearly eight miles, the 125 forage-filled wagons slowed him down in the undulating terrain as he neared the Mason-Dixon Line. Stuart's attempt to locate Ewell's corps was further delayed when on June 30 he encountered some of Pleasonton's Union cavalry at Hanover. Stuart fought a sharp battle there before swinging east and north for Carlisle in an effort to locate Ewell, a movement that precluded his involvement in the subsequent fighting at Gettysburg on July 1 and 2. Stuart, however, does not bear all of the blame for his cavalry's disappearance and failure

---

44 USGS MRC 39076E8 and 39076F8. Although the reconnaissance took place on June 29-30, the circular was not released until July 1. It was a contingency and not a formal plan because Longstreet's exact positions had yet to be verified. Reynolds agreed with Meade that they did not want to be flanked as Hooker had been at Chancellorsville.

45 *OR* 27, pt. 3, 400.

to return to Lee on a timely basis. Lee must assume at least some of the responsibility because he issued discretionary orders. A scholarly study conducted in recent years by the U. S. Marine Corps Command and Staff College concluded Stuart's ride kept away from Lee the most important asset to the invasion: information regarding the enemy. "The cavalry brigades that remained with the main body," argued this report, "did not possess the experience or discipline to remain flexible to the changing situation and perform reconnaissance and security expected by the leadership of the Army of Northern Virginia. Even though Lee, Stuart, Ewell, and Longstreet had reservations about these units' capabilities, sufficient measures were not taken in preparation or execution to make them more effective."[46]

A major engagement loomed somewhere in south-central Pennsylvania and neither opposing commander was fully prepared for it.

---

46 Major Louis J. Lartigue, "Shared Blame (Inertial Leadership, Indiscipline, and Horse Blinders): The Failure of the 'Other' Confederate Cavalry Brigades during the Gettysburg Campaign (20 May-1 July 1863)" Masters of Military Studies (Quantico, Va.: United States Marine Corps Command and Staff College, Marine Corps University, 2002). For a detailed analysis of Stuart's performance and the opinions of his peers and later historians, see Eric J. Wittenberg and J. David Petruzzi, *Plenty of Blame to Go Around: Jeb Stuart's Controversial Ride to Gettysburg* (El Dorado Hills, CA, 2011).

Chapter Two

"I had gained positive information of the enemy's position and movements, and my arrangements were made for entertaining him until General Reynolds could reach the scene."

— *Brig. Gen. John Buford, First Division, Cavalry Corps*[1]

One Mistake Begets Another

Long before dawn on Monday, June 29, hundreds of campfires crackled in the morning mist near Fayetteville, Pennsylvania. Confederate soldiers from General Heth's division of A. P. Hill's Third Corps were boiling coffee and preparing their breakfasts. Orders to move out coursed through the camps and within a few minutes a long column of gray was tramping eastward along the macadamized gravel turnpike stretching between Chambersburg, Gettysburg, and York. General Hill had orders "to move on this road in the direction of York, and to cross the Susquehanna menacing the communications of Harrisburg and Philadelphia, and to cooperate with General Ewell, acting as circumstances might require."[2]

After crossing the South Mountain passes these Rebels reached the west-central Adams County village of Cashtown before sunset. Heth deployed scouts to watch his flanks and foraging parties moved out to gather supplies from the countryside. Shortly after arriving, he sent two regiments with artillery support down the Orrtanna Road toward Fairfield. In the early evening this force secured the village without incident before plundering and (allegedly) threatening its residents. Pulling back beyond the northern and eastern outskirts of Fairfield, the Rebels formed a strong picket line with two cannon placed to cover both the town and the strategic road to Cashtown and Bullfrog Road, which intersected to the southeast with the Emmitsburg Road near Gettysburg. The other two divisions of

---

1   OR 27, pt. 3, 416. Circular dated June 30, 1863. See also USGS MRC 39077F2 and 39077G2.

2   Ibid.

Hill's Third Corps under Major Generals Anderson and Pender remained in Fayetteville.[3]

While the Third Corps threatened Franklin and Adams counties, Second Corps commander Ewell had Harrisburg on his mind as he continued his expedition to the Susquehanna River. However, his advance proved short-lived. Once near Carlisle, he sent his chief engineer, Capt. Henry B. Richardson, along with Brig. Gen. Albert G. Jenkins' cavalry, to reconnoiter Harrisburg's defenses. Soon thereafter, Lee's orders arrived for Ewell to join the main body of the army at Cashtown, west of Gettysburg.[4]

Two of Ewell's divisions, those of Maj. Gens. Robert E. Rodes and Edward Johnson, halted mid-morning about six miles northeast of Carlisle and reversed their march. Johnson's division led the way back south through Carlisle to Cashtown via the roads to Green Village and Scotland. With the road jammed with Johnson's long columns, three artillery battalions, and accompanying trains, Rodes' division had to detour southeast toward Petersburg (Pennsylvania) ten miles distant and roughly 25 miles north and west of Gettysburg.[5]

Concurrently in York, some 35 miles northeast of Cashtown along the turnpike, the bulk of Early's division rested while foragers scoured the prosperous region for supplies, food, and horses. Civic officials, fearing that provocation might result in the burning of their town of 8,600 people, had "surrendered" York to Brig. Gen. John B. Gordon, allowing for a peaceful occupation on the 28th. Gordon's Georgians had marched on to Wrightsville, a dozen miles east of York, where they failed to seize the mile-and-a-quarter-long covered bridge over the Susquehanna River. Inexperienced state emergency militia defended the crossing in a relatively bloodless skirmish before retreating into Lancaster County. They burned the massive wooden toll-bridge behind them, denying its use to the Rebels.[6]

Division leader Jubal Early was trying to collect a $100,000 tribute levied upon York's residents when Capt. Elliott Johnson, one of Ewell's aides, arrived late on Monday with Lee's orders to rejoin the rest of the corps near the eastern base of South Mountain. At dawn on Tuesday, June 30, Early moved west toward Heidlersburg, from which point he "could move either to Shippensburg or to

---

3   OR 27, pt. 2, 607. Buford reported the presence of two Mississippi regiments. However, neither division commander Heth nor Brig. Gen. Joseph Davis, commander of the brigade with the Mississippi regiments at Cashtown, reported detaching two regiments to Fairfield. USGS MRC 39077F3 and 39077G4 (present-day State Route 3011).

4   OR 27, pt. 2, 443.

5   Ibid., 552; USGS MRC 40077B2, 40077A1, 40077A2.

6   For details on this activity see, generally, Mingus, *Flames Beyond Gettysburg*.

Greenwood by way of Arendtsville, as circumstances might require." Early also sent Lt. Col. Elijah V. White's 35th Battalion, Virginia Cavalry on the pike from York toward Gettysburg to look for any signs of the enemy in that direction.[7]

Also on the morning of June 30, as Early marched toward Heidlersburg, the soldiers of Allegheny Johnson's division left their camp at Green Village and headed east on Black Gap Road. After passing through Scotland, the men could see South Mountain looming off their left-front. The narrow road upon which they marched skirted its base, winding southeast toward Fayetteville another 10 miles away. At the end of his 15-mile march Johnson bivouacked north of Fayetteville within sight of Anderson's division, with John Bell Hood's and Lafayette McLaws' divisions of Longstreet's corps camped but a few miles farther west. Cashtown lay roughly a dozen miles due east.[8]

*   *   *

That evening, as Lee's army was settling down for its morning push toward Cashtown, Union staff officers and couriers distributed a circular to General Meade's corps commanders: "The following is the order of march for to-morrow: Twelfth Corps to Littlestown, passing the Third Corps. Fifth Corps, Pipe Creek Crossing, on the road between Littlestown and Westminster. Sixth Corps, through Westminster to Manchester. First Corps, half way to Gettysburg, on crossing Marsh Creek. Headquarters at Taneytown to-morrow night. Headquarters train will move at 8 a.m. to-morrow. The Artillery Reserve," continued the order, "will move to Piney Run Crossing, on the road between Littlestown and the Taneytown, following the Twelfth Corps. Engineers and bridge train to the vicinity of the Fifth Corps. Headquarters train will have the right of way when it moves."[9]

Although Lee did not order his corps leaders to specifically consolidate at Gettysburg, he nevertheless realized the town was important enough to direct Ewell to use it as a throughway on the last day of June. Brigadier General J. Johnston Pettigrew, who led a brigade in Heth's division, requested permission to march his men the nine miles from Cashtown to Gettysburg in the morning to get provisions thought to be there in abundance (despite White's and Early's visit there on June 26). The foray to Gettysburg would double as a reconnaissance-in-force.

There was enough information on hand that Tuesday for Meade to realize Lee would almost certainly recall and consolidate his army somewhere between South

7   OR 27, pt. 2, 467-68.

8   Ibid., 503; USGS MRC 39077H5, 39077H6, 39077G6.

9   Ibid., pt. 3, 402.

Brig. Gen. John Buford,
1st Division, Cavalry Corps,
Army of the Potomac. *LOC*

Mountain and the Susquehanna River south of Carlisle, most likely in Adams or York counties. Meade knew it would be unwise to confront Lee on his terms. He also fully realized, as did the War Department, that the Army of Northern Virginia could only spend so much time in Pennsylvania before it would have to withdraw south of the Potomac River. The Confederacy simply did not have the logistical support a prolonged stay in Pennsylvania would require. The information Department of the Susquehanna commander Darius Couch's scouts passed on to Washington about Lee's widely separated state was relayed hourly to the Army of the Potomac. The first bit of startling news arrived at 6:30 a.m. on June 29: Couch had no idea where Longstreet's and Hill's corps were located.[10]

Meade and his staff arrived at Taneytown, 13 miles south of Gettysburg, by midmorning on the 30th. Unbeknownst to Meade, General Buford with two brigades of cavalry had just entered Gettysburg after leaving Fairfield shortly after sunrise. Buford had led his tired column through Monterey Pass the night before with orders to reconnoiter and, if possible, hold Gettysburg. The quickest way there ran through the Carroll Valley, where several shortcuts existed via Fairfield. Buford's troopers moved into the picturesque valley using a rural lane that intersected the old Waynesboro Pike about six miles northwest of Emmitsburg. The horsemen passed over Tom's Creek before calling a halt, and resumed their march the next morning.[11]

Buford woke well before dawn that Tuesday and, approaching Fairfield, discovered Confederate artillery and a reinforced picket line. "I determined to feel it

10 Ibid., pt. 2, 407.

11 Ibid., 407; USGS MRC 39077F3, 39077G3.

Gettysburg's center square. Buford upon his arrival found
the townspeople to be "in a terrible state of excitement." *ACHS*

and drive it, if possible," the Kentucky-born cavalryman wrote, "but, after a little
skirmishing, found that his own artillery" would have to be used. Convinced
cannonading "from that quarter might disarrange the plans of the general
commanding," Buford went on to explain, "Fairfield was 4 or 5 miles west of the
route (Emmitsburg Road), assigned me, and I did not want to bring on a general
engagement so far from the road I was expected to be following." With orders to
not bring on a general engagement, he recalled his skirmishers, formed his men in
column of fours, and, with Lt. John H. Calef's Battery A, 2nd U.S. Light Artillery in
tow, moved back toward the old Waynesboro Pike following the old Fairfield Road
paralleling Tom's Creek. "I immediately turned my column toward Emmitsburg
without serious molestation," Buford continued, "and was soon on my proper road
and moving on Gettysburg."[12]

     While Buford was recalling his troopers from their skirmish at Fairfield,
General Pettigrew's large Confederate brigade was beginning its fateful march from
Cashtown to Gettysburg. When it reached the western outskirts of town, the
vanguard could clearly see Union troopers approaching from the south. Like
Buford, Pettigrew had strict orders not to bring on a general engagement. Without
making contact, the well-educated North Carolinian reversed the direction of his
command and tramped back west, disappearing over the ridges with his 17 wagons
still empty. "I entered this place to-day at 11 a.m.," Buford later wrote. "Found

12 Ibid., 926.

everybody in a terrible state of excitement on account of the enemy's advance upon this place. He had approached to within half a mile of the town when the head of my column entered."[13]

Sending couriers galloping south to Meade, Buford at 12:20 p.m. relayed this news and more: "My extreme left reports a large force coming from toward Fairfield, in the direction to strike Emmitsburg Road this side of Marsh Creek."[14] This could only mean Buford's advanced left-flank vedettes patrolling the roads south of Gettysburg (between the Emmitsburg Road and town of Fairfield) happened upon the enemy in numbers moving eastward somewhere north of Marsh Creek. Although Buford never mentioned the force, its numbers, or what roads the enemy were using, it suggested the Rebels may strike the Emmitsburg Road somewhere between Gettysburg south to Marsh Creek. General Reynolds likewise passed on this information, stating, "Buford also sent a regiment to Fairfield, on road leading to Moritz Tavern." Major General Oliver O. Howard corroborated this, adding, "The enemy are reported moving on Gettysburg from Fairfield to Cashtown."[15]

Although Buford was positive the troops he had seen retiring toward Cashtown would eventually return on the same road, he remained concerned about being flanked south of the pike via the numerous rural crossroads connecting Fairfield to Gettysburg. It would have taken an entire brigade to sufficiently patrol the sprawling sector between the Cashtown Pike southward to the Millerstown Road, which linked Fairfield and Gettysburg via the Emmitsburg Road. The loss of the Emmitsburg Road south of the latter was not an option.[16]

Although Buford's headquarters was in the saddle, a review of his correspondence allows one to fully appreciate the outstanding job of intelligence-gathering and reconnaissance Meade's cavalry was performing—especially when compared to General Lee's Confederate horsemen. At 5:30 a.m. while en route to Emmitsburg, Buford received a useful message he forwarded on to Reynolds and Meade: "The enemy has increased his forces considerably. His strong position is just behind Cashtown. My party toward Mummasburg met a superior force, strongly posted. Another party that went up the road due north, 3 miles out, met a strong picket; had a skirmish, and captured a prisoner of Rodes' division. Another

13 Ibid., pt. 1, 923.

14 Ibid., 922.

15 Ibid.; OR 27, pt. 3, 417, 418.

16 Ibid., pt. 1, 922; USGS MRC 39077F3, 39077G3.

party that went to Littlestown heard that Gregg or Kilpatrick had a fight with Stuart, and drove him from Hanover."[17]

The timing of the above correspondence (5:30 a.m., June 30) suggests Buford sent his scouting parties north and east of Gettysburg shortly after his command descended Monterey Pass the previous day. It is also obvious those parties returned with their news early on the 30th and met Buford somewhere on the road near Emmitsburg. It would not have been unusual for all-night patrols to have ridden and reached their destinations and returned to Buford at or near Emmitsburg by 5:30 a.m. Only some 14 miles separated Emmitsburg from Gettysburg, it was about 18 miles to Littlestown, and a little less than 19 to Mummasburg. How far out the Mummasburg Road Buford's patrol ventured is hard to say. They may have scouted as far as three miles north of Gettysburg on the old Harrisburg Road, because all these patrols could have easily ridden the distances mentioned and returned to Emmitsburg in a timely manner. There was no logical reason for Buford to have reached Gettysburg in the early afternoon and then write a note to Reynolds and Meade backdated to 5:30 a.m.[18]

Both armies spent June 30 redeploying their forces and supply trains to positions best suited to their specific needs. Neither general was exactly sure what the other might do, so each order sending any given unit on a particular route or to a certain town was somewhat of a gamble. Lee also had to deal with an extended and crowded supply line. Longstreet spent most of the day with General Lee. About noon, Hill's corps and Ewell's wagon trains blocked the Cashtown Pike in front of the First Corps. Longstreet received orders to allow these trains to pass, and that he should camp at Greenwood, about 10 miles east of Chambersburg.[19]

Both Heth and Hill considered Pettigrew's report of Union troops in Gettysburg as unreliable or inadequate. Pettigrew could not offer information concerning the enemy's identification or its strength. His aide-de-camp, Capt. Louis G. Young, had traveled with the brigade to Gettysburg and suggested the enemy appeared "well-trained." Hill, however, refused to believe the Army of the Potomac had advanced so far north, and he supposedly suggested the enemy was most likely a "home guard." Relaying this information and his opinion to Lee, Hill concluded Meade's army was still in central Maryland between Frederick and

---

17 Ibid. At 5:30 a.m. Buford was either approaching or already at Emmitsburg, having left Carroll Valley which he had entered from the direction of Monterey Pass. OR 27, pt. 1, 922. He was not in Gettysburg at that early hour.

18 Ibid.

19 Longstreet, *SHSP*, vol. 5. His infantry would have no choice but to remain there until late on the afternoon of July 1. The artillery did not get onto the road until 2:00 a.m. on July 2.

Middleburg. With that in mind, Heth inquired of his corps commander whether he had any objections if his entire division marched to Gettysburg on the morning of July 1, to which Hill supposedly remarked, "None in the world."[20]

Brigadier General James J. Archer learned his small veteran brigade of Alabamians and Tennesseans would lead the division toward Gettysburg. Captain Young reportedly briefed Archer that Yankee cavalry was spotted there the evening before, and that the enemy could use several intersecting lanes he would march pass to flank his column. Beyond Cashtown, however, there were no signs or reports of the enemy in strength. "Everyone was relaxed, and the conversation was unusually careless & jolly," wrote First Corps artillerist Col. Edward Porter Alexander, who was visiting Lee's headquarters at Greenwood that night. "Certainly there was no premonition that the next morning was to open the great battle of the campaign."[21]

At some point after Buford's briefing on June 30, Meade's headquarters at Taneytown revised the earlier marching circular. In its place came a new order to send the Third Corps to Emmitsburg, the Second to Taneytown, the Fifth to Hanover, the Twelfth to Two Taverns, the First to Gettysburg, and the Sixth to Manchester. An amendment soon followed: "The commanding general has received information [from Buford] that the enemy are advancing, probably in strong force, on Gettysburg. It is the intention to hold this army pretty nearly in the position it now occupies until the plans of the enemy shall have been more fully developed." Given the lack of solid intelligence on the whereabouts of the various elements of the Confederate army, Meade's decision was prudent. But, as he had written his wife a few days previously, he was committed to going straight at Lee and would, one way or another, offer battle.[22]

Meade's latest order became necessary after Buford's far-reaching patrols ran into reinforced enemy picket lines along the major throughways north of Gettysburg. On several occasions the light skirmishing resulted in the capture of prisoners. The appearance of Robert Rodes' division triggered a flood of communications between Meade and Buford—far more than flowed from Pettigrew to Heth to Hill and then Lee. Reynolds sent a late-night message from his headquarters at the Moritz Tavern to Meade: "I do not believe the report of their marching on [East] Berlin, which would lead them direct to York. The enemy are

---

20 Louis Gurdin Young, Walter Clark, ed., "Pettigrew's Brigade at Gettysburg," in *Histories of Several Regiments and Battalions from North Carolina in the Great War, 1861-1865*, 5 vols. (Raleigh, NC, 1901), vol. 5, 115-20. See also Henry Heth, *SHSP*, vol. 4, 156-57. Heth's account dates from well after the war and is suspect in several regards.

21 Heth, *SHSP*, vol. 4, 156-57; Alexander, *Fighting for the Confederacy*, 230.

22 *OR* 27, pt. 3, 416.

evidentially marching out into this Valley, but whether it is for the purpose of going to York to give us battle, I cannot say." Reynolds' late statement was more than either Ewell or Hill offered Lee.[23]

Why did A. P. Hill dispatch an entire infantry division with artillery to gather provisions on July 1 in a town allegedly occupied by a few poorly trained home guardsmen? This was especially curious given that General Early had driven out almost 1,000 state emergency militiamen on June 26 with only White's cavalry battalion and the mere threat of an advance by Gordon's infantry brigade.[24] It appears the only high-ranking officer of either side fairly confident that a momentous battle was about to erupt at Gettysburg was John Buford. The Union general deployed his two brigades fronting west and north that evening, and ordered Lieutenant Calef to park his six rifled guns between the Lutheran Theological Seminary on Seminary Ridge west of town, and McPherson's Ridge about 800 yards farther west. This would allow the guns to be moved to any threatened part of the line within a moment's notice. Buford's advance pickets and vedettes, some as far as four miles beyond his main force, kept watch throughout the night. "By daylight on July 1," he later reported, "I had gained positive information of the enemy's position and movements, and my arrangements were made for entertaining him until General Reynolds could reach the scene."[25]

Hooker's initial blunder in allowing Lee to get a one-week head start, and then his decision to drag his feet in pursuit, was inexcusable. However, Jeb Stuart's lengthy ride around the Union army, combined with exceptional intelligence work within the U. S. War Department (coupled with Pleasonton's redesigned cavalry command) had by this time offset Lee's initial advantage. Resting Longstreet and Hill at Culpeper for so long did not help Lee's position in Pennsylvania. His decision to stop again at Chambersburg to rest and gather supplies likewise proved beneficial to the Federals. But Lee's men were spirited and confident, and he was equally sure of success. The primary issue confronting Lee in the early hours of July 1 was not so much the Federals, but how to get five of his of nine divisions through the narrow Cashtown Gap before Meade's army could assemble and block Ewell from reuniting with Lee's main forces.[26]

---

23 Ibid.

24 For much more on the skirmishing near Gettysburg on June 26, and how it may have impacted subsequent events on July 1, see generally, Mingus, *Flames Beyond Gettysburg*. General Early captured about 175 of these emergency men, whom he labeled "utterly inefficient."

25 *OR* 27, pt. 1, 927.

26 Colonel Charles Marshall to Jubal Early, letter dated 1876, Box 8, Jubal Early Papers, Manuscript Division, Library of Congress, Washington, DC.

Longstreet's entire corps of three divisions plus that of Anderson (Third Corps) and Johnson (Second Corps) could not possibly move as one single column through the Cashtown Gap. Many historians now support Colonel Alexander's assertion that, on the night of June 30, Lee did not foresee the forthcoming battle. If he had, he would have continued marching his troops from Fayetteville and Greenwood to Cashtown throughout the night. A further complication arose when Longstreet had no choice but to leave Pickett's division near Chambersburg until Brig. Gen. John Imboden's troopers could relieve it. This did not sit well with Longstreet, and Lee already knew his chief subordinate did not approve of his invasion plan. "We discussed it over and over," Longstreet later complained, "and I discovered that his main objection to it was that it would, if adopted, force him to divide his army. He left no room to doubt, however, that he believed the idea of an offensive campaign was not only important but necessary."[27]

Thus far, Lee's actions had indeed been strategically aggressive. Sending General Ewell's corps racing ahead was quite bold, but time was not on Lee's side. "At length, while we were discussing the idea of a western forward movement [to relieve the Union siege at Vicksburg]," Longstreet recalled, "he asked me if I did not think an invasion of Maryland and Pennsylvania by his own army would accomplish the same result, and I replied that I did not see that it would, because this movement would be too hazardous, and the campaign in thoroughly Union States would require more time and greater preparation than one through Tennessee and Kentucky. I soon discovered," continued Longstreet, "that he had determined that he would make some forward movement, and I finally assented that the Pennsylvania campaign might be brought to a successful issue if he could make it offensive in strategy, but defensive in tactics. This point was urged with great persistency."[28]

Longstreet's persistence was obvious to many. His staff officer Moxley Sorrel mused that Longstreet appeared melancholy and convinced the recent reorganization of the army was unsuitable for such an invasion. Pender's division, for example, largely formed from unassigned or reserve commands around Richmond, was new and had never collectively seen combat.[29] Longstreet thought a defensive posture more practical: "I suggested that, after piercing Pennsylvania and menacing Washington, we should choose a strong position and force the Federals to attack us, observing that the popular clamor throughout the North would speedily force the Federal General to attempt to drive us out. I recalled to him the

27 Longstreet, *SHSP*, vol. 5.

28 Ibid.

29 Sorrel, *Recollections*, 160.

battle of Fredericksburg as an instance of a defensive battle, when, with a few thousand men, we hurled the whole Federal army back, crippling and demoralizing it, with trifling loss to our own troops; and Chancellorsville as an instance of an offensive battle, where we dislodged the Federals, it is true, but at such a terrible sacrifice that half a dozen such victories would have ruined us."[30]

Although Lee pitched his tent in proximity to Longstreet's headquarters at Greenwood on the evening of June 30, the record is silent as to whether the two generals discussed a pending battle on the morrow. "Getting his infantry through to Cashtown in one piece was one thing," explained Pennsylvania College professor Michael Jacobs, an eyewitness to the invasion, but "getting the artillery and trains there was yet another. Lee had natural and physical issues to deal with that night as well. Throughout the period of the invasion the weather was uncharacteristically cool with clouds and rain. Bodies of water that were normally low, even dry, at this time of year were running high," he continued. "The usually dry roads would become muddy and slippery during the showers then turn to pan-hard clay afterward. Unshod horses became lame. The soles of the infantrymen's footwear rotted, disintegrated, with many continuing barefoot."[31] "No incident worthy of notice occurred on the march to this place [Fayetteville]," wrote Capt. Edward B. Brunson, the commander of a battalion of reserve artillery in Hill's Third Corps, "and I may say it was most successfully conducted, especially when we consider the miserable condition of the horses feet, for lack of shoes, on the limestone pikes, over which a large portion of our march was made."[32]

In order to move artillery, ordnance, and matériel and have it maintain pace in column with an army on the move, draft animals had to be kept healthy. Captain Brunson's single battalion used about 150 horses during the campaign and battle, of which 20 broken-down animals were turned loose on June 29. Lee's army needed tens of thousands of horses and mules to operate effectively. Although strong and resilient, these sturdy animals were trained to work in fields followed by close care and, more importantly, a good night's rest under the warm roof of a barn or stable. They were not used to the stressful pace of forced marches and the rationing of forage. Not even the vast quantities procured along the march could fill the stomachs of the number of fresh horses needed daily to keep Lee's massive trains moving without long periods of rest.

30 Longstreet, *SHSP*, vol. 5.

31 Michael Jacobs, *Notes from the Invasion of Maryland and Pennsylvania June 15th until July 22nd, 1863* (Philadelphia, PA, 1864).

32 OR 27, pt. 2, 677.

Early morning at Fayetteville saw Richard Anderson's eastbound division of A. P. Hill's corps hit the road soon after daylight. With his front blocked by a long train, his column came to an abrupt stop for some 30 minutes until the ponderous wagons had cleared the road. This was just the beginning of the difficulties his division would confront during the next few days.[33]

Thirty-eight miles southeast of Lee's tent, Meade's headquarters at Taneytown was a beehive of activity. In the short time since Meade assumed command, he had unknowingly taken advantage of Lee's misfortunes, pacing his infantry on short forced marches that sent them to strategic points along their routes, mostly within a half-day of one another. The far right wing of Henry Slocum's Twelfth Corps, however, was still a good day's march from Gettysburg. On the night of June 30, Meade received news (which Lee did not) that Brig. Gen. H. Judson Kilpatrick's cavalry division had battled Jeb Stuart's cavalry that day at Hanover in southwestern York County. Although a tactical stalemate, Stuart disappeared eastward into the night before continuing his move north in the general direction of York in search of Lee's army.[34]

Combined with Buford's earlier reports, this fresh intelligence convinced Meade his army's hard march was coming to an end. The Rebels were not far off. In contrast to Lee's less urgent movements and clogged roads because of his extended supply line of wagon trains, Meade issued the following order: "Corps commanders will hold their commands in readiness at moment's notice, and, upon receiving orders march against the enemy, their trains must be parked in the rear of the place of concentration. Ammunition wagons and ambulances will alone be permitted to accompany the troops. The men must be provided with three day's rations in haversacks, and with 60 rounds of ammunition in the boxes and upon the person." General Reynolds replied: "At all events, an engineer officer ought to be sent up [north] to reconnoiter this position, as we have reason to believe that the main force of the enemy is in the vicinity of Cashtown, or debouching from the Cumberland Valley above it." Meade confirmed the receipt of Reynolds' dispatch and added, "The enemy undoubtedly occupy the Cumberland Valley, from Chambersburg, in force; whether the holding of the Cashtown Gap is to prevent our entrance, or is their advance against us, remains to be seen. With Buford at Gettysburg and Mechanicsburg, and a regiment in front of Emmitsburg, you ought to be advised in time of their approach."[35]

---

33 Ibid., 613, 677.

34 Philip Laino, *Gettysburg Campaign Atlas* (Dayton, OH, 2009), 74-75. See also Wittenberg and Petruzzi, *Plenty of Blame To Go Around*, 65-117.

35 *OR* 27, pt. 3, 417, 419, 421.

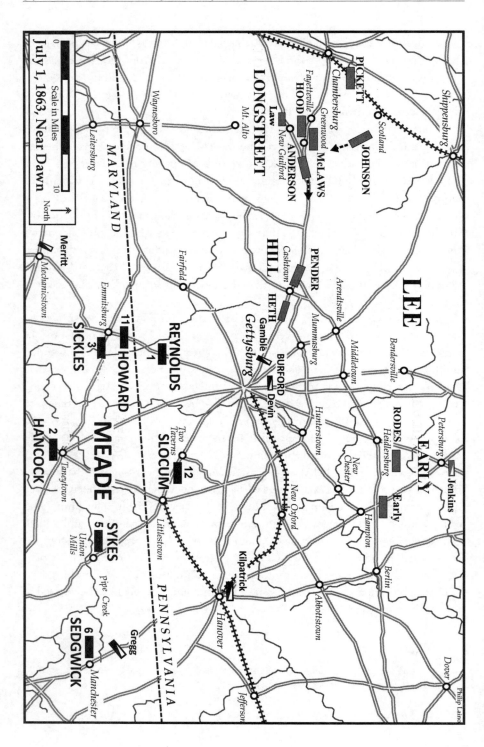

July 1, 1863, Near Dawn

General Lee wanted to consolidate his army around Cashtown on June 30, some seven miles west of Gettysburg. The quiet hamlet was strategically located at the entrance to the mountain pass connecting Lee's scattered forces to the Cumberland Valley and his vital supply lines, as well as the Potomac River. *ACHS*

From about 1:00 p.m. until midnight, the dispatches sent to Meade all but pointed to either Gettysburg or Emmitsburg as Lee's potential target. Meade knew from Couch's reports several pieces of useful intelligence: (1) Lee's Harrisburg adventure was over; (2) Ewell was retiring from York and Carlisle; (3) Jeb Stuart was heading north, detached from Lee's main army, and; (4) Lee would likely turn and fight after his army concentrated east of the Cumberland Valley. With that in mind, Reynolds' concern that Lee would move to Fairfield and then Emmitsburg remained a viable threat.[36]

Meade's staff was both aware and worried that Lee could divide his forces as he had at Chancellorsville, and as he had recently done with Ewell's corps. Reynolds foresaw Lee sending part of his army to Gettysburg while simultaneously flanking him through Emmitsburg. Unless Lee withdrew his entire army into the Cumberland Valley, neither Reynolds nor Meade expected Lee to fortify and wait near Cashtown. That would be uncharacteristic of the aggressive Southern commander. Meade anticipated instead that Lee would move toward him. Like

36 USGS MRC 39077G3.

Longstreet, Meade was thinking in defensive terms (hence the Pipe Creek circular). For the third time Meade's staff revised the planned destinations for the morning of July 1: "Eleventh Corps to Gettysburg, Third Corps to Emmitsburg, Second to Taneytown, Fifth to Hanover, Twelfth to Two Taverns and Sixth to stay near Manchester."[37]

As Meade pondered his options, Lee ordered his corps commanders to concentrate near Cashtown. Ewell also received a discretionary note suggesting the most favorable route for him to follow. He would heed the advice. When he learned the enemy vanguard was near Frederick, Maryland, and that Meade was now in command of the Army of the Potomac, a conversation ensued in Rebel headquarters about whether Meade might turn west toward the Cumberland Valley in an effort to cut off Lee's supply routes and communication with Richmond. This, however, seemed unlikely since it would require Meade to turn opposite Harrisburg or leave an open road to Baltimore.[38]

Lee's personal secretary, Lt. Col. Charles Marshall, later discussed why General Lee decided to concentrate around Cashtown: "You will thus see that the movement to Gettysburg was the result of the want of information, which the cavalry alone could obtain for us, Lee was compelled to march through the mountains from Chambersburg eastward without the slightest knowledge of the enemy's movements, except brought by the scout [Harrison]. While making this march the only information he possessed led him to believe that the army of the enemy was moving westward from Frederick to throw itself upon his line of communication with Virginia, and the object of the movement, as I have stated, was simply to arrest the execution of this supposed plan of the enemy, and keep his army on the east side of the Blue Ridge."[39]

"Supposed" is the key word in Marshall's observation. Nothing in any of Lee's post-battle reports or later correspondence reflects the notion he was worried on June 30 about his communication lines west of South Mountain. "It would have been entirely within the power of General Lee," Marshall continued, "to have met the army of the enemy while it was moving on the road between Frederick and Gettysburg, or to have remained west of the mountain."[40] Marshall's comments suggest that as late as 5:00 a.m. on July 1, when Anderson's division took to the road from near Fayetteville to Cashtown, Lee was still unsure exactly how and where

37 OR 27, pt. 3, 416-17, 421-22, 426.

38 R. A. Brock, ed., "Events Leading up to the Battle of Gettysburg: Address of Charles Marshall," in *SHSP*, vol. 22, 1895, 225-27.

39 Ibid.

40 Ibid.

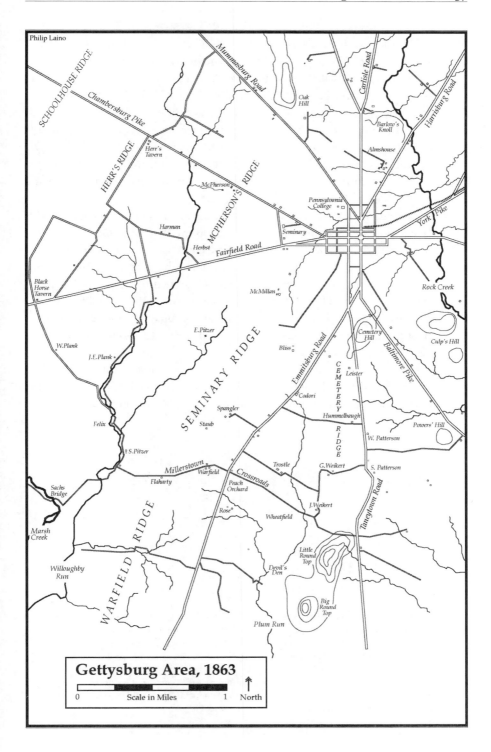

Philip Laino

SCHOOLHOUSE RIDGE

Chambersburg Pike

Mummasburg Road

Carlisle Road

Harrisburg Road

Oak Hill

Barlow's Knoll

Almshouse

HERR'S RIDGE

Herr's Tavern

McPherson's

MCPHERSON'S RIDGE

Pennsylvania College

York Pike

Harman

Seminary

Herbst   Fairfield Road

Black Horse Tavern

McMillan

Rock Creek

E.Pitzer

SEMINARY RIDGE

Cemetery Hill

Culp's Hill

W.Plank

Bliss

Emmitsburg Road

Baltimore Pike

J.E.Plank

CEMETERY RIDGE

Leister

Felix

Spangler

Codori

Staub

Hummelbaugh

Powers' Hill

W. Patterson

S.Pitzer

Millerstown

Warfield   Crossroads

Trostle

G.Weikert

S. Patterson

Flaharty

Peach Orchard

Taneytown Road

Sachs Bridge

Rose

Wheatfield

J.Weikert

WARFIELD RIDGE

Marsh Creek

Little Round Top

Willoughby Run

Devil's Den

Big Round Top

Plum Run

Gettysburg Area, 1863

0   Scale in Miles   1   ↑ North

Meade had positioned his army. His gamble to head east and concentrate would pay off in ways he was not quite prepared to manage or efficiently handle.

Shortly after A. P. Hill received Pettigrew's news on June 30 about an enemy presence at Gettysburg, Hill wrongly surmised it was likely, but not positively, Pennsylvania militia. The corps commander sent couriers galloping eastward to Ewell with the same information. "A courier was then dispatched with this information to the general commanding, and with orders to start Anderson's early," reported Hill, and "also to General Ewell, informing him, and that I intended to advance the next morning [toward Gettysburg] and discover what was in my front."[41]

Hill's determination to discover exactly what was in his front, coupled with Meade's decision to send the First Corps, supported by Maj. Gen. Oliver O. Howard's Eleventh Corps, northward to Gettysburg set the two armies on a collision course. The subsequent battle resulted from these orders of June 30 and not from an accidental meeting as Confederates searched for shoes, as has often been reported based on Heth's dubious postwar account. It was Hill's choice to reconnoiter eastward in force to a town he thought occupied by nothing more than inexperienced home guard troops—which posed barely a nuisance and certainly not a credible military threat.

Lee's order that a "general engagement was to be avoided until the arrival of the rest of the army" was about to be cast aside, and the previously obscure Adams County crossroads town of Gettysburg would never again be the same.[42]

---

41 *OR* 27, pt. 2, 607.

42 Stephen W. Sears, *Gettysburg* (New York, 2002), 196. Author J. D. Petruzzi argues that technically speaking, Heth's engagement with Buford on July 1 was not a violation of General Lee's order to avoid bringing on a "general engagement." Other similar engagements had taken place during the campaign. Heth's supporters argue he did exactly what he should have done: engage to develop what was in his front. When the fighting became more general and John Reynolds' I Corps was discovered, Heth properly disengaged. There was a lull in the fighting thereafter until Ewell's Second Corps arrived from the north and General Lee sanctioned an all-out attack. Email from Petruzzi to author, October 3, 2013.

Chapter Three

> "The army, therefore, moved forward as a man might walk
> over strange ground with his eyes shut."
>
> — *Lt. Gen. James Longstreet, C.S.A.*[1]

July 1: The Battle is Joined

Long before General Anderson's division of Hill's Third Corps filed onto the Cashtown Pike early that fateful July 1 morning, First Corps commander General Longstreet had repeatedly voiced his opinion on how best to proceed with the campaign.

Shortly after the battle of Chancellorsville, he proposed a summer offensive plan to President Jefferson Davis and Gen. Robert E. Lee to relieve the pressure against Vicksburg, Mississippi. Longstreet suggested his entire corps, or portions thereof, be detached and shipped west while Lee's Army of Northern Virginia, bolstered by fresh troops from the Carolinas, maintained its line along the Rappahannock River. Davis rejected his plan and Longstreet remained part of Lee's reorganized army.[2]

Once Lee decided to march the army into Pennsylvania, Longstreet complained it "became useless and improper to offer suggestions leading to a different course." He later wrote, as touched upon earlier, that he suggested the offensive campaign be conducted with defensive tactics, with the goal of forcing the enemy to attack the army in an advantageous position. In his opinion, this "might assure us of a grand triumph." According to Longstreet, Lee "readily assented" to his request "as an important and material adjunct to his general plan."[3]

---

1 James Longstreet, *From Manassas to Appomattox: Memoirs of the Civil War in America* (Philadelphia, 1895), 330-31.

2 Longstreet, *SHSP*, vol. 5.

3 Ibid.

Longstreet's mindset was the opposite of Lee's successful gamble at Chancellorsville, where Lee split his army in the face of the enemy. This, however, was not Chancellorsville, let alone Virginia. Longstreet's doubts increased when he learned of Lee's orders to General Stuart. As Longstreet was leaving the Blue Ridge, he instructed Stuart to follow him and cross the Potomac River at Shepherdstown while Longstreet used the ford at Williamsport 10 miles upstream. Longstreet withdrew his orders after Stuart informed him that Lee had granted him "discretionary powers" over the cavalry's movements. "General Stuart held the Gap for awhile," Longstreet later wrote, "and then hurried around beyond Hooker's army, and we saw nothing more of him until the evening of the 2d of July, when he came down from York and joined us, having made a complete circuit of the Federal army. The absence of Stuart's cavalry from the main body of the army during the march," continued Longstreet, "is claimed to have been a fatal error, as General Lee says: 'No report had been received (on the 27th) that the enemy had crossed the Potomac, and the absence of the cavalry rendered it impossible to obtain accurate information.'" As Longstreet put it, "The army, therefore, moved forward as a man might walk over strange ground with his eyes shut."[4]

Ironically, Longstreet's rejected plan mirrored concerns passed by General Buford to John Reynolds that Lee might try moving around his Left Wing from the southwest. Longstreet wanted to seek suitable ground between the Army of the Potomac and Baltimore-Washington and force Meade to attack. Unbeknownst to Longstreet, however, Meade was prepared for this very scenario. The suggestion to move south, find suitable terrain, and offer battle in a defensive posture would have been essentially the same as his "walk over strange ground with eyes shut."[5]

A. P. Hill's morning move toward Gettysburg on July 1 negated both Longstreet's desire to move south and assume the defensive, as well as Lee's goal to reunite his widely scattered columns around Cashtown. It also put to rest the possibility of using the Cashtown Gap to return to Chambersburg and the Cumberland Valley. While Anderson's division of 7,132 men and trains filled that vital mountain gap heading east, Longstreet's fitful movement continued. General Edward "Allegheny" Johnson's division of Ewell's Second Corps had orders to follow Anderson. The rest of the First Corps would follow Johnson later that day, giving Longstreet ample time to not only gather his command and be ready to move, but to also ponder a host of possibilities—especially those he had suggested

---

4   Ibid.

5   Ibid.

and assumed had fallen upon deaf ears. Simply put, Longstreet was not happy with his move to Cashtown or with Hill's decision to continue on to Gettysburg.[6]

When the sun rose on July 1, General Ewell was accompanying Maj. Gen. Robert E. Rodes' division about 13 miles northeast of Cashtown, having reached Heidlersburg the previous night. Rodes had an open but narrow pike through Middletown (now Biglerville) that would have placed his division at Cashtown no later than 4:00 p.m. Instead, after receiving Hill's communiqué concerning moving south to see what was in his front, Ewell adopted Lee's June 30 suggestion by continuing down the Harrisburg Pike to Gettysburg, 11 miles distant. Doing so would place Rodes within supporting distance of General Heth's division, and more importantly reunite Rodes with Maj. Gen. Jubal Early, who was then en route with his division to Gettysburg from East Berlin, a 19-mile march.[7]

Sandwiched between Hill's divisions of Heth and Anderson on South Mountain, Maj. Gen. Dorsey Pender continued marching his division toward Cashtown at about 8:00 a.m., and reached that place shortly after Heth's command departed from it. Pender's assistant adjutant-general, Maj. Joseph A. Engelhard, later recorded, "The light division of Maj. Gen. W. D. Pender, consisting of the brigades of Gens. J. H. Lane, E. L. Thomas, A. M. Scales, and S. McGowan, the latter under command of Col. A. Perrin, Fourteenth South Carolina Volunteers, which had encamped on the afternoon of June 30, on the north side of South Mountain, Pennsylvania, moved from that position at 8 o'clock on the morning of July 1 along the turnpike through Cashtown, the direction of Gettysburg, in rear of Major-General Heth."[8]

About 8:00 a.m. Colonel Perrin, an antebellum South Carolina attorney with Mexican War experience, received orders to get his men under arms. Leaving Capt. William M. Hadden and the 1st South Carolina (Orr's) Rifles to guard the wagon train, Perrin led the rest of his brigade eastward on the turnpike toward Gettysburg, with the rest of Pender's division trailing behind them. Well ahead, his men could occasionally catch a glimpse of the tail end of Heth's division, leading the long Confederate column along the undulating terrain.[9]

After receiving Hill's notification that Heth's entire division would march to Gettysburg, General Lee was in the saddle shortly after Anderson's division took to the road. He was under the impression Pender would be at Cashtown when he

---

6   Ibid.

7   OR 27, pt. 2, 445; USGS MRC 39077G2, 39077H2. See also Jubal Early, *SHSP*, vol. 4, 1877, 49-66, and Walter H. Taylor, *Four Years with General Lee* (New York, NY, 1877), 124-39.

8   OR 27, pt. 2, 656.

9   Ibid., 661.

arrived with Anderson. Heth's securing of Gettysburg would make it much easier for Ewell's two divisions to pass through the gap and then march to Cashtown. This would also allow Johnson the necessary time to march unabated through the gap with his trains. Longstreet would follow with Lafayette McLaws' and John Hood's divisions, leaving General Pickett's division west of the gap until it was relieved by General Imboden's cavalry. The timing of the various movements was intended to avert a serious traffic jam in the narrow mountain pass.[10]

The small Franklin County communities of Greenwood and Fayetteville came alive at sunrise that first of July when more than 26,000 men, ordnance and trains rolling with them, began stirring. Before leaving Greenwood, Lee penned a letter to General Imboden, who was still south of Chambersburg with his cavalry: "Upon arriving at Chambersburg to-day I desire you to relieve General Pickett, who will move toward this place. You must turn off everybody belonging to the army on the road to Gettysburg, the reserve trains of the army are parked between Greenwood and Cashtown on said road, and to-morrow," continued Lee, "I desire you to move up to this place, establish yourself as to command the cross-roads and roads leading in to town [Chambersburg]. . . . My headquarters for the present will be at Cashtown east of the mountain."[11]

In Gettysburg, meanwhile, scouts informed General Buford of the Confederate presence in the mountains off to the west. Accordingly, he posted vedettes nearly four miles out the Cashtown (Chambersburg) Pike near its intersection with Knoxlyn Road. Although Confederate pickets were only a half-mile beyond Buford's vedettes, not a shot was fired as the sun broke the horizon. Both advanced lines opted to lay low and await developments. Shortly after 7:00 a.m., however, a rustling to the west brought the Federal troopers to their feet. Rebel skirmishers were advancing. "Between 8 and 9 a.m.," Buford recalled, "reports came in from the First Brigade that the enemy was coming down from toward Cashtown in force." Lieutenant Marcellus Jones of the 8th Illinois Cavalry borrowed a breech-loading carbine from one of his men and, by some accounts, leveled it, took aim, and squeezed off the battle's first shot. It was about 7:30 a.m.[12]

Messengers from the advance skirmish line dashed back west to warn Brig. Gen. James J. Archer that the enemy was waiting ahead. The veteran brigadier formed his brigade into line of battle below the Cashtown Pike. He had no idea what or who awaited him beyond the wooded ridges. "Colonel [William] Gamble

---

10 USGS MRC 394352077225001-AD-808.

11 OR 27, pt. 2, 947-48. See also John W. Busey and David G. Martin, *Regimental Strengths and Losses at Gettysburg* (Hightstown, NJ, 1986).

12 *OR* 27, pt 1, 967.

made an admirable line of battle, and moved off proudly to meet him," Buford later reported. "The two lines soon became hotly engaged, we having the advantage of position, he of numbers." Heth's skirmishers were soon absorbed into the main line as it ever so slowly pressed eastward, held back by the superior firepower of the Yankee troopers' fast-loading carbines and excellent artillery.[13]

Effective support from Calef's six 3-inch Ordnance Rifles of Battery A, 2nd U.S. Artillery enabled Gamble to hold his first position for more than an hour. Despite what evolved into a three-to-one advantage in manpower, Harry Heth was unable to advance quickly in any meaningful way. Colonel Birkett D. Fry, one of Archer's regimental commanders, understated the stubborn resistance displayed by Gamble's troopers atop Belmont Schoolhouse and Herr's ridges, but touched on something else quite important when he observed, "As Colonel of the 13th Alabama Infantry I was then attached to Archer's brigade, Heth's division. That brigade as you know opened the battle on the morning of the July 1, by driving in some small detachments of cavalry and attacking Genl. Reynolds' troops near Gettysburg, unaware of, or unheeding the vastly superior force in its front, the brigade rushed impetuously forward."[14]

Although Fry's recollection came 14 years after the fact, it reflected key issues that would plague Lee's commanders for three full days: insufficient reconnaissance, uncertain or conflicting information, and an overall lack of tactical coordination. It appears as though the only useful information gleaned from Pettigrew's foraging move the previous day was Major Young's assessment that the enemy troops looked to be professional and not Pennsylvania militia. One might suggest that Archer's and Brig. Gen. Joseph R. Davis's brigades were advancing over "strange ground with eyes shut," as Longstreet later scribed. It is not hard to understand why Archer and Davis exercised considerable caution during this stage of the advance.[15]

"The First Brigade held its own for more than two hours," John Buford later noted, "and had to be literally dragged back a few hundred yards to a position [Herr's Ridge] more secure and better sheltered. Tidball's battery, commanded by Lieutenant Calef, Second U.S. Artillery, fought extremely well." At one point the Rebels managed to position a dozen guns at relatively short range to achieve a concentric fire upon the battery. Calef held his own and worked his guns

13 Ibid.; Busey and Martin, *Regimental Strengths and Losses*, 16-207.

14 Birkett D. Fry to John Bachelder, Dec. 27, 1877, in David L. and Audrey J. Ladd, ed. *The Bachelder Papers*, 3 vols. (Dayton, OH, 1994), 1:517.

15 Joe Davis was Jefferson Davis's nephew.

deliberately and with steady judgment and skill, hammering the Southern guns with Union metal "with wonderful effect."[16]

What Colonel Fry failed to mention was the superior and overwhelming firepower that Calef's six rifled cannon provided in support of the so-called "small detachment" of cavalry that morning. Outgunned as he was, and while facing the aforementioned fire, Calef's pieces drove away individual Rebel guns, and in one instance forced an entire battery to retire.[17]

Fry witnessed this opening duel as Calef's gunners systematically disrupted the Confederate fire, which in turn allowed several Federal guns to train their tubes upon Archer's advancing and vulnerable infantry. Rather than recall Archer and Davis (who was advancing east north of the pike) to avoid bringing on a general engagement per Lee's orders, Heth ordered his two leading brigades to press ahead. Despite the raining shell fragments, the Southern troops eased back Buford's dismounted cavalry up and over Herr's Ridge and down toward Willoughby Run. "On nearing Gettysburg," Heth later reported, "it was evident that the enemy was in the vicinity of the town in some force. It may not be improper to remark at this time—9 o'clock on the morning of July 1—I was ignorant what force was at or near Gettysburg, and supposed it consisted of cavalry, most probably supported by a brigade or two of infantry."[18]

General Pettigrew reported on the evening of June 30 that a sizeable Union force was in Gettysburg. Whether home guard or tested veterans no one knew with certainty, but A. P. Hill—without sufficient reconnaissance—allowed Heth's entire division to move forward supported by two battalions of artillery. Heth's postwar suggestion that he knew a force was there, but did not know its composition, does not excuse the *manner* in which he advanced. The mistakes made by both Hill and Heth combined to trigger a sizeable combat the Confederate army was not ready to wage or exploit.

---

16 *OR* 27, pt. 1, 927.

17 Warren W. Hassler, *Crisis at the Crossroads: The First Day at Gettysburg* (Tuscaloosa, AL, 1970), 33. See also Samuel P. Bates, *Battle of Gettysburg* (Philadelphia, 1875), 56-58 and James K. P. Scott, *The Story of the Battles at Gettysburg* (Harrisburg, PA, 1927), 123, 133. Contrary to popular belief, it was not Calef who opened the artillery engagement on July 1 but Capt. Edward A. Marye's Fredericksburg Artillery, which deployed south of the pike on Belmont School House Ridge west of town. Marye opened with two 3-inch Ordnance Rifles while Union Lt. John W. Roder and Sgt. Joseph Newman wheeled their respective sections about at "reverse trot" atop McPherson's Ridge. The first two Confederate rounds passed harmlessly overhead while Calef was busy deploying his sections. Apparently three rounds passed over Roder's position before he could reply with the first Union shell. In all likelihood, the mounted men Roder targeted belonged to Marye's battery, and were not part of a Confederate cavalry command.

18 *OR* 27, pt. 2, 537.

Unfortunately for General Archer and his men, an unexpected impediment south of the Chambersburg Pike confronted the left elements of his brigade as it descended the eastern slope of Herr's Ridge. A working rock quarry cut into the western slope of McPherson's Ridge immediately east of Willoughby Run about 250 yards south of Cashtown (Chambersburg) Pike. This man-made obstacle with three horizontal sides confronted his left wing as Archer's line of battle approached the run. Archer had few alternatives to maneuver, for Roder's and Newman's combined four pieces were sweeping the ground between the Cashtown Pike and the quarry.[19]

For the first time at Gettysburg, a geographical impediment demanded a change of plans, and the consequences that followed for Archer and his men proved dreadful. With orders to advance, Archer had little choice but to press directly forward. Because of the quarry, however, his left wing veered (or obliqued) south-southeast. This, in turn, pressed his center as the battle line splashed across Willoughby Run in front and immediately south of the quarry. Archer's exposed right flank forded the creek several hundred yards farther south. From the quarry's top rim, Buford's troopers fired essentially unopposed into Archer's men. Farther south of the Herbst Woods, Colonel Gamble's dismounted troopers faced about on the military crest in support of Calef's third section. The advance and losses had already exhausted and weakened Archer's brigade by the time it began ascending the ridge toward Herbst Woods and the crest of McPherson's wooded ridge.[20]

By this time, General Reynolds was deploying his leading infantry elements to relieve Buford's hard-pressed troopers. "It was General Reynolds' intention to dispute the enemy's advance at this point," Maj. Gen. Abner Doubleday later reported, "falling back, however, in case of a serious attack, to ground already chosen at Emmitsburg."[21]

After breaking camp about 8:00 a.m., John Reynolds led his First Division toward Gettysburg and the distant thumping artillery fire. By the time Brig. Gen. James S. Wadsworth's forward elements approached the battleground it was closing in on 10:30 a.m. With a rush forward, Reynolds personally led Brig. Gen. Solomon Meredith's famed "Iron Brigade of the West" toward Herbst Woods. The reinforcements approached from the southeast. Meredith's men surprised Archer's Rebels as they struggled up the slope east of Willoughby Run. The Union volley cut through the Confederate ranks and a desperate battle ensued at point-blank range.

---

19 USGS MRC 39077G2. See also the John Bachelder map, *Battlefield of Gettysburg: Early July 1* (Washington, DC, 1876).

20 Ibid.

21 *OR* 27, pt. 1, 244.

Meredith's left pressed forward and outflanked Archer to the south, rolling up his line from right to left. The surprised and decimated Rebels collapsed and fell back down the slope toward Willoughby Run in abject chaos, vigorously followed by the jubilant enemy. The Iron Brigade captured scores of men including the disgusted and enervated James Archer—the first general officer taken as a prisoner in battle since General Lee assumed command of the Army of Northern Virginia.[22]

Joe Davis's command north of the Chambersburg Pike suffered a similar fate riddled with surprise and blood. Although the initial advance went relatively well, part of his brigade jumped into an unfinished railroad cut. Although it appeared to offer an outstanding defensive advantage, in fact the cut was too deep along much of its length to be effectively used. Many of the hundreds of Rebels jammed into it could not even see the approaching enemy, let along fire at them. A sharp battle south of the cut ensued, and when the 6th Wisconsin of the Iron Brigade reached the lip and fired into the milling Mississippians and Tar Heels, most threw down their weapons and surrendered while those who could ran out of either end in an effort to escape captivity. Heth's initial advance met a sharp and bloody repulse. North of town, General Ewell, who could hear the battle, received a message from A. P. Hill that Heth's division had run up against stiff resistance.

Although Lee could ill afford to lose such a capable veteran like Archer, Meade and the Union army fared much worse that morning. During the early minutes of the fighting, Reynolds dropped dead from his horse with a bullet to head. By 11:45 a.m., a lull fell over the fields west of town. Taking advantage of the brief respite, Buford, with help from Wadsworth's and General Cutler's infantry brigade, saw to it that the lines were reformed in anticipation of renewed Rebel assaults. More reinforcements arrived in the form of General Doubleday and the Second and Third Divisions of the First Corps. With Reynolds dead, Doubleday temporarily assumed overall command. He positioned the two fresh divisions a bit farther west on Oak Ridge.[23]

Arriving on the field shortly after 10:30 a.m. from Emmitsburg, Maj. Gen. Oliver O. Howard of the hard-marching Eleventh Corps quickly seized upon the importance of the heights south of Gettysburg. Couriers galloped back south down the Emmitsburg Road with orders for Brig. Gen. Francis C. Barlow to hurry along the First Division. The firing farther west was slowing down when Howard, who did not yet know of Reynolds' death, dispatched an aide to inform Reynolds that he was now on the field. Inside Gettysburg, the one-armed corps commander studied the battlefield from an enclosed observatory atop the Fahnestock Brothers store on

22 Lt. Col. John Collis, in *Bachelder Papers*, 1:140-41.

23 Ibid., 141-44. See also *Bachelder Maps, First Day*.

Baltimore Street. It was there he learned of Reynolds' fate, that Ewell was approaching from the north with his corps, and that Jubal Early was advancing toward Gettysburg from York.[24]

There is no record of Howard riding either west to Seminary Ridge or north of town for personal on-the-field observations. An experienced soldier, he knew good ground when he saw it. Howard returned to Cemetery Hill to establish headquarters and await Barlow's arrival. Like Buford and Reynolds before him, Howard appreciated that the heights south of town were critical. He also realized that his corps could be overwhelmed at any moment. His plan mirrored Reynolds', which was to hold the Rebels in check until help arrived.[25]

Having left Emmitsburg about 8:00 a.m., Barlow, commanding the First Division of the Eleventh Corps, received Howard's order to hurry along as he neared Marsh Creek via the Emmitsburg Road, the same route Reynolds and Doubleday had taken earlier that day with most of the First Corps. Unfortunately for Barlow, his column slowed to a crawl as it approached the creek and encountered the First Corps reserve trains. A nearly impassable, low-lying muddy road did not help matters. The column had to snake around stalled trains for much of the way and would not arrive below Cemetery Hill until nearly noon.[26]

Off to Barlow's east, Howard's couriers were also racing to reach Maj. Gen. Carl Schurz's Third Division as it marched north via the Taneytown Road, having detoured through Horner's Mill. Ordered to press on with haste, Schurz detached the 45th New York to march ahead and secure Cemetery Hill, where Maj. Thomas W. Osborn would join them with an artillery battery. Commanding the corps' artillery, the 30-year-old Osborn rode to the rear of Schurz's division and secured Capt. Hubert Dilger's Battery I, 1st Ohio Light Artillery. The German-born, professionally trained Captain Dilger was one of the best artillerymen in either army.[27]

When he reached the base of West Cemetery Hill, Osborn noted that the 45th New York had double-timed the entire distance, leaving many stragglers along the

---

24 OR 27, pt. 1, 696, 701-702. According to Tim Smith, Senior Licensed Battlefield Guide, "Gen. Howard was on top of that building when he learned that Gen. Reynolds was killed in the first day's fighting and that he had assumed Reynolds' command." *New 1863 Gettysburg Images Surface: The Center For Civil War Photography*, vol. 3, June 2005, www.civilwar photography.org/newsletters/118.

25 OR 27, pt. 1, 701.

26 Edwin B. Coddington, *The Gettysburg Campaign: A Study in Command* (New York, 1968), 278-80. See also OR 27, pt. 1, 701-703, 712, 715.

27 OR 27, pt. 1, 727, 754. After the war during Reconstruction, Osborn served as a Republican U.S. Senator representing Florida.

route. Dilger's six guns, angling to the northeast, ascended the gentle slope above the strategic intersection where the Taneytown Road met the Emmitsburg Road and Washington Street. Osborn learned of General Reynolds' death as he deployed his 12-pounder bronze Napoleons atop West Cemetery Hill between that intersection and the Baltimore Pike. Once deployed, all the pieces fronted to the northwest.[28]

While Osborn oversaw the placement of Dilger's artillery, General Schurz reported to Howard in Gettysburg, where he observed through his field glasses Doubleday's right flank atop Oak Ridge northwest of town. Howard ordered Schurz to take the First and Third Divisions through the town and gain possession of the eastern spur of the ridge that was then partly held by elements of the First Corps. Howard would hold Brig. Gen. Adolph Von Steinwehr's Second Division when it arrived, and the remaining artillery, on Cemetery and Culp's hills as a strategic reserve.[29]

Shortly thereafter, the forward elements of Barlow's division appeared. Passing through the intersection, Barlow continued up the Emmitsburg Road to Baltimore Street, which he followed north through town and out Carlisle Street before turning onto the Harrisburg Road. When Battery G, 4th U. S. appeared at the rear of the column, Major Osborn rode down from Cemetery Hill to meet the youthful Lt. Bayard Wilkeson, leaving Dilger's six pieces unlimbered on the military crest. Even though General Howard knew of Ewell's overpowering numbers approaching from the north, his decision to hold the heights south of town, instead of committing all of his effective troops northward, verifies his willingness to continue

---

28 Ibid., 747, 754, 756. See also Thomas W. Osborn, "Artillery at Gettysburg," *Philadelphia Weekly Times*, May 3, 1876.

29 Ibid., 727.

Looking east and southeast beyond Gettysburg toward the high ground. This postwar photo demonstrates the imposing terrain below and beyond the town. *LOC*

Reynolds' plan by holding the enemy in check while preparing a suitable defensive position immediately below town.[30]

Within moments of the major's departure, the lead elements of Schurz's Third Division appeared. Shortly after noon Schurz ordered Dilger's 1st Ohio Light and the 45th New York to rejoin the division as it double-timed through the intersection, having turned right toward Baltimore Street. Shortly after Dilger's departure, Lt. William Wheeler's 13th New York Light Artillery arrived on the scene and reported for duty atop the hill. Wheeler had raced forward via the Taneytown Road from his position in the rear of Von Steinwehr's division which was still several miles south of town.[31]

The defensive plan south of Gettysburg was well-conceived. Wheeler assumed Dilger's vacated position on top of Cemetery Hill, west of the Baltimore Pike, until the forward elements of Von Steinwehr's Second Division came into view. He was

30 Ibid.

31 Osborn, "Artillery at Gettysburg," *OR* 27, pt. 1, 752.

then ordered off the hill with instructions to report to Dilger north of town. By then, the latter was already engaged with several enemy batteries planted on top of and below Oak Hill. He had separated his command, with one two-gun section engaging north along the Carlisle Pike, and the other two sections battling enemy guns to the west.[32]

Captain Michael Wiedrich's Battery I, 1st New York Artillery rolled into position atop East Cemetery Hill northeast of the Evergreen Cemetery gatehouse, after ascending West Cemetery Hill with Col. Charles Coster's First Brigade of the Second Division. "On arriving at Gettysburg," Coster recounted, "General Steinwehr, the division commander, halted the brigade and formed it in line of battle, by battalions in mass, in rear of Cemetery Hill, the rest of the corps, except Wiedrich's battery, having passed through the town and engaged the enemy in the open fields on the farther side."[33]

Howard placed Col. Orland Smith's brigade, part of the Second Division, in line of battle fronting north, stretching from the Baltimore Pike through Dilger's and Wheeler's vacated positions to the Taneytown Road below. Captain Lewis Heckman's Battery K, 1st Ohio Light Artillery passed through Von Steinwehr's lines to the intersection below and parked along the northern base of Cemetery Hill. With the battle to the west once again heating up, and with the tempo of the fighting north of town increasing with each passing minute, Howard's preparations to hold the heights south of town would be both challenged and amended to meet the developing threat.[34]

Meanwhile, Confederate General Anderson's movement toward Cashtown was uneventful until he began hearing distant artillery. "Shortly before our arrival at Cashtown," he reported, "the sound of brisk cannonading near Gettysburg announced an engagement in our front. After waiting an hour at Cashtown, orders were received from General Hill to move forward to Gettysburg." Anderson's column stretched back through the pass for more than three miles, with one of his brigades separated behind his attached artillery battalion, two reserve artillery battalions, and a massive wagon train. Behind them trailed General Lee and his staff, accompanied by Longstreet and staff and Harrison the spy.[35]

Behind the command group, Ed Johnson's division fell in ahead of Longstreet's own infantry. As suggested, even with Hill's move to Gettysburg to

32 Wheeler unlimbered fronting north between Dilger's two commands.

33 Osborn, "Artillery at Gettysburg"; *New York Monuments Commission, Final Report on the Battlefield of Gettysburg*, in 2 vols. (Albany, NY, 1900), 1:14.

34 *OR* 27, pt. 1, 724. See also Howard to Bates, Sept. 14, 1875.

35 *OR* 27, pt. 2, 613.

see what lay in his front, Lee seems not to have expected a serious fight. He allowed Johnson to take to the road with not only his attached artillery battalion, but his entire supply train. "Instead of ordering his trains to the rear as Meade had done," explained historian Harry Pfanz, "Lee allowed them to move east of the mountains with their corps. Obviously he did not expect a battle that would limit his army's ability to maneuver on 1 July." Longstreet's leading division under General McLaws would not depart from Fayetteville until as late as 4:00 p.m.[36]

Anderson, who would play a decisive role in the attack of Cemetery Ridge on July 2, commanded five brigades, each from a different Southern state. Brigadier General William Mahone's Virginians led the way, followed closely by Brig. Gen. Ambrose R. Wright's Georgians. Brigadier General Carnot Posey's Mississippians and Brig. Gen. Cadmus M. Wilcox's brigade of Alabamians were next in line, followed by Maj. John Lane's artillery battalion, trailed by a mile-long wagon train. Colonel David Lang's small brigade of Floridians brought up the rear.[37]

Lee had chosen the Cashtown Gap to turn east because it was wide and the pike that ran through it was a good and well-maintained road. He surmised Hill and Longstreet could pass through with their attached artillery and trains with ease and with few, if any, issues. The gap cut miles off an already long march that otherwise would have had to continue north of South Mountain, as had Rodes and Johnson, toward Carlisle. Heading south around the mountain range was out of the question with enemy forces reported to be approaching. The incline of the Cashtown Gap Road approaching the summit from west to east was not too severe, so the men and animals could move easily up it. However, snarled traffic behind Anderson took its toll. Four of his brigades moved easily up and over the pass, but those caught behind the trains, including Lang's Floridians, frequently halted in stop-and-go traffic that did not wear well on nerves. Johnson's unplanned and untimely intervention between Hill and Longstreet compounded the issue.[38]

It was not until Lee passed the burned-out Caledonia Iron Works that he too picked up the sounds of distant artillery.[39] As he descended the widening eastern basin of the pass, the long deep-throated booming grew louder and more defined.

---

36 Harry Pfanz, *Gettysburg: The Second Day* (Chapel Hill, NC, 1987), 22; OR 27, pt. 2, 366.

37 OR 27, pt. 2, 622, 631. Brigadier General Edward Perry, the commander of the Florida Brigade, was suffering from typhoid fever, so command fell to its senior colonel, David Lang. To avoid confusion, "Lang's brigade" will be used throughout this narrative.

38 Andrew Brown, *Geology and the Gettysburg Campaign* (Harrisburg, PA, 1962).

39 When he came across the Caledonia Iron Works on June 26 and learned the owner was "Radical Republican" Congressman Thaddeus Stevens, Jubal Early ordered his cavalry to burn the complex. He spared only the homes of the workers and a blacksmith shop. Mingus, *Flames Beyond Gettysburg*, 103-104.

A significant engagement, rather than a fight with some trifling cavalry or local home guard troops, was underway. Lee, Longstreet, and their staffs spurred their horses eastward. In the meantime, Anderson had wisely ordered the wagon trains off the road to make way for Lang's Florida brigade. "On July 1," Lang later recorded, "while on the march from Fayetteville to Gettysburg, this brigade being the rear guard of Anderson's division, heavy firing was heard to the front, and I received orders from Major-General Anderson to pass ahead of the wagon train, and close up on General Wilcox's brigade."[40]

Lang caught up with some of Anderson's men just east of Cashtown, where they had moved into a field for a well-earned rest while the officers conferred. General Wright recalled, "In a few minutes after I halted, the report of artillery was heard in the direction of Gettysburg." Like Lee, Anderson and his men knew this was more than light skirmishing. While Anderson's men rested on either side of the pike, Lee and his chief of artillery, Brig. Gen. William N. Pendleton, accompanied by their staffs, arrived. When Anderson's men recognized or learned the identity of the mounted men, they rose, waved their hats, and cheered. Lee acknowledged them as he rode past, but he was clearly distracted and gravely concerned. After he passed, the men regarded each other uneasily. The cannon fire grew louder.[41]

Lee's appearance at Cashtown about noon may have been premature and unexpected. There are no records indicating that A. P. Hill was there, or that he had sent information back to Lee while the latter was en route. History suggests the ailing Hill was somewhere between Cashtown and Gettysburg in his ambulance, possibly following Pender's division. After learning of the thrashing of Archer and Davis, however, Hill had sent riders galloping back to General Anderson, whose division was at that time resting around Cashtown. Lee was also there when Hill's message arrived requesting the division continue on to Gettysburg.[42]

According to Anderson, Lee was visibly disturbed to learn of the situation. "Marse Robert" allegedly remarked, "I cannot think what become of Stuart; I ought to have heard from him long before now. He may have met with disaster, but, I hope not. In the absence of reports from him," continued Lee, "I am in ignorance as to what we have in front of us here. It may be the whole Federal army, or it may be only a detachment. If the whole federal force we must fight a battle here; if we do

40 *OR* 27, pt. 2, 631.

41 Ibid., 622, 661; Thomas Mann Randolph Talcott, letter dated Richmond, Va., March 7, 1910, *SHSP*, vol. 37; Larry Tagg, *The Generals of Gettysburg: The Leaders of the Greatest Battle* (New York, 2003), 306-307.

42 Arthur J. L. Fremantle, *Three Months in the Southern States: April-June 1863* (New York, 1864), 255-56.

not gain a victory, those defiles and gorges through which we passed this morning will shelter us from disaster." Lee's supposed statement to Anderson suggests that even before he knew what Hill was facing, his mind was made up that if in fact those opposing Hill belonged to the Army of the Potomac, he was going to fight a battle.[43]

Prior to the arrival that morning of Anderson's division and Lee at Cashtown, Pender's division had passed through the village about 9:00 a.m. after breaking camp an hour earlier. As Colonel Perrin later reported, "About 8 o'clock on the morning of July 1, I received orders to get under arms, and the brigade . . . commenced the march on the turnpike leading to Gettysburg, at the head of the division, just in the rear of the division of Major-General Heth." The rural crossroad community quickly transformed into a huge military park all the way to Caledonia, with trains from both divisions scattered across open fields on either side of the macadamized pike. Fortunately on this morning, General Hill had ordered both Heth's and Pender's trains to stay off the road for easier and faster marching.[44]

Perrin's subsequent arrival west of Gettysburg roughly coincided with General Archer's and General Davis's bloody repulse about 11:00 a.m. Instead of pressing his attack immediately forward, however, Heth ordered up his remaining two brigades while Pender formed his division into line of battle in support. In the meantime, the artillery duel continued unabated through the noon hour and dragged on past 1:00 p.m., when it finally began diminishing until it fell away into a fitful exchange. By this time the forward elements of Ewell's Second Corps were approaching the field of battle from north of Gettysburg, some of it taking possession of Oak Hill.[45]

Although Hill failed to interact with Lee in the early morning, the message he sent to Ewell concerning "finding out was in his front" the night before reached Ewell between 8:00 and 9:00 a.m., after Rodes had started his morning march toward Cashtown. "The next morning," Ewell later recalled, "I moved with Rodes' division toward Cashtown, ordering Early to follow to Hunterstown. Before reaching Middletown, I received notice from General Hill that he was advancing upon Gettysburg, and turned the head of Rodes' column toward that place, by the Middletown road. I notified the general commanding of my movement, and was informed by him that, in case we found the enemy's force very large, he did not

---

43 James Longstreet, *Annals of the War: Leading Participants North and South* (Philadelphia, 1879), 419-21.

44 OR 27, pt. 2, 656, 661, 664-65.

45 *Bachelder Maps, First Day.*

want to bring on a general engagement." Ewell added, almost as an afterthought, "By the time this message reached me, General A. P. Hill had already been warmly engaged with a large body of the enemy in his front, and Carter's artillery battalion, of Rodes' division, had opened with fine effect on the flank of the same body, which was preparing to attack me."[46]

The timing of Ewell's remarks, however, does not coincide with the chronology of events on July 1. If Hill's message had reached Ewell after Lt. Col. Thomas H. Carter's artillery battalion opened from Oak Hill, the time would have been between 12:30 and 1:00 p.m., not sometime between 8:00 and 9:00 a.m. as Ewell later reported.[47]

It appears that Carter had not been informed that the commanding general did not wish "to bring on a general engagement" if opposing forces appeared superior in numbers. Once again, without proper reconnaissance Ewell sent a detachment forward, just as Hill had done on June 30 and again on the morning of July 1 (or as Longstreet suggested, "as a man might walk over strange ground with his eyes shut"). Rodes, whose men took up positions on and behind Oak Hill, later wrote, "When within 4 miles of town, to my surprise, the presence of enemy there in force was announced by the sound of a sharp cannonade." Ewell finished with, "It was too late to avoid an engagement without abandoning the position taken up, and I determined to push the attack vigorously."[48]

When General Lee left Cashtown, he must have known he was riding toward a situation that, if played correctly, might offer the chance to secure yet another major victory. He had three divisions moving in unison toward Gettysburg in a potential envelopment from the west, north, and east-northeast. The possibilities were not unlike those at Chancellorsville. What bothered Lee, however, was not his own concentrating forces, but the identity and strength of the enemy troops Heth had encountered. The artillery firing Lee first heard while still west of Cashtown now told him, as he approached Belmont School Ridge, that the Federal forces were in significant number, just as Rodes had suggested as he approached from the north.[49]

Carter's unexpected arrival and artillery barrage from the north atop Oak Hill surprised the Union forces deployed along Oak Ridge and those then deploying in the verdant fields north of town. His opening north of the salient separating the

---

46 OR 27, pt. 2, 444. See also Coddington, *The Gettysburg Campaign*, 281.

47 OR 27, pt. 2, 552.

48 Ibid. See also Longstreet, *From Manassas to Appomattox*, 330-31.

49 Fremantle, *Three Months in the Southern States*, 255. See also *Bachelder Maps, Second Day*; OR 27, pt. 2, 444, 552.

Brig. Gen. William N. Pendleton,
Chief of Artillery,
Army of Northern Virginia
NA

wings of the Union First and Eleventh corps served to confirm Buford's repeated earlier warnings to Howard about Rebels approaching from the north. Within a few moments of Carter's opening rounds, the entire Union artillery then on line responded. Off to the southwest, A. P. Hill's artillerists opened to counter this fire. This firing was the bombardment clearly heard by both Lee and Rodes.

While en route to Cashtown, General Pendleton, who was both the army's chief of artillery and Lee's personal friend, rode with the army commander. Lee expressed concern about the roaring artillery coming from the direction of Gettysburg. "After a brief pause near Cashtown, to see how it would prove," Pendleton wrote, "the commanding general, finding the cannonade to continue and increase, moved rapidly forward. I did the same, and at his request rode near him for instructions." Pendleton did not recount Lee's instructions, but certainly Lee wanted information about the enemy force, its size, the terrain, the approaches, and potential fields of fire. More importantly, he wanted to know who he was facing. As the two generals approached Belmont Schoolhouse Ridge, neither had a clear idea of what lay beyond the gathering smoke billowing up from beyond the next rise.[50]

By the time Lee and Pendleton dismounted west of and below the crest of Herr's Ridge, Heth's and Pender's infantry were engaged on either side of the Cashtown Pike along the length of Willoughby Run. To the northeast, Rodes' infantry had appeared and were battling along Rock Creek from the Harrisburg Road west to Oak Hill. "Arriving near the crest of an eminence more than a mile west of town," Pendleton reported, "dismounting and leaving horses under cover, on foot we took position overlooking the field." It did not take Lee long to seize the

---

50 OR 27, pt. 2, 348. See also *Bachelder Maps, Second Day.*

Gen. Henry J. Hunt,
Chief of Artillery,
Army of the Potomac
LOC

opportunity once he realized he was facing part of the enemy army. His superior position and numbers could be used to advantage, and he was not going to wait for Meade's entire Federal army to arrive.[51]

While Lee attended to the infantry and studied the situation, Pendleton turned his attention to his artillery. He would spend the next several hours riding up and down Herr's Ridge overseeing the batteries and their supporting elements, placing them as they arrived. However, his work was sloppy and haphazard. He never coordinated the guns or attempted to centralize their fire onto any given point. From the moment Marye's Fredericksburg Artillery had opened on Buford earlier that morning, Pendleton's artillerists were outgunned by their Union counterparts—even when the former possessed overwhelming numbers. Pendleton's failure along the Herr's Ridge line was just the beginning of the ineptitude he would demonstrate anew at Gettysburg.

Unfortunately for the Confederates, this was the first battle in which their gunners faced off against General Hunt's reorganized, retrained, and resupplied artillery corps. The Rebel artillerists were outgunned from the first shot. The Federal gunners' superb handling of their pieces against superior numbers on July 1 helped alleviate what could have been an even bigger victory for Lee. A closer look at what occurred along Herr's Ridge evidences an equally important story. Several batteries were brought on line and unlimbered within range of enemy guns, but never fired a round. Some parked west of the ridge still limbered. When the Union

---

51 Ibid. According to Pendleton, it was approaching 2:00 p.m. when Lee finally ordered the general advance.

line collapsed later that afternoon, Pendleton, accompanied by Lt. Col. John J. Garnett with three of his four batteries, crossed Willoughby Run to Seminary Ridge, where he placed them under the cover of the Lutheran Seminary instead of unlimbering in "Action Front" to continue the battle. The fourth battery was returned to Garnett after engaging and was likewise placed in sanctuary, or as Garnett later wrote, it "remained in park until the following morning, protected from the enemy's fire by a high [Cemetery] Hill."[52]

At the very height of the Union collapse, when Lee could have used Garnett's 15 guns (of which nine were rifled) to bombard Cemetery Hill, they instead remained silent. To make matters worse, the Confederate infantry then south of the Fairfield Road would have benefited from Garnett's support as they continued east toward Cemetery Hill under a terrible artillery fire from the new Union line assembling atop it. This Southern infantry was called back before being slaughtered in the center of the so-called "Broad Open Plain." The failure of Pendleton's artillery to help secure the full victory Lee wanted and needed on July 1 would continue through July 2 and July 3. Garnett's failure to provide firepower when needed was not entirely his fault; the problem began at the highest field command level.

Lee was about to learn the hard way that Henry Hunt had refined Union artillery command, logistics, and organization, into something approaching a fine art.[53]

---

52 Ibid., 642.

53 Five CSA artillery battalions (Carter, Jones, Garnett, McIntosh, Pegram) numbering 83 cannon failed to outgun the combined 58 Federal pieces.

Chapter Four

"Had we taken the Hill that evening it is hardly possible to say how
great our victory would have been."

— *Capt. John Gorman, C. S. A.*[1]

July 1: Union Collapse

1:00 p.m. on July 1, Major General Anderson's Confederate division was back on the dusty gravel Cashtown (Chambersburg) Pike heading east toward Gettysburg. The men marched to the reverberating sound of the distant gunfire, although without perhaps the intense urgency one might have expected. Generally speaking, that was Anderson's way of doing things.

The men pressed forward without much banter, their anxiety growing with each step. "The echoing sounds were well understood," confirmed the 10th Alabama's Bailey G. McClellan, part of Wilcox's brigade, "and that numbers of our boys would never return from the Pennsylvania soil back to the good Dominion state. No soldier was gifted with prophecy so as to say who would be the next of his company's comrades to miss roll call," continued McClellan, "[but] there was a secret inspiration of hope in each one's heart that 'I will escape the dangers so prevalent in battle.'" Despite their rising tension, Anderson's veterans believed they were ready for the fight each man knew was coming. "Let me remark," penned Capt. John Lewis of the 16th Mississippi of Posey's command, "all were perfectly certain of a great victory whenever we should meet the enemy, as no army that we ever had, nor would any which we may be able to get, have been able to stand up before us." Lewis's expression of invincibility ran not just within his company or even Anderson's division, but throughout the entire Army of Northern Virginia. What neither the young Mississippi captain nor anyone else marching with him that

---

1 John Gorman to his mother, letter of unknown date, from a newspaper clipping in the Gorman Family Collection, Box Three, North Carolina State Archives, Raleigh, N.C.

morning realized was that they were about to meet an army led by a new and more resolute general than Joe Hooker. They also did not know that they would avoid combat on this day, but play a major role in the army's center on the morrow.[2]

Following Lee and his staff down the Cashtown Pike, Anderson's men trod east-southeast, traversing at right angles a series of low ridges and valleys. As the column crested each rise, the men could see the billowing smoke ahead and hear ever more clearly the roar of the big guns. Once they dipped back into the swales between the parallel ridges, however, they could see nothing beyond the crest of the next rise and the sound of artillery became muffled and at times diminished altogether.[3]

Like many of his peers, Richard Heron Anderson was a career military officer. He graduated from West Point in the 1842 class that included James Longstreet and Lafayette McLaws. Anderson was a tall man—sturdy, bearded, 41 years old—from South Carolina, though hardly the sort of firebrand often associated with the Palmetto State. Longstreet staff officer Moxley Sorrel went so far as to call him "indolent." Anderson fought in the Mexican War and his service on the frontier included active duty in the Utah Territory during the Mormon Rebellion of 1858 and in "Bloody Kansas." When the Civil War opened, he resigned his commission to take command of the 1st South Carolina Infantry. The twice-wounded Anderson performed well at the head of a division that May at Chancellorsville. When Lee reorganized his army, he briefly considered him for command of the new Third Corps. Anderson's reputation for humility and a certain lack of assertiveness, however, convinced Lee to pass on him and choose instead the more aggressive Virginian, Ambrose "Little Powell" Hill.[4]

As Anderson's dusty column drew closer to Gettysburg, a steady stream of small arms fire opened. By 2:30 p.m., the incessant rattle had risen in intensity to a continuous roar. A courier from General Heth drew in his mount somewhere east of Belmont Schoolhouse Ridge to pass along new instructions to the division commander. "Upon approaching Gettysburg, I was directed to occupy the position in line of battle which had just been vacated by Pender's division," explained Anderson, "and to place a brigade and a battery of artillery a mile or more on the

2   Bailey G. McClellan, "Civil War History of Company D, 10th Alabama Regiment," in *Anniston (Al.) Star*, January 2-March 7, 1901, transcription in the vertical files of the Gettysburg National Military Park Library. Hereafter cited as GNMP; John Lewis to Mother, July 21, 1863, "The Battle of Gettysburg," in *Lee Republican*, July 19, 1924, GNMP.

3   Christian G. Samit, "Battle of Gettysburg: Day Two," in *America's Civil War*, August 29, 2006.

4   Tagg, *Generals of Gettysburg*, 306-307; Sorrel, *Recollections*, 128, 301.

right of the line, in a direction at a right angle with it and facing to the right [south]."[5]

For Anderson's men, thus far the battle was little more than a cacophony of distant sounds and pillars of smoke in the distance. All that changed once they crossed Belmont Schoolhouse Ridge, where the panorama of combat unfolded before their eyes. A steady stream of walking wounded, friend and foe alike, were descending the next ridge and heading toward them. A sluggish creek in the center of a swale between the William H. Wierman and David Whisler farms provided water for several hastily established field hospitals. Bisected by the pike, Whisler's home—occupied by a tenant named James Grimes—and farmyard overflowed with injured and dying men. Anderson's foot soldiers passed by largely in silence as litter bearers and ambulance drivers hauled their mangled loads past the advancing column for all to see. Surgeons and assistants tended to the casualties as best they could in these crude hospitals. Wagons and artillery parks likewise surrounded the hospitals in clusters in the open swale between Belmont Schoolhouse and Herr's ridges. Sullen Union prisoners milled about in groups just beyond the pike's stout rail fence, watched closely by Confederates with fixed bayonets.[6]

Anderson's men were seeing the detritus of the earlier fighting between Wadsworth's and Doubleday's Union divisions and A. P. Hill's other two Third Corps divisions, one under Henry Heth, who had opened the battle that morning, and the other under William Pender, whose division was about a mile ahead of Anderson attacking a makeshift final Yankee line atop Seminary Ridge.

Continuing through the shallow valley, Anderson and his staff rode to the crest of Herr's Ridge while guides diverted the column to the southeast toward Frederick Herr's country tavern, which had been turned into a field hospital. Gazing eastward, Anderson could see the distant spires of Gettysburg where the fighting still raged. A group of red brick buildings—the Lutheran Theological Seminary— loomed about a mile away atop a low (Seminary) ridge. Directly across a shallow brush-lined creek, less than 800 yards distant, smoke billowed from a burning barn belonging to John Herbst. It was about 4:00 p.m.

By this time Anderson's five brigades had topped the ridge above Willoughby Run, near where Pender's division had been prior to its advance earlier in the day. Everywhere Anderson's men looked the scene was frightful, but nowhere was it worse than on Herr's Ridge as it sloped down toward the creek, on ground

---

5   OR 27, pt. 2, 613.

6   *Bachelder Maps, First Day.* See also Gregory A. Coco, *A Vast Sea Of Misery: A History and Guide to the Union and Confederate Hospitals at Gettysburg July 1-November 20, 1863* (Gettysburg, PA, 1988), 135. Wierman was one of the founders of the Adams County Bank in 1864.

belonging to the John Herbst family. There, the dead and dying carpeted the earth where lines of men, sometimes no more than a handful of yards apart, had fired into one another. Carcasses of slain horses were scattered about the slope. The nauseous smell of death filled the air.[7]

*   *   *

Earlier in the afternoon, while Anderson was still approaching Belmont School Ridge from the west, two of Ewell's divisions had arrived north and northeast of Gettysburg. Lee had suggested to Ewell on June 30 that he send Robert Rodes' division to Cashtown via Gettysburg rather than risk it becoming entangled with Edward Johnson's slow-moving column to its front. Although this detour was longer, the main road south to Gettysburg from Papertown (now Mount Holly Springs) was in good shape and relatively free of military traffic. Rodes had camped for the night north of Heidlersburg (a mere 11 miles above Gettysburg) with Jubal Early's division three miles farther east after having marched southwest from York all that day. At dawn on July 1, neither Ewell, Rodes, nor Early were yet aware A. P. Hill had given Heth permission to march into Gettysburg. However, Early captured a Union cavalryman from the Army of the Potomac at East Berlin, Pennsylvania—a clear indication the enemy was operating in the vicinity.

Shortly after 10:00 a.m., Ewell urged Rodes forward and dispatched couriers to inform Early of a change in plans. Cashtown was no longer the destination; now it was Gettysburg. Rodes and Early reached the northern and northeastern outskirts of town, respectively, between 2:00 and 3:00 p.m. Ewell's divisions faced parts of Howard's Eleventh Corps. As noted earlier, Howard had arrived from the south, surveyed the region from Cemetery Hill, anchored that piece of high ground with Col. Orland Smith's infantry brigade and some artillery, and then sent forward the bulk of his 9,300-man corps north of town.

Howard deployed General Schurz's division northwest of Gettysburg toward the flank of Reynolds' First Corps while General Barlow's division moved north. Barlow had advanced to Rock Creek, well forward of Howard's intended position. His exposed position offered an inviting target for Jubal Early, who quickly seized the opportunity by forming his men into line of battle. He also allowed his division's chief of artillery, Lt. Col. H. P. Jones, the luxury of choosing his own artillery platform. Jones was doing that when Early's infantry started forward

---

7   Seward R. Osborne, ed., Theodore Gates, *Holding the Left at Gettysburg: The 20th New York State Militia on July 1, 1863* (Hightstown, NJ, 1990), 8-12. Companies G and K advanced across Willoughby Run to the Emanuel Harmon farm. Some of the casualties were a detachment from the 80th New York, which crossed west of the run and was cut off when Pender attacked.

without initial artillery support. Within a few minutes Jones' battalion opened upon an exposed battery Barlow had placed in harm's way. At roughly the same time Jones opened, Rodes' division atop Oak Hill attacked Schurz's division and Barlow's left, with his line overlapping Brig. Gen. John Robinson's First Corps division on Oak Ridge and along the Mummasburg Road. The surging waves of Confederates were initially thrown, but a renewed effort began rolling up the Federal flanks and exploiting the gap between the First and Eleventh corps. At the same time, Pender's division renewed its attacks from the west.[8]

At first, the Eleventh Corps' retreat was undertaken with some order and discipline. Pressed back toward town through undulating open fields, however, Howard's individual brigades began converging on three avenues that forced the retiring troops into one giant milling mass. Hundreds of others, however, turned to wage a stout, if relatively brief, defensive effort. In truth, Howard's stubborn retreat was draining both energy and cohesion from Ewell's two attacking divisions.[9]

South of the Chambersburg Pike beyond Doubleday's left, meanwhile, Pender's division outflanked Col. Chapman Biddle's Union brigade after a long and hard fight that included hand-to-hand combat. Doubleday's left wing did not have the town impeding its immediate retreat. The open fields west of Gettysburg made for a bit more orderly retreat once Seminary and Oak ridges were lost. The Broad Open Plain west and south of town became a right of way, with Washington Street the principle avenue for the shattered First Corps' withdrawal through Gettysburg.

Thousands of Union men jammed every avenue and alley in a frantic effort to gain Baltimore Street and Cemetery Hill. Many Federals surrendered or were captured in the chaos and ensuing melee. Although most made it, more than 2,500 men from both broken Union corps became prisoners. One good omen for Meade's retreating men was the fact that, once clear of town, they could see a Federal line atop Cemetery Hill replete with deployed artillery. Regimental and national colors studded the position. With few exceptions, everyone from both corps knew where to go. Getting there safely, however, was another matter.[10]

Fortunately for the routed Union troops, A. P. Hill's infantry pouring in from the west were just as disorganized and exhausted as Ewell's troops. The pursuing

---

8   William Calder to mother, July 8, 1863, Calder Family Papers, Southern Historical Society Collection, Louis R. Wilson Special Collections Library, Collection No. 00125, UNC; Captain M. Brown to John Bachelder, April 8, 1864, *Bachelder Papers*, 1:148-49. See also *OR* 27, pt. 2, 445, 552, 566-67, 579.

9   George Campbell Brown, "Military Reminiscences 1861-1863," in Campbell Brown-Ewell Papers, Box No. 2, Tennessee State Library Special Collections Department, Nashville.

10   *Bachelder Maps, Second Day*; Walter L. Owens to John Bachelder, August 6, 1866, *Bachelder Papers*, 1:268-69. See also *Cincinnati Daily Gazette*, July 8, 1863, and *OR* 27, pt. 1, 724.

Confederates lost most of whatever cohesion they had left once they entered Gettysburg. From brigade command down to individual companies, many became so entangled it took well into the early hours of July 2 to get fully reorganized. The need to collect and guard thousands of prisoners and care for the wounded of both sides only added to the confusion. Generals Howard, Doubleday, and Winfield Hancock, meanwhile, who upon Meade's orders now commanded all the Federal troops then on the field, took advantage of the chaos and precious time to solidify the heights south of town.[11]

This high ground was a series of low hills and ridges stretching from the outskirts of Gettysburg. The immediate concern was the imposing Cemetery Hill, which rose about 80 feet above the town center. A distinctive brick gatehouse framed the entrance to the town's public cemetery, which gave the high ground its name. The Baltimore Pike, Taneytown Road, and Emmitsburg Road all passed over or near the hill, so control of it was critical to protecting the supply lines and routes of reinforcements. The terrain south of the hill descended in a long low spine called Cemetery Ridge to the lower and occasionally marshy ground below Little Round Top. East of Cemetery Hill were larger and more imposing heights, the mostly wooded twin summits of Culp's Hill. Few Union troops would occupy the latter elevation on July 1.

*   *   *

Earlier, between 4:00 and 5:00 p.m. as Pender's division was storming Seminary Ridge, Dick Anderson's division was preparing for an assault most were certain would soon be ordered. The lead brigade under General Mahone filed south out of the Chambersburg Pike using Herr's Ridge Road, a small rural lane connecting the pike with the Fairfield Road a mile south of the tavern. Along the way they passed dead and wounded men—many from James Archer's overrun brigade—who had been carried to the tavern grounds or had simply fallen there during the earlier cannonading. Once off the pike, Mahone's Virginians faced left and advanced away from the road, clearing the right-of-way for the next brigade before forming a line of battle facing east. Each of Anderson's succeeding brigades passed by Mahone and also fronted east. The resulting line ran north to south

---

11 OR 27, pt. 2, 670-71. For an exceptional account of the Rebel attack from the west, see D. Scott Hartwig, "Never Have I Seen Such a Charge": Pender's Light Division at Gettysburg, July 1," Gettysburg Seminar Papers, National Park Service, on-line at http://www.nps.gov/history/history/online_books/gett/gettysburg_seminars/7/contents.htm. For a full account of the fighting on July 1, see Pfanz, Gettysburg: The First Day.

parallel to Herr's Ridge with the right flank resting near David Finnefrock's farm just north of the Fairfield Road.[12]

As Anderson's division deployed, the artillery attached to Heth's and Pender's divisions, which had been firing from the tree line on Herr's Ridge, limbered and galloped east to Seminary Ridge. Anderson's five brigades dressed ranks, anticipating the order that would send them forward into battle while Maj. John Lane's Sumter Artillery Battalion, attached to Anderson, parked in reserve west of and below the crest. "No event worthy of mention occurred during the march," remembered the young West Point-educated artillerist, "and it was made without loss on the part of the command, except a few horses broken down and left on the roadside." Cemetery Hill was in plain view and already known to be the Union strategic strongpoint. There was plenty of daylight left, but Lane's 17 artillery pieces remained limbered rather than moved forward and deployed with Anderson or sent elsewhere to be gainfully employed.[13]

Despite the horrific carnage, Anderson's veterans sensed that the army was on the verge of a great victory. The Yankees had been driven away with heavy losses. McPherson's Ridge had been cleared. Heth and Pender had recently taken Seminary Ridge. The friendly artillery that had galloped off when Anderson appeared was now redeploying along Seminary Ridge even before the small arms fire subsided. Hundreds of blue uniformed men were falling back in the fields around town and converging on the hill south of it, where brightly colored Union flags fluttered on the heights. Between 5:00 and 6:00 p.m., when more Federals were streaming out of and around town than Confederates were entering it, many in Anderson's division believed that one last all-out assault on the heights past the town would secure a decisive victory. No order to advance, however, arrived.

At some point soon after Seminary Ridge was secure, General Pendleton and Col. R. Lindsay Walker, the commander of A. P. Hill's artillery reserve, led Maj. David G. McIntosh's artillery battalion forward. Of the four batteries comprising the battalion, three were lightly engaged from positions north of the Chambersburg Pike, firing intermittently throughout the afternoon and early evening. Captain Marmaduke Johnson's Richmond battery, however, was detached and placed off Anderson's right flank near the Fairfield Road fronting southeast toward Buford's cavalry and Calef's Battery A, 2nd U.S. Artillery. Johnson soon had six guns with

---

12 *Bachelder Maps, Day One.* See also USGS MRC 39077G2, and Osborne, *Holding the Left,* 8-10.

13 OR 27, pt. 2, 635. Major John Lane was an anomaly in the Confederate army. He was born and raised in Indiana, but expressed strong states's rights views. His father, Joseph Lane, was John C. Breckinridge's running mate in the 1860 presidential election. John Lane resigned from West Point in February 1861 and joined the Confederate army.

him after receiving a brace (pair) of 3-inch Ordnance Rifles from Capt. W. B. Hurt's battery.[14]

Placed somewhere between the Finnefrock farm and the Fairfield Road, probably off Lang's right flank, Johnson's artillerists had a view similar to that of Anderson's right wing. Because the battle was less intense in this sector, Johnson's gunners were probably better equipped to see Cemetery Hill and the fields below than those positioned farther north. Johnson's six rifles not only had the range and an exquisite open field of fire to reach Cemetery Hill, but commanded the entire swale between Herr's Ridge and South Seminary Ridge, including all of the southern half of McPherson's Ridge from the burning Herbst barn south to the Edward Plank farm (the latter a half-mile south of the Fairfield Road just west of and above Willoughby Run).[15]

Marmaduke Johnson almost certainly took note of Calef's quintet of guns arrayed in battery in a small wheatfield just west of the Shultz Woods, with the Yankees' rightmost cannon just south of the Fairfield Road and the remaining pieces spread southward for 100 yards. Supported by both mounted and dismounted cavalry, the enemy battery, about 1,000 yards distant, was not enough to spur Johnson into a concerted counterbattery bombardment. Instead, both batteries fired slowly and deliberately as if to avoid bringing on a general engagement. Not even when a dismounted Federal skirmish line opened an enfilading fire on the right wing of Brig. Gen. James H. Lane's advancing North Carolinians did Johnson respond, opting instead to lob occasional rounds at Calef.[16]

The sudden enfilading of his lines forced Lane to detach 40 men to take care of this threat to his right flank. His advance slowed when Lieutenant Calef's guns sent shells screaming into his left wing. A mounted cavalry feint off his right compounded Lane's problems by forcing the brigadier to take additional defensive measures. This, however, did not stall the left, which kept up a cautious eastward march under the relatively uncontested fire from the Yankee guns. Finally, Lane's far left and Abner Perrin's far right, moving down and north of the Fairfield Road, respectively, flanked Calef's right piece, forcing the Union gunners to cease fire and retire, followed soon by Buford's supporting cavalry.[17]

---

14 Ibid., 674. See also Busey & Martin, *Regimental Strengths and Losses*, 192. The 36-year-old Johnson, a prewar attorney and politician from Richmond, was the uncle of fellow ANV artillerist Willie Pegram.

15 Ibid. See also *Bachelder Maps, Day One* and USGS MRC 39077G2.

16 Ibid.

17 Ibid., 660-61. See also *Bachelder Maps, Day One* and USGS MRC 39077G2.

Johnson's guns did not engage Buford or Calef to their full potential during any of Lane's assault on July 1, and Johnson did not contest Buford's withdrawal from Seminary Ridge. The Army of Northern Virginia frowned upon firing above friendly advancing lines in close support because Southern fixed ammunition was predictably unreliable. A good example of this defect took place earlier that day when a shell prematurely detonated and killed a crewman and several horses. To be fair to the captain, the sudden explosion likely took some of the fight out of his handlers, loaders, and gunners. Unfortunately, this was not unusual or uncommon. Inferior Confederate ordnance would plague General Lee's long-arm throughout the battle.[18]

Shortly after Seminary Ridge had been cleared, McIntosh's artillery battalion, followed by General Lane's infantry, moved onto McPherson's Ridge and picked its way southeast over the field. Continuing across the open plain, the battalion ascended Seminary Ridge between the Lutheran Seminary and Fairfield Road. With the order "Reverse, Trot," the teams hauling the guns swung around in a tight 180-degree turn that brought the guns to bear on distant Cemetery Hill. McIntosh unlimbered his pieces south of the road in a line extending south about a quarter of a mile. Major John Lane's battalion continued several hundred yards farther and deployed. His gun line extended from Shultz's woodlot some 300 yards south to the McMillan Woods. Two of Lane's batteries—those of Capt. H. T. Ross and Capt. John Wingfield—opened fire briefly with no recorded results. Captain George M. Patterson's battery formed behind them as the reserve.[19]

The cannonade that followed was both uncoordinated and ineffective. Anderson's unengaged brigades, meanwhile, watched the action from Herr's Ridge. Several men expressed surprise and frustration that they were not ordered to join in the day's fighting. They had quietly waited in line of battle for almost two hours west of Gettysburg, watching as smoke rose in the distance and the sounds of battle filled the air. "The query was in our minds," admitted the 8th Alabama's Lt. Col. Hilary A. Herbert. "Why are we not put in? And we answered ourselves by saying, if we were needed, 'Marse Bob' would have us there."[20]

---

18 Ibid, 675. See also Richard Rollins, "The Failure of Confederate Artillery at Gettysburg: Ordnance and Logistics," in *North & South*, vol. 3, no. 2, January 2000, 48-50.

19 *Bachelder Maps, First Day*. Herman Haupt built Oakridge, the house owned during the battle by Mrs. Schultz. He sold it in 1852. During the Gettysburg campaign he commanded the U. S. Military Railroad and was instrumental in repairing the substantial damage done to the railroad bridges by Jubal Early's cavalry from June 27-30 in York and Adams counties.

20 Hilary A. Herbert and Maurice S. Fortin, ed., "Col. Hilary A. Herbert's 'History of the Eighth Alabama Volunteer Regiment, C.S.A.'" in *The Alabama Historical Quarterly*, vol. 39, no. 1, 2, 3 and 4, 1977.

With the sun setting behind them beyond South Mountain, it became obvious no attack would come. Colonel Perrin later wrote that after carrying Seminary Ridge, General Pender told him he had sent for reinforcements, "But neither Anderson nor his Division could be found." Perrin complained that "the very batteries which we had driven off through Gettysburg were the first to fire a shot from their new position. . . . The first shell fired by them . . . was aimed at my Brigade."[21]

Unbeknownst to Perrin, General Lee had sent a note to Ewell suggesting that he take Cemetery Hill "if practicable." Ewell studied the terrain and enemy from his perspective and decided it was not "practicable" for a host of reasons and did not assault. One reason was that Ewell had earlier received information that a considerable enemy force was approaching from the east. This threat proved to be true. Brigadier General Alpheus S. Williams, in temporary command of the Union Twelfth Corps, was leading his division north using a rural lane connecting the Baltimore Pike with Hanover Road. Paralleling Rock Creek, the lane was screened from view by Wolf Hill and Benner's Hill, as well as connecting woods and a small rise. Williams' two brigades, some 3,700 men accompanied by ten Napoleons in two batteries, successfully gained Ewell's left flank. For the most part, this movement went undetected.[22]

According to Brig. Gen. Thomas H. Ruger, who was temporarily in charge of Williams' division, "The First Division leaving the [Baltimore] turnpike and bearing to the right [north] at a point about 2 miles [southeast] from Gettysburg, gained a position threatening the left flank of the enemy, who had compelled the First and Eleventh Corps to retire toward Gettysburg. The appearance of the division in this position at the time it occurred," added Ruger, "was apparently a timely diversion in favor of our forces, as the farther advance of the enemy ceased."[23]

Ruger commanded two brigades, Col. Archibald L. MacDougall's and his own now under Col. Silas Colgrove. They formed two lines of battle east of Benner's Run with unlimbered batteries fronting west on either side of the Hanover Road. Confederates watching from atop Benner's Hill hustled off when Union skirmishers began ascending the height about 6:00 p.m. Generals Williams and Ruger and their staffs followed, and from the crest surveyed the situation unfolding to the west.[24]

---

21 Abner Perrin to Governor Milledge L. Bonham, July 29, 1863, GNMP.

22 OR 27, pt. 1, 771, 773, 777; pt. 2, 349, 445.

23 Ibid., pt. 1, 777.

24 Bachelder Maps, First Day and USGS MRC 39077G2.

Fortunately for Ewell, General Slocum, commanding Meade's Right Wing, ordered Williams not to engage. After firing only a few rounds and taking no casualties in return, Ruger's two brigades reversed their ascent and descended the hill. It was dusk by the time Ewell's scouts returned to Benner's Hill. The threat to the flank remained, however, as an enemy regiment was still visible in the shadows along the lower heights east of Benner's Run. The question, however, was where the remaining 3,000 enemy infantry and reported artillery had gone.[25]

Division commander Jubal Early decided the threat needed addressing. "General [William] Smith's son, who was acting as his [Smith's] aide, came to me with a message from the general," Early later wrote, "stating that a large force of the enemy, consisting of infantry, artillery, and cavalry, was advancing on the York road, and that we were about to be flanked; and though I had no faith in this report, I thought proper to send General Gordon with his brigade to take charge of Smith's also, and to keep a lookout on the York [and Hanover] road, and stop any further alarm."[26]

The unexpected Federal appearance on Benner's Hill could not have been better timed for Union fortunes. Much of the day's battle had been choreographed by chance and luck, nearly all of it bad for Meade and the Army of the Potomac. In this instance, however, fortune smiled on Northern arms. Ewell's decision to order General Gordon east took pressure off Howard's reorganizing forces on Cemetery Hill. Soon thereafter, Ewell sent his last division under Edward Johnson to relieve Gordon. Johnson arrived late (between 7:30 and 8:00 p.m.) after getting stuck behind Anderson's column and trains. Although a bit footsore, his division was relatively fresh and had not suffered any losses that day.

Johnson's division was delayed, but Robert Rodes' division had suffered heavy losses and was severely disorganized and still mired mostly in town. If the hill was to be carried, Jubal Early's men would have to do it. His division, however, was divided and had also suffered sizeable losses. The brigades of Gordon and William "Extra Billy" Smith were off to the east protecting the flanks—a job normally tasked to cavalry—and the understrength brigades of Harry Hays and Isaac Avery were disorganized and too small to do much of lasting value without additional coordinated support. By 7:00 p.m., it would have been very difficult to successfully organize and attack south against the reinforced heights without help from Anderson's fresh division. Anderson, however, never received an order to advance that evening. Many Rebels expressed frustration at what they believed was a lost opportunity. "Had we taken the Hill that evening," claimed the 2nd North

25 *OR* 27, pt. 1, 771, 773; pt. 2, 445, 469.

26 Ibid., pt. 2, 469.

Carolina's Capt. John C. Gorman, who went on to make several exaggerated claims, "it is hardly possible to say, how great our victory would have been. Washington would have been evacuated, Baltimore would have been free, Maryland unfettered, the enemy discomforted, and our victorious banner flaunting defiantly, before the panic-stricken North." Such overconfidence and wishful thinking still abounded in the Confederate ranks in the early evening of July 1.[27]

Some in the ranks (as well as in the Southern press) cast the blame for not taking Cemetery Hill on Anderson's shoulders. "The addition of Anderson's force to that already engaged on our side would have enabled us to get possession of the mountain range upon which the subsequent battles were fought by the enemy," penned a reporter for the *Richmond Examiner*. "Had our army succeeded in getting possession of this range there can be no doubt that the whole Yankee army would have been destroyed." The delay in getting Anderson's division into the fight, he continued, "prevented Heth and Pender from taking possession of this important position, and permitted it to fall into the enemy's hands." He went on to claim that "this fatal blunder" had the "most disastrous consequences to our arms, [and that] all of the brigadier commanders in Anderson's division were anxious to advance, but the major general would not consent." He presumed Lee would have the whole matter investigated.[28]

*   *   *

While Ewell was evaluating his options for striking at Cemetery Hill, Anderson's frustrated infantry went into bivouac on Herr's Ridge. They remained confident of victory on the morrow. "We all knew that one day's work could not decide the contest between two such powerful armies," related the 9th Alabama's Edmund Patterson. "Our noble army, flushed with a long series of victories and feeling unlimited confidence in the ability of General Lee and the justice of the cause for which we were fighting, were eager for the fray." What many did not fully appreciate, however was that General Lee was operating blind without solid intelligence from his cavalry as to position of the Union army. His remark to Anderson earlier in the day, "I cannot think what has become of Stuart," not only demonstrated concern for Stuart's well-being, but for the loss of his services and the impact that had on his operations.[29]

---

27 John Gorman to his mother, North Carolina State Archives.

28 *London Evening Herald*, Aug. 13, 1863, citing the *Richmond Examiner*.

29 John G. Barrett, ed., *Yankee Rebel: The Civil War Journal of Edmund Dewitt* Patterson (Chapel Hill, NC, 1966), 114; Longstreet, *From Manassas to Appomattox*, 357.

About 6:00 p.m. Anderson sent an order to Cadmus Wilcox to march his brigade south down the Herr's Ridge Road, which broke off perpendicular to the Chambersburg Pike. By 7:00 p.m., about the same time Gordon's brigade was moving to cover the army's far left, Wilcox's brigade withdrew from Anderson's line to protect the right side of the Southern army. Its destination was about one mile southwest, to the right and rear of Anderson's east- by southeast-facing right flank, where a farm lane intersected the Fairfield Road above Marsh Creek.[30]

Dusk was settling in when Lee sought more information on the enemy's disposition. Calling for Pendleton, the army leader asked his artillery chief to ride south and reconnoiter the ground well of the army's right flank. Concerned about both flanks, and knowing the left was being attended to by Ewell, Lee asked Pendleton to see what lay beyond the distant (Shultz-McMillan-Spangler-Pitzer) woods. Lee was already looking beyond Cemetery Hill for other opportunities to attack the enemy gathering on the ridges and higher ground to the west.[31]

"When I overtook General Lee at 5 o'clock that afternoon," wrote Longstreet after the war, "he said, to my surprise, that he thought of attacking Meade upon the heights the next day." Longstreet suggested that this course was at variance with the campaign plan agreed upon before leaving Fredericksburg. According to the corps leader, Lee firmly replied, "If the enemy is there to-morrow, we must attack him." Taken aback, the corps commander retorted, "If he is there, it will be because he is anxious that we should attack him—a good reason in my judgment for not doing so." He urged Lee to move to the right and put the army between Meade and Washington. By threatening the Federal left and rear, Meade would be forced "to attack us in such position as we might select." Longstreet added, "it seemed to me that if, during our council at Fredericksburg, we had described the position in which we desired to get the two armies, we could not have expected to get the enemy in a better position for us than that he then occupied."[32]

The object of Pendleton's evening reconnaissance was not to look for easily defensible terrain, as Longstreet desired, but to find a route to outflank the Yankee-held higher ground. Pendleton, however, was an odd choice for the mission. He was not the experienced or dynamic leader needed to manage an artillery corps in the field, let alone conduct a daring reconnaissance of such importance. Lee's top artillerist graduated from West Point fifth in the Class of 1830, but resigned his commission three years later to pursue a career in higher education. In 1847, he gave up public teaching to become an Episcopal priest and educator. Ten years later

---

30 *OR* 27, pt. 2, 616.

31 Ibid., 318.

32 Longstreet, *SHSP*, vol. 5, 54-86.

he became rector of All Saints Church in Lexington, Virginia, a position he was still holding when the war broke out. Why Lee believed three years of military service that ended three decades earlier qualified Pendleton to command an extensive artillery corps—one that younger officers strove to make as progressive as the enemy's—or conduct a reliable field reconnaissance defies both logic and reason. Pendleton later reported sending "members of my staff to reconnoiter the woods on the right, and explore, as well as they might be able, a road observed along a ravine back of the woods."[33]

While staffers trotted south along Willoughby Run, Pendleton returned to McIntosh's and Capt. E. B. Brunson's newly formed line on Seminary Ridge. The Episcopal educator dismounted on the Fairfield Road and surveyed the terrain to the east through his field glasses. "The position [Cemetery Ridge] was within range of the hill beyond the town," he later reported, "to which the enemy was retreating, and where he was massing his batteries." Brigadier General Stephen Ramseur, who led a brigade in Rodes' division, had just occupied Gettysburg with his command. He met Pendleton on Seminary Ridge and requested that the batteries not open because they would draw a concentrated fire upon his men, some of whom were exposed. Pendleton agreed: "Unless as part of a combined assault, I at once saw it would be worse than useless to open fire there."[34]

The silent Rebel batteries provided yet another stroke of luck not only for Meade's generals on Cemetery Hill, but for John Buford, whose cavalry division was reforming along the lower western base of the high ground. Beginning at the three-way intersection where Washington and Taneytown streets intersect the Emmitsburg Road, this elongated base (actually a low ridge) stretched southward for nearly two miles. This ground—Cemetery Ridge—petered out with Little Round Top and Big Round Top towering over the lower terrain.[35]

*   *   *

Atop Cemetery Hill, meanwhile, Maj. Gen. Winfield Scott Hancock was now in command of the Union forces that were then on the field. When word reached Meade at Taneytown earlier that afternoon that John Reynolds was dead, the Union army leader directed Hancock to ride with speed to Gettysburg "and assume

---

33 Robert K. Krick, "A Stupid Old, Useless Fool," in *Civil War Times*, June 2008, 46l; OR 27, pt. 2, 349.

34 *OR 27*, pt. 2, 249. Brunson commanded Maj. William J. Pegram's reserve artillery battalion.

35 *Bachelder Maps, Day One* and USGS MRC 39077G2.

command of the First, Third, and Eleventh Corps in consequence of the death of Major General Reynolds."[36]

Tall, sturdy, blue-eyed, and tough, Hancock was easily recognized by his characteristic black slouch hat and, even more so, by his unmatched profanity. "The air was blue all around him," an admirer once wrote. He fought in the Mexican War, served on the frontier, and commanded the Presidio at Los Angeles, California. Hancock had officially assumed leadership of the Second Corps just a few days before Meade replaced Hooker, and was one of Meade's early favorites. Hancock was ferocious in combat and preferred to personally place his men into position, often accompanied by a flow of invectives as intimidating as any Rebel threat, rather than send adjutants to relay his orders. He was a native of nearby Norristown, Pennsylvania, and had an identical twin brother who worked as an attorney in Minnesota. The charismatic Hancock, an 1844 West Point graduate, was well-known throughout both armies and had many close friends fighting for the Confederacy.

After receiving Meade's orders, Hancock left Taneytown and headed north, leaving his corps in the capable hands of the Second Division commander, Brig. Gen. John Gibbon. He reached the battlefield at 3:00 p.m. Despite the fact that General Howard was his senior, it was Hancock who commanded at Cemetery Hill that afternoon—a tribute both to his leadership abilities and to Meade's intervention at a time of high drama and crisis. Hancock's arrival helped calm the demoralized men. He immediately worked to stabilize the position and build on Howard's good work there. The high ground dominated the surrounding terrain. Hancock, Howard, and Doubleday reformed battle lines and deployed artillery to cover every avenue of approach. General Schurz, a German-born political general from Wisconsin and a better judge of men than he was a military tactician, would later write, "His [Hancock's] mere presence was a reinforcement, and everybody on the field felt stronger for his being there."[37]

One of Hancock's first orders redeployed Buford's two cavalry brigades from beneath the shadows of the hill one mile south toward the Millerstown-Emmitsburg Road intersection to cover the southern and western approaches. Hancock, who had a keen eye for ground, took note of the two small mountains west of the Taneytown Road on his ride north to Gettysburg and recognized that they, together with the low ridge north of them, had to be held. He moved immediately to secure the Round Tops, as he described in his report: "Brigadier-General [John W.] Geary's division, of the Twelfth Corps, arriving on the ground

---

36 OR 27, pt. 1, 367-68.

37 Carl Schurz, *The Reminiscences of Carl Schurz*, 3 vols. (New York, NY, 1908), 2:14.

Brig. Gen. John Gibbon, commander, 2nd Division, Second Corps. *LOC*

subsequently, and not being able to communicate with Major-General Slocum, I ordered the division to the high ground [South Cemetery Ridge] to the right of and rear of and near Round Top Mountain, commanding the Gettysburg and Emmitsburg Road, as well as commanding the Gettysburg and Taneytown Road to our rear."[38]

"We have now taken up a position in the cemetery, and cannot well be taken," Hancock wrote Meade at 5:25 p.m. "It is a position, however, easily turned. Slocum is now coming on the ground and is taking position to the right, which will protect the right. But we have, as yet, no troops on the left, the Third Corps not having yet reported; but I suppose that it is marching up. If so," continued Hancock, "its flank march will in a degree protect our left flank. In the meantime Gibbon had better march on so as to take position on our right or left, to our rear, as may be necessary, in some commanding position."[39]

Meade replied to Hancock about 6:00 p.m., copying Doubleday but not (for reasons that remain unclear) Oliver Howard: "If General Slocum is on the field, and I hope he is, of course he takes command," explained Meade. "Say to him I thought it prudent to leave a division of the Third Corps at Emmitsburg, to hold in check any force attempting to come through there." Howard was not pleased with Hancock's arrival or that he assumed command at the front. He was, however, a professional and did not make an issue of it at that time. Instead, Howard worked with Hancock to solidify the position that Reynolds and he (not Hancock) had

38 Ibid., pt. 1, 369. See also *Bachelder Maps, Day One* and USGS MRC 39077G2. These two low heights are known today as Big Round Top and Little Round Top. Hancock took note of them because they were the highest ground he passed.

39 Ibid., 366. General Geary's placement on the Union left was not accomplished without protest. Geary thought Howard was in command, and refused to deploy until Slocum ordered him to do so.

Maj. Gen. Winfield S. Hancock,
commander of the Second Corps.
LOC

chosen. Meade's 6:00 p.m. note excluding him, however, proved one brick too many to bear. He appealed to Army headquarters, "General Hancock's order, in writing to assume command reached here at 7. At that time, General Slocum being present, having just arrived at this point, I turned the command to him. . . . The above has mortified me and will disgrace me. Please inform me frankly if you disapprove of my conduct to-day, that I may know what to do."[40]

Slocum arrived sometime between 6:00 and 7:00 p.m. and, after consulting with Hancock and Howard, placed Williams' division on the right flank "some distance to the right and rear" of Wadsworth's shattered First Corps division survivors. Looking west through the waning light, Slocum observed the enemy battle lines drawn up in the shadows of the woods and along the ridge south of the seminary and west and northwest beyond the town. More Confederates filled the town almost due north with a large column [Johnson's division] moving eastward beyond it.[41]

The tenuous position on Cemetery Hill was now as secure as Howard, Doubleday, Hancock, and Slocum could make it with the largely exhausted troops at hand. With Slocum now in command and the capable Williams addressing the right flank issue, Hancock turned his attention south to Cemetery Ridge, the Round

40 Ibid., pt. 2, 696-97; pt. 3, 466, 468. Why Meade excluded Howard's name remains a mystery. The situation was somewhat defused at 9:30 p.m. when his chief of staff, Maj. Gen. Daniel A. Butterfield, sent a message to Maj. Gen. Daniel Sickles of the Third Corps that included, "General Hancock is not in command—General Howard commands." When Sickles arrived at the Evergreen Cemetery gatehouse shortly after 10:00 p.m., he reported to Slocum but without a doubt also spoke to Howard. It likewise appears that when Meade arrived, amends were made in the best interests of the current situation.

41 Ibid., pt. 2, 758-59; pt. 1, 366-69.

Tops, and Taneytown Road in their immediate rear. Although the Round Tops on the far left loomed above the Emmitsburg Road, they were too far east to control it or block passage along it. He knew there were not yet enough men and guns up and available to control that area. With Lee's army in possession of the ridges opposite him, Hancock also suspected (as had Howard) that any attack would probably come from that direction and thus across the open fields, and not so much from the south. He also had a vivid memory of Chancellorsville, where unexpected Rebel flank attacks had created so much consternation. Hancock's next chore was to ensure that General Geary's division had sufficient support, and that the two small mountains anchoring the Union left could not be flanked during the night.

Although the Emmitsburg Road weighed heavily on Hancock's mind, so did the Taneytown Road. If the former could not be secured, it became all the more critical to retain control of the latter. This Taneytown artery not only connected the elements of the Army of the Potomac already on the field with those still on the march, but with their supplies, artillery, reserves, and hospital wagons. With both the Second and Third Corps approaching from the south, it became even more vital. In Hancock's view, the distinct possibility of portions of Lee's army executing a flanking move around Big Round Top, like the one Stonewall Jackson had undertaken at Chancellorsville two months earlier, was reason enough to cover and hold the Taneytown Road from east of the Round Tops.

*   *   *

And so the primary goal of the Army of the Potomac expanded to not only holding Cemetery Hill, Culp's Hill, and the Baltimore Pike, but now also Cemetery Ridge and the Round Tops to control the Taneytown Road angling behind them. All of this, in turn made the Emmitsburg Road the dividing line between the armies, with the reconstituted Union line on Cemetery Ridge defending against any Rebel movement from the west. The Federal center was now located midway between Cemetery Hill and Big Round Top, near Jacob Hummelbaugh's well-worn farm lane.

On the morrow, Hancock's men in that vicinity would be sorely tested. So would Dick Anderson's.[42]

42 Ibid., pt. 1, 366-368, 405. See also Elmira Russell Hancock, *Reminiscences of Winfield Scott Hancock* (New York, 1887), 187-95; *Bachelder Maps, Day One* and USGS MRC 39077G2.

Chapter Five

"The ground southwest of the town was carefully examined by
me after the engagement on July 1st."

— *Brig. Gen. William N. Pendleton, C. S. A.*[1]

Evening, July 1: Lee Reconnoiters and Meade Makes a Stand

The evening sun was settling behind South Mountain and the shadows were lengthening when General Wilcox led his brigade of Anderson's division along a dirt road atop Herr's Ridge a couple of miles west of Gettysburg. While there is no detailed record of Wilcox's exact route, he likely marched his 1,700 Alabamians down Herr's Ridge Road as it angled west-southwest toward its intersection with the Fairfield Road, immediately east of Marsh Creek and Francis Bream's Black Horse Tavern. Wilcox's departure left a large gap in the right-center of Anderson's division, but there was no immediate enemy threat so no one overly worried about it. The right flank of the army was another matter. Because the main body of the Army of the Potomac was known to be coming up from the south, the primary threat would probably come from that direction (which partially explains General Lee's earlier request that General Pendleton reconnoiter in that direction).[2]

Wilcox was in a hurry. He was not merely moving troops to establish a bivouac, but seeking a tactical position that would allow him to picket and guard the army's dangerously exposed right and rear. Apparently, his scouts did not descend the steep incline of the ridge down to Marsh Creek or the bridge on the Fairfield Road. The gathering darkness and a screen of timber and underbrush prevented them

---

1 Jefferson Davis, *The Rise and Fall of the Confederate Government*, 2 vols. (New York, 1881), 2:441-42.

2 USGS MRC 39077G3.

This modern photo shows the third-growth timber and brush that concealed Bream's Black Horse Tavern from Wilcox's marching Alabama troops. *Sal Prezioso*

from even learning of the existence of Bream's country tavern directly below their route.[3]

Wilcox's column had been on the move most of the day since leaving Fayetteville early that morning. It was now dark, the men were traversing unfamiliar ground, and doing so without support. Any troops encountered would likely be hostile. After advancing a little more than a mile, the column halted and formed into line along the length of Butt's Schoolhouse Road 700 yards east of the intersection. This small rural lane was 400 yards long and connected with Herr's Ridge Road and the Fairfield Road well east of the crest. A belt of light woods separated it from both the intersection and creek below.[4]

While not ideal, Wilcox's position on this elevated ground seemed at least tenable. He anchored his left flank south of the Fairfield Road near the Samuel

---

3 Ibid. Wilcox did not mention anything concerning his position above or the creek, bridge, and tavern. The old bridge dated from 1809.

4 *Bachelder Maps, Day One* and USGS MRC 39077G3.

Brig. Gen. Cadmus M. Wilcox,
a brigade commander in
Richard Anderson's division.
LOC

Johns farm. The rest of the line extended up Butt's Schoolhouse Road some 300 yards northward to the Adam Butt farm. Concealed in Butt's woodlot, Wilcox's pickets spread out south and west on the high ground above Marsh Creek with his far left opposite the Fairfield Road. They were so close to the tavern that Francis Bream, one of Gettysburg's wealthiest merchants, could hear the pickets conversing.[5]

Cadmus Marcellus Wilcox was a seasoned soldier with a distinguished record in Lee's Virginia army. A nervous man with close-cropped hair and a full mustache, precise in the field but amiable in camp, he was known as "Old Billy Fixin'" because of his characteristic jumpiness. Born in 1824 in North Carolina but raised in Tennessee, he graduated from West Point in 1846 in a class that included such future notables as Thomas J. Jackson, George McClellan, and John Buford. He fought gallantly in the Mexican War and returned to West Point to teach military tactics. Wilcox authored a book entitled *Rifles and Rifle Practice* that became the U.S. Army's standard training manual before serving on the Western frontier. After Tennessee seceded, he resigned his commission and traveled to Richmond, where in July 1861 he became colonel of the 9th Alabama. Wilcox entered the Gettysburg campaign frustrated that he was still only a brigadier general. He had informed Lee that he intended to leave the army over the rank issue, which he perceived as a slight.[6]

Wilcox's brigade had begun its march north from the Fredericksburg region with 1,830 enlisted men, plus officers. It consisted of five infantry regiments—the 8th, 9th, 10th, 11th, and 14th Alabama—all formed in the summer of 1861. Back

---

5   OR 27, pt. 1, 366. The foragers may have been deserters or had left without permission, and so did not report the tavern's existence to Wilcox's headquarters.

6   Cadmus M. Wilcox, "Four Years With General Lee—A Review by C. M. Wilcox," *SHSP*, 6:71-85; Tagg, *Generals at Gettysburg*, 310-13. See also Gerard A. Patterson, *Rebels from West Point* (Mechanicsburg, PA, 1987), 51-52, and his *From Blue to Gray: The Life of Confederate General Cadmus M. Wilcox* (Mechanicsburg, PA, 2001), 26-27.

then, each individual regiment numbered about 1,200 men. However, losses, including killed, wounded, missing, those who had transferred, and others who deserted, cut regimental numbers in half. Reinforcements eventually replenished the ranks, which were then cut in half again by subsequent campaigning. By the time they reached Gettysburg, each regiment was a tried and tested veteran unit.[7]

The largest of Wilcox's regiments, by far, was the 8th Alabama under the capable command of Lt. Col. Hilary A. Herbert. The outfit was the first Alabama regiment to enlist "for the war," meaning that the men would stay for its duration, unlike regiments mustered in for fixed periods of time. The 29-year-old Herbert, a prewar attorney from Greenville, took 506 men north. The 9th Alabama was organized in July 1861 with Wilcox as its first colonel. It and the other three regiments were all smaller than the 8th, with each numbering from 325 to 335 men—a quarter of their original sizes—and included wounded men who had recovered enough to rejoin the ranks. They hailed from across the state, farmers and sharecroppers by and large, but some came from Montgomery and Auburn and smaller towns. The poor comprised most of the enlisted men, and the officers were largely men of wealth. That was true for most regiments in both armies, although as the war dragged on, death and incompetence weeded out many of the incompetent field officers. Debilitating disease, devastating casualties, and changes in command led to four of the five regiments being rebuilt, reorganized, and then brigaded under General Wilcox. He had led a mixed brigade of regiments from Alabama, Mississippi, and Virginia in the fall of 1861 in what was then Longstreet's division, before taking command of the all-Alabama brigade.[8]

The past September at Harpers Ferry, Wilcox's quartet of regiments followed Joe Kershaw's brigade through the Union line to participate in the capitulation and capture of the garrison. A few months later, the 14th Alabama joined the brigade and, during the last hours of Chancellorsville fought in the fierce and often overlooked combat at Salem Church. The command was cut up during its advance on the Union line along the Plank Road. The 14th Alabama had "seen the elephant" under trying and desperate conditions and was now part of a brigade of veterans.

While the Alabamians were marching southwest down Herr's Ridge Road, Brig. Gen. Edward L. Thomas's Georgia brigade of Pender's division was moving southeast beyond the Fairfield Road. Having been placed in reserve, Thomas's four regiments followed the division's battle line off Herr's Ridge, his right flank

---

7   8th, 9th, 10th, 11th, and 14th Alabama Muster Rolls, Alabama Department of Archives and History, Montgomery. See also Busey and Martin, *Regimental Strengths and Losses*, 185-86.

8   Ibid. Hilary Herbert would serve as the secretary of the Navy under President Grover Cleveland from 1893-97.

somewhere north of the Fairfield Road as it advanced toward McPherson's Ridge and then Seminary Ridge. When he stopped west of and below the Lutheran Seminary, Thomas later reported that his brigade remained there until near sunset, when he moved it "near Gettysburg, on the right of the town, in support of the artillery."[9]

The Georgians moved into the swale around Stevens' Run south of the Fairfield Road, east of and below David McMillan's farm orchard on South Seminary Ridge. Their advanced picket line secured a sunken farm lane 200 yards farther east opposite and above Stevens' Run. This dirt lane would play a critical role on July 2 and 3 because it was within easy rifle range of upper Cemetery Ridge and subject to artillery fire from Cemetery Hill and elsewhere. No one at senior command level informed Wilcox that a friendly unit would be picketing nearby, and the terrain did not allow for visual contact, especially at night, since some two miles as the crow flies separated Thomas's right from Wilcox's left.[10]

The terrain between Wilcox above Marsh Creek to the west and Thomas to the east, stretching south to Sachs' covered bridge beyond the Millerstown Road, would confound both armies and frustrate the plans of both commanders over the next 24 hours. Confederates would reconnoiter the ground at least three times within a 14-hour span, but their lines of march would still be difficult and slow. A Federal column would nearly come to grief on the night of July 1, and a veteran Union major general would defy Meade's orders on July 2 because of what he could not see beyond McMillan's, Spangler's, and Pitzer's woods to Thomas's immediate rear and right-rear.[11]

This patch of ground was barely two square miles and roughly rectangular, but understanding it is crucial to understanding so much of what follows. Most of the few roads and rural lanes that crossed it were unsuited for military movements because in many instances it was impossible to see beyond the next rise or through the woods they bisected. In other places, however, these roads and lanes were completely exposed. Though Lee would be assuming the offensive and Meade attempting to defend his long line, but commanders would have to move large bodies of men quickly, and at the same time conceal or detect those movements. Movement meant roads or open fields, because fences, stone walls, brooks, and standing water broke up formations and cost time and effort that neither

---

9   OR 27, pt. 2, 668. See also Busey & Martin, *Regimental Strengths and Losses*, 183.

10 USGS MRC 39077G3. Pitzer's farm should not be mistaken for Pitzer's schoolhouse, which was located nearly one mile south.

11 Ibid. In some period accounts, the locals spelled this Sauches Bridge after its construction in 1854.

commander could afford. As a result, parts of their armies would follow these roads and rural lanes, other parts would not, and neither man knew the ground.[12]

A body of woods running north-south for a distance of about one mile began at a dirt farm lane (today's West Confederate Avenue) leading from the Shultz farm along the Fairfield Road. The timber traversed the property lines of the Shultz, McMillan, Spangler, and Pitzer homesteads. This unbroken stand of old growth tracked along Seminary Ridge west of the crest, dropping several hundred yards to the opposite side of Willoughby Run. From the eastern bank of Willoughby Run, just south of the Meals farm below Fairfield Road, the woods angled southeast. The thick line of trees stretched through the extensive holdings of the Emanuel Pitzer family and ended along the banks of a sluggish creek known locally as Pitzer's Run. Buford's Union cavalrymen had held these woods for most of the morning until Dorsey Pender's far right flank forced them back. (For simplicity and clarity, we refer to the entire unbroken line of timber in this area as "Pitzer's Woods") Buford's left flank elements occupied the northernmost tract on the Shultz farm earlier in the day after being pressed back from another stand of timber on McPherson's Ridge 850 yards to the west. In the afternoon, Buford's right and Calef's supporting battery occupied these woods. Once south of Pitzer's Run, the wood line ascended East Seminary Ridge on farmland belonging to Samuel Pitzer, where it widened to several hundred yards. From the crest of Seminary Ridge, Pitzer's Woods continued south past the Samuel Pitzer farm, ending 500 yards farther south at the Millerstown Road just east of a country schoolhouse at the Blackhorse Tavern Road intersection.

North of Fairfield Road, the narrow Willoughby Run ravine widened into an open swale as the creek angled to the south-southwest away from the woods. Flowing just east of the George Culp farm, the watercourse continued southwest toward the John Edward Plank farm 1,000 yards downstream. About 100 yards south of the Plank farm, the creek turned southeast into Pitzer's Woods, passed under the Black Horse Tavern Road 200 yards farther downstream, and continued another 1,000 yards to the Millerstown Road, where it flowed south toward its confluence with Marsh Creek several miles distant.[13]

A well-traveled farm lane referred to locally as Willoughby Run Road intersected the Fairfield Road at the Meals family farm just west of the bridge. Following the western bank of the run, it connected the George Culp and John

---

12 Ibid.

13 Warren W. Hassler, Jr., *First Day at Gettysburg: Crisis at the Crossroads* (Gaithersburg, MD, 1998), 37; USGS MRC 39077G3. Pitzer's Woods extended some 3,200 yards. See also *Bachelder Maps, Day One.*

Approaching Pitzer's Woods from lower South Herr's Ridge above and west of Willoughby Run and the Edward Plank Farm. The Black Horse Tavern Road enters Pitzer's Woods on the left after descending the open slope from the right. *Sal Prezioso*

Plank farms before fording the run just north of Pitzer's Woods. From the eastern bank, the dirt lane continued south following the creek into the small wood, where it intersected the Black Horse Tavern Road near the Felix homestead, just opposite the bridge over which Black Horse Tavern Road spanned Willoughby Run. A sizeable open field varying in width from 400 to 600 yards separated Willoughby Run at the Plank farm from Pitzer's Woods on the crest of Seminary Ridge. This field paralleled the woods all the way south to the Samuel Pitzer farm and the Millerstown Road beyond. Like most open meadows in the area, it was crisscrossed by rail fences separating properties and bordered by stone walls.[14]

The old Black Horse Tavern Road (actually a crossroad, or shortcut) intersected the Fairfield Road east of Marsh Creek at the bridge directly south of Bream's country tavern. Angling northwest to southeast, it passed over the crest of Herr's Ridge, but not before ascending a prominent knob 200 yards due south of the William Plank farm. The road intersected a small lane linking William's property to his brother John's just north of the knob east of and below the crest along Willoughby Run. Once over this soon-to-be-famous knob, the Black Horse Tavern Road continued its descent, angling east by southeast toward Willoughby Run. Passing through open fields dotted with orchards and small woods, the road entered the tree line of the aforementioned woods south of the John Plank farm and crossed Willoughby Run via the old wooden bridge. Once east of the creek, the Black Horse Tavern Road veered south where it intersected the Willoughby Run Road near the Felix farm. Continuing south through the woods, it passed into open

14 *Bachelder Maps, Second Day.* The stone span was built in the 1880s.

fields west of Samuel Pitzer's farmyard and intersected the Millerstown Road at the schoolhouse. This was the complex ground over which the Rebels would operate.[15]

General Lee was concerned about his exposed right flank from the moment he arrived and scanned the ridges in that direction. According to General Pendleton, "Observing the course of events, the commanding general suggested whether positions on the right could not be found to enfilade the valley between our position and the town and the enemy's batteries next to the town [on Cemetery Hill]. My services were immediately tendered, and the endeavor made." Lee's trust in Pendleton is evident, but many issues surrounding the important reconnaissance (including his selection of Pendleton) remain shrouded in no little mystery.

With many younger men available, many better suited to conduct such a reconnaissance, Lee settled on Pendleton, his chief of artillery, friend of three decades, member of his class at West Point, and the Episcopalian minister of his vestry. With his graying hair and beard Pendleton resembled Lee, at least at first glance, though he was shorter than the army leader and not quite as sturdy. He also suffered from recurring bouts of depression, but no lack of cheer affected his devotion to the commanding general.[16]

At best Pendleton was little more than a figurehead, and the February 1863 reorganization of the Army of Northern Virginia's artillery was something of a substantive demotion for him. It was Pendleton who proposed the reorganization to Lee with the support of, among others, artillery battalion commander Colonel Alexander. When the dust settled, the pious preacher, nicknamed "Parson" Pendleton, remained Lee's chief of artillery. His order from Lee to reconnoiter south was comparable to Meade's order to General Hunt, Pendleton's Army of the Potomac counterpart, to reconnoiter Pipe Creek. Hunt, however, had ample time to perform his task and was competent in every regard; Pendleton was militarily incompetent and in the midst of a battle, to boot.[17]

Had Lee's favorite engineer, Colonel Alexander, been on hand, perhaps he would have tapped him for the task, but Alexander was still west of Cashtown bringing up his reserve artillery battalion. He would not reach the field until after midnight. Lee could have selected Capt. Samuel R. Johnston, an experienced civil engineer and officer assigned to his staff. Johnston was already well known for his

15 Ibid. The old Fairfield Road east of Marsh Creek can be seen to the north of and above the present day cut-out and should not be confused with the modern highway.

16 OR pt. 2, 349; Tagg, *Generals at Gettysburg*, 371-73; Robert K. Krick, "A Stupid Old, Useless Fool," in *Civil War Times*, vol. 46, June 2008.

17 Coddington, *The Gettysburg Campaign*, 384; OR pt. 2, 614-18; Alexander, *Fighting for the Confederacy*, 230.

extensive reconnoitering service and for a keen eye and common sense, at least according to his own postwar recollections. Lee found Johnston an expert and effective subordinate, but for reasons that remain unexplained, put his trust instead in Pendleton.[18]

Pendleton, in turn, assigned this critically important mission to several younger aides, including perhaps Captain Johnston. We do not know where General Pendleton initially briefed the small scouting party before leaving. He probably corralled these men somewhere near the Lutheran Seminary on Seminary Ridge and led them southward. We know Pendleton personally rode at least as far south as the David McMillan farm because he encountered several artillery battalions unlimbering while en route. He personally helped Capt. Victor Maurin, commanding the Donaldson (Louisiana) Artillery of Garnett's battalion, place several batteries of guns south of the McMillan house. In all probability, Pendleton directed the soldiers selected for the patrol to begin their assignment from near that point.[19]

While Pendleton assisted Maurin, his reconnaissance party probably rode down South Seminary Ridge, making sure to keep on the west side of the belt of woods and below its crest to remain unseen. Common sense dictates the most likely route thereafter was south down Pitzer's Run to its confluence with Willoughby Run, about 400 yards north of the Samuel Pitzer farm. No one in the scouting party could see beyond the distant Spangler's Woods, and no one knew that an opening existed between that Spangler's Woods and East Pitzer's Woods. In the waning twilight, the timber looked like nothing more than one single forest. The Plank farm and Willoughby Run, however, were quite visible to the southwest, as was the old Willoughby Run Road where it crossed the stream. Once inside the northern edge of Pitzer's Woods, the Rebel officers happened upon a wooden bridge over the run where the Willoughby Run Road intersected the Black Horse Tavern Road at the Felix homestead.[20]

Keeping to the left, the patrol entered and continued down Black Horse Tavern Road. Heading due south several hundred yards, the riders splashed across Pitzer's Run, at its confluence with Willoughby Run. The riders continued 400 yards and passed the Samuel Pitzer farm on their left, with his large home and barn situated in the middle of an expansive field surrounded by thin woods. After

18 *OR* pt. 2, 349; David Powell, "A Reconnaissance Gone Awry: Capt. Samuel R. Johnston's Fateful Trip to Little Round Top," *Gettysburg Magazine* (July 2000), Issue 23, 88-99.

19 Ibid. The discussion that follows is quite detailed, but to date no one has tracked or described this route, which would play a very important role in the upcoming battle.

20 *Bachelder Maps, Day One* and USGS MRC 39077G3.

another quarter of a mile, the party came upon the Pitzer schoolhouse on their right, tucked between the road and Willoughby Run. Thirty yards distant was a three-way intersection as the run continued southerly off to their right. One leg of the junction was the Millerstown Road, an extension of the Fairfield Crossroad cutoff. To the east was a gentle rise with the Millerstown Road angling to the northeast across Warfield Ridge. They also took note of J. Flaharty's farm, his dirt trace forming the third leg of the Y-intersection. At least one of the scouts rode east to and observed the trace to the south of the farm followed a narrow belt of woods angling southeast toward Biesecker's Woods. Looking due south from the Y-intersection, the Millerstown Road curved to the southwest toward Willoughby Run.[21]

After traveling an additional quarter-mile, the men reached another wooden bridge where the Old Fairfield Crossroad (or Millerstown Road) crossed Willoughby Run as it angled southwest toward Marsh Creek and Sachs Bridge. Here the patrol turned east and headed toward the crest of South Seminary Ridge. The riders reached it somewhere south of the Samuel Pitzer farm, possibly cresting it on the Millerstown Road. Although by this time it was dark, they could still make out high ground and woods across the open field directly to their front. Beyond that was still higher ground and the shadowy top of a rugged mountain. The belt of woods on either side of the Millerstown Road that fell away to the east offered cover that could conceal troop movements in the Willoughby Run depression to their immediate rear.[22]

It appears that at some point the scouting party broke into two groups—one riding farther south to see what lay in that direction, and the other back toward the field of battle. The former continued down the Millerstown Road where it came upon yet another rural lane at the wooden bridge where the former road passed over Willoughby Run. Referred to today as Red Rock Road, this southerly narrow lane paralleled the eastern bank of Willoughby Run. More importantly, two intersecting farm lanes (within half a mile of the Millerstown Road) ascended Warfield Ridge. One could easily move troops unseen between this newly found narrow road and the two farm lanes up the ridges on either side of the Millerstown Road. At some point, one or more members of the scouting team scaled Warfield Ridge and spotted the darkened shadow of a small mountain looming beyond the wooded crest.[23]

21 Not to be confused with today's avenues. See map entitled "Probable Routes."

22 Pitzer's and Biesecker's woods.

23 USGS MRC 39077G3. Present day Red Rock Road.

This modern view shows the narrow rural trace angling up East Warfield Ridge through Biesecker's Woods, giving a good idea of the nature of these rural routes. *Sal Prezioso*

The latter or second group, meanwhile, rode back toward army headquarters and found General Pendleton somewhere near the Fairfield Road deep in conference with Colonel Walker, the commander of A. P. Hill's Third Corps artillery reserve. "Having further examined this ridge and communicated with Colonel Walker, chief of artillery Third Corps," General Pendleton would soon report to General Lee, "I returned across the battlefield, and sent to inform the commanding general of the state of facts, especially of the [Willoughby Run] road to the right, believed to be important toward a flank movement against the enemy in his new position."[24]

The riders reported that a large force could remain hidden from view if it used the Willoughby Run ravine. Because darkness curtailed further scouting, there was no way to know with any reasonable certainty what lay south of Millerstown Road. "The ground southwest of the town was carefully examined by me after the engagement on July 1st," Pendleton later added. "Being found much less difficult

24 *OR* 27, pt. 2, 349.

than the steep ascent fronting the troops already up, the practicable character was reported to our commanding general."[25]

Pendleton did not elaborate on the narrowness of the Willoughby Run Road or the bottomland around the meandering creek. His suggestion that he carefully examined it is at best questionable, especially since he did not accompany the scouting party to Millerstown Road. Had the party followed the Millerstown Road south, on the west side of Willoughby Run, it would have found Sachs Bridge at Marsh Creek not three-quarters of a mile away. However, in this event, they likely would have missed discovering Red Rock Road and both Biesecker's and Douglas's farm lanes. Although the rise separating Marsh Creek from Willoughby Run is wide, it is lower than both Seminary and Warfield ridges, making it impossible to see both it and the bridge from beyond the ridges to the east. Had the patrol ventured west, it would have learned of another rural lane or shortcut connecting Sachs Bridge at Millerstown Road with Warfield Ridge by a shallow ford across Willoughby Run. This poorly maintained and seldom used shortcut was an extension of farmer Douglas's lane.[26] These riders would also have seen two well-worn roads paralleling Marsh Creek northward above either bank. Union troops would use these two avenues moving north in the dark toward the Cashtown Pike in an attempt to reach the gathering army just south and east of Gettysburg.

*   *   *

With his picket lines extended in a broad arc and his brigade finally deployed, Cadmus Wilcox awaited the battery of guns promised him by his division commander. Anderson kept his word, and Maj. John Lane selected Company B, Sumter Light Artillery under George Patterson, to report to the Alabama brigadier. "Early in the morning of July 2," Major Lane wrote, "in compliance with an order, I sent Captain Patterson's battery, consisting at that time of two Napoleon guns and four 12-pounder howitzers, with one 12-pounder howitzer of Captain Ross's battery, to report to Brigadier-General Wilcox."[27]

The precise time Patterson reported to Wilcox passed unrecorded, for the general only mentioned "being joined by a battery of artillery." According to Lane it was after midnight when he issued the orders to Patterson to move out. With a full moon to light the way, Patterson led his six pieces, plus a howitzer detached from

25 Davis, *Rise and Fall*, 2:441-42.

26 This rural crossroad can be accessed today via a path and a steel span bridge over Willoughby Run used for walking and biking.

27 OR 27, pt. 2, 635.

Ross's battery, out of Shultz's Woods. Because Lane's position on Seminary Ridge was just south of Fairfield Road and east of Willoughby Run, it is almost certain that Patterson would have returned to that road and then headed back across Willoughby Run.

Patterson likely ascended Herr's Ridge before reporting to Wilcox. If he had he attempted this route during daylight, he surely would have been detected during his approach on Butt's Schoolhouse Road because the Fairfield Road was clearly visible from the towering Round Tops. The battery, however, reported without mishap. The gun crews bivouacked somewhere north of the pike with their horses almost certainly left in their traces, the guns limbered and at the ready to move. If Patterson followed general practice, he would have divided the battery in two, one-half to support the right wing, and the remaining pieces deployed to protect the left wing. Exactly where Patterson placed his artillery, however, has also gone unrecorded.[28]

*   *   *

Meanwhile, well east of Seminary Ridge, Union soldiers from Maj. Gen. Daniel E. Sickles' Third Corps began arriving in the vicinity of Gettysburg. Captain A. Judson Clark, commanding Battery B, 1st New Jersey Light Artillery, ordered his column to the side of the Emmitsburg Road some time after 7:00 p.m. "About sundown we emerged from a belt of woods [Biesecker's] into clear fields; the road was on a ridge," recalled Clark. "Looking to the westward we saw the wooded slopes of Seminary Ridge, and the valley below. To the eastward was the wide diversified landscape stretched away to the foot of the Round Tops."[29]

Battery C led Brig. Gen. Hobart Ward's Second Brigade of the First Division northward from Emmitsburg. Ordered to halt in Sherfy's peach orchard while Ward's brigade closed up, Clark watched as troopers and Regular Army artillerymen cooked their evening meals around small campfires. Buford's dismounted cavalry lounged with studied calm, their horses picketed as far north as Clark could see. He continued: "On our front and left were our cavalry, who were protecting our left flank, engaged in getting their suppers. On the ridge to the

---

28 Captains William French, William Barry, and Henry J. Hunt, U.S.A., *Instruction for Field Artillery* (Philadelphia, PA, 1860), 40-44; James L. Speicher, *The Sumter Artillery: A Civil War History of the Eleventh Battalion Georgia Light Artillery* (Gretna, LA, 2009) 337-42.

29 Adoniram Clark to Michael Hanifen, in *History of Battery "B" First New Jersey Artillery* (Ottawa, IL, 1905), 135.

Maj. Gen. Daniel E. Sickles,
commander of the Third Corps.
LOC

northwest I could see the smoke of the enemy's camp fires. To the northeast, on Cemetery Ridge, we could see the bivouac fires of our army."[30]

The campfires Clark saw from the Emmitsburg Road were not from Wilcox's Confederate brigade but from Dorsey Pender's division, spread alongside and below McIntosh's and Lane's artillery line along Seminary Ridge. Anderson's campfires on Herr's Ridge could also be easily seen. Wilcox was aware of the proximity of the enemy, for he had witnessed them retiring and was informed of their general location on the heights south of town. He may have been ignorant of the Third Corps troops arriving on the southern end of the field. Because his picket line was well west of the crest of Seminary Ridge, his men could not see these newcomers. By 9:00 p.m., an odd circumstance was at hand. Union and Rebel soldiers on the southern end of the field could see campfires of opposing units farther north, but they could not see (and so were unaware of) one another.

*   *   *

Shortly after sunset, Winfield Scott Hancock left Cemetery Hill and rode south toward Taneytown and General Meade's headquarters. At some point during this 14-mile ride he encountered the vanguard of his Second Corps marching north. Hancock stopped to speak with his trusted subordinate, Brig. Gen. John Gibbon, and directed the division leader to bivouac the corps near "Round Top Mountain" in order to cover that exposed left flank. The army's flank on the Emmitsburg Road was temporarily secured by John Buford's cavalry and the better part of Brig. Gen. John Geary's infantry division of Slocum's Twelfth Corps. Hancock expected Sickles' Third Corps to soon move up to support them. His next concern was the

30 Ibid.

Taneytown Road, which had to be kept open; Gibbon would have to see to it. If the Confederates attempted a strike south of the Round Tops, Hancock wanted his Second Corps in position to meet it.

Aside from Hancock's own corps, by 8:30 p.m. portions of three other Union divisions accompanied by three batteries (plus a section of a fourth) were camped west of the Taneytown Road just two miles from Wilcox's bivouac on Herr's Ridge. Buford's cavalry division formed a strong picket line on the Emmitsburg Road at the Peach Orchard, with more troopers pushed west across the road. It appears that none of Wilcox's pickets or Buford's vedettes crossed paths. Portions of Geary's "White Star Division" stretched from Little Round Top northward along lower Cemetery Ridge, and to their immediate right camped David Birney's First Division of the Third Corps. By the time the sun disappeared behind South Mountain, some 7,500 Union cavalry, infantry, and artillerymen were in position west of Taneytown Road to help Hancock block any enemy effort to flank the "mountains on the left" during the night.[31]

John Geary was a grizzly of a man. He stood six-and-a-half-feet tall and weighed more than 200 pounds, a physique matched by a violent temper, piercing black eyes, and thick full beard. The 43-year-old Pennsylvania-born general had done and seen much. A former mayor of San Francisco and later the governor of Kansas, Geary had already been wounded nine times in this war and five times before that in Mexico. In command of the Second Division of the Twelfth Corps, he placed the majority of his men along Cemetery Ridge extending north from Little Round Top to meet an attack from the west. He also placed several regiments in reserve east of Little Round Top, facing south. With Knap's Battery E, 1st Independent Pennsylvania Light Artillery in support, his role was to hold the Taneytown Road and check any effort by the enemy to roll up the Union position with a flank attack from the south.

Geary was unaware as he arranged his lines that Hancock's Second Corps (under John Gibbon) had moved into open fields on either side of Taneytown Road just one mile farther south. The Second Corps line stretched along the crest of a low ridge running from the southern base of Big Round Top east across the Taneytown Road. When they arrived about 9:00 p.m. from Taneytown, Brig. Gen. John Caldwell and his First Division turned east, Gibbon's Second Division turned west, and Brig. Gen. Alexander Hays' Third Division deployed straddling the road. Hays ordered a battery of guns to unlimber training north. If Meade decided to

---

31 The brigades were aligned, from south to north: Candy and Greene from the Twelfth Corps, Ward and Humphreys from the Third Corps, and Devin and Gamble from Buford's First Cavalry Division. The batteries were the Second U.S., Battery A; Fifth U. S., Battery K; First New Jersey, Battery B; and First Rhode Island, Battery E.

withdraw his gather army, the Second Corps' job was to keep the back door open and block Confederate pursuit. By 10:00 p.m. on July 1, all three divisions were hard at work building earthen and wooden breastworks below the eastern slope of Big Round Top, silhouetted now in the clear moonlight.

An unending stream of citizens fleeing Gettysburg, Confederate prisoners under guard, and Union walking wounded flooded the Taneytown Road. Most of them shared tales of the battle and the day's sad ending. "At 3 [p.m.] o'clock," according to Cpl. James Stewart, "we were ordered up to the front, took position on the extreme left. A great many women and children passed us, being ordered out of town. Large numbers of wounded were lying on the road sides. Slept by our Guns all night, nothing transpired."[32]

Deployed in the shape of an elongated "L" with its base west of Taneytown Road, Gibbon's division fronted the forbidding rough ground south of and below Big Round Top. From the northern end of his division, the line took a right turn, running due east with Hays' division in column of brigades—the three brigades stacked behind each other—astride the Taneytown Road and Caldwell's division continuing the line eastward toward the Baltimore Pike where his pickets connected with men from Geary's Second Brigade under the command of Brig. Gen. Thomas S. Kane. "At 4 p.m. I passed over the Pennsylvania line," one of Caldwell's officers recounted. "There was heavy cannonading in my front. At nightfall, I received orders to bivouac and immediately after was ordered to march my regiment to the right on picket. I did so. My line of outposts covered the right flank of the [Caldwell's] First Division and connected with the picket line of the Twelfth Corps." Hancock's Second Corps moved about 14 miles on July 1, a comparatively easy march and shorter than Anderson's Rebel division across the way, and less trying than Brig. Gen. A. A. Humphreys' Federal division of Sickles' Third Corps experienced. By midnight, Hancock's line (including Capt. John Hazard's Second Corps batteries) was in place and its men resting under arms.[33]

*   *   *

While Meade, Hancock, and Hunt discussed their strategy in Taneytown, farther north in Gettysburg, General Lee formulated his plans. After digesting Pendleton's incomplete report on the evening's reconnaissance patrol, Lee issued a

---

32 Corporal James P. Stewart, Knap's Battery "E" Independent PA. Light Artillery, Letters, 1861-1863, James P. Brady Collection, Gettysburg, PA. See also James P. Brady, *Hurray for the Artillery! Knap's Independent Battery "E" Pennsylvania Light Artillery* (Gettysburg, PA, 1992), 252.

33 OR 27, pt. 1, 411.

directive (as noted earlier) instructing his artillery chief to continue scouting downstream at first light.

In his after-action report, Lee would explain that once he drove the enemy through town, the attack was not pressed due to failing light and uncertainty about the enemy's location and strength. By that time it was already impossible to withdraw back through the mountains, he continued, and so a battle "thus became, in a measure, unavoidable." Now that the fight was on, it must be won. In his headquarters near Mary Thompson's stone house on the Chambersburg Pike, Lee worked late into the early morning hours of July 2 planning his morning troop dispositions. He decided to find the Union left flank and, if possible, crush it.[34]

Though neither could know it, Hancock's actions to shore up the Union left and center checked Lee's plans. From Pender's division on the right flank to Edward Johnson's on the far left, Lee's fishhook-shaped exterior line extended at that time more than three miles. Now, he proposed to stretch it even farther south —just as Hancock thought he might and prepared to meet. "The remainder of Ewell's and Hill's corps having arrived, and two divisions of Longstreet's," explained Lee after the fact, "our preparations were made accordingly." Longstreet had two divisions on hand under Maj. Gens. Lafayette McLaws and John Bell Hood. His third division under Maj. Gen. George Pickett was still well to the rear with the trains.[35]

On the night of June 30, both McLaws and Hood bivouacked in and around Greenwood a short distance behind Johnson's division. Ordered to follow Johnson's column the next day, they moved at a snail's pace, stuck in a trail of dust behind not only Johnson but his wagons and the artillery reserve and ammunition trains of Hill's Third Corps. According to Longstreet, McLaws reached Marsh Creek at dusk. As he recounted, "Our march was greatly delayed on this day by Johnson's division, of the Second Corps, which came into the road at Shippensburg, and the long wagon trains that followed him. McLaws' division reached Marsh Creek, 4 miles from Gettysburg, a little after dark, and Hood's division got within the same distance of the town about 12 o'clock at night."[36]

Brigadier General Joseph B. Kershaw led a brigade, and after the campaign would write General McLaws' division report. "Anderson's and Johnson's divisions and General Ewell's wagon train occupied the road until 4 p.m., when we

34 Ibid., pt. 2, 309. In a small touch of irony, Radical Republican congressman Thaddeus Stevens owned the house that the widow Mary Thompson occupied on the Chambersburg Pike.

35 Ibid.

36 Ibid., pt. 2, 358.

marched to a point on the Gettysburg Road, some 2 miles from that place," explained Kershaw, "going into camp at 12 p.m." By the time these units arrived, Lee had already designated them to extend his line south. McLaws and Hood would be placed in the morning to attack north and northeast up the Emmitsburg Road, severing that avenue while driving a wedge into the Union position below and to the southwest of Cemetery Hill. This, Lee believed, would cut the Union line in half, isolating those on Cemetery Hill.

Supply replenishment aside, Lee's primary purpose in marching north had always been to confront the Army of the Potomac and whip it. In his view, putting it off after a smashing victory on July 1 would not only be demoralizing to his army but also grant time for the Union forces to consolidate. In attempting this, Lee faced a number of quandaries. His plan lacked the basic intelligence required, information that normally would have been provided by Jeb Stuart's cavalry. Stuart's absence—the loss of the army's "eyes and ears"—confounded him, but his commitment to continue the fight outweighed his absence of military intelligence. He would make do. If he did not have Stuart, he would use Pendleton. At Chancellorsville, Lee operated on familiar territory in the midst of a sympathetic populace. In Pennsylvania, he had neither.

Lee did, however, have James Longstreet back with the army, and for the moment at least, a rare superiority of numbers. He could not account for the terrain features beyond his immediate line of sight nor the strength or exact location of his enemy, but his belief that he had more men on hand than Meade, coupled with his desire to keep the initiative, made him anxious to plan an attack for the next day. And he would do so as soon as possible, before the enemy could fully gather. The urge to attack quickly made him overly sanguine about his chances. Perhaps he was spoiled by the clumsy and often hesitant movements of many of the Federal army's former commanders and anticipated more of the same.

Still, Lee must have known by this time that his army was not the sole occupant of the roads leading into town. Hundreds of campfires glowing along Cemetery Ridge and near Little Round Top offered ample proof of this fact. Buford's cavalry line could clearly be seen from Seminary Ridge. Without Stuart to advise him, Lee was improvising and, to some extent, floundering. As July 1 turned into July 2, he knew with certainty that two Union infantry corps were present, although perhaps three and even a fourth may have arrived. He felt certain he outnumbered Meade— but for how long? His preferred tactic was a strong flank attack, which had been so successful at Second Manassas and Chancellorsville. Lee consulted his maps and ordered a further reconnaissance with the intent of repeating the maneuver that had worked so well just two months earlier. General Pendleton would arise at 3:00 a.m. to prepare for another ride down Willoughby Run, but this time several engineers from Longstreet's corps would accompany him. The orders from Lee to Pendleton were simple to articulate, if difficult to accomplish: "survey the enemy's position toward some estimate of the ground and best mode of attack."[37]

One significant problem with Lee's plan was that his senior subordinate still firmly opposed it. The army had marched north to force a battle on ground of their choosing, argued Longstreet, with the intent to employ a general offensive strategy but with defensive tactics. According to Old Pete, Lee was changing the plan midstream and proposing to go over to the tactical offensive—and he did not like it. Meade, a careful engineer, would be working throughout the night to bolster his lines. Union troops still south of Gettysburg would be hurrying to join their comrades at Gettysburg. The two generals could see campfires across the way. Longstreet argued with his commander that all of this was clear evidence Yankees occupied the ridge in strength. He strenuously objected to Lee's plan, arguing it was best to disengage and move the army south and around the Union left, secure a defensive position between the Army of the Potomac and Washington, and force them to attack. In its simplest form, Lee was seeking to repeat Chancellorsville, while Longstreet was looking to reprise Fredericksburg.[38]

According to Lee's military secretary, Col. Armistead Long, the commanding general objected to Longstreet's idea, describing it as "impractical." How could they walk away from such a victory as this day? How would the men react if Lee withdrew for any reason? When Longstreet disagreed a second time, Lee reportedly remarked, "No, the enemy is there, and I am going to attack him there." Longstreet once again objected and repeated that it was best to disengage the army and march south. Lee responded, "If the enemy is there tomorrow, we must attack him," to which Longstreet later claimed he replied, "If he is there, it will be because he is anxious that we should attack him—a good reason in my judgment for not doing so."[39]

With that exchange, the discussion ended and Longstreet rode off, leaving Lee and his staff to iron out their plans for the morrow. It was well after midnight when Lee finally retired to his tent and cot. Although we do not know what he was thinking, it is reasonable to assume he believed Longstreet would be up and moving his divisions before dawn, in time to situate themselves for whatever was required as early as possible. He looked forward to Pendleton's early return with favorable news. Everything planned thus far relied upon vague information presented by men who had no real idea of what was transpiring east of the Emmitsburg Road.

---

37 Ibid., pt. 2, 350.

38 Long, *Memoirs of R. E. Lee*, 276-77.

39 Ibid. See also Longstreet, "The Gettysburg Campaign," *Philadelphia Weekly Times*, November 1877.

Unbeknownst to General Lee, by the time he finally fell asleep that humid summer Pennsylvania night, his ambitious plans to crush the Union left were already unraveling.

Chapter Six

"I found myself in the immediate vicinity of the enemy."

— *Brig. Gen. Andrew A. Humphreys, U. S. A.*[1]

Night, July 1-2:
The Army of the Potomac
Comes Together

As night deepened on July 1, more Union Third Corps regiments arrived from the south. They passed unnoticed by Confederate Brig. Gen. Cadmus M. Wilcox and his Alabamians who for all practical purposes had been ordered to pay attention to such things. In a startling display of ineptitude or inattention, Wilcox's advanced pickets along the Fairfield Road and above Marsh Creek failed to notice two entire brigades of enemy infantry, supported by noisy rumbling artillery and wagons, approach within a few hundred yards of their line.[2]

The Federal column moving past Wilcox's outmost position near the landmark Black Horse Tavern consisted of Brig. Gen. Andrew A. Humphreys' Second Division, part of Daniel Sickles' Third Corps. Earlier in the day, about 1:00 p.m., Humphreys had marched his men through Emmitsburg, Maryland, on the main road running north to Gettysburg before halting a mile above the former town for a much-needed rest. Humphreys rode off to conduct "a careful examination of the ground in front of Emmitsburg," leaving Brig. Gen. Joseph B. Carr of the First Brigade temporarily in command of the halted division. Orders arrived about 3:00 p.m. to move north up to Gettysburg, still about a dozen miles distant, where John

---

1 OR 27, pt. 1, 531.

2 Ibid, pt. 2, 613, 616-17.

Brig. Gen. Andrew A. Humphreys,
2nd Division, Third Corps,
Army of the Potomac.
LOC

Reynolds' and Oliver Howard's two corps had been heavily engaged with the enemy.[3]

Humphreys sent Lt. Col. Julius Hayden, the Third Corps' inspector general, back to General Carr with instructions to lead the division toward Gettysburg. Carr, in turn, ordered his own brigade and Col. William Brewster's Second Brigade onto the Emmitsburg Road and left Col. George C. Burling and his Third Brigade in reserve to help hold Emmitsburg. Burling's men would be useful in any battle fought around Gettysburg, but if the Confederates succeeded in driving the army back, or if they sent troops in a flanking movement, it was critical that the route through Emmitsburg remain open.[4]

Hayden had personal instructions from army headquarters on how best to proceed to the Gettysburg area. He employed Dr. Annan, a prominent local citizen and Union sympathizer, to help guide him. Because Maj. Gen. David B. Birney's First Division was also using the Emmitsburg Road, it was thought best to send Humphreys' men on side roads to avoid traffic delays.[5] Carr's brigade led the way northeast through southern Adams County, followed by Lt. Francis W. Seeley's six Napoleons of Battery K, 4th U.S. Light Artillery. Brewster's brigade brought up the rear, followed by the wagons, including ambulances, for both brigades. Starting

---

3 Ibid., pt. 1, 530.

4 Ibid., 541-43.

5 Ibid. See also T. J. C. Williams and Folger McKinsey, *History of Frederick County, Maryland*, 2 vols. (Frederick, MD, 1910), 1:585. This guide was probably Dr. Robert L. Annan and not his aging father, Andrew, who was also a local physician. It was certainly not Andrew's half-brother Samuel, who was a Confederate surgeon, though not part of the Army of Northern Virginia. Daniel D. Hartzler, *Medical Doctors of Maryland in the C.S.A.* (Westminster, MD, 2007), 11.

Brig. Gen. Joseph B. Carr,
1st Brigade, 2nd Division, Third Corps,
Army of the Potomac.
LOC

northward about 3:30 p.m., Carr's pioneers fell in behind Annan, Hayden, and an escort from the 6th New York Cavalry detached from Third Corps headquarters.[6]

After advancing about a mile north from the short-lived campsite, the head of the long column reached the red brick Moritz Tavern. There, Dr. Annan directed the advance guard onto a rural road angling northwest, roughly parallel to the Emmitsburg Road. This was the same route Brig. Gen. Thomas Rowley's First Corps division traversed that morning. This avenue, called Bullfrog Road by some and Ross White's Crossroad by others, was a well-traveled cutoff used by locals to reach the Black Horse Tavern on the Fairfield Road at Marsh Creek. Gettysburg lay three miles east of the latter inn.[7]

Carr, who could clearly hear the booming artillery as he marched toward Gettysburg, proceeded with caution. He had no idea what lay around the next bend, beyond the next stand of woods, or over the next rise. To his relief, about 4:30 p.m. that July 1, General Humphreys caught up with his column and assumed command. Reassured by the Dr. Annan that, other than the already crowded Emmitsburg Road this was the surest way to Gettysburg, Humphreys settled in with the understanding that the doctor and Hayden knew where they were going.[8]

Like Winfield Hancock, "Old Goggle Eyes" Humphreys was a man of "distinguished and brilliant profanity." At age 52 and relatively old for field command, he was the only general in Sickles' Third Corps to have graduated from West Point, a career soldier who found himself among political cronies and

6   Ibid., pt. 1, 531.

7   USGS MRC 39077F3. The intersection, now in Fairplay, PA., is seven miles south of Gettysburg. The tavern opened in 1802. General Reynolds spent the last night of his life there.

8   OR 27, pt. 1, 531.

appointees. A Philadelphian and grandson of the designer of "Old Ironsides" (the U.S.S. *Constitution*), he had served as a military and civilian engineer for 30 years. Humphreys was not a popular man. Many of his troops considered him to be "an unfeeling, bow-legged tyrant" with a reputation as a strict disciplinarian. Humphreys was strict, and his veneer tough and often cold. He was, however, an officer of substantial competence and personal bravery.[9]

At some point after Humphreys' division passed onto Bullfrog Road, Capt. John McBlair, attached to Third Corps headquarters, reached the column with a dispatch. The message originated on the battlefield from General Howard, who sent it to General Sickles to warn him to "look-out for his left in coming up to Gettysburg." Sickles forwarded the warning on to Humphreys. Shortly thereafter the advance cavalry scouts encountered a civilian traveling south who had guided some of the First Corps to Gettysburg that morning. The man corroborated the dispatch, stating "that our troops occupied no ground near Gettysburg west of the road from that town to Emmitsburg." This reinforced Humphreys' determination, as instructed by Sickles' staff officer McBlair, to take position on the left of Gettysburg as soon as he could arrive. The problem was that Bullfrog Road was a longer, more circuitous route than the Emmitsburg Road, traffic or not.[10]

Humphreys had enough information now to justify changing the prescribed marching route, but allowed Hayden to continue leading the column northwest in the fading sunlight—steadily diverging from the Emmitsburg Road. Sometime about dusk the vanguard reached a four-way rural intersection referred to then as the Millerstown Crossroad. Bullfrog Road continued well to the northwest toward Fairfield. The column turned northeast (or right) onto present-day Pumping Station Road. The head of Humphreys' column was now about two miles southwest of Sachs Bridge.[11]

The advance to Marsh Creek was slow, tense, and tedious. The thunder of artillery had faded with the dying light, but by now the Rebels surely were close and the division was tramping along a strange road. When they reached the creek, the Third Corps men faced a three-way intersection. Humphreys decided they should turn right and head east back toward the main road. Staff officer Hayden protested, arguing that "General Sickles had instructed him to guide the division by way of Black Horse Tavern, on the road from Fairfield to Gettysburg." It was an awkward situation for the veteran general. A lieutenant colonel, junior in rank but sporting

---

9   Ezra J. Warner, *Generals in Blue* (Baton Rouge, LA, 1964), 240-42. Humphreys received his unusual nickname for his penchant for wearing eyeglasses.

10 *OR* 27, pt. 1, 531.

11 USGS MRC 39077G3.

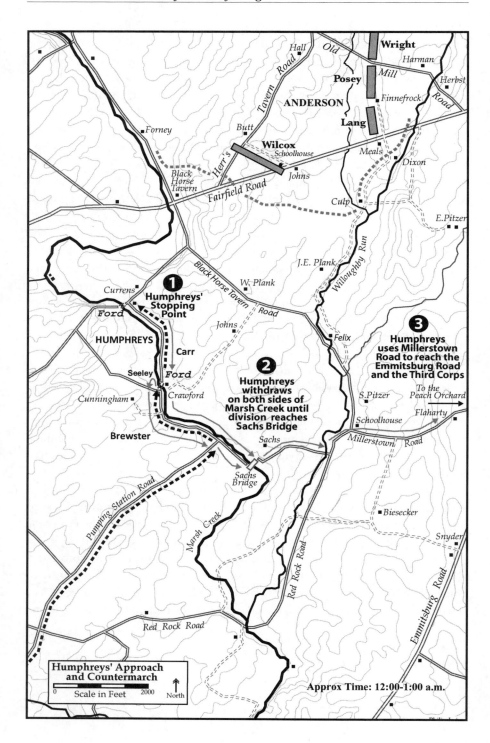

Humphreys' Approach and Countermarch

0   Scale in Feet   2000   North

Approx Time: 12:00-1:00 a.m.

Sickles' authority, was ordering him to turn again to the northwest, opposite the direction leading to the Emmitsburg Road and the supposed left of Howard's line south of Gettysburg. Reluctantly, Humphreys agreed and motioned for Carr's column to turn left (today's Scott Road). Hayden with his 6th New York Cavalry escort led the way through the intersection in the twilight.[12]

The road followed the curving western bank of Marsh Creek before turning sharply to the northwest and cutting through open farmland. Knowing this route would lead farther away from their ultimate destination (making a connection with the Union left somewhere south of Gettysburg), Humphreys became more cautious. With the enemy in proximity, he ordered complete silence and began seeking a suitable path across the stream to head for the Black Horse Tavern, as instructed by Sickles.[13]

There were two fords between Sachs Bridge and Fairfield Road to the north. The first was at the John Crawford farm a little more than 1,000 yards upstream from the covered bridge. This extensive homestead sat east of the creek above a bend and beyond a belt of woods, making it impossible to see either the covered bridge or the Millerstown Road from the ford. The other shallow crossing was a half-mile farther north opposite the spillway at Bream's gristmill below Currens' expansive farm. Situated below Herr's Ridge along the creek's eastern bank, it sat roughly 1,000 yards south of the tavern Lieutenant Colonel Hayden was trying to locate. Like the Crawford farm, the Currens property lay below the military crest of Herr's Ridge, with farm lanes running not only north and south along the creek, but also ascending the ridge east and northeast toward the Black Horse Tavern Road.[14]

According to Humphreys, he reached Marsh Creek and followed its west bank for some time before crossing. He never mentioned how far north he traveled or if he knew of the second, or upper, crossing. Common sense suggests Hayden, Dr. Annan, and their cavalry escort forded the stream at the Crawford farm simply because it was the first passage north of Sachs Bridge. Once east of the creek, Hayden's party headed north again, following the eastern bank roughly 1,000 yards until they reached Bream's mill spillway. Once there they had two options: continue up the eastern bank to the Fairfield Road, or turn right and ascend the ridge by passing eastward through the Curren homestead, following its lane to the Black

---

12 *OR* 27, pt. 1, 531. It is unknown whether the civilian guide Dr. Annan voiced an opinion.

13 Osborn, *Holding the Left*, (see map), 2. See also Pfanz, *Gettysburg: The Second Day*, 44-46, and Adolph F. Cavada, *Personal Diary: Company C, 23rd Pennsylvania Volunteer Infantry Regiment, 1861-1863*, Collection #6956, HSP.

14 Ibid. This latter lane is today's Plank Road. See also Andrew A. Humphreys to Archibald Campbell, August 1863, A. A. Humphreys Papers, Collection #304, HSP.

Bream's Black Horse Tavern west of Gettysburg was a popular local watering hole.
GNMP

Horse Tavern Road. The former route is the most probable as it looked like the most direct route to the Fairfield Road and beyond. Wilcox's pickets were but a quarter-mile away and none of the Unionists had an inkling of their presence.[15]

Selecting the direct road, Hayden avoided attracting the attention of the Confederate picket line strung out east of and above Marsh Creek. Almost certainly he approached the tavern via the lower lane paralleling the creek. This farm lane intersected the Fairfield Road near an old bridge over Marsh Creek, and the long-sought tavern was but a few yards beyond, its lights beckoning a bright welcome. Having volunteered to ride ahead, Hayden, with Dr. Annan and couple escorts in tow, picked their way to the Fairfield Road. Seeing no one about, they urged their mounts across the dark road. After entering the Black Horse Tavern Road north of the Fairfield Road, they turned onto the grounds of proprietor Francis Bream's establishment, a 2 1/2-story fieldstone edifice with a massive bank barn and numerous nearby outbuildings. All was quiet from the tavern, as well as from Wilcox's pickets on

15 USGS MRC 39077G3. See also *Bachelder Maps, Second Day*.

the high ground some 200 yards away. The staff officer dismounted, walked into the popular tavern, and spoke with its owner—Cumberland Township's wealthiest citizen. When the 56-year-old Bream told Hayden there was a Rebel picket post just 200 feet away, the stunned officer remounted and returned to General Humphreys. First, though, he left his escort to guard the innkeeper and two of his sons, threatened them to keep quiet, and allegedly ordered food for the general.[16]

Hayden met Humphreys about a quarter-mile south of the Fairfield Road near the mill, the general and the head of his column having since forded the creek. When he heard the news about the enemy picket post, Humphreys stopped his command and repeated his order for complete silence. Leaving the column under Carr's care, Humphreys and a few aides, including his son Henry, followed the lieutenant colonel back to the tavern to confirm the story. Once inside, Humphreys questioned Bream and his boys. "It must have been Colonel Hayden who threatened them and ordered supper," Humphreys later speculated, "I did not do either; and, indeed the more intelligent of the two sons mentioned told me that the enemy's picket line was about two hundred feet from us, and would have given the alarm in ample time to the main body, had I attempted to surprise them. I was right in not attempting it."[17]

It is hard to fathom how 2,145 infantrymen in two brigades, a full battery of limbered Napoleons, caissons, hundreds of horses, and supporting wagons carrying weapons, ammunition, materiél, and accouterments, plus an additional 30 or so mounted men of various ranks and duties could move so close to an armed picket line and not once be detected. The partially cloudy skies that somewhat obscured the full moon (which rose at 8:07 p.m.) does not explain how the Confederates missed the sounds of a fully equipped infantry column on the move, crossing a waist-deep stream on an otherwise still evening.

Several things contributed to Humphreys' good fortune in avoiding what would have been a difficult night fight with Wilcox's command. The first was the possible effect of an acoustic shadow (an area through which sound waves fail to propagate because of topographical obstructions). Once Carr's column halted east

---

16 Humphreys to Campbell, August 1863, HSP. William McClellan built the bridge in 1809.

17 Ibid. While visiting the area again in 1869, the general had a candid conversation with Francis Bream. The innkeeper told Humphreys his troops made "a great noise" coming up, talking loudly, but had later slipped away so quietly that he did not hear them leave. Humphreys replied that the report of loud conversations was not true; he had ordered his men to use "caution to be quiet" on the approach because he knew he was coming upon the enemy. He believed Bream heard the unavoidable noise of the horses, artillery, and ambulances as they crossed the rocky-bottomed Marsh Creek. Bream and his wife Elizabeth had six sons and a daughter. He filed a damage claim for $7,000 damage after the battle, but was never paid. He died in 1882 at his home.

of the creek (it may have forded at the Crawford farm), it remained as quiet as possible, but Seeley's battery made a considerable amount of noise when it crossed behind Carr (Brewster's brigade remained west of the stream). The slope of Herr's Ridge immediately east of the tavern rises steeply, ascending more than 40 feet in a little more than 100 yards, with Bream's tavern located near the ravine's lowest point along the creek. The Rebels closest to and above the inn were picketed in some woods beyond the military crest. From this position, they could not see the base of the ridge or the tavern below; the intervening ground and woods likely muffled the sound.[18]

Unbeknownst to Humphreys or Hayden, the Rebel line south of the Fairfield Road arched back to the east and faced south with advanced pickets pushed as far east as Willoughby Run and south as far as the J. E. Plank farm. Although Wilcox's men had an unobstructed view across the open, if somewhat undulating, eastern slope of South Herr's Ridge, they could not see beyond the Black Horse Tavern Road as it passed along the crest to their right and front, angling to the southeast. The terrain likely muted most of the noise, but did not eliminate it. Humphreys' second stroke of good fortune was that the Rebel pickets may well have heard the commotion, but mistook it for General Longstreet's arriving troops. For example, a Confederate forager named George Weaver, a private with Lane's Georgia artillery battalion, heard a bugler in Seeley's battery signal "Halt," and, mistaking the call for his own, blundered into the Union line to be captured.[19]

Inside the comfortable country inn, meanwhile, Andrew Humphreys decided not to linger for the home-cooked meal Hayden had ordered. He returned on the lower road and met the head of the divisional column, still stationary near the Currens farm. Humphreys faced it about, sending Seeley's battery and some infantry back across Marsh Creek to rejoin Brewster. Most of Carr's men "did not cross but kept along the [east] bank."[20]

Humphreys' brief visit to Francis Bream's tavern that night lasted only a few minutes, but it was much more dangerous than the general knew at the time. As he learned six years later, "The sons (indeed Bream himself) mentioned that I had not been gone ten minutes when a party of twenty or thirty of the enemy came into the

---

18 USGS MRC 39077G3.

19 Speicher, *The Sumter Artillery*, 188. As with so many things, most bugle calls for the two armies were identical. Researcher Dean Shultz suggests the soldier was captured near the ford at "Old Bream's Mill," near the Currens farm. The creek had a spillway and the water level was shallow. See Frassanito, *Gettysburg Hospitals*, 140-145; *Bachelder Maps, Second Day*.

20 A. A. Humphreys, "The Gettysburg Campaign of 1863," in *The Historical Magazine and Notes and Queries: Concerning the Antiquities, History and Biography of America*, vol. VI, Second Series, No. 1, July 1869 (Morrison, NY, 1869).

tavern and passed the night there." The Philadelphia-born general went on to say that the day had been rainy and sultry, and his men longed for a few more minutes at each stop along the lengthy march. But, if he had conceded to their wishes, perhaps his small "virtually unarmed" party of five escorts might have arrived at the tavern fifteen minutes later, after the Rebels had occupied the inn. "What might not have been the result of a deliberate volley from twenty or thirty muskets or rifles at the distance of twenty feet?" he postulated.[21]

While Wilcox's Alabamians engaged the services of the Bream family, Humphreys' and Carr's men headed back south to find the Millerstown Road. Passing southward through the Crawford and Sachs farms, the new leading regiment reached the Millerstown Road roughly 950 yards downstream from where the column had reversed course. The portion of the division that had remained west of the creek now moved south along that bank, likely passing through the John Cunningham property before tramping across Sachs Bridge and rejoining the column. Of his misguided detour Humphreys later reported, "Upon reaching the Black Horse Tavern I found myself in the immediate vicinity of the enemy, who occupied that road in strong force." He maintained that the enemy remained unaware of his presence and suggested that he could have attacked them at daylight "with the certainty of at least temporary success." He rationalized that he was "three miles distant from the remainder of the army, and I believed such as course would have been inconsistent with the general plan of operations of the commanding general."[22]

Lieutenant Colonel Clark Baldwin, commanding the 1st Massachusetts in Carr's brigade, thought the route hiccup was Hayden's fault. "July 1. Moved at 8:30 a.m. raining hard, marched to Emmitsburg where we arrived about 2:30 p.m.," he penned in his diary. "At 4:30 p.m. hearing heavy firing on right and front, we again moved forward, the column being led by a staff officer who was more noted for froth and foam than for common sense, although a West Pointer and on a Major General's staff; got on the wrong road and got lost. About 10 p.m. our advance guard came upon the enemy's pickets. The column consisting of the Second Division, Third Corps, was soon as our position ascertained, faced about and

---

21 Ibid. Humphreys recalled that the small party consisted of "Myself, Captain [Carswell] McClellan, my son Harry, Colonel Hayden, and Doctor Annan, of Emmitsburg, and my orderly, [Pvt. James F.] Diamond." The latter, detached from the 6th U. S. Cavalry, would die in the fighting on July 2; his body was never identified.

22 OR 27, pt. 1, 531; Humphreys, *The Historical Magazine*, vol. VI. Carr also left a brief account of these events. See also Coddington, *The Gettysburg Campaign*, 328, and USGS MRC 39077-G2-TF-024.

quietly retraced our steps about four miles where the right road was found."[23] On July 29, Capt. Mathew Donovan, who by then was commanding the remnants of the 11th Massachusetts, admitted the brigade "got on wrong road; about-faced, and marched toward Gettysburg, arriving some 3 miles from it at 1 a.m.; lay down and slept."

What many Gettysburg students fail to fully realize or appreciate is that General Humphreys, using his experience and talent as a commander, extracted his two brigades safely out of harm's way in the darkness. He did so with a minimum of noise and confusion and no casualties. His was a very nice piece of troop maneuvering under difficult circumstances. Much of the time the officers and men worked in near-pitch blackness. What very easily could have been a disaster was instead nothing more than a delay.

Once back on the move, those in front guided those to their rear as the silhouetted column snaked its way eastward out the Millerstown Road. Humphreys' vanguard passed over Willoughby Run, where earlier that evening Pendleton's reconnaissance party had ascended South Seminary Ridge. Continuing in silence the last mile, Humphreys finally reached the Emmitsburg Road shortly after midnight. There, the column was probably directed north by Birney, Geary, or Buford, or possibly one of the latter's subordinates such as Col. William Gamble or Col. Thomas Devin, the commanders of Buford's two brigades then on the field.

Humphreys' division marched several hundred yards past the Sherfy homestead before being directed to the right (east) onto Abraham Trostle's farm lane, another rural avenue used to connect major throughways by cutting across private lands. In this case, the east-west Trostle lane connected the much-traveled Emmitsburg Road with the Taneytown Road, traversing an unimposing low ridge 1,200 yards east of the farmyard. A shallow swale with farms, homesteads, orchards, woods, wood lots, pastures, and rocky fields, all crisscrossed by rail and stone fences, lay between the lesser ridge to the east and the Emmitsburg Road Rise to the west.[24]

Turning east on the Trostle lane, Carr's lead regiment was directed over the crest of the Emmitsburg Road Rise 200 yards east of the pike. At some point between the crest and Trostle's farmyard below, an additional 200 yards east, Carr turned his brigade north into an open meadow where, after continuing 600 yards his vanguard stopped north of Daniel F. Klingle's farm. Pickets from each regiment

23 Lt. Col. Clark Baldwin to Col. John B. Bachelder, March 20, 1865, John P. Nicholson Collection, Bachelder Papers, Huntington Library, San Marino, CA; OR 27, pt. 1, 551; USGS MRC 39077G3.

24 Ibid. See also *Bachelder Maps, Second Day*.

This 1880 photo looks northwest toward the eastern slope of the Emmitsburg Road rise. The buildings (from left to right) are the Klingle, Rogers, and Codori farms. The road in the foreground is where present-day Sickles Avenue intersects United States Avenue (the Trostle farm lane). Humphreys deployed the brigades of Brewster (on the left) and Carr (on the right) in the fields adjacent to the Abraham Trostle and Daniel Klingle farms between 1:00-2:00 a.m. on July 2. *GNMP*

were sent east, up the Emmitsburg Road Rise, passing through the farmyards and turnpike before dropping into the open fields belonging to Henry Spangler. Brewster's command did the same. By this time it was well past 1:00 a.m. on July 2.[25]

Brewster's brigade settled in south of Carr, his bivouac encompassing most of Trostle's rolling farm. To his immediate rear was marshy bottom land, strewn with rocks and boulders, uprooted and felled trees, a weak growth of junk timber and thick underbrush. Plum Run, a small meandering watercourse, ran through this soggy terrain. Beyond the creek Humphreys could see campfires belonging to Ward's brigade, also part of the Third Corps, bivouacked on a low ridge opposite the creek. Two parks of artillery, one belonging to Captain Clark, sat to his right and rear below the ridge nearer the run.

Although thoroughly exhausted, Humphreys assessed his new position. "At an early hour of the morning," he wrote in his report, "my division was massed in the vicinity of its bivouac, facing the Emmitsburg road, near the crest of the ridge

25 USGS MRC 39077G3.

running from the cemetery of Gettysburg, in a southerly direction, to a rugged conical-shape hill, which I find goes by the name of Round Top, about 2 miles south of Gettysburg." It did not take him long to decide he did not like it. It was not a strong military position, reasoned Humphreys, and it was almost certainly untenable if pressed by the enemy. He knew a sizeable Confederate force was in his immediate front a couple thousand yards distant, though he did not know its full complement or its exact location. All he could do under the circumstances was send a reinforced picket line west across the Emmitsburg Road.[26]

"The distance marched this day was over 30 miles," recalled the 1st Massachusetts's commander Lieutenant Colonel Baldwin. "The brigade was at once formed in columns of regts., the men nearly exhausted lay down upon their arms and were soon lost in sleep, many too tired to eat their supper." The lengthy maneuvering averted a collision between Humphreys' division and Wilcox's brigade, but only for about 15 hours, when they would meet along the Emmitsburg Road.[27]

*   *   *

About the time General Lee was retiring to his tent, his opponent arrived at the base of West Cemetery Hill. It had been a long and tiring day for General Meade, who with his escort had departed Taneytown about 10:00 p.m. The ride up the Taneytown Road required he and his party to occasionally swing off the road and pick their way in the darkness through fields, fences, and orchards to move around stalled traffic. The group reached Hancock's Second Corps bivouac about 11:30 p.m. Meade stopped long enough to speak with the corps leader and his subordinate John Gibbon, the former having rejoined his corps just an hour earlier. Meade instructed Hancock to move the Second Corps toward Gettysburg before dawn.

Meade continued north accompanied by his chief of artillery, General Hunt, Capts. George Meade, Jr., William H. Paine, and Charles Cadwalader, his orderly Sgt. William Waters, and a portion of Company C of the 2nd Pennsylvania Cavalry. He passed Lieutenant Atwell's Independent Battery E and the sleeping Lt. Edward Geary. Meade reached West Cemetery Hill sometime after 12:30 a.m. The general and his party ascended the gently sloping plateau above Zeigler's Grove and passed over the crest into Evergreen Cemetery, arriving at its gatehouse about 1:00 a.m. At

---

26 OR 27, pt. 1, 531.

27 Baldwin to Bachelder, March 20, 1865, *Bachelder Papers*.

roughly the same time, General Humphreys' division was settling in from its 30-mile trek from Maryland.[28]

Meade had slept but little since assuming command of the Army of the Potomac three nights earlier. Although the toll was beginning to affect his appearance, his wits remained as sharp as ever. Luck, skill, or a little of both, the element of good timing now swung to Meade's side of the ledger. He had telegraphed Washington at 6:00 p.m., stating in part, "I see no other course than to hazard a general battle. Circumstances during the night may alter this decision, of which I will try to advise you." Near the gatehouse Meade was greeted by Slocum, Howard, Sickles, Birney, and chief engineer Brig. Gen. Gouverneur K. Warren. When they told him that the position they held was favorable, the laconic Meade remarked that this was good news because it was too late to leave.[29]

Meade's firm commitment to battle after part of his army was routed, in a position fraught with uncertainty and flux, had few precedents in the war's Eastern Theater. The army's previous commanders had been cautious, timid, even intimidated—bold one moment, frozen into inaction the next. The aggressive Lee had taken advantage of many tactical blunders. Repeated Union command errors built upon a collective lack of heart and commitment to battle, mistakes further compounded by indecision. Being overly cautious in front of the opportunistic Lee (as Maj. Gen. George McClellan found out on Richmond's doorstep) was every bit as dangerous as being too aggressive (as Maj. Gen. John Pope discovered at Second Bull Run). Now it was George Meade's turn to make decisions with Lee's army gathering around him. The dour Philadelphian would use this night to bolster his position in the event that Lee attacked in the morning. Grizzled, leathery, near-sighted, and overly fatigued, the new commander possessed the one thing many of his predecessors lacked: grit and stamina. If the position was adequate, he would stay and fight. His greatest concern at 1:00 a.m., however, was that Lee would attack before all of his infantry corps were up and situated. Meade needed time.[30]

While there is no record of the exact duration of this short council of war that early morning, the energetic Meade, still fully functional despite his lack of rest, was back in the saddle before 2:00 a.m. Accompanied by generals Howard and Hunt,

28 OR 27, pt. 1, 115. Meade placed his arrival at 1:00 a.m.; Hunt about 2:00 a.m. See also Pfanz, *Gettysburg, Second Day*, 42-45, and Hunt, "Second Day," *B&L*, vol. 3, 291.

29 Longstreet, "The Gettysburg Campaign," *Philadelphia Weekly Times,* November 1877; OR 27, pt. 1, 72.

30 Gallagher, Gary W., ed., *Three Days at Gettysburg: Essays on Confederate and Union Leadership* (Kent, OH, 1999), 25, 39-42. See also William Paine to George G. Meade, June 20, 1886, Gettysburg Letter Book, Meade Collection, HSP.

aides George Meade Jr. and Captain Paine (who was also his engineer and cartographer), and Lt. Charles Bissell, Meade spurred his horse back over the crest to lead his small reconnaissance party down the slope toward Taneytown Road and Zeigler's Grove beyond it.[31] The group stopped near the grove, where they encountered Brig. Gen. George J. Stannard, the general duty officer who also commanded the Third Brigade, Third Division, First Corps. Stannard's "Paper Collar Brigade" of Vermonters had only arrived a few hours earlier, after the first day's fighting had ceased. However, he was up to speed on the latest positions and deployments, and quickly relayed the desired information to Meade and the others.[32]

Under what was now a full moon with the clouds having given way, Howard pointed out Confederate positions across the way to Hunt and commented on how the Union-held open plateau around Zeigler's Grove was a tremendous artillery platform. It commanded not only the entire field to the west, but also the Emmitsburg Road as far south as the eye could see. Hunt, the Army of the Potomac's premier artillerist, immediately grasped what Howard was telling him. Although not an engineer, Hunt's keen eye and past feats as the Army of the Potomac's chief artillery officer were well known throughout both armies. As a fine engineer himself, Meade shared Howard's and Hunt's point of view. If Meade had been uncertain of his decision to stand fast, their report clinched it. This was good ground for defense. The army would stay put.[33]

The party remounted and rode past Abraham Bryan's small farm on Cemetery Ridge before continuing south. The riders stopped near a copse of junk timber and thick underbrush littered with the odd bits of farm debris and rubble. The Union position here was weak, with only small groups of men to cover the 800 yards from Zeigler's Grove south to Birney's right flank below Jacob Hummelbaugh's farm lane. Excluding Buford's vedettes along Emmitsburg Road, this portion of Cemetery Ridge, including what would come to be known as "the Copse of Trees," was devoid of any sizeable force all the way to Geary's position near Little Round Top.[34]

The officers continued their reconnaissance, stopping briefly to discuss positions, make notes, and move on. Paine and Bissell trailed behind in the

---

31 Ibid.

32 The brigade's mocking nickname arose from its spanking new blue uniforms and the general contempt the Army of the Potomac's veterans had for new units that had not seen combat.

33 Henry Hunt to O. O. Howard, Aug. 21, 1876, Hunt Papers, Box 4, LoC; *OR* 27, pt. 1, 349.

34 *Bachelder Maps, Second Day.*

company of Hunt, sketching what they could see of Cemetery Ridge. Perhaps they dismounted occasionally to steady their hands as they followed Meade all the way to Birney's line. There is no record of Meade speaking to General Sickles after leaving the gatehouse. Their disagreements would become widely publicized almost immediately after the smoke cleared; had they met that night, surely one or the other would have mentioned it. Sickles had not met with Humphreys earlier, and it seems that now he likewise did not meet with Meade. Rather, he retired to his tent, where he remained through the night.[35]

After passing through positions held by the Third Corps and Twelfth Corps Meade reached the base of Little Round Top, where the Millerstown Road passed over the ridge. While Meade talked with Howard and Geary, Hunt strolled over to Lt. John Egan's section of guns from Battery K, 5th U.S., unlimbered to cover the road, and struck up a conversation with Lt. John Kinzie, the battery's commander. When Hunt inquired about the ground, Kinzie replied that he had looked it over and believed it to be too broken, rocky, and uneven for an attack in either direction. Advancing over such ground would ruin formations and break up the battle lines. "If we are to be attacked," opined the lieutenant, "it will not be across my front but from the direction of town to the right, where the ground is open, where the enemy campfires were."[36]

These were bold words from an obscure young officer to a general, but Kinzie was right about the nature of the terrain to his front and south. It was very rough, broken up by numerous rock formations and great stone slabs, rocky wooded ledges, stone walls, and a myriad of rail fences. The ground to the north and west, by contrast, was open rolling fields over which masses of men could easily advance. Beyond those open fields flickered the campfires of Dorsey Pender's division along the length of Seminary Ridge some 1,200 yards due west of Cemetery Hill.[37]

With their conversation and reconnaissance ended, Meade and Howard departed about 3:30 a.m., riding east over the crest of Cemetery Ridge to the Taneytown Road. Meade left Hunt to oversee Paine and Bissell as they finished their sketches. Once done, Hunt escorted them back over the same route Meade had taken up the Taneytown Road. They dismounted at a small white clapboard house, the army's new headquarters, on the west side of Taneytown Road south of Cemetery Hill. The Copse of Trees they had visited earlier was 270 yards to the

---

35 There are no viable reports or correspondences that suggest Sickles and Meade spoke after meeting at the gatehouse about 1:00 a.m.

36 Hunt to Howard, December 29, 1876, Hunt Papers, Box 4, LoC. Kinsey, a West Point graduate, survived the war and retired a brigadier general shortly after the turn of the century.

37 USGS MRC 39077G3; *Bachelder Maps, Second Day*.

west. The trio wearily walked into the house, which belonged to a widow named Lydia Leister. It was now after 4:00 a.m. The first hint of dawn glimmered over the low ridges to the east. It had been a long night for Meade and his officers. It would be an even longer day.[38]

*   *   *

Once Meade completed his Cemetery Ridge reconnaissance, he had a general plan as to where he would deploy each of his corps. Seated at a small table and working by flickering lantern light, Paine and Bissell fleshed out their crude, but relatively accurate, copies of the sketches they had drawn while accompanying Meade down the ridge. With Howard's assistance, they roughed out the major features of the terrain east of the Baltimore Pike. This would have to do until daylight permitted more detailed revisions. Meade personally indicated to his cartographers where he wanted each corps placed. Once he was satisfied they understood, Meade stepped outside to find Hunt drinking coffee after a short nap.[39]

The bulk of Hunt's artillery reserve, under Brig. Gen. Robert O. Tyler, was still in northern Maryland. Meade had already inquired as to the whereabouts of Hunt's trains and the available supply of fixed ammunition. When asked again, Hunt told him that two reserve artillery brigades were less than an hour away and the rest would arrive by mid-morning, and that he had just sent riders south to guide them forward. This satisfied Meade, who was still standing outside the Leister house when General Slocum and several aides galloped up.[40]

The men entered the farmhouse headquarters, where Meade showed him the maps and proposed troop dispositions. Hunt sat down and leaned back against a small sapling, his eyes heavy from lack of proper sleep. Hunt's earlier short nap was the only rest he had managed in 24 hours. Even with a cup of coffee he dozed in semi-consciousness. His fitful respite was interrupted when Meade and Slocum stepped onto the porch and discussed the Twelfth Corps' positions along the Baltimore Pike. Slocum expressed concern about a 1,000-yard gap in his line facing Rock Creek east of the turnpike (south of Cemetery Hill and east of wooded Culp's Hill).[41]

38 Hunt, "The Second Day," *B&L*, 3:295-96.

39 Ibid.

40 Hunt to Howard, December 29, 1876, Hunt Papers, Box 4, LoC.

41 *OR* 27, pt. 1, 290-91; USGS MRC 39077G2; *Bachelder Maps, Second Day*.

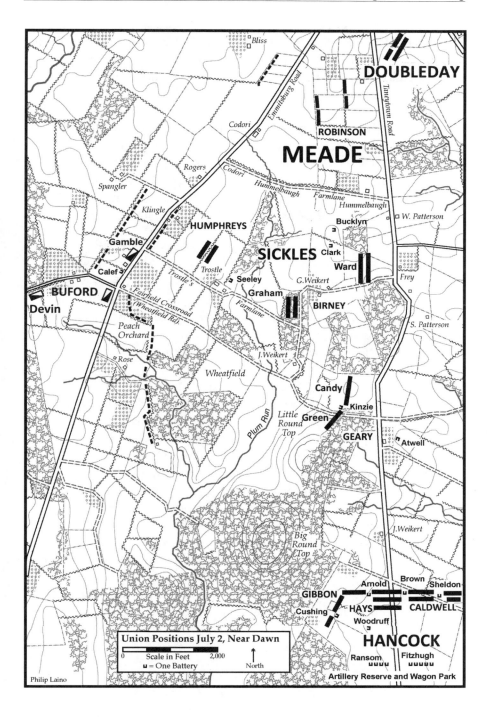

Union Positions July 2, Near Dawn
0   Scale in Feet   2,000
■ = One Battery   North

Philip Laino

Generals Hancock, Howard, and Doubleday had attended to the approaches from the north and west. In his usual thoroughness, Hancock had also seen to it that Generals Geary and Buford picketed the approaches from the south and southwest, and aligned his own Second Corps to guard against a possible enemy flanking sweep around the Round Tops. Now, hours later and in the early morning darkness, the gap pointed out by Slocum to the east appeared to offer an unguarded avenue of enemy approach through a lightly wooded and largely open meadow. When he spotted his chief of artillery resting, Meade chastised Hunt while he and Slocum conferred. Hunt opened his eyes and retorted, "I have heard all that has passed between you." Meade ordered the artillerist to inspect the gap, take whatever measures were available to correct the problem, and report back with his findings.[42]

Thus far Meade had been lucky. He was getting what he had hoped for and desperately needed: time. There were no reports of current enemy activity. Slocum's report about a gap on his eastern flank brought up concerns about last evening's sighting of a large enemy column passing eastward north of town. The column in question was Edward Johnson's Confederate division on its way east to cover Lee's exposed left flank. Meade had no way to know Johnson's current position, and so was understandably concerned about the Union right flank beyond Culp's Hill.[43]

Hunt called for his horse and set off for the Baltimore Pike accompanied by Col. Charles Warner and two couriers. They followed a dirt lane belonging to Catherine Guinn eastward to the Baltimore Pike just south of and below Cemetery Hill, a few hundred yards north of Abraham Spangler's farm. Hunt swung left into Spangler's narrow lane, where the quartet of riders followed the path east as it dropped off the pike and entered thick woods south-southeast of and below Culp's Hill. It was at the edge of these woods that Hunt stopped and looking eastward in disbelief. The full moon revealed a huge open meadow owned by farmer Henry Spangler. The ground stretched out below Culp's Hill for nearly 1,000 yards toward Rock Creek and Wolf's Hill beyond. Other than a pair of Napoleon guns covering the meadow from the Spangler farmyard, no one except a few pickets was in position to defend the all-critical Baltimore Pike against an assault from this direction. Hunt and his small party could plainly hear Union axes felling trees to erect fortifications on top of Culp's Hill, but all that work would be to no avail if the

---

42 Ibid.; Hunt, *Philadelphia Weekly Times*, May 31, 1879; Hunt to Bachelder, January 20, 1873, *Bachelder Papers,* 2:426.

43 Thomas Osborn, in Herb Crumb, ed., *The Eleventh Corps Artillery at Gettysburg: Papers of Major Thomas Ward Osborn, Chief of Artillery* (Hamilton, NY, 1991), 231.

hill was flanked on the right and the critical turnpike below it lost to the Confederates.[44]

The majority of Lee's army might be north and west of the Union position, but the enemy column that had passed to the east at nightfall was suddenly a very serious threat. Late on July 1, the disappearance of Brig. Gen. Alpheus Williams' division of the Union Twelfth Corps, east of Benner's Hill, had baffled General Ewell. Now, the whereabouts of Johnson's division likewise worried General Slocum. Hunt could visualize Slocum's concern about Ewell's veteran infantry pouring into this gap. The artillerist rode into the meadow and questioned a few of the pickets assigned there. Nearby, a number of pioneers wielding axes and shovels pointed Hunt to an old logging path they were busy widening. The artillery chief ascended the rudimentary trail up Culp's Hill a short distance to see if it would allow the movement of men and guns, and then spurred his horse back toward the Baltimore Pike.

Meanwhile, Meade set out on another reconnaissance, this time to inspect his eastern flank. At some point during his ride he again encountered the Twelfth Corps' Slocum. With Geary's division removed from his immediate command to its position near Little Round Top, Slocum now had only General Williams' division to hold a mile-long stretch of the Baltimore Pike between Rock Creek and the meadow, and Williams did not have nearly enough men and guns to do the job.[45]

The substance of Meade's conversation with Slocum went unrecorded. Still, since neither man was sure when George Sykes' Fifth Corps or John Sedgwick's Sixth Corps would arrive, Slocum apparently asked for the return of Geary's division from its current position on the distant Union left. Meade either approved Slocum's request on the spot, banking on Sickles' Third Corps and his missing brigades to fill the void Geary would leave, or he gave personal instructions to Geary himself while visiting that command below Little Round Top. The former is more likely. Meade had to weigh two threats at this point and, while he surely disliked weakening his left flank at this hour, he had to plug the yawning gap on his right. In his after-battle report, Geary reported no contact with Meade authorizing his movement, mentioning only that Slocum ordered him to Culp's Hill.[46]

It is reasonable to believe that Meade and Geary discussed in some form the White Star Division's return to the Baltimore Pike when the commanding general

---

44 USGS MRC 39077G2; David Shultz and Richard Rollins, *The Baltimore Pike Artillery Line and Kinzie's Knoll* (Redondo Beach, CA, 1997), 7-8.

45 Ibid.

46 *OR* 27, pt. 1, 825; Pfanz, *Gettysburg: Second Day*, 60.

visited Geary near Little Round Top that morning. The fact that neither Geary, Meade, nor Howard noted it in their reports is enough to suggest that Geary's withdrawal about 5:00 a.m. went without a hitch as he suggested, and that Slocum alone ordered it. Howard would have reflected on the move if it had been brought up because he played a key role in most of the activities and decisions then being made concerning the Baltimore Pike and Cemetery and Culp's hills.

Besides Geary's two brigades stirring below Little Round Top between 4:00 and 4:30 a.m., Hancock's Second Corps was likewise being prodded awake east of the high ground. At 4:15 a.m., just about the same time General Lee was briefing General Pendleton and Captain Johnston on Seminary Ridge prior to their reconnaissance, Hancock's weary men were lighting small campfires to boil coffee. By 4:45 a.m. their fires were extinguished, leftover coffee poured out, and whatever meal was being consumed hastily placed inside haversacks. Assembly sounded and the footsore men of the Second Corps fell in. By 5:00 a.m. Hays' division was moving north again, marching straight toward Captain Atwell's limbering Independent Pennsylvania Battery E, which at that time, along with the two supporting regiments, were preparing to file back onto the Taneytown Road to rejoin Geary's division heading east toward the Baltimore Pike.[47]

Hemmed in by low stone walls, fenced lots, farmyards, and orchards, Hancock's move north stalled on the Taneytown Road within minutes of Hays' troops taking to it. Fence-lined intersecting rural lanes running perpendicular to the road, coupled with uneven rock-strewn and wooded terrain, made cross-country marching nearly impossible. It only got worse when the column ground to a near standstill when Geary's division crossed Hays' path. The head of Hays' column struggled up the road for more than an hour before it was halted a quarter-mile south of its goal. Directed to the right, off the road, Hays' men filed into open fields as the first rays of the sun broke beyond the ridges to the east.[48]

Both armies had their share of miscues and mix-ups on the morning of July 2. The timing of the Second Corps' march north and that of Geary's division to the east impacted one, and likely both, columns. Hancock's northward movement occurred about 5:00 a.m., while Geary's movement took place from as early as 5:00 to as late as 6:00 a.m. Had Meade known this, he likely would have taken additional precautions to protect his exposed left flank. When Meade finally learned of these movements, he ordered Hancock's corps to march to the right, or east, of the

47 John Gibbon, *Personal Recollections of the Civil War* (Dayton OH, 1988), 271-73.

48 *OR* 27, pt. 1, 379, 381, 386. Major Leman W. Bradley, commanding the 64th New York, Fourth Brigade, Caldwell's First Division, recalled, "At 4:10 A.M. we moved about 1 mile to the front, and at 5:45 A.M. halted in a wood."

Taneytown Road to await further developments. Meade ordered this, argued one historian, because "action was expected on the right flank of the army."[49]

The head of Hays' column became somewhat entangled with Geary in gridlock where the present-day Wheatfield and Blacksmith Shop roads intersect the Taneytown Road. Geary's recall to the Baltimore Pike supports the theory that Meade, Slocum, Howard, Hunt, and Williams all thought the Union right was the weak point. Hancock's placement east of the Taneytown Road, however, has never been rationally or fully explained. When Meade discovered what had occurred on his left, he likely had no choice but to stop Hancock's northward progression until army headquarters could coordinate that movement with Geary's departure east, Sickles' redeployment, and the pending arrival of Maj. Gen. George Sykes' Fifth Corps. It was about this time, roughly 6:00-6:15 a.m., that Meade sent his son, Capt. George Meade Jr., south to Sickles' headquarters to find out what the Tammany Hall general was up to. Sickles' reply placated General Meade when he sent word in back that Brig. Gen. J. W. Hobart Ward's brigade would redeploy toward Little Round Top. Nothing, however, suggested what Sickles had in mind for General Humphreys' division.[50]

Maintaining control of the Taneytown Road was imperative to the operation of Army of the Potomac. If Meade's army was to hold the positions he had laid out that morning, the Taneytown Road and Cemetery Ridge had to be held at all costs. The long low ridge was the key element to Meade's planned deployment because it screened his troops, reinforcements, supplies, numbers, and movements. It also screened his direct link to Frederick City, Westminster, and Baltimore beyond, via the Taneytown Road, and was critical to his ability to move troops, matériel, and supplies. Holding the round-topped hills anchoring his left, or southern, end of the line was as important as holding Cemetery Ridge. If the hills fell, so too would Cemetery Ridge and the important avenue east of it. If any of the ridges or heights —Cemetery Hill, Culp's Hill, Cemetery Ridge, or the Round Tops—were to be lost, even for a brief period of time, the vital Taneytown Road would almost certainly become untenable. This, in turn, would place too much pressure on the already overcrowded Baltimore Pike, Meade's foremost concern on the army's right flank. Leaving his left flank so vulnerable makes little sense, but that was what was done. Meade stayed calm for the time being, knowing that Sickles was taking action to shore up the miscue when Geary departed. Whatever the case, the Second

---

49 Eric Campbell, "Caldwell Clears the Wheatfield," *Gettysburg Magazine,* Issue 3, 29.

50 Ibid. Sickles temporarily placated Meade by sending one infantry brigade toward Little Round Top.

Corps' move north at that hour was within the scope of Meade's initial mapped plan.[51]

*   *   *

Once he completed his pre-dawn reconnaissance of the Culp's Hill-Spangler's Meadow area and subsequent debriefing with Meade, General Hunt rode back toward Cemetery Hill for the sole purpose of placing artillery along the Baltimore Pike to cover the gap that so worried General Slocum. The sun was beginning to rise above the ridges to the east when Hunt encountered artillery commander Maj. Thomas Osborn near the gatehouse. Ordering Osborn to join him, Hunt headed south down the Baltimore Pike toward Spangler's farm lane and the unprotected gap in the Union line 2,000 yards east of the Baltimore Pike beyond Spangler's expansive meadow.

Hunt and Osborn had not ridden far when Hunt noticed several smoothbore guns in battery along the pike some 500 to 600 yards north and northwest of the meadow. Obviously taken by surprise, Hunt abruptly turned to Osborn and pointedly asked, "What are those batteries doing there?" The Eleventh Corps artillery commander explained that he had just placed them at General Howard's discretion to guard this opening in the line. Despite being sent by Meade to expedite this exact deployment, Hunt retorted, "Batteries should not be so exposed without support." When Osborn replied that General Howard had no troops to spare, Hunt asked, "Whose plan was it in putting them there?" Osborn explained that he had reconnoitered the pass, found it open, and volunteered to Howard to guard it with more guns. Hunt completed his inspection and was about to ride off when Osborn asked him what instructions he had to give. "None," replied the apparently satisfied artillery chief.[52]

Six Napoleons belonging to Lt. Eugene A. Bancroft's Battery G, 4th U.S. had unlimbered west of and above the Baltimore Pike 500 yards northwest of Spangler's Meadow at a slight angle to the road. Fronting southeast, Bancroft's guns sat in perfect left-enfilade (with the advantage of elevation) to the meadow, allowing each piece to rake the approaches over most of the nearby open ground. With an effective range of about 1,700 yards at a five-degree muzzle elevation, the smoothbores could easily cover all but 300 yards of the main avenue of approach for any Confederates coming from the east.[53]

51 USGS MRC 39077G2, *Bachelder Maps, Second Day.*

52 Osborn, *Eleventh Corps Artillery,* 22.

53 Ibid., 21; Shultz and Rollins, *The Baltimore Pike Arty Line,* 10-12; USGS MRC 39077G2.

A little farther northeast of the Baltimore Pike on the same extended rise that held Bancroft's battery west of the pike was Capt. Hubert Dilger's Battery I, 1st Ohio Light Artillery. While they did not enjoy Bancroft's field of fire, Dilger's half-battery of smoothbores nevertheless enfiladed much of Spangler's Meadow, including the stretch from Spangler's Spring southeast to Rock Creek and south toward McAllister's Hill. Thus, an attacking force moving from east to west toward the turnpike would have to advance through eleven pieces of smoothbore artillery and a well-placed and consolidated crossfire. The Napoleons, though lacking the distance of rifled guns, were devastating at these relatively short ranges against infantry in the open. A substantial part of the slaughter visited on Brig. Gen. Alfred Scales' North Carolina brigade the previous afternoon south of the Chambersburg Pike came from just such pieces.[54]

Although Meade, Hunt, and Slocum shared concerns about the gap, it was Major Osborn who had taken the initiative, approached Howard, and received permission to shift the better part of two batteries to cover it—despite leaving West Cemetery Hill vulnerable. This was but another example of how time favored Meade while capable subordinates assumed responsibilities in the field, covering issues and concerns that were still being discussed at army headquarters. Osborn's gamble to shift guns from the already undermanned West Cemetery Hill line would in time pay off. Hunt departed Cemetery Hill for army headquarters after telling Osborn to draw whatever ammunition he needed when the Artillery Reserve and its reserve train under General Tyler arrived. Osborn would do so and, when the Rebels renewed their attacks through Spangler's Meadow 24 hours later, several of his guns were on hand to help knock the attacking infantry into bloody heaps.[55]

Hunt returned to army headquarters and informed Meade that he had visited Cemetery Hill and instructed Osborn to send batteries to plug the gap that worried Slocum. This information—coupled with news from General Tyler that an ample supply of ammunition was but a few miles south—relieved Meade. Hunt walked outside the small Leister house, stretched out under a small tree, and fell asleep. Hancock was already napping nearby. This would be their last good rest for quite some time.[56]

*   *   *

---

54 Shultz and Rollins, *The Baltimore Pike Arty Line*, 12-13.

55 *OR* 27, pt. 1, 232; Shultz and Rollins, *The Baltimore Pike Arty Line*, 12-13. Edward G. Longacre, *The Man Behind the Guns: A Military Biography of General Henry J. Hunt, Commander of Artillery, Army of the Potomac* (Cranbury, NJ, 1977), 187.

56 Longacre, *The Man Behind the Guns*, 187.

On the other side of the field, General Pendleton and Capt. Samuel Johnston were sitting on their mounts in Biesecker's Woods just west of the Emmitsburg Road. After having successfully crested Warfield Ridge sight unseen, south of and below John Buford's cavalry, they planned to scout east of the Emmitsburg Road —just as Ward readied his brigade to redeploy southward.

An inevitable clash was in the making, one that promised to be large and unrelenting. Hancock, Humphreys, Anderson, and Wilcox would play major roles in the upcoming fight—all based on the rather sketchy and often inaccurate information provided by reconnaissance patrols dispatched by their respective commanders.

Chapter Seven

"[We] rode along the base of round top to beyond the ground that was occupied by General Hood, and where there was later a cavalry fight."

— *Capt. Samuel R. Johnston, C. S. A.*[1]

Early Morning, July 2:
The Pendleton-Johnston Reconnaissance

About the same time the Union men of Gen. Winfield Hancock's Second Corps were rising southeast of the Round Tops, Gen. Richard Anderson's Rebel division was beginning to stir in the pre-dawn stillness atop Herr's Ridge west of Gettysburg. A half-mile to Anderson's front and right, General Pender's division was likewise rising. Thomas's and Perrin's brigades, the latter devastated in battle the day before, began relieving and reinforcing their picket line in an old sunken farm lane that connected William Bliss's property with Breckenridge Street south of town. By the light of the full moon, advanced skirmishers and sharpshooters crawled forward to a split-rail fence a few yards east of and above the sunken farm lane to reinforce those already there. From this advanced position they could hear and see enemy pickets behind another rail fence 300 yards away. The opposing skirmishers warily eyed one another, but no one pulled a trigger. The rest of Thomas's Georgians, sheltered in the McMillan orchard west of the wall, listened to the creaking of artillery wheels as several batteries redeployed west of an above them.[2]

On Thomas's right was a relatively fresh brigade of Tar Heel infantry. Brigadier General James H. Lane, a prewar professor at VMI and the North Carolina Military

---

1   Samuel R. Johnston letter to Lafayette McLaws, June 27, 1892, *SHSP,* 5:183-184.

2   OR 27, pt. 2, 664-65. The old sunken road is also known as Long Lane. The second farm lane is today's West Confederate Avenue. The McMillian orchards were all west of the wall on both sides of the farm.

This modern photo shows the northern entrance to the William Bliss farmyard looking south from the dog-leg section of the Sunken (Long Lane) Road. The Bliss house once stood to the right of the gate with the barn beyond it. Spangler's Woods are clearly visible in the distance. *Todd C. Wiley*

Institute, ordered the bulk of his force to pull back westward, away from both the wall and the rutted farm lane in order to allow arriving artillery to move into position. His skirmishers, however, stayed put in the sunken lane and connected with the right flank of Thomas's picket line at the point where the lane abruptly turned west 90 degrees before passing over upper Stevens Run. Instead of following the lane west and forming a salient, Lane's pickets continued southeast across it, following the narrow hollow housing Stevens Run as it skirted the eastern edge of the Bliss farm. To the immediate east of Stevens Run, an elongated knoll rose up to 10 feet above the depression before gradually descending eastward toward the Emmitsburg Road some 350 yards away. To the south, this low rise melted into the southern edge of the plain before reaching the Bliss farm lane and gate along the Emmitsburg Road.[3]

Lane's men controlled both the shallow hollow and Bliss farm and the north-south running rail fence atop the rise east of and above Stevens Run. This old wooden fence, however, was overgrown with thick and tall brush and other assorted vines that obstructed both easy passage and view. If not well-maintained,

3   USGS MRC 39077G2; *Bachelder Maps, Second Day.*

Pennsylvania bush honeysuckle grows in clumps from six feet to as tall as 15 feet and half again as thick, a dense hedgerow that covers any and all obstacles in its way. As Lane's men quickly learned, each fencepost acted as an anchor for the wild vines that grew in abundance, fed by the nutrients and moisture in the hollow around Stevens Run. At least head high in spots, at first blush the tangled growth appeared to be a perfect location for Rebel marksmen to ply their trade. It would soon also become a hindrance. Until then it was a safe haven for Lane's advance pickets, who could hear their adversaries talking several hundred yards away along the Emmitsburg Road.[4]

Youthful Col. William Lowrance, the commander of the 34th North Carolina, assumed command of Alfred Scales's shattered brigade after that general's painful wounding the previous day. Ordered to the extreme right of Lee's line, Lowrance sent out a strong picket to the east and south to guard against any surprises. It was not until about 1:00 a.m. that he ordered the few men still in the ranks to stack arms for the night. His effective strength was so small that nearly all of his men were out on the skirmish line. His left flank connected with Lane's on the Bliss farm, and thinly stretched 500 yards south toward the northeastern point of Henry Spangler's woods. Lowrance did not have enough men to adequately cover such a large front, but he did the best with the limited manpower he had at his disposal.[5]

About dawn on July 2, Lowrance received orders to reposition his brigade by extending his right. He was to hold that position "at all hazards." The colonel was not overly excited about this assignment because his command was the only force available to guard the guns on that exposed flank. "I considered it hazardous in the extreme," he explained. Lowrance planned to throw out a strong line of skirmishers under Lt. A. J. Brown of the 38th North Carolina. In order to fill Brown's line, however, the 26-year-old colonel had to use nearly all his available manpower. Hugging the stone wall paralleling the eastern edge of Spangler's Woods, Brown stretched his line another 700 yards south, where he refused it to the right to front south to face the Millerstown Road.[6]

Between 1:00 a.m. and early dawn, McIntosh's and Lane's artillery battalions were parceled out south of the Fairfield Road. Although McIntosh still held his position in Shultz's Woods, his 14 pieces were spread farther south to make up for Captain Patterson's departure to support Wilcox's brigade. Major John Lane's ten guns extended this line southward several hundred yards to a point just north of the

---

4   Ibid. Northern bush honeysuckle (*Diervilla Ionicera*), native to south-central Pennsylvania, is an arching shrub with twining vines in the family *Caprifoliaceae*.

5   OR 27, pt. 2, 671.

6   Ibid.; USGS MRC 39077G2; *Bachelder Maps, Second Day*.

McMillan farm. Around the same time Colonel Lowrance was redeploying his skirmishers southward, Maj. Charles Richardson from Lt. Col. John J. Garnett's battalion of Heth's division arrived with nine additional rifled cannon. He had orders to send all of his rifles to a position opposite Cemetery Hill and south of the Fairfield Road. Richardson was placed to the right of Lane, with his cannons unlimbered within the belt of timber atop the crest. His rightmost piece was very near the northern edge of Spangler's Woods.[7]

The Confederate gunners had little initial opposition when dawn finally broke. As the darkness ebbed, each gun's chief of the piece sighted his charge at fixed positions across the way using landmarks such as a grouping of trees atop Cemetery Hill, Zeigler's Grove, Bryan's orchard, or a coppice along the low ridge, the latter about 1,200 yards distant from the McMillan farm. They could see some Yankee infantry stirring across the way, but the gunners held their fire so as not to draw counterbattery interest. Unknown to anyone on Seminary Ridge at 5:00 a.m., nine of the guns that had been seen unlimbering atop Cemetery Hill the previous evening had been redeployed elsewhere.[8]

General Ewell's Second Corps artillery formed an irregular crescent from northwest of Gettysburg around to the right of Cemetery Hill. On the extreme Confederate left near Benner's Hill was Lt. Col. R. Snowden Andrews' battalion of guns under a teenage major named Joseph W. Latimer (Andrews was wounded at the Second Battle of Winchester). The Rebel position extended progressively westward past Blocher's Knoll to Oak Hill before turning due south toward the Lutheran Seminary, where Capt. Willis J. Dance's 1st Virginia Artillery Battalion of the Second Corps Reserve Artillery deployed. On Dance's right, extending down Seminary Ridge, was nearly all of A. P. Hill's Third Corps Reserve Artillery. It was a formidable line of guns, all of which were aimed at known Union positions south of Gettysburg. Cemetery Hill was the primary target, with little if any immediate reference to the lower ridge south of it.[9]

The rising sun illuminated the outline of Cemetery Ridge for the Rebel artillerists. From Zeigler's Grove 500 yards south to the Copse of Trees, the darkened crest and the lower western brow above the Emmitsburg Road appeared open except perhaps for the Emanuel Trostle farm. The setting appeared perfect for raking the lower ridge from top to bottom (Zeigler's Grove in the north to the Hummelbaugh farm lane farther south). Although Colonel Walker's reserve batteries near the Fairfield Road had a good right-front enfilade, a careful look at a

---

7   OR 27, pt. 2, 635, 652.

8   Thomas W. Osborn, "The Artillery at Gettysburg," *Philadelphia Weekly Press*, May 31, 1879.

9   OR 27, pt. 2, 349; *Bachelder Maps, Second Day*.

map suggests that any and all of his batteries might readily become targets for Union gunners posted on Cemetery Hill. Unless that piece of high ground was neutralized early, the magnificent fields of fire presented at sunrise could quickly vanish.[10]

*   *   *

Between 4:00-4:15 a.m., Hancock's Second Corps was stirring beyond Little Round Top while Confederate General Pendleton, about three miles distant, was being briefed by General Lee on Seminary Ridge before setting out on an early morning reconnaissance. Unbeknownst to either Lee or Pendleton, and well out of their detection, two enemy brigades belonging to Geary's division were likewise brewing their morning coffee. Both Hancock's and Geary's commands would be on the move northward and eastward, respectively, by the time Pendleton and his escort started on their sunrise journey southward to discover the location of the Union left flank and a suitable route to get there.[11]

Meeting at General Lee's headquarters south of the Chambersburg Pike, a hand-picked group of some of the army's most capable artillerists and engineers listened as their commanding general explained his desire for them to "survey the enemy's position toward some estimate of the ground and best mode of attack." Members from Pendleton's staff (including, as earlier noted, probably Captain Johnston), had ventured down Willoughby Run as far as the Millerstown Road the night before, but dusk overtook them before they could finish their work. It was believed that several rural lanes south of Millerstown Road might offer enough cover to mask a large move south. This morning's objective was to scout south of the Millerstown Road.[12]

The size of Pendleton's group on the morning of July 2 is unclear. Almost certainly it was quite small, for its objective was to reconnoiter, and do so without being seen. We know he was accompanied by reserve artillery colonels R. Lindsay Walker and A. L. Long, engineers Maj. John J. Clarke and Capt. Samuel R. Johnston, and a detachment of cavalry. Pendleton led his scouting party south from Lee's headquarters past the Lutheran Seminary along the lane paralleling the crest. Once across the Fairfield Road the party continued south toward the McMillan residence, where the farm lane was unkempt, narrow, and rutted. Turning out of it,

---

they probably headed south by southwest down the gentle slope angling toward Willoughby Run, as had the previous evening's reconnoitering party.[13]

Still guided by the full moon, and mindful of the previous evening's sortie, Pendleton made sure he stayed well below the crest of South Seminary Ridge. John Buford's Union cavalry was known to be picketing the Emmitsburg Road near where it intersected the Millerstown Road. Generals Thomas and Lane had both watched the dislodged Union troopers redeploy along Cemetery Ridge after the July 1 fight, and then watched again when they redeployed, unchallenged, farther south. When the sun set that first day, Confederate pickets could see Buford's troopers along the Emmitsburg Road on property belonging to Joseph Sherfy.[14]

Continuing down the Willoughby Run ravine, the riders splashed across the shallow run and in all likelihood followed Pitzer's Run through East Pitzer's Woods. By this time the Confederates knew Pitzer's Run was the shortest route to the Millerstown Road. Reaching the Black Horse Tavern Road just north of the confluence of Pitzer's Run and Willoughby Run, the reconnaissance party headed south below Samuel Pitzer's farm and arrived at the Pitzer Schoolhouse. Once again, a small body of Confederate riders had reached this place unseen, and were once again gazing at the terrain across the Millerstown Road unopposed.[15]

Although we do not know for sure, it is likely Pendleton ordered the riders to stop under cover of the woods while a scout or two rode out to check the Millerstown Road. At some point during this phase of the operation dawn began to break. It is probable that one of the scouts who had been on the reconnaissance the night before led the detachment southeast onto the small trace that intersected the Millerstown Road at the Flaharty farmyard just east of Willoughby Run near present-day Red Rock Road.[16] Angling unseen up Warfield Ridge through Biesecker's Woods, the party crested the ridge well south of the undulating open meadows surrounding the Millerstown Road intersection on the rise anchoring Buford's left flank. Reining in at the Philip Snyder homestead west of the Emmitsburg Road, the belt of woods there would have hidden their presence and the trace they had followed from Buford's observation.[17]

---

13 Davis, *Rise and Fall of the Confederate Govt.*, 2:441-42; USGS MRC 39077G2; *Bachelder Maps, Second Day.*

14 USGS MRC 39077G2; *Bachelder Maps, Second Day.*

15 Ibid.

16 McLaws described this sortie as consisting of 200 men. Captain Samuel Johnston described it as three or four. Pfanz, *Gettysburg: The Second Day*, 106, fn. 11; USGS MRC 39077G2; *Bachelder Maps, Second Day.*

17 USGS MRC 39077G2, *Bachelder Maps, Second Day.*

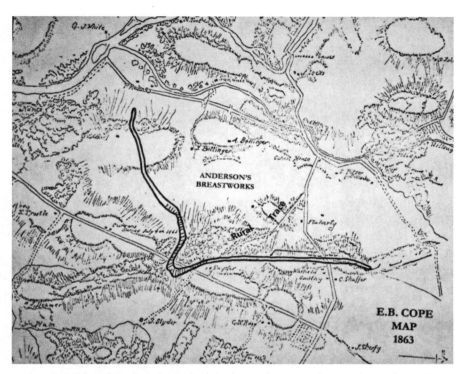

This 1868 Edward D. Cope map displays the rural trace angling southeast along West Warfield Ridge though Biesecker's Woods. It was crucial to concealing Longstreet's artillery. Note the surrounding terrain including the Pitzer, Rose, Sherfy, Snyder, Slyder, and Bushman farms along Old Red Rock Road paralleling Willoughby Run. The old Bollinger property is today's Eisenhower National Historical Site. Also note the old Willoughby Run Road intersecting the Black Horse Tavern Road at the Felix homestead in Pitzer's Woods. *LOC*

Once they reached the Snyder farm, Pendleton, Walker, Long, Clarke, and Johnston probably rested their horses and discussed their options. They apparently stayed back from the Emmitsburg Road watching and planning while several locals passed the Snyder house in an effort to get away from the battlefield. What they could not see, however, were Union troops to the south, north or east. Evidently, Pendleton and company believed they had arrived beyond the southern end (the left flank) of Meade's line.[18]

---

18 Johnston to Fitzhugh Lee, Feb. 16, 1878, Freeman Papers, Box 173, LoC. See also USGS MRC 39077G2 and *Bachelder Maps, Second Day*.

The Confederates would have noted that the ground to the east was much higher and much more rugged than the rolling and more open terrain off to the north. Unable to see far in either direction, however, and knowing General Meade's line of battle was somewhere out that way (to the east), engineers Clarke and Johnston were either ordered, or they volunteered, to guide their horses across the Emmitsburg Road and into the unknown to have a better look at what lay beyond the low ridge (Houck's) to their front. There is no record of how long General Pendleton, Walker, and Long waited in Biesecker's Woods for the engineers to return.

It was probably approaching 7:00 a.m. when the two-man scouting party returned to the Emmitsburg Road from its potentially perilous ride farther east. They were forced to wait in cover while Union cavalry riding north trotted past without detecting them. When the route was clear, Clarke and Johnston re-crossed the road and rejoined the others.[19] Whatever time it was when they returned, it was obviously before Brig. Gen. J. H. Hobart Ward's brigade of David Birney's division secured Little Round Top, Houck's Ridge, and the Rose Woods. That movement took place between 7:00 and 7:30 a.m.—long before the brigades of Cols. Burling and de Trobriand appeared a couple of hours later (about 9:00 a.m. and 10:00 a.m., respectively).[20]

The citizens Pendleton saw heading south also spotted his party, because they reported it to Col. Regis de Trobriand, a brigade commander in Birney's division, Sickles' Third Corps, when they crossed paths with his northbound brigade south of Marsh Creek. Colonel George Burling, whose brigade preceded de Trobriand's, never mentioned encountering any citizens, nor did he report receiving any information of an enemy presence in the general area. However, Capt. George Winslow of Battery K, 1st New York Artillery, supported de Trobriand's account, writing, "When within about three miles of [Gettysburg], the command halted for a brief rest, but, being informed by citizens the enemy's skirmishers were only a mile distant, and advancing toward the [Emmitsburg] road upon which we were marching, was immediately pushed on." Colonel de Trobriand's nearly four-mile slow and deliberate march to Gettysburg took an additional three hours to

---

19 Ibid. This reconnaissance was of critical importance to General Lee, so it is worth pondering why a relatively junior captain like Johnston was put in command of the small party that ventured across the Emmitsburg Road, when Major Clarke, a seasoned army engineer, was present and available. It is possible that special instructions from General Lee set the chain of command in advance, but to date no evidence either way has surfaced.

20 C. R. Page to Pendleton, Feb. 22, 1878, Pendleton Papers, Louis R. Round Special Collections Library, UNC; Johnston to McLaws, June 27, 1892, Freeman Papers, Box 173, LoC.

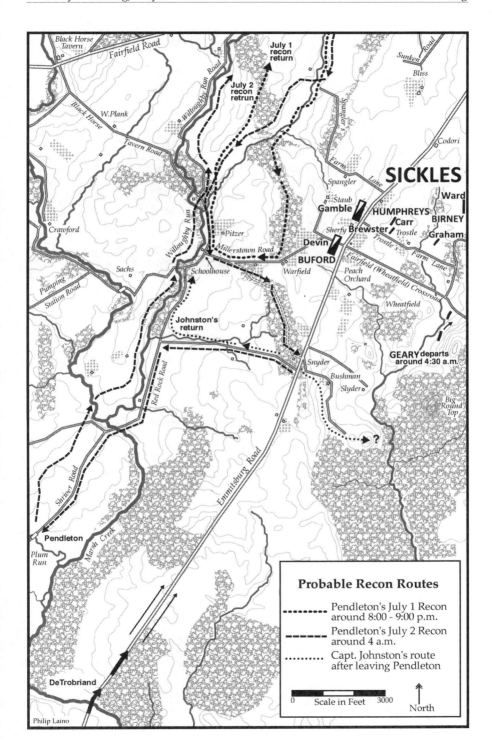

Black Horse Tavern

Fairfield Road

July 1 recon return

Sunken Road

Bliss

Black Horse

W. Plank

Willoughby Run Road

July 2 recon retrun

Codori

Tavern Road

Spangler's Spring

Spangler Lane

SICKLES

Farm

Spangler

Ward

Crawford

Willoughby Run

Pitzer

Staub

Gamble

HUMPHREYS

BIRNEY

Carr

Sherfy **Brewster**

Trostle

Millerstown Road

Devin

BUFORD

Warfield

Peach Orchard

Fairfield (Wheatfield) Crossroad

Graham

Trostle's Farm Lane

Sachs

Schoolhouse

Pumping Station Road

Johnston's return

Wheatfield

Snyder

GEARY departs around 4:30 a.m.

Bushman

Slyder

Big Round Top

Red Rock Road

Emmitsburg Road

?

Shriner Road

Pendleton

Plum Run

Marsh Creek

DeTrobriand

Philip Laino

Probable Recon Routes

▪▪▪▪▪▪▪ Pendleton's July 1 Recon around 8:00 - 9:00 p.m.

━ ━ ━ Pendleton's July 2 Recon around 4 a.m.

·········· Capt. Johnston's route after leaving Pendleton

0   Scale in Feet   3000

North

This 1904 photo was taken where present-day West Confederate Avenue intersects the Emmitsburg Road. Philip Snyder's farmyard is in the middle-right distance atop Warfield Ridge surrounded by the white picket fence with Biesecker's Woods beyond it. General Pendleton's reconnaissance party waited here for Captain Johnston to return from east of the Emmitsburg Road. The NPS demolished the post-battle house on the left. *NPS*

complete. However, the brigade did not encounter or spot any Rebels because Pendleton's party was long gone by the time de Trobriand's lead elements reached the Snyder farm.[21]

With the certain knowledge that civilians had seen them, and with the intelligence his group had gathered, Pendleton knew he had to get word quickly back to General Lee. Pendleton had to be pleased that he had secured information about the general location of the Army of the Potomac's left flank, but he may have been troubled by the fact that he was still unsure of the route Lee could use to execute a large scale flanking maneuver. It appears that once Johnston and Clarke safely returned west of the Emmitsburg Road, they rode northward to report back to Lee, while Pendleton continued farther south.[22]

21 OR 27, pt. 1, 519-20, 523, 570, 587. Most reports and descriptions of Pendleton's reconnaissance suggest a small party. The civilian report of a "column" suggests a larger party, giving some credence to General McLaws' recollection that it was 200 men, supra, note 16.

22 Samuel R. Johnston to Lafayette McLaws, June 27, 1892, in Johnston Notes, Lafayette McLaws Papers, Duke University. See also David A. Powell, "A Reconnaissance Gone Awry," *Gettysburg Magazine*, Issue 23, 88-99.

The question Pendleton had to resolve was whether massed troops could be brought up unobserved. With so many stone walls and rail fences crisscrossing the fields and meadows, it is almost certain that Pendleton would have followed the lanes or stream beds wherever possible during this part of his patrol. The faster he could gather his information, the more quickly he could return. Sticking to the available byways was by far the least time-consuming way to travel, and because part of his mission was to find a route by which to move large numbers of troops and artillery trains, he had a particular interest in the roads.[23]

What remained of Pendleton's scouting party dropped back into the Willoughby Run ravine, probably following present-day Red Rock Road, while Johnston and Clarke rode back north. Continuing south paralleling the eastern bank of Willoughby Run, Pendleton's party reached the confluence of the meandering run with Marsh Creek three miles distant. They forded the creek and continued down Red Rock Road as far as present-day Shriver Road, where they turned east toward the Emmitsburg Road before ending their lengthy ride at the Shriver farm overlooking (West) Plum Run, a small tributary 1,000 yards west of and below the Emmitsburg Road. The Shriver farm was well hidden west of and below a wide cultivated rise with the south-flowing Marsh Creek in the low ground some 500 feet west of the road. (West) Plum Run flowed due east before emptying into Marsh Creek near the Emmitsburg Road bridge. Somewhere likely near Shriver's farm, Pendleton's group encountered two dismounted Union cavalrymen who promptly surrendered. "Having satisfied myself of the course and character of this road [known variously as Willoughby Run, Black Horse Tavern, and Red Rock]," Pendleton later wrote, "I returned to an elevated point on the Fairfield road . . . and dispatched messengers to General Longstreet and the commanding general."[24]

In a letter to Lafayette McLaws almost three decades later, Captain Johnston described how he crossed the Emmitsburg Road, from which he said he had a commanding view but could see no Union soldiers. He noted that he, Maj. John Clarke, and two others conducted the reconnaissance (he made no mention of Pendleton), and that they crossed the creek [Willoughby Run] and "turned to the left at once and got on the ridge where you formed your line, following along that ridge in the direction of the round top across the Emmetsburg [sic] Road and got up on the slopes where I had a commanding view, then rode along the base of

23 OR 27, pt. 2, 349; USGS MRC 39077G2. The scouting party likely returned to Willoughby Run via present day Eisenhower Farm Road, which at the time was a rural farm lane.

24 Samuel R. Johnston letter to Fitz Lee, February 11, 1878, Johnston letter to Lafayette McLaws, June 27, 1892, Douglas S. Freeman Collection, LoC. See also SHSP, 5:182-184.

round top to beyond the ground that was occupied by General Hood, and where there was later a cavalry fight."[25]

Johnston never claimed to have scaled either of the Round Tops. Rather, he wrote that he moved up the slope skirting the base of Big Round Top. Passing over a ridge with a commanding view, he suggested that he rode over the same ground where on July 3, troopers from Brig. Gen. Elon J. Farnsworth's brigade of Judson Kilpatrick's cavalry division battled for their lives on land belonging to farmers John Slyder and George Bushman. The so-called "ridge" he probably scaled was west-southwest of both Round Tops and Houck's Ridge, where the Slyder and Bushman farms are located [today referred to as Bushman's Hill]. There are numerous outcropping and rises that comprise part of Houck's Ridge referred to as Devil's Den and Gate, where Plum Run separates lower western Big Round Top from that of South Houck's Ridge. From his position, Johnston almost certainly could have seen the shadow-covered western face of Little Round Top from either the Slyder or Bushman farms without actually scaling Big Round Top. Geary's White Star Division was almost certainly already gone and Ward's brigade had yet to arrive, but was stirring to the north and by 7:00 a.m. was in transit south.[26]

However far Pendleton and his riders traveled, by any measure this reconnaissance was an abysmal failure. Its primary purpose was to positively identify the Union left, and this it failed to do. Had Johnston really enjoyed the "commanding view" he would later claim, he surely would have noted Ward's brigade below Little Round Top in the Valley of Death, with its skirmishers on Houck's Ridge north of today's Slaughter Pen and Devil's Den. He would also have seen two enemy batteries unlimbered below the base of Little Round Top in what today is referred to as "the Valley of Death," stretching from Devil's Den north to beyond Wheatfield Road. The reconnaissance team had somehow failed to notice 8,500 Union soldiers—including more than 2,000 cavalrymen and horses—north of them opposite the crest less than one mile away. Even a six-gun Union battery aligned along the Emmitsburg Road stretching some 150 yards was somehow missed.

First Captain Johnston and later General Pendleton would explain in detail to General Lee that they had indeed discovered a route that would allow the army to move large bodies of troops and artillery beyond the Union left unseen. One

---

25 Ibid. The Shriver Plum Run farm is located east of and above Plum Run on Shriver Road west of Greenmount. This Plum Run should not be confused with the Plum Run farther north that flows through the battlefield. Johnston's claims have been the subject of controversy and speculation since the battle. He may have reached Bushman's Hill, but not by the route he described. It seems unlikely he reached the slopes of the Round Tops.

26 USGS MRC 39077G2.

Gettysburg authority summarized it this way: "It must be concluded that when Johnston's reconnaissance party failed to detect Federal units in the area between the Peach Orchard and the Round Tops and on the lower end of Cemetery Ridge, it was somehow the victim of grave misfortune. As a result of this failure, Captain Johnston made an incorrect report to his commanding general that was to have serious consequences later in the day."[27]

Pendleton's returning party passed back over Millerstown Road unnoticed and continued north unmolested. Reentering Pitzer's Woods, the riders retraced their route. This time they encountered pickets belonging to the 10th Alabama of Wilcox's brigade, sent there to secure the vital woods and army's right flank. Continuing north, Pendleton and his patrol returned unscathed to the Fairfield Road two prisoners richer, but not before noticing Union troop movement along and east of the Emmitsburg Road. Somewhere after cresting South Seminary Ridge (possibly from a position near the McMillan farm) they spotted significant numbers of Federal troops on line or moving up, including Hancock's Second Corps. By the time Pendleton reached the Fairfield Road, his artillery was engaging some of Hancock's men as the Second Corps deployed along Cemetery Ridge and the Emmitsburg Road.[28]

* * *

Between 5:00-5:30 a.m. on July 2, the Taneytown Road south of Gettysburg experienced a flurry of activity. With Geary's two brigades heading east, combined with Hancock's entire corps moving north, it is a wonder gridlock did not ensue, creating what Meade did not want or need—an unexpected waste of time. Colonel Charles Candy's brigade left Little Round Top and Cemetery Ridge via the crossroad with Lt. John Egan's section of bronze smoothbores in tow, while Brig. Gen. George Greene's brigade exited Cemetery Ridge to the north using several rural lanes that passed through Sarah Patterson's Woods. Turning east on Blacksmith Shop Road, Greene led the way, followed by Candy's brigade, with Kinzie's and Atwell's eight combined guns bringing up the rear. Although Geary's departure from South Cemetery Ridge did not significantly impact Hancock's

27 Johnston to George Peterskin, undated letter, Johnston Papers, HSC. For a complete guide to the July 2 Johnston-Pendleton affair, see Powell, "A Reconnaissance Gone Awry," and Pfanz, *Gettysburg: The Second Day*, 107.

28 Ibid.

march north, it would, however, impact the redeployment of Sickles' Third Corps.[29]

Even though Birney's division of the Third Corps was directed to replace the departing Geary, Birney did not receive notice from Sickles until 7:00 a.m.—a full two hours after Geary vacated South Cemetery Ridge. "On the morning of July 2, about 7 a.m. under orders from Major-General Sickles," Birney later wrote, "I relieved Geary's division, and formed a line, resting its left on the Sugar Loaf Mountain [Little Round Top] and the right thrown in a direct line toward the cemetery, connecting on the right with the Second Corps."[30]

Birney was correct with his time, but wrong about his right flank and Hancock's Second Corps. Since its arrival the previous evening, Ward's brigade had served as Birney's right flank along the line atop Cemetery Ridge. When Ward and the two attached batteries, Bucklyn and Clark, headed south about 7:00 a.m., Cemetery Ridge was devoid of Union infantry from Zeigler's Grove south about a mile to beyond the George Weikert farm. By the time Hancock's Second Corps began arriving 90 minutes later, Ward was still repositioning his brigade west of Little Round Top. At that moment, the impromptu plan was for Humphreys' brigades under Carr and Brewster to fill at least a portion of the void from Birney's division in the shadows of Little Round Top north to where Hancock would deploy on southern Cemetery Ridge. Later, the balance of Birney's men and Humphreys' late-arriving brigade under Colonel Burling would further fill the large gap that from 7:00 to 8:30 a.m. had sat wide open. Luckily for the Third Corps, there was no Rebel attack until well after the gap was closed.[31]

Meanwhile, Meade was banking on keeping all the roads leading to Gettysburg open in order to expedite the arrival of not only Burling and de Trobriand, but the Fifth Corps and Sixth Corps, which were still four to ten miles distant, respectively. Not only were all trains ordered off the Taneytown Road and Baltimore Pike, but many were sent back toward Westminster, some 25 miles distant. Although this would allow more rapid movement by the infantry approaching from the east, south, and southeast, the army would have make do with the loss of vital supplies such as food stores, medical stores, equipment, and personal baggage. The fields and meadows on either side of the Taneytown Road north to Cemetery Hill clogged with ambulances and wagons carrying the army's mainstay, including

---

29 USGS MRC 39077G2.

30 *OR* 27, pt. 1, 482.

31 Birney's right flank was nowhere near the Second Corps after Ward vacated his position atop Cemetery Ridge at 7:00 a.m. to move south in conjunction with that division's movement toward the Round Tops, or "Sugar Loaf Mountain," as Birney suggested.

ordnance and munitions. Although these trains had priority over those considered superfluous, they too were ordered off the roads until further notice.[32]

As the dawn began to break above the wooded ridge to the east, Union Capt. Dunbar R. Ransom, commander of the First Regular Brigade of Reserve Artillery, raised a pair of field glasses to his eyes. Though born in North Carolina, Ransom grew up in Vermont, the eldest son in a military family that reached back to the American Revolution. He fought bravely at Antietam and was singled out by both Meade and Hunt. When the artillery arm was reorganized following Chancellorsville, Ransom was promoted to brigade command. Dawn on July 2 found him standing near the crest of Cemetery Ridge above the Jacob Hummelbaugh barn, where moments earlier General Tyler, commanding the Artillery Reserve, was ousted from his newly acquired headquarters by Second Corps medical staff that had arrived in advance of that corps to set up shop.[33]

West from his position Ransom spotted another wooded ridge nearly a mile distant. Visible west to northwest was the white cupola atop the Lutheran Seminary nestled in a grove of trees on the low crest of Seminary Ridge. This rise stretched as far south as the eye could see paralleling the higher ground where Ransom stood. The Emmitsburg Road running between the ridges undulated over the wide valley before disappearing during its run southward over the high ground where Buford's cavalrymen were still posted. The red morning sun had not yet cleared the next eastern ridge, so the valley floor and Taneytown Road below him remained partially concealed in early morning shadows. A blanket of mist and lingering campfire smoke drifted through hollows, wood lots, and orchards. The distinctive smells of battle and of an army in camp permeated the sultry morning air. Unbeknownst to the captain, not far beyond the cupola-topped building to Ransom's northwest, General Lee was in a heated discussion with his "old war horse," General Longstreet, about how to wage the upcoming battle.[34]

Sometime between 5:00 and 6:00 a.m. several companies of pioneers from Hancock's Second Corps double-timed through the Hummelbaugh intersection. Detached from the 14th Indiana, Capt. Nathan Willard set his men to work dismantling Hummelbaugh's rail and snake fences and, north of his property, those belonging to a tenant named Peter Frey. Clearing the fences and partially dismantling the low stone wall would allow other troops to move easily and quickly

32 Ibid., 128-29.

33 Wyllys Cadwell Ransom, *Historical Outline of the Ransom Family of America* (Ann Arbor, MI, 1903), 29; Obituary of Dunbar R. Ransom, *Dallas Morning News,* July 12, 1897.

34 USGS MRC39077G2.

once they left the road to angle up the gentle eastern slope of East Cemetery Ridge.[35]

South of Willard's busy pioneers, Hancock's Second Corps was on the move again. The column had left its bivouac and been trudging up the road for more than an hour when the vanguard division under Brig. Gen. Alexander Hays was ordered off the road to the right. Apparently the entire corps stopped prior to committing itself to Cemetery Ridge, possibly until General Slocum had secured the Baltimore Pike. With Slocum appeased on notice of Geary's arrival, the Second Corps moved out again with the end of its delayed march just a quarter-mile or so ahead. Hancock's men were worn down. Except for a couple hours of rest at Uniontown, Maryland, on June 29 to let the corps close up, his footsore infantry had force-marched 30 of the past 48 hours. Nearly three-quarters of his men had either fallen or lagged so far behind that he had no choice but to stop at Uniontown to let them catch up. They had been slogging through rain, heat, ankle-deep mud, and even heavy dust for the better part of five days, rarely resting more than a few hours at a time. The efforts of Captain Willard's pioneers would help make the last leg of their journey up the eastern slope of Cemetery Ridge a bit easier.

"I was so completely worn out & exhausted that I groaned at every step," one private wrote of the march to Gettysburg. "When we halted last night, there was not 2 whole companies left in the regiment. The boys had marched just as far as they were able and then fell out. The road was lined with men for 5 miles. We lost 2 boys that I know of out of the regiment that died yesterday." The endless marching was nearly over. The dying, however, was just beginning.[36]

Conspicuous by its absence, as Ransom duly noted, was wagon traffic. It was evident that everything with wheels except artillery carriages and caissons had been ordered off the road. Artillery baggage wagons and ambulances were no exception. As of 4:30 a.m., the Taneytown Road had been declared off-limits to most wheeled traffic. Even the much-needed ammunition train that accompanied Ransom's Regular Artillery Brigade—which had been promised to Howard's Eleventh Corps —would sit for four hours in its park south of Little Round Top. Meade had ordered the expediting of this small ammunition train but, without clearing it with him, Hancock dispatched a verbal communiqué to clear the road of all wagon traffic—with no exceptions—prior to his corps' taking to that avenue that

---

35 *OR* 27, pt. 1, 459. Willard was detached from the 14th Indiana to command the Second Corps pioneers. They likely arrived between 5:45-6:00 a.m. in order to clear the fences and dismantle the wall.

36 Private Manley Stacey to father, June 30, 1863, in Civil War Letters, Manley Stacey Collection Historical Society of Oak Park and River Forest, IL; *OR* 27, pt. 1, 407. He gives a very precise account of his regiment's movements and their times.

morning. No one dared challenge the fiery Hancock, however informally, least of all Ransom, who had ridden ahead of his column to await the ammunition train. Like others, he had no choice but to mark time.[37]

While Captain Willard's pioneers dismantled fences and cleared a path, Hays' Third Division reentered the Taneytown Road after its short stay south of the Granite Schoolhouse Road. This column of soldiers—their dark blue blouses, kepis, and hats coated with fine Pennsylvania dust—closed on Hummelbaugh's farm lane 500 yards distant, while Gibbon's men took to the avenue to their rear. Although it had been daylight for nearly an hour, the sun had yet to crest the ridge east of Taneytown Road as Hays' column quietly marched north. After having heard Meade's proclamation concerning the shirking of duties, aside from the occasional barking of an officer all that could be heard was the tramping of feet, the rattling of accouterments, the jingling and clanking of equipment, and a cough or faint remark here and there. Two of Alexander Hays' three brigades knew little of their general, who had taken command only a few days before. They could see that he cut a good figure, a six-footer with reddish hair and a graying beard.[38] The Third Brigade, comprised of three relatively inexperienced and one veteran New York regiments, however, knew him to be loud, fiery, and aggressive. They were devoted to him, for up until the previous week he had been their trusted brigade commander. And just a week earlier neither Hays nor the Third Brigade had been part of the Army of the Potomac, serving instead on guard duty in Centreville, Virginia. Now, finally, they were back with the army. The men had full confidence in both Hays and Hancock, and it was well-placed on both counts.[39]

Hancock was engaged in an animated conversation at army headquarters about where each corps should be positioned. Meade set forth his plan of how he expected to hold the Taneytown Road and, more importantly, the Baltimore Pike. Hancock at this early hour already had some doubts after finding out Geary had departed for the east. As Hancock already knew, Meade expected the defeated First

---

37 OR 27, pt. 1, 368. Not all orders were passed down through the chain of command, which at times created confusion. Osborn's shortage of ammunition atop Cemetery Hill would last until afternoon after Hancock's early morning order concerning wagon traffic upset the timetable, or expectations, of Generals Hunt and Tyler. Hancock's order delaying Tyler's reserve ammunition, including Captain Ransom's, would spark a polite feud between Hancock and Hunt that would last until Hancock's death in 1886. Artillery pieces and their accompanying caissons were the exception to this order.

38 Wayne Mayhood, *Alexander "Fighting Elleck" Hays: The Life of a Civil War General from West Point to the Wilderness* (Jefferson, NC, 2005), 5, 100-10.

39 Ibid. Gilbert Adams Hays, George T. Fleming, ed., *Life and Letters of Alexander Hays: Brevet Colonel, United States Army, Brigadier General and Brevet Major General United States Volunteers*, 195-216; OR 27, pt. 1, 453-54.

Corps and Eleventh Corps to hold Cemetery Hill with help from Twelfth Corps on their right and rear. Hancock's own Second Corps would connect with the First Corps' left west of Cemetery Hill, and stretch as far south as the terrain and his strength permitted. Dan Sickles' Third Corps, meanwhile, would connect with Hancock's left flank near the Hummelbaugh farm lane (the Union center) while George Sykes' Fifth Corps would join up with Sickles' left somewhere north of Little Round Top. Alfred Pleasonton's cavalry would patrol the army's far left, with mounted vedettes reaching as far west, north, and south as practicable. The arriving Sixth Corps under John Sedgwick would be held in reserve along the Baltimore Pike within striking distance of any part of Meade's anticipated fishhook-shaped line.[40]

As Meade, Hancock, and others continued their discussions, a noted absentee from the meeting, Maj. Gen. Daniel E. Sickles, was conducting his own Third Corps staff briefing. The New York general worried that his six small brigades, numbering 10,675, were too few to hold the lengthy low ridge Meade had instructed him to occupy. When Meade dismounted at the Evergreen Gatehouse near midnight, he suggested to Sickles that his corps hold the ridge connecting the two hills on the left currently occupied by Geary's division. He could place his arriving brigades as he saw fit as long as they were in position to block any and all attempts of the enemy to flank the position. Because he entrusted his subordinates to make necessary decisions, Meade was not worried about Sickles or his intentions at 6:00 a.m. on July 2; his orders had been clearly communicated the previous night—or so Meade thought.[41]

Besides the fact that much of his corps was on relatively low and swampy ground, Sickles believed his thinly stretched front was not sufficient to secure his line. His left flank was in the air and thus exposed. It was unclear to him at that hour where, exactly, his left flank was supposed to be located. Sickles worried about both what he could not see, and what the cavalry was not telling him. Simply put, he did not trust Meade's word that Sykes' Fifth Corps would be up in time to support him. Chancellorsville was fresh in his mind. His left flank loomed large as an issue that, to him, seemed insoluble. As the minutes ticked past, however, the general became even more concerned about his front, convinced the higher Emmitsburg Road was

---

40 *Bachelder Maps, Second Day*. The old Fairfield Crossroad, a rural wagon road known today as the Wheatfield Road, needed to be controlled, as did Abraham Trostle's farm lane 500 yards to the north and the Codori-Hummelbaugh farm lane an additional 1,000 yards farther north. All of these lanes intersected Taneytown Road. Hancock knew all of them had to be maintained if he was to hold Cemetery Ridge.

41 Freeman Cleves, *Meade of Gettysburg*, 146; U. S. Congress, *Report of the Joint Committee on the Conduct of the War*, A. A. Humphreys Testimony, 389-90.

the proper line to man and vigorously defend. Call it foolishness, insubordination, or military boldness, but Sickles on his own made up his mind that he was not going to occupy the inferior ground of lower Cemetery Ridge. This process started with his placement of A. A. Humphreys' arriving two brigades along the Emmitsburg Road—shortly after listening to Meade at the Evergreen Cemetery gatehouse— instead of linking up with Ward's brigade on the ridge. Hancock was concerned about his own left, because unless he could connect with Sickles' right flank, the Second Corps was open to a turning operation. After receiving Meade's assurance that Sickles would adhere to his plan, Hancock focused instead on his arriving corps.[42]

*   *   *

Several issues had plagued General Meade since the opening of the battle on July 1. Like his adversary Robert E. Lee, Meade was in the midst of a breakdown in command communications with subordinate generals who arguably placed their personal opinion, political issues, and/or selfish ambition ahead of their assigned and sworn martial duty. Meade's newness as army commander should have warranted closer cooperation from his senior lieutenants. Instead, some of them, in particular the Third Corps' General Sickles, seemed intent to act upon their own accord and ignore orders for their own interests. And Dan Sickles was not the only one.[43]

Another example is Twelfth Corps leader Maj. Gen. Henry Slocum, who made the questionable decision the previous evening to pull Brig. Gen. Alpheus Williams' division back from Benner's Hill. Slocum apparently did not want to dirty his hands, particularly considering his unusual decision that night to allow a junior-ranking officer, General Hancock, to place Brig. Gen. John Geary's division of Slocum's corps south of Cemetery Hill. It was not Slocum's first controversial decision. Had he personally ridden forward to oversee his two divisions during the early action on July 1, Slocum would have inherited command of all the troops then on the field. That night, with General Reynolds dead and the first day's fighting in the books as another in a seemingly endless string of Union defeats, Slocum apparently did not want to assume the role of field commander nor take the corresponding personal responsibility. He and his staff had, by all appearances,

42 OR 27, pt. 1, 368-70; *Bachelder Maps, Second Day.*

43 Mark P. Oreb, S. Littlejohn, & K. Foss, eds., "Phenomenology," in *Encyclopedia of Communication Theory* (Thousand Oaks, CA: SAGE Publications, 2009), 750-52.

remained a safe distance from the front until any and all responsibility for the failure of that day's battle had passed.[44]

"General Slocum's personal behavior compounds the indictment against his generalship," argues one modern Civil War historian. "Howard's calls [note the plural] for help contained implicit and explicit requests for Slocum to ride forward and consult with him. Slocum ignored these entreaties, although he did canter ahead of his men when he met Capt. Addison G. Mason of Meade's staff. Mason informed Slocum of Reynolds' death and passed on Meade's desire to the 'push forward with all dispatch.'" Slocum's inactivity also frustrated the Eleventh Corps' General Howard, as it did General Sickles, who had previously received the same response as Howard even after Meade had informed his generals to send help if called upon.[45]

Now, on what would prove to be a fateful Thursday, July 2, basic fundamental battlefield principles—such as reconnaissance to gain a reasonable knowledge of the foe and terrain—generally did not exist for either army. The shifting and unplanned courses of action, such as that brought on by Slocum's questionable generalship, that had hindered both Meade and Lee on July 1 would continue throughout July 2. Politics within the command structure likewise hampered both leaders, who themselves lacked a solid course of action or goal. Robert E. Lee only knew that, "The enemy was there and I am going to attack him there;" his logic being "they are in position, and I am going to whip them or they are going to whip me." Even though it appears Lee had a planned course of action as early as nine o'clock on the evening of July 1, for one reason or another nothing had since materialized that could be deemed as a reliable or satisfactory reconnaissance. Lee knew the enemy was out there somewhere east of the Emmitsburg Road along Cemetery Ridge, but that was about the extent of his initial working knowledge of the tactical situation south of the Copse of Trees. He had no solid intelligence about the enemy's current forces on the field and their disposition. General Lee also lacked a solid grasp of the terrain and how who or how many other Union forces were converging on his army.

Concurrently, Meade knew little more than Lee except for the fact the Army of Northern Virginia could not possibly continue to operate so far from its home base in Virginia while subsiding off the land without risking its extensively long supply lines. Meade knew Lee had to make a move; he could not sit idle in Pennsylvania

---

44   OR 27, pt. 1, 758; Oreb, *Encyclopedia of Communication Theory,* 750-52.

45   Gallagher, *The Second Day at Gettysburg,* 100; Oreb, *Encyclopedia of Communication Theory,* 750-52.

very long. With that in mind, Meade had a slight advantage as his remaining corps converged on Gettysburg from the south and southeast.[46]

A significant part of Lee's dilemma was the fact that he had lost his "ears and eyes" when Jeb Stuart's cavalry column disappeared while moving through north Northern Virginia and into Maryland. Solely dependent on General Imboden's cavalry, which was spread thinly along his supply lines and routes of march, Lee could ill-afford to pull the Virginia horsemen away for the kind of major reconnaissance needed for an operation of the size he was undertaking. Depending upon the local citizenry for reliable intelligence was problematic at best. All Lee had as he approached Gettysburg to gather much-needed information on Meade's whereabouts were isolated roving bands of cavalry and partisans, foraging parties, skulkers, and a few spies. Without Stuart's cavalry, Lee's awareness of his opponents' movements suffered considerably.[47]

"In its semi-independent status," wrote one historian about Imboden's brigade, "the command served in an auxiliary capacity during the Gettysburg Campaign." Imboden's force was ill-prepared for such a large undertaking and was inferior to any of the brigades of cavalry currently under Jeb Stuart's command. Still, Imboden did what he could under present and dangerous circumstances. The result, however, was the "lack of carefully appraised intelligence of enemy movements and intents." And this was something General Lee desperately needed as he passed over the Mason-Dixon Line. Well before any communication failure took place at Gettysburg, the seeds of its preempted breakdown were already planted and blossoming.[48]

The general perception of Robert E. Lee is that he was a superb strategist and tactical genius on the battlefield, but that he tended to give indirect orders and "suggestions" to his subordinates rather than firm directives. He expected his lieutenants to act on their own initiative to carry out the spirit of his intentions. It was, in hindsight, ineffective with some of his leading lieutenants, including General Stuart, whose somewhat self-serving interpretation of Lee's concession to his desire to break free and roam at will during the army's march toward Maryland and Pennsylvania did not serve the army well at Gettysburg. Lee believed his gifted, but often independent-minded cavalry chieftain would understand and follow his instructions about keeping contact with the army. It apparently never entered Lee's mind that Stuart would assume this meant he could do what he wanted. Thus, Lee

---

46 Longstreet, "The Mistakes of Gettysburg, "*Philadelphia Weekly Times,* Feb. 23, 1878; Pfanz, *Gettysburg: The Second Day,* 26.

47 Coddington, *Gettysburg: A Study in Command,* 17-18.

48 Ibid.

gave the charismatic cavalryman the permission he requested. Perhaps the best general at understanding and acting on Lee's intentions had been Thomas J. Jackson, but Stonewall was dead. A. P. Hill and Richard Ewell had formally replaced the already legendary general in the new command structure of the Army of Northern Virginia, but not in the ability to really understand the army commander's desires and objectives and how to carry them out.

Major General Jubal Early, one of Ewell's division commanders, later stated that General Lee conducted his staff meetings with a very participatory style, soliciting input and comment from everyone present before reaching a decision, and that Lee held both Jackson and Longstreet in high regard. "Longstreet seemed to Lee to be steady and dependable, the consummate professional," Early opined. "Jackson was a killer, possessed of the same sorts of aggressive instincts which obsessed Lee." After Jackson was mortally wounded at Chancellorsville, Lee lamented, "I have but to show him my design, and I know that if it can be done it will be done." Lee, however, always had the last word and demanded loyalty above and beyond one's own design and/or expectations.

There was every reason for Lee to believe that, on July 2, Generals Longstreet, Hill, and Ewell would act exactly as he expected: Longstreet to attack "up the Emmitsburg Road" with cooperation from the other two corps leaders. For reasons that have never been fully explained, his corps commanders failed to execute these plans in a timely or effective manner. Lee did not call a council of war with Longstreet, Ewell, and Hill to discuss his intentions for July 2, and perhaps he should have. There is nothing, however, to suggest that Lee's lieutenants purposely dismantled his plans and objectives. On the contrary, the evidence demonstrates that all three generals participated (to varying degrees) in the planning and operations of their troops, even if their execution proved sorely lacking.

Lee, of course, spoke with all three of his corps commanders on the evening of July 1 and morning of July 2. We will never know the full nature of these conversations but, as one writer aptly put it, it left "an illusion of unanimity."[49]

---

49 Chuck May, "A Historical Perspective on Organizational Communication: Lee and his Lieutenants at Gettysburg," Thesis, University of Maryland, College Park, 1998.

Chapter Eight

"[T]he brigade rejoined the division then in front, and advanced bearing to the right,
for the purpose of taking position in line of battle."

— *Brig. Gen. Cadmus M. Wilcox, C. S. A.*[1]

Morning, July 2: Preparations

Between 8:30 and 9:00 a.m. on July 2, everyone who had ridden with General Pendleton on the lengthy dawn reconnaissance patrol had safely returned to Confederate headquarters on Seminary Ridge. General Lee received the intelligence first from Capt. Samuel R. Johnston, and next from his military secretary, Col. Armistead L. Long, who offered Lee both Pendleton's report as well as his own. All three reconnaissance accounts agreed: the Union left was nowhere to be seen south or east of Buford's cavalry bivouac along the Emmitsburg Road. The combined effect of these reports reinforced Lee's commitment to roll up the Emmitsburg Road and strike the enemy's left, which apparently was not anchored on the high ground and so was probably "up in the air." This ambitious plan would be primarily executed with Longstreet's First Corps, with portions of A. P. Hill's Third Corps going in thereafter against the Union center farther north. Hill's thrust would support and exploit Longstreet's effort. Lee was so eager to press this attack that, by the time he received Long's morning report, he had already offered his plan to Generals Ewell, Hill, Longstreet, Hood, and McLaws.[2]

When, exactly, John Hood and Lafayette McLaws issued marching orders to their respective First Corps divisions passed unrecorded. They likely received instructions from Lee's staff sometime before 7:00 a.m. because A. P. Hill completed his dispositions before nine that morning. Longstreet, however, worried

1 OR 27, pt. 2, 617.

2 Long, *Memoirs of R. E. Lee,* 280-82.

that his force was too weak to make the attack Lee wanted and, with Lee's permission, decided early on to forgo moving any troops until Brig. Gen. Evander M. Law's Alabama brigade rejoined Hood's division. Law, along with Bachman's German battery, had camped the previous night several miles to the west near New Guilford in the Cumberland Valley to protect the Confederate rear. "As soon after his arrival as we could make our preparations," Longstreet later recorded, "the movement was begun."[3]

Much has been written about the late hour Longstreet began what would be a meandering march to the army's right flank and the opening of his assault. In all likelihood, we will never fully understand or agree why this aspect of the battle evolved as it did. We do know that General Lee knew of Longstreet's desire to wait for Law and reluctantly agreed. Law's brigade did not leave New Guilford, almost 25 miles away near Fayetteville, until 3:00 a.m. Even with a relentless uninterrupted march, Law's 1,900 men could not cross South Mountain and reach the battlefield before 1:00 p.m., and Longstreet knew this when he visited Lee that morning. Lee would have known it, too. More Union troops reached the field during these intervening hours, so any increase Law's brigade contributed to the attack was more than offset by enemy arrivals. Longstreet did not send Col. E. Porter Alexander south on yet another reconnaissance to seek a route for his artillery and infantry until after 9:00 a.m., which means Longstreet could not have expected Alexander to return much before 11:00 a.m. Whatever the case, while Longstreet impatiently waited for his brigade to arrive from New Guilford and stewed about having to go over to the offensive, the timing of Lee's initial plan collapsed.[4]

Unlike Longstreet, A. P. Hill immediately moved to implement his orders. Sometime after midnight, he shifted his headquarters closer to the front to Emanuel Pitzer's barn west of McMillan's Woods along Willoughby Run. Hill also sent orders to Richard Anderson to bring his division forward from Herr's Ridge as soon as possible. For reasons that remain unexplained, however, Hill failed to share with Anderson the commanding general's intentions to attack the enemy later that day. "[I] received orders to take up a new line of battle on the right of Pender's division, about a mile and a half forward," reported the division leader. "Lane's battalion of artillery was detached from my command this morning, and did not rejoin it." Anderson did not mention that General Wilcox's brigade was still detached off his right and rear and would not quickly rejoin the division. Wilcox later claimed that he did not receive orders to rejoin Anderson's division at its new

---

3   OR 27, pt. 2, 858. Captain William Bachman's battery from Charleston, South Carolina, was originally part of the Hampton Legion.

4   Ibid., 391, 394.

Maj. Gen. Richard H. Anderson, a division commander in Lt. Gen. A. P. Hill's Third Corps. *LOC*

location until about 7:00 a.m. By that time Anderson's other brigades under Mahone, Wright, Posey, and Lang had orders to support Pender's division along Seminary Ridge.[5]

A. P. Hill's activities on that important morning remain largely undocumented, but it is likely the Third Corps commander oversaw his duties from the shade of the large Pitzer barn below the crest of Seminary Ridge. From there, Hill could easily see the changeover of picket duties when Anderson arrived with his four brigades. Between 6:00 and 7:00 a.m., Billy Mahone's Virginians entered McMillan's Woods to the immediate right of General Thomas's brigade (Pender's division). Some of Mahone's Virginians relieved Lowrance's Tar Heel pickets in Long Lane to the west of Stevens Run, with their advanced line connecting with Thomas's Georgians. Likewise, Carnot Posey's Mississippians relieved Lowrance's pickets at the Bliss farm, as did Ambrose Wright's Georgians south of that place. David Lang's Florida Brigade took control of Spangler's Woods with his pickets supporting Lt. Alsa J. Brown, the latter's right flank still refused somewhere near the Spangler homestead. Looking across the valley for the first time, Anderson's infantry saw an open Cemetery Ridge devoid of any substantial body of Union troops.[6]

The men on both sides of the line were already hot. The temperature never rose out of the 80s on July 1, but the thermometer was already at 80 degrees by 7:00 a.m. that sultry July 2 Thursday. The scattered clouds that had offered a few cooling showers were beginning to drift away and bright sunshine baked the open fields between Seminary and Cemetery ridges. Aside from the fortunate Mississippians

5   Ibid., 613, 617. As noted in Chapter 3, Col. David Lang was in command of Perry's Florida Brigade because of the latter's illness.

6   *Bachelder Maps, Second Day.*

from Posey's brigade who had taken up positions in the Bliss home and barn, most of the other pickets had to endure the rising heat and humidity with little shade or breeze. Even the coolest woodlot or orchard offered little respite, and the day would only get hotter and muggier. Despite the shimmering haze enveloping the Bliss farm, Union observers in Samuel Zeigler's grove could readily discern two things: the farm was within rifle range from Cemetery Ridge, and Confederates were swarming through it. Shortly after Posey's skirmishers arrived on the Bliss propery, a light spattering of fire broke out between the pickets. When the eight o'clock hour struck, it was still relatively quiet on Wright's and Lang's front.[7]

An hour or so earlier, Cadmus Wilcox assembled his brigade in its bivouac above the Black Horse Tavern. With orders to rejoin Anderson's division south of Pender's position, Wilcox put his column in motion using the most direct route to reach his destination. Leaving Butt's farm lane, Wilcox led his Alabamians northeast back down Fairfield Road to its intersection with the Old Willoughby Run Road. Off in the distance the Alabamians could see the vanguard of the rest of Anderson's division (Lang's Floridians) moving south toward them.

Lang's brigade moved through the intersection past Henry Meals' 82-acre farm and continued south on the Old Willoughby Run Road toward the Samuel Dickson and George Culp farms (the latter tenant-farmed by John Horner). Wilcox probably altered his course by cutting cross-country and heading east toward the Dickson and Culp farms. His Alabamians arrived at the Culp farm ahead of Lang, who had been redirected across Willoughby Run. Reunited, Anderson's division began ascending West Seminary Ridge about the same time A. P. Hill's staff was setting up the Third Corps headquarters 1,000 yards ahead of Anderson at the Emanuel Pitzer farm.[8]

The brigade "advanced bearing to the right, for the purpose of taking position in line of battle," reported Wilcox. "The major-general commanding [Anderson] indicated to me the position to be occupied by my brigade. The right of my line, as thus directed was thrown forward, resting against a heavy and thick woods, and ran thence back obliquely to the rear across an open field, terminating at a stone fence 100 yards from the right of Lang's brigade. Not knowing whether the woods against which the right of my line was to rest was occupied by the enemy," Wilcox

7   John J. Garnett, *Gettysburg: A Complete Historical Narrative of the Battle of Gettysburg and Campaign Preceding It* (New York, 1888), 247.

8   USGS MRC 39077G2; *Bachelder Maps, Second Day*; Herbert, "History of the Eighth Alabama." Emanuel Pitzer Sr. died on June 18, 1863. One story suggests his son Samuel hid $5,000 in gold and silver under a bake oven. Rebels supposedly located and kept the hoard. The sprawling homestead is now known as Brown's Ranch.

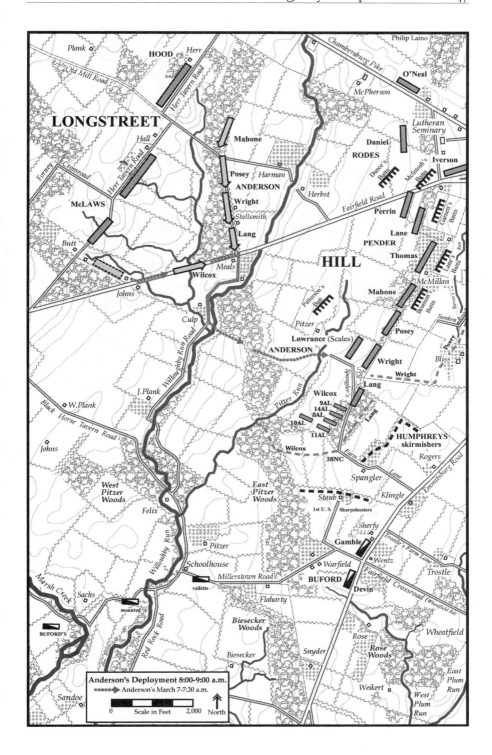

Anderson's Deployment 8:00-9:00 a.m.
▪▪▪▪▪▶ Anderson's March 7-7:30 a.m.

0   Scale in Feet   2,000   North

Richard Anderson's east-facing right flank deployed in Henry Spangler's woods behind his farmyard. With the farmyard controlled by Union skirmishers, General Wilcox's and Colonel Lang's men reinforced Colonel Lowrance's North Carolinians holding the stone wall paralleling the base of the woods barely visible beyond the farmyard. *GettysburgDaily.com*

continued, he advanced the 10th and 11th Alabama regiments into the timber to screen the rest of the brigade.[9]

The 100 yards separating Wilcox's left from Lang's right was initially covered when Lieutenant Brown and a company from Lowrance's brigade remained on line. Instead of retiring with the rest of the brigade, Brown stretched his already thin line in both directions, supporting not only Lang and Wilcox but Wright's brigade to Lang's left. Brown's posture at the angle in Spangler's farm lane protected Wilcox's otherwise exposed left flank until reinforcements from the 11th Alabama arrived. The real threat, as Wilcox had been warned, was to the south beyond his right. As a result, Wilcox's skirmish line was fronted in that direction with his brigade aligned *en masse* behind the skirmishers.[10]

---

9   OR 27, pt. 2, 617. According to Lt. Colonel Herbert, the 8th Alabama was next in line behind the 10th and 11th. Patterson's battery was detached from the brigade and sent back to Maj. John Lane, for there is no record of Patterson's guns supporting Wilcox at this time.

10 USGS MRC 390772G; *Bachelder Maps, Second Day*. Brown stayed on the picket line with a company of men supporting Lang's Florida Brigade near the Spangler farm, but in time would

Wilcox's east-facing skirmish line stepped over a low stone wall in a shallow depression bordering the eastern edge of Henry Spangler's woods. The Alabamians continued, passing through Col. W. L. J. Lowrance's thin and overly extended line of North Carolinians before ascending a low rise to reach Henry Spangler's farmyard. The Spangler property sat atop the highest elevation between the Emmitsburg Road and Seminary Ridge north of the Millerstown Road. A few advanced Union pickets from Sickles' Third Corps quickly and quietly retired, leaving the farmyard and buildings in Confederate hands. Wilcox was more much successful than Lieutenant Brown, who had earlier led some of Colonel Lowrance's skirmishers forward in a failed attempt to force their way into the farmyard.[11]

These retiring Union skirmishers were under the command of Col. Elijah Walker of the 4th Maine of Ward's brigade. Walker had established a main line 300 yards east of the Spangler farm and about 200 yards west of the Emmitsburg Road. "I knew the enemy were there in force on my front," Colonel Walker later wrote. Fearing a major attack, he relayed his concerns to Third Corps and divisional headquarters and asked for support. His pleas were dismissed; no one in a position to do anything about it seemed to believe the Confederates were across the way in the woods in large numbers. Instead, they claimed the main force "had fallen back."[12]

Though seemingly minor, these events evidenced a potential breakdown in Union communication and judgment at various command levels early on July 2. Colonel Walker initially (and erroneously) believed the Rebels in his front were much stronger than the 200 Tar Heels who had been pestering him that morning. His concerns about a major attack coming from this direction, however, turned out to be warranted, with a sneak peek coming in the form of Wilcox's strong skirmish line advancing toward the Spangler farm. The Third Corps and divisional staff officers were victims of the failure the previous night to properly picket the front and conduct deeper scouting and reconnaissance work with any available cavalry. General Humphreys had already reported his division's close encounter with Rebels the previous night. The relevant staff officers knew or should have known

---

migrate north toward the Bliss farm in support Wright's Georgians and later Posey's Mississippians.

11 *OR 27*, pt. 2, 617; USGS MRC 390772G; *Bachelder Maps, Second Day; Charlotte Daily Observer*, March 31, 1895 (Davis Library, UNC Chapel Hill). Lieutenant Brown stayed on the picket line with a company of men, including sharpshooters, supporting Lang's and Wilcox's brigades near the Spangler farmyard, but in time they would migrate north toward the Bliss farm to support Wright's Georgians and later Posey's Mississippians. See Laino, *Gettysburg Campaign Atlas*, 309.

12 Elijah Walker to Bachelder, *Bachelder Papers*, 2: 1093-94.

of Humphreys' report and used it to judge Colonel Walker's claims that Rebels were in his front in sizeable force and preparing to attack.[13]

While the frustrated Walker withdrew, General Wilcox established a new skirmish line to confront the Yankees. The Alabamians stretched across a front 400 yards long behind a snake rail fence. A small apple orchard north of the yard offered some shade and shelter. Meanwhile, Lieutenant Brown advanced some of the remaining North Carolinians (including skilled sharpshooters) from the woods to join Wilcox's line atop the rise. Brown spread his mountain marksmen along the length of Wilcox's skirmish line. Some of these Tar Heels filled the gap along the stone wall between Lang's right and Wilcox's left, while others moved forward into the apple orchard and farmyard.[14]

Most of the right flank of Wilcox's advanced skirmish line manned the western edge of Spangler's farm facing east, while the rest bent back almost 90 degrees behind the barn fronting south. From there, the line continued west toward the woods where Lowrance's Tar Heels had earlier taken shelter. From this farmyard salient, the Alabamians took a few potshots at some of Colonel Walker's late-leaving Yankee skirmishers who had taken their time falling back. They were wearing the distinctive green uniforms of the U. S. Sharpshooters.

The green-clad Federals rejoined Colonel Walker's main skirmish line only 300 yards from Wilcox's position. Walker later noted that his line was "30 or 40 rods west of the Emmitsburg Road," running the length of a stout rail fence atop the first rise west of the roadway. A shallow, trough-like depression separated Walker's men from Wilcox's and Brown's (Lowrance's) men. Walker's 4th Maine men and most of the other blue-uniformed skirmishers were either prone behind the lowest fence rail or in position farther down the eastern brow of this rise. The green-uniformed sharpshooters, along with a few marksmen from Wisconsin, plied their trade in a fitful manner with a few well-aimed offerings. In response, Brown's expert mountain riflemen from his 38th North Carolina made sure the Federals knew they were equal to the task. Within minutes each side earned respect for the other's accuracy and the firing waned to almost nothing.

Spangler's farm was an especially strategic piece of ground because it provided Confederate observers with a bird's-eye view of the surrounding countryside from the second-story windows of the house and the loft of the huge barn. Spangler's

---

13 Ibid. Neither Humphreys nor any of his officers later mentioned any cavalry screening their approach or guiding the column. Walker's intelligence seems to have triggered someone to push out 100 U. S. Sharpshooters, a fact Walker seems to have forgotten or perhaps had never known. See below for more information.

14 *Charlotte Daily Observer*, March 31, 1895.

farm lane connected the Emmitsburg Road Rise with Seminary Ridge and all points west of it, making it tactically important for moving troops, artillery, materiel, and equipage. Intersecting the Emmitsurg Road 40 yards north of Daniel F. Klingle's 15-acre farmyard, the fence-lined Spangler lane undulated westward nearly 1,000 yards through mostly open cultivated fields to the crest of Seminary Ridge.[15]

Located 340 yards south of Spangler's lane (and 500 yards southwest of the farm) was the John and Catherine (Codori) Staub's two-story home, small barn, and outbuildings. This small farm and adjoining rail fences housed several Union sharpshooters who, for one reason or another, had allowed Wilcox and Lowrance to swap skirmish lines without interference. The 600 yards between the Staub farm west to Spangler's Woods was an especially dangerous place for the Alabamians and Brown's handful of Tar Heels. Their figures (and the fence partially sheltering them) were silhouetted against the northern horizon, clearly revealing their position to the Federal marksmen, who eventually resumed their fire. Most of Wilcox's skirmishers were on their stomachs along this fence line. The extreme left of Wilcox's skirmish line was tucked behind the fence in the shelter of Spangler's Woods. That relatively dense woodlot concealed the bulk of the Alabama brigade.[16]

A few Union sharpshooters, hard to see in their forest green garb, along with a dozen or so men in blue, held the snake-rail fence just west of the Staub farm. This fence paralleled the Spangler's farm lane 320 yards to the south and ascended Seminary Ridge, where it terminated at a rail-topped low stone wall dividing the properties. Eventually, superior Confederate firepower forced the Yankees back down the gentle slope to the Staub farmyard. Apparently no one on either side was injured during this brief, but intense, exchange of powder and lead.[17]

Just east of the Staub premises was yet another Union-held rail fence. This one snaked its way eastward into the deepest part of the trough-like swale west of the Emmitsburg Road before ascending the rise, where it intersected the sturdier rail fence sheltering Colonel Walker's skirmishers. This Staub fence line was important because it controlled Spangler's lane eastward to the farm, including the tactically important salient. The Union troops holding the reverse salient where the two fences intersected had a centralized crossfire onto the front portion of the Spangler farmyard, which is why most of Wilcox's and Brown's men remained well-hidden behind the buildings. The most immediate threat came from the handful of 2nd U.

15 USGS MRC 390772G; *Bachelder Maps, Second Day.*

16 *OR* 27, pt. 2, 617; USGS MRC 390772G; *Bachelder Maps, Second Day.*

17 *OR* 27, pt. 1, 482, 514-18; James L. Speicher, *The Sumter Flying Artillery: A Civil War History of the Eleventh Battalion Georgia Light Artillery* (Gretna, La.: Pelican Publishing, 2009), 188; Coddington, *Gettysburg: A Study in Command,* 420; *Bachelder Papers,* 2:1055.

Col. Hiram C. Berdan,
1st U. S. Sharpshooters
LOC

S. Sharpshooters on Staub's farm and behind his fences who enjoyed a good crossfire toward the Rebel salient in Spangler's lane and a right-enfilade down the stone wall along the eastern edge of Spangler's Woods. These sharpshooters also had a grand view of Pitzer's and Spangler's woods, both of which seemingly brimmed with Rebels.[18]

Likewise, the Rebels lining the Spangler lane along the edge of the woods could see almost a mile, giving them a clear view of Union troop dispositions to their front. When they spotted enemy positions, they passed the word along the line. Tactics on the opposing skirmish lines that morning varied. Aside from a few specially designated separate commands, most Southern sharpshooters were common infantrymen who demonstrated a keen eye, steady hand, and patience. By July 2, 1863, most of these marksmen had learned their trade through trial and error, earning the designation "sharpshooter" via on-the-job training. This was not the case for Hiram Berdan's specially trained and equipped U. S. Sharpshooters, who specifically trained for their assignments. The Federals tended to work best in teams, with one man firing while two to three comrades played the roll of spotters looking for tell-tale puffs of smoke from the hidden Rebel marksmen. In contrast, Confederate sharpshooters usually worked independently. Many tended to conserve their ammunition, seemingly always in short supply, waiting for that right moment to dispatch some unsuspecting distant Yankee skirmisher.[19]

The old rutted dirt road through the McMillan Woods angled southward through Spangler's Woods and intersected the Spangler lane near the southern edge

18 Also referred to as "backward bulge." *Bachelder Maps, Second Day.*

19 USGS MRC 390772G; *Bachelder Maps, Second Day*; Dean S. Thomas, *Ready, Aim, Fire: Small Arms Ammunition in the Battle of Gettysburg* (Arendtsville, Pa.: Thomas Publications, 1981).

of the woods. This latter lane continued into the open fields toward the Staub farmyard, clearly visible 570 yards from the Rebel marksmen near the road intersection. Once clear of Spangler's Woods, the lane passed through a narrow belt of trees part way toward the Staub farm. This tree line was also in Rebel hands. There, Wilcox's riflemen had a relatively clear, though distant, shot at the Yankees around the Staub farmhouse and outbuildings. Adding to Colonel Walker's concerns were the skirmishers of the 11th Alabama on Wilcox's far right flank, who now controlled the low stone wall paralleling the eastern brow of Seminary Ridge near the spot where the west-running rail fence ascended the ridge.[20]

An outcropping of timber adjoining East Pitzer's Woods 150 yards southwest of Spangler's lane offered ample cover along the stone wall. Combining fire with the Alabamians in the thin belt of woods near the Staub farm, Rebels behind the stone wall enjoyed a perfect cross-fire into Walker's line. "At about 7:30 a.m. I received orders to send forward a detachment of 100 sharpshooters to discover, if possible, what the enemy was doing," Union Col. Hiram Berdan later explained. "I went out with the detail, and posted them on the crest of the hill beyond the Emmitsburg road, and where they kept up a constant fire nearly all day upon the enemy in the woods beyond." Most of the sharpshooters were scattered along the length of Walker's line except for a dozen or so who were on the Staub property. They responded to the crossfire in an effort to neutralize Wilcox's men holding the thin belt of woods. Meanwhile, word reached Third Corps commander Sickles that the Confederates were stirring. Reports arrived before 8:00 a.m. that something was brewing out west, even as Anderson's division was taking position along Seminary Ridge.[21]

Behind Wilcox's lengthy skirmish line, the general had arrayed his five Alabama regiments (10th, 11th, 8th, 14th, and 9th) all poised to advance as needed. The brigade at this time faced south in column of battalions. Within about an hour of deploying his main body, Wilcox decided to shift Colonel Pinckard's 14th Alabama and Captain King's 9th Alabama into the center of Spangler's Woods, where they faced east along the old rutted farm road 100 yards behind the skirmishers lining the low stone wall.[22]

---

20 Ibid.

21 *OR* 27, pt. 1, 515-16; *Bachelder Maps, Second Day*. Berdan's recollection seems to refute (at least partially) Colonel Walker's accusation written in 1885 that Third Corps staff officers had ignored his repeated pleas for help; someone had the foresight to send forward the colonel and his 100 trained men from Maj. Homer Stoughton's 2nd U. S. Sharpshooters.

22 *OR* 27, pt. 2, 671-72.

When he was warned that Union cavalry was in his front along the Millerstown Road, Wilcox sent a rider north toward the Emanuel Pitzer farm to inform General Anderson. Within a quarter-hour, Anderson and an aide arrived to see firsthand what was happening and oversee the redeployment of Wilcox's remaining three regiments. Colonel William Forney's 8th Alabama was sent farther west and south, with its right flank resting above Pitzer's Run. Forney sent a reinforced skirmish line forward with orders to watch the Yankees, but avoid bringing on a general engagement. Anderson and Wilcox also moved Col. J. C. C. Sanders' 11th Alabama forward and westward, with its right wing overlapping Forney's left and rear. About 50 yards separated the two regiments. Sanders's skirmishers quickly and quietly linked up with those of the 10th Alabama. With Wilcox's line set to Anderson's satisfaction, the division commander rode away. There is no evidence Anderson made another appearance south of McMillan Woods for the rest of the day.[23]

Wilcox's new arrangement meant the 8th, 11th, and 10th Alabama regiments were slightly *en echelon* of one another. "The right of my line, as thus directed, was thrown forward," recalled Wilcox, who continued:

> resting against a heavy and thick woods, and ran thence back obliquely to the rear across an open field, terminating at a stone fence 100 yards from the right of Perry's [Lang's] brigade, the ground occupied by the left of my line being lower than the right, and ascending slightly in the latter direction. In front of my line in the open fields were several farm-houses, with barns, orchards, and the usual inclosures [sic]. The enemy's pickets were seen about these, and some 600 or 700 yards distant. Not knowing whether the woods against which the right of my line was to rest was occupied by the enemy, the Tenth Alabama Regiment (Colonel Forney) was ordered to occupy the woods, and the Eleventh Alabama Regiment (Colonel Sanders) formed in line in the open field to the left of the Tenth. The regiments, being preceded by skirmishers, were ordered to advance, the Eleventh to its position in line in rear of a fence, and the Tenth to keep on a line with the Eleventh, to protect it from the enemy's fire should he be found in the woods, the remaining regiments being held in rear till it should be ascertained if the enemy were in the woods.[24]

Across the way, meanwhile, Colonel Walker readied his 4th Maine and its supports. Even though his concern of a major attack after repulsing Brown's Tar Heels proved premature, it was fortunate and prudent as events would soon demonstrate. About sunrise, Walker had worried the Rebels were so strong that

---

23 USGS MRC 390772G; *Bachelder Maps, Second Day*, Tagg, *Generals of Gettysburg*, 311.

24 *OR* 27, pt. 2, 613, Wilcox, *SHSP*, vol. 4 (1877), 111-17.

General Birney's entire 6,000-man division could not push them out of the woods. Wilcox's arrival, believed Walker, confirmed the Rebels were indeed in strength and planning an assault. By 8:00 a.m, however, General Sickles, armed now with both Humphreys' report and Walker's pleas, became convinced his primary threat was waiting just beyond the low wooded ridge a bit more than a mile to the west.

By the time Colonel Berdan informed Birney about detaching Major Stoughton's marksmen to strengthen Walker's line, General Hancock's Second Corps was beginning its ascent of the eastern slope of Cemetery Ridge. Hancock fully expected Sickles would comply with General Meade's general order to defend the ridge and thus pull back and redeploy off Hancock's left flank to help secure a more formidable line. Like Sickles, Hancock was also concerned about was what lay beyond the forbidding wood line to the west, and what time the Rebels would storm out trees in an effort to crush their front. Hancock's plan was straightforward: form a strong line with Sickles to his immediate left and Doubleday's battered First Corps on his right and destroy any Rebels foolhardy enough to try and cross the wide expanse separating the armies. Unbeknownst to Hancock and Meade, however, Dan Sickles was already formulating plans of his own that did not include linking his corps with Hancock's.[25]

*   *   *

Union artillery brigadiers Hunt and Tyler were near the Hummelbaugh farm lane's intersection with the Taneytown Road when Capt. John G. Hazard, commander of the Second Corps artillery, joined them. As the officers conversed, the vanguard of Col. Samuel S. Carroll's First Brigade, Third Division, Second Corps, appeared off to the south. A flurry of activity ensued as staff officers and aides galloped past. Pioneers from Hays' division had already dismantled the split rails along the low walls west of the Taneytown Road. General Hays preceded his command and was somewhere atop the crest west of Meade's headquarters (probably near the Copse of Trees) inspecting the position he would occupy while scanning Seminary Ridge a mile west. Hays was already figuring out where to position his skirmishers, so he had sent aides galloping south to fetch Carroll's leading regiment.[26]

---

25 Coddington, *Gettysburg: A Study in Command*, 333-35, 339; USGS MRC 39077G, *Bachelder Maps, Second Day*.

26 Hays and Fleming, *Life and Letters of Alexander Hays*, 430. Carroll's brigade consisted of the 14th Indiana, 4th and 8th Ohio, and 7th West Virginia infantry. Three great-great uncles of co-author Scott Mingus served in the 7th West Virginia.

Jacob Hummelbaugh house and yard east of the crest of Cemetery Ridge (with a contemporary inset photo taken from the Taneytown Road intersection 100 yards south of the farmyard). *LOC*

Passing through the intersection, Hunt and his party watched as "Red" Carroll redirected the head of his column with a left-oblique into the fields west of Taneytown Road. Angling to the northwest, Carroll's veterans of the "Gibraltar Brigade" began ascending Cemetery Ridge toward the Copse of Trees about 700 yards distant. The head of Carroll's brigade disappeared northward when Col. Thomas Smyth's Second Brigade appeared. Hummelbaugh's meadow was gentle in its ascent, and the numerous small orchards, low walls (some crumbling), and split rail fences posed but little interruption. The troops moved easily up the slope, largely indifferent to the surrounding landscape. It was shortly after 8:00 a.m. when the telltale boom of a distant artillery piece echoed in from the west.[27]

27 *OR* 27, pt. 1, 457. Carroll placed his arrival on the crest at 8:00 a.m. See also pt. 2, 678. Captain Brunson places his opening at an "early hour." In the summer of 1863, the famous Copse of Trees was nothing more than a small twisted grove of a few small scrub oaks (12-15 feet high), second growth timber, and underbrush. The immediate area was used as a dumping ground for rocks, boulders, probably old wood, and possibly discarded farm equipment. Gibbon detailed men to Cushing's front to clear a field of fire through the rubble and slashing (second growth). There are more written references to the "big gray stone house" (the Peter Frey residence) by Union soldiers than to the Copse of Trees.

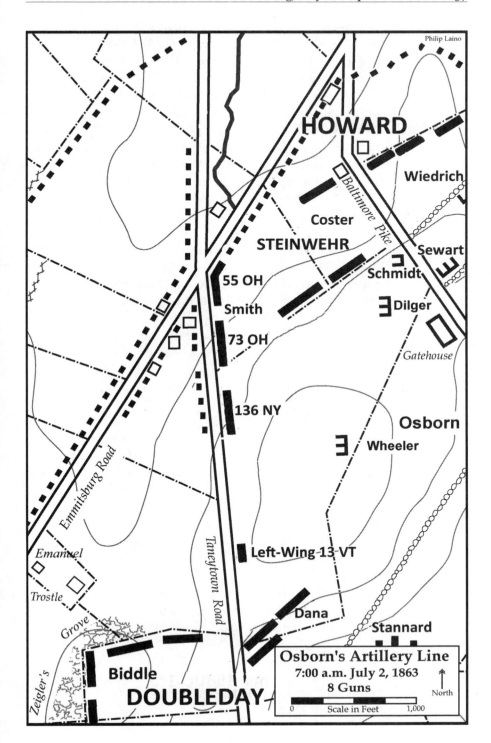

Philip Laino

HOWARD

Wiedrich

Coster

STEINWEHR

Baltimore Pike

Sewart

55 OH

Schmidt

73 OH

Smith

Dilger

Gatehouse

136 NY

Osborn

Wheeler

Emmitsburg Road

Left-Wing 13 VT

Taneytown Road

Dana

Emanuel

Stannard

Trostle

Osborn's Artillery Line
7:00 a.m. July 2, 1863
8 Guns

Grove

Biddle

DOUBLEDAY

Zeigler's

0   Scale in Feet   1,000

North

The first Confederate shell of the morning arced toward Cemetery Ridge just as Col. George L. Willard's Third Brigade paused in the road to allow the last of Smyth's column to clear the intersection. Many in Willard's ranks hoped to redeem their unfortunate reputation earned the previous September at Harpers Ferry. The Army of the Potomac was full of tough units and capable soldiers who had fought well and bravely, but who had not always been well or bravely led. Perhaps more than any other units in this army, Willard's four regiments felt they had something to prove—especially the seasoned 39th New York, also called the Garibaldi Guards. These veterans had four battles under their belts by the time of Harpers Ferry. The 111th New York, 125th New York, and 126th New York, on the other hand, had been in uniform only three weeks when they were thrown into action on September 12, 1862.

By the end of September 15 the siege of Harpers Ferry was over. On that dismal day, all four of Willard's New York regiments had surrendered their arms along with their honor. Nine months later, they still bore the stigma of that surrender and the humiliating nickname "Harpers Ferry Cowards." Every man in the more experienced 39th New York felt betrayed by the new recruits. The 39th had been engaged at First Bull Run, Cross Keys, and Middletown—the latter pair of fights in the Shenandoah Valley—and had fought well. It was a trusted veteran regiment whose surrender at Harpers Ferry, together with the 111th, 125th, and 126th regiments, was a bitter blow that still stung as they tramped their way toward Gettysburg.

Although the 111th New York had not been singled out for any particular acts of cowardice at Harpers Ferry, it still shared the hated nickname with the 125th and 126th. Organized as an overflow unit of enlisted men from Cayuga and Wayne counties, it mustered into service at Albany on August 20, 1862. The command placed 368 men armed with .58 caliber Enfield rifle muskets and 22 officers on the forming Cemetery Ridge line.[28]

Colonel Clinton MacDougall commanded the 111th New York when it surrendered at Harpers Ferry. While he shared in his men's disgrace, he rejected the idea that he or they were cowards. He knew they were good men. Educated, light-hearted, and forceful, the dashing MacDougall had taken his capture and parole somewhat philosophically. He knew the 111th, 125th, and 126th should not have been in the front lines after negligible training and only three weeks of service. At the same time, he refused to make any excuses. Like Maj. Hugo Hildebrandt,

---

28 Busey & Martin, *Regimental Strengths and Losses;* 44, 203. See also Edmund J. Raus Jr., *A Generation on the March: The Union Army at Gettysburg* (Lynchburg, Va.: H. E. Howard, Inc. 1987), 58.

commander of the 39th New York, MacDougall was looking for redemption and peace of mind.[29]

Any lingering thoughts of their previous embarrassment, together with the boredom and fatigue of the long march into Pennsylvania, instantly fell away with the distant crack of man-made thunder from the west. After the first round came another, separated by a short interval, and then a third. While Willard's New Yorkers waited, two of Captain Hazard's batteries pulled out of line behind them and, with cannoneers running, hustled through the brigade as it separated to make way for the rumbling guns. Lieutenant George A. Woodruff's Battery I, 1st U.S. led the way with its sextet of smoothbore Napoleons, followed by the six 3-inch rifles of Capt. William A. Arnold's Battery A, 1st Rhode Island. Lieutenant Colonel Edward R. Warner, the army's inspector of artillery and General Hunt's chief of staff, led the limbers and caissons past the Hummelbaugh farm lane and through the large swath created first by first Colonel Carroll's men and now Colonel Smyth's brigade.[30]

The youthful Warner led his charges to a farm lane heading west, passing Peter Frey's stone house and his massive bank barn. Within seconds the first gun passed through Smyth's grumbling infantry and topped the crest of Cemetery Ridge just south of the Copse of trees. Warner, an 1857 graduate of West Point who had served in California before the war, was acting on his own initiative. When he found the road closed to traffic, Warner "thought it best to bring at least two batteries forward immediately," as he later informed his superior Henry Hunt. "Not knowing where Capt. Hazard was I assumed responsibility and in your name and removed them from the Second Division. I sent Capt. [J. N.] Craig to Gen. Gibbon to inform him of my intentions. They were to report to you at headquarters with the guns. I turned off the road near the stone house," he continued, "passing through the lane running perpendicular to the ridge. Not finding you I reported to Gen. Hays who took possession of the guns."[31]

Hays gladly took possession of the twelve pieces when Hazard approached him on horseback. With the bright morning sun behind them, Hazard's batteries were clearly visible to the enemy gunners on Seminary Ridge, who promptly opened on them as they wheeled their pieces into line. Smyth's column was moving

---

29 Personal Military and Pension Records of C. D. MacDougall (Washington, D.C., NNRG-NA). See also *The Union Army at Gettysburg*, 77. Hildebrandt and MacDougall openly disliked one another. MacDougall thought that Hildebrant was a braggart and a rather contemptuous individual.

30 Edward Warner to Henry Hunt, July 6 1863, Hunt Papers, LoC.

31 Ibid. This "stone house" was likely the Peter Frey home.

Abraham Bryan's (sometimes spelled Brien or Brian) farm on northern Cemetery Ridge in a modern view taken from west of the Emmitsburg Road. Note the sloping nature of the ridge here. Zeigler's Grove is clearly visible in the left-distance just to the immediate north of the farm, and Bryan's small peach orchard is on the right side of the photo south of the house. *Todd C. Wiley*

past the small umbrella of trees at that moment, and both his brigade and Hazard's guns came under enemy fire.[32]

Colonel Carroll's four regiments had by this time moved north along the crest. They relieved fatigued First Corps pickets in Zeigler's Grove above Abraham Bryan's small farm, about 300 yards north of the clump of trees. Once there, Carroll's men deployed in Bryan's farmyard and orchard, leaving room so they did not interfere with Woodruff's battery when his guns rode up and unlimbered immediately west of Zeigler's Grove. Giving the lieutenant's command a wide berth to complete its maneuver, the Gibraltar Brigade entered the grove from the south, immediately east of and below the Bryan house. Under General Hays' orders, Carroll formed his veterans in line of regiments "right in front, between Woodruff's battery on the left and the Taneytown Road on the right." Smyth's 1,100-man brigade formed into battle line south of Carroll's command in the Bryan

---

32 Ibid. "Action Front, forward into battery, reverse trot," was the order, with "Action Front" the trumpet call.

This view looks north–northwest from the old Zeigler's Grove observation tower toward Emanuel Trostle's farm in the center of picture (circa 1880s). The house along the Emmitsburg Road and adjoining farmyard in the left forefront was erected after the battle and has been removed. *National Archives*

peach orchard, his skirmishers taking control of a stone wall on Arnold's right stretching north to Bryan's small clapboard barn.[33]

Zeigler's Grove was a crescent-shaped stand of mature hardwoods covering about ten acres. The apex, or corner, extended west-northwest into the lower open fields belonging to Emanuel G. Trostle, a young local shoemaker whose farm ran the length of the Emmitsburg Road from the Bryan farm lane north to the Washington Street-Taneytown Road intersection. Everyone from the south, west, and northwest could see Zeigler's striking body of timber on the lower reaches of Cemetery Hill. From afar, a small copse southwest of Zeigler's Grove appeared larger than it really was. A closer look revealed that an open plain ascending toward the crest of Cemetery Hill separated the two woodlots. This group of scrub oaks would soon became the battle's most enduring landmark. Confederate positions to

33 OR 27, pt. 1, 456; Annual Report of the Gettysburg National Military Park Commission to the Secretary of War, Oct. 21, 1896, GNMP; Rollins and Shultz, "Measuring Pickett's Charge," 108-16. Smyth's brigade consisted of the 14th Connecticut, 1st Delaware, 12th New Jersey, and 108th New York.

the north and west used it to measure distance. Carroll's official report indicates his brigade fronted both west and north, his center angling with the grove some 250 yards above the Trostle homestead, or due north fronting open fields between the Emmitsburg and Taneytown roads east of the farmyard. His Gibraltar Brigade was the northernmost unit of the Second Corps.[34]

In order to fully understand the Cemetery Ridge line, explained Maj. Francis A. Walker, the Second Corps adjutant, "It will be necessary . . . to describe the nature of this position with some fullness. Separating Cemetery Hill, so called, from Cemetery Ridge is a small wood, known as Zeigler's Grove, to which is posted Battery I of the First Artillery, under Lieutenant Woodruff. This battery, well advanced to the front, holds the right of the Second Corps line." Walker went on to describe the position in some detail, noting that the 108th New York supported Woodruff. Next in line was Hays' division, arrayed in two lines with the front line posted behind a low stone wall. Perhaps 350 yards from the grove, this old stone wall ran westward (toward the Confederate position) to enclose another more advanced ridge. "Here the wall is lower," Walker noted, "and is surmounted by a country post-and-rail fence." Deployed on Hays' left was Smyth's infantry and Arnold's Rhode Island battery, with Brig. Gen. Alexander S. Webb's "Philadelphia Brigade" of John Gibbon's division connecting with Hays' left at the angle in the stone wall. Lieutenant Alonzo H. Cushing's Battery A, 4th U.S. unlimbered its six 3-inch rifles in support. Colonel Norman J. Hall's brigade, also of Gibbon's division, continued the line south, supported by Brown's Rhode Island battery of six smoothbore Napoleons. Next in line was Brig. Gen. William Harrow's brigade, accompanied by Rorty's New York battery of 10-pounder Parrott Rifles. "On his front and Hall's," Walker finished, "the stone wall is replaced by an ordinary rail fence, which has been thrown down by the troops to gain some slight cover. Still farther to the south, in a clump of trees and bushes, lies Stannard's Vermont brigade of Doubleday's division." It was a formidable line on favorable terrain, with clear fields of fire. The position would present a significant challenge to any attacking force.[35]

Between 8:00 and 8:30 a.m. the number of Union guns fronting west from the Copse of Trees north to Washington Street jumped from seven to 19. By 9:00 a.m., the tally of cannon had increased to 31, still just half the number arrayed across the way along the Rebel line. At that time, a total of 62 Confederate guns, with converging fields of fire, extended in a wide arc from just north of the Fairfield

---

34 *Bachelder Maps, Second Day.*

35 Francis Walker, *History of the Second Army Corps in the Army of the Potomac* (New York, 1886), 291-92.

Road south to Spangler's Woods. All of these had been in position for at least 30 minutes prior to the first appearance of Hancock's Second Corps on Cemetery Ridge, and many had been in position well before first light. With such a marked superiority in firepower, Lee's gunners should have been able to dominate the field, but they had been unable to do so the day before, and they would fail to do so on this day and the next. The inability of Pendleton's artillery to work in unison was evident on July 1 when his guns failed to control the field. Entire batteries sat idle when they should have been engaged. Most of those that did fire selected targets at random. Cooperation between batteries was almost non-existent. Unfortunately for Southern fortunes, July 2 began much the same way.[36]

By the time all five Union Second Corps batteries unlimbered on Cemetery Ridge, an additional 18 guns attached to Sickles' Third Corps had likewise assumed positions or were available in park. Add in horse artillerist Lt. John H. Calef's five remaining 3-inch rifles, and the total number of Union guns fronting west numbered 61, just one piece shy of the total number Lee had on line. Even though the Southern gunners had a sweeping field of fire, Union artillerists had their counterparts in an enfilading crossfire that, if centralized and synchronized, could and would be devastating. There were several other reasons why General Pendleton's superior numbers failed to overpower the arriving Second Corps's artillery early on and were never able to achieve dominance during the day. Simply put, they were overmatched by a combination of difficult terrain, insufficient and faulty ammunition, and superior Union training, cooperation, and tactics.[37]

The "bible" for gunners in both armies was the 1860 U.S. Army artillery instruction manual *Field Artillery Tactics*, which incorporated advances in light field artillery tactics from the Mexican War and the numerous conflicts in Europe since the previous manual's issuance in 1845. Experiences during the first two years of the Civil War led to further revisions and the army published a new edition in 1863. Its authors were William H. French, William F. Barry, and Henry J. Hunt, the latter Meade's chief of artillery and arguably the preeminent artillerist in either army. The manual detailed the actions of artillerists in every conceivable way, assigning responsibilities, discussing proper deployment, the number of horses to a battery, duties in camp, and duties on the march. "As it is impossible to point a piece exactly without knowing the distance of the object," the authors wrote in the chapter "Pointing and Ranges," "artillerymen should be frequently practiced in estimating

---

36 Busey & Martin, *Regimental Strengths and Losses*. See aggregate compiled numbers.

37 Mark R. Gilmore, Maj. USA, Ret., "Artillery Employment at the Battle of Gettysburg," Master of Military Art and Science Thesis, Fort Leavenworth, Kansas, 1989, 39-45; *Bachelder Maps, Second Day*.

distances by the eye alone, and verifying the estimate afterwards, either by pacing the distance, or by actual measurement with a tape-line or chain, until they acquire the habit of estimating correctly."[38]

It was of course difficult to pre-measure unfamiliar terrain on a battlefield. Artillerymen would rely on their best guess, a range-finding instrument known as a Pendulum-Hausse, and, best of all, by ranging fire, whereby they shoot, observe the fall of the shot, and then adjust accordingly. The disparity in experience also came into play. Generally speaking, Confederate artillerymen did not possess enough ammunition to practice while in camp. By contrast, Union gun crews were allocated a sufficient supply of solid shot, bolt (recoverable afterward), shell, and case shot to practice and drill. Further, after the fight at Chancellorsville, Union artillery officers and gunners assigned to the Army of the Potomac were sent to General Barry's school of artillery training for a crash course in basic practice and gunnery. Hunt purged those he deemed unfit, unreliable, and/or unskilled in both artillery practice and leadership.[39]

As a result, the newly arrived Second Corps gunners who sighted down the tubes of their pieces tended to be more practiced, more recently trained, and better equipped than their Southern counterparts across the way. Most of the Rebel gunners had learned their trade in the field and in many cases only practiced during live combat. Although a few Confederate cannoneers had indeed targeted the Copse of Trees and Zeigler's Grove for range shortly after dawn, there is no evidence they shared their findings with other batteries. While this was in part a command failure that should have been corrected by some level of initiative between battery commanders, there is no evidence such cooperation existed within the Army of Northern Virginia.

By the time Capt. John Hazard arrived on Cemetery Ridge, General Hays had already directed Woodruff and Arnold where to place their guns. With little to say about it, Captain Hazard oversaw the placement of Battery I as it wheeled around in front of Zeigler's Grove. Woodruff's men and guns would not be silhouetted against a rising sun, and for the most part the horses, limbers, and caissons would be sheltered in the grove. Still, placing batteries in front of infantry—woods or no woods—in the face of the enemy almost always invited a concentrated

38 Wm. H. French, Wm. F. Barry, and H. J. Hunt, *Field Artillery Tactics* (Washington, DC, 1859), 28-30.

39 *OR* 25, pt. 1, 471-72, Special Order No. 129, May 12, 1863. Sections I-IV explain in detail the exact procedure of the artillery reorganization. See page 585 for verification of Hunt's elevation to chief of artillery of the entire army as well as the latest order of battle, dated May 31, 1863. See also, Alan Nevins, *A Diary of Battle: The Personal Journals of Colonel Charles S. Wainwright, 1861-1865* (Gettysburg, PA, 1962), 107-14 and 129-31.

counterbattery fire that frequently passed through or over the intended target to strike troops in the rear. This morning was no exception, except that the enemy's counterbattery fire never amounted to much. Hays' first two infantry brigades assumed their positions without serious incident.[40]

Woodruff's 1st U.S. Light Artillery unlimbered its six bronze Napoleons without mishap, with his left piece some distance north of Bryan's whitewashed clapboard barn and his right piece several hundred yards southeast of Trostle's farm. His deployment brought on a flurry of enemy counterbattery fire that passed well over Woodruff's gun line, as well as the grove behind him. A few rounds, however, exploded in or above the woods.[41]

Despite Woodruff's front being exposed, his position was well chosen. Emanuel Trostle's farm screened his right and front from numerous enemy batteries posted near the Lutheran Seminary and along the Fairfield Road. This, in turn, allowed his Union gunners to concentrate on the Emmitsburg Road, the Broad Open Plain beyond, and Seminary Ridge to Woodruff's immediate front and left. However, distant Confederate marksmen hidden west of the Emmitsburg Road soon began to pluck away with some success against the artillerists. This threat proved to be short-lived, for the Rebels pulled back when Hays deployed his skirmishers, relieving those of the First Corps while at the same time connecting with the left flank of Col. Orland Smith's brigade near the Trostle house.[42]

While Hazard oversaw Woodruff's placement, Hays personally placed Arnold's six 3-inch Ordnance Rifles 250 yards south of Battery I, with Smyth's brigade filling the vacancy between the batteries. Smyth moved portions of his command to a crumbling stone wall, with his right resting at the barn and his left near Arnold's right piece about 100 yards distant. The rest of Arnold's battery stretched southward an additional 100 yards across the front of Bryan's peach orchard toward the inner angle, with the Copse of Trees another 100 yards beyond that. The same crumbling stone wall that Smyth's New Yorkers occupied ran the length of Arnold's front, giving his men a small but comfortable redoubt in the open plain.[43]

---

40 Ibid., pt. 2, 453, 478. See also Blake Magner, "Hancock's Line at Gettysburg," in *Blue & Gray*, vol. 26, No. 4.

41 Tully McCrea, Letters to Belle, U. S. Military Academy Special Collections Library, Box 6, West Point, New York.

42 Rollins and Shultz, "Measuring Pickett's Charge," 108-16.

43 Elwood Christ, *The Struggle for the Bliss Farm at Gettysburg* (Baltimore, MD, 1994), 15-16. Bryan's name was spelled with a "y" when he filed his claim against the government in 1863. The authors believe the file was written out by someone other than Bryan, a clerk perhaps, and

While Woodruff and Arnold readied their batteries, Willard's arriving infantry brigade was placed "by battalions en masse" in an open area north of the Bryan peach orchard, with his right resting near Smyth's left-center and rear. First to stack arms east of the crest was the 126th New York, separated from Arnold's parked caissons by a stone wall paralleling the eastern brow of the ridge. The 125th, 111th, and 39th settled in behind them in that order. In all, the four regiments numbered 1,508 officers and men. Placed in the immediate rear of Arnold's caissons, the brigade members lay down while the opening guns thundered beyond their view west of the crest. Ironically, they could still hear a distant band playing inspiring tunes.[44]

Once the two batteries were planted, Hays left their further handling to Captain Hazard. It is almost certain Hazard picked out targets for each unlimbered battery, directing them to concentrate their combined firepower on individual Confederate batteries, sections, even single guns. As the gunners quickly acquired the range, the information was passed from battery to battery. This was Hunt's prescribed method of engagement, and it would become common practice for all of the Army of the Potomac's artillery at Gettysburg. Within moments of opening the Confederate guns fell silent.

The distance between the opposing gun lines varied between 1,200 and 1,600 yards. The greatest difficulty for both sides was the terrain, which played a singular role in the opening exchange of fire. When the gunner's target is beyond point-blank range, the barrel of the piece has to be elevated above the target. Allowance has to be made not only for distance, but for windage and elevation, with each individual gun handled differently depending on direct location to the target. Targeting an object involves measuring or at least estimating the distance between the piece and the point on the horizontal plain where the round first strikes the ground or object, with adjustments made thereafter. Further corrections had to be made for the type of ammunition used. According to the manual, "Shells are intended to burst in the object aimed at; spherical case shot are intended to burst from fifty to seventy-five yards short of it."[45]

Application of this theory was made harder because the ground over which the opposing artillery engaged (a fairly even elevation) was the most difficult type to

---

that Bryan himself was illiterate. The name could be Brian, but the fact remains it is signed Bryan on the official document.

44 Ibid., 15-16. See also New York Monuments, *Final Report on the Battlefield of Gettysburg*, 2:800; Benjamin Thompson, "This Hell of Destruction, Part Two," *Civil War Times Illustrated*, Vol. 12, No. 6 (1973), 13-23.

45 French, Barry, and Hunt, *Field Artillery Tactics*, 28.

target with positive results. The undulating open ground, natural low rises, ridges, swells and knolls, separated by small woods, orchards, fences, and various buildings, made it nearly impossible to estimate the distances with the naked eye. The range-finder of the day, the Pendulum-Hausse tool to measure distance and elevation, was virtually useless once the firing started. Even direct observation of a projectile was at times impossible. In many places, especially between the ridges, the rises and uneven ground either obscured the fall of a shot or offered an optical illusion as to where the round actually hit. It did not take much of a misjudgment to render one's gun inaccurate, and perhaps hundreds of feet off the mark.[46] It appears Woodruff's and Arnold's chiefs sighted their pieces relatively quickly and easily, but Confederate gunners struggled from the outset to guess and gain their range. Powder smoke quickly rendered the Pendulum- Hausse meaningless. This was made all the harder when Union guns unlimbered and fired, enshrouding and masking their own position.[47]

Within moments of Woodruff's and Arnold's opening, the few Confederate gunners who may have had their range lost it. Every round recoils a gun several feet or more from its original positions. Unless the wheels were chocked or marked, the next round would be well off the mark, and progressively more so with each succeeding shot. Six inches forward or back of the gun's original position made a significant difference in elevation, and six inches left or right would send the next shot as much as hundreds of yards wide of the previous round. The Union tactic of concentrating fire on one or two batteries at a time began to take effect with these opening shots, and every Confederate battery so targeted grew less effective with each passing minute.[48]

The big guns atop West Cemetery Hill under the Eleventh Corps' Maj. Thomas Osborn did not open in support of Hazard's artillery. The reason seems to be Special Order No. 129, which made it a possible court-martial offense to run out of ammunition while engaged on line. The order was issued by General Joe Hooker on May 12 while he was still in command of the army. Failure to keep adequate ammunition on hand was but one of the numerous penalties General Hunt enacted with John Reynolds' (and Hooker's) approval. The order also gave Hunt sole and independent command over that entire branch of service. In other words, every gun attached to every battery in every corps, including the horse artillery attached to General Pleasonton's cavalry, was under Hunt's authority. Hunt was also free to

---

46 Ibid.; USGS MRC 39077-G2-TF-024.

47 John Gibbon, *The Artillerist's Manual* (New York, 1863), 356-63; French, Barry, and Hunt, *Field Artillery Tactics*, 51, 186.

48 Ibid.

amend what could and could not be done while engaged. Never running out of ammunition in battle was but one of the new rules.[49]

Hunt and Reynolds got to work in mid-May and within two weeks had reorganized the entire artillery corps and re-instituted a code of conduct for battery and brigade commanders while under fire. It was now against army regulations to engage uncertain targets without direct confirmation. It was also forbidden to run out of ammunition while deployed in battery and engaged or to withdraw from any line while engaged because of a lack of ammunition. Ammunition was no longer to be stacked on the ground or placed loosely in spring wagons. Any munitions considered wasted would be charged to the section and battery commanders and even artillery brigade commanders, with the cost of that ordnance deducted from their pay. Accountability extended beyond ordnance to equipment. From lost tools to harnesses and traces, to carriage wheels and disabled wagons, all equipment would be accounted for, or a special headquarters committee would look into the waste and administer penalties. All of this accounts in large part why Union artillery reports and returns filed after Gettysburg are very specific about what was used, what was damaged, and what was lost and how, especially ordnance.[50]

Major Osborn's Eleventh Corps guns were low on ammunition with no knowledge exactly when a delivery was to be made. Even though Hunt had promised Osborn a fresh supply, the major was still uneasy as the sun rose above Cemetery Hill. He was aware that Hancock had ordered all his trains off the roads leading to Gettysburg. Howard ordered both Osborn and the First Corps' Col. Charles Wainwright to conserve what they had in case the anticipated infantry attack began before either his or Hunt's ammunition trains arrived. As a result, when Hancock's corps was deploying farther south, Osborn could do nothing more than watch while Rebel guns opened on Hazard's unlimbering batteries.

With the ground now chosen, everyone knew that something major could break out with each passing moment. Thus far, however, the day had been fairly quiet. "The morning was a busy and some respects an anxious one," Hunt wrote. "[I]t was believed that the whole Confederate army was assembled, and it was equal if not superior to our own numbers, and that battle would commence before our troops were up." Although there had been some discussion regarding sending portions of Slocum's Twelfth Corps on an end-around flank movement to the north, nothing came of it. "After an examination," Hunt continued, "Slocum reported the ground as unfavorable, in which Warren concurred and advised against an attack there. The project was abandoned, and Meade postponed all

49 OR 25, pt. 1, 471-72.

50 Ibid.

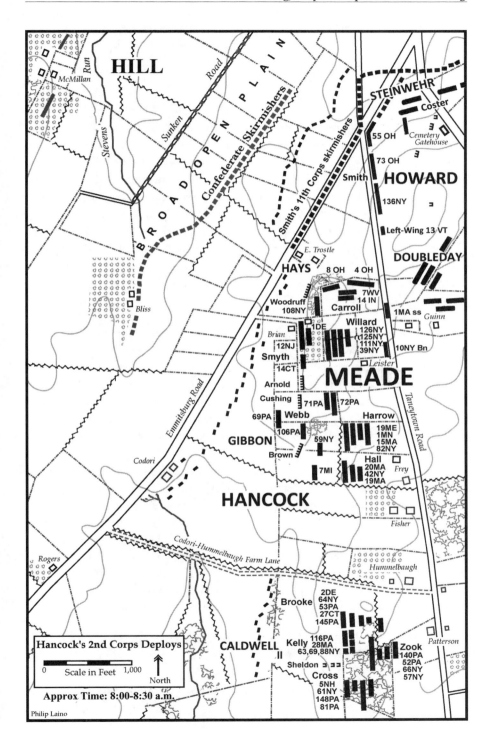

HILL

McMillan

Run

Road

Sunken

Stevens

BROAD OPEN PLAIN

Confederate Skirmishers

Smith's 11th Corps skirmishers

STEINWEHR

Coster

55 OH

73 OH

Smith

Cemetery Gatehouse

HOWARD

136NY

Left-Wing 13 VT

DOUBLEDAY

E. Trostle

HAYS

8 OH   4 OH

7WV
14 IN

Woodruff
108NY

Carroll

1MA ss   *Guinn*

Willard
126NY
125NY
111NY
39NY

Brian

1DE

12NJ

Smyth

14CT

10NY Bn

Leister

MEADE

Arnold

Cushing

71PA   72PA

69PA   Webb

Harrow

106PA   59NY

19ME
1MN
15MA
82NY

GIBBON

Brown

Codori

Hall
20MA
42NY
19MA

Frey

7MI

HANCOCK

Fisher

Codori-Hummelbaugh Farm Lane

Rogers

Hummelbaugh

Patterson

Brooke

2DE
64NY
53PA
27CT
145PA

CALDWELL

Kelly

116PA
28MA
63,69,88NY

Zook
140PA
52PA
66NY
57NY

Sheldon

Cross

5NH
61NY
148PA
81PA

Hancock's 2nd Corps Deploys

0   Scale in Feet   1,000

North

Approx Time: 8:00-8:30 a.m.

Philip Laino

offensive operations until the enemy's intentions should be more clearly developed."[51]

*   *   *

While relatively quiet, the morning was an anxious one for the naturally aggressive General Lee. He spent the hours of 7:00 to 9:00 a.m. trying to determine his enemy's intentions. The early hours slipped away, as did any hope of a morning attack. On the previous evening, Lee told both Longstreet and A. P. Hill, "Gentlemen, we will attack the enemy in the morning as early as practicable." Even though Hill's divisions were in position to assist, it remained Lee's responsibility to determine why Longstreet was not yet up and ready to assault. As Lee's staff officer, Col. Armistead Long, later explained it, "as early as practicable" did not mean sunrise nor even 7:00 a.m. What was practicable to Lee at that time may not have been practicable with Longstreet, who had made it clear that he wanted to wait for the rest of Hood's division (Law's large brigade) to come up before anything was put into motion.[52]

Lee rose early enough to brief Pendleton and Johnston prior to their dawn reconnaissance ride. While they were gone, he held early morning meetings with many officers, and was available when Johnston arrived and when Colonel Long brought back Pendleton's report. Pendleton suggested that on several occasions he sent word to Longstreet to hurry along, but it is not clear whether Lee did the same. Whatever the case, it was too late to take advantage of the overpowering numbers the Army of Northern Virginia enjoyed until Hancock's corps arrived on the opposite ridge.[53]

Major Osborn, meanwhile, watched from Cemetery Hill as the crackling of small arms fire intensified between the lines. Hays' skirmishers were pushing across the Emmitsburg Road toward the Rebels. At issue was the relatively flat and open ground west of the road. Within minutes it was much more difficult to identify single shots as the firing escalated into a steady clatter. The Rebel riflemen grew bolder, firing so often that the wafting smoke gave away their once-secret positions. From the Washington Street intersection south to the Bliss farm lane, Confederates fired from windows of buildings and barns, from behind trees and stumps, fence posts and hillocks, taking advantage of whatever cover they could find or erect. By

---

51 Hunt, "The Second Day at Gettysburg," in *B&L*, 297.

52 Long, *Memoirs of R. E. Lee*, 277.

53 Longstreet, "Lee's Right Wing at Gettysburg," *B&L*, 339-40; Col. William Allan, "A Reply to General Longstreet," *B&L*, 355 and Osborn, *Eleventh Corps Artillery*, 22.

9:00 a.m., whatever relative safely there had been from the sunken farm lane to upper Cemetery Ridge had vanished. The sprawling terrain west of the Emmitsburg Road was now a no-man's-land.[54]

Just hours earlier, many of the soldiers positioned along this contested line had formed an uneasy truce along two parallel fence lines running from Washington Street south toward the Bliss farm. Blue-clad warriors hugged the eastern fence of the sunken Emmitsburg Road, while several Rebels crept up to the western fencing. The handful of yards separating the opposing soldiers did not deter them from trading coffee for tobacco, or newspapers for dime novels. The brush and honeysuckle choking both fence lines provided cover that shielded the men not only from each other, but from observation by their officers. Young soldiers crawled into the space between the lines to trade and barter, talk about the war, and swap stories. This truce had continued throughout the early morning hours on July 2 until well after sunrise.

By the time Woodruff's and Arnold's batteries ceased firing that morning, however, no one unlucky enough to be manning the picket line dared raise his head above the top rail of either fence.[55]

54 USGS MRC 39077G2; *Bachelder Maps, Second Day*.

55 William Cline Diary, 73rd Ohio Volunteers, "Gettysburg Account," University of Notre Dame Rare Books and Special Collections Library, South Bend, Indiana.

Chapter Nine

"This is to be the great battle of the war and that any soldier leaving ranks without leave will be instantly put to death."

— *Maj. Gen. George G. Meade, Army of the Potomac*[1]

Morning, July 2: Fighting on the Bliss Farm

Crickets were still loudly chirping when Brig. Gen. Joseph B. Kershaw's South Carolinians awoke at 4:00 a.m. near Marsh Creek west of Gettysburg. Theirs had been a short night. Like the rest of Maj. Gen. Lafayette McLaws' division, Kershaw's men did not get into camp until about midnight after a long tramp across South Mountain from Franklin County. They had a few minutes to boil morning coffee and converse over a quick breakfast, much of it appropriated over the past few days from Pennsylvania farmers. The riflemen had enjoyed the leisurely march into the Keystone State. Many related humorous stories of recent interactions with terrified residents who freely offered foodstuffs to the passing soldiers in the hope of avoiding the rumored destruction of their homes and barns. The time for serious fighting, however, was now at hand. According to Kershaw, his men left camp after sunrise and marched eastward on the Chambersburg Pike in the morning mists a short distance toward Gettysburg, with "only a slight detention from trains in the way." Meanwhile, Hood's division also re-entered the macadamized pike, following it east to Herr's Ridge Road where he turned south, passing the inviting country tavern as had Anderson's division the previous afternoon. Hood halted his vanguard at the intersection with present-day Old Mill Road.[2]

---

1 Patrick H. Taylor diary, July 2, 1863, in *Bachelder Papers*, 2:962.

2 OR 27, pt. 2, 366; USGS MRC 39077G2; *Bachelder Maps, Second Day*.

In order to expedite his movement and keep traffic flowing, McLaws directed his long column off the turnpike to the south using present-day Knoxlyn Road. Turning due east on the lower Old Mill Road, his men marched through gently rolling meadows under a beautiful full moon. At the head of the division, Kershaw's South Carolinians arrived in front of Gettysburg "about one half hour after sunrise." Kershaw added, "We debouched from the main road by a by-road [Knoxlyn Road to Old Mill Road] that traversed an open common for a few hundred yards, and there halted, the head of the column having reached the Hoss [Haas] house."[3]

Ascending West Herr's Ridge midway between the Chambersburg Pike and Fairfield Road, the Old Mill Road passed over the crest and bisected Dr. Samuel E. Hall's 135-acre tract of land, his residence located next to the Haas home southwest of the avenue's intersection with Herr's Ridge Road. Fronting east, Hood's right flank was just north of this intersection. The Old Mill Road continued over Herr's Ridge through unkempt woods before dropping down into the bottomland and crossing Willoughby Run at the Harmon homestead. The road arched southeast past the John Herbst farm, where it intersected with the Fairfield Road in the middle of the swale separating Herr's and lower McPherson's Ridges from Seminary Ridge.[4]

Kershaw later stated he saw a large body of Union infantry moving north, with flankers out, on what he thought was the Emmitsburg Road. In order to see that main thoroughfare at its intersection with the Millerstown Road, as the general suggested, he could have used several vantage points south of Dr. Hall's house nearer Butt's farm lane and school where Wilcox's Alabama brigade had bivouacked the night before.[5] The identity of the enemy troops Kershaw spotted is uncertain. Besides Buford's cavalry troopers, two of Humphreys' brigades would also arrive from that direction, as well as Hancock's Second Corps, which would be

---

3   Kershaw to John Bachelder, March 20, 1876, Camden, SC, in *Bachelder Papers*, 2:453. The 1858 map of Adams County shows this as the "A. Haas" home.

4   USGS MRC 39077G2. The Harmon (or Harman) farm in recent years has been the Gettysburg Country Club. About 95 acres of the old homestead have been saved and are now part of the National Park Service's holdings.

5   Ibid. See also USGS MRC 399077G2 and Gregory Coco, *A Vast Sea of Misery: A History and Guide to Union and Confederate Field Hospitals at Gettysburg July 1-20, 1863* (Gettysburg, PA, 1988), 141. Shown on some period maps as the Samuel Herbst farm, researcher Greg Coco believed that by 1863 Adam and Nancy Butt owned this particular farm. The high ground would have provided a good vantage point for a general on horseback to view the distant Emmitsburg Road.

Col. Edward Porter Alexander,
artillery battalion commander,
Longstreet's First Corps,
Army of Northern Virginia.
Richard Rollins

using that route between 8:30 and 9:00 a.m. In all likelihood, Joe Kershaw spotted Burling's Third Corps brigade shortly before 9:00 a.m.[6]

By this time, Lafayette McLaws' and John B. Hood's divisions were in position south of the Chambersburg Pike on Herr's Ridge, but their corps commander, James Longstreet, remained very skeptical about the reconnaissance results he heard from General Pendleton, Colonel Long, and Captain Johnston. Also to his substantial discomfort, his third division under George Pickett was not yet up. It was about 8:30 a.m. or so when Old Pete sent Col. James B. Walton, the chief of his artillery reserve, racing back to Marsh Creek to fetch Col. E. Porter Alexander.

A brilliant artillery officer and equally impressive engineer, the 28-year-old Alexander was a West Point-educated professional. After the battle of Chancellorsville, the Georgia artilleryman had proposed and drafted a plan to reorganize and refit the Army of Northern Virginia's entire "long arm." Longstreet applauded the gunner's idea, but Lee and Pendleton thought it too progressive, too wasteful and quite possibly too demoralizing to several officers and so rejected the proposal. As far as Longstreet was concerned, Alexander was the best-suited and most capable officer in the army to command all of the artillery. Longstreet's favorite colonel, however, led but one of two battalions of his reserve artillery under the overall command of Colonel Walton.[7]

---

6   OR 27, pt. 2, 531, 570, 577. See also Kevin Coughenour, "Andrew Atkinson Humphreys: Divisional Command in the Army of the Potomac," Gettysburg Seminar Papers, "Mr. Lincoln's Army: The AOP in the Gettysburg Campaign," GNMP Library.

7   For more on Lee's artillery, see Jennings C. Wise, *The Long Arm of Lee, or, the History of the Artillery of the Army of Northern Virginia*, 2 vols. (Lynchburg, VA, 1915).

While Alexander was en route from Marsh Creek, Lee, Longstreet, McLaws, and Hood debated the potential tactics and deployments based upon the sketchy reconnaissance reports. Ultimately Lee as the army commander had his way. Assured by Johnston and Long that the Union left was accessible, Lee refused to change or amend his previous plans. Longstreet would hit the Union left with his two extant divisions and drive up the Emmitsburg Road. With A. P. Hill's Third Corps supporting the assault, Lee remained certain his strong army could sever the Union center below Cemetery Hill. Lee was so certain of what he wanted that when Longstreet explained to McLaws how he wanted his division deployed, Lee overrode him and said, "No General, I wish it placed just the opposite."[8]

After listening to Lee, it appears Longstreet was more convinced than ever that he needed Alexander. The colonel later stated he had not looked at his watch, but that it was near 9:00 a.m. when he rode forward to find Longstreet with Lee on Seminary Ridge. "In Gen. Lee's presence," Alexander later wrote, "Longstreet pointed out the enemy's position and said that we would attack his left flank." Longstreet told him to take command of all the artillery on the field and ride at once south to study the ground, after which he was to bring up his artillery battalion. The corps commander specifically cautioned the young colonel to "keep all movements carefully out of view" of a distant signal station, where Federal flags were wig-wagging on Little Round Top. Within ten minutes after arriving at headquarters, Alexander had his orders and was off to examine the various roads and routes leading to the right and front. He would do his best to understand the Union position and, as he later wrote, "how and where we could best get at it."[9]

*   *   *

Just about the time Colonel Alexander was galloping to meet with Lee and Longstreet on Seminary Ridge, not two miles to the southeast Union Brig. Gen. Alexander Hays' final brigade was advancing up Cemetery Ridge with the lead elements of Gibbon's Second Division closing on its rear. Like the men of Hays' division, Gibbon's columns had been temporarily placed east of the Taneytown Road below the Granite Schoolhouse Road intersection in open fields belonging to

---

8   Lafayette McLaws, "Gettysburg," in *SHSP*, 1869, 7:68-69; "The Battle of Gettysburg," *Philadelphia Weekly Times*, April 21, 1886. After further questioning by Lee, Captain Johnston headed south again to recheck the proposed routes. It is not clear if Kershaw relayed the information concerning the Union troops he saw arriving. McLaws never made mention of it.

9   Gallagher, *Fighting for the Confederacy*, 235. It was probably around 8:30 a.m. when E. P. Alexander arrived, because Hancock's Second Corps had yet to fully deploy and skirmishing was still quite light.

farmers Michael Frey and Jacob Swisher. Roused from their bivouac east of the Round Tops before sunrise, by 6:00 a.m. Gibbon's men had heard their officers read Meade's manifest to them and they were not pleased with what they heard.[10]

To their immediate south was Sarah Patterson's extensive farm, where Brig. Gen. John C. Caldwell's trailing First Division patiently waited for orders. Unlike the open meadows Hays' and Gibbon's divisions occupied farther north, Caldwell's column moved into semi-wooded rolling terrain, much of it rocky and uneven. Besides her land stretching eastward from the Taneytown Road, Patterson also owned a significant belt of woods west of the avenue that paralleled it for several hundred yards.[11]

Patterson's Woods west of the Taneytown Road would in time become as important and strategic to the Second Corps as Zeigler's Grove to the north. Early on July 2 it meant nothing to any of Caldwell's men, who filed right off the road directly across from it. Colonel Arthur F. Devereux, commanding the 19th Massachusetts (Harrow's brigade, Gibbon's division), recalled his regiment's stay east of the Taneytown Road: "At daybreak of the 2nd we marched to the front, this division forming in columns of regiment by brigade on the right of the road, with its front toward the right of the position held by our army [fronting north]."[12]

When Gibbon's command arrived at the Frey property, his regiments stacked arms to the south of Alexander Hays' division, with Woodruff's and Arnold's batteries parked between them. Gibbon's artillery support—Lt. Alonzo Cushing's Battery A, 4th U.S. and Lt. Thomas Frederick Brown's Battery B, 1st Rhode Island—pulled off the road, stopping in column of sections behind the division. Stretching themselves on the grass, infantrymen and artillerymen alike opened haversacks and produced an astonishing selection of fresh food and drink. "While waiting we improved the time," Sgt. John Rhodes of Battery B recalled fondly. "Small fires were built and a pot of hot coffee soon made to refresh the inner man for the work ahead."[13]

No regiment in Gibbon's division was tougher or more seasoned than the veteran 1st Minnesota. Its commander, a 33-year-old lawyer-turned-journalist named William Colvill, mustered in with the regiment on April 29, 1861, as a brevet captain in command of Company F. Two years later, Colvill was as rough as his northern Red-Wings and, at 6' 5" towered over all of them. Unlike many volunteer

---

10 *OR* 27, pt. 1, 442.

11 USGS MRC 39077G2; *Bachelder Maps, Second Day*.

12 *OR* 27, pt. 1, 442.

13 John H. Rhodes, *History of Battery B First Regiment Rhode Island Light Artillery in The War to Preserve the Union 1861-1865* (Providence, RI, 1914), 200.

officers who disdained the company of enlisted personnel, Colvill relished it and demanded no more of his enlisted men than he did of himself or his junior officers. Colvill sat with his men in the field enjoying his first decent meal in days, and he did so while under informal arrest. On the march through Maryland, he allowed a few of his boys to cross Monocacy Creek single-file on a log instead of wading through the chest-deep water. Lieutenant Colonel Charles H. Morgan, General Hancock's 28-year-old chief of staff, spotted the infraction and charged Colvill with insubordination. The charge meant that Gibbon had little choice but to place the Minnesota regimental commander under arrest for disobeying orders and wasting time. And so Colvill sat and waited amongst his men for his brigade commander, Brig. Gen. William Harrow, to rescind the pending charge and put the ridiculous issue in the past.[14]

Instead of the hearing that the charge was being thrown out, however, Colonel Colvill and his Minnesotans learned what many men of the Second Corps already knew. "Order from Gen. Gibbon read at 5:50 A.M. to us," Sgt. Patrick H. Taylor of the 1st Minnesota vividly recalled, "in which he says this is to be the great battle of the war and that any soldier leaving ranks without leave will be instantly put to death." The pleasant respite in Frey's fields was cut short when repeated bugle calls of "Assembly" from Hays' division to the north pierced the air.[15]

Within moments the buglers of Gibbon's division were also sounding "Assembly," as did Caldwell's buglers to the south a minute or so later. Food not yet stuffed into hungry mouths quickly vanished back into haversacks. Unconsumed coffee was dumped onto the small kindling fires, ashes kicked and spread, and individual weapons removed from the stack. The crewmen of Cushing's and Brown's batteries dressed ranks to the rear of their respective pieces. The assembly was systematic and orderly, and within a few minutes Gibbon's well-drilled soldiers were ready to move. Once in column, however, they would wait standing in the fields east of the Taneytown Road for nearly three-quarters of an hour.[16]

When Woodruff's and Arnold's batteries pulled in behind Willard's brigade, Brig. Gen. Alexander Webb's Second Brigade, leading Gibbon's division, moved onto the road behind them. Shortly thereafter both of Hays' attached batteries were called forward while Webb's column closed that gap. Colonel Norman Hall's Third

14 Return I. Holcombe, *History of the First Regiment, Minnesota Volunteer Infantry* (Stillwater, MN, 1916), 52.

15 Taylor Diary, July 2, 1863, *Bachelder Papers*, 2:962.

16 Ibid.

Brigade, with Harrow's First Brigade and Cushing's and Brown's batteries in tow, was attached to Gibbon's division and followed Webb.[17]

Within minutes of Hays' division topping the crest of Cemetery Ridge, both of Gibbon's attached batteries, with their cannoneers mounted, made their way to the front by rumbling up the narrow Taneytown Road, scattering cursing infantrymen slow to yield the right of way. Turning onto a dirt farm lane—possibly Hummelbaugh's—they hurried toward the ridge crest while Webb's leading regiment angled through the meadow following the well-defined swath cut by Hays' column. Artillery Captain Hazard met Cushing's and Brown's batteries before they reached the crest. Cushing hurried his Regulars past the Copse of Trees, where Battery A wheeled about at "Reverse Trot" to the left of Arnold, the low crumbling stone wall separating the commands. Rebel artillery rounds fired from beneath the canopy of trees lining Seminary Ridge greeted Cushing's arrival. Within moments of unlimbering, two of Cushing's crewmen went down. Brown's battery fared better when Hazard ordered it deployed about 100 yards south of Cushing opposite the Copse of Trees, his right piece not 40 paces south of the soon-to-be-famous grove. Although Brown's position appeared weak and unsupported, the trees and brush to his immediate right screened his men and guns so that he did not attract the same level of attention from the Confederate gunners as did Woodruff, Arnold, and Cushing. Sergeant Rhodes penned the time Battery B unlimbered as "about ten o'clock," but it was likely closer to 9:00 a.m., about the same time Alexander was riding south for Longstreet.[18]

The energetic General Gibbon was on scene barking orders when Webb's brigade reached its designated area east of and below Cushing's unlimbered battery. Gibbon placed the 71st and 72nd Pennsylvania regiments behind Battery A, and ordered the 69th and 106th Pennsylvania to move toward the Copse of Trees on the left of Cushing's gun line. Webb placed the 69th along the stone wall to Cushing's front and left, its line bisecting an unkempt connecting wall that intersected the north-south running wall passing under the copse of trees. The 106th's line was posted 80 yards behind the 69th's left and center, its immediate left flank just north of Brown's right section. Colonel Hall extended Gibbon's line south by placing the 59th New York behind Brown's battery. The 7th Michigan's left flank was resting under the Copse of Trees. When the distant Confederate gunners saw Brown unlimbering and Webb and Hall deploying, they unleashed another short barrage toward the tree clump just as they had showered Cushing

---

17   OR 27, pt. 1, 416.

18   OR 27, pt. 1, 476. See also Rhodes, *History of Battery B*, 200.

This 1902 image was taken south of the Copse of Trees and looks southwest across the Codori farm toward the distant Spangler's and Pitzer's woods. The Codori barn is visible on the right, the Rogers farm is just left of the monument, and the Klingle farm is on the far left. Capt. James M. Rorty's Battery B, 1st New York Light Artillery, unlimbered here on the early evening of July 2. Lang's Floridians advanced (right to left) across this part of the field, as did the right side of Wright's Georgia brigade. Caldwell's Union division, which moved south to support Sickles' Third Corps, was supposed to cover this part of Cemetery Ridge below the Union Center. Once Caldwell left, it was basically unguarded. *LOC*

moments before. Most of these rounds overshot the crest and dropped amid Harrow's brigade as it arrived opposite the crest.[19]

Within moments of Webb posting his regiments, Capt. John J. Sperry, commanding Companies A and B, 106th Pennsylvania, supported by Companies A and I, 72nd Pennsylvania, descended the western slope toward the Codori farm and orchard with the fence-lined Emmitsburg Road as their goal. Sperry's strung-out quartet of companies passed over the plank fences and dropped into a shallow swale west of the road. Sperry's men could hear firing increasing off to the north.[20]

It was nearly 9:00 a.m. by the time General Harrow's 1,366-man brigade swung into Hummelbaugh's well-trampled field. A pre-war Indiana lawyer of questionable

19 USGS MRC 39077G2; *Bachelder Maps, Second Day.* For information concerning Confederate artillery, see Richard Rollins's three-part essay, "The Guns Of Gettysburg," in *North & South,* vols. 2, 3, and 4. It should be noted the Emmitsburg Road Rise near the Klingle House and Sherfy Peach Orchard rise is higher than South Cemetery Ridge. Captain Judson Clark, commanding Battery B, 1st New Jersey Light, Third Corps Artillery Brigade, realized and took note of it.

20 *OR* 27, pt. 1, 416; *Bachelder Maps, Second Day.*

sobriety, Harrow had been ill during much of the march. Despite not being able to walk or ride for much of the past five days, he was quite certain he had the energy for the impending battle. After announcing he was not about to "play it safe during a fight," the 40-year-old brigadier led his men up the eastern slope of Cemetery Ridge under an indirect shelling that proved fatal to a few soldiers. The last of Gibbon's three brigades to arrive, Harrow's men were placed in reserve on the eastern slope with Webb's 71st and 72nd Pennsylvania regiments in their immediate right and front.[21]

Harrow posted his brigade in regiments by battalion, as had Willard to the north. They stacked arms under a "terrific and severe" artillery barrage intended for Cushing, Brown, Arnold, Hall, and Webb. The Copse of Trees, a conspicuous landmark used by Confederate gunners, stood stark atop the crest 100 yards to Harrow's front, with Meade's headquarters near the Taneytown Road about 200 yards off his right.[22]

The 19th Maine had led Harrow's brigade up the slope after the 15th Massachusetts was detached and directed to continue north on the Taneytown Road. Commanded by Col. Francis Edward Heath, a well-respected and gracious officer, his 543 soldiers of the 19th Maine were a no-nonsense bunch of woodsmen, small farmers, tradesmen, fishermen, and college students. Although their regiment was not yet a year old, it had participated in the major battles of Fredericksburg and Chancellorsville as well as several smaller skirmishes. Heath's men quietly stacked arms and lay down while solid shot and rifled bolt intended for Cushing's gun line passed overhead. The solid rifled bolts were morale busters that tumbled as they lost velocity and fell toward earth.[23] The real killer, however, was shrapnel, which exploded above the ground to disperse jagged chunks of searing hot iron earthward over a large area. For Heath's soldiers hugging the ground, it was a trying time. "The Confederates made no attack in front of the position we were holding in the forenoon," Sgt. Silas Adams described, "but they evidently knew we were there. Every now and then they would pitch a shell over among us, which

---

21 According to General Harrow, "The division arrived upon the battle-field on the morning of the 2nd, and was ordered into position by Brig. Gen. John Gibbon, as follows: The Second Brigade [Webb]—occupied the right of the division—The Third Brigade [Hall] connected with the left of Gen. Webb's brigade, and continued the line in the direction of Round Top Mountain to the left, their two brigades covering a front of 500 yards. The First brigade, my own command, was placed in reserve 100 yards in rear of the Second [Webb] and Third [Hall] Brigades and opposite the center of the line." *OR* 27, pt. 1, 419.

22 Shultz and Rollins, *Measuring Pickett's Charge*, 108-16.

23 John Day Smith, *The History of the Nineteenth Regiment of Maine Volunteer Infantry, 1862-1865* (Gaithersburg, MD, 1909), 58. See also *OR* 27, pt. 2, 629.

would strike in our midst, killing and wounding a number of men. All we could do was lie there and guess where the next one would strike, or who the next victim would be. We were near enough to the crest of the hill [ridge] to get the full benefit of their fireworks."[24]

The 1st Minnesota paused a short distance behind Heath's 19th Maine. Two hundred yards north, just outside Bryan's peach orchard, Colonel Colvill could see the stacked arms of the 111th New York and, a little nearer, those of Webb's 71st and 72nd Pennsylvania regiments. Colvill's 329 men and officers stacked arms while the 15th Massachusetts, moving at double-quick to their left, crested the ridge near the Copse. The Bay State troops had earlier been detached, but now rejoined Harrow's brigade using the Peter Frey farm lane. After dropping their packs and personal belongings, they continued up and over the crest and tramped down the western slope toward the Codori farmyard. Sperry's four companies of the 72nd and 106th Pennsylvania, meanwhile, disappeared from view, seemingly swallowed up beyond the road west of that farm.[25]

Within moments of the 15th disappearing over the crest, a bugle sounded "Assembly" calling the 82nd New Yorkers to their feet. Colvill's Minnesotans and Heath's men paid little attention as the 82nd formed and dressed ranks. Within moments the New Yorkers were winding their way west, passing through the 1st Minnesota and then the 19th Maine. Turning left at the stone wall, they passed behind Cushing's caissons and turned west again, following the 15th Massachusetts to the Codori farm. Continuing down the undulating plain to the Emmitsburg Road, both the 15th and 82nd formed a battle line supporting Sperry's Pennsylvanians, whose sparse line was by now suffering under an intense artillery fire. With the 15th and 82nd detached, Harrow was down to two regiments mustering some 769 effectives. Webb had even fewer effectives, perhaps 700 between his two remaining regiments, the 71st and 72nd Pennsylvania. In all, Gibbon's division had roughly 1,400 men in reserve along Cemetery Ridge.[26]

* * *

---

24 Ibid., 70.

25 The 15th Massachusetts continued north on the Taneytown Road, moving onto the ridge via the Peter Frey farm. It is clear the column was stopped somewhere near the road because these men were the last of Harrow's regiments to arrive. OR 27, pt. 1, 416; *Bachelder Maps, Second Day*. Sperry's men descended into the swale.

26 Ibid., pt. 2, 423, 426.

While the trailing First Division of Caldwell's Second Corps closed on the Hummelbaugh's farm lane, Maj. Gen. George Sykes' Fifth Corps approached on the Baltimore Pike after a grueling 14-mile march from Hanover in neighboring York County. Previous events, such as the uncertainly over Johnson's Rebel division's exact whereabouts, combined with General Slocum's continued concern about the Union army's exposed right flank, convinced General Meade to alter his plans. Instead of sending Sykes to reinforce the vulnerable right, Meade ordered the Fifth Corps into reserve. "[I] reach[ed] the field of Gettysburg, via Liberty, Union Mills, Hanover &c., about 8 a.m.," Sykes reported. "My troops took position on the right of our line [near Hanover Road], but being thought too extended, they were subsequently massed near the bridge over Rock Creek, on the Baltimore and Gettysburg pike, within reach of the Twelfth Army Corps. While thus situated, I was directed to support the Third Corps, General Sickles commanding, with a brigade should it be required."[27]

Sykes' exhausted men stacked arms in the fields surrounding George Musser's farm about three-quarters of a mile east of Little Round Top. This was well within supporting distance of Meade's left flank. It is unclear whether Third Corps commander General Sickles was aware of this information at that early hour. His subsequent actions appear as if he had no knowledge of Sykes' proximity or that it was a temporary position as Sedgwick's Sixth Corps arrived. While Sykes was taking up this position, Sickles was fretting about his western front and the lack of information being relayed his way by John Buford's troopers picketing the Emmitsburg Road Rise.[28]

Instead of continuing north through Hummelbaugh's intersection, Caldwell's division was directed up the slope. Before reaching the crest, Col. Edward E. Cross's leading brigade was ushered south through an uneven rock-strewn field bordered on his left by the Patterson Woods with the low open crest of Cemetery Ridge not 150 yards off his right flank. Placed in "column of regiments by brigades" for quick deployment, Caldwell saw to it his men remained opposite the low crest with his rear regiments safely tucked into the woods. Caldwell meant well, but his division was clearly visible to the Rebels watching across the way. Looking west from Caldwell's initial deployment area on Cemetery Ridge, the Emmitsburg Road appears as high as the ridge itself. Although his masses were visible to Rebel eyes, this natural illusion made it hard for the Confederates to gauge his position clearly

---

27 Ibid., pt. 1, 592.

28 USGS MRC 39077G2; *Bachelder Maps, Second Day*. Sykes would later report that he did not speak to Sickles until later in the day.

or estimate its distance.[29] Lieutenant Albert Sheldon, commanding Battery B, 1st New York with the 14th New York (Brooklyn Battery) Independent attached, followed Col. John R. Brooke's trailing brigade up the avenue. When Brooke deployed in column of regiments nearest the Hummelbaugh farm lane, Sheldon swung his guns wide and placed them in battery along the front center of the division. Caldwell ordered Sheldon to also remain below the crest.[30]

Within a few minutes of their arrival, several detachments from each of Caldwell's regiments began dismantling rail and plank fences in the depression between Cemetery Ridge and the Emmitsburg Road. Unlike Gibbon's men near the Copse of Trees who were openly exposed, most of Caldwell's soldiers had the luxury of lying in the shade of the western belt of Sarah Patterson's woods. Although the ground was rough and in places rocky, it was better than resting under a rising sun behind artillery engaged in counter-battery action. Still, a few errant rounds fired from across the valley found their mark within Caldwell's ranks. Rather than respond to this shelling, however, Caldwell ordered Lieutenant Sheldon to keep his four 10-pounders concealed east of the crest. He knew that exposing Sheldon's pieces or worse still, letting them return fire, would bring on a more intense response from the enemy.[31]

About a mile or so to the west, meanwhile, E. P. Alexander conducted a reconnaissance wholly unlike General Pendleton's prior ride. Lee's chief of artillery had led his party down an inactive line before sunrise, passing as he did so a few scattered North Carolinians. The circumstances had changed considerably the moment Hancock's Second Corps showed itself atop Cemetery Ridge. Between 8:00 and 8:30 a.m., with the picket truce at an end, a spattering of fire between Lowrance's North Carolinians and Union skirmishers turned deadly when the Rebel marksmen switched their attention to Hays' arriving division. Even now, alongside Lowrance's skirmishers, a few of Anderson's early arrivals began harassing Hays' men, and immediately to the south Gibbon's line came under artillery fire as he oversaw his deployment from near the Copse. To his left front,

29 OR 27, pt. 1, 384; Thomas L. Livermore, *Days and Events* (Cambridge, MA, 1920), 755-57; New York Monuments Commission, *Final Report on the Battlefield of Gettysburg*, 1:420; 2:475, 480-81, 491-92, 515.

30 Ibid.; USGS MRC 39077G2.

31 Ibid., pt. 1, 386, 379. Colonel Patrick Kelly, commanding the 68th New York as well as the brigade, remembered, "Arriving on the heights near the village, and in view of the enemy's pickets, we took a position in two lines on the right of the First Brigade, stacked arms, and allowed the men to rest." Caldwell reported, "My command arrived on the field of battle on the morning of July Second, and was placed in position by General Hancock on the left of the Second (Gibbon's) Division, in columns of brigades."

Humphreys' advanced skirmish line—bolstered by the arrival of 100 of Maj. Homer R. Stoughton's green-clad 2nd U.S. Sharpshooters—renewed the contest from the Spangler and Staub farmyards behind any rail fence offering cover. Lowrance's thin line was exhaling its harassing fire when Alexander began riding down Willoughby Run.[32]

From Washington Street south to the Henry Spangler farm lane, a distance of about a mile and a half, the Emmitsburg Road line erupted into a deadly contest fed by Generals Carnot Posey and Ambrose Wright, who sent heavy waves of skirmishers forward. An acceleration of the fighting here was not what Meade wanted. He needed time for the Fifth Corps and Sixth Corps to arrive and deploy, secure his flanks, and establish a proper reserve. Likewise, this was not what Lee wanted or expected because it did not fit his attack plan. Once south of the Fairfield Road, Colonel Alexander could not see Lowrance's advanced pickets or Anderson's men. He could, however, hear the level of musketry increase as he rode south toward Pitzer's Woods. The individual crack of a sharpshooter's weapon was now nearly impossible to distinguish from the increased crash of steady trigger-pulling along the length of the line.[33]

Rebel sharpshooters planted along the fences between the Bliss property and the Emmitsburg Road became so deadly they were knocking men down in Woodruff's gun line west of Zeigler's Grove, as well as men behind them in the 108th New York. Sharpshooters using the Bliss barn and house continued hitting artillerists in Arnold's battery along with men in the 14th Connecticut and 12th New Jersey to their right. An exasperated General Hays, watching from the crest, had seen enough. He issued orders to Lt. Col. Edward P. Harris, commanding the 1st Delaware of Smyth's brigade, to storm the Bliss property. Confederate Colonel Alexander, meanwhile, was somewhere west of the wooded crest beyond the Bliss farm.[34]

As Alexander followed Willoughby Run southward he concluded, just as Pendleton had, that this would be the protected route his artillery battalions would use to reach the far right. Heeding Longstreet's instructions to keep out of view, he remained below the crest of Seminary Ridge while the battle heated up on the opposite side. Alexander picked his horse along the shallow watercourse to its ford with Willoughby Run Road south of the J. Plank Farm and proceeded east on that

---

32 USGS MRC 39077G2, *Bachelder Maps, Second Day.*

33 Clark, *History of the Several Regiments,* 2:678-79; USGS MRC 39077G2.

34 Christ, *The Struggle for the Bliss Farm,* 14-15. It was against general military regulations and standing orders to knowingly target a private citizen's home. See also Gallagher, *Fighting for the Confederacy,* 235-36.

avenue toward Pitzer's Woods, where he surely took note of Wilcox's forward pickets. At some point near there, Alexander reported hearing firing to his right as well as to the east. If this is correct, he was probably hearing the skirmishing between Wilcox's advanced right-most regiment (the 10th Alabama) and Devin's dismounted cavalrymen beyond the western portion of Pitzer's Woods near present-day Pumping Station Road.[35]

It is also likely Alexander noticed the Black Horse Tavern Road where it bridged Willoughby Run near the Felix homestead. Up to this time it is doubtful he knew that road existed. Had he scanned the terrain west, he would have seen it skirting the northern edge of the western branch of Pitzer's Woods above the opposite bank of Willoughby Run. Once clear of the thin wood line the dirt road angled west-northwest, traversing the gentle slope of South Herr's Ridge where it disappeared over the crest of the W. Plank farm along the creek. However, Alexander could not see that this road skirted the open crest for nearly 800 yards before descending toward Marsh Creek, leaving several hundred men in full view of the Union signal station atop the "mountain on the left."[36]

At some point the increased firing to the east got the best of the artillery colonel. Ascending the crest of Seminary Ridge somewhere west of the Staub farm, a sweeping panorama unfolded before Alexander as he drew near the eastern edge of Pitzer's Woods. It was in his opinion an excellent platform to view the field. Looking north he could see the fight for the Bliss farm escalating as the 1st Delaware was by then likely advancing or already directly embroiled with Lowrance's men. He not only watched Gibbon's men deploying forward, but also portions of another enemy force whose pioneers were hard at work dismantling fences between the Emmitsburg Road and the low ridgeline beyond it—likely Caldwell's division or men from Humphreys' division of Sickles' Third Corps.[37]

Directly east, Alexander's eye may have caught Humphreys' division resting on the eastern slope of the Emmitsburg Road Rise in Trostle's open meadow. He would have clearly seen Humphreys' reinforced skirmish line, including the specialized sharpshooters, not 400 yards away. Continuing south, his gaze would have picked up Buford's cavalry videttes as well as a battery of horse artillery. The distance to Sherfy's Peach Orchard from just inside the eastern edge of Pitzer's

---

35 Ibid. This was near where the present-day Longstreet statue is located off West Confederate Avenue. It is possible Pendleton rode with him to this observation point.

36 USGS MRC 39077G2. As a trained engineer and artillerist, Alexander must have noted this road was more direct thus a much shorter route. At some point Alexander changed or reconsidered his route south.

37 Ibid.

Woods was about 1,200 yards, and according to Alexander that area was devoid of enemy infantry. The artillery officer scanned in that direction before the arrival of Burling's and de Trobriand's Third Corps brigades. Like Pendleton, Long, and Johnston before him, Alexander never claimed he pinpointed the location of the Union left flank.[38]

Alexander's stay atop the crest was brief. Dropping back down to Willoughby Run, he continued southward to the Millerstown Road. Across that lane above the eastern bank of the creek was the entrance to the rural trace that angled up the slope of West Warfield Ridge through Biesecker's Woods. This was the same route Pendleton, Long, and Johnston reported and that Longstreet probably had second thoughts about using. Alexander later specified that his ride lasted a little over an hour. Had he stayed longer, he would have spied Burling's brigade moving past the Peach Orchard, but he departed before the arrival of those troops.

For all practical purposes Alexander achieved what was expected, but while doing so wasted precious time for the army's commanding general. Although he managed to find a route out of view of prying Union eyes, Alexander had nothing more to report than what Captain Johnston and Colonel Long had already turned in. Alexander sent riders to all concerned that the Willoughby Run ravine would allow easy travel for artillery while the stream bed and open fields on either side could easily handle massed infantry. As long as Wilcox's brigade controlled Pitzer's Woods on either side of the run—through which all of Longstreet's command would pass—this route would work despite the Union signal corps atop Little Round Top "wig wagging" their flags.[39]

Alexander returned north believing the Union left flank, wherever it actually was, could be bypassed without detection via the trace he had found opposite the Millerstown Road. His plan was to precede the infantry with his battalion of artillery to the Pitzer schoolhouse, where he would await the rest of the artillery prior to deploying it up that avenue. Galloping back up Willoughby Run, Alexander paid scant attention to the escalating Bliss farm fight, which by that time had turned into a raging no-man's-land struggle. What the colonel did not divulge at this time was the fact that he had spied a new route above Willoughby Run that beckoned him.[40]

*   *   *

38 Gallagher, *Fighting for the Confederacy,* 235-36; USGS MRC 39077G2; *Bachelder Maps, Second Day.*

39 USGS MRC 39077G2; *Bachelder Maps, Second Day.*

40 Gallagher, *Fighting for the Confederacy,* 235-36; USGS MRC 39077G2; *Bachelder Maps, Second Day;* Christ, *The Struggle for the Bliss Farm,* 16.

While E. P. Alexander was reconnoitering, part of Alexander Hays' Union division was spreading out on northern Cemetery Ridge across a tidy farm belonging to Abraham Bryan, a black widower with five children. Bryan purchased the 12-acre tract in 1857 shortly before marrying Elizabeth, his third wife. In addition to his peach orchard atop the crest, Bryan cultivated barley, wheat, and timothy. The northern perimeter of the farm was bounded by a low stone wall extending east 200 yards toward the Taneytown Road. Beyond that wall lay the Emanuel Trostle farm and Zeigler's Woods. To the south, the widow Lydia Leister's smaller 10-acre farm extended west from the Taneytown Road to the crest of Cemetery Ridge, where it intersected Bryan's property line. Meade, as noted earlier, had appropriated the white-washed Leister home as his headquarters.[41]

Skirmishers from Carroll's and Smyth's brigades eased their way west, but before they could deploy, Lowrance's well-practiced Rebel riflemen pitched into them from beyond the Emmitsburg Road. Those Southerners hugging the brush-choked rail fence east of and above Stevens Run opened a deadly fire that brought down many Federals. The stout plank fence along the Emmitsburg Road, along with the Bryan house and Trostle's barn to the north, helped the Union First and Eleventh corps skirmishers holding that vital road. When Hays' reinforcements reached the Bryan house and passed through the gate, they spread out both north and south, lending their firepower to the skirmishers along the road from the First Corps. Unable to dislodge the Rebel riflemen from the rail fence (as well as those supporting them from the Bliss farm), something more aggressive had to done.

The Bliss buildings sat almost midway between the lines, roughly 600 yards from the Bryan barn and 600 or so yards from the stone wall paralleling the eastern brow of Seminary Ridge, with an expansive orchard between the Bliss yard and the ridge. The first Union troops to cross the Emmitsburg Road in force from the Second Corps on July 2 belonged to Lt. Col. Edward P. Harris's 1st Delaware. Numbering roughly 250 men, they double-timed down the Bryan farm lane with arms at "right shoulder shift," descending Cemetery Ridge toward the Emmitsburg Road. When he reached the road, Harris led his column out the Bliss farm lane under a hail of small arms fire erupting from a rail fence about 200 yards distant, as well as the brush-choked fence line on the rise farther north.[42]

Harris's objective was the Bliss farm between the ridges. Chaplain Henry S. Stevens of the 14th Connecticut, also part of Smyth's brigade, left a good description of the Bliss farm buildings: "In front of our skirmish line were two buildings . . . one was a large barn almost citadel in itself, it was extensive and

41 USGS MRC 39077G2-TF-024.

42 Christ, *The Struggle for the Bliss Farm*, 15-18.

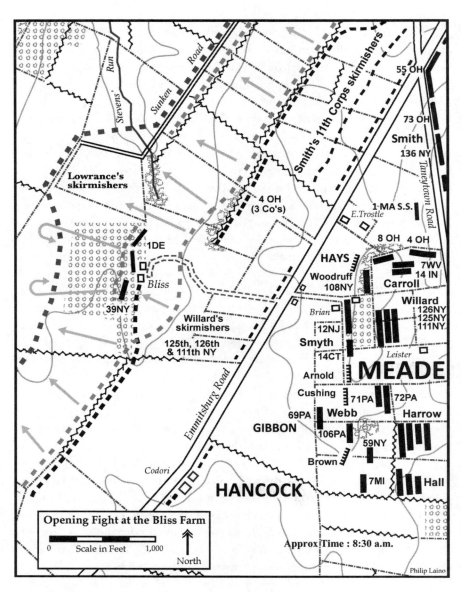

Opening Fight at the Bliss Farm

0   Scale in Feet   1,000

North

Approx Time : 8:30 a.m.

Philip Laino

elaborately built structure, as barns go, 75 feet long and 33 feet wide, its lower story .
. . 10 feet high, constructed of stone, and its upper part, 16 feet high to the eves, of
bricks, the wall being gables," he continued. "There was an overhang 10 feet long
across the entire front for the shelter of cattle, and the rear was banked to the first
floor—whence the name bank barn—furnishing a driveway for loads to that floor.
There were 5 doors in the front wall of the basement and 3 windows in each end;

Loooking east from the Bliss farm. The camera is positioned on the strategic rise just east of and above Stevens Run, about 200 yards west of the Emmitsburg Road. Abraham Bryan's white house is in the center-distance below what was once Zeigler's Grove. *Todd C. Wiley*

several vertical slits in the upper story and 2 rows of windows in each end. Ninety paces north of the barn was the mansion, a frame building, two stories in height."[43]

Scales' North Carolina brigade (now under Colonel Lowrance) was so badly mauled on July 1 that its advanced skirmishers quickly gave way near the Bliss farm lane when Harris's vanguard closed on them. They retired from the fence line north of the farm lane as well as the fence-lined rectangular lots south of it; Lt. Alsa Brown of the 38th North Carolina rallied the fleeing skirmishers in the farmyard. The mounting pressure from the advancing "First Staters," however, soon forced them farther west toward the Bliss orchard.[44]

Brown reluctantly withdrew from the farmyard when the 1st Delaware spread out after passing to the west of the boxed lots and into the farmyard, with the Federal right flank moving northwest toward the house and Stevens Run beyond, and the left flank moving south and west to storm the barn and outbuildings.

---

43 Henry S. Stevens, "Address at Dedication to Monument, 14th Connecticut Volunteers, Gettysburg PA, July 3, 1884," in *The 14th Connecticut Volunteers At Gettysburg, 1863-84*, LOC, 0-013-709-117-3).

44 Ibid.

Brown pulled his men back to a second rail fence west of the yard, where his men sent streams of deadly lead missiles into the ranks of the advancing 1st Delaware. Fortunately for Harris, the barn and house acted like buffers as his line due east of both passed through the farmyard without taking any casualties. Lieutenant Brown gave up his rail fence and withdrew another 100 yards toward the Bliss orchard. The retreating Tar Heels met knots of other determined Rebels moving up through the widely spaced fruit trees to lend support: Carnot Posey's Mississippians had arrived.[45]

While Harris seized the Bliss farm, Union Second Corps gunners on Cemetery Ridge opened fire to silence the Confederate batteries firing from various points along wooded Seminary Ridge. The 1st Delaware was not alone west of the Emmitsburg Road by the time Posey's Mississippi troops moved east to join Brown's sharp fight. After receiving personal instructions from General Webb, Captain Sperry led his four Pennsylvania companies up and out of the western slope of their sheltering swale. Their line angled slightly away from Harris's left flank in the Bliss farmyard. Cresting the rise, Sperry's small detachment overran a few of Brown's North Carolinians who were either too exhausted to flee or simply not paying attention when their comrades around them withdrew from the Bliss farmyard.[46]

With his men now in control of the fence line, Sperry's right flank was about 100 yards south of Capt. M. W. B. Ellegood's Company E (the 1st Delaware's left flank) just south of the bank barn. Those Tar Heels who did not surrender to Sperry likewise fell back to the southern edge of the orchard, joining those men who had already retreated there from the barn and farmyard. Fortunately for Ellegood's company and Sperry's Keystoners, Arnold's and Cushing's rifled batteries along with Brown's six smoothbores just south of the copse of trees suppressed the enemy fire.[47]

With the left flank of the 1st Delaware positioned around the Bliss barn, Harris's right wing was able to drive Lowrance's skirmishers out of the northern part of the farm, forcing them back into the orchard west of it above the dogleg of the sunken lane. With the 1st Delaware now in complete possession of the farmyard, and with Sperry south of it, more Federals began streaming across the Emmitsburg Road, especially toward the brush-choked fence above Stevens Run. Skirmishers from both Carroll's and Smyth's brigades, as well as sharpshooters

45 Clark, *History of the Several Regiments*, 2:678-79.

46 *OR 27*, pt. 1, 465.

47 John L. Brady to Col. John Bachelder, May 24, 1886, *Bachelder Papers*, 3:1387-88.

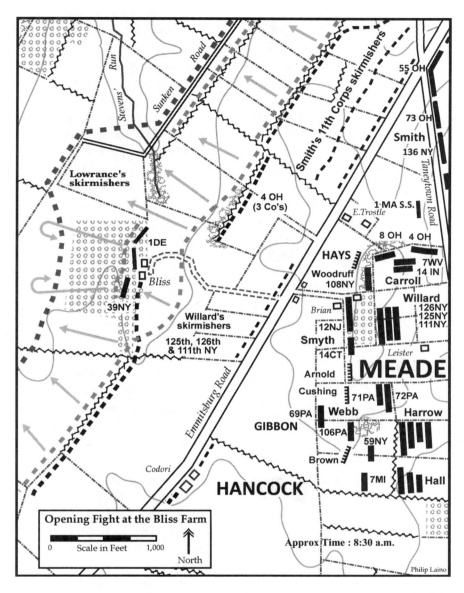

Opening Fight at the Bliss Farm

Scale in Feet

0   1,000

North

Approx Time : 8:30 a.m.

Philip Laino

from various units, joined Col. James Wood, Jr.'s 136th New Yorkers north of the Bliss farm in their attempt to hold the Emmitsburg Road.[48]

In an effort to counter the Federal buildup, Confederate infantry from Edward Thomas's and James Lane's brigades were detached southward in an attempt to

48 OR 27, pt. 1, 460.

support the arriving troops under Posey and William Mahone, and the hard-pressed Lowrance. Dressing ranks in the relative safety of a depression west of the sunken road, this impromptu line of Georgians and North Carolinians, supported by a few Virginians from Mahone's outfit, began advancing from the depression east of the McMillan orchard, angling toward the Bliss farm. Union fire from the brush-covered fence above Stevens Run raked the far left end of the Rebel line. At that moment there were not enough Confederate rifles within range to effectively stop the enemy fire. Thomas's Georgians in the sunken road did their best to support the counterattack to the south, and at the same time neutralize the Union fire from the fence as the fighting erupted into a heavy and sustained musketry fight.[49]

The lines slugged it out for about half an hour before the heavier Confederate numbers to north began to tell in the orchard. Captain Ellegood and Lt. John L. Brady, also of the 1st Delaware's Company E, discovered that the right wing, suffering under a galling fire from numerically superior Rebels, was slowly being pressed backward toward the regimental center at the Bliss barn. After a brief and rather hurried conversation, Brady, who "had lost sight of" Harris, rode down the line in search of the regimental commander. He located the officer in the basement of the barn, where he had established his headquarters. Brady "at once explained to him the state of affairs, as existing on the right."

What came next was nearly unheard of within the ranks of either army. According to a stunned Brady, "[Harris] after carefully venturing from his safe retreat, and taking a very hasty glance over the situation, turned and fled precipitately, toward our lines." His apparent cowardice left that portion of the field to the command of Brady and 1st Lt. Charles B. Tanner. By then, the right wing was somewhat disorganized, but a portion had reached the northern fence line parallel to the east-west dogleg of the sunken lane.[50]

With the Bliss farmhouse anchoring and protecting the Delaware regiment's far right, Brady and Tanner pulled the line back and using the rail fence due north of the house, poured a devastating fire into the Rebel left flank. These volleys, together with help from those on their own right holding the brush-choked rail fence, stopped the Rebel advance. The advancing Confederate line coming from the northwest beyond the dogleg soon joined up with Posey's Mississippians advancing through the orchard. This combined line easily manhandled not only Harris's center, but also that of Captain Ellegood's company on the far left. The 1st

---

49 Brady to Bachelder, May 24, 1886, *Bachelder Papers*, 3:1387-88. Thomas had about 1,200 men in action at Gettysburg, of whom 34 were killed, 179 wounded, and another 57 missing. Manning the sunken lane between the armies proved a mixed blessing. Gettysburg monument.

50 Brady to Bachelder, May 24, 1886, *Bachelder Papers*, 3:1387-88.

Delaware unwound from house to barn, or north to south, as its line withdrew from the rail fence along the eastern edge of the orchard. The troops in the house were the first to fall, followed by those in the barn and the farmyard as the advance line melted away.[51]

Brady and Tanner rallied the few remaining men on hand and formed them into a new defensive line along the southern side of the fence. When Lieutenant Tanner received a painful wound and had to retire from the field to seek aid, Brady remained as the last officer in the sector. The small group managed to squeeze off "a few well-direct shots into the now rapidly advancing enemy," wrote Brady, which "caused him to swerve obliquely to his right [west-southwest] and at the same time to pass between our left flank [at the farmhouse], and barn." Realizing the enemy had received reinforcements and was now passing to his left and rear (south of the farmhouse & barn), Brady "deemed it prudent to retire." It proved to be a wise decision, for at the same time he issued the order, Rebel infantry flanked and surrounded the regiment's left wing.[52]

Before the hard-pressed 1st Delaware departed the body-strewn farmyard, Posey's Mississippians, accompanied by Lieutenant Brown and a few of his North Carolinians, reoccupied the barn and house and immediately opened fire from within the shelter of the structures. Their fire forced Captain Sperry to leave his advance position. He and his Pennsylvanians retired eastward to another rail fence where his men met arriving skirmishers from Harrow's brigade supported by a small detachment of sharpshooters from Minnesota and Massachusetts. With Posey still firmly in control of the farmyard and rail fence, a new squabble erupted when enough men from the 1st Delaware faced back along the rectangular fields north of Sperry.[53]

Prior to Harris's premature and controversial departure from the Bliss farmyard, General Hays had already organized support for the beleaguered 1st Delaware. He ordered Col. Leonard W. Carpenter, commanding the 4th Ohio of Carroll's Gibraltar Brigade, to detach four companies to bolster the skirmish line north of the Bliss farm. Fronting due north, the Buckeyes' right rested just below the Taneytown Road in Zeigler's Grove. "At 9:30 a.m. I received orders to advance four companies of my regiment to support the line of pickets," Carpenter reported, "which I did, under the command of Major [Gordon A.] Stewart." Major Stewart moved his four companies left-oblique into the upper or western reaches of the Emanuel Trostle farm. Moving at the double-quick toward the Trostle farm and the

51 Christ, *The Struggle for the Bliss Farm*, 15-18.

52 Brady to Bachelder, May 24, 1888, *Bachelder Papers*, 3:1387-88.

53 Christ, *The Struggle for the Bliss Farm*, 15-18.

Emmitsburg Road, they passed the front of the 8th Ohio on the 4th's immediate left.[54]

As Major Stewart's left flank companies passed through the farm, several marksmen from the 1st Company, Massachusetts Sharpshooters joined them as they pushed uncontested across the road. Reaching the brush-covered rail fence well north of the Bliss farm lane, Stewart's men provided additional firepower which helped check the Confederates' southward advance. The Rebels seemingly melted back into the earth as they took refuge in the sunken road. It was too late, however; because by that time Posey's fresh Mississippians had consolidated their control of the Bliss farm. Unfortunately for many of those newly arrived Rebels, they had to contend with Capt. William Plumer's 1st Company, Massachusetts Sharpshooters with their Sharps and Merrill rifles. Aside from those who had joined Stewart along the rail fence, these marksmen engaged from the Bryan tenant house as well as from Emanuel Trostle's large bank barn.[55]

Colonel Willard's veterans of Harpers Ferry were also called upon for help. The battle-tested 39th New York, accompanied by several companies from the 125th and 126th New York regiments, formed and went forward. Deploying into a lengthy skirmish line, with their left flank near Arnold's rightmost gun and their right near Bryan's small barn, they passed through the peach orchard and then crested the rise before descending toward Smyth's brigade and the stone wall to their front. Moving at double-quick with arms at "right shoulder shift," they made it to the eastern plank fence without a single casualty and immediately engaged the Confederate riflemen harassing the reforming 1st Delaware.[56]

Taking advantage of the chaos west of the road, Maj. Hugo Hildebrand ordered his 39th New York through the Bliss gate and over the fences west of the pike. Within moments Willard's skirmish line seized command of the rail fence to the immediate left of the shaky 1st Delaware. Hildebrandt's bold move not only allowed Sperry to consolidate his men, thus strengthening his line and grip on the rail fence south of the barnyard, but also allowed Capt. Thomas B. Hizar, now commanding the 1st Delaware with Harris missing, the time he needed to steady his

---

54 Brady to Bachelder, May 24, 1886, *Bachelder Papers*, 3:1387-88.

55 Ibid.; Christ, *The Struggle for the Bliss Farm*, 19-20. See also OR 27, pt.1, 456, 460.

56 Raus, *The Union Army at Gettysburg*, 58. Captain Aaron P. Seeley of the 111th New York recalled, "We lay in this position until 5 p.m. most of the afternoon under a furious shelling from the enemy."

shaken regiment. Posey, however, was not yet finished as the fight became a stalemate, his numbers slowly increasing as the minutes ticked past.[57]

*   *   *

Meanwhile to the west, Colonel Alexander returned from his reconnaissance. However, he neither reported to Longstreet nor personally relayed the new route he spied to anyone except perhaps the bewildered Captain Johnston or someone close to him. Given the best available evidence, it appears Alexander was trying to figure out how he could detour Colonel Walton's batteries into the Willoughby Run valley using the alternative route he had discovered. Without authorization to do so, Alexander dispatched riders in search of Col. Henry G. Cabell's artillery battalion with orders to meet him at the Pitzer schoolhouse near the Millerstown Road. He also personally hooked up Maj. M. W. Henry's artillery battalion parked near his own along Marsh Creek.[58]

By the time Alexander reached his own and Major Eshleman's Washington Artillery bivouacs, much of the Bliss farm fighting he could clearly hear was pouring out of rifled muskets held by Major Hildebrandt's 39th New York, which was fully embroiled in a difficult combat with Posey's Mississippians for possession of the Bliss farm. The open salvo aimed at redemption for Willard's "Harpers Ferry Cowards" rested on their shoulders.

57 New York Monuments Commission, *Final report on the Battlefield of Gettysburg*, 1:278; Fleming, *Life and Letters of Alexander Hays*, 431-41, Clinton MacDougall to Hays, November 29, 1909, Auburn, New York.

58 Gallagher, *Fighting for the Confederacy*, 235-36; USGS MRC 39077G2-TF-024.

Chapter Ten

"The skirmishing was the heaviest I have ever heard of, being almost equal to a pitch[ed]
battle all the time. . . . I think twas the hottest place I have yet been."

— *Capt. Charles A. Conn, Thomas' brigade, Army of Northern Virginia*[1]

Morning, July 2:
Union Uncertainties Across the Front

By the time Confederate Colonel Alexander completed his lengthy morning reconnaissance south of Gettysburg, the firing along the length of the Broad Open Plain from Washington Street south to the William Bliss farm was in full fury. Muskets crackled, artillery roared, bugles blared, and soldiers far from home died or fell injured in sun-baked Pennsylvania fields.

Although control of the Bliss farm midway between the ridges was vital to the fortunes of both armies, the brush-covered fence above Stevens Run and the northern portion of the Bliss farm would, in time, become more strategic for Meade's men in blue. Unfortunately for General Posey's Mississippians defending the farm, Union gunners rained so much shot and shell into the orchard and woods it became nearly impossible for Posey and General Wright to reinforce their advanced lines—but reinforce them they did. From afar it appeared to Rebel division commander Anderson and his staff that as many Confederates were retiring westward as were moving east. As a steady stream of wounded or exhausted men made their way back to Seminary Ridge, many more dashed forward between the wood line, orchard, and yard—all under the sustained Union artillery crossfire.[2]

---

1   Letters from Charles A. Conn, *Georgia Historical Quarterly*, Georgia Historical Society Library and Archives, Vol. 46, 187-88.

2   OR 27, pt. 2, 668, 671-672. USGS MRC 39077G2; *Bachelder Maps, Second Day*.

At some point between 9:30 and 10:00 a.m., Colonel Lowrance received orders from division commander Pender to pull Scales' brigade off line and take refuge west of Seminary Ridge. This withdrawal was almost certainly the steady stream of men Anderson spotted retiring west toward the wood line. Leaving Lt. Alsa Brown with a few courageous volunteers from the 38th North Carolina, the remainder of Lowrance's weary soldiers made their back toward the safety of Seminary Ridge and McMillan's Woods. Excepting Brown's detachment, Lowrance would not fully complete his withdrawal until well after 1:00 p.m. Like Brown's men near the Bliss farm, a few of Lowrance's more rugged individuals stayed on line to support Anderson's right flank in Spangler's Woods.[3]

The lively fight at the Bliss farm initially played badly for the Union as the 39th New York began taking significant casualties, much more so than the remnants of the 1st Delaware to its right. With little cover except the wooden rail fence, the enemy fire emanating from the farmyard and orchard into the "Garibaldi Guards" was a testimony to the dogged persistence of Posey's Mississippians and Brown's supporting North Carolinians, all of whom were taking fire from at least two, and perhaps as many as three, Union batteries. Supported by several companies from the 125th and 126th New York, Major Hildebrandt's 39th New York held its own against enemy numbers that were slowly but steadily increasing.[4]

To the north of the 1st Delaware and the immediate right of Maj. Gordon Stewart's four companies of the 4th Ohio, the 136th New York's reinforced skirmishers continued to hold the rail fence atop the rise west of the Emmitsburg Road. The balance of Col. James Wood's Eleventh Corps regiment rested in the Emmitsburg Road depression that separated the rise from the Emanuel Trostle farm. Confederate Brig. Gen. Edward L. Thomas's failed attempt to secure the north end of the Bliss farm and the rise northeast of it would in time impede him and others confronting Wood's New Yorkers. "The skirmishing was the heaviest I have ever heard of, being almost equal to a pitch [sic] battle all the time," the 45th Georgia's Capt. Charles A. Conn recalled the struggle, "I think twas the hottest place I have yet been."[5]

"We lie down in line of Battle to keep the enemys Batterys from having such affect on us," penned the 14th Georgia's George W. Hall. "Cannon balls, bombs, grape and canister fall thick and fast among us killing and wounding several of our

---

3   Ibid., 671. Although Lowrance incorrectly assumed the time relieved was 1:00 p.m. he eventually aligned with Gen. James Lane's brigade on the far left.

4   Christ, *The Struggle for the Bliss Farm*, 19-20; Clark, *History of the Several Regiments and Battalions from North Carolina*, 2:678-79.

5   Conn, *Georgia Historical Quarterly*, 46:187-88.

regt." Caught between the fire of Woodruff's six Napoleons near Zeigler's Grove and Major Osborn's gunners on Cemetery Hill above and beyond them, Thomas's prone Georgians found themselves locked in a desperate and deadly situation.[6]

North of Thomas, Col. Abner Perrin's and Brig. Gen. James Lane's skirmishers were not much better off. Farther north, the soldiers of Brig. Gen. S. D. Ramseur's brigade (Robert Rodes' division, Ewell's corps) opted for the most part to keep their heads down, allowing a few of their most skilled marksmen to trade shots with the 73rd and 55th Ohio regiments just south of town. A wisp of powder smoke from a musket along this sector usually invited a shell or two from the Union guns that enjoyed remarkable fields of fire the entire length of the Broad Open Plain. "July 2, remained in line of battle all day," Ramseur simply reported, "with very heavy skirmishing in front." Major General Robert E. Rodes' three other brigades under Daniels, Iverson, and Doles had suffered considerably on July 1. They contributed nothing of significance this morning, lying in reserve behind and north of the sunken road. Rodes' line stretched as far north as the Lutheran Seminary.[7]

Unlike the torpor that seemed to have seized many of the Confederate commanders along this sector, their Union counterparts generally remained quite active. With the artillery steadily banging away and the rattle of musketry growing louder, Col. Clinton MacDougall of the 111th New York of Colonel Willard's brigade, Hays' division, grew restless. Accompanied by his aide Lt. Col. Isaac Lusk and several company commanders, MacDougall walked to the crest of the ridge to observe the unfolding action. This was their first view of the sprawling battlefield, and an alarming panorama unfolded before them as they topped the ridge north of Arnold's battery. Across the Emmitsburg Road, the fight centered on the Bliss property intensified with each passing minute, the steady crackling of musketry indicating the 39th New York and 1st Delaware faced heavy opposition. Confederate skirmishers, sheltered by the Bliss orchard, barn, and fences, were standing firm.

As MacDougall and the others watched, members of the 39th New York rushed forward in an effort to take control of the eastern edge of the farm, but were promptly driven back. Not to be outdone, the Confederates took advantage of this and countercharged along that part of the line before the 39th New York repeated the favor and sharply repulsed them. Shortly thereafter, the entire Confederate line south of the Bliss house moved in unison toward the 39th. Major Hildebrandt's

---

6 George Washington Hall Diary, July 2, 1863, Gettysburg, LoC; USGS MRC 39077G2; *Bachelder Maps, Second Day.*

7 Ibid.; *OR* 27, pt. 2, 665, 669, 671.

thin line began to waver. This did not sit well with men from the 1st Delaware, who also became nervous when the right of the 39th began to buckle.

Fortunately, Major Stewart's four companies of the 4th Ohio along the brush-covered rail fence suddenly stood up. At Stewart's emphatic command to fire, the Buckeyes delivered a crippling volley into Posey's advancing left flank, stopping the advance in its tracks. The Buckeyes proceeded to fire in an organized drill, sending volley after volley across Stevens Run down into the Bliss farmyard east and north of the house. This allowed the 1st Delaware to hang on as the fight south of them, nearer the barn, intensified. Watching from Cemetery Ridge, division commander Hays impetuously galloped down the slope of the ridge toward Hildebrandt's still-wavering 39th New York. This was Hays' combat of battle with his good friend and commanding officer Hancock, and he was not about to let the general down.[8]

Accompanied by his aide Corporal Carroll of the 5th New York Cavalry—"a reckless, devil-may-care Irishman"—and a few others from his staff, Hays met the few retreating Garibaldi Guards when they arrived near the road, and none too warmly. Hays, together with Brig. Gen. Samuel "Red" Carroll fervently waving the divisional flag, galloped from north to south rallying the 1st Delaware and 39th New York. The men of the latter regiment, their confidence restored, faced about and countercharged, retaking the rail fence on the east edge of the farm. This sudden action drove the Rebels back to the rail fence near the Bliss barn, but could not dislodge them from it or from the unfortunate family's bullet-pierced dwelling. This countercharge, combined with an advance by Major Stewart's heroic four small companies north of the 1st Delaware, enabled Capt. Thomas B. Hizar to establish a precarious grip on the farm lane and rail fence east and north of the house.[9]

From his impromptu observation post on Cemetery Ridge, the 111th New York's Colonel MacDougall watched General Hays' personal display of "superb gallantry." As MacDougall later observed, "The line of skirmishers on our right was hard pressed and gave way. In an instant the general rode down at a gallop mounted on his fine bay 'Dan,' with an orderly carrying his division flag, followed by other

---

8   Clinton D. MacDougall to Gilbert A. Hays, Nov. 29, 1909, in Hays and Fleming, *Life and Letters of Alexander Hays*, 431.

9   Richardson to Bachelder, June 18, 1867, in *Bachelder Papers*, 1:315, 319. A watching Capt. Charles Richardson, 126th New York, later wrote, "Here a lively skirmish took place, and the enemy's reinforcements to their line, coming from the northwest [McMillan Woods] through the orchard close to the barn, began to drive back the 39th New York, but, Gen. Alex Hays, accompanied by his adjutant general and the division flag dashed down on horseback to the line, rallied the men under a shower of bullets, reestablished the line and rode back unharmed." Richardson described Hays' flag as a "plain white square with blue trefoil."

Early 1900s image taken from the Zeigler's Grove tower looking due south down Cemetery Ridge toward the Round Tops. The protruding salient in the Union center followed the natural contour of Cemetery Ridge. The Bloody Angle, the general focal point of the Pickett-Pettigrew-Trimble Charge on July 3, is on the center right, with the umbrella-shaped Copse of Trees in the center. *Tipton, GNMP*

orderlies. The line was at once re-established and never broke again. It was," MacDougall went on to say, "the first and last time I ever saw a division commander with his flag and staff on the skirmish line—they were targets for hundreds of sharpshooters." Upon his return to Cemetery Ridge, Hays called upon Colonel Willard to have MacDougall send a pair of companies from his regiment to reinforce the 39th New York and the detachments belonging to the 125th and 126th New York regiments. The Pennsylvania-born general also sent forward Company I of the 12th New Jersey (Smyth's brigade) to bolster Captain Hizar's tenuous hold on the farm lane east of the Bliss house. Hays was managing the fight, and he was enjoying it.[10]

Hancock was certainly satisfied with his old West Point roommate Hays, and learned early in the fight that his right flank on Cemetery Ridge was in good hands. However, the Second Corps commander had arrived in time to witness the initial retreat of the 1st Delaware. He expressed his keen displeasure with Lieutenant

10 MacDougall to Hays, 300. According to Colonel MacDougall, "The two companies were detailed as skirmishers not long after arriving."

Colonel Harris upon the latter's return to Cemetery Ridge. Although Hays was occupied shoring up Harris's failure at the Bliss farm, Hancock was angry enough to take the time to chastise the unfortunate Delaware officer, dismissing him and placing him under arrest. Hancock also ordered Capt. John Hazard to pour on artillery fire to support Hays' and Gibbon's fight west of the Emmitsburg Road. Hancock had no qualms about completely disregarding General Hunt's special standing orders concerning the waste of fixed ammunition. Not one to question any general—let alone the fiery Hancock—Hazard obediently complied and poured it on.[11]

Hancock displayed firm command and control of all of the batteries attached to his corps. It should be noted that those crews assigned to his Second Corps were the only ones allowed to stack live ammunition on the ground near their gun line at Gettysburg without interference from artillery commander Henry Hunt or anyone else. This used to be common practice but by June 1863 had largely been discouraged. When ordered to leave their position during battle, most cannoneers had simply hitched their guns to the limbers and rumbled away with little or no thought to the ordnance left piled on the ground. It was also quite dangerous. Hunt's recent directive made it punishable by court-martial, a stiff fine, or both. Alexander Hays' aide-de-camp, Capt. David Shields, wrote that the 108th New York (deployed in Zeigler's Woods) "can tell how I restored confidence, when they were so shook up by the explosion of shells that our artillerymen [Woodruff's battery] had piled up nearer the guns than the caissons and close beside the 108th. It was an appalling sight and to this day is a horrible one to think of."[12]

* * *

To the rear, fresh Union troops were still approaching the battlefield. Within a few minutes of Harrow's brigade vacating Hummelbaugh's intersection, Caldwell's First Division entered the Hummelbaugh's intersection after temporarily placing his men east of the Taneytown Road. As noted earlier, his command took cover in a thick belt of woods belonging to Sarah Patterson north of the Blacksmith Shop Road, the easternmost extension of the system of lanes that made up the "Fairfield

---

11 The Confederate guns ranged from the McMillan Woods south to Spangler's Woods on South Seminary Ridge. Most likely these guns belonged to Brander, Zimmerman, Marye, Wingfield, and Ross. They outnumbered Batteries A and B, 20 guns to 12.

12 David Shields to Bachelder, letter dated Sewickley, Allegheny Co., PA, Aug. 27, 1884, in *Bachelder Papers*, 2:1069-70.

Cross Roads" linking the crucial Baltimore Pike with that borough in western Adams County.[13]

At this juncture both Meade and Hancock assumed that A. A. Humphreys' division of Sickles' Third Corps would deploy back onto lower Cemetery Ridge due east from where the men bivouacked and still rested. Their orders were to pull back south of the Hummelbaugh farm lane and connect with Hancock's left. Major General David B. Birney would then redeploy his division to the north to connect with Humphreys' left as soon as the Fifth Corps arrived to relieve him near the Little Round Top. If Hancock thought Caldwell was alone and detached, at this early hour he did not show it. One can assume he was busy a quarter-mile to the north and hadn't the time to note that Caldwell was indeed isolated and in a poor position to support either Gibbon or Hays.[14]

Captain George G. Meade, Jr., the 19-year-old, reed-thin, wispy-mustachioed son of the Army of the Potomac's leader, stood outside the Third Corps command tent talking with Capt. George E. Randolph, Sickles' 23-year-old chief of artillery. Seven months after dropping out of West Point and just five weeks in his new rank, young Meade now had a problem: he had orders from his father for Sickles to report to army headquarters right away, but the latter would not speak with him nor would he come out of his tent. Meade Jr. could hardly force his way into the tent of so senior an officer, thus the somewhat stockier Randolph, with sideburns as wispy as Meade's mustache, volunteered to convey the order. He soon disappeared into the tent to relay what General Meade, via his son, had to say to the Sickles.

Sickles chose to obey only Meade's instructions that he relieve John Geary's two brigades near Little Round Top. Even then, he managed to do it in such a manner as to defy Meade. When Meade sent his son to see Sickles about 9:00 a.m., he thought the Third Corps had already taken its assigned position on Cemetery Ridge, tucked neatly between Little Round Top to the south and Hancock's Second Corps to the north. The young captain did not speak directly to Sickles on this occasion, subjected instead to an astonishing demonstration of pique and ill manners, as Sickles remained hidden. It was not until his son returned to

---

13 There was a blacksmith shop operating on that portion of the Fairfield Cross Road, hence the name Blacksmith Shop Road. The terrain Caldwell's division occupied was near the farm belonging to Sarah Patterson, sister of William Patterson, whose own property was occupied by Hays' division a quarter-mile farther north. Sarah's farm was separated from William's by the Michael Frey and Jacob Swisher farms, which held portions of Hays', Gibbon's, and Caldwell's divisions, from left to right facing east. The woods holding Caldwell's division was just north of Sarah's house directly east of and across the Taneytown Road from the Patterson Woods, with Cemetery Ridge less than 300 yards distant.

14 USGS MRC 39077G2; *Bachelder Maps, Second Day.*

headquarters that Meade learned that, while Ward's brigade had indeed replaced Geary, the rest of the Third Corps was still scattered west of the ridge all the way to the Emmitsburg Road. In the years to come, Sickles would accuse Meade of issuing unclear and conflicting orders.[15]

Captain Meade soon returned to his father, who by now was furious. He instructed his son to return to Sickles with strict orders for his corps to connect with Hancock's left while at the same time securing Little Round Top. On his return to the Third Corps, the captain was able to catch Sickles outside his tent and relay the orders word-for-word. Sickles sent him back to army headquarters with the odd reply that "the corps would be posted shortly; however, insofar as he knew, General Geary's division had no position but was massed." This, of course, made no sense whatsoever. The Third Corps commander had earlier sent Ward's brigade, plus two artillery batteries, to relieve General Geary near Little Round Top at 7:00 a.m. Geary, however, had already marched away with his division and was nowhere to be seen.[16]

Why Sickles would send such an inappropriate misleading message to his commander is worth comment. While never good, his relationship with Meade had deteriorated over the past few days after the latter replaced General Hooker. Sickles and Hooker had been close friends; tales of their heavy drinking and womanizing were already the stuff of army legend. A few days earlier, Sickles had been one of the Army of the Potomac's inner circle, where his inexperience at senior command mattered less than his talent for carousing and his political connections. With Hooker gone, Sickles found himself on the outside of a command circle made up of trained, professional soldiers. At the best of times Sickles was a man with but little restraint, and on the evening of July 1 he retreated to his tent after sunset without paying much attention to the positioning of his troops. He did not emerge either to confer with Humphreys after his post-midnight arrival or to report to Meade on his reconnaissance two hours thereafter, nor did he speak directly to young Captain Meade on his first visit on the morning of July 2. He did manage to make it as far as Union headquarters at the Evergreen Cemetery gatehouse around midnight, but when Meade arrived he promptly set his spurs and rode off. Whether Sickles spent this time drinking, sulking, or sleeping (as some critics suggest), his resentment had

---

15 James A. Hessler, *Sickles at Gettysburg: The Controversial Civil War General Who Committed Murder, Abandoned Little Round Top, and Declared Himself the Hero of Gettysburg* (New York, NY, 2010), 79-80.

16 George Meade Jr. to Alexander Webb, December 2, 1885, in Webb Papers File 0053-3, Yale University, Special Collections Library. See also: George Meade III, ed., *Life and Letters of George Gordon Meade*, 2 vols. (New York, NY, 1913), 1:65-66.

caused him to abandon his duties, reprehensible at any time, but disgraceful in a period of crisis.[17]

Meade had demonstrated no great confidence in Sickles. The orders to scout the ground in front of Emmitsburg, Maryland, on the morning of July 1 had gone from Meade directly to Humphreys and not through his Third Corps commander. Sickles had taken this departure from the chain of command as an insult, though it may not have been intended as one. Under great pressure and in the first days of command of an army on the march, Meade had sent orders to a trained veteran soldier (Humphreys) without regard for niceties. Meade made it clear that his circular, which was distributed and read at sunrise on July 2, was meant for officers of every rank as well as the enlisted men.[18]

In accordance with orders, Birney had redeployed Ward's brigade south and west to Houck's Ridge, while the two attached batteries, Capt. A. Judson Clark's and Lt. John K. Bucklyn's, respectively, were repositioned near Sickles' headquarters tent. Captain Meade had made the commanding general's wishes very clear to Sickles, even when Randolph intervened as a go-between. Dan Sickles' stubborn actions thus far on July 2 smacked of insubordination, or a feeling of superiority versus the newly appointed army commander. Ward was now 800 yards west of and below Cemetery Ridge, having moved in exactly the opposite direction from where Meade wanted him, and the two batteries were well forward of the ridge, in low ground, "unprotected, and commanded by Emmitsburg Road Rise" to their front. Dismayed by the placement of these guns, Randolph asked Captain Meade on his second visit to request that Hunt come inspect the Third Corps artillery positions and parks. It was about 10:00 a.m. when Meade Jr. departed Sickles' headquarters for the second time.[19]

It was about this time when Hancock became seriously concerned about the Second Corps' left flank. With Hays and Gibbon in control to the north, Hancock was able to ride south and visit Caldwell's division. While there he noted that Humphreys had still not taken his expected position on the ridge south of Caldwell, and there were no indications he would do so anytime soon. As a result, Caldwell's left flank remained completely exposed, with a large gap between his right flank and Gibbon's already weakened left flank running along the Emmitsburg Road and atop the low ridge south of the Copse of Trees. Hancock dispatched one of his aides back to army headquarters to inform Meade of the situation, at which point several couriers again galloped to Sickles instructing him to correct the problem and

17 Ibid.

18 Hessler, *Sickles at Gettysburg*, 79-80; OR 27, pt. 1, 531.

19 Ibid., 580-81. See also pt. 1, 482.

This modern image taken from the Pennsylvania State Monument looks north above the Union center. Present-day Hancock Avenue (far left) parallels the crest running north toward the Copse of Trees. The wide open nature of the crest from Pleasonton Avenue in the foreground (historic Hummelbaugh farm lane) north to Zeigler's Grove (timber in the center-distance) is evident. Much of this part of the Union line was stripped nearly bare on the afternoon of July 2. The Peter Frey barn is on the right, and the guns on the left along Hancock Avenue represent Weir's 5th U.S. Battery C and Rorty's 1st New York Battery B. Rebel infantry attacked left to right across this terrain. *Utica College*

adhere to general orders. However, instead of complying with Meade's orders to return Birney's and Humphreys' brigades back to Cemetery Ridge, Sickles opted to reply with notes describing the high ground along the Emmitsburg Road Rise.[20]

By 10:00 a.m. Humphreys' precarious position had become a serious issue. He had not yet established a line along the road and his men were now too far forward to be of any material use in defending the prescribed Cemetery Ridge line. Except for the fact that his reinforced skirmish line was keeping the enemy skirmishers at bay, Humphreys was utterly alone and isolated. The arrival of Burling's brigade might have helped improve the situation had general orders been followed, but Sickles instead placed the newly arrived brigade west of Plum Run near his headquarters above the Abraham Trostle house. Sickles did this despite full knowledge of Meade's orders. Sickles was well aware that Humphreys' right wing was supposed to connect with Hancock's left. Burling's placement, followed by de

20 USGS MRC 39077G2; *Bachelder Maps, Second Day.*

Trobriand's advance placement, infuriated Hancock, who reportedly sent Meade yet another message suggesting Sickles was not going to comply.[21]

As 11:00 a.m. neared it was evident that Caldwell's division now was the left flank of the Union forces then occupying Cemetery Ridge. When the younger Meade delivered his report and relayed Randolph's request, the commanding general suggested it was time for his chief of artillery to take a personal look at the situation. Henry Hunt, however, had just returned from another reconnaissance, having ridden the entire length of the line to spend a good thirty minutes or so at the signal station atop Little Round Top. He must have witnessed the arrival of Colonel de Trobriand's brigade, and perhaps Colonel Burling's as well. It also appears Hunt was atop the low mountain when General Birney redeployed Ward to Houck's Ridge and Graham toward the Peach Orchard. With an impromptu meeting about to begin, Hunt however placed his southward return on hold.[22]

In addition to Hunt, Generals Hancock, Warren, Slocum, Sykes, and Newton were in attendance at Meade's headquarters. They discussed several issues of importance, including the Sickles dilemma and the location of the army's right flank. Meade instructed Sykes to hold tight, but remain in readiness for whatever might occur. Slocum again reminded Meade that he still needed both artillery and infantry support. Meade asked Warren to help Slocum by riding over the terrain and then reporting back to him. He gave Hancock instructions to take whatever measures he could until Sickles complied with general orders and also told him that General Hunt was on his way to help correct the problem. Meade also shook up his command structure, assigning a division leader from the Sixth Corps, Maj. Gen. John Newton, to replace the more senior Maj. Gen. Abner Doubleday as the First Corps' commander. Meade also grilled Hunt about artillery ammunition and reserve batteries and ordered him to lend Hancock a few batteries to bolster the line between Gibbon's and Caldwell's divisions. When the meeting ended, Meade called Hunt aside and again inquired about ammunition stocks. Meade likely gave his chief of artillery last-minute instructions on his errand as Hunt prepared to ride south to see Sickles.[23]

Until midmorning, it appears Hancock remained unaware of any significant Confederate activity on his front and the demonstrations then taking place in and beyond Pitzer's Woods. Although he could see that Humphreys' skirmish line was active to Caldwell's front and left, he never tied the two enemy actions together. He

21 Ibid. Peter Trostle owned this house and 134-acre farm. His son Abraham's large family occupied it at the time of the battle.

22 Ibid.

23 OR 27, pt. 3, 1086; Meade Jr., *Life and Letters*, 71-72.

did not know that Buford had thus far failed to provide adequate information to Sickles about the enemy presence in Pitzer's Woods, or the fact that Devin's troopers were trading shots with the enemy beyond the ridge to his left. Sickles, however, was well aware of both facts and was rightly concerned that a Confederate force of undetermined strength had moved into the woodlot. Humphreys' line still rested in the low ground east of and below the Emmitsburg Road with both flanks in the air and open to direct enfilade. The angle of the terrain left his men with their backs at a slight left oblique to Caldwell's west-facing line. In so doing, Sickles not only placed Humphreys in jeopardy, but Hancock's entire Second Corps.[24]

To add to the worsening situation, Birney, as Hunt had probably witnessed from Little Round Top, received orders from Sickles to send Brig. Gen. Charles K. Graham's First Brigade farther west, taking up a position on the reverse, or eastern slope of the Emmitsburg Road Rise east of the Millerstown Road intersection. He likewise placed de Trobriand's newly arrived Third Brigade north of the Stony Hill to the rear of Graham, roughly 500 yards south of Burling's brigade, which by now had been detached from Humphreys' division. Sickles made no effort to pull any of these brigades back toward Cemetery Ridge or the small round-topped mountain on the left. Despite his professed interest in the high ground to his front, Sickles had placed one of his artillery batteries above his headquarters at the Trostle farm just west of the ravine, with another below it. Two others sat in the ravine around Plum Run, with a fifth battery in the low ground to the south near a large wheatfield to de Trobriand's left and rear. Cemetery Ridge was alarmingly devoid of Federal troops from Little Round Top on the left, all the way north to Caldwell's left flank, a distance just short of a mile.[25]

Hunt, leading a small party of aides including Col. Edward Warner and Capt. J. N. Craig, hurried south angling toward Trostle's farmyard beyond the Plum Run ravine. Like Hancock, he was appalled to see both Caldwell's and Humphreys' divisions isolated and exposed. From his viewpoint the Third Corps appeared badly scattered, disconnected in individual clumps with none of them remotely near the position Meade had originally assigned to Sickles. Humphreys' division was still where it had bivouacked the night before, with Burling's recently arrived brigade resting to the immediate south of Brewster. Ward's brigade of Birney's division was nowhere to be seen as Hunt's party dropped into the ravine. Upon passing over the creek onto Trostle's farm lane, Hunt could see de Trobriand's brigade off to the

---

24 Sickles Testimony, U. S. Congressional Report of the Joint Committee on the Conduct of the War, 228-29; USGS MRC 39077G2; *Bachelder Maps, Second Day.*

25 Referred to today as Houck's Ridge.

left, some 800-1,000 yards away resting on the lower eastern slope of the Peach Orchard, with Graham's brigade nearer the crest.[26]

Once across the run, Hunt could see nothing to his immediate front except the eastern slope of the Emmitsburg Road Rise with the farm lane ascending it. He noted three batteries in park near Sickles' headquarters, with the caissons of one sitting idle on the eastern brow west of and above it. How long, if at all, Hunt stayed at Third Corps headquarters is not known. What is certain is that General Sickles and Major Tremain mounted their horses and joined Hunt. Continuing up the rise, the trio passed Bucklyn's Rhode Island Battery, his unlimbered gun line and caissons separated by the crest of the rise. Sickles and Hunt reined in somewhere on the Emmitsburg Road near Sherfy's farm. They could see some of the specialized U. S. Sharpshooters to the front, clearly identifiable in their distinctive dark green uniforms. Colonel Elijah Walker's 4th Maine Volunteers were likewise engaged along a nearer rise some 400 yards west of Calef's battery, drawing fire from enemy skirmishers and sharpshooters alike.[27]

Dan Sickles had been fretting about his position all morning. Now, warned by Walker about the enemy's increasing activity to his front—including a reinforced picket line with troops in Pitzer's Woods—Sickles decided he had to learn more. From where the generals sat on their horses, the woods to the west could hold a sizeable force and, with little information from Buford, Sickles decided that a second reconnaissance toward Pitzer's Woods was warranted. Looking about, Hunt could see that Buford's cavalry, Calef's guns included, was beginning to pack up. Sickles expressed the idea of a reconnaissance to Hunt, who readily agreed. What is unique about this is the fact Hunt could not only hear Buford's cavalry engaged beyond Pitzer's Woods, but he could see that one of Calef's sections had been detached and was unlimbered in "Action Front" south-southwest of the Millerstown Road intersection after having been called forward. Clearly the situation was uncertain.[28]

For some reason Hunt never sent any of his aides galloping back to warn Meade about the cavalry withdrawal or to report that some of Buford's troopers were engaged alongside Sickles' advanced skirmishers near and beyond Pitzer's Woods. At 9:30 a.m. Signal Officer Capt. James Hall on Little Round Top had

26 USGS MRC 39077G2; *Bachelder Maps, Second Day.*

27 Ibid.; Tremain, "Great Speech of General Sickles on the Battlefield, July 2," *National Tribune,* July 15, 1886.

28 Elijah Walker to Bachelder, Jan. 5, 1885, *Bachelder Papers,* 2:1093-95. Sergeant William Bradshaw, 9th New York Cavalry, reportedly spotted Wilcox advancing earlier that morning. "Action Front" was when in battery and prepared to open.

wig-wagged a message to Meade's chief of staff, General Butterfield: "The enemy are moving a brigade of five regiments from in front of our center to our right, at a point east-southeast of the Second Division, Twelfth Corps, and is in easy range. A heavy line of enemy's infantry on our right. Very small force of infantry—enemy's infantry visible in front of our center."[29]

After reading Hall's message and given the reported Confederate movement, General Butterfield, and perhaps Meade as well, focused on the right. Lieutenant Aaron B. Jerome, who was under Hall's immediate command, followed up with another seemingly meaningless message concerning the Union center at 11:45 a.m. "Enemy's skirmishers are advancing from the west, 1 mile from here." That was the extent of the messages from Little Round Top concerning Sickles' front prior to Buford's withdrawal during the forenoon hours. Meade had every reason to cast his attention toward his right flank where Slocum continued to demand him to take action. With his trusted chief of artillery heading south to meet with Sickles, he had no reason to suspect that Sickles would not comply with his general orders.

Buford's failure to provide adequate information to both Meade and Sickles weighs heavily within the scope of a controversy that lingers to this day.[30]

29 OR 27, pt. 3, 488-89.

30 Ibid.

Chapter Eleven

"I immediately dismounted and deployed two squadrons in support of
Berdan's Sharpshooters and formed the brigade into line. . . .
With one section of Tidball's [Calef's] battery in position."

— *Col. Thomas C. Devin, Army of the Potomac*[1]

Noon, July 2: A "Mostly Insignificant Affair" Shapes the Battle

In the mid-1800s many American sportsmen considered the annual champion of the New York Rifle Club to be the best shot in the country. For fifteen consecutive years preceding the Civil War, that title belonged to Ontario County, New York, native Hiram Berdan. Short and sturdy with mutton-chop sideburns, the Hobart College graduate was an accomplished mechanical engineer and prolific inventor. His string of successful new products included a commercial amalgamating machine that separated gold from ore, a novel collapsible boat, a reaper, and, of all things, a bread slicer. His ingenuity and keen sense of fulfilling customer needs made him rich. Berdan also invented the Berdan repeating rifle and center-fire primer he used in shooting competitions across the world. Berdan's wealth and international fame placed him within the tight circle of politically connected cronies of New York City's infamous Tammany Hall political machine.[2]

Shortly after the war broke out in April 1861, Berdan, with the support and encouragement of President Lincoln and Gen. Winfield Scott, recruited and organized a regiment of sharpshooters with him as their colonel. He drew men from all across the Union. At a time when recruits were herded into companies,

---

1   OR 27, pt. 1, 939.

2   C. A. Stevens, *Berdan's United States Sharpshooters in the Army of the Potomac, 1861-1865* (St. Paul, Minnesota, 1892), 2.

drilled to march and execute martial maneuvers, but rarely taught to shoot, Berdan insisted that all of his handpicked soldiers be top marksmen. "No man is to be mustered in who cannot, when firing at a distance of 200 yards," he declared, "putten consecutive shots in a target, the average distance not to exceed five inches from the bull's-eye."[3]

So popular was his idea that instead of one regiment of crack shots Berdan received a budget appropriation for two, which became the 1st and 2nd United States Sharpshooters. His name alone attracted the best of the best as gentlemen, frontiersmen, farmers, and merchants flocked to his call and earnestly competed to join his two elite units. Many brought their own weapons, but Berdan rearmed those who succeeded in passing the rigorous shooting trials with his choice of weapon, the .52-caliber Sharps Model 1859 breech-loading rifle. Berdan wanted repeatability in every aspect, including sharing cartridges, if necessary, on the battlefield during combat. By the time his two regiments marched north to Gettysburg, his elite command boasted some of the finest marksmen in either army.[4]

Under pristine conditions, the average muzzle-loading rifleman could shoot no more than three rounds per minute. Many of Berdan's experts, however, could fire up to eight shots in the same time time with their breech-loaders. They received training to shoot from cover, and often targeted enemy officers. The Confederates soon came to despise these marksmen calling them "snakes in the grass." Wearing forest green uniforms and hats, the sharpshooters received specialized training in the art of concealment. They learned to use the prevailing terrain and any cover to protect themselves and allow a reasonable vantage at the target without overly exposing their location. When in formal battle line, this concealment was less necessary because the sharpshooters' high rate of fire mostly kept the enemy troops at bay.[5]

Colonel Berdan and his hand-picked men would play a key role at Gettysburg on July 2. Early that morning, Union artillery chief Henry Hunt had reconnoitered the Baltimore Pike, completing his journey just east of Little Round Top. Before returning to army headquarters, Hunt scaled the low mountain using an old logging path that intersected the present-day Wheatfield Road at the hill's northeastern base. Once atop the rocky height, Hunt dismounted and undoubtedly chatted with the signal officers who would have pointed out key terrain features pertinent to Hunt's interests and questions. The general's keen eyes examined the high ground

3   Ibid.

4   Ibid.

5   Busey & Martin, *Regimental Strengths and Losses,* 203.

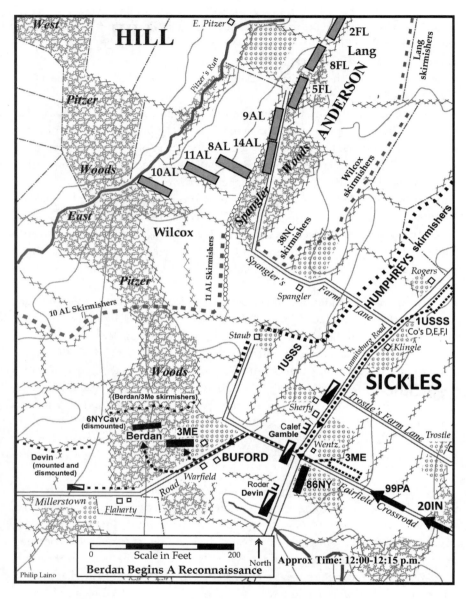

Berdan Begins A Reconnaissance

Approx Time: 12:00-12:15 p.m.

Scale in Feet   0 — 200

North

Philip Laino

due west beyond intervening Houck's Ridge and a dense tract of timber on George Rose's farm. Rose's Woods, later explained Hunt, "constituted a favorable position for the enemy to hold." He was thus pleased when he learned John Buford was in force about 8:00 a.m. guarding that flank, with Maj. Gen. David Birney's Third Corps infantry division protecting the rugged ground below. Birney had advanced a picket line to the Emmitsburg Road, with his skimishers some 300 yards beyond

Union Generals Sickles, Birney, and Hunt knew Confederates occupied Pitzer's and Spangler's woods (in the distance), but had no idea as to their strength. This view looks northwest toward Spangler's farm (distant left) and woods from the Emmitsburg and Millerstown road intersection, with the Sherfy farm on the right. *Gettysburgdaily.com*

the pickets.[6] To Hunt's immediate north, however, lower Cemetery Ridge was still devoid of troops, a fact he reported to Meade upon his return. When Meade learned that fact at that early hour, he likely believed Hancock and Sickles would work out the matter. Knowing Buford was on line in force with patrols out and about must have offered some reassurance that his left was in good hands, allowing the army commander to focus more attention on his right flank.[7]

However, Dan Sickles remained quite concerned about the timbered, rolling ground west of the Emmitsburg Road Rise which could mask thousands of oncoming Confederates. In the late morning he sent aides scurrying with orders for Birney to reconnoiter Pitzer's Woods. Birney, in turn, ordered Colonel Berdan to

6   OR 27, pt. 1, 482.

7   Henry E. Tremain to Daniel Sickles, June 26, 1886, *National Tribune*, July 15, 1876; Longacre, *Man Behind the Guns*, 162.

This modern view looks west toward Pitzer's Woods from the Millerstown–Emmitsburg Road intersection. Behind the camera position is the Sherfy Peach Orchard. Three of Barksdale's Mississippi regiments advanced on the right side of this road, and his fourth, the 21st Mississippi, on the left. A southern portion of Spangler's Woods is to the right (north) behind the rail fence encasing Spangler's farm lane. *Gettysburg Daily*

lead this reconnaissance. Tellingly, Birney assigned his aide-de-camp, Capt. Joseph C. Briscoe, to accompany him. This was no accident. Although Berdan was a favorite of the president and an ambitious and relentless self-promoter, many observers believed he was militarily incompetent and somewhat of a coward on the battlefield. The 1st U.S. Sharpshooters' Lt. Col. Casper Trepp, a Swiss-born veteran of the Crimean War, had little use for the man. Just a month earlier, Trepp had written to Secretary of War Edwin Stanton to warn him about Berdan, whom he described as "most unscrupulous and totally unfit for command." Stanton, however, decided against making a change in leadership.[8]

Trepp was not alone in his poor perception of Hiram Berdan. Other sharpshooters demonstrated open contempt for their famous colonel and accused him of never being at the front during battle. Berdan himself had inflamed the underlying acrimony when he brought court-martial proceedings against Trepp and

8   Colonel Trepp to Edwin Stanton, June 1, 1863, Casper Trepp Papers, New York Historical Society, Patricia D. Klingenstein Library.

John and Catherine Staub's original farmhouse. Union sharpshooters and skirmishers fired from both the first and second-story windows as they engaged Rebels along the edges of Pitzer's and Spangler's woods. The structure was relocated to east side of the Emmitsburg Road just north of present-day United States Avenue (Trostle farm lane) near the turn of the 20th century. It was demolished by the NPS in mid 1960s. *LOC*

four other veteran officers, all of whom were acquitted. The morale and command efficiency of the green-clad sharpshooters left much to be desired. When Birney assigned Captain Briscoe to accompany him, Berdan understood exactly what that meant: tactical decisions would have to be cleared with the staff officer and, more importantly to Hiram Berdan, high-ranking officers in the Third Corps questioned his leadership and personal courage.[9]

Birney instructed Colonel Berdan to take 100 sharpshooters out the Millerstown Road beyond the line of skirmishers he had advanced earlier that morning. Berdan pulled his column together from his 1st Regiment and, despite warnings from Humphreys and a local citizen that the woods to the west were full of Rebels, marched his sharpshooters in columns of fours down the Trostle dirt

9 Roy Marcot, "Berdan Sharpshooters at Gettysburg," *Gettysburg Magazine,* 1:36-37.

lane to the Emmitsburg Road intersection. There, in full view of the enemy pickets in Pitzer's Woods, he snappily turned the green-clad column south as calmly as if on dress parade. The men passed through Col. William Gamble's retiring cavalry brigade and Calef's limbering artillery battery. Turning west, Berdan and his company continued out the Millerstown Road, passing Col. Thomas Devin's dismounted troopers as the sharpshooters closed on Staub's farm lane intersection and the distant Pitzer's Woods.[10]

Casper Trepp followed Captain Briscoe along the road, upset that his men were voluntarily exposed "in plain view of the enemy." He fumed about Berdan's unnecessary showmanship, and later complained that his detachment could have marched forward "perfectly concealed from view of the enemy and without loss of time." Trepp believed the Confederates must have seen every man from the time they reached the Emmitsburg Road until they entered the woods on the Millerstown Road, which gave the Confederates more than enough time to counter the approaching Union sharpshooters. The enemy gained even more time because Trepp's support, the 3rd Maine under Col. Moses Lakeman (part of Ward's brigade) had received instructions to halt at the Millerstown Road. The sharpshooters continued on unsupported. "For this violation of rules to secret expeditions we paid dearly," added Trepp, "for when we [subsequently] entered the woods, advancing as skirmishers, we met the enemy's skirmishers very soon after crossing the road."[11]

Once clear of the open field between the Staub homestead and the nearby woods, Berdan gave the order "half-right-march." By making this 45-degree turn in unison, the regiment transformed from a road column of fours into a battle line approaching the woods at a slight angle. Skirmishers hurried out in advance of the main line, their maneuver performed in full view of a handful of Confederate skirmishers of Lowrance's 38th North Carolina and Wilcox's 10th Alabama. There were not enough advance Rebels, however, to discourage the thrust, but they held their positions while the 3rd Maine finally began deploying to the right and rear of Berdan's company. Once it became obvious they were heavily outnumbered, the distant Southerners fired a few spiteful rounds and quietly vanished into the timber. Berdan's skirmishers picked up the pace as they hurried toward the recently held Rebel position behind a low stone wall. There, they met up with some of

10 For a more extensive discussion of the Pitzer's Wood fight, see Pfanz, *Gettysburg Second Day*, 97-102, 102; Elijah Walker to Bachelder, Somerville, MA, Jan. 5, 1885, *Bachelder Papers*, 3:1092-93.

11 Ibid.

Col. William Forney,
10th Alabama Infantry,
Wilcox's brigade, Anderson's
division, A. P. Hill's Third Corps.
LOC

Stoughton's 2nd U.S. Sharp-shooters who had left the safety of the Staub farm to join in the bold advance.[12]

Forewarned of Berdan's pompous approach, General Wilcox's regimental commanders readied themselves. The first two of his regiments to answer the call were Col. William Forney's 10th Alabama and Col. J. C. C. Sanders' 11th Alabama. Forney guided his regiment south through Pitzer's Woods while Sanders' men tramped across the open meadow on Forney's left flank. Within minutes, the 10th Alabama skirmishers who had fallen back faced about and opened fire at the advancing Union skirmishers now just 100 yards distant. While Berdan was advancing west, other Federals in the vicinity were preparing to leave.[13]

John Buford had received directions to retire from the field and take a post at Westminster, Maryland, to assist in guarding the army's wagon trains parked there. Gamble's brigade pulled out first, leaving Devin's brigade still on line temporarily as Berdan moved forward. The pertinent correspondence suggests simple miscommunication by all concerned. Meade's chief of staff, General Butterfield, summed up the confusion when he penned a note to cavalry chief Alfred Pleasonton at 12:50 p.m., just 90 minutes after Buford's departure: "The major-general commanding directs me to say that he has not authorized the entire withdrawal of Buford's force from the direction of the Emmitsburg [Road], and did not so understand when he gave the permission to Buford to go to Westminster; that the patrols and pickets upon the Emmitsburg road be kept on as long as our

12 Wiley Sword, *Sharpshooter: Hiram Berdan, His Famous Sharpshooters and their Sharps Rifles* (Lincoln, RI, 1988), 25-26.

13 Marcot, "Berdan Sharpshooters at Gettysburg"; USGS MRC 390772G.

troops are in position." Butterfield admitted his own misunderstanding, adding "my note, written five minutes since, is a little confused, I find. The general expected, when Buford's force was sent to Westminster, that a force should be sent to replace it, picketing and patrolling the Emmitsburg road."[14]

Hunt, Sickles, or both sent someone galloping to army headquarters to explain that the left front was no longer protected. "Buford's cavalry, which had been on the left, had been withdrawn," Sickles later testified. "I remonstrated against that, and expressed the hope that the cavalry, or some portion of it, at all events, might be allowed to remain there." The confusion over what was transpiring on the left also struck Colonel Devin, who may have mistaken Sickles' redeployment of General Ward's skirmishers westward past the Emmitsburg Road as the vanguard of his designated replacement. The concerned Sickles went on to later report, "I was informed that it was not the intention to remove the whole of the cavalry, and that a portion of it would be returned. It did not return, however." Buford's withdrawal and Hunt's realignment of some of his artillery evaporated any reasonable possibility that Sickles' two divisions would reassemble along southern Cemetery Ridge on Hancock's left flank. All of this, in turn, made an encounter with the enemy well west of Meade's desired position for Sickles' Third Corps more likely.[15]

Buford's cavalry had been busily scouting the lanes and ridges to the west since before dawn. Scouting parties from Devin's brigade had ventured beyond Marsh Creek and as far south as Bullfrog Road, and his troopers had been fitfully engaged with Colonel Forney's advance Alabama skirmishers around the Samuel Pitzer farm for several hours. Two of Devin's squadrons were still near that property when Berdan's advancing sharpshooters began exchanging shots with Wilcox's skirmishers in Pitzer's Woods. When Berdan's "sharpshooters became engaged with a division of the enemy advancing to feel our lines in front on my position (Millerstown Road)," reported Devin, "I immediately dismounted and deployed two squadrons in support of Berdan's Sharpshooters (who were engaged in my front) and formed the brigade into line on the left of the First." All of this contact and combat was taking place while Devin was preparing the balance of his cavalry brigade for departure.[16]

---

14 OR 27, pt 3, 490. The replacement force mentioned by General Butterfield was sent south too late to be of any service July 2.

15 Bill Hyde, ed., *The Union Generals Speak: The Meade Hearings on the Battle of Gettysburg* (Baton Rouge, 2003), 42; OR 27, pt. 1, 939; Hyde, *The Union Generals Speak*, 42; *Bachelder Maps, Second Day*.

16 OR 27, pt. 1, 939.

According to Lieutenant Calef, who was supporting Devin, the attack opened "directly in front of where my battery was parked. . . . We had hardly got into position when an order came from General Buford for me to follow with my battery the First Brigade, of his division, and march with it to Taneytown, Md., for supplies and forage."[17] There is little doubt Devin's brigade, or portions thereof, supported by Calef's battery, were prepared to give battle when word arrived to pull out. The experienced Buford apparently failed to realize a pending battle was underway in Pitzer's Woods, let alone its importance. His report tersely noted: "July 2, the division became engaged with enemy sharpshooters on our left, and held its own until relieved by General Sickles' corps, after which it [his division] moved to Taneytown, and bivouacked for the night."[18]

For all the sour words and negative comments penned about Daniel Sickles (many of which are justified), few writers have assigned any blame to Pleasonton or Buford for how the fighting on this front unfolded. Sickles (or Meade or Hunt, for that matter) had little direct influence over the apparent mishandling of mounted operations along the Emmitsburg Road on July 2. Failure to provide adequate information concerning the enemy and what lay beyond Pitzer's Woods, let alone the Emmitsburg Road, rested with the cavalry's senior leadership, particularly Pleasonton. Buford's unexpected withdrawal, brought about by a major failure in communications along the chain of command, left Sickles' Third Corps exposed and in a vacuum in terms of intelligence on enemy strength and positions.

Hunt and Sickles, accompanied by several staff officers and aides, ventured as far west as the Sherfy farm to observe Berdan's movement. From somewhere near Trostle's cherry orchard, near where Hunt placed Clark's New Jersey battery, the artillery general watched Berdan's sharpshooters disappear into the woods the 3rd Maine advanced in his right-rear. The subsequent crashing volleys and rising smoke made it clear this was not a small skirmish between a handful of pickets.[19]

When Berdan made contact with the Confederates, his force included the 100 men from his 1st U.S. Sharpshooters, Lakeman's 3rd Maine (14 officers and 196 men), and several dozen of Homer Stoughton's 2nd U.S. Sharpshooters. Adding in Devin's two remaining small squadrons of dismounted cavalry troopers, Berdan's available strength likely was about 500 muskets and carbines. There is no evidence Devin's remaining dismounted troopers west of the woods advanced in earnest with Berdan. Although it appears some troopers may have moved north through

17 Ibid., 1032. Calef's battery reached Taneytown about 4:00 p.m. and immediately encamped.

18 Ibid., 928.

19 Michael Hanifen, *History of Battery B, First New Jersey Light Artillery* (Ottawa, IL, 1905), 67; Marcot, "Berdan Sharpshooters at Gettysburg."

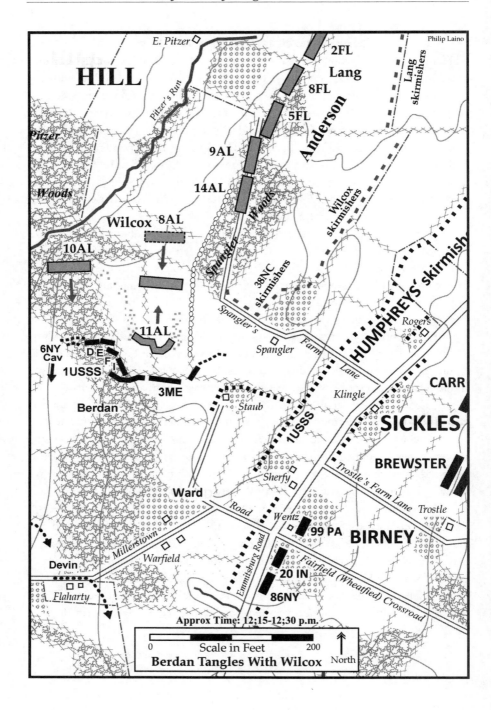

Philip Laino

E. Pitzer

HILL

Pitzer's Run

Pitzer

Woods

2FL

Lang

8FL

5FL

9AL

14AL

Anderson

Lang skirmishers

Wilcox skirmishers

Wilcox   8AL

10AL

11AL

Spangler Woods

38NC skirmishers

6NY Cav

D E F

1USSS

3ME

Berdan

Spangler's   Farm   Lane

Spangler

HUMPHREYS' skirmishers

Rogers

Staub

Klingle

CARR

SICKLES

BREWSTER

Ward

1USSS

Sherfy

Road

Wentz

Millerstown

Warfield

99 PA

Trostle's Farm Lane

Trostle

BIRNEY

Devin

Emmitsburg Road

20 IN

86NY

Fairfield (Wheatfield) Crossroad

Flaharty

Approx Time: 12:15-12:30 p.m.

0   Scale in Feet   200

Berdan Tangles With Wilcox   North

the western skirt of the woods, most remained behind a rail fence west of the trees. Their unique firepower, however, helped neutralize skirmishers from the 10th Alabama's right wing firing from behind a parallel rail fence 100 yards away. This suppressing fire allowed Berdan's left flank to move through the stand of old oak and chestnut trees, where the Sharpshooters received little opposition as they drove back the skirmishers comprising Colonel Forney's right wing. Contrary to what is recited in many works on Gettysburg, the Pitzer's Woods fight was not a surprise. Wilcox had been receiving routine updates all morning. He had been sent there to cover the army's right flank with his brigade, and he was deployed to do just that. Sickles, Birney, and Hunt all knew that Rebels in some strength were within that tract of timber. The only question was how many and for what purpose. But make no mistake, no one was surprised that Berdan's probing force made contact with more than a few pickets.[20]

With Devin's support off to their left, Berdan's sharpshooters tramped through the woods quicker than the men of the 3rd Maine could advance in the open under fire. Within a few moments of engaging, Berdan's line surged about 50 yards ahead of Colonel Lakeman's troops. Immediately north of the 3rd Maine, the exact opposite occurred when the Confederates moved forward. Advancing in an open field, Sanders' 11th Alabama outdistanced Forney's 10th Alabama. This was unfortunate for Sanders and his men. By this time the 3rd Maine, concealed behind trees and rock ledges, delivered a crippling volley that stopped Sanders' regiment in its tracks after it had advanced some 300 yards. Adding to Sanders' misfortune, Companies F and I of the 1st U.S. Sharpshooters pivoted half-right and advanced to the eastern edge of the timber. There, from 75 yards away at point-blank range, Berdan's troops delivered a crushing enfilading volley. The blast knocked a number of men off their feet. Sanders' right flank fell apart and the troops took refuge behind a rail fence that offered scant cover.[21]

The Alabamians could not stand long in the face of this overpowering firepower from Union breech-loading Sharps rifles and the muskets of Lakeman's New Englanders near the stone wall, and within a few minutes retreated pell-mell, even as the fresh 8th Alabama approached in support. The 8th's commander, Lt. Col. Hilary Herbert, recalled the chaotic scene: "Its [the 11th's] gallant commander, attempted to swing it around facing the wall, but the fire was too severe, and the 11th fell back over the 8th, which by this time occupied a road running parallel with,

---

20 *OR* 27, pt. 1, 234, 516; pt. 2, 616.

21 Ibid., pt. 2, 617.

and about two hundred yards from the wall. The 8th was ordered to lie down until the 11th passed to the rear of it."[22]

At some point during the fighting, most and perhaps all of Devin's dismounted cavalry unexpectedly disappeared. "The enemy not pressing his advance," Colonel Devin later wrote, "and the Third Corps coming in to position, we were ordered to march to Taneytown." It appears Devin pulled back his two squadrons under orders while the fight was still in progress. This helps explain Herbert's relatively easy advance across the open meadow. As Herbert described it, "The 8th [Alabama] marched up to it, and took the stone wall, which was not very vigorously defended." The sudden removal of Devin's carbines was the stroke of luck Wilcox needed. The success of the 8th Alabama's advance, combined with Devin's departure, allowed the 11th Alabama to rally and press back Berdan's left wing, helping the 8th in its quest to drive the Yankee right wing from the field.[23]

After gaining the stone wall and driving back the right flank of the 3rd Maine, Herbert's 8th Alabama turned its attention to Berdan's center. Wheeling to front in that direction, Herbert's veterans delivered a murderous crossfire down the length of Lakeman's line toward the eastern edge of the woods while the 8th's left flank became entwined with part of Forney's 10th Alabama. For a few frenzied minutes the fighting in Samuel Pitzer's smoke-canopied woodlot was intense and brutal.

When the 8th Alabama pivoted to front southwest and delivered what would be a crippling blow to the 3rd Maine, the end was in sight for the Pitzer's Woods combat. Berdan's outnumbered and outflanked line was no match for Wilcox's seasoned veterans, and they began to retire. "Col. H. Berdan then gave the order to fall back firing, which was done in good order, the enemy pursuing a short distance," Trepp confirmed in his report for the 2nd U.S. Sharpshooters. "This command was collected and formed on the Emmitsburg road." "It was a trying occasion for our men," admitted Sgt. Charles Stevens of the 1st U.S. Sharpshooters, "but Colonel Berdan, riding in front of the line quickly took in the situation, and knowing that the time gained was everything, dispatched Captain Briscoe to our Generals Birney and Sickles, a mile away, to warn them of the danger —that threatened assault upon our left." No one would accuse Hiram Berdan of cowardice in the face of the enemy on July 2.[24]

The men of the 3rd Maine also fired as they retired in relatively good order toward the Staub farm. Once along the Emmitsburg Road, Lakeman faced all his men west once more and redressed his thinned ranks. "I was obliged to leave my

22 *Bachelder Papers,* 3:1056.

23 *OR* 27, pt. 1, 939; *Bachelder Papers,* 2:1056.

24 Marcot, "Berdan Sharpshooters at Gettysburg."

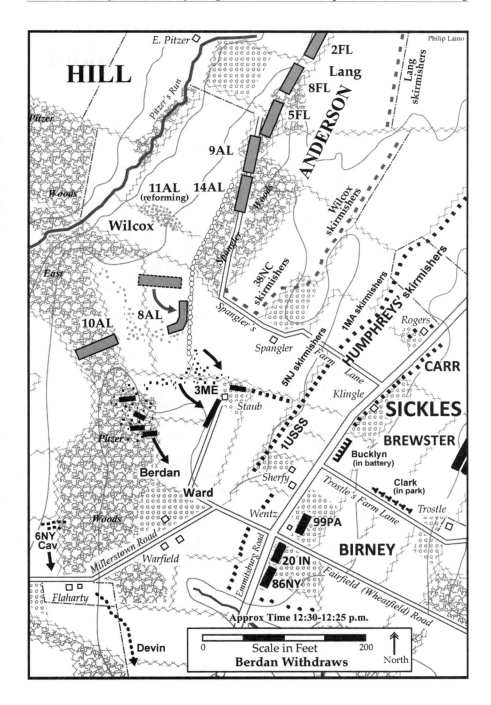

Philip Laino

HILL

E. Pitzer

2FL
Lang
8FL
5FL

ANDERSON

9AL

Lang skirmishers

11AL 14AL
(reforming)

Wilcox

Pitzer

Woods

East

Wilcox skirmishers

38NC skirmishers

8AL

10AL

Spangler's

Spangler

5NJ skirmishers

1MA skirmishers

HUMPHREYS' skirmishers

Rogers

CARR

3ME

Staub

Klingle

Farm Lane

SICKLES

1USSS

BREWSTER

Pitzer

Bucklyn
(in battery)

Clark
(in park)

Berdan

Sherfy

Ward

Wentz

99PA

Trostle's Farm Lane

Trostle

Woods

6NY
Cav

Millerstown Road

Warfield

Emmitsburg Road

20 IN

86NY

BIRNEY

Fairfield (Wheatfield) Road

Flaharty

Devin

Approx Time 12:30-12:25 p.m.

0   Scale in Feet   200
Berdan Withdraws

North

dead and seriously wounded on the field," he reported, "and on arriving back at the road formed my regiment, which had gotten somewhat confused from loss of men and obstructions in our retreat. This engagement was short but very severe, and serves to give me a renewal of confidence in the men I command." Lakeman had sustained a loss of 48 killed, wounded, and missing from his 210 men engaged.[25]

The sharpshooters also suffered significant losses during the firefight with the Alabamians. According to Trepp, his 2nd regiment "lost 1 commissioned officer killed, 2 officers wounded, and 16 enlisted men killed, wounded and missing" of his roughly 100 men. In total, Berdan suffered at least 67 casualties, all within a quarter of an hour of entering the woods. Wilcox's losses were also high, about 70 killed or wounded (none missing). In one sense the Pitzer's Woods fight ended on a positive note for both Generals Lee and Meade. For the Confederates, Wilcox succeeded in doing exactly what his brigade had been sent south to do: protect the right flank of the Army of Northern Virginia. For the Union army, Sickles' deep reconnaissance discovered that the heavy woods was playing host to a sizeable Confederate force less than a mile west of his position.[26]

Meade trusted his immediate subordinates would follow orders and in certain circumstances used his office, rank, and name recognition to enforce them. Artillery chief Henry Hunt's role on this part of the field has long been misunderstood. Meade had sent him south to see what Sickles wanted and then report back to headquarters. Instead, Hunt remained with Sickles watching Berdan's reconnaissance get underway. This should not be surprising because it was Hunt who had suggested it. "At my instance General Sickles ordered a reconnaissance to ascertain if the [Pitzer's] wood was occupied," he later reported. Hunt redeployed two batteries forward to support the operation. Once that was done, he rode with Captain Randolph to point out potential artillery positions that could work in concert to support Ward's brigade on Houck's Ridge.[27]

If Hunt was supposed to sell Sickles on Meade's general plan and make sure he complied (i.e., deploy his corps on lower Cemetery Ridge to the left of Hancock), advancing his artillery west to a forward position on higher ground along the Emmitsburg Road was no way to go about it. Although Hunt denied it until the day he died, the evidence suggests he and Sickles independently arrived at the same conclusion: a forward position well to the west along on the Emmitsburg Road Rise was preferable to a withdrawal to a lower position back on Cemetery Ridge.

25 *OR* 27, pt. 1, 507.

26 Ibid., pt. 1, 507, 517; pt.2, 517; USGS MRC 390772G.

27 Hunt, *Battles & Leaders,* 3:302.

Unbeknownst to Hunt, Sickles had sent his aide, Maj. Henry E. Tremain, to army headquarters around 1:00 p.m. with a full report of what had just transpired—including Buford's departure, the results of the sharp fight in Pitzer's Woods, and the forward redeployment of Birney's infantry division. Instead of summoning Hunt to headquarters or riding south himself, however, Meade sought out Pleasonton to determine why he had withdrawn Buford's two cavalry brigades.[28]

Major Tremain later claimed that when he reported this information to Meade, the army commander seemed disinterested. He repeated it a second time to be sure the general heard him, but Meade allegedly again ignored it. If Tremain's memory is accurate, perhaps there was good reason for it: Meade had a lot on his mind and he already had Hunt overseeing the army's left flank in general and Sickles' situation in particular. According to Tremain, the only news that seemed to spark any concern in Meade was Buford's unexpected departure. When Tremain inquired about the Third Corps supply trains, Meade abruptly ended the short meeting. By the time Hunt reported to Meade, 1:00 p.m. had passed and Hunt received new orders to return south to Sickles' front. Tremain, of course, had already returned and reported his meeting with Meade to Sickles, who apparently mistook Meade's lack of curiosity or concern to as agreement with the redeployment of Birney's infantry westward. Sickles sent instructions to Humphreys to also advance west to the Emmitsburg Road.[29]

On the other side of the field, General Wilcox referred to Pitzer's Woods as a "spirited but mostly insignificant affair," little realizing, even after the campaign ended, how this "spirited" if short fight helped mold the forthcoming battle below the Union center. Although it lasted no longer than 20 minutes, the Pitzer's Woods engagement was the excuse Sickles wanted and needed once he watched Buford's troopers mount up and retire south down the Emmitsburg Road. Buford's premature departure propelled Hunt to provide the information that may have convinced Sickles that he approved the Third Corps' new forward position. Meade's chief of artillery had not only suggested and authorized Berdan's reconnaissance that triggered the Pitzer's Woods fight, but also redeployed Bucklyn's and Clark's two batteries to provide support.[30]

28 Henry E. Tremain to Daniel Sickles, June 26, 1886, *National Tribune*, July 15, 1876.

29 Ibid.; Sickles, "Testimony," *JCCW*, 298, as noted in Pfanz, *Gettysburg The Second Day*, 102-103. Hunt had already departed for army headquarters when Sickles ordered Humphreys' division forward, thus he allegedly did not know of that division's deployment to the Emmitsburg Road.

30 *OR* 27, pt. 3, 617; Hunt, *Battles & Leaders*, 3:302; USGS MRC 390772G. While Berdan was beginning his movement, about 11:45 a.m. Meade's assistant-adjutant general, Seth Williams, issued a circular requesting that all corps commanders send headquarters a drawing of their

Pre-battle watercolor looking west from Cemetery Ridge toward Seminary Ridge. The Bliss farm and barn are in the center, with the Abraham Bryan house on the far right. GNMP

While Colonel Berdan was preparing his troops for their Pitzer's Woods reconnaissance, another incident ensued at the Bliss farm 1,500 yards to the north. Soon after the fighting there had stabilized, a few bold Mississippians moved through the orchard and reentered the bank barn under the noses of Union skirmishers not 100 yards away. Moving to the upper floor, they began firing through the slatted breeze ways, "whence they picked off our men with impunity from the loop-holed windows," reported a Federal officer. General Hays dispatched three fresh companies from Willard's 126th New York to clear the structure. Captain Charles Wheeler, commanding Company K, led the detachment in a successful seizure of the barn and several enemy sharpshooters within. By the

position, including the pertinent roads. Only a few officers, including Gibbon, saw this notice before it was withdrawn. Gibbon allegedly exploded, "Great God! General Meade does not intend to leave this position?" In response to his questioning, Butterfield retracted the circular, stating "Meade had no notion of falling back," but rather "wanted the army to be prepared, in case it should be necessary to leave." Gibbon later testified to the Joint Committee on the Conduct of War, "I was firmly convinced General Meade had no notion of falling back from his position and it was very remarkable that his chief of staff should be making out an order to retreat." OR 27, pt. 3, 487; *JCCW*, Vol. 1. 298, 436; and Meade, *Life and Letters,* 2:168-71.

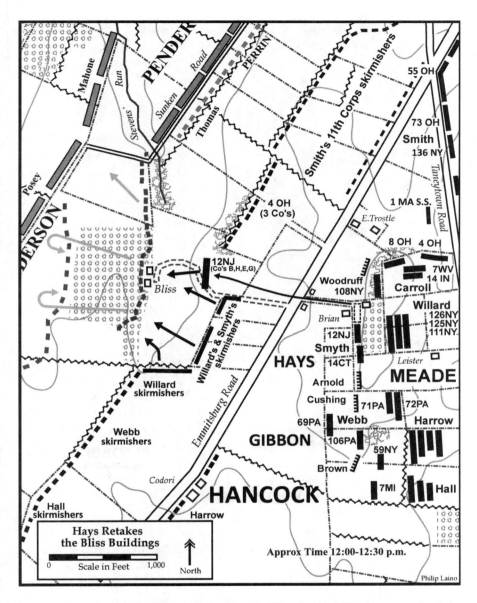

Hays Retakes the Bliss Buildings

0   Scale in Feet   1,000   North

Approx Time 12:00-12:30 p.m.

Philip Laino

time Berdan's troops withdrew from Pitzer's Woods, the Bliss barn was back in Union hands and the fighting had once again quieted down.[31]

31 *New York at Gettysburg*, 10; Charles A. Richardson to Bachelder, August 8, 1886, New Hampshire Historical Society, Concord, copy on file at GNMP.

Lt. Gen. James Longstreet
Commander of the First Corps,
Army of Northern Virginia
LOC

While Union officers reviewed their lines, Berdan and Wilcox skirmished for a strategic tract of woods, and Hays continued fighting for the Bliss farm, Rebel Colonel Alexander readied his reserve artillery battalion for a march that would spark one of the major controversies in a day filled with them. What exactly transpired at Lee's headquarters at that hour remains unclear. After digesting reports first from Captain Johnston and later Colonel Long regarding the perceived location of the Union left flank, Lee was positive that Longstreet's drive up the Emmitsburg Road would roll up and crush the vulnerable Federal army. A drive northward against Meade's line on Cemetery Ridge would be easier to support because it would necessarily spill into A. P. Hill's sector and better allow Richard Ewell to coordinate his supporting attack. Rather than further separate his army (as a move beyond and perhaps around Meade's left would do), Lee sought to shorten his exterior line, which in turn would bring his legions closer together in a manner that best utilized the information he had gained through the various reconnaissance patrols.[32]

Longstreet, however, did not trust the scouting reports. He was adamant—some writers suggest insubordinate—in his open disagreement with Lee in front of others. After lengthy discussions, during which sketches were drawn in the dirt, Longstreet finally relented. "Longstreet did not want wish to take the offensive," explained Colonel Alexander. "His objection was not based at all upon the particular strength of the enemy's position for that was not yet recognized, but solely on the general's [Lee] principles—perhaps the same referred to implied in Gen. Lee's report where he says that he ' had not designed to give battle so far from his base unless attacked.' Then Longstreet," continued Alexander, "asked permission to delay it [the attack] until one of the brigades of Hoods' division—Laws'—which had been left on picket duty the day before at Gilford Ct House could rejoin the division. It is doubtful Gen. Lee would have consented had he realized the length of said delay."[33]

Alexander, a generally reliable source, penned his account many years after the war. He suggests why Lee allowed Longstreet to send the artilleryman on yet a third reconnaissance that morning. If the attack was going to be delayed, explained the artillerist, reconnoitering the Union left yet again made sense. There was no viable reason, however, for Longstreet to keep the men he had on hand marking time, and yet that is precisely what he did. His divisions under Hood and McLaws did not march a step toward their jump-off position. Instead, they spent several hours sitting atop Herr's Ridge while Alexander hurried down Willoughby Run.[34]

Estimates of how long it took for Alexander to complete his last reconnaissance and gallop back north along Willoughby Run vary from one to as long as three hours. He later wrote that it was after 9:00 a.m. when Colonel Walton fetched him, and he started his ride south 10 minutes after reporting to General Longstreet. Alexander "rode fast—having a courier or two with me, & I don't think it took me much over an hour to get a very fair idea of the ground & roads to find Cabell's & Henry's battalions, & give them what instructions were needed."[35] He had encountered General Pendleton somewhere south of the Fairfield Road and continued on, dropping down toward Willoughby Run to follow the creek as Pendleton had before him. At some point along his meandering journey he heard heavy musket fire and his curiosity got the best of him. Turning roughly east, Alexander had crested southern Seminary Ridge, where a stunning panorama greeted him. Although Alexander never explained his exact location, he probably emerged on or near that Staub farm near Wilcox's right flank, because the colonel mentioned seeing enemy sharpshooters spread out in the distance in force. How long he remained is unknown, but when he had seen enough, he turned his horse around and rode back to bring up his artillery battalion.[36]

---

33 Gallagher, ed., *Fighting for the Confederacy*, 236-37.

34 Ibid.; *Battles & Leaders,* 3:359. Accounts vary as to both the time the march actually began, and the length of Alexander's reconnaissance. Estimates range as to the latter range from one to three hours.

35 Pfanz, *Gettysburg: Second Day*, 117. Pfanz suggests Pendleton possibly joined Alexander on this ride. The firing Alexander heard to the southwest was skirmishing between Union cavalry and Wilcox's advanced pickets beyond the S. Pitzer farm southwest of Pitzer's Woods.

36 E. P. Alexander to Rev. J. William Jones, March 17, 1877; "E. P. Alexander at Gettysburg," *SHSP*, vol. 4, No. 3, Sept. 1877.

This modern image was taken from West McMillan Woods atop Seminary Ridge looking west toward the Emanuel Pitzer farm. Willoughby Run is an additional 600 yards beyond. Lt. Gen. A. P. Hill, commander of the Third Corps, located his headquarters here shortly after 7:00 a.m. on July 2, as did Maj. Gen. Richard Anderson, one of Hill's division leaders. Although strategically located, neither commander seems to have spent much time at the front. *Richard Rollins Collection*

All three of Longstreet's artillery battalions (Alexander's, Cabell's, and Henry's) were bivouacked along Marsh Creek west of and below Herr's Ridge between the Fairfield Road and Cashtown Pike, with Alexander's battalion parked the farthest north. Having met Longstreet near the Seminary prior to reconnoitering down Willoughby Run, Alexander was somewhat familiar with Herr's, McPherson's, and Seminary ridges—at least in relation to the locations of Hood's and McLaws' divisions and their probable artillery parks. Although he knew where Maj. Benjamin F. Eshleman's Washington Artillery was bivouacked, Alexander did not know precisely where Cabell's and Henry's parks were located, except that they were somewhere south of his own. He later stated he did not have a watch nor did he know the time, but it was certainly before Berdan advanced his men to Pitzer's Woods when Alexander rode in search of Cabell's battalion during his journey back north.[37]

Alexander never explained his precise route to Marsh Creek. He could have ridden any number of rural farm lanes and avenues traversing Herr's Ridge. He must have envisioned a shorter route, having noted the Black Horse Tavern Road above the William Plank farm. Whatever route Alexander and his aides took, they

37 USGS MRC 39077G2-TF-024; *Bachelder Maps, Second Day.*

found Cabell's and Henry's battalions west of Marsh Creek where the Old Mill Road passed over the watercourse. It is probable that once north of the Fairfield Road he passed over Herr's Ridge using the Old Mill Road, which by chance separated Hood's right flank from McLaws' left atop the crest. Although Alexander never mentioned encountering either infantry division on his return, the Old Mill Road would have led him directly to both of the division's artillery parks below and to their rear, for the road bisected their commands.[38]

As a possible alternative, the Black Horse Tavern Road (north of the Fairfield Road) was equally as easy to reach Marsh Creek as the Old Mill Road, though a bit longer. This west-to-southwest running farm lane intersected Herr's Ridge Road some 200 yards south of Dr. Hall's house, or halfway between the Fairfield and Old Mill roads. It descended west 200 yards before angling southwest toward Marsh Creek, where it intersected the Black Horse Tavern Road at Mark Forney's farm. Whatever route the colonel used, he passed over Marsh Creek using Old Mill Road, where a right turn on Knoxlyn Road took him to Cabell's bivouac.[39]

His stay was a short one. Continuing north on Knoxlyn Road toward his own battalion, Alexander relayed the same instructions to Major Henry, who was parked just north of Cabell. The exact nature of these instructions remains a mystery. What we do know is that Cabell and Henry were preparing to use a different route. According to Alexander, Longstreet ordered him, in Lee's presence, "to take command of all the artillery on the field, for the attack, & suggested that I go at once, first, & get an idea of the ground, & then go and bring up my own battalion. But he told me to leave the Washington Arty. in bivouac where they were."[40]

When he reached his own battalion, Alexander ordered "boots and saddles. And then my men had their revenge for marching in the rear, for we had to file our whole length along by the W. A. [Eshleman's Washington Artillery] men & guns. And every man of ours was strutting and telling his neighbor [to the south], I told you so. We got the front at last." It appears Alexander's battalion passed Henry's and Cabell's battalions, from north to south respectively, to begin the march. Turning east on Old Mill Road, Alexander's column passed over the bridge spanning Marsh Creek. Instead of ascending Herr's Ridge, Alexander made an immediate right south on Black Horse Tavern Road. A short ride paralleling the creek above its eastern bank found his battalion passing the Mark Forney farm.

---

38 Gallagher, ed., *Fighting for the Confederacy*, 236; USGS MRC 39077-G2-TF-024. Near Knoxlyn Road.

39 Ibid.

40 Ibid., 235. Perhaps Alexander was referring to Longstreet's Reserve Artillery.

Within five minutes they closed on Bream's Tavern, 500 yards farther downstream, near where the Fairfield Road passed over Marsh Creek.

It is unclear when Alexander decided this alternate route was better for the movement south. He never mentioned it to Cabell or Henry, for they marched on a different route, one more in tune with Pendleton's, Long's, and Johnston's earlier recommendations concerning the Willoughby Run Road. Alexander knew that route and that it would hide his column from the enemy's prying eyes. The more direct route he was then using had yet to be sufficiently reconnoitered, and was thus something of a gamble.[41]

Shortly after Alexander disappeared down the Black Horse Tavern Road, both Cabell and Henry fell in and moved across the bridge following the Old Mill Road. "When we commenced to ascend the road leading to the crest of the hill," Cabell reported, "where the battle was subsequently fought my battalion moved to the head of the column." With Cabell in the lead they halted their column in sections by battalion in line, facing east in the narrow road. The column consisted of 35 cannon of varying calibers and types, plus attached limbers and caissons. This line would have stretched for more than a quarter-mile, plugging the west-to-east running Old Mill Road as it passed over Herr's Ridge and blocking all traffic. Protocol would have deemed it necessary to report the delay to their respective commanding generals: Cabell to McLaws and Henry to Hood. Eshleman's reserve battalion, as ordered, remained in park along Marsh Creek.[42]

Porter Alexander, meanwhile, continued marching his battalion down the Black Horse Tavern Road, passing over the Fairfield Road where it spans Marsh Creek at the tavern. Once south of the Fairfield Road, Alexander kept to the left ascending South Herr's Ridge on the old Black Horse Tavern Road as it traversed the rise above Marsh Creek angling up the slightly precipitous slope.[43] When he reached the crest, Alexander stopped his column somewhere near the Curren farm lane intersection, 500 yards shy of the William Plank farm. He and a couple of aides rode forward past the farmyard, where to their dismay they learned the route was visible to the Union signal station atop Little Round Top. From this cleared elevated position the colonel could clearly see the Edward Plank farm below where the Black Horse Tavern Road curved around it before entering the northwestern

---

41 Ibid., 236.

42 OR 27, pt. 3, 375, 433; USGS MRC 390772G; *Bachelder Maps, Second Day*.

43 USGS MRC 390772G. There are other possible routes the colonel may have taken that need not be explained, because this approach is the most direct route to reach Pitzer's Woods from any and all points near Francis Bream's Black Horse Tavern. It is interesting to note that the lower right fork road paralleled Marsh Creek, and was the one Union General Humphreys had taken to reach Bream's Tavern the previous night.

belt of Pitzer's Woods. He could likewise see Willoughby Run and the nearby road, with A. P. Hill's headquarters beyond, followed by Seminary Ridge.[44]

"I had come here [Pitzer's Schoolhouse] by a short & quite direct road," Alexander wrote, "which at one point passed over a high bare place where it was in full view of the federal station. But I avoided that part of the road by turning out to the left, and going through fields & hallows, & getting back to the [Black Horse Tavern] road again one quarter mile or so beyond." The colonel's route is not only easy to understand but makes perfect sense. Leaving the Black Horse Tavern Road from a point just north of the Edward Plank farm, he descended the eastern slope traversing through fields belonging to both Edward and his older brother William, whose farm rested above Willoughby Run a quarter-mile southeast. [45]

Before continuing on, Alexander likely sent an aide galloping back to Generals Hood and McLaws with news and fresh directions concerning this more direct route. Alexander's news must have stirred a tremendous amount of discussion and activity atop Herr's Ridge, for between 1:00 and 1:30 p.m., movement there caught the attention of the Union signal corps and Meade's engineers on Little Round Top. Plans were redrawn for the march south as McLaws readied his division to lead the way. It was agreed Cabell and Henry would accompany their respective divisions, which meant there had to be a lot of re-planning and rearranging for such significant changes. It could also be the reason why Longstreet's march remained stalled even longer than necessary. By now, the general was more than frustrated. He suggested that Captain Johnston, who had not reconnoitered this new route, continue leading the column as Lee's adjutant and liaison.[46]

In the meantime, Alexander's battalion found its detour through Plank's fields rewarding. Having dropped off the crest of Herr's Ridge, his column traversed the gentle eastern slope undetected by Union eyes. Reentering the Black Horse Tavern Road near the William Plank farm, a short ride through the woods brought his column to the schoolhouse where, as ordered, they pulled off the road to await the arrival of Cabell's and Henry's battalions.[47]

*   *   *

44 Ibid.

45 Gallagher, ed., *Fighting for the Confederacy*, 236.

46 *OR* 27, pt. 3, 375.

47 USGS MRC 390772G; *Bachelder Maps, Second Day*.

While Alexander's column rumbled south, General Wilcox's Alabama infantry moved in force back up to the tree line, retaking the stone wall south of Spangler's farm lane. With this done, the nearby Union skirmishers in the farmyard had no choice but to vacate it for fear of being cut off. A few daring Confederates crept forward to establish firing positions from within the farmyard, while their Union counterparts reformed along Humphreys' skirmish line not 200 yards distant. The now-isolated left wing of the 8th Alabama fronted east from west of the wall at the edge of the woods, while the right for the most past continued fronting south. Leaving a sizable skirmish line to the right of the 8th that stretched the width of the woods, Colonel Forney removed the balance of his regiment back to Spangler's Woods, where it linked with Sanders' 11th Alabama.[48]

Thus far, the 11th Alabama had taken more casualties than the 8th and 10th combined in Wilcox's sharp but short combat with Berdan and the 3rd Maine. However, within a half-hour of its mauling in the open field, Colonel Sanders was able to regroup his command, take care of his wounded and dead, and shelter his healthy remaining combatants in Spangler's Woods. Placed to the right of the 14th, Sanders' men enjoyed some rest and shade while Forney's 10th Alabama extended the line to the right. With Forney's right flank resting near Spangler's farmyard, a significant gap of perhaps 400 yards existed between that regiment and the left of Herbert's 8th Alabama. Artillery support would be needed if the isolated 8th was to continue holding Pitzer's Woods, so Wilcox sent a courier to fetch Captain Patterson's battery. Still detached from Major Lane's Sumter Artillery, Patterson's Company B had parked near A. P. Hill's headquarters when Wilcox took up his southern-facing position earlier that morning. Rumbling forward, Patterson swung about at reverse trot with his five 12-pounder howitzers and two Napoleons securing the gap. A low stone wall stood several feet beyond the wood line, but Patterson decided to place his guns under the sheltering canopy of timber. His crewmen soon surely appreciated the cover, for the heat was becoming more oppressive as the humidity soared to near 85 percent, with the temperature reaching a similar number.

From their positions south of the Spangler farm lane, Herbert's infantry and Patterson's gunners could see everything taking place along the Emmitsburg Road, including the ominous presence of Bucklyn's and Clark's repositioned Union batteries 1,200 yards distant. Some of Herbert's soldiers began exchanging shots with Federal skirmishers to their front, while others policed the wooded battlefield behind Patterson, all the while watching as the enemy dispositions across the way changed from minute to minute as dark blue columns, large and small, marched this

---

48 Ibid.

way and that. One would disappear into a patch of woods only to seemingly reappear back where it began. What these Confederates did not know was that Sickles' Third Corps was on the move.

In the meantime, when word of General Sickles' Pitzer's Woods affair reached army headquarters, a near-panic ensued. It was bad enough that Sickles had not yet complied with Meade's general order to relocate east to Cemetery Ridge, but now his already undersized command was scattered into groups of battalions and brigades with little resemblance of an effective force arranged to receive an attack. The Pitzer's Woods fight had convinced Sickles to further isolate his corps, spreading it even thinner. Both flanks were in the air with a skirmish line stretching from just north of the Rogers farm one mile south beyond John Sherfy's peach orchard. A clear main battle line did not exist at this time, as both Birney's First and Humphreys' Second divisions were irregularly placed, with many units detached to either participate in or to help cover the Pitzer's Woods reconnaissance. Cemetery Ridge was not on Sickles' mind. All of this suggests that Sickles' advance "disrupted Meade's overall defensive scheme," explained one historian, "and significantly degraded Union combat effectiveness.[49]

To make matters worst, Birney's division had been given the difficult task of not only guarding the "mountain on the left" (Little Round Top), but also supplying the forces that participated in the Pitzer's Woods fight, as well as those placed in reserve west of the Emmitsburg Road. Birney's undermanned division was unstable at best, and hosted a pair of dangerous salients—the first at Sherfy's peach orchard fronting west to south, with the second apex some 1,100 yards east where it again turned south to front west paralleling Houck's Ridge and Plum Run where the latter flowed south through what would become the "Valley of Death" (the area separating Little Round Top from Houck's Ridge). Birney's line, from his far left flank resting atop southern Houck's Ridge west to Sherfy's Peach Orchard and then north 500 yards, was about twice as long as what he should have been ordered to hold.[50]

Humphreys' Second Division was not much better off. Although somewhat intact, his three brigades were placed in brigades by battalion across a 1,000-yard stretch of rolling terrain. The whittling down of Col. George Burling's brigade began shortly after the Pitzer's Woods fight in order to help bolster Birney's irregular and thinly held line. From the Rogers house south to Abraham Trostle's farm, Humphreys' small division was readying itself for what many already figured

---

49 David Powell, "Advance to Disaster: Sickles, Longstreet, and July 2nd 1863," *Gettysburg Magazine*, Issue 28. USGS MRC 390772G; *Bachelder Maps, Second Day*.

50 USGS MRC 390772G; *Bachelder Maps, Second Day*.

was about to occur. Attached artillery was alerted with calls for reserve batteries to be ushered into play. "The overall length of the two lines should have been a critical concern," explained historian David Powell. "The Third Corps' intended line was just under a mile in length, about 1,600 yards. Sickles claimed that the Third Corps' 10,000 men were not sufficient to hold that length of line effectively. This claim does not bear up to scrutiny," continued Powell. "10,000 troops were sufficient to fully man the mile-long length of the intended line while still leaving Third Corps strength for reserves. The line he finally adopted, however, was twice as long at nearly 3500 yards."[51]

It was at this time that Sickles became concerned that his irregular thin front was inviting disaster. Both flanks were well advanced and in the air. He sent messenger after messenger galloping off to Meade and Sykes pleading for support. Birney's left wing was in a terrible posture, sitting several hundred yards west of and below unoccupied Little Round Top. With large breaks between individual commands, and with most of his men holding uneven terrain choked with thick brush and timber, stone walls, rocks, and rail fences, Birney called for more artillery support. He was also alarmed about his right flank positioned east of the Emmitsburg Road Rise because Humphreys' division north of it was not clearly visible as it disappeared into swales and low ground paralleling Plum Run north of Trostle's farm. Birney's refused center was in extreme danger as Colonel De Trobriand's small brigade spread itself thin to the right and front of Ward's line atop Houck's Ridge. A large gap located between de Trobriand's right and that of General Graham's left near the "stony knoll" ran some 800 yards and was but lightly defended. Ward's detached regiments had been called back from beyond the Emmitsburg Road and redeployed east of and opposite the rise in Sherfy's peach orchard, with skirmishers along and west of the Emmitsburg Road.[52]

The pieces were in place, and the stage ready for one of the most hotly contested confrontations of the entire Civil War.

---

51 David Powell, "Advance to Disaster: Sickles, Longstreet, and July 2nd 1863"; USGS MRC 390772G; *Bachelder Maps, Second Day.*

52 *OR 27*, pt. 1, 493, 501, 510, 511. This was the rough ground that Lt. David Kinzie of Battery K, 5th U. S. had pointed out to Generals Meade, Howard, and Hunt on their early morning reconnaissance.

Chapter Twelve

"The column was awaiting the movements of Colonel [sic] Johnston, who was trying to lead
it by some route by which it could pursue its march without falling
under view of the Federal signal station."

— *Lt. Gen. James Longstreet, C.S.A.*[1]

Afternoon, July 2: The March and Final Preparations

From High Street south to Breckenridge and from Franklin Street east to Stratton, sporadic skirmishing and sharpshooting continued on the southern edge of Gettysburg until well into the early afternoon. Major Thomas Osborn's First Corps and Eleventh Corps artillerists atop West Cemetery Hill had kept a careful eye in that direction all day, and for good reason.

Off in the distance beyond Gettysburg to the west, they watched as a seemingly unending line of enemy trains and columns moved along the Chambersburg Pike. The Federal gunners occasionally fired long-range iron greetings at them, as they did the Confederate infantrymen moving near the Lutheran Theological Seminary. Frustrated with the pesky sniping from the town, several Eleventh Corps infantry commanders called upon Major Osborn with requests that he engage individual sharpshooters plying their trade from the presumed safety of buildings dotting the southern outskirts of town. Osborn directed Capt. Michael Wiedrich to train his pieces of Battery I, 1st New York Light Artillery on these targets, all of which were private dwellings. Under normal circumstances this was against military regulations. This situation, however, was anything but normal. General Howard accordingly

---

1   James Longstreet, "General James Longstreet's Account of the Campaign and Battle," *SHSP*, vol. V, nos. 1-2, January-February 1878, 54-85.

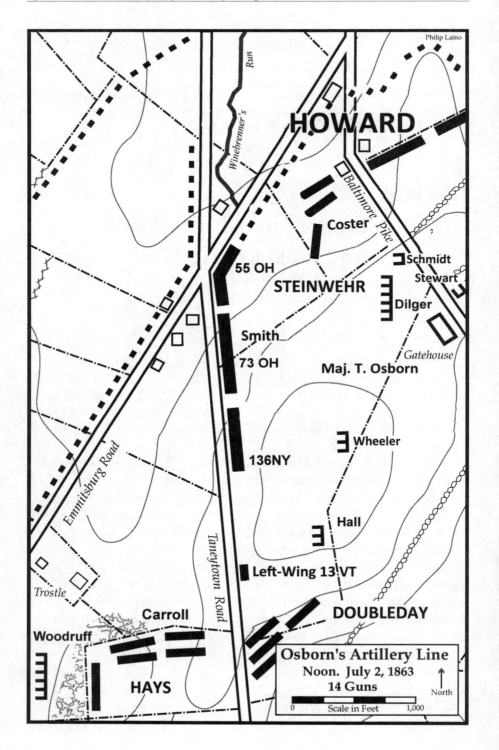

Philip Laino

HOWARD

Winebrenner's Run

Baltimore Pike

Coster

55 OH

Schmidt

Stewart

STEINWEHR

Dilger

Smith

73 OH

Gatehouse

Maj. T. Osborn

Wheeler

136NY

Emmitsburg Road

Hall

Taneytown Road

Left-Wing 13 VT

DOUBLEDAY

Trostle

Carroll

Woodruff

HAYS

Osborn's Artillery Line
Noon. July 2, 1863
14 Guns

North

0   Scale in Feet   1,000

looked the other way as the guns discharged, scattering the Rebel sharpshooters, at least temporarily.[2]

Prolonged Confederate activity west, northwest, and north of the Union "fishhook" line garnered the attention of nearly every man wearing blue, including General Meade. As Howard pointed out to him and General Hunt during their pre-dawn reconnaissance, the next major Confederate attack would most likely come from the west. The previous evening Howard had watched a long Rebel column (portions of General Pender's division and its supporting artillery) slide south of the Fairfield Road, where they deployed for the night. Howard noted that their skirmishers had been inching eastward closer to the Emmitsburg Road since early that morning. The one-armed Eleventh Corps commander suggested to Meade that General Lee would not hesitate to attack. He worried that the Confederate commander would support an attack from the west with troops he suspected remained hidden beyond Seminary Ridge, where hundreds of campfires had been visible during the night.[3]

Howard and his chief of artillery, Major Osborn, agreed they needed to keep watch on the sectors west and north of Gettysburg and track as close as possible any distant troops disappearing into or around town. Watching the day's slow progress of Rebels redeploying field guns to various points west and northwest of Cemetery Hill, Osborn decided to recall Capt. Hubert Dilger's half-battery from its temporary position along the Baltimore Pike. "As soon as the enemy developed the position he would probably occupy with his batteries," Osborn later explained, "I placed mine in position to command them." To counter such possibilities, he proactively targeted specific knolls, open fields, elevated rises, and wood that the enemy could potentially utilize as artillery platforms. Both he and Howard readily realized their dominant position on Cemetery Hill was the key to Meade's entire line.[4]

In addition to the continuing sniping from the edges of the town and the arrival of trains and fresh troops west and north of it, several other incidents captured Meade's attention. The Pitzer's Woods fight had brought on another new unexpected threat. With Buford's cavalry gone from the field and no other body of horsemen then in motion to replace them, Meade could only speculate what lay beyond Seminary Ridge south of the Fairfield Road. If this wasn't bad enough, new messages coming in from the northeast beyond Benner's Hill were equally

2   Thomas W. Osborn, "The Artillery at Gettysburg," *Philadelphia Weekly Times,* May 31, 1879.

3   USGS MRC 39077G2.

4   OR 27, pt. 1, 749; Thomas W. Osborn, "The Artillery at Gettysburg," *Philadelphia Weekly Times,* May 31, 1879.

It was not until 3:00 p.m. that Meade's ongoing fixation with his right flank diminished. This post-battle image of Zephaniah Taney's farm east of Rock Creek was taken from the lower fields of the Peter Baker farm, north of and below present-day "Lost Avenue" off the Baltimore Pike. The "gap" that so worried Slocum and Meade until late on the afternoon of July 2 directly influenced the outcome of events that day. LOC

disturbing. Skirmishers from Brig. Gen. David M. Gregg's Second Cavalry Division had been plucking away at enemy skirmishers on Brinkerhoff's Ridge east of Gettysburg along the Hanover Road. By 1:00 p.m. the fire had intensified and reinforcements added until a smart little fight was in progress. It became cyclical as the afternoon wore on—the firing would die down to occasional individual shots and then flare up again. From a Union perspective, the sharp engagement in Pitzer's Woods to the south and the continued action at Brinkerhoff's Ridge to the northeast of Cemetery Hill made it seem as if Lee was feeling for Meade's flanks.[5]

Adding to Meade's concerns about his right flank, in the early afternoon he heard a sudden boom to the northeast from the direction of Benner's Hill, followed

---

5 Eric J. Wittenberg, "Mount Up! Cavalry Operations of the Gettysburg Campaign." In the early afternoon Gregg's cavalry division arrived in the vicinity of Gettysburg from Hanover in southwestern York County. His men engaged Confederate infantry at Brinkerhoff's Ridge, disallowing a brigade of veteran soldiers from participating in the twin assaults on Culp's Hill and East Cemetery Hill that night. Gregg did a superb job of protecting the Union right flank.

by another. Within seconds both rounds from Capt. Archibald Graham's Rockbridge (Virginia) Artillery exploded above Evergreen Cemetery east of the Baltimore Pike. Graham used the landmark cemetery gatehouse to direct the fire of his four 20-pounder Parrott Rifles. Moments later, all four of his large-bore rifles were sending shrapnel, shell, and solid bolts west and southwest in an attempt to break up the Union batteries and regiments on the hilltop. Unbeknownst to either Captain Graham or his battalion commander, Maj. Joseph W. Latimer (who oversaw the opening salvo), there were no Federal artillery pieces at that time atop Cemetery Hill or Culp's Hill that could directly challenge Graham.[6]

The effective range of Union Col. Charles Wainwright's 3-inch Ordnance Rifles on East Cemetery Hill was about 2,400 yards, about 400 yards short of Graham's position on North Benner's Hill. With the elevations nearly equal, Graham's 20-pounders had a decided advantage until the Union leaders could bring up their own heavy guns in response. Within minutes, Latimer and Graham called out corrections and the four guns began pounding away. Graham's initial bombardment proved erratic, with rounds flying as far south as Slocum's headquarters down the Baltimore Pike and as far west as Zeigler's Grove along the Taneytown Road. However, enough rounds soon struck home to annoy Osborn's and Wainwright's infantry support. Several shells struck limbers and caissons, disrupting the counterbattery fire that Colonel Wainwright was attempting despite the lack of effective range.[7]

Another concern for Meade was where to place Maj. Gen. George Sykes' Fifth Corps to parry the anticipated Confederate assault. Meade spent the morning and early afternoon personally or through his staff officers rectifying his lines, positioning various commands, watching the distant enemy movements, and studying the field. Artillery commander General Hunt noted, "This was made more difficult as the day wore on due to misinformation including supposed expectations from numerous worried general officers including Maj. Gen. Doubleday and Howard who kept a watch on the build up west and north of town." The heavy

---

6   OR 27, pt. 1, 592, 759, 761; Richard Rollins and David Shultz, *The Baltimore Pike and Artillery Line and Kinzie's Knoll* (Redondo Beach, California: Rank and File Publications, 1997), 10. Lieutenant William Hardwick's section of 20-pounders of Capt. Charles I. Raine's Virginia Battery joined Graham during the afternoon.

7   *Ibid.*; Jennings Cooper Wise, *The Long Arm of Lee, or The History of the Artillery of the Army of Northern Virginia With a Brief Account of the Confederate Bureau of Ordnance,* 2 vols. (Lynchburg, Virginia: 1915; reprint, Richmond: Owens Publishing Co., 1988), 2:623-26. Although Graham's fire slowed down considerably in the early afternoon, it would not cease until nearly 2:30 p.m. when it became necessary to regroup and resupply.

Taken from the Baltimore Pike looking southwest. General Sykes placed his weary Fifth Corps in the fields and woods surrounding George Musser's farm. This central position enabled his 10,907 infantry and attached artillery to be used wherever Meade needed them. They could be used as a whole or piecemealed to either flank within 30 minutes marching quick-time. *Rosemary G. Oreb*

enemy traffic and the unlimbering of fresh batteries in the distant west continued to bother Doubleday and Howard in particular, as well as Major Osborn.

To the northeast, Captain Graham, with no effective Yankee counterbattery fire, periodically continued hurling shells at Cemetery Hill, adding to Meade's uncertainty as to where exactly Lee intended to strike him. Although relatively few in number, Graham's rounds at times passed well beyond the hill and took a mental toll, if not a physical one, on the Union troops on the western slope along the Taneytown Road, those ensconced in and around Zeigler's Grove, and the lines on the Emanuel Trostle and Bryan farms. Apprehension remained especially high immediately west of and below Cemetery Hill. Keeping an eye to the west was one thing; not knowing what was taking place beyond East Cemetery Hill was another entirely. It raised the distinct possibility that Lee might try a pincer movement from two directions aimed at capturing the critical high ground hinge of Meade's line.[8]

8   Henry Hunt, "The Second Day at Gettysburg," *Battles & Leaders,* vol. III, 296-297; USGS MRC 39077G2.

Along Cemetery Ridge, Winfield Hancock's veteran officers of his Second and Third Divisions surely knew their predicament. They could not only hear the artillery firing to their right and rear, but could also see the affairs to the west and southwest. What made looking south a bit easier for them to swallow was the fact they could see General Humphreys' Second Division, Third Corps off to their left and front. There was almost a mile between their Second Corps line and the ominous woods on Seminary Ridge, which offered plenty of warning in the event of a major assault from that direction. Hancock's officers had watched the Pitzer's Woods fight develop from afar and knew blue-clad infantry remained in force throughout the fields, orchards, and woodlots west and south of them. They also knew Hancock had dispatched General Caldwell's First Division as a mobile reserve. Caldwell was a veteran, competent officer who was tough-minded in a fight, which made Gibbon's and Hays' seemingly isolated positions feel a bit more secure. However, Hays' men had reservations about their supports to the north of Zeigler's Grove—Doubleday's battered remnants of the First Corps and Howard's so-called "Flying Dutchmen" whose reputation had suffered so much at Chancellorsville back in May. However, for Hancock and Meade, the more troubling immediate concern was Sickles' Third Corps and its advanced position. The left-flank corps's location and arrangement clearly spelled potential trouble.[9]

To the professional and volunteer officers who understood the basic military tactics of that era (and especially to those senior leaders who knew of Meade's general order to defend the Cemetery Ridge/Cemetery Hill/Culp's Hill position with its vital roads), Sickles' new irregular line, or what could be seen of it, was too far advanced to be of any real value to Hays' or Gibbon's troops in case of a determined enemy assault against the center. With Caldwell's move south and Sickles' forward position, the exact location of the Second Corps' left flank was in some doubt. Was it off Gibbon's left in the center of Cemetery Ridge north of the Hummelbaugh farm lane, or farther south off the left of Caldwell's detached division? Where was the Second Corps most vulnerable?[10]

A yawning gap stretching a third of a mile now existed between Gibbon's and Caldwell's divisions atop Cemetery Ridge. Although the far right of Humphreys' Third Corps division masked a portion of this dangerous opening, it was nevertheless at least 800 yards in front of Gibbon's left flank and the soldiers were still resting in battalions by brigade with their arms stacked. Its members did not seem concerned about a potential attack. The gap was wide enough for the enemy

9   USGS MRC 39077G2; see troop dispositions, *Bachelder Maps: Second Day.*

10 Ibid.; James Woods, *Gettysburg July 2: The Ebb and Flow of Battle* (Gillette, NJ: Canister Publishing, 2012), 112-19.

to easily exploit Humphreys' flank and then drive relatively unopposed toward Cemetery Ridge, and Sickles' reserves were not visible. None of it made sense to Hancock's field officers. Had Sickles taken the time to visit army headquarters and consult with his good friend General Butterfield, Meade's acting chief of staff, he would have been privy to the latest information, including reports from the signal stations and mounted scouts. However, there is no evidence Sickles actively sought any headquarters information concerning troop dispositions, either Union or Confederate. Except for communicating with General Hunt, he depended upon his own credentials and expertise to formulate and execute his unauthorized forward movement.[11]

At some point shortly after Sickles' fight at Pitzer's Woods ended, the chief signal officers of the Second Corps (Capt. Peter Taylor) and the Twelfth Corps (Capt. Lemuel Norton) contributed to Meade's ongoing concerns about Lee's intentions. From their lofty vantage point on Little Round Top, they informed Capt. James S. Hall, General Warren's chief signal officer who was then visiting army headquarters, that they "saw a column of the enemy's infantry move into woods on a ridge, three miles west of town, near the Millerstown Road. Wagon teams, parked in an open field beyond the ridge, moved to the rear behind woods. More wagons can be seen moving up and down on the Chambersburg pike, at Spangler's. Think the enemy occupies the range of hills three miles west of town in considerable force." Norton later offered a clarification to what was likely a direct question from army headquarters concerning the "Millerstown road." He explained, "General Meade: Millerstown Cross-Road is about 8 miles, a little south and west from this signal station 1½ miles to the south of this house [Leister]."[12]

In the meantime, Meade's headquarters sent a pair of messages to Union cavalry commander General Pleasonton, the first arriving at 12:50 p.m. Five minutes later a second directive demanded corrective action after Buford's premature departure. About 1:50 p.m. Pleasonton finally ordered General Gregg, commanding the Second Cavalry Division off the right near the Hanover Road, to send a regiment to the far left. Despite having his hands full with the ongoing engagement on Brinkerhoff's Ridge with James Walker's Stonewall Brigade, Pleasonton dispatched the 4th Pennsylvania south. However, "by the time they

---

11 David J. Eicher, *The Longest Night: A Military History of the Civil War* (New York: Simon & Schuster, 2001), 533-35.

12 *OR* 27, pt. 3, 489; Noah Andre Trudeau, *Gettysburg: A Testing of Courage* (New York: Harper Collins, 2002), 306. Exactly what Confederate troops these were remain unknown because no Rebel infantry at this time was near the Millerstown Road in force. Perhaps Taylor and Norton spied Wilcox's brigade west of Pitzer's Woods, or Longstreet's troops massed atop Herr's Ridge between the Old Mill Road and Chambersburg Pike south of Herr's Tavern.

arrived, it was too little, too late, as Longstreet was about to unleash his sledgehammer blow on the Army of the Potomac's left flank and center," cavalry expert Eric J. Wittenberg opined. "It is unclear where the responsibility for the failure to replace Buford's departing troopers lies, but it ultimately must fall upon the Cavalry Corps commander, Pleasonton, for failing to recognize the need to protect the army's position with a cavalry screen." Pleasonton also detached Lt. Edward Heaton's Consolidated Batteries B/L, 2nd U. S. The horse artillery took position along the Granite Schoolhouse Road near its intersection with the Old Blacksmith Shop Road. Strategically placed on the crossroad between the Baltimore Pike and Taneytown Road, Heaton's four Ordnance Rifles initially fronted south to challenge any potential Confederate flanking move around the Round Tops.[13]

By mid-afternoon, things had calmed down somewhat south of Cemetery Hill except for Graham's periodic fire from Benner's Hill. Officers on both sides used the lull to reinforce their already strong skirmish lines, feel one another's positions, redeploy units to new locations thought to be of importance, or rest their men for the major action everyone sensed was fast approaching. Some Federal officers tried to reassure their men that help was on the way. According to the 69th Pennsylvania's Lt. Anthony McDermott, "General Webb walked along his brigade assuring his men that General McClellan soon would be in the rear of the Rebels at the head of 30,000 troops, and their defeat would be easily accomplished." The rumor, of course, was untrue. All manner of false suggestions circulated that afternoon in the Army of the Potomac, including unfounded tales of powerful Federal columns heading south and west from Harrisburg and Philadelphia, respectively.[14]

With the popping of skirmishers west of Cemetery Ridge dwindling and the mid-afternoon heat increasing, many of Hancock's men took the opportunity to doze off. In Alexander Webb's Philadelphia Brigade, men played dominos, shared food, and discussed how nice it was to be home again in Pennsylvania, even under such trying circumstances. Across the verdant fields to the west, their Rebel opponents also rested while awaiting the certain order to advance. The Floridians of Colonel Lang's brigade lay behind the eastern stone wall bordering Spangler's Woods, enjoying the canopy of shade, sleeping, resting, or playing cards. Many

13 OR 27, pt. 3, 490; Eric J. Wittenberg, "The Truth about the Withdrawal of Brig. Gen. John Buford's Cavalry, July 2, 1863; *Bachelder Maps, Second Day*.

14 Anthony W. McDermott to John Bachelder, June 2, 1886, *Bachelder Papers*, 3:1408. Webb was a protégé of Meade from their days together in the Fifth Corps. Both were initially considered as "McClellanites."

young men in both armies took care to write what they hoped would not be a last letter, scribe a quick note, or pen a simple "I love you" to the folks back home. Some anxious soldiers penciled their names on scraps of paper and tucked them into their pockets—just in case.[15]

As was the case with most common soldiers, they spoke little if anything of battle while not engaged. Most of those men in Gibbon's Second Division paid little attention to what was occurring a quarter-mile away to the south, or north for that matter, let alone a mile distant to the west. If it did not affect them directly, it was none of their business. Most were simply grateful to not be out on the skirmish line or detailed to some "junket officer" for a meaningless or mundane purpose. Most of Meade's rank and file were in good spirits and happy to be out of Virginia. Although the rigorous march had taken its toll, once they crossed the Mason-Dixon Line their spirits soared as they tread upon Northern soil. As Hancock's men rested, most fretted little despite the enemy rounds occasionally striking within their forward ranks.[16]

General Alexander Webb, one of John Gibbon's brigade commanders, again did his best to boost morale in his command by continually reassuring his soldiers that reinforcements were indeed en route to join them. However, like most others in the Army of the Potomac, Webb's Philadelphians did not need more morale-building speeches. They had all heard General Meade's earlier circular condemning them if they shirked their duty on the battlefield. They did not have to be cajoled to fight. They did not need army headquarters threatening them. They were on their home soil, and fight they would. From Sickles' far left to Slocum's far right, George Meade's men knew what was expected this day. But, for now, it was time to rest and mentally prepare for the coming storm.[17]

General Lee's gray- and butternut-clad soldiers across the way on Seminary Ridge also relaxed as best they could, suspecting the orders to advance would soon be forthcoming. They had entered Pennsylvania eager to fill their haversacks with the rich bounty of Keystone farmers and defeat the Army of the Potomac.

15 J. B. Johnson, "A Limited Review of What One Man Saw at the Battle of Gettysburg," GNMP; Alexander Webb interview with Alexander Kelly, May 15, 1899, GNMP; *Bachelder Map, Second Day*.

16 A "junket officer" was a term for a political or social appointee, with many holding commissions for no other reason than they were born into wealthy families. For the most part, these young staffers were along for the adventure and to build their resumes, at least in the opinion of many serving in the rank and file. However, at Gettysburg many of these junior officers, despite a lack of formal military training, displayed tremendous courage and competency.

17 "The Battle of Gettysburg: The Part Taken by the Philadelphia Brigade in the Battle," *Gettysburg Compiler*, June 7, 1887, GNMP.

However, the time for foraging and picnicking had ended. They were ready and eager to pitch into the hated Yankees. The battle-tested veterans had been in these kinds of situations before, and most were ready for another successful fight. Even after days of fatiguing marches, with many having already fought a large battle the previous day, most simply wanted to get it over in the usual manner: hit the Yankees hard and drive them off the field in abject defeat. That's the way it had almost always worked in previous encounters. Southern confidence abounded. The results of the previous day had been costly, but the nature of the successful fight had spread through the ranks. Many Southerners thought their Army of Northern Virginia invincible, and with that mindset had the false notion they could lick the Yankees no matter what.

For the most part, Lee's rank and file could care less about their general's extended exterior line (and most didn't even know the nature of the army's full configuration). Nor did they know, or particularly care, that General Stuart and his cavalry were not yet present. Nearly all command-and-control issues that plagued Lee and his chief subordinates at Gettysburg remained unknown to the common infantryman and artilleryman. Hood's and McLaws' men patiently waiting on Herr's Ridge to deploy had no clue Generals Longstreet and Hill were not communicating, or that Lee, Longstreet, McLaws, and Hood disagreed about how to handle the attack against the Yankee lines across the way. They simply waited for their orders, paying little if any regard to matters outside their personal field of vision.[18]

While the opposing men poised in the center of the battlefield marked time and pondered their immediate destinies, General Meade's chief of staff, General Butterfield, fired off a message to the commander of the Reserve Artillery, Brig. Gen. Robert O. Tyler: "Send a battery to report to General Sickles on the left." Butterfield was attempting to solicit any additional help he could for his Tammany Hall mentor and friend. General Hunt had already sent orders for several reserve batteries to move to Sickles' aid, and Caldwell's division had been sent south to offer some infantry support. However, Butterfield's simple request indicated that at least some individuals at army headquarters suspected Sickles and his corps were in imminent danger. Although he lacked military professional military training, it was Butterfield's obligation to press his commanding officer on such subjects, help define and clarify situations and opportunities, and clear up any and all misunderstandings.[19]

---

18 John Heiser, "Soldier Life in the Civil War," May 1, 1998, GNMP.

19 Woods, *Ebb and Flow*, 115.

And there was plenty to set straight. Between 1:00 and 2:00 p.m. there was more bustling activity underway south of Trostle's farm lane than along the entire length of Meade's remaining intact line. Moving troops anywhere took time, even those traversing a short distance under good conditions. For example, Col. P. Regis de Trobriand of Birney's division needed three-quarters of an hour to move three regiments a distance of only 400-600 yards from their position near the old Jacob Weikert log cabin east of Trostle's woods to the Wheatfield, where they rejoined the 5th Michigan and 110th Pennsylvania. General Ward of the same division needed even longer to redeploy his detached command to several points needing additional troops. According to Colonel Elijah Walker, commanding the 4th Maine on Ward's skirmish line, "From 9:30 until 2:30 there was but little firing from my men or by the enemy in our front . . . it took one hour to relieve and get my men [back] to where I had my headquarters" (near the Weikert homestead, a distance of roughly 1,000 yards).[20]

By 2:00 p.m. the first of Hunt's promised support for Sickles' advanced line arrived from the artillery park. Captain Nelson Ames' Battery G, 1st New York arrived and parked in reserve in the low ground near Trostle's farm. Sickles and his artillery chief Major Randolph used the afternoon lull wisely to redistribute the forward Third Corps artillery to those positions General Hunt had earlier suggested. They moved Capt. James E. Smith's six 10-pounder Parrott rifles from their park near the old Weikert homestead south a quarter of a mile along the Plum Run valley. Smith subsequently deployed four guns atop Houck's Ridge fronting west-southwest with an unobstructed view toward the Emmitsburg Road, and kept the remaining section in reserve behind closer to the Millerstown Road. Fronting south down Plum Run valley, this pair of rifles enjoyed a very limited, but very important, field of fire.[21]

At some time after 2:00 p.m. General Hunt's second promised battery arrived in the Third Corps sector. Captain James Thompson's Consolidated Pennsylvania Light Batteries C/F parked his six 3-inch Ordnance Rifles near meandering Plum Run east of and below the Trostle farm. All told, with these reinforcements Hunt had now detached a full dozen artillery pieces for Sickles' use along on his extended new line well to the west of General Meade's original intended line on southern Cemetery Ridge. Hunt was well aware Sickles was not in the right position, but the Third Corps commander clearly believed Hunt approved of his advanced line from the first moment Meade's chief of artillery called upon Captain Clark's New Jersey

---

20 Elijah Walker to John Bachelder, January 5, 1885, *Bachelder Papers,* 2:1094.

21 OR 27, pt. 1, 588; Woods, *Ebb and Flow,* 119-133. Ames' battery had been detached from Fitzhugh's 4th Volunteer Reserve Brigade.

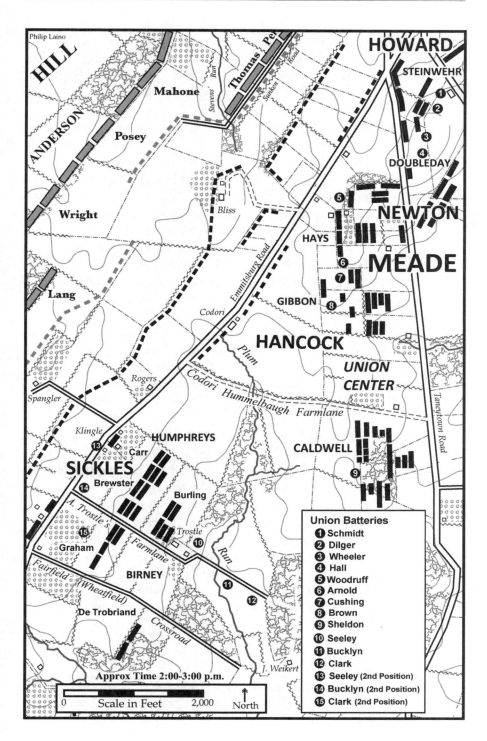

Philip Laino

HILL

ANDERSON

Mahone

Posey

Wright

Bliss

Lang

Codori

Plum

Spangler

Rogers

Codori *Hummelbaugh Farmlane*

Klingle

HUMPHREYS

Carr

SICKLES

Brewster

A. Trostle's

Graham

Fairfield *(Wheatfield)*

BIRNEY

De Trobriand

Burling

Trostle

Farmlane

Run

Crossroad

J. Weikert

HOWARD

STEINWEHR

DOUBLEDAY

NEWTON

HAYS

MEADE

GIBBON

HANCOCK

UNION
CENTER

CALDWELL

Taneytown Road

Union Batteries
❶ Schmidt
❷ Dilger
❸ Wheeler
❹ Hall
❺ Woodruff
❻ Arnold
❼ Cushing
❽ Brown
❾ Sheldon
❿ Seeley
⓫ Bucklyn
⓬ Clark
⓭ Seeley (2nd Position)
⓮ Bucklyn (2nd Position)
⓯ Clark (2nd Position)

Approx Time 2:00-3:00 p.m.

0   Scale in Feet   2,000   North

battery to move forward and support him. General Hunt had also kept his word about sending additional support from the artillery reserves, and yet at the same time denounced Sickles' position as untenable and too far west. To Sickles, however, Hunt's redeployment of the reserve guns indicated tacit approval at the very least.

Meade, for his part, also continued to take advantage of the delay in the Confederate attack. However, the nagging uneasiness—especially from the observers on Little Round Top—handcuffed the Army of the Potomac's hierarchy. Lieutenant Norton's report, though reliable, was not enough by itself to convince Meade, Slocum, or even Butterfield that the army's left flank and center were more susceptible to an attack than the right flank, as those generals then strongly believed. Graham's ongoing slow but methodical bombardment from North Benner's Hill, the Rebel skirmishing with David Gregg's cavalrymen along Brinkerhoff's Ridge, and more importantly Confederate demonstrations north of town only reinforced the idea that the main attack would come against the Union right. In addition, a large Confederate force (Edward Johnson's entire division) lurked in the area north and east of Culp's Hill and additional enemy troops (Smith's and Gordon's brigades of Early's division) had taken position near the railroad tracks and York Road, fronted by two brigades (Hays and Avery) stretching from Middle Street eastward to the Culp farm. Thus, it would take much more than the ominous reports from Little Round Top to convince headquarters to deploy Sykes' Fifth Corps to reinforce the Union left. Sickles, at least for the time being, was on his own.[22]

At some point before 2:30 p.m., Meade ordered his chief engineer, General Warren, to accompany General Slocum toward the right flank on a scouting mission to see what lay beyond that sector once and for all. This was Slocum's second visit to the vicinity, having taken a quick look during the morning. Meade's deep interest in his right flank went far beyond what many students believe. He had toyed for quite some time with the idea of a preemptive strike in that sector. Shortly after 9:00 a.m., he had sent word through Butterfield to Slocum "to make your arrangements for an attack from your front on the enemy, to be made by the Twelfth Corps, supported by the Fifth. He wishes this a strong and decisive attack, which he will order as soon as he gets definite information of the approach of the Sixth Corps, which will also be directed to co-operate in this attack. For this

---

22 Union observers also spotted the movement of some of Johnson's regiments which had stopped for the night north of town now being deployed into position to support the rest of the division.

purpose, he has sent an officer to ascertain the whereabouts of General Sedgwick, and report."[23]

Slocum responded with, "I have already made a better examination of the position in my front than I am able to now that we have taken up a new line. If it is true that the enemy are massing troops on our right, I do not think we could detach enough troops for an attack in insure success. I do not think the ground in my front, held by the enemy, possesses any particular advantage to him." Still, the idea of an attack from the Culp's Hill sector percolated in Meade's mind.[24]

Now, in mid-afternoon, Meade continued to fret about his right. He had not sent Sykes to support Sickles as the latter had requested numerous times. It is unclear what Meade was thinking when it came to Gregg's Second Cavalry Division, which up to this time was in control of both his front and army's far right flank. He needed these troopers to provide early warning of any Confederate aggressiveness. "Without doubt, General Meade's mind, initially was not on his left," explained one historian of the battle, "and his vaunted staff served him poorly [Hunt included] with respect to the Third Corps' activities." This assessment concluded, "General Meade's lack of concern for his left must have resulted in part from information provided by his signalmen."[25]

"Still there was no hostile movement of the enemy," Henry Hunt later wrote, "and General Meade directed Slocum to hold himself in readiness to attack Ewell with the Fifth and Twelfth, as soon as the Sixth Corps should arrive." Meade was anticipating the timely arrival of John Sedgwick's Sixth Corps, hoping Lee would not launch an attack before its arrival. Hall's and Jerome's messages regarding enemy movement toward the army's right may have prompted Meade's consideration of launching his own attack. Whatever the reason, Meade shortly thereafter discarded the idea when Slocum and Warren returned from their reconnaissance. According to General Hunt, Warren's and Slocum's short quick ride to the right was conclusive: "After an examination Slocum reported (again) the ground as unfavorable, in which Warren concurred and advised against an attack there."[26]

23 *Congressional Set: The Miscellaneous Documents of the House of Representatives for the First Session of the Fifty-First Congress, 1889-90. Correspondences, Orders, and Returns Relating to Operations in North Carolina, Virginia, West Virginia, Maryland Pennsylvania and the Department of the East from June 3 to August 3, 1863* in 47 volumes. Hereafter cited as *CS*, vol. 22, pt 3. See also OR 27, pt 3 486-487 which is part of this larger set of documents.

24 Ibid.

25 Pfanz, *Gettysburg, Second Day*, 141.

26 Hunt, "The Second Day at Gettysburg," *B&L*, 3:297.

This "unfavorable" ground worked both ways: if it was unsuitable for a Union offensive attack as Slocum reported, it was most assuredly unsuited for a Confederate attack from the north. With this second reconnaissance and Slocum's repeated counsel against an attack, Meade's concern of an enemy assault from that direction diminished, as did his thought about launching his own offensive. Based upon Slocum's and Warren's input "the project was then abandoned," in Henry Hunt's words, "and Meade postponed all offensive operations [on the right] until the enemy's intentions should be more clearly developed." However, Meade still thought it prudent to keep Sykes' Fifth Corps in readiness along the Baltimore Pike until Sedgwick's Sixth Corps arrived.[27]

On the other end of the line, Dan Sickles was still busy realigning his brigades. He had thus far placed his men as best he could under trying conditions and unfavorable terrain. From Devil's Den north the length of Houck's Ridge and then west to the Peach Orchard, General Birney and his staff had managed to piece together a thin defensive line across rough terrain, a remarkable feat given the circumstances and lack of time for proper reconnaissance. General Hunt had approved Randolph's hastily stitched together artillery positions, with the two reserve batteries in park to support the quintet of Third Corps batteries. What was now missing was the cavalry screen Buford's troopers had earlier provided. To balance that out, Sickles again called upon several companies of Maj. Homer Stoughton's 2nd U. S. Sharpshooters. "I remained in position until about 2:00 p.m.," Stoughton later reported, "when General Ward directed that I should deploy my regiment across the ravine and through woods on the right, and advance." He accordingly moved several companies from the vicinity of Trostle's Woods near the Jacob Weikert homestead south down the Plum Run valley. At some point he moved the right of his line southwest over Houck's Ridge near Devil's Den while the left continued through the Plum Run ravine to the area separating today's "Slaughter Pen" from the Den toward present-day Devil's Gate. Once beyond the maze of jumbled rocks and boulders and the ravine, Stoughton led his green-clad sharpshooters into the fields south and west of Big Round Top. This difficult deployment consumed more than an hour. All this activity perhaps explains why Sickles personally opted to forgo Butterfield's memorandum calling for his attendance at army headquarters at 3:00 p.m. This action alone was insubordination as the circular was a direct order, not an invitation.[28]

---

27   USGS MRC 39077G2; *Bachelder Maps*, Second Day; Hunt, "The Second Day at Gettysburg," *B&L*, 3:297.

28   OR 27, pt. 1, 518; USGS MRC 39077G2.

While all this was transpiring between two and three o'clock in the afternoon, Maj. Gen. John Sedgwick's 15,600-man Sixth Corps continued to close in on the battlefield from the south. With no rest stops or unforeseen delays, Meade expected Sedgwick to arrive between 4:00 and 5:00 p.m. He would be in good shape if only the Rebels would delay their attack until then.[29]

*   *   *

From the moment Berdan's and Wilcox's fight in Pitzer's Woods ended and Sickles began finalizing and fortifying his advanced line, some of General Longstreet's officers had found convenient vantage points from which to observe the distant Yankees deployed along the Emmitsburg Road. Brigadier General Joseph Kershaw, commanding his veteran South Carolina brigade, found such a spot. In a postwar letter to battle researcher John Bachelder, he discussed what he saw from atop Herr's Ridge near Dr. Hall's house before being ordered to take up the march. Kershaw recalled seeing long lines of Union soldiers in the open ground "some distance to the right of the point where we afterwards joined the battle." They were clearly visible, he stated. Kershaw's claim contradicts some postwar suggestions that the Confederates did not know the whereabouts of the Union left flank that afternoon when they launched their assault.[30]

Although heavily timbered in places, Herr's Ridge offered for a fine view of Cemetery Hill southward down Cemetery Ridge beyond Hummelbaugh's farm lane. From that point, the Emmitsburg Road Rise, stretching from just south of the Codori farm to Sherfy's peach orchard, was the dominant rise in Kershaw's sweeping panorama to the southeast. The South Carolina general could see the wigwagging signal flags atop Little Round Top, but Kershaw could not see the base of Little Round Top, Plum Run Valley, or Houck's Ridge. It is doubtful he fully realized just how rough the terrain was that he would be ordered to traverse. From Kershaw's vantage point at Dr. Hall's, the distance to the Millerstown-Emmitsburg Road intersection, as the crow flies, was about three and one-half miles. Whatever he saw, he almost certainly forwarded the intelligence to General McLaws, his commanding officer.[31]

29 Ibid., 665, 669, 673, 675; Coddington, *The Gettysburg Campaign*, 344-45.

30 Kershaw to Bachelder, March 20, 1876, *Bachelder Papers,* 1:452-58; USGS MRC 39077G2. Kershaw likely spotted the distant Union infantry from a vantage point where the Fairfield Road crossed over Herr's Ridge. Today, modern Route 116 passes through this ridge via a deep cut that has obliterated Kershaw's presumed 1863 vista.

31 Ibid.; USGS MRC 39077G2; *Bachelder Maps, Second Day*.

While Kershaw and others surveyed the terrain and observed Union activity, Longstreet temporized, "fearing that my force was too weak to venture to make an attack." As Old Pete later explained it, "I delayed until General Law's brigade joined its (Hood's) division." The First Corps commander had General Lee's permission to await the arrival of Brig. Gen. Evander Law's brigade before moving out. When Law's Alabamians finally arrived between 1:15 and 1:30 p.m., there was no time to allow them to rest. Short on water, the fagged Alabamians fell in on Hood's far left without complaint, nearly a half-mile north of the Old Mill Road. With no reason to prolong his march it was time for Longstreet to begin moving. Law's men would be the last brigade—the first was Kershaw's South Carolina command—in a long column heading south. Longstreet finally set of shortly after 1:30 p.m.[32]

Under the guidance of Capt. Samuel R. Johnston, McLaws' division led the way south down Herr's Tavern Road toward the Fairfield Road. There, the head of the column stopped at a rural farm lane that angled southwest down Herr's Ridge toward farmer Mark Forney's tract of land bordering the Black Horse Tavern Road, with Marsh Creek beyond it. "We were then directed to move under cover of the hills toward the right," Kershaw later mentioned, "with a view to flanking the enemy in that direction, if cover could be found to conceal the movement." He did not follow the farm lane down the slope with his men marching in column, but instead ordered his leading regiment either half-right or right as the men descended west Herr's Ridge by the right flank or half-right (either north of or bisecting Forney's farm lane). This move would have screened the entire column from view, as each following regiment perpetuated the movement. Kershaw explained, "About one and a half o'clock (I speak from memory) we moved by flank from the head of column perpendicular to the rear, passed back of the hill, filed under its cover to the left, passed to the right of the building afterwards used as hospital, and between it and the bridge across a creek at that point. This building I suppose to be the Black Horse Tavern."[33]

Kershaw specifically suggested that once they filed (by column) to the left on Black Horse Tavern Road, his men were once again heading south. "The road, which we had just previously left [Forney farm lane], I think, led through the lane [Black Horse Tavern Road] and to this bridge. The bridge is the same across which the army retreated after the battle. Some three hundred yards from the hospital [the Black Horse Tavern] when the head of column was about to reach the top of a hill

---

32 Kershaw to Bachelder, March 20, 1876, *Bachelder Papers*, 1:452-58; John Bell Hood's unofficial Gettysburg report, June 28, 1875, GNMP; USGS MRC 39077G2.

33 Ibid.

Maj. Gen. John B. Hood,
division commander, First Corps,
Army of Northern Virginia
LOC

where it would be seen," he continued, "McLaws halted the troops and with Longstreet went over the hill along the road we were on [Black Horse Tavern Road south of Fairfield Road]." It did not take long for General Kershaw's vanguard to negotiate the nearly 2,000 yards from just south of Dr. Hall's residence on Herr's Ridge down to where the brigade stopped on Black Horse Tavern Road.[34]

Hood's division, however, was temporarily held up because of other columns, ambulances, and wagons using Herr's Tavern Road. Of all the confusing issues surrounding Longstreet's chaotic march that afternoon, one is the whereabouts at this time of Colonel Cabell's and Major Henry's artillery battalions. Assigned to McLaws' division, Cabell's four batteries waited on the Old Mill Road west of its intersection with Herr's Tavern Road near Dr. Hall's residence. They were to fall in behind the division. Henry's four batteries

Maj. Gen. Lafayette McLaws,
division commander, First Corps,
Army of Northern Virginia
LOC

34 Ibid.

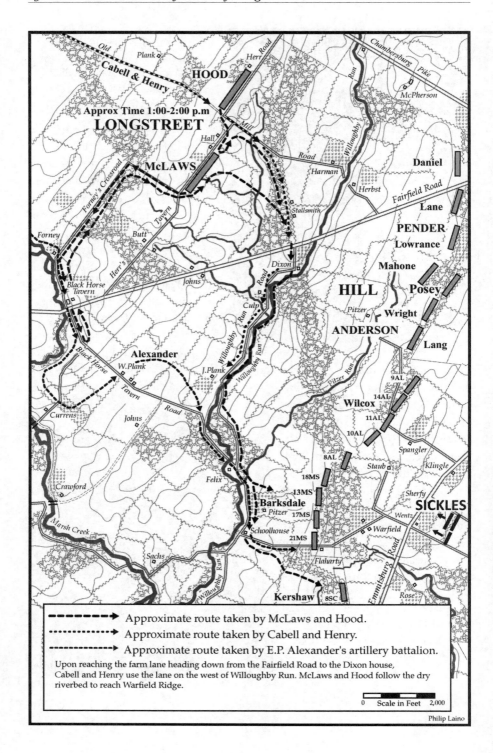

Approx Time 1:00-2:00 p.m

- - - - - → Approximate route taken by McLaws and Hood.
················→ Approximate route taken by Cabell and Henry.
- - - - - → Approximate route taken by E.P. Alexander's artillery battalion.

Upon reaching the farm lane heading down from the Fairfield Road to the Dixon house,
Cabell and Henry use the lane on the west of Willoughby Run. McLaws and Hood follow the dry
riverbed to reach Warfield Ridge.

0   Scale in Feet   2,000

Philip Laino

likewise waited behind Cabell to join Hood. Neither plan, however, materialized due to an unforeseen issue created when McLaws' leading regiment came to a complete stop, piling up all the traffic behind it. Both artillery battalions stayed put until further notice. When Hood finally got moving to the rear of McLaws, the head of his column likewise stopped somewhere south of the Old Mill Road intersection. Cabell's battalion was apparently still parked to the west of the intersection with Henry's farther down the slope somewhere east of and above Marsh Creek.[35]

General McLaws and Captain Johnston, accompanied by a few aides, spurred their horses south and disappeared up the dirt road as it angled south-southeast and ascended South Herr's Ridge from its intersection with the Fairfield Road. Stopping near the William Plank farm, they slowly moved toward the crest where McLaws immediately ascertained they would be spotted if they continued. The men of Kershaw's brigade, having stopped near the bridge, watched as Longstreet and his staff galloped past only to meet the returning McLaws somewhere opposite the road.[36]

General Longstreet presumed McLaws' halted column would soon move forward. When it did not, he sent a courier riding to the front to inquire as to the reason for the unexpected delay. His messenger returned with a report that the column was awaiting direction from Captain Johnston, who was trying to find a suitable route for the march that did not fall under the view of the Federal signal station. Looking across the way at Little Round Top, Longstreet could see the signal station was clearly visible, which meant that enemy observers could also see his large scale movement of troops and guns. The sight must have triggered both frustration and anger with Lee's corps commander. In his opinion, "further efforts to conceal ourselves would be a waste of time. I became very impatient at this delay, and determined to take upon myself the responsibility of hurrying the troops forward. I did not order General McLaws forward because, as the head of the column, he had direct orders from Lee to follow the conduct of Colonel [sic] Johnston."[37]

At the time, Lafayette McLaws and his staff were riding well out in front of his division, which had slowly resumed its march. As the road crested a small hill, Little Round Top "was plainly visible, with the flags of the signal men in rapid motion." After sending a rider back to halt his division, McLaws rode with Johnston rapidly around the vicinity to see if there was an alternative road which might conceal their planned movement from the distant Yankee signal men. Not finding any, McLaws

---

35 *Bachelder Maps, Second Day.*

36 Kershaw to Bachelder, March 20, 1876, *Bachelder Papers*, 1:452-58; USGS MRC 39077G2.

37 "Longstreet's Account of the Campaign and Battle," *SHSP.*

This modern photo looks south down present-day Black Horse Tavern Road from atop "Longstreet's Bald Knob" toward West Pitzer's Woods. *Sal Prezioso Collection*

rejoined his command, where he encountered General Longstreet. "What is the matter?" Longstreet demanded. McLaws replied, "Ride with me and I will show you that we can't go on the route, according to instruction, without being seen by the enemy." They rode to the top of the hill, where Longstreet realized the predicament. "Why this won't do," he remarked. "Is there no way to avoid it?" McLaws told him of his morning reconnaissance, mentioning that the only way to get to that safe route to Willoughby Run was by countermarching. "Then all right," the corps commander responded. Exactly how long Longstreet and McLaws were gone has never been ascertained. Kershaw noted that "those gentlemen" (Longstreet and McLaws) returned to the halted column, with "both manifesting considerable irritation." "McLaws ordered 'Countermarch,'" Kershaw recalled, "and we filed to the rear passing nearly on the same ground as before."[38]

Instead of facing about his entire division to avoid congestion, McLaws likely ordered Kershaw to have the leading 3rd South Carolina perform two column lefts to complete a 180-degree reverse direction. By doing this, the 3rd headed north back up the Black Horse Tavern Road, passing the rest of the brigade which was facing southward. The regiment followed Forney's farm lane up Herr's Ridge until

38   Lafayette McLaws, "Gettysburg," *SHSP,* 3:391-92; Kershaw to Bachelder, March 20, 1876, *Bachelder Papers,* 1:452-58.

it reached Herr's Tavern Road. It finally passed Brig. Gen. William T. Wofford's halted Georgians, the last of McLaws' four brigades. Instead of continuing to the intersection of Herr's Tavern Road with the Old Mill Road, Captain Johnston and General McLaws ushered the South Carolinians southeast down an unnamed trace well south of Dr. Hall's house. Using thick timber to screen their movement, they continued down the eastern slope of Herr's Ridge some 900 yards to the Stallsmith residence.[39]

General Kershaw's column began marching along the Old Mill Road, passing Hood's division. It proved chaotic, with two divisions and two artillery battalions all clogging the same road. "The brigade moved back to the place where we had rested in the morning," Kershaw continued, "and thence by a country road to Willoughby Run, then dry, and down that to the school-house beyond Pitzer's Woods." This "country road" shortcut allowed McLaws' division to hold its position in the lead.[40]

However, Longstreet's decision to allow McLaws, Cabell, and Henry to use the same road as Hood infuriated the former, who later blamed Hood for pressing his division forward "so that it lapped considerably, creating confusion in the countermarch." According to McLaws, Longstreet rode over to him and said, "General, there is so much confusion, owing to Hood's division being mixed up with yours, suppose you let him countermarch first and lead in the attack." McLaws, perhaps feeling this would slight his and his men's honor, implored, "General, as I started in the lead, let me continue so." Longstreet supposedly agreed and then rode off. Here again the reasoning on Longstreet's part to redirect his column as he did during the countermarch was sound. He did so not to appease McLaws, as his estranged subordinate later claimed, but because he did not want to entangle eight batteries of artillery on narrow routes in timber behind slow-moving infantry.[41]

With the artillerists mounted atop limbers and caissons the detached battalions rumbled down the Old Mill Road as Kershaw's men used the "country road" to the south. Moving at a steady clip, Colonel Cabell led his guns south off the Old Mill Road at the Harmon farm toward the Stallsmith house. Throwing out flankers for protection and continuing south past Kershaw's front, Cabell's column rolled past the Finnefrock home. Passing over the "old road to Hagerstown," Cabell directed

39 Ibid.

40 Ibid.

41 McLaws, "Gettysburg," *SHSP,* vol. VII, 69.

This 19th century view along Willoughby Run looks southwest. Once General Longstreet's countermarch was underway, both McLaws' and Hood's divisions, accompanied by Cabell's and Henry's artillery battalions, were redirected down Willoughby Run. *Sal Prezioso Collection*

his guns onto the rural Willoughby Run Road just west of and above the run heading south toward the Samuel Dixon farm 100 yards distant.[42]

Once Cabell and Henry had cleared the way, a clearly agitated Hood was finally able to turn the head of his column south on Old Mill Road trailing the guns. However, he again had to halt and his vanguard became tangled with Kershaw's rearmost regiments. This unfortunate mishap created another short, confusing delay and was the straw that broke the camel's back, at least as far as Hood was concerned. It still made perfect sense to him that if McLaws was to support his advance "up the Emmitsburg Road" off his left flank, it would be prudent that his division lead the way. It is uncertain exactly how long it took to get the two divisions back on track, but more time was being wasted and the afternoon sun dipped lower.[43]

In the lead, the 3rd South Carolina continued its slow march down the "country road," becoming the first infantry regiment in McLaws' division to pass over the Fairfield Road about 2:15 p.m. As they entered the relatively dry creek bed

42   Ibid.

43   USGS MRC 39077G2.

south of the road somewhere near the Samuel Dixon farm, Kershaw's remaining troops spread out using both the creek bed and the Willoughby Run Road as the column moved toward Pitzer's Woods. They believed they had remained unseen since they began the countermarch. The "gamecocks," however, were wrong.[44]

Captain James Hall, one of the Union signal officers on Little Round Top, had noticed large numbers of Confederates moving atop Herr's Ridge near Dr. Hall's residence. Captain Hall reported that "a heavy column of the enemy's infantry, about 10,000 strong, is moving from opposite our extreme left toward our right." At 2:10 p.m. Hall verified his report and added, "Those troops were passing on a by-road [Herr's Tavern Road] from Dr. Hall's house to Herr's Tavern on the Chambersburg Pike. A train of ambulances is following them." What Captain Hall undoubtedly observed was McLaws countermarching his legions atop Herr's Ridge before they disappeared into the timber south of the Hall residence. The captain, of course, had no clue McLaws had subsequently turned eastward and passed through the concealing woods down to the Old Mill Road. He naturally assumed the Rebels had continued north to the Chambersburg Pike.[45]

Hall's alarming report did not help General Sickles' situation at headquarters because it reinforced Meade's earlier supposition that Lee would feint against the Union left and then strike on the right around Culp's Hill. Lee was apparently moving troops into position for such an attack, or perhaps he intended them to be used to hit the Union right-center from across the wide open plain with support from units fronting the town. General Slocum remained steadfast in his belief that Lee would strike the far right, while Eleventh Corps commander Oliver Howard readied the remnants of his battered corps for either contingency.[46]

While Longstreet was busy counter-marching his men for miles under the bright afternoon sunshine, Meade had taken steps to bolster his line further. Lieutenant Colonel Freeman McGilvery had arrived in Gettysburg in the forenoon with his First Volunteer Artillery Reserve Brigade as well as Capt. Elijah D. Taft's Second and Capt. James F. Huntington's Third—a total of 52 guns of various calibers and capabilities. Behind them rumbled First Lt. Cornelius Gillett's artillery reserve ammunition train including Henry Hunt's so-called "ghost train" of more than 70 wagons filled with ammunition and other artillery supplies. Hunt had secretly authorized this extra materiel back when Joe Hooker commanded the army, exceeding the army's table of allowances for artillery commands.

44   Ibid.; Kershaw to Bachelder, March 20, 1876, *Bachelder Papers*, 1:452-58.

45   *OR* 27, pt. 3, 488.

46   *Bachelder Maps, Second Day.*

McGilvery had reported for duty between 11:00 and 11:30 a.m., parking all three volunteer brigades in a strategic location near the Taneytown Road on the William Patterson farm, near several other reserve batteries belonging to Capt. Dunbar Ransom's First Regular Brigade. General Tyler, under Meade's orders, had subsequently directed Lieutenant Gillett to move his reserve ammunition train toward the Old Blacksmith Shop Road, where it was turned into an open field south and west of the intersection with the Taneytown Road. The lieutenant's train was so large that staff officers and aides from Tyler's headquarters had to begin sorting out the trailing wagons. They placed the wagons in blocks, or parks, by priority in an area that spread three miles southward to the east side of the Round Tops. More than 100 of Gillett's heavy and light wagons filled a 380-acre parcel of rock-strewn, undulating meadows belonging to farmers William Patterson, Jacob Swisher, and George Spangler. Their central location, however, would allow Meade, Tyler, and/or Hunt to replenish ammunition quickly to the front-line batteries, if necessary.[47]

Gillett parked Hunt's "ghost train" somewhere east of the Round Tops where the unreported wagons quietly blended in alongside the ammunition trains of the First, Second, and Eleventh corps. The caravan contained not only ordnance and materiel for the artillery battalions, but copious amounts of provisions for the campaign trail. After serving under McClellan, Burnside, and Hooker, Henry Hunt had learned the hard way that he could not fully depend upon headquarters to sustain the needs of his artillery. Meade, however, was different in that Hunt respected both his character and his truthful disposition. While Longstreet countermarched, Hunt readied his 114 cannon of various calibers, together with the associated limbers, caissons, forges, supply wagons, and 1,717 men and 1,785 horses. It was an imposing and powerful display of a well-planned, highly efficient artillery support function.[48]

General Tyler's artillery park was perfectly situated for any contingency. Three important routes intersecting the Taneytown Road provided convenient transport lanes to get ammunition and supplies quickly to Hancock's line on Cemetery Ridge or southward to Sickles. These routes were, from south to north, the Millerstown Crossroad (present-day Wheatfield Road), the George Weikert farm lane through Patterson's Woods, and the Hummelbaugh farm lane (now Pleasonton Avenue) near the Union center. In addition, other routes led eastward to the Baltimore Pike to move materiel efficiently to Howard's forces on Cemetery Hill. Tyler could move guns or caissons along Granite Schoolhouse Road or Old Blacksmith Shop

---

47 OR 27, pt. 1, 872, 878, 891-92; USGS MRC 39077G2.

48 USGS MRC 390772G; *Bachelder Maps, Second Day.*

Road, which merged into what is now Hospital Road. The latter intersected the Baltimore Pike below Power's Hill across from McAllister's Mill. Any battery then in Tyler's expansive park could reach any part of Meade's interior line within 15-30 minutes.[49]

To ease congestion in his extensive park, Tyler ordered all working battery forges and supporting wagons to move north of the Granite Schoolhouse Road. He established a repair and restoration park beyond the country schoolhouse along a sluggish brook some 700 yards east of the Taneytown Road. The tradesmen who shod horses and repaired wheels, axles, limbers, caissons, and guns worked as one team to get damaged ordnance and hardware back in the battle, no matter from which command. It was a novel, and effective, concept. Lieutenant Gulian Weir of Battery C, 5th U. S. noted he had seen numerous artillery parks before, "but this was different, big and being quiet." The afternoon passed in relative peace as the batteries rested and waited.[50]

The efficiency and innovation of the artillery organization traced its origins to the past winter when Hunt and Maj. Gen. John F. Reynolds had spent hours while encamped near Falmouth, Virginia, writing or rewording a series of documents for Hooker in an attempt to increase the authority of the role of the army's chief of artillery. They needed to cut red tape, quickly, in order to expedite ammunition to front-line batteries that needed to be resupplied. Hunt, with Reynolds' blessing, introduced a general order that would authorize a single signature from an ordnance officer, adjutant, or even a caisson teamster to requisition ordnance, materiel, and/or ammunition. Hooker accepted and signed the order on May 17. The first officers to take advantage of this new procedure during the battle of Gettysburg were Colonel Wainwright and Major Osborn, whose empty caissons had been parked off Baltimore Pike south of Evergreen Cemetery since before dawn.[51]

Although they had been issued a few rounds from Captain Ransom's Regular Reserve Brigade, Wainwright and Osborn had welcomed the chance to resupply from Gillett's reserve ammunition wagons and caissons. Every battery then on line atop Cemetery Hill over time had sent limbers and caissons rumbling southward to the park. Using both the Baltimore Pike and the Taneytown Road, they rolled into

---

49 OR 27, pt. 1, 872, 878, 891-92; USGS MRC 39077G2.

50 Gulian Weir to father, July 5, 1863, copy in GNMP; David Shultz, "Gulian V. Weir's 5th U. S. Artillery, Battery C," *Gettysburg Magazine,* no. 18, 82. Tyler would establish a secondary reserve ammunition park the night of July 2 along a sluggish creek east of army headquarters near the location of the present-day Gettysburg Visitor's Center.

51 OR 27, pt. 1, 233; Longacre, *Man Behind the Guns,* 178.

Gillett's ammunition park and filled their chests having had someone other than a senior officer sign for the received ordnance. When the heavily-laden caissons returned to Cemetery Hill, the drivers discovered that General Tyler, anticipating the need, had already sent wagons full of ammunition to their respective parks. Crews were busy loading the ammunition into limbers and any wagons that could hold it.[52]

By contrast, as the afternoon wore on and Hunt's guns readied for action, across the battlefield the Confederate artillerists did not enjoy the same foresight, innovation, and efficiency. Although their operations appeared to be moving as well as possible under the present circumstances, the artillery officers could not proactively institute independent orders like their Federal counterparts. Lee's chain of command for his "long arm" was too demanding and too old in its ways and procedures. There was no way General Pendleton could have assumed the same responsibilities as Hunt. First and foremost, Pendleton's position was imbedded within Lee's staff. He could not and did not demonstrate his own opinions and initiatives, let alone issue orders to anyone without Lee's direct consent. On the contrary, the aggressive Hunt influenced many outside his immediate command by invoking Meade's name, and was seldom, if ever, questioned about it. On his own authority and without consulting Meade, Hunt had sent his aide galloping to Tyler's artillery park for reinforcements for Sickles' advanced front. Pendleton enjoyed no such autonomy.

For example, unlike Hunt, Parson Pendleton had no direct control over his own artillery. All Army of Northern Virginia artillery reserve batteries and trains formally belonged to the three corps, each with its own artillery reserve commander, none of whom held the rank of general. Hence, the ultimate authority for their usage and deployment lay with Longstreet, Ewell, or Hill, respectively. Although titled the "Chief of Artillery of the Army," General Pendleton lacked the specific authority to commandeer any of the three corps' artillery battalions, brigades, or guns without the corps commander's consultation and specific agreement. Pendleton also lacked an efficient ammunition specialist such as Lieutenant Gillett or a trusted subordinate such as Hunt enjoyed with General Tyler. Lee's artillery reserve would have been better used had it been under the command of one good officer in an organized, independent corps.

Hunt had already had an active and efficient day, even before the Rebels slowly moved into position for a late-afternoon assault. Many of his activities demonstrated leadership and initiative outside of his normal duties as chief of

---

52 Ibid.; Thomas W. Osborn, "The Artillery at Gettysburg," *Philadelphia Weekly Times,* May 31, 1879.

artillery. He had quickly dispatched Colonel Warner to inform Meade of Buford's premature departure. Later, before Colonel Berdan had returned from his foray into Pitzer's Woods, Hunt had dispatched aides to army headquarters with the news of the Rebel advance. And, Hunt had spotted and reported the Rebel movement west of Seminary Ridge before G. K. Warren's signal officers atop Little Round Top flashed their messages. Hunt had been magnificent thus far this day, but Meade had not seemed overly concerned about his reports, nor had the army commander openly fretted over Sickles' forward position.[53]

After Capt. Elijah Taft arrived at Gettysburg in the early afternoon with his New York battery of six 20-pounder Parrott Rifles, they had contested Graham's guns on North Benner's Hill. Shortly before 2:30, a masked Rebel battery opened fire from north of town. Meade quickly dispatched Hunt to determine the source of this new disturbance. Arriving near the cemetery gatehouse, Hunt noted that Taft had repositioned his left section to front almost due north to silence the fresh enemy position. Returning to the Leister house, he informed Meade about the tactical situation. Meade began asking various questions about the artillery, especially the available supply of ammunition. Hunt assured him all was well, especially the ammunition, and for the first time mentioned his special train. Without hesitation, Meade handed Hunt full rein of the Army of the Potomac's artillery. "I considered this . . . Order . . . as a recognition," a grateful Hunt later related, "for the present, at least, of the position I had held at Antietam and Fredericksburg, as commander of the artillery of the army, and proceeded to make the necessary dispositions and to give all directions I considered necessary during the rest of the battle."[54]

Not far from where Meade and Hunt were chatting, General Hancock and Lieutenant Colonel Morgan mounted and rode south to review the precarious situation of the left flank of the Second Corps. With south Cemetery Ridge unoccupied between Gibbon's and Caldwell's divisions, the Union center was in jeopardy if the Rebels exploited the yawning gap. Hancock found Caldwell enjoying the shade of Patterson's Woods south of the Hummelbaugh farm lane. Hancock reportedly pointed south toward George Weikert's stone house and ordered Caldwell to be ready to take his division down that way. It was a gamble, as it would widen the opening. "The Third Corps having advanced far beyond the original line

---

53 Ibid.; George Meade Jr. to Henry Hunt, July 22, 1886, LOC; Longacre, *The Man Behind the Guns*, 162-63; *OR* 27, pt. 1, 891.

54 Hunt, "The Second Day at Gettysburg," *B & L*, vol. III, 293; *JCCW*, 448; *OR* 27, pt. 1, 232; Pfanz, *Gettysburg: Second Day*, 140-42; USGS MRC 39077G2; George Meade Jr. to Henry Hunt, July 22, 1886, LOC. Meade never made nor offered a change in Hunt's official status. He remained a brevet brigadier for the entire war.

of battle," Hancock later penned, "and Caldwell's division having been detached, a larger interval remained on the left of the Second [Gibbon's] division without troops."[55]

For all he tried, Hancock, like Hunt, could not persuade Meade to ride to the crest of Cemetery Ridge and see for himself what was occurring, particularly the danger Sickles' move presented. With Buford gone there was little if any reliable information making its way back to Pleasonton or army headquarters from the far left. Aside from the reports from Warren's signal station on Little Round Top, one could easily get comfortable in believing from the lack of information that all was well. The problem was a lack of good visuals on the most likely jump-off points for any Confederate attacks on the far left. Hobart Ward did have skirmishers spread south of Millerstown Road several hundred yards west of the Emmitsburg Road, but other potential Rebel avenues of attack were out of sight of Union eyes, other than the signal station. Hancock's problem was no different than that of Sickles or Hunt. No one quite knew if the Rebels would try the left or left-center, and Meade was still somewhat concerned about his right.

That worry soon increase. Lieutenant Aaron Jerome relayed another message from Little Round Top: "Over a division of rebels is making a flank movement on our right, the line extends over a mile and is advancing, skirmishing. There is nothing but cavalry to oppose them." Jerome's warning captured Meade's attention. Jerome likely saw Confederate infantry pressing back Gregg's cavalry at the William Storrick and Henry Brinkerhoff farms on Brinkerhoff's Ridge. Confronted by superior numbers, the slowly-retiring Southern riflemen opposite Gregg had received reinforcements from Walker's "Stonewall Brigade," which took the offensive and pushed Gregg back. Stretched thin from just south of the Hanover Road northward to the York Pike, this was almost certainly the "mile-long" line of skirmishers Jerome reported seeing.[56]

While Meade looked again to his right flank, Hancock remained seriously concerned about his Second Corps' position. His ride southward with Morgan revealed many faults, among them that the declining ground between the Emmitsburg Road and southern Cemetery Ridge was open and suitable for an enemy offensive drive from the west, with plenty of undulating cover to negate artillery fire. Humphreys' division was apparently in no hurry to assume its expected position back on the ridge, which would have released Caldwell's division

---

55 OR 27, pt. 1, 370.

56 OR 27, pt. 3, 489; Hall, *The Stand of the United States Army at Gettysburg*, 284-88; USGS MRC 39077G2; *Bachelder Maps, Second Day*.

to return to its initial position bisecting the Codori meadow-Hummelbaugh farm lane.[57]

As a result Hancock's center remained exposed, with Caldwell's First Division now entirely isolated and unable to support his Second and Third divisions to the north. They remained vulnerable to an attack coming through the gap in the lines if Caldwell could not be returned as desired. At least Caldwell himself was not in imminent danger. Any attack from the west on his position would first run into Birney's and Humphreys' Third Corps divisions, buffering the immediate impact. Off to Caldwell's rear, the Fifth Corps could provide additional relief if needed.[58]

It was Gibbon's left, exposed by the gap in the line, that most concerned Hancock. The position would become even weaker if Sickles fed regiments to the west-southwest toward the Sherfy peach orchard. The bulk of Brig. Gen. Joseph Carr's brigade of Humphreys' division still rested above Plum Run. However, Hancock could see Carr detaching individual regiments to the southwest and west as skirmishers, and so sent an aide galloping back to headquarters to inform Meade about these new issues. When Hancock learned that Brewster's and Burling's brigades were likewise sitting idle to the left of Carr, the frustrated Second Corps commander had had enough. Spurring his horse toward Meade's headquarters, he disappeared over Cemetery Ridge.[59]

Meanwhile, Meade called a council to convene at 3:00 p.m. It is difficult to believe that he was still unaware of the vulnerable gap to Hancock's left. Hunt had explained the situation several times as 3:00 p.m. drew near. Hancock and Hunt likely knew that potential help was on the way if the Confederates continued to dawdle, with the head of Sedgwick's Sixth Corps reportedly just a few miles away trudging up Baltimore Pike. However, their value in a pitched fight later in the afternoon was questionable. Sedgwick's soldiers would need some rest after enduring an all-night forced march during which hundreds of men dropped by the wayside. Meade informed Major General Halleck, "The Sixth Corps is just coming in, very much worn out. I have awaited the attack of the enemy [and] I have a strong position for defensive. . . . He has been moving on both my flanks apparently. Expecting a battle, I have ordered the trains to the rear."[60]

* * *

57 Ibid.

58 OR 27, pt. 1, 531; "Humphreys Testimony," *JCCW,* 391; USGS MRC 39077G2.

59 Cleaves, *Meade of Gettysburg,* 147.

60 OR 27, pt. 1, 27.

Hancock would have been even more worried had he known that little more than a mile to the west, Longstreet's two divisions were marching to prepare for a massive assault. Sometime between 2:15 and 2:30 p.m., Col. James Walton, Longstreet's chief of reserve artillery, and his staff galloped past Kershaw's brigade as it entered Pitzer's Woods. Making his way around the foot-soldiers, Walton reached Pitzer's Schoolhouse where Cabell, Alexander, and Major Henry waited. Dismounting, Walton relayed Longstreet's latest plans to his fellow artillery officers. Longstreet had instructed Walton to surge ahead of the deploying infantry. Likely armed with details from Pendleton's and Johnston's earlier reconnaissance patrols, Walton knew of the rural trace ascending Warfield Ridge angling east-southeast through Biesecker's Woods. He would lead Cabell's and Henry's guns forward, leaving Alexander to tend to his own battalion as he followed in their wake. He warned Alexander to stay under cover until Cabell and Henry opened so they could cover his deployment.[61]

Colonel Walton led his three battalions back onto the old Willoughby Run Road as the men from McLaws' last two brigades, Barkdales' and Wofford's, made way for the passing artillery. With Cabell's battalion leading the way, Walton headed south toward the old Millerstown Road and then east before splashing across Willoughby Run. At John Flaharty's farm, Walton and Cabell led the column up the rural trace that intersected Millerstown Road east of Willoughby Run. Angling up Warfield Ridge, they passed Kershaw's and Semmes' brigades to their right advancing toward Biesecker's Woods. Behind the guns, Hood's column had to wait for the last of Alexander's caissons to clear the road before the infantry could continue moving south beyond McLaws' division, as planned.[62]

Luckily for Walton, no Yankee pickets occupied the thick belt of hardwood trees. As both Pendleton and Johnston had reported, the woods would provide excellent cover for artillery and infantry columns to ascend Warfield Ridge undetected. Reaching the wide wooded crest, Walton and Cabell halted their column and went forward to reconnoiter. A dirt road paralleled the crest, paralleled with a stone wall. They crossed over and gained good vantage points to survey the terrain to the east. To their astonishment, they learned that masses of Yankees were waiting for them. They watched in disbelief as enemy troops in large number moved along the Emmitsburg Road Rise. No Yankees were supposed to be there, at least according to the earlier reports. Ahead of them, an intersecting farm lane led

---

61   OR 27, pt. 2, 429; USGS MRC 39077G2; *Bachelder Maps, Second Day.* Alexander specifically stated that he and his battalion received orders to accompany McLaws' and Hood's divisions without as much as one word regarding Cabell's or Henry's battalions.

62   USGS MRC 39077G2; *Bachelder Maps, Second Day.*

east toward Philip Snyder's small farmyard; beyond it some 200 yards lay the Emmitsburg Road. Taking a few moments to ponder the changed tactical situation, Walton and Cabell agreed that Cabell would lead his column into an open field due north of Snyder's residence, while Walton continued down the trace with Henry's battalion angling southeast toward that avenue's intersection with the Emmitsburg Road.[63]

As the guns began rumbling into position and Longstreet's infantry advanced eastward, out of their sight at the modest Leister house on the Taneytown Road, General Meade convened his 3:00 p.m. council of war. Early arrivals included Warren and Slocum, who were inside the home discussing the situation with new First Corps commander Maj. Gen. John Newton. They did not believe retreat was a viable option, but agreed to hold off any offensive movement for the time being. Howard did not offer an opinion. Outside of the house, Sykes was conferring with his closest staff officers when Hancock arrived, dismounted, and relayed news of the Third Corps' ever-precarious position. Meade was already aware of Hancock's dissatisfaction, for he had recently met with Lieutenant Colonel Morgan. The timing could not have been better for Hancock when one of General Warren's aides reined in his lathered horse and rushed to Warren's side. After listening to him, Warren ushered the young man to Meade, where he repeated that Sickles had advanced about three-quarters of a mile in front of Cemetery Ridge. The multiple reports left no doubt that the left was now in jeopardy.[64]

Meade cancelled the meeting, and all corps commanders except Sykes headed back to their respective commands. The new army commander had been thrown into his position of responsibility without warning, and had moved to counter Lee's invasion, obeying his orders to cover both Baltimore and Washington. He had the Baltimore Pike well covered and his road network secure. If the Confederates did not attack, he anticipated Lee would attempt to turn or roll up one of his flanks. The defensive position he had adopted was on good defensive terrain, and his fishhook-shaped line gave him the advantage of the interior position. Meade had, observed one historian, "reunited divisions of the same corps, moved two weakened First Corps divisions into reserve, and systematically strengthened his line from the far left to the far right. The army staff, including the Signal Corps, was in full operation. Meade was not sure of Lee's specific intentions, but he was aware of dangerous activity on both flanks. To cover probable attack areas, he had two battle weary First Corps divisions in reserve on his right center and with the Fifth in

63 Ibid.; Pfanz, *Gettysburg: The Second Day*, 116-21; Wise, *The Long Arm of Lee*, 756, 851.

64 Cleaves, *Meade at Gettysburg*, 147.

rear of his left." Everything was in hand except for Dan Sickles and his Third Corps. Meade had to rectify his left—and fast.[65]

Within a few moments of General Sykes' departure, Henry Hunt rode up after completing yet another inspection of Cemetery Hill. While there, he, Wainwright, and Osborn agreed to move a few batteries around to better cover the hill's western and eastern slopes, while at the same time keeping watch and ample firepower trained northward. After exchanging a few words with Meade concerning artillery placements, Hunt received an update on the situation with Sickles and ordered to ride to him again and instruct him to return to his designated position on lower Cemetery Ridge.[66]

Before Hunt could depart Sickles himself arrived at the Leister house in company with Major Tremain and Capt. Alexander Moore. Ordered not to dismount, Sickles exchanged a few words with the irritated army commander before inviting him to ride back and see things for himself. Meade informed his subordinate that he had other things to do, but would be along when he finished. When Sickles asked if General Warren could join him, Meade rejected that proposition as well: Warren would be attending to other duties. Meade instead offered his chief of artillery. With Hunt and Colonel Warner in tow, Sickles swung his horse around and put spurs to its flank, departing the Leister house after accomplishing nothing that would boost his standing, at least as far as Meade was concerned.[67]

On his journey southwest toward the army's left flank, Hunt surely noticed that the Union center just north of Hummelbaugh's farm lane had been left unprotected. Gibbon's division at the time was but an empty shell of its former self, with many of his regiments either forward on picket duty or detached south to cover the gap and support batteries. What he could not see was the growing presence of the Rebels across the fields on the wooded ridges to the west. McLaws had begun deploying his forward regiments near the crest of South Seminary Ridge and North Warfield Ridge (with the Millerstown Road bisecting the ridges and McLaws' division as it deployed). Hunt also, of course, did not know that Hood's two brigades were even then passing over the Millerstown Road heading south to

---

65 Ibid.; David B. Downs, "His Left Was Worth a Glance: Meade and the Union Left on July 2, 1863," *Gettysburg Magazine*, no. 7, 1992.

66 Hunt, "The Second Day at Gettysburg," *Battles & Leaders*, vol. III, 297.

67 Tremain to Sickles, June 26, 1886, *National Tribune*, July 15, 1876.

get into position to sweep up the Emmitsburg Road as ordered, or that Colonel Walton was busy selecting favorable firing platforms for his guns.[68]

Arriving at Third Corps headquarters, Hunt was astonished to see how quickly Sickles had redeveloped his forward line since his last visit. Sickles had secured the Emmitsburg Road Rise and its intersection with the Millerstown Road. General Birney had redeployed several of Ward's regiments elsewhere, moving Graham's brigade and detached regiments from Burling's brigade to replace them. Hunt could see Birney's first line of skirmishers, including some of Colonel Berdan's green-clad sharpshooters, some 200 yards west of the Emmitsburg Road, with a formidable second skirmish line in the roadway. The main battle line rested from 100 to 300 yards east of the plank fence paralleling the road. Looking due south, he could see other regiments of Graham's brigade moving forward into position.[69]

Colonel Calvin A. Craig was moving his 105th Pennsylvania west-northwest in the general direction of Hunt and Sickles, with Col. Peter Sides' 57th Pennsylvania in tow. The two veteran regiments halted short of the Emmitsburg Road and the men went prone in an open field east of the thoroughfare. Meanwhile, forward pioneers busily dismantled the plank fence north of Sherfy's farm, tearing apart every other section to facilitate easy passage for troops and guns if needed. To Hunt, sitting in his saddle at the intersection of Trostle's farm lane and the Emmitsburg Road, the lane appeared to be the dividing line between Birney's and Humphreys' commands.[70]

To the north of Hunt, Bucklyn's Rhode Island battery occupied the ground to his immediate right. Beyond the six gleaming Napoleons lay Humphreys' division, which also boasted a second line of reinforced skirmishers along the road. He had deployed in long double line with regiments both east and west of the road. About 400 yards north of the intersection sat Seeley's Battery K, 4th U. S. Artillery, which had unlimbered immediately south of Klingle's farm. Several companies from Carr's and Brewster's brigades occupied the yard and orchards. Beyond them, Humphreys' line continued another 400 or so yards north toward the Rogers house.[71]

For the second time this day, Sickles asked Hunt what he thought of the position. Hunt replied that it was not his decision, and that Meade's general order was for Sickles to have deployed both of his divisions on Cemetery Ridge. Hunt's

68 USGS MRC 39077G2; *Bachelder Maps, Second Day;* Hessler, *Sickles at Gettysburg,* 119.

69 Ibid.

70 Ibid.

71 Ibid.; Woods, *Ebb and Flow,* 146-47.

reply surely dismayed Sickles. After all, it was Hunt who had earlier positioned Clark's New Jersey battery atop the crest to support Ward's brigade. Hunt had ridden the proposed line with Captain Randolph suggesting battery placements, not to mention demanding infantry support for them. Hunt had not only promised two batteries from the reserve park, but had urged Sickles to send Berdan's reconnaissance to Pitzer's Woods. Lastly, it was Hunt who agreed that Ward's brigade should replace Buford's retiring cavalry. And now, Hunt had the audacity to inform Sickles that none of this was his decision—even as his two promised batteries sat not 300 yards away to the east. Whatever specifically transpired between Sickles and Hunt at this time, the latter made it clear he was not responsible for anything contrary to Meade's general plan.[72]

"The primary disadvantage of Sickles' position was that the Third Corps was too far in advance of Meade's army to receive support," explained James Hessler in his award-winning study *Sickles at Gettysburg*. "Meade's reinforcements had to cover ½ mile of open ground and Sickles negated Meade's interior lines. The essentially straight line along Cemetery Ridge, which Meade intended Sickles to occupy, was approximately 1,600 yards in length. Sickles' Third Corps had roughly 10,675 effectives and he would later claim that he lacked sufficient strength to man Meade's front. Yet the new position covered a front that was nearly twice as long; approximately 3,500 yards. Despite his efforts to refuse them, his flanks were in the air."[73] Hunt knew all this, and perhaps as the hour of combat drew near, was having second thoughts himself.

Although Hunt tried disassociating himself from Sickles' decision to move forward, it was too late now to withdraw. He knew the Third Corps needed even more artillery support to hold the line, and that the seven batteries then in position could not properly cover the 3,500-yard line, especially considering the stands of timber and many hollows and ravines between the regiments. Descending the rise with Sickles, Hunt returned to the Third Corps headquarters, where he found artillery chief Captain Randolph. After a few minutes discussion, Hunt and Colonel Warner joined Randolph on an inspection of each battery's position. Although Hunt could readily see Clark's, Bucklyn's, and Seeley's batteries along the Emmitsburg Road (as well as Thompson's and Ames' reserve batteries in park), he had no clue where Randolph had placed Winslow's Battery D, 1st New York or Smith's 4th New York.[74]

---

72   "Sickles' Testimony," *JCCW*, 299.

73   Hessler, "Sickles at Gettysburg Sketch," GNMP.

74   "Sickles' Testimony," *JCCW*, 299.

Maj. Gen. George Sykes,
commanding Fifth Corps,
Army of the Potomac
LOC

Within a quarter-hour or so of Sickles' departure from army headquarters following Meade's aborted council, General Warren returned to the Leister house after visiting his signal station east of the Taneytown Road. He never had a chance to dismount, because Meade invited him to ride with him to see Sickles. With several aides, guards, and staff officers in tow, the party headed southward along the crest of Cemetery Ridge. Shortly after passing over Hummelbaugh's farm lane, Warren offered his opinion, "This is where [Sickles'] line should be." According to Warren, this was the first time Meade became fully aware of just how far west Sickles had moved. While descending the ridge southwest, Meade's group must have noticed Lieutenant Sheldon's Battery B, 1st New York to their left as they rode past Caldwell's front.[75]

Meade sent several couriers galloping off to Sykes to hurry him along. Unknown to Meade, Sickles had already sent an aide seeking support from the Fifth Corps' commander. Sickles' rider apparently reached Sykes first, but the general again refused to move his division strictly on Sickles' request without authorization from headquarters. Some observers have speculated that Sykes, a veteran Regular Army officer, did not respect the request of the volunteer political general, one with a shady past and questionable leadership qualities. He finally began moving his men in Sickles' direction only after Meade's courier arrived with the requisite order.[76]

Back at Sickles' headquarters at the Trostle farm, word arrived that Meade was approaching with his entourage. Riding out to meet him, Sickles and his staff halted

75 Eugene Gifford Taylor, *Gouverneur Kemble Warren: The Life and Letters of an American Soldier* (Boston: 1932), 122; USGS MRC 39077G2; *Bachelder Maps, Second Day*.

76 OR 27, pt. 1, 592; Earl Schenck Miers and Richard A. Brown, *Gettysburg* (New Brunswick, NJ: Rutgers University Press, 1948), 133-35; Cleaves, *Meade of Gettysburg*, 148.

east of Plum Run, where the rising ground offered a decent vista of his position. Meade immediately chastised Sickles: "General, I am afraid you are too far out." When Sickles attempted to explain the favorable topography, Meade abruptly stopped him. "General Sickles, this is in some respects higher ground than that to the rear, but there is still higher in front of you, and if you keep advancing you will find it constantly higher ground all the way to the mountains."[77]

While Meade and Sickles conversed, off to the west Longstreet prepared to attack. Sometime between 3:45 and 4:15 p.m., Colonel Cabell led his artillery battalion through the woods toward an open field north of Snyder's farm lane. A stone wall blocked immediate access (although Cabell could have used the farm lane to enter the field farther eastward), his gunners spent time moving enough rocks to create several passageways to file through by section. Fanning out in the meadow between the wood line and the Emmitsburg Road, Cabell's battalion formed a ragged crescent facing north by northeast. From north to south (left to right from the colonel's perspective) Cabell aligned as follows: a section of Capt. H. H. Carlton's Troup (Georgia) Artillery (two 12-pounder howitzers); Capt. B. C. Manley's 1st North Carolina (Ellis's) Artillery (two Napoleons and two Ordnance Rifles); Carlton's second section of two 10-pounder Parrott Rifles; Capt. E. S. McCarthy's 1st Richmond Howitzers (two Napoleons and two Ordnance Rifles); and finally nearest the Emmitsburg Road, Capt. J. C. Fraser's Pulaski (Georgia) Artillery (two Ordnance Rifles and two 10-pounder Parrotts). Cabell ran all 16 caissons up to the stone wall, where they remained under the cover of the canopy of trees. It was a formidable gun line, capable of both long- and short-range support for the impending infantry assault. Gun chiefs began sighting the distant Yankee positions and judging ranges.[78]

Having followed Colonel Walton's column toward the Emmitsburg Road some 400 yards south of Captain Fraser's Georgians, Major Henry stopped his battalion long enough for him and Walton to assess the situation. As Cabell unlimbered to the north, Walton and Henry led Capt. James Reilly's Rowan (North Carolina) Artillery across the Emmitsburg Road onto the country lane that Colonel Long and Captain Johnston had used on their reconnaissance earlier that morning. Leaving Reilly's two 12-pounder Napoleons in Biesecker's Woods as a reserve, Walton placed Reilly's two 3-inch Ordnance Rifles 300 yards east of the road atop a

77 Isaac R. Pennypacker, *Great Commanders: General Meade* (New York: D. Appleton and Co., 1901), 169.

78 Samuel Ringgold, *School of Battery: Instruction for Field Artillery: Horse and Foot* (Washington: U. S. Government Printing Office, 1845), 118-46; *Bachelder Maps, Second Day*; Murray, "E. P. Alexander and the Artillery Action in the Peach Orchard," 42-43.

low elongated rise. For the time being, Reilly's right piece marked the far right of Lee's Army of Northern Virginia.[79]

Captain H. R. Garden unlimbered his Palmetto (South Carolina) Artillery's two Napoleons and two 10-pounder Parrotts Rifles left of Reilly. Captain W. K. Bachman dropped his four smoothbores of the German (South Carolina) Artillery to the left of Garden, with Capt. A. C. Latham's Branch (North Carolina) Artillery remaining west of the road 50 yards to Bachman's left. Reilly's remaining two Parrotts unlimbered in line west of the road with Latham's trio of Napoleons.[80]

Trailing Henry's battalion up the Millerstown Road to the Flaharty farmyard, Porter Alexander's battalion had the shortest distance to travel to reach position. After following the trace perhaps 200 yards, Alexander halted his limbered guns in a field just east of and above Flaharty's farm. Like Cabell to the south, several of Alexander's men walked through the woods and began disassembling portions of the bordering stone wall to clear a right of way for the limbered guns to file through by section.[81]

After getting his guns through the various openings, Alexander spread out his battalion to maximize their net field of fire. He established his right flank some 70-80 yards north of Cabell's leftmost guns (a section of Carlton's battery). Alexander's line from south to north (right to left, continuing the Confederate gun line northward) with Capt. W. W. Parker's Virginia Battery (four 12-pounder howitzers) anchoring his right; Capt. O. B. Taylor's four Napoleons near the Warfield house; and then Capt. Pichegru Woolfolk's Ashland Battery's two Napoleons and two 20-pounder Parrotts in Warfield's orchard north of the barn. Captain T. C. Jordan's four ordnance rifles were next in line and then Capt. George V. Moody's Madison Louisiana Artillery (four 24-pounder howitzers). The four 12-pounder howitzers of Lt. S. C. Gilbert's Brooks (South Carolina) Battery anchored Alexander's left. Moody and Gilbert were about 75 yards to Jordan's left

---

79 Ibid.

80 Ibid.; OR 27, pt. 2, 375, 428; Pfanz, Gettysburg: Second Day, 160-61. Confederate batteries at Gettysburg typically had four guns, often of mixed types, while all but one of Henry Hunt's Union batteries utilized the same type of cannon. (Sterling's 2nd Connecticut was the only Federal battery without the same caliber of guns.) For example, James Reilly commanded six guns, two more than the usual Confederate battery, but each section had different calibers— two 12-pounder Napoleons in one section, two ordnance rifles in the second, and two 10-pounder Parrott rifles in the other section. Almost all Federal batteries had the distinct advantage of needing to carry only one type of ammunition into action.

81 Ringgold, School of Battery; USGS MRC 39077G2; Bachelder Maps, Second Day.

and rear, and about 40 yards east of Pitzer's Woods. The left of Alexander's gun line unlimbered some 900 yards northwest of the Millerstown Road.[82]

As the gunners prepared their pieces, Longstreet's infantry began taking up their assault positions. Hood's column continued moving south beyond the Millerstown Road as McLaws began forming his battle line. Barksdale's Mississippi brigade filed through the woods toward the stone wall where Porter Alexander had parked his reserve caissons. Jordan's, Moody's and Gilbert's dozen combined pieces were out of their view beyond the edge of the woods. The men settled down to rest in the welcome shade of the trees. McLaws and Kershaw spurred their horses onto the wooded crest of Warfield Ridge as Alexander unlimbered the last of his guns. While Kershaw's and General Paul Semmes' brigades settled in the fields east of Biesecker's Woods and south of the Millerstown Road, McLaws later claimed to be astonished to see thousands of Union troops before him. He should not have been surprised, because Kershaw had earlier watched Yankees strengthening this very position from his vantage point at Dr. Hall's place, and would have informed him so.[83]

Meanwhile, John Bell Hood had taken his veteran division down present-day Red Rock Road before ordering it up Warfield Ridge by the left flank. As Hood and his men ascended the slope, his scouts returned from a recent reconnaissance of the terrain east of the Emmitsburg Road. They indicated that if he continued east and bypassed the mountain (Big Round Top), he would not only come in on the left and rear of the Union army, but would also be among their parked trains (Tyler and Gillett, as well as those of the First, Second, and Eleventh Corps). The Taneytown Road was wide open for the taking. Accordingly, Hood sent a few Texan runners ahead to verify the scouts' report while he sent a courier galloping to inform Longstreet of this new development.[84]

On Hood's left, McLaws, instead of sending a rider to inform Longstreet that Yankees were not where they were supposed to be, decided to report in person. He found the corps commander somewhere north of the Millerstown Road and explained his unexpected predicament. Longstreet reiterated General Lee's expectations of an attack up the Emmitsburg Road. McLaws tried reasoning with the general about alternative options, but Old Peter refused his entreaties. Leaving

82 OR 27, pt. 2, 375, 379-382, 384-385; Busey and Martin, *Regimental Strengths*, 136, 142, 149; *Bachelder Maps, Second Day*.

83 McLaws, "Gettysburg," *SHSP,* Vol. 7, 1879; USGS MRC 39077G2; *Bachelder Maps, Second Day*.

84 Hood, "John Bell Hood Gettysburg Battle Report," GNMP.

Longstreet, the frustrated McLaws returned to the Warfield house to prepare his division for the attack.[85]

Within a few minutes a sudden boom rang out, followed in quick succession by another. A plume of gray smoke drifted skyward above Colonel Cabell's right flank, and all eyes turned in that direction. Across the way, no sooner had General Meade finishing lashing out at Sickles when Cabell's two opening rounds passed over Birney's line along the Emmitsburg Road and exploded in the air north of the Trostle farm lane. When Sickles muttered something about returning to Cemetery Ridge, Meade responded, "I wish to God you could, but those people will not permit it. If you need artillery call on the Reserve."

By that time Confederate missiles of every description filled the late-afternoon sky. Solid shot and bolts ricocheted and bounded across the landscape, while spherical case and shrapnel exploded overhead. Timed case and percussion shells exploded on impact or rolled along before detonating. Unfortunately for Walton and Cabell, far too many of these rounds failed to explode properly, if they exploded all. However, unbeknownst to the gun crews, a shell exploded behind Meade and showered him with debris. Luckily for the Union army commander, he and his horse galloped away unscathed.[86]

If Lee was at fault for not being at or near the front at the time he expected Longstreet to launch his attack, then General Meade should be considered equally at fault for not earlier viewing his left flank, especially with his headquarters less than a few minute's ride away. From the Copse of Trees, he could easily viewed the Emmitsburg Road south all the way to Sherfy's peach orchard and Little Round Top. He could have watched firsthand as Berdan's reconnaissance advanced into Pitzer's Woods and fought there. Instead, he sent couriers, including his son, southward each and every time a complaint reached him that Sickles' Third Corps was not in the correct position. Only belatedly had he responded in person, and now it was too late to do much about it.

---

85 McLaws, "Gettysburg," *SHSP,* Vol. 7, 1879. It should be noted that before the campaign commenced, Longstreet had debated with Lee as to how it should be conducted. What bothered Longstreet more than Lee's disagreement was the latter's silence afterward. Lee's nature was that once finished the subject was closed; it was time move on. This characterization remained true when Longstreet disagreed about how best to launch his attack on July 2, thus allegedly delaying Lee's planned offensive operation. Rather than go see in person about the delay, General Lee instead wondered aloud to subordinates, "what is taking Longstreet so long." Now, here it was after 4:00 p.m. and the delay had allowed the Union army to bolster its defenses even if Meade's right flank was in an unorthodox position. Coddington, *Gettysburg: A Study in Command,* 378-79.

86 George G. Meade, *Gettysburg Letterbook,* Meade Collection, HSP; Cleaves, *Meade of Gettysburg,* 148.

Unlike Lee whose decision and word was final, Meade in turn appears to have tried his best to appease his lieutenants. The first lengthy detailed work of the battle at Gettysburg, war correspondent William Swinton's 1886 book *Campaigns of the Army of the Potomac*, blasted Sickles for his move, but with the same pen Swinton chastised Meade for being like General Lee, who was not firm enough with his commanders when it counted. Newspaper editor Horace Greeley also noted Meade's lack of clear orders and Sickles' misinterpretation of them on July 2.[87]

Nineteenth-century author Samuel P. Bates, Pennsylvania's state historian, was blunt, stating, "It was inexplicable that General Meade did not issue specific orders to Sickles and see about the positioning of the 3d Corps in person." Sickles' later explanations for the "misunderstanding" attempted to paint Meade as incompetent, suggesting he had no choice but to move forward because of the terrible position in which Meade had originally placed him.[88]

The opening of Cabell's signal gun on July 2 confirmed the worst: Meade indeed had run out of time. Even with the lengthy delays provided by Longstreet and Lee, Meade and his immediate subordinates did not communicate well enough to take advantage of that extra time. Union correspondence within the *Official Reports* suggest a series of mishaps and miscues that at least arguably helped Lee with his own struggling plan. Even with the efficient signal stations manned by professionals, Meade and his generals did not take full advantage of all their opportunities.[89]

---

87 William Swinton, *Campaigns of the Army of the Potomac: A Critical History of the operations in Virginia, Maryland, and Pennsylvania from the Commencements to the Close of War* (New York: Charles B. Richardson, 1866), 345-56; Horace Greeley, *The American Conflict: A History of the Great War in 2 vols.* (New York: Dick and Fitzgerald, 1867), 2:381. A case in point occurred moments shortly after Captain Cabell's Confederate artillery battalion had opened the ball. When General Sickles asked, "Should I retire to the ridge?" Meade did not give him a direct and specific order. Instead of a decisive answer, Meade merely commented on the enemy. Sickles may have ridden away with a false assumption that his forward line was okay—at least that is what he later suggested to the Joint Committee on the Conduct of War. In his in-depth 20th-century study concerning July 2, historian Harry Pfanz opined, "Meade's staff poorly served their chief by not keeping him informed of all the messages received from his troops." Although it is probably true Meade did not receive all the information sent his way, it is hard to fathom that the two officers who primarily visited Sickles on his behalf that day—George Meade, Jr. and Chief of Artillery Henry Hunt—did not report back to him. Pfanz, *Gettysburg: The Second Day*, 106-107; Samuel P. Bates, *The Battle of Gettysburg* (Philadelphia: T. H. Davis & Co., 1875), 108-112.

88 Ibid. The Meade-Sickles controversy can be better understood by studying Licensed Battlefield Guide James A. Hessler's fine work *Sickles at Gettysburg*. Compounded by politics flamed by New York City's Tammany Hall members, Meade later had to defend his action and decisions before the Joint Committee on the Conduct of War.

89 OR 27, pt. 3, 489, 490.

General Warren had not accompanied Meade all the way to Sickles' headquarters. He had instead headed toward his signal station on Little Round Top, where he could see signalmen frantically wigwagging messages. Warren realized they had no infantry support if the Rebels swept in their direction. As Warren galloped southward to join his signalers, Meade met with General Caldwell, who was observing the incoming artillery barrage. He sent couriers scurrying to hurry along Sykes and to inform Slocum, Newton, and Howard of the situation. Another rider headed to General Tyler to request support from the reserve artillery park. The latter proved to be redundant, because the ever-alert Colonel Warner had raced east to fetch the rest of Freeman McGilvery's batteries and whatever else might be available.[90]

Unceremoniously put in his place, the prideful Sickles was now inclined to show Meade he could indeed remove his command back to South Cemetery Ridge whether the enemy allowed it or not. He rode over to General Humphreys with orders to move in battalions by brigade east toward the ridge behind them. Humphreys complied by issuing orders to Carr and Brewster at the same time. Both brigades began moving in unison southward before obliquing southeast in order to link with Birney's division. Other officers within view paused to watch the grand spectacle, with Brewster's men leading Carr's in battalions en mass, flags waving while drummers beat cadence. Both brigades were at the time under strength, having earlier dispatched nearly one-third of their combined firepower to support other positions along the extended Third Corps line. It was a textbook field maneuver, and one that elicited admiration from most observers.[91]

George Meade was not one of them. From his position with Caldwell, he could see what Sickles was attempting, and was livid. He realized it was now far too late to pull back, something that should have been done much earlier given the circumstances. Meade sent Maj. Benjamin Ludlow racing west to intercept Humphreys and inquire what he was doing. The surprised Humphreys was simply obeying Sickles' order to fall back, and so questioned the nature of this new order. Ludlow galloped back to Meade, who reissued the instructions as a firm directive: Humphreys would move back to the Emmitsburg Road, which he did under the general's distant eye and in splendid style.

As always, terrain played a key role. As young Union artillerist Lt. David Kinsey of Battery K, 5th U.S. had earlier pointed out, he doubted an advance would come from the west or southwest because the ground fronting Little Round Top was unfavorable, with an abundance of obstacles that would break up formations and

90 Ibid.; Pfanz, *Gettysburg: The Second Day*, 116-21.

91 "Sickles' Testimony," *JCCW*, 299; Cleaves, *Meade of Gettysburg*, 148.

create chaos for both attackers and defenders, with many places both impenetrable and indefensible. Many Union officers in the vicinity knew this fact, but across the field Lee's subordinates had no such detailed knowledge of the terrain they would soon attempt to cross. Neither Pendleton nor Johnston had included this intelligence in their earlier reports to Lee, the information he needed to formulate (and rationalize) his attack plan. The Emmitsburg Road Rise at the Sherfy farm was the only viable real estate suitable for massed military operations.[92]

West of the Emmitsburg Road, Longstreet's immediate concern was the terrain immediately in front of his assault lines. The fence-lined Millerstown Road separated McLaws' division into two parts. That could play a role in any subsequent need to reunite the brigades. It might not have been as big an issue if the Yankees were farther north and east as the early reconnaissances indicated. But now, with Sickles' front line blocking the way, McLaws realized that fusing his separated wings would be difficult. There was no way he could simply swing north up the Emmitsburg Road as originally anticipated. First, he would have to oust the thousands of blue-clad troops planted along the rise, along with their artillery supports.

Another critical terrain feature would come into play—the south branch of Plum Rum. This small, meandering tributary flowed through a shallow depression west of the Emmitsburg Road some 150 yards south of Millerstown Road. Once east of the roadway, the shallow depression became quite irregular with fairly steep banks on either side as it flowed toward the Rose Woods. Union troops and artillery on the rise in Sherfy's peach orchard enjoyed a good field of fire toward any enemy columns along the creek in that sector. Compounding the issue for McLaws, as the run continued eastward toward the Stony Hill, the ravine became deeper and rocks and timber lined the banks, potentially disrupting his formations. A 300-yard gap existed between Kershaw's left flank and Barksdale's right. The depression housing the south branch of Plum Creek ran through this gap, compounding issues of coordination.

McLaws front offered serious problems, but General Hood's were even worse. Facing the harsh terrain toward Houck's Ridge and Little Round Top, Hood studied his situation carefully with his trained eye. Isolated pockets of Union troops moved through the fields west of and below Big Round Top, some bunched together and others in small groups or individually. He realized it would be impossible to envelope the enemy's left, let alone aggressively drive up the Emmitsburg Road as Lee planned. The uneven ground would be difficult to traverse in line of battle, even if uncontested. That, of course, would not happen

---

92 USGS MRC 39077G2; *Bachelder Maps, Second Day.*

because he too had spotted Sickles' advanced position prior to his division passing over the Millerstown Road.[93]

News from his Texas scouts verified that a flank move around Big Round Top appeared viable, and Hood decided to act on it. "The reconnaissance by my Texas scouts and the development of the Federal lines were effected in a very short space of time," he later wrote to Longstreet, "in truth, shorter than I have taken to recall and jot down these facts, although the scenes and events of that day are as clear to my mind as if the great battle had been fought yesterday." Reeling from the thought of advancing into the teeth of the new Yankee position, Hood knew that even if he was successful, he would suffer heavy casualties.[94]

"I was in possession of these important facts," he added, "so shortly after reaching the Emmettsburg [sic] road, that I considered it my duty to report to you at once my opinion, that it was unwise to attack up the Emmitsburg road, as ordered, and to urge that you allow me to turn Round Top and attack the enemy in flank and rear." By now Longstreet's cannonade had been in progress about 15 minutes, and Hood realized orders to attack could come at any minute. He again tried to convince Longstreet to change plans. Accordingly, he dispatched a staff officer to relay his request to be allowed to execute the proposed flanking movement. The courier returned with Longstreet's terse reply, "General Lee's orders are to attack up the Emmitsburg road." A discouraged Hood dispatched a second officer to say that he feared an attack would accomplish nothing and to renew his request to turn Big Round Top. Again, Longstreet replied, "General Lee's orders are to attack up the Emmitsburg road."[95]

The rate of Union counterbattery fire confirmed the Union position was much stronger than Lee or Longstreet had expected. Within moments of Longstreet's second response, Hood for a third time dispatched one of his staff officers to explain fully the situation and suggest that Longstreet "had better come and look for yourself." For this important last-ditch plea, he sent his highly regarded adjutant general, Col. Harry Sellers, a man Longstreet would know as "not only an officer of great courage, but also of marked ability." However, to Hood's dismay, Sellers also returned bearing the same curt response from Longstreet. Almost simultaneously, Maj. John W. Fairfax of Longstreet's own staff rode up to Hood and verbally repeated the orders to "attack up the Emmitsburg Road." After Hood formally protested the order—the first and only time he ever lodged such a protest in his

93   Ibid.

94   Hood, "John Bell Hood Gettysburg Battle Report," GNMP.

95   Ibid.

entire military career—he reluctantly instructed his subordinates to prepare to advance.[96]

Both Hood and McLaws, even before Cabell's opening salvo, knew that General Lee had not only underestimated the enemy's strength, but troop dispositions as well. They later suspected that Longstreet realized the situation but was too proud to protest, having been earlier chastised by Lee. They could both see the enemy gaining strength by the minute and that the bombardment was having but little effect. Indeed, the Union batteries seemed to be gaining the upper hand. Both of Longstreet's divisions had already lost men to this fire, which was increasing in intensity by the minute. McLaws' skirmishers were already engaged, particularly those from Anderson's division (Wilcox's Alabama and Lang's Florida brigades). Despite the radically changed circumstances, other than an unexpected change in direction, Lee's general plan, as historian Harry Pfanz later put it, "was not changed, not greatly at any rate. The attack would be made as planned."[97]

While Hood and his subordinates reluctantly prepared their brigades for the impending assault, McLaws attempted one more time to gain Longstreet's ear. He again reported that a strong Federal force was to his front and an attack as planned would be disastrous, even if they won the day. He anxiously awaited his commander's reply, which soon came in the form of Maj. Osmun Latrobe, one of Longstreet's veteran staff officers. The major asked why the attack had not begun, especially because "there is but one regiment of infantry and a battery of artillery to your front." Latrobe's comment made no sense, for McLaws was under orders to wait for Hood's attack to begin on his immediate right before moving forward. The general responded by telling Latrobe that a large force with artillery support confronted him, not just a single regiment or one battery, and that an ill-prepared attack would in all probability fail. He sent the major galloping back to Longstreet with this fresh information. Longstreet was being inundated with various messages and requests, and time was running out to cancel or postpone the attack.[98]

Once again there was a breakdown in Confederate preparations and communications, coupled with unexpected tactical misunderstandings and insufficient field intelligence. Hood was clearly upset at not being allowed to sweep around Big Round Top and gain access to the Union army's left rear and supply line. McLaws was bothered by what he perceived as botched orders, and a Union corps that was not supposed to be there was only 700 yards opposite his center.

---

96 Ibid.

97 Pfanz, *Gettysburg: Second Day,* 167.

98 McLaws, "Gettysburg," *SHSP,* vol. 7, 1879; USGS MRC 39077G2; *Bachelder Maps, Second Day.*

Longstreet, too, was agitated after Lee had rejected his alternative plan. What is unique about all this is that Longstreet was in consultation with Lee when both McLaws and Hood formally requested amendments to the stated plan to attack up the Emmitsburg Road. It was not Longstreet's decision alone to proceed with the "close-order formation" assault that would be required in order to carry the enemy position.[99]

While the Confederate senior commanders exchanged messages, the Yankee artillery responded well to Walton's and Cabell's opening cannonade. The first Union unit to respond was Capt. Judson Clark's 1st New Jersey, Battery B in the northern belt of Sherfy's peach orchard near the Emmitsburg Road-Millerstown Road intersection. The six Parrotts there quickly drew a storm of return fire. The captain's first inclination was to get the hell off the hilltop and down to the military crest to front south instead of west. General Hunt, who had arrived within minutes of Cabell's opening, directed Clark's redeployment. The battery rumbled southeast off the dangerous hill, with each gun crew acting independently for now. Clark resumed "battery" immediately north of present-day Wheatfield Road in a new position high enough for his ensuing fire to clear the orchard south of the road, but low enough to screen his guns visually from those enemy batteries off to the west. The ground behind him rose to the north. It was a much better position that offered considerably more shelter while still giving him a field of fire toward any enemy approaching via the Rose farm and the south branch of Plum Run. The only harassment at this early phase came from indirect solid shots that occasionally bounded over the crest from the west and northwest. Once out of the direct crossfire, Clark's veteran artillerists went back to work.[100]

Hunt had ordered all six Parrott tubes loaded with shell and shrapnel. As the well-trained New Jersey gun crews rammed the rounds into the rifled muzzles, their captain chose a target 1,400 yards to the south—one of Cabell's batteries. Clark ordered all six guns trained upon a single section in a "deliberate consolidated crossfire." Spanning some 60-odd yards, Clark's compact line enabled him to keep tight control. When he ordered "Open Fire," each gunner pulled his lanyard

99 Longstreet, "The Campaign of Gettysburg," *Philadelphia Weekly Times,* November 3, 1877; McLaws, "Longstreet at Gettysburg," *Philadelphia Weekly Times,* February 15, 1888; John B. Hood, *Advance and Retreat: Personal Experiences in the United States and Confederate States Armies* (New Orleans: 1880), 56-58, copy available at Huntington Library, San Marino, California; Karleton D. Smith, "'To Consider Every Contingency': Lt. Gen. James Longstreet, Capt. Samuel R. Johnston, and Factors That Affected the Reconnaissance and Countermarch, July 2, 1863," *Gettysburg Seminar Papers: The Second Day at Gettysburg,* GNMP, 2006. Close-order formation is a military tactical formation wherein soldiers are close together and regularly arranged for the tactical concentration of force.

100 Clark to Michael Hanifen, in *History of Battery "B",* 135.

simultaneously. Before each piece settled in place after having recoiled several feet, Clark's crews were already moving toward their respective piece. Clark's report was a simple affair: "Nothing transpired until about 3 p.m. [actually 4:30] when a rebel battery, which had just been placed in position near a house [Philip Snyder's home] on the Emmitsburg road, about 1,400 yards to our front, opened fire on my position."[101]

The defense of the Emmitsburg Road Rise and, by extension, Hancock's center between the farm lanes, was now underway. It would prove to be a perilous and deadly fight, and one that would end Sickles' active field service and validate his counterpart's sobriquet as "Hancock the Superb."

101 Ibid.; OR 27, pt. 1, 586.

Chapter Thirteen

"Never mind the left, boys; look out for your own front."
— *Maj. Gen. Oliver O. Howard, Eleventh Corps, Army of the Potomac*[1]

Late Afternoon, July 2:
Longstreet Attacks Sickles' Salient

After watching General Humphreys make his hasty countermarch back to the Emmitsburg Road, Winfield Hancock, together with his trusted subordinate Gibbon, mounted his horse and with several aides and adjutants in tow headed back northward. As they closed on Hummelbaugh's farm lane, they noticed several Regular batteries approaching the crest from the east. These were two of the four batteries General Hunt had promised Hancock prior to Meade's 3:00 p.m. council of war. Leading the way was Battery C, 4th U. S. under the command of 19-year-old Lt. Evan Thomas. The son of Lorenzo Thomas, the U. S. Army's adjutant general, the younger Thomas enjoyed many connections within the Regular Army. He was young, but he was also talented and a veteran of Antietam and several other battles. The other oncoming unit was Battery C, 5th U. S., under 25-year-old Gulian Verplanck Weir, son of Professor Robert Weir, the Head Instructor of Drawing at West Point.[2]

As the guns reached the wide crest above Hummelbaugh's small clapboard barn, Hancock spurred his horse forward and waved them to a halt. The generals

---

1   William Wheeler, letter to family, Warrenton Junction, Virginia, July 26, 1863, GNMP, 13th NY Battery vertical file.

2   Evan Thomas & Gulian Weir Personal Military and Pension Records (NNRA-AGO, Washington, D.C.) The generals probably used the Peter Frey farm lane that passed by the big gray stone house. In April 1873 Evan Thomas would die in combat against the Modoc Indians in California.

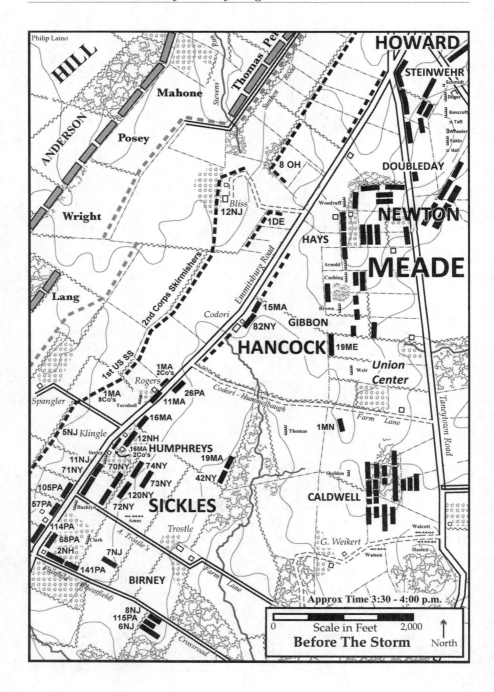

listened intently as Lieutenant Thomas explained that he and Weir had orders to report to the Second Corps. Hancock turned to Gibbon and suggested he place Weir's battery wherever he saw fit. Hancock wheeled about, ordering Thomas to follow him. He ushered Battery C south down an old farm lane that paralleled the crest for perhaps 200 yards before turning south-southwest and descending the slope toward the rocky, thicket-covered rough ground east of Plum Run 300 yards distant. Just northwest of this area, the Codori and Hummelbaugh farm lanes intersected near Plum Run. Hummelbaugh's lane was a much-used shortcut connecting the Emmitsburg and Taneytown roads. It would soon become critical to Hancock's entire position. This road had to be held at all costs. The Second Corps leader ordered Thomas into "action front" south of the lane and the nearby rock-strewn thickets.[3]

At first sight, Thomas's new position appeared a terrible one as he unlimbered and prepared for battle about 75 yards east of and about 10 feet above Plum Run. The brush and thickets lining its banks were higher than a mounted officer; not that this mattered because the rise beyond Plum Run blocked most of Thomas's view to the west anyway. To his left, a gentle open meadow gradually descended toward the watercourse, which bent in toward his gun line before curving away. The creek disappeared from the lieutenant's view below some higher ground opposite a small ravine, or wash, which emptied into the Plum Run ravine. Beyond this depression the undulating meadow gradually ascended to an open crest (where Caldwell's First Division had initially been placed).[4]

The high ground west of Plum Run masked a portion of Thomas's left section's field of fire, but not his center or right. He could see clearly the Emmitsburg Road from his right section, but lost sight of it as he moved south toward his center section. From the left flank brace of guns, all that he could see was the rising slope and the Klingle farm, several snake rail fences, and portions of the plank fence paralleling the eastern edge of Emmitsburg Road. It was a limited field of fire in case of a Rebel attack from that direction. Young Thomas, or so it appears, was most concerned about the wash to the immediate south in that it widened significantly as it neared Plum Run ravine, thus forming a natural byway that led directly toward Cemetery Ridge and Thomas's rear. If the enemy took possession of either the dry wash to his left or the elongated knoll opposite the creek bed to the west, his position would soon become untenable.[5]

---

3   OR 27, pt. 1, 873; USGS MRC 39077G2.

4   USGS MRC 39077G2.

5   Ibid.; *Bachelder Maps, Second Day.*

The cannoneers of Thomas's right section could see the white picket fence surrounding Peter Rogers' dwellings 500 yards to their immediate front and right. Well beyond that they could see the wood line, but not much of the intervening undulating fields. The Emmitsburg Road Rise was slightly higher than Thomas's position, thus blocking his field of fire in that direction. Thomas could see several Union infantrymen moving around the Emmitsburg Road Rise, but not enough to sufficiently convince him his flank was safely covered. Almost the exact distance to the northwest (about a 45-degree angle to his right flank) stood Codori's massive red barn. About 800 yards beyond it, he could see the Bliss barn encased in powder smoke. From his battery's position, he also could clearly see the 82nd New York and 15th Massachusetts clustered in Codori's farmyard, the former's left flank resting at the barn. For the time being, the space separating the Rogers and Codori homesteads appeared void of any significant concentration of Union troops. Thomas grew uneasy about his prospects in case of a determined enemy assault. He was lucky, however, in that none of the enemy's artillery fire was at this time directed directly at him.[6]

To Thomas's immediate right, the low rough ground formed a natural barrier resembling a thickly wooded, rock- and brush-covered amphitheater. A few sharpshooters enjoyed the shade of its thin canopy. A very low elongated rise, perhaps three feet high, whose southernmost part housed Thomas's right section, wound through rough, boggy ground paralleling the run. However, to his good fortune, his position was so low that Confederate gunners could not see his gun line, so he was safe from any counterbattery fire.[7]

Looking about, it was obvious to Thomas his battery was well forward and isolated. Accordingly, the 19-year-old lieutenant, perhaps impertinently, requested infantry support directly from Hancock, who readily agreed. Hancock decided to send one or more units from Caldwell's division to support Thomas, a sound decision both tactically and politically. Only a fool would leave the son of the Adjutant General of the U. S. Army in an isolated pocket.[8]

While Thomas was planning his potential avenues of fire, to the north General Gibbon deployed Gulian Weir's six 12-pounder Napoleons on the wide crest of Cemetery Ridge approximately 200 yards north of the Hummelbaugh farm lane and 350 or so yards south of the Copse of Trees. Gibbon told Weir to hold his fire until he received orders to open. Unlike Thomas's masked position south of the farm lane, Weir's field of fire north of it was spectacularly open. He could pivot his

---

6 Ibid.

7 Ibid.

8 Thomas's father, Brig. Gen. Lorenzo Thomas, was a personal friend of President Lincoln.

guns up to 160 degrees and sweep any enemy columns approaching Cemetery Ridge. The only major obstacle was Codori's massive barn and outbuildings 500 yards west of his battery. If Weir's gunners elevated their fire to clear the Codori farm, they could attack several of the enemy gun positions along southern Seminary Ridge.[9]

By 4:00 p.m. Thomas's and Weir's combined dozen smoothbores were the main Union guns in position to guard the Union center along Hummelbaugh's farm line on Cemetery Ridge. They did have some distant support. Some 300 yards north of Weir's right flank, Lt. Fred Brown's Rhode Island battery manned a position just south of the Copse of Trees. Gibbon, one of the Old Army's premier artillerists, had positioned Weir's guns with explicit orders to avoid drawing counter-battery fire. He also instructed Weir not to take orders from anyone except himself or Hancock. As they waited and watched, Weir's veterans witnessed several volunteer reserve batteries ascend the ridge using Hummelbaugh's farm lane en route to bolster Sickles' front. Turning south, these reinforcements followed the lane along the crest and disappeared in a dust cloud heading toward Caldwell's position 800 yards away.[10]

Soon, more Regular Army guns (Batteries F & K Consolidated, 3rd U. S.) thundered over the crest of Cemetery Ridge. Hancock and Gibbon were busy placing Thomas's and Weir's batteries south and north of the intersection, respectively, when Lt. John Turnbull's battery crested the ridge. His was the third battery to top Cemetery Ridge during Hancock's deployment of Thomas. The first two, Capt. Charles Phillips' 5th Maine and Capt. John Bigelow's 9th Massachusetts, turned south down the lane paralleling the ridge while Turnbull passed through the intersection heading west. Unable to corral them, General Gibbon watched the latter bumped its way down the fence-lined farm lane dividing Codori's meadow. Unfortunately for Hancock, Lt. Henry C. Christiancy, one of Humphreys' young staff officers, happened upon Turnbull, who promptly agreed to follow him. At some point after Humphreys had reversed his flank march, he had sent Christiancy scurrying about in search of artillery batteries. The logical place to find fresh batteries was east of and below Cemetery Ridge.[11]

9   OR 27, pt. 1, 881; Francis Walker, *History of the Second Army Corps in the Army of the Potomac* (New York, 1886), 745-48; Shultz, "Gulian V. Weir's 5th Artillery Battery C," *Gettysburg Magazine,* Issue 18, 78, 83; USGS MRC 39077G2; *Bachelder Maps, Second Day.*

10   Ibid.; Phillips' 5th and Bigelow's 9th Massachusetts Batteries file GNMP; USGS MRC 39077G2; *Bachelder Maps, Second Day.*

11   OR 27, pt. 1, 532; Carlswell McClellan to A. A. Humphreys, File 22, 8-9; Humphreys Papers, HSP.

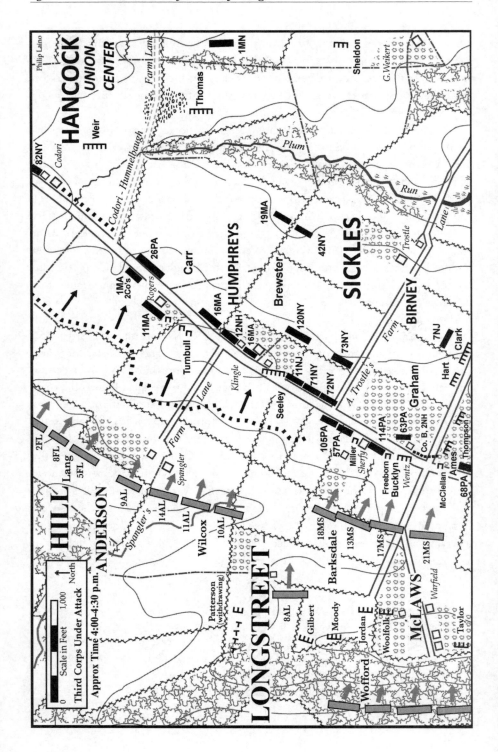

There is no record of how Christiancy happened upon Lieutenant Turnbull, who at the time had parked his battery below the Hummelbaugh farm near the Taneytown Road. It is also unknown whether Turnbull was still in park or still en route, or if General Tyler had changed his orders. That is possible, but doubtful as Colonel Warner, Hunt's chief of staff, was the one who was escorting Phillips' and Bigelow's batteries out of the park via the Hummelbaugh farm lane. It was also Warner who had previously ordered Captain Ransom to send his four Regular batteries to reinforce Hancock. Whatever the case, Turnbull found himself moving west up Cemetery Ridge led by Lieutenant Christiancy and behind Phillips and Bigelow. Turnbull's column splashed across Plum Run southwest into the fields toward the waiting Humphreys and Carr, who were delighted to see him and his fresh guns.[12]

At this moment the Union center was virtually devoid of sufficient reinforcements to simultaneously support Hancock, Sickles, and Slocum. Longstreet's delay in arriving in his attack position had allowed Humphreys' two brigades to successfully return to the Emmitsburg Road north of Birney's division, and the reinforcing batteries to head for and reach the front. Sickles' extended line now measured about 1.6 miles from Captain Smith's 4th New York Independent Battery atop Houck's Ridge on the left west to the Emmitsburg Road and then north to Humphreys' right flank near the Codori farm lane-Emmitsburg Road intersection.[13]

As noted earlier, Sickles' defensive line was much longer than than his original intended position on lower Cemetery Ridge, which in turn diluted his firepower and absorbed most of his available reserves into the new front line. As luck had it, Humphreys was busy placing troops along the Emmitsburg Road near the Peter Rogers house when Christiancy and Turnbull arrived. After Humphreys pointed out the desired position immediately south of the Rogers' farm, Turnbull began his deployment by ordering "action front." Before his subordinates could execute this order, dozens of infantrymen under Christancy's supervision began dismantling the sturdy wooden fences along both sides of the road to make way. When the path was clear, Turnbull's right section swung about and unlimbered in Rogers' small apple orchard, with his left section slightly to the rear of the center in the Emmitsburg

12 *Bachelder Maps, Second Day.*

13 Ibid.; USGS MRC 39077G2.

The modern view of Codori's meadow below and west of the Union center just north of where the Codori-Hummelbaugh farm lane passes over Plum Run. It looks southeast toward lower Cemetery Ridge and Patterson's Woods, where Humphreys' division was expected to be before moving west toward the Emmitsburg Road. Instead, Hancock detached Caldwell's division from the Second Corps to cover the meadow beyond the rail-lined crossroad, leaving the Union center on Cemetery Ridge virtually unoccupied.
Rosemary G. Oreb

Road. Turnbull's gun line was somewhat compact, stretching some 50-70 yards from Rogers' orchard southward.[14]

Meanwhile, someone had informed Captain Ransom that only two of his batteries had arrived at their intended destination to support Hancock's Second Corps. Lieutenant Chandler P. Eakins had been sent to Cemetery Hill earlier that afternoon and attached to James Huntington's Third Volunteer Brigade. Reporting to Maj. Thomas Osborn, Eakin managed his guns independently of Huntington. The second missing battery was of course Turnbull, but Ransom knew exactly where to find him. When he reined his horse in along the Emmitsburg Road, one look was all it took, and Ransom began assisting Turnbull in the placement of his guns to counter the growing threat from the west.

14 Ibid.; Pfanz, *Gettysburg Second Day*, 364; USGS MRC 39077G2. See also A. A. Humphreys to John W. DePeyster, August 11, 1869, Licensed Battlefield Guide File, 03-25m Resource Material, GNMP.

This 1901 view looks west up Hummelbaugh's rutted farm lane toward the crest of Cemetery Ridge 400 yards beyond the farmyard. The wide open nature of the deep Union center, and rough road conditions that would have existed during the battle, are clearly evident. This was the route Capt. Dunbar Ransom's 1st Regular Brigade Reserve Artillery used to report to General Hancock. *GNMP, Richard Rollins Collection*

Hancock, meanwhile, had returned to the crest of Cemetery Ridge where he located Gibbon somewhere north of the Hummelbaugh farm lane near Weir's guns. Hancock made a mental note of this battery's location. Realizing that he had no choice, Hancock further piecemealed Gibbon's division to meet existing needs. Without hesitating, he ordered two regiments be sent toward Humphreys' division along a route that would send them west of Plum Run, where they could from a distance support Evan Thomas's battery. He also directed Gibbon to send a third regiment south to directly support Thomas's guns. A fourth regiment would march over the crest to bolster the relatively thin line just south of the Copse of Trees.[15]

With these instructions confirmed, Hancock turned his horse and disappeared over the crest in search of Meade. His mission took on a new urgency when in about 15 minutes John Bell Hood's far right wing stepped out from a belt of timber

15 *OR* 27, pt. 1, 370-371, 416-417, 419.

This turn-of-the-century photo depicts the intersection of present-day Sickles Avenue and the Emmitsburg Road 50 yards south of the Rogers house. Lieutenant John Turnbull's Consolidated Batteries F & K, 3rd U.S. unlimbered west of this road to support General Humphreys' weakened right flank. *GNMP, Richard Rollins Collection*

in rear of Henry's gun line, the barrels of their muskets glistening in the bright afternoon sunshine. General Warren on Little Round Top and General Hunt on Houck's Ridge both noticed the Rebels stepping off, even as the nearly one-hour artillery bombardment showed no sign of abating.[16]

Shortly after Hancock's departure to seek Meade, Gibbon relayed orders to Brig. Gen. William Harrow, who in turn instructed Col. Francis E. Heath to bring forward his 19th Maine. Heath's veteran New Englanders redeployed over the crest and took their place in line south of the left flank of Brown's Rhode Island battery, roughly 250-300 yards south of the Copse. Meanwhile, Col. William Colvill received orders to lead his 1st Minnesota due south to support Thomas's Battery C, 3rd U. S.[17]

---

16 Norton, *Attack and Defense of Little Round Top*, 309-10; Hunt, *B&L*, 3:305-307.

17 First Minnesota Memorial inscription, GNMP.

Moving south in column of fours, Colvill's men snaked their way past Weir's parked Battery C, 5th U. S. before crossing the Hummelbaugh lane. The colonel formed his regiment into two lines of battle. His men could probably see Caldwell's division as it redeployed farther south, with its right flank nearly a quarter of a mile beyond Colvill's left. Colvill ordered his soldiers to lay down, with their right flank between 100-200 yards south of the farm lane, but well out of supporting range of the 19th Maine. As a result, many of Heath's infantrymen believed they formed the end of Gibbon's line. Despite being in the very middle of the patchwork Union line on Cemetery Ridge, the 19th Maine had become, in the words of one of its members, "particularly alone on that . . . part of the field."[18]

Except for officers and a few sergeants who were busy observing the distant enemy, Colvill's 224 effectives lay for the most part concealed on the low crest where today's Pennsylvania Monument now rests, some 100 yards east of Evan Thomas's caissons parked on the gentle western brow. Thomas's limbers and his gun line were well below the crest, with a recently dismantled rail fence separating the pieces from Plum Run a short 70-100 yards distant. When he stood up, Colvill had the same vantage as that of Caldwell before him. Looking south-southwest, he could see the billowing smoke of battle drifting upward from beyond some woods a mile distant. The faint nonstop crackle of small arms, punctuated with the deep boom of artillery increased as the fighting escalated. To Colvill's and Thomas's front, Andrew Humphreys readied his division along the Emmitsburg Road Rise.[19]

While Henry's, Cabell's, and Alexander's Confederate artillery battalions settled into an artillery brawl with the Yankee gunners, the batteries of A. P. Hill's Third Corps remained mostly silent. Except for Captain Patterson ensconced in Pitzer's Woods, the battalion commanders north of him chose not to engage in an effort to avoid provoking a lethal Union response. There was no doubt the

---

18 Smith, *Nineteenth Maine*, 69; *OR* 27, pt. 1, 419. John Smith, the 19th Maine's historian, recalled, "About five [4:00 PM] o'clock the First Minnesota was taken from the Brigade and conducted a short distance to the left, to support Battery C, Fourth United States Artillery." Colonel Harrow wrote, "The First Minnesota Volunteers, Colonel Colvill commanding, by the direction of General Gibbon, were moved from their original position in the rear, to the left of a battery commanded by Lieutenant Thomas, and stationed on the high ground a short distance to the left of the division line of battle. The Nineteenth Maine Volunteers, Colonel Heath commanding, moved to the left front of the division line, and placed in position to the right of a battery commanded by Lieutenant [Captain] Brown." According to Smith, "That left the Nineteenth Maine particularly alone on that particular part of the field it then occupied."

19 William Lochren, "Narrative of the First Regiment," in *Minnesota in the Civil War and Indian Wars, 1861-1865,* 2 vols. (St. Paul, MN, 1891), 2:34-35; USGS MRC 39077G2; J. S. McNeily, "Barksdale's Mississippi Brigade at Gettysburg: Most Magnificent Charge of the War," in Franklin L. Riley, ed., *Publications of the Mississippi Historical Society* (J. D. Williams Special Collection Library, University of Mississippi, 1914), 14:233-35.

stalemate that had begun along Hancock's front about 2:00 p.m. was coming to an end. To the west and north of Gibbon, Capt. George Price of the 1st Delaware noted, "As the roar of battle to the south rose [Capt. Henry F.] Chew [12th NJ] discovered that [Carnot] Posey had steadily been reinforcing his skirmish line so that our attention was not to be attracted until they had enough men to drive us away from the [Bliss] barn."[20]

Chew, after reporting this to Maj. John T. Hill, readied his companies knowing the news would quickly reach his brigade commander, Brig. Gen. Alexander Hays. Chew knew Hays, an impatient man, would not wait while Posey's Mississippians gained control of the strategically important Bliss farmyard. At about the same time Colonel Colvill was leading the 1st Minnesota south, Hays' men west of the Emmitsburg Road renewed their duel with Posey. From the perspective of Confederates deployed along Seminary Ridge, the main fight still seemed a long distance away, although within easy earshot and mostly within eyesight.[21]

However, there was little collaboration between A. P. Hill and Longstreet as Hays' renewed his bloody little fight along Hill's center with vigor. Hays ordered Captain Chew with his men of the 12th New Jersey, with portions of the 1st Delaware, 39th New York, and others in support, swept the farmyard and took possession of the barn and its garrison of Rebels. Unknown to Chew, however, Posey had committed several hundred soldiers to his skirmish line in the Bliss orchard, so when an additional 300-odd rifles from the 16th Mississippi showed up, they easily drove back the Federals.[22]

Before they withdrew, however, Hays' command had blunted and then halted Posey's counterattack, containing it within the Bliss farm with assistance from Captain Hazard's Second Corps batteries. Posey's Mississippians were more than willing to hang onto the house and barn and western portion of the yard, including both orchards, leaving the Yankees the eastern plank fence and fields beyond it. A spirited duel soon erupted along the length of the Bliss farm, picking up in volume off both flanks until an unending line of musket flashes were visible from just beyond the Rogers house northward to well beyond the Bliss property and on into the wide open plain.[23]

---

20 Henry's, Cabell's, and Alexander's battalions spent most of their time waging counterbattery actions, with but little time to focus on Meade's infantry. John M. Archer, *Fury on the Bliss Farm at Gettysburg* (Gettysburg: Ten Roads Publishing, 1995), 36.

21 Ibid.; OR 27, pt. 1 470-71; Gilbert A. Hays & George T. Fleming, ed., *Life and Letters of Alexander Hays* (Pittsburgh, 1919). 411-12.

22 OR 27, pt. 1, 465, 469; pt 2, 2 633.

23 Hays, *Life and Letters,* 412-13.

Brig. Gen. William Barksdale,
McLaws' division,
Longstreet's First Corps,
Army of Northern Virginia
LOC

Confederate gunners deployed between Spangler's and McMillan's woods had no choice but to open in counterbattery fire. The long-arm fire quickly escalated up and down Hill's line from the Fairfield Road south to Spangler's Woods. From atop West Cemetery Hill, Major Osborn's gunners opened in support of Hazard's Second Corps guns, which in turn forced A. P. Hill to bring forth his reserve guns. The cannonade along Hill's front developed into independent skirmishes between individual batteries that bore little resemblance to standard Confederate bombardment prior to an infantry assault. Longstreet's First Corps batteries to the south had their hands full battling enemy batteries, but nevertheless they alone would have to carry the load of supporting the sweeping infantry assault south of Anderson's division.[24]

Moving unhindered into the thin strip of woods atop South Seminary Ridge, Brig. Gen. William Barksdale's Mississippians were just glad to be out of the hot sun and in the shade. Anchoring the left front of McLaws' division, the feisty lawyer, newspaper publisher, and state representative had deployed his men in what he considered a good position behind friendly artillery. Captain Patterson's Sumter Artillery remained in position 200 yards to Barksdale's left and front. Moody's and Gilbert's commands were to his immediate front. Within minutes of Barksdale's resting his brigade in the tranquil woods, Cabell had opened the ball. Within a short moment every Confederate gun within sight of his regiments had likewise opened. After Seeley's battery replied, Turnbull's Consolidated 3rd U.S. off to his right joined in. Both Seeley and Captain Ransom saw they had an enemy battery

---

24 Thomas W. Osborn, "The Artillery at Gettysburg," *Philadelphia Weekly Times*, Vol. III, No. 14, May 31, 1879; Longstreet, "General James Longstreet's Account of the Campaign and Battle," *SHSP*, Vol. 5, Nos. 1-2, Jan.-Feb. 1878, 54-85.

(Patterson's Company B, Sumter Light Artillery) west of Pitzer's Woods in partial and near full left enfilade at about 1,000 and 1,500 yards respectively.[25]

Within a few minutes, Seeley's and Turnbull's gunners had Patterson's exact range. What followed was a decisive one-sided artillery duel. Patterson's gun crews did not stand a chance as the incoming enfilading crossfire disrupted his gun crews while disabling two of his six pieces. Unfortunately, Barksdale's men to Patterson's right and rear suffered from this fire as well, especially from 12-pounder solid shot. These cast iron balls bounded and bumped across the landscape, creating havoc in their path. Just as lethal were the spherical shot that exploded overhead, tearing trees to pieces and raining jagged shrapnel and splintered timber toward the troops below.

Soon, at least three Union batteries had opened from along the Emmitsburg Road, placing Barksdale's battalions in a deadly crossfire. Frustrated and filled with anxiety, Barksdale walked along his brigade line, speaking at the top of voice and cheering on Colonel Alexander's gunners while tossing profanities at the distant Yankees. "Impatient" is the word many of his peers used to describe the excitable Barksdale. He itched to get his men moving forward away from the murderous incoming artillery rounds.[26]

With the artillery duel in process, Humphreys, even while sustaining casualties, completed setting his divisional line along the Emmitsburg Road, including placing stretcher-bearers and ambulances to the rear. To his immediate left, Brig. Gen. Charles K. Graham's Pennsylvania brigade of Birney's division held an irregular position fronting both south and west, the apex of Sickles' defensive salient being the southern portion of Sherfy's peach orchard along the Emmitsburg Road. Colonel Byron R. Pierce's 3rd Michigan of Colonel de Trobriand's brigade fronted due west, while Col. Edward L. Bailey's 2nd New Hampshire, from Burling's brigade, faced due south. However, they were both vulnerable to an enfilading crossfire from south and west. Even though most of Longstreet's batteries were engaged in counterbattery fire within 15-20 minutes of Cabell's opening, plenty of their rounds landed within the ranks of several of Sickles' regiments, especially those forming the salient in the Peach Orchard.[27]

Because the focus of this study is the attack and defense of the Union center well to the north, discussions of the fighting south of Millerstown Road and east to Little Round Top will only encompass important issues and events that directly

---

25 *OR* 27, pt. 1 591.

26 Philip T. Tucker, *Barksdale's Charge* (Philadelphia: Casemate, 2013), 77; Freeman, *Lee's Lieutenants*, 117-18; Alexander, *Fighting for the Confederacy*, 237-50.

27 *Bachelder Maps, Second Day.*

affected Hancock's and Humphreys' positions. One of the distant units that had a material impact on the defense of the Emmitsburg Road and south Cemetery Ridge was Col. Andrew H. Tippin's 68th Pennsylvania, part of Charles Graham's brigade of Birney's division. Fronting west, Tippin's left flank was to the immediate right and rear of the 3rd Michigan, with his right flank stretching beyond and below two of Capt. Nelson Ames' south-facing artillery sections. A detached third section under 2nd Lt. Samuel McClellan was 40 yards off the 68th's right flank, fronting west.[28]

To the right and rear of McClellan's section lay Lt. William W. Ballard's detached Company B, 2nd New Hampshire (better known as the "Goodwin Rifles"). Ballard, who was in temporary command, placed about 40 of his sharpshooters along a plank fence in a line stretching from just south of Millerstown Road northward to the Wentz house. Bucklyn's left gun was about 30 yards to the front and right of Ballard's line. To Bucklyn's right, Lt. Col. Frederick F. Cavada's 114th Pennsylvania waited east of the Emmitsburg Road with its advance line to the west in Sherfy's farm. Cavada's 259-man regiment stretched the length of the farmyard with its right holding the barn. A section of 3-inch Ordnance Rifles under Lt. Joseph L. Miller (Hampton's Battery F Pennsylvania Independent) was next in line.[29]

Nathaniel Irish, one Capt. Robert Hampton's original lieutenants at the time the battery formed, had led his section brilliantly since January 1862. Promoted to captain on May 24, 1863, for conspicuous and meritorious duty at Chancellorsville, Irish refused to serve under senior officer James Thompson, a captain Irish claimed had shirked his duty at Chancellorsville. Even after Reynolds and Hunt intervened, Irish refused and threatened to resign. Hunt temporarily assigned him to his staff, so Irish arrived at Gettysburg without a direct command. In the meantime, Lieutenant Miller had tough shoes to fill. Miller's cannoneers, with help from Cavada's red-trousered Zouaves, hand-pushed the brace of Rodman rifles through the right-center of the 114th Pennsylvania. The youthful Miller took position

28 USGS MRC 39077G2; *Bachelder Maps, Second Day.* Ames' New York battery was one of the units first called to the front around noon. Lt. Samuel A. McClellan commanded Ames' west-facing section.

29 Martin A. Haynes, *A History of the Second Regiment, New Hampshire Volunteer Infantry in the War of the Rebellion* (Lakeport, NH, 1896), 170-72; Samuel G. Griffin, *A History of the Town of Keene, New Hampshire* (Keene, NH, 1904). Raus, *A Generation on the March*, 141-142. Collis' Zouaves was the original nickname of the 114th PA. See Chapter XVIII, *Civil War*, 477-79.

between Sherfy's house and barn, surrounded by brethren from the Keystone State.[30]

To the north of Cavada and Miller, opposite the Sherfy barn, skirmishers from Col. Peter Sides' 57th Pennsylvania held the southern half of a narrow peach orchard. To their immediate right, Col. Calvin A. Craig's 105th Pennsylvania's advance line of skirmishers held the northern end, with his right flank stretching slightly past the Trostle farm lane intersection. Both main regimental lines were still east of the Emmitsburg Road. They formed the end of Graham's west-facing brigade line south of Trostle's farm lane. From flank to flank, including the 3rd Michigan on the left, the Union line numbered approximately 1,307 men compared to Barksdale's 1,720 attackers. Unfortunately for Graham, the enfilading artillery crossfire that had plagued his men for an hour had taken a toll. The high morale his men arrived with at Gettysburg plummeted along the entire length of his line with each discharge of an enemy gun. Casualties climbed. Across the way, the white-haired General Barksdale continued to watch the early stages of the combat. He and his men ushered in a cheer every now and then, and with his good nature he continued urging the nearby Mississippians who could hear him to be ready. He believed the Yankees were about to get handed a whipping. As 4:30 p.m. Drew near, the Confederate brigades south of Millerstown Road finally began stepping off in a line from south to north.[31]

North of the Trostle farm lane intersection, Col. William R. Brewster's brigade anchored Humphreys' left flank. Colonel John S. Austin's 72nd New York was east of the Emmitsburg Road with his left flank resting near Trostle's farm lane (directly behind the right of the 105th Pennsylvania). To Austin's immediate right stood Col. Henry L. Potter's 71st New York. Waiting behind a rail fence some distance to the rear, Maj. Michael W. Burns' 73rd New York anchored Brewster's second line. A hundred yards to his right was Lt. Col. Cornelius Westbrook's 120th New York. Brewster's two front regiments totaled 748 effectives, while his second line had more firepower with 943 muskets.[32]

For some unexplained reason, Lieutenant Seeley's Battery K received orders to gallop to the Rogers house to support Brig. Gen. Joseph Carr's right flank. Seeley moved approximately 80 yards north of Klingle's modest log house, so as not to impede Turnbull's battery another 100 yards northward. Within a few moments

30 William Clark, *History of Hampton's Battery F, Independent Pennsylvania Light Artillery* (Pittsburgh, 1909), 58-60.

31 Busey & Martin, *Regimental Strengths and Losses*, 49, 139; McNeily, "Barksdale's Mississippi Brigade at Gettysburg."

32 *New York at Gettysburg*, 1:103, 108.

Capt. Carswell McClellan, one of Humphreys' aides, arrived and thundered at Seeley, "What in Hell are you doing?" He immediately ordered Seeley back to his former position, a move Seeley accomplished without hesitation or casualties. With the New Hampshire battery having recently unlimbered in the Peach Orchard and with Turnbull firmly planted on the right, Humphreys needed Seeley's firepower closer to the Trostle lane intersection.[33]

This minor issue created two related incidents. When Seeley ceased firing, Captain Patterson was able to pull his Rebel battery out of the deadly pocket in which it had been trapped. Retiring west away from the wall, he reopened with several guns using the edge of Pitzer's Woods for cover while the remaining four pieces rejoined his caisson park in a clearing west of the woods. Secondly, Seeley's move from in front of Klingle's orchard was one thing, but on his return he deployed in the fruit trees, forcing the infantry already there to redeploy, including the right wing of Col. Robert McAllister's 11th New Jersey and the left of Lt. Col. Waldo Merriam's 16th Massachusetts. Both regiments had helped tear down the plank fences east and west of the Emmitsburg Road for Seeley's entrance, as well as to clear his field of fire. "Before reaching the crest of the hill [Emmitsburg Road Rise] occupied by our line of pickets, on the summit of which stood a little farm house and garden, we were halted," McAllister later recalled, "with the right of my regiment in the orchard in front of the house, and ordered to lie down. In a short time a rebel battery secured our range, when I received orders to move by my left flank in front of the One hundred and twentieth New York Regiment, so as to give room for one of our batteries to take position on the crest of the hill." Within moments of unlimbering, Seeley's gunners were back at work from the orchard, targeting Patterson's surviving gun crews.[34]

The 16th Massachusetts, having advanced up the slope of the Emmitsburg Road Rise, stopped short of the crest to the right and rear of the 11th New Jersey. As Merriam's men lay on the reverse slope—with his left wing anchored in the eastern portion of the Klingle orchard—the entire regiment endured relentless left-flank enfilade fire from Henry's and Cabell's battalions, which swept down the line killing and wounded a number of men. Seeley's arrival brought on a vigorous increase in counterbattery fire that smashed through the orchard sheltering Seeley's caissons. Redeploying to make room for the carriages, Merriam separated his command. Several companies from his left flank moved forward to secure Klingle's log house while the balance of the regiment slid north, marching around Capt. John

33 *OR* 27, pt. 1, 532, 551.

34 Ibid.; 590-91; USGS MRC 39077G2; McNeily, "Barksdale's Mississippi Brigade at Gettysburg;" A. A. Humphreys to John W. DePeyster, August 11, 1869, GNMP.

F. Langley's 12th New Hampshire. These two regiments crowded into Klingle's farm, covering a front roughly 150 yards from flank to flank. Seeley was to their left firing from the edge of the orchard.[35]

Confederate infantrymen across the way were not much better off than Merriam's Bay Staters. Although Union gunners were targeting enemy batteries, plenty of their missiles, especially bounding solid shot and tumbling bolts, tore into woods concealing Lieutenant Colonel Herbert's 8th Alabama (Wilcox's brigade, Anderson's division). Several hundred yards off Herbert's right flank, from left to right (north to south), Barksdale's 18th, 13th, 17th, and 21st Mississippi continued absorbing a bloody pounding. Most of the incoming fire came from Lieutenant Miller's two Ordnance Rifles east on the Sherfy's farm, and Barksdale took it personally. Allegedly, he ran into Longstreet and pleaded, "I wish you would let me go in, General; I would take that battery in five minutes." Longstreet reportedly replied, "Wait a little, we are all going in presently."[36]

Most everything that Miller's two iron guns lobbed at Alexander's batteries passed above Moody and Gilbert and into the woods beyond their gun line. Bucklyn's and Ames' combined eight Napoleons added to Barksdale's misery as their rounds also slammed the woods with telling effect. Neither Pitzer's nor North Biesecker's Woods offered much respite for the Rebels, especially when the old growth timber exploded overhead, showering the men below with slivers and chunks of iron and wood.[37]

Turnbull's six Napoleon tubes were burning hot to the touch, actively engaging Patterson and Alexander with outstanding marksmanship, at least according to General Hunt. The lieutenant's left gun was either in or near the Emmitsburg Road, with his right piece west of it in a small apple orchard south of the Rogers house. Their limbers were east of the road, with the caissons parked beyond them. To Turnbull's left and front, the right flank of Col. William Sewell's 5th New Jersey occupied the opposite rise west of the road, just beyond a deep wide swell to the battery's immediate front. The 5th covered the length of Carr's front, with their left flank passing over Spangler's intersecting farm lane. Company G of the 1st Wisconsin Sharpshooters and portions of Lt. Col. Clark Baldwin's 1st

35 USGS MRC 39077G2; *Bachelder Maps, Second Day*.

36 Douglas S. Freeman, *R. E. Lee: A Biography*, 4 vols. (New York, 1935), 2:532-33; USGS MRC 39077G2: *Bachelder Maps, Second Day*.

37 Edward Porter Alexander, "Gettysburg," Edward Porter Alexander Papers, UNC; Pfanz, *Gettysburg: Second Day*, 310-12; McNeily, "Barksdale's Mississippi Brigade at Gettysburg," 234-36.

Massachusetts were intermixed to the north stretching Carr's skirmish line beyond the Rogers homestead.[38]

To Turnbull's immediate right, the 11th Massachusetts secured the Rogers buildings and yard. Lieutenant Colonel Porter Tripp's men enjoyed the perceived security of not only the house, but a small barn and several outbuildings along with various fences and two small orchards. To Tripp's immediate right and rear east of the road was Maj. Robert L. Bodine's 26th Pennsylvania. The next troops north of the Rogers house comprised the remainder of Baldwin's 1st Massachusetts. With eight of his ten companies out on the skirmish line, Baldwin's remaining two companies were spread thinly along the Emmitsburg Road with the larger 26th Pennsylvania deployed to their rear. With Sewell's 5th New Jersey (about 206 muskets supported by at least 200 specialized sharpshooters, including Company G) to his front, Carr's effectives now exceeded 2,000 rifles. Supported by a dozen 12-pounder Napoleons, his line appeared strong.[39]

Geographically speaking, the Union center was 1,100 yards northeast of the 26th Pennsylvania's right flank and rear, and 800 yards from the left-rear of Lt. Col. James Huston's 82nd New York occupying the Codori farmyard. Colonel Heath's 19th Maine and Colvill's 1st Minnesota were the only two infantry regiments posted at this time to cover the gap on the military crest of Cemetery Ridge. With Caldwell's entire division redeployed southward, covering the entire Union center was in real jeopardy. Hancock sent more riders galloping off to find reinforcements.

Off to the south, another of Longstreet's brigades stepped off. Several minutes passed before Longstreet allowed Lafayette McLaws to join the fight, and Joe Kershaw advanced his South Carolinians into action. The brigade rose, dressed ranks, and his first line passed over a nearby sheltering stone wall. Hundreds of yards to the east, thousands of nervous Yankees awaited their advance.[40]

* * *

Captain William Wheeler's 13th New York Independent Battery had been posted west of the Baltimore Pike fronting the Broad Open Plain since the night of July 1. "At about two [3:00] o'clock in the afternoon the artillery of the Second Corps became hotly engaged on the [Union] left," Wheeler recalled, "and our boys

---

38 USGS MRC 39077G2; *Bachelder Maps, Second Day.*

39 Busey & Martin, *Regimental Strengths and Losses*, 49, 139. This was the 82nd New York from Harrow's brigade in the Codori farmyard.

40 USGS MRC 39077G2; *Bachelder Maps, Second Day.*

This modern photo was taken from Sherfy's Peach Orchard looking west by northwest. General Barksdale's Mississippians surged out of Pitzer's (in the right-distance) and Biesecker's Woods (in the left-distance) with one regiment south of the Millerstown Road (pictured) and three to the north. They passed through E. P. Alexander's artillery battalion, which filled the meadow where the tree line now stands between the homesteads of J. Snyder (to the north) and free black James Warfield (to the south, obscured by woods).
Richard Rollins Collection

all stood on tiptoe to watch the contest. Just then General Howard rode along and said, 'Never mind the left, boys; look out for your own front'; and sure enough, a few minutes afterward, we saw puffs of smoke—which we knew well enough arose from the hills opposite to us—then the boom of the guns and the bursting of the shells among us."[41]

General A. P. Hill's artillery north of Patterson's battery, meanwhile, failed miserably when their chance to prove themselves arrived. Their primary task was to support Henry, Cabell, and Alexander. Except for a few scattered rounds, these Southern guns did not even begin firing until after Hancock's batteries had reopened in support of Alexander Hays' advance on the Bliss farm. Hill's late cannonade was also short-lived because Captain Hazard's better equipped, better trained, and better disciplined Union gunners quickly gained the upper hand. Unfortunately for Hill's artillery battalions, Major Osborn on West Cemetery Hill also ordered his batteries to open fire in support of Hazard. The result was a deadly iron crossfire along Seminary Ridge from the McMillan house north to the Lutheran Seminary.[42]

By the time Osborn's gun line opened, Hood's infantry division was already east of the Emmitsburg Road and McLaws' division was launching its attack. Longstreet's infantry, continued Captain Wheeler of the 13th New York

41 Ibid.; William Wheeler, letter to family, Warrenton Junction, Virginia, July 26, 1863, GNMP, 13th NY Battery vertical file; *Bachelder Maps, Second Day*.

42 Rollins & Shultz, "A Combined and Concentrated Fire."

Independent Battery, "soon got an answer from us; we had nine three-inch rifled guns in a row there, from Hall's Second Maine Battery, Wiedrick's [sic] Battery, and mine. Beside these, there were the bronze guns of Dilger's Ohio Battery, and 'G' of the Fourth Regulars, although they were of more service at close quarters. We did not fire very rapidly, but every shot was aimed with deliberation and judgment, as my corporals were cool and skillful." Over the next half-hour, Osborn would refocus his fire against the distant Confederate batteries.[43]

Many modern historians believe A. P. Hill's guns failed to provide Longstreet's advance with adequate artillery support, but the truth is that he was simply outgunned. His artillery line of at least 53 pieces of various calibers stretched from Patterson's Company A of Capt Hugh M. Ross's Sumter Light Artillery, whose right gun rested near the northern edge of the Spangler's Woods, all the way north to Lt. John Cunningham's Virginians, whose right gun was unlimbered just north of the Fairfield Road. Across the field, Major Osborn, outnumbered two to one, relished the support offered by Captain Hazard's three right-wing batteries. This support enabled Osborn to focus on the enemy batteries to his immediate front, leaving Woodruff's, Arnold's, and Cushing's batteries to deal with those directly west of Hays' and Gibbon's divisions. Superior ordnance and materiel, combined with better trained and equipped personnel enjoying an elevated field of fire upended General Hill's long-arm.[44]

Northeast of Cemetery Hill, shortly after 4:00 p.m., Maj. Gen. Edward Johnson ordered Lt. Col. Snowden R. Andrews' artillery battalion, temporarily under 19-year-old Maj. Joseph W. Latimer since Andrews' wounding at Second Winchester, to get into position on Benner's Hill. The plan was simple. General Ewell wanted Latimer to soften up the defenses of East Cemetery Hill and Culp's Hill before Early's and Johnson's infantry charged each hill, respectively—all theoretically taking place while Longstreet drove his divisions up the Emmitsburg Road. Latimer had searched all morning for a suitable artillery platform north and east of Gettysburg, but Benner's Hill was the only viable spot. It was also an exposed position that would put his own men in grave danger.[45] Latimer deployed his batteries from north to south atop the elongated hill, passing Captain Graham who was again unlimbering atop North Benner's Hill. Unfortunately for the Rebels, the middle and southern parts of Benner's Hill were well within range of Colonel

43 Ibid.; USGS MRC 39077G2; *Bachelder Maps, Second Day.*

44 Busey & Martin, *Regimental Strengths and Losses,* 290-95.

45 Pfanz, *Culp's Hill & Cemetery Hill,* 67-70; Shultz, "Benner's Hill: What Value?", 57-60.

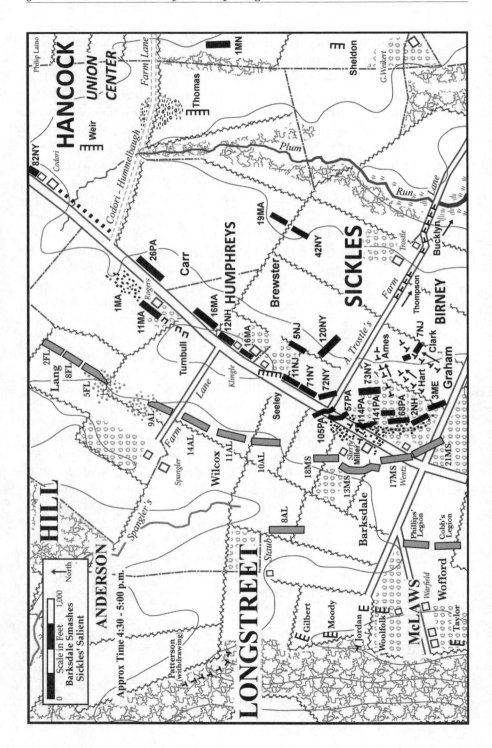

Scale in Feet
Barksdale Smashes
Sickles' Salient
Approx Time 4:30 - 5:00 p.m.

Wainwright's rifled guns on East Cemetery Hill, with South Benner's Hill also within easy reach of the Federal smoothbores.[46]

To add to Latimer's woes, the first two Yankee rifled guns to open on him (Lt. John Geary's section of Knap's Battery E, First Pennsylvania Independent) fired from Culp's Hill not 900 yards distant with an enfilade fire. Within a few seconds all of the guns on East Cemetery Hill joined in. Even Captain Wheeler's west-facing 10-pounder Parrotts were wheeled about to participate in the attack against Latimer's badly exposed guns. Just a few weeks after the battle, Wheeler wrote a letter home to his family describing the artillery exchange:

> Soon they opened again, more fiercely than ever, but we quickly got their new range and punished them severely. They placed one battery of very long range on our right flank, and completely enfiladed [Graham's 20-pounder Parrotts on North Benner's Hill]; luckily for us they did not get the range for some time. A twenty-pounder Parrott battery was brought up from the Reserve, and this kept them very quiet. By 4½ P.M. my ammunition was exhausted, and Major Osborn, our new Chief of Artillery, relieved my Battery with another, and sent mine back to replenish; at the same time he asked me to remain with him and assist him in his very arduous duties, as he had charge of all the batteries on Cemetery Hill, and his regular adjutant was completely used up. This exactly suited me, as my blood was up, and I did not like the idea of going back with my Battery. Until nightfall I was hardly out of fire once, and I was raised to the highest pitch of excitement; the danger was so great and so constant that, at last, it took away the sense of danger. I placed several batteries on the hill, under the Major's orders, and at length I went back to the Artillery Reserve to bring up a supply of ammunition.[47]

Unfortunately for Major Latimer and his men, there were no nearby woods to conceal their caissons and limbers, which were hammered almost from the very beginning of the exchange. During the heaviest moments of the one-sided artillery duel, Maj. Robert Stiles of the 1st Richmond Howitzers, detached as an aide, found his way to Benner's Hill with orders for General Johnson. When he reached the Daniel Lady farm east of the crest, Stiles observed the destruction of Latimer's battalion. "Never, before, or after did I see fifteen or twenty guns in such condition of wreck and destruction as this battalion was," he recalled. "It had been hurled backward, as it were, by the very weight and impact of metal from the position it

---

46 Ibid.; David Martin, *Confederate Monuments at Gettysburg,* 78, 89, 104; C. F. J. Cook, *The Chesapeake Battery–Maryland Troops In The Confederacy,* 182. See also William F. Hatton Memoirs, LOC and GNMP, 454-455; Wainwright journal, July 2, 1863, San Marino, California: The Huntington Library. Wainwright estimated Latimer's guns were spaced at 30-yard intervals.

47 William Wheeler, letter to family, Warrenton Junction, Virginia, July 26, 1863, GNMP.

had occupied on the crest of a little ridge, into a saucer-shaped depression behind it; and such a scene it presented—guns dismounted and disabled, carriages splintered and crushed, ammunition chests exploded, limbers upset." One of the casualties was the youthful Latimer, who fell with a mortal wound. Captain Charles I. Raine assumed battalion command, its third leader since June 14.[48] Unable to sustain its perch atop Benner's narrow open crest, what was left of Latimer's artillery battalion, including Graham's and Hardwick's 20-pounder Parrott Rifles to the north, were withdrawn before General Ewell's Second Corps infantry advanced. Lee's and Ewell's plan for Latimer's guns to support the overall assault plan proved a costly failure.[49]

If Longstreet (or A. P. Hill) expected Ewell to pitch in with infantry between 4:00 and 5:00 p.m., he was sadly mistaken. Instead, Ewell did little except order "Allegheny" Johnson to open fire from Benner's Hill the moment he heard Longstreet's signal guns. From Lee's headquarters three miles to the west opposite Gettysburg, Latimer's opening signaled that Ewell was engaged. Because their observers could see the artillery bombardment with field glasses from the Lutheran Seminary, Lee and staff reasonably believed the plan, or at least its concept, was underway. Lee expected "a simultaneous demonstration" on the Confederate left, but thus far nothing had evolved beyond the artillery fire, something General Lee did not yet realize.[50]

Off to the south, the Confederate right continued to step off at intervals. By now, a key leader in Longstreet's assault was out of action. A half-mile south of the Millerstown Road, beyond Lafayette McLaws' right wing, General Hood was seriously wounded when an enemy shell exploded overhead, with some of its metal shards ripping into Hood's left arm. Aides placed the stricken division commander on a stretcher in one of George Bushman's orchards and carried him away. With him passed the best opportunity for unified action with McLaws' division on his left. Hood's own attack began drifting more easterly than northward, moving steadily away from McLaws.[51]

With Hood suddenly unavailable, the entire division headed away from Lee's intended target, the planned assault northward "up the Emmitsburg Road." Again, the natural topography worked against Lee just as young Union artillery Lieutenant Kinsey had envisioned that morning. The terrain made it impossible to advance in

---

48 Stiles, *Four Years Under Marse Robert*, 217-18.

49 Pfanz, *Culp's Hill & Cemetery Hill*, 67-70; Shultz, "Benner's Hill: What Value?"; USGS MRC 39077G2; *Bachelder Maps, Second Day*.

50 Ibid.

51 Pfanz, *Gettysburg: Second Day*, 170-73.

cohesion as expected. It soon became apparent that McLaws' division would mostly be fighting independently of Hood's command. In effort to keep his own division moving in a cohesive manner and not risk further isolating Kershaw's and Semmes' brigades, McLaws sent Capt. Gazaway B. Lamar, Jr. galloping north with orders for Barksdale to advance.[52]

"The noise of hard battle, when Hood's division opened the fight, was heard far to our right soon after 4 o'clock," Pvt. John S. McNeily of the 18th Mississippi later wrote. "The resistance was more obstinate, and the wave of attack was longer in reaching us, than calculated. The brigades of Kershaw and Semmes, South Carolina and Georgia, of our division, McLaws, went in soon after 5 o'clock on our immediate right, but hidden from view by rolling ground." The attack did not begin well, continued the private. "The 'bad luck' that threaded Gettysburg for the Confederates outcropped at the outset of Longstreet's attack, in the wounding of Hood," he wrote with the benefit of hindsight. "The loss of his consummate and daring leadership in attack at such a crisis may not be measured. But it is easily imaginable that it was of serious adverse effect."[53]

With attack orders in hand, Barksdale quickly and effectively formed his men. He was rewarded with hearty cheers and a drum roll calling assembly. Soon his first line stepped out of the wood line and over the wall, advancing only far enough for the second line to appear. There, in the open, Barksdale dressed his four regiments before riding nearly the length of his line from left to right. Waving his broad-brimmed hat, he ordered his Mississippians forward. A resounding Rebel Yell let everyone know his brigade was on the move. E. P. Alexander's batteries gave Barksdale's line a welcoming hurrah as the Mississippians passed through, receiving in return an even more resounding Rebel Yell. With the batteries behind the advancing long gray line, the distant Union gunners redirected much of their fire onto the 21st and 17th Mississippi from right to left, respectively. After opening with shrapnel and solid shot, they turned to canister as the Rebels closed on the Emmitsburg Road. Colonel Holder's 17th, with its right flank anchored in the Millerstown Road, likely was the first of Barksdale's regiments to pause, aim their muskets, and open fire. The ensuing volley drove the advanced Union skirmishers back toward a rail fence and then beyond to a supporting line of infantry. With everyone but himself on foot, Barksdale, still with hat in hand, urged his men forward. "The line before you must be broken," he had earlier urged his officers,

---

52 Gazaway B. Lamar Papers, University of Georgia, Hargrett Rare Book & Manuscript Library, Athens; McNeily, "Barksdale's Mississippi Brigade at Gettysburg," 234-35; USGS MRC 39077G2; *Bachelder Maps, Second Day.*

53 McNeily, "Barksdale's Brigade at Gettysburg," 234-36.

"To do so let every officer and man animate his comrades by his personal presence in the front line."[54]

"[Barksdale's] brigade was placed in line—formed with the 21st, Col. B. G. Humphreys, on the right, then the 17th, Col. W. D. Holder, next the 13th, Col. J. W. Carter, with the 18th, Col. Thos. M. Griffin, on the left—under the crown of a low ridge, five or six hundred yards distant from the position of assault," wrote Private McNeily. "Open fields, fences and scattered farm houses lay between. Parallel with our line, and at the base of the Peach Orchard, ran the Emmitsburg Road, between two high rail fences. Farther to the left a picket fence lay beyond the road."[55]

Joe Kershaw's woes, unwinding beyond Barksdale's view, began within moments of passing through Cabell's and Alexander's artillery lines. Isolated with both flanks in the air, his South Carolinians descended the undulating, but otherwise open meadow toward the Emmitsburg Road 350-400 yards distant. His Palmetto regiments were aligned, from left to right as follows: 8th, 3rd (James) Battalion, 2nd, 3rd, 7th, and 15th. His right flank was closer to the road, which angled eastward away from Kershaw's left units. Several braces of Union 12-pounder Napoleons planted opposite the ravine along the Emmitsburg Road began hitting the Rebels with spherical case and solid shot, punching large holes in Col. John W. Henagan's 8th South Carolina command on Kershaw's far left. When Lt. Samuel McClellan's advanced a section of Battery G, 1st New York and switched to canister, the 8th's left flank began melting away as if a heavy wind had blown through its ranks. McClellan's pair of guns unloaded with a left-front enfilade, and Henagan's men were unable to close with them because of the ravine cutting across their front.[56]

From east of the road, the other four smoothbores of Ames' New York battery supported McClellan's pair of guns. Fronting southwest and west, they hammered Cabell's and Alexander's batteries, along with Kershaw's advancing center and right wing. Despite the bold front Alexander later reported, his battalion failed to knock McClellan's two smoothbores off their advanced perch, and the Union lieutenant with a dozen or so crewmen continued to mow down the 8th South Carolina. Within moments of the advance of Colonel Humphreys' 21st Mississippi toward McClellan's section, however, the artillery lieutenant had little choice but to pull

---

54 Ibid.; Benjamin G. Humphreys, "Sunflower Guards—21st Mississippi Volunteer Regiment," 11-12, in J. F. H. Claiborne Papers, SHSC Collection, UNC.

55 Ibid.

56 Joseph B. Kershaw to John Bachelder, Camden, SC, April 3, 1876, and August 7, 1888; *Bachelder Papers,* 1:470-71, 2:900-901; OR 27, pt. 1, 818; USGS MRC 39077G2; *Bachelder Maps, Second Day.*

back at fixed prolonge to the Emmitsburg Road. Had Barksdale advanced within a few minutes of Kershaw, the deadly effects of this pair of Union guns would not have been possible. The quarter-hour that passed between the time Henagan's 8th South Carolina (on Kershaw's left) stepped off, and the advance of Colonel Humphreys' 21st Mississippi (anchoring Barksdale's right) had a tremendous effect on Kershaw's advance.[57]

Without infantry support off his left, McClellan's guns hammering into his flank pressed Henagan's South Carolinians southeast away from the Peach Orchard. Within minutes they were crowding the left side of Lt. Col. W. G. Rice's 3rd "James" Battalion. By the time Kershaw's right wing reached the Emmitsburg Road, his left wing was already unraveling. Caught up in the fencing and slammed by 32 Union guns, Colonels Henagan and Rice bravely led their regiments across the splintered fence-lined road, losing heavily as they did so. Once again Union artillerists enjoyed a perfect left-front enfilade down much of the length of Kershaw's long brigade line, with the far left elements absorbing the brunt of the pounding.[58]

Union infantry, starting with the 2nd New Hampshire of Burling's brigade and the 141st Pennsylvania of Graham's brigade soon pitched in. When portions of the 3rd Maine of Ward's brigade joined in the escalating musketry, Kershaw's left wing veered even farther south. At some point after having moved several hundred yards into farmer Rose's meadows, the entire line north of the Rose farm was finally forced to find cover, or as Kershaw described it, "[F]or a short time the left wing halted about the walls and fences left [north] of the Rose's and [was] then ordered to attack the battery." Although this respite was short-lived, it allowed the right wing elements time to reach a line of woods 200 yards east of the Rose house. With orders to commence his advance, Col. John Kennedy of the 2nd South Carolina led the left wing forward. Soon, Kershaw's left wing (8th, 3rd Battalion, and 2nd) was moving almost due north, attacking the Peach Orchard from the south, while his right regiments (3rd, 7th, and 15th) were attacking eastward. As a result, the once small gap between Kershaw's wings widened to the point that each portion became isolated from the other and vulnerable to defeat in detail. Within minutes the three right regiments were hit with such a devastating fire from the Union Third Corps guns arrayed along the Millerstown Road that they fell back [59]

57 OR 27, pt. 1, 818; Pfanz, *Gettysburg: The Second Day*, 254-55.

58 Kershaw to Bachelder, April 3, 1876, and August 7, 1888; *Bachelder Papers*, 1:470-471, 2:900-901.

59 Ibid.; USGS MRC 39077G2; *Bachelder Maps, Second Day*.

East and south of the Peach Orchard, meanwhile, Kennedy's 2nd South Carolina finally reached the West Plum Run ravine that divided these South Carolinians from their Union opponents. Raked by small arms and artillery fire, they passed over the small creek only to be met by a terrible and sustained fire of canister and shrapnel combined with small arms. At some point shortly after descending into the ravine, Kennedy turned his regiment toward the east, either as the result of an order lost to history or on his own initiative. Kennedy's move drew the other two regiments with him also eastward, further disjointing Kershaw's battle lines. However, this move east allowed Union batteries fronting south along the Peach Orchard line to pulverize the entire line, chopping it to bits as it tried to move in the open out of the ravine. "Kennedy confesses that the troops 'huddled' into the woods in some disorder," recorded Kershaw, "and I have no doubt some went back to Rose's house."[60]

Taking cover as best they could, the Palmetto soldiers regrouped for another go at it. The breaking of Kershaw's command into two wings, followed by their bloody pounding and withdrawal, however, made it impossible for the South Carolinians to advance with Barksdale's Mississippians to their north and support that portion of Longstreet's attack. The difficult terrain, coupled with a stout Union defensive effort, forced Kershaw to amend his attack plan to coincide with the existing situation. With his right wing on the move once more, the logical thing for the left portion to do was to move in unison with it. As a result, instead of continuing due north, the new focus for the 8th, 3rd Battalion, and 2nd South Carolina was the rock- and brush-strewn stony hill northeast of their position.[61]

During their short stay under cover somewhere north of the Rose house, Kennedy and Henagan could see Benjamin Humphreys' 21st Mississippi battling for possession of the Peach Orchard. With Lieutenant McClellan's Union artillery section finally out of the way, the 21st had easily pushed aside the Federal skirmishers who had created so much havoc for Kershaw. Retiring to the Emmitsburg Road, these men rejoined the ranks of that portion of Sickles' thin blue line then fronting west. Humphreys' regiment of more than 400 effectives advanced toward the waiting 68th Pennsylvania of Graham's brigade. These defenders enjoyed the support of portions of the 2nd New Hampshire and 3rd Maine, numbering some 450 rifles. The planned linkage of Kershaw's left and Barksdale's right would never occur. The original gap that existed between the brigades when they were initially placed into position was never a matter of much

---

60 D. Augustus Dickert, *History of Kershaw's Brigade* (Dayton OH: Morningside, 1988), 237-39.

61 Ibid.

The gap in the line. This view, which Joe Kershaw's left regiment (8th South Carolina) would have had on the afternoon of July 2, was taken from the Emmitsburg Road south of the ravine through which runs West Plum Run. On the high ground sits the Sherfy Peach Orchard. The depression was a serious impediment for the South Carolinians, and the pounding they took here kept Kershaw from wheeling north up the Emmitsburg Road in support of Barkdale's Mississippians, which were well off his left flank. *Richard Rollins collection*

concern, and it may have even passed unnoticed. The consequences of that alignment were now bearing fruit—for the Union defenders.[62]

As noted, Barksdale's Mississippians had stepped off about 15 minutes after Kershaw's right flank started forward. Taking advantage of that quarter-hour, the three south-facing Union regiments (the 2nd New Hampshire, 141st Pennsylvania, and 7th New Jersey), supported by Captain Clark's Battery B, 1st New Jersey, initially concentrated their firepower against the 8th South Carolina without interference from either Humphreys' 21st Mississippi or General Wofford's trailing brigade of Georgians. If the Mississippians had advanced sooner, this would not have been possible. This, in turn, also resulted in Kershaw generally heading east instead of wheeling north behind the Peach Orchard and driving up the Emmitsburg Road, as originally intended.[63]

62 Ibid.; McNeily, "Barksdale's Brigade at Gettysburg," 234-36; Busey & Martin, *Regimental Strengths and Losses*, 245-46, 282.

63 Martin Alonzo Haynes, *A History of the Second Regiment New Hampshire Volunteer Infantry in the War of the Rebellion* (Lakeport, NH: s. n. 1896), 175-78.

As was becoming readily apparent, much of Longstreet's attack was breaking apart into separate brigade- and regimental-sized actions. A lack of communication, questionable timing, and unforeseen terrain issues combined to break down the anticipated unified, mutually supporting attack front. When General Semmes' Georgia brigade, which had deployed behind the South Carolinians, moved to advance on Kershaw's right, any hope of salvaging the planned move up the Emmitsburg Road en masse entirely disappeared. Committed to the Rose Woods fight, Semmes' four regiments would be bogged down there in bloody combat for more than an hour before extracting themselves. When Colonel Humphreys' Mississippians of the 21at regiment wheeled north to take the Union defenders in the flank, the fight south of them degenerated into an entirely separate contest for possession of Little Round Top, the Rose Farm, Stony Hill, the Wheatfield, and Devil's Den—none of which was a major sweep north and northeast up the Emmitsburg Road as originally intended.[64]

With Barksdale now well underway, the initiative to advance moved north into A. P. Hill's sector, where Cadmus Wilcox's Alabama brigade, part of Richard Anderson's division, stood next in line. Off to the east, beyond the Emmitsburg Road and Plum Run, Union Generals Hancock and Gibbon were busily preparing to meet the threat they knew was heading their way.

The fight for the Union center was about to begin in earnest.

---

64 McNeily, "Barksdale's Brigade at Gettysburg," 234-36.

Chapter Fourteen

"When they appeared at point blank range they were a compact mass of humanity.
Although our shooting was good, there wasn't enough of it."

— *History of the Second Regiment New Hampshire Volunteer Infantry*[1]

Late Afternoon, July 2:
Wilcox Joins Longstreet's Attack

Most of James Longstreet's First Corps Rebel brigades were busy engaging the Union lines south of the Millerstown (Wheatfield) Road when Maj. Gen. Richard Anderson's division of A. P. Hill's Second Corps prepared to continue the planned *en echelon* assault against Union troops arrayed in the L-shaped salient along the Millerstown and Emmitsburg roads. Northeast of that salient on Cemetery Ridge, Winfield Hancock redeployed some of his Union Second Corps regiments to cover perceived weak points in the center of the Army of the Potomac's loosely defined "fishhook" line.

"About 5:00 p.m., some time after the Third Corps had been engaged on our left," recalled Col. Arthur F. Devereux of the 19th Massachusetts, "Colonel [James E.] Mallon, commanding the Forty-second New York, and myself were ordered by the brigade commander [Col. Norman Hall] to follow a staff officer, whom he pointed out, but whose name and rank I do not know, which was done, my regiment leading." Devereux's Bay State boys, with Mallon's New Yorkers in tow, tramped southwest off Cemetery Ridge angling toward the low rough ground and Lt. Evan Thomas's nearby Battery C, 4th U. S. Passing to the front of Lieutenant Thomas's gun line, Devereux moved both infantry regiments (about 360 effectives) across the sluggish stream and positioned them just east of and below the crest of

---

1   Martin A. Haynes, *History of the Second Regiment New Hampshire Volunteer Infantry, in the War of the Rebellion* (Lakeport, NH, 1896), 185-87.

the elongated knoll west of the Plum Run ravine. The 19th Massachusetts was on the right and the 42nd New York on the left, the latter's right flank about 300 yards in front of and to the left of Thomas's left section.[2]

Showers of hot shrapnel fired by enemy guns along Warfield Ridge filled the afternoon sky south of Devereux's new position. On Cemetery Ridge, several more volunteer reserve batteries destined for Sickles' Peach Orchard salient drove past Colonel Colvill's 1st Minnesota, which was still resting in rear of the crest not far from Thomas's caissons. Many of Colvill's northwoodsmen had dozed off in the afternoon heat despite the noise and commotion of a dozen pieces of artillery and their associated limbers and caissons rumbling past their position. Nearby, Thomas's artillerymen relaxed as best as they could near their silent guns. Many passed the time chatting, napping, and relaxing.[3]

Although the combined 690 rifles of the 19th Massachusetts, 42nd New York, and 1st Minnesota had helped reinforce the vulnerable Union center, General Hancock still lacked sufficient men and guns to send substantial help southward to Sickles. Several of Hancock's subordinates had already stripped their brigades of much-needed firepower in an effort to bolster gaps in other parts of the disjointed Federal line. Brigadier General William Harrow had dispatched Col. George H. Ward's 15th Massachusetts (304 men) and Lt. Col. James Huston's 82nd New York (394 men) to the Codori farm to reinforce John Gibbon's engaged picket line. Harrow had no more regiments to spare. Division commander Gibbon had deployed Col. Francis Heath's 19th Maine to the immediate left of Lt. Thomas F. Brown's Rhode Island artillery battery, with Brown's right gun located about 30 yards south of the Copse of Trees. Gibbon ordered Brown to shift his guns forward in front of the stone wall west and southwest of the copse to make room for part of General Webb's oncoming Philadelphia Brigade. Gibbon also called up the 20th Massachusetts and 71st and 72nd Pennsylvania from his reserves to bolster the 106th Pennsylvania and 7th Michigan. This left Colonel Willard's New York brigade as the only viable Second Corps reserve unit east of Cemetery Ridge.[4]

---

2   OR 27, pt. 1,442; USGS MRC 39077G2.

3   Ibid.

4   Ibid., 419. "The First Minnesota Volunteers, Colonel Colvill commanding," Colonel Harrow wrote, "by the direction of General Gibbon, were moved from their original position in the rear, to the left of a battery commanded by Lieutenant Thomas, and stationed on the high ground a short distance to the left of the division line of battle. The Nineteenth Maine Volunteers, Colonel Heath commanding, moved to the left front of the division line and placed in position to the right [left] of a battery commanded by Lieutenant Brown." See also Smith, *Nineteenth Maine*, 69; USGS MRC 39077G2; *Bachelder Maps, Second Day.*

This modern view from Cemetery Ridge (west of today's Pennsylvania Monument) depicts the approximate position held by the right wing of the 1st Minnesota as it lay behind Lt. Evan Thomas's Battery C, 4th U.S. Thomas's gun line was west of the pictured horizontal rail fence, with the caissons stretched from the rough ground (noted by the trees south of the crossroad) across the open field toward the left frame of the photo. Plum Run can be seen flowing southward (distinguishable by the line of brush below where the slope drops away). Thomas's guns were atop that drop-off. They were perhaps the best-placed Union battery on July 2. *Rosemary G. Oreb*

Lieutenant Brown moved his guns as ordered, relocating them west of his initial position in front and south of some rough ground 60 yards southwest of the Copse of Trees. His artillerymen dismantled one of farmer Nicholas Codori's wooden rail fences that ran perpendicular to their new gun line. Brown's movement, however, left both of the 19th Maine's flanks unsupported. Colonel Heath's left flank in particular hung in the air with the nearest assistance, Lt. Gulian Weir's Battery C, 5th U. S., well off to his left and rear. The nearest practical support for Heath's left flank was the 1st Minnesota, which was nearly a quarter of a mile away to the south. The situation was disconcerting for Hancock and Gibbon because it was now clear the Rebels were preparing to advance in strength toward their position if they overran Sickles' salient—and maybe even if they did not.[5]

Meanwhile, the battle raged with wild abandon as far south as Hancock and Gibbon could see. What they could not yet see was another looming threat, one much closer to their own lines. In Spangler's Woods across the fields west of the

5 Smith, *Nineteenth Maine,* 69. The 7th Michigan and portions of the 20th Massachusetts filled Brown's initial position off the right flank of the 19th Maine.

two veteran West Point-educated Union generals, the infantry of Brig. Gen. Cadmus Wilcox's Alabama brigade readied themselves to join the attack. Unfortunately for the Rebels, however, Wilcox was not properly deployed, and now had to quickly scramble at the last minute to get into the correct position. "My instructions were to advance when the troops on my right [Barksdale] should advance, and to report to the division commander, in order that the other brigades [to the north] should advance in proper time," recalled Wilcox. "In order that I should advance with those on my right, it became necessary for me to move off by the left flank so as to uncover the ground over which they had to advance. This was done as rapidly as the nature of the ground with its obstacles would admit." Wilcox estimated he moved 400-500 yards to his left. The time required by this shift, however, mean that Barksdale's brigade advanced without any direct support from Wilcox on its left flank.[6]

Wilcox and General Lee had talked at some point prior to the opening of Hood's assault. Although the exact location of their discussion remains uncertain, it likely occurred near Pitzer's Woods. Moving into position near Warfield Ridge for the planned assault, General McLaws' division had filed past the generals during that late afternoon conversation. What is certain is that Lee informed Wilcox of his expectations for the impending assault. Lee believed the Federal flank still rested 600 to 800 yards in front of McLaws' left, an indication that he had not ridden to the front to see for himself. Not one to point out such information, Wilcox confirmed that he would carry out the order. Satisfied, Lee left Wilcox to ready his men and rode north in the direction of A. P. Hill's Third Corps headquarters.[7]

Wilcox's superior, General Anderson, seems not to have been on hand during this brief exchange. "Shortly after the line had been formed," as "Fighting Dick" later penned, "I received notice that Lieutenant-General Longstreet would occupy the ground on the right; that this line would in a direction nearly at right angles with mine, that he would assault the extreme left of the enemy and drive him toward Gettysburg, and I was at the same time ordered to put troops of my division into action by brigades as soon as General Longstreet's corps had progressed so far in their assault as to be connected with my right flank."[8]

Lee's assaulting forces were arranged, to use Wilcox's verbiage, in "close order formation." This called for the brigades to be deployed with little space between them so that once underway, they would be nearly elbow-to-elbow advancing toward a common goal with little space separating the commands. This was a

---

6   OR 27, pt. 2, 618; USGS MRC 39077G2; *Bachelder Maps, Second Day.*

7   Ibid.

8   Ibid.; Wilcox, "General Wilcox on the Battle of Gettysburg," *SHSP*, 1878, 6:97-104.

Lt. Gen. A. P. Hill,
commander, Third Corps,
Army of Northern Virginia. *USAHEC*

typical formation in the modern army of that era. Unfortunately for Lee, what young Union artillerist Lt. David Kinzie had relayed to Generals Meade, Howard, and Hunt earlier that morning from below Little Round Top—that the ground was not favorable for a large scale attack because the terrain was too rough and broken—would prove true. The rocky wooded ground was wholly unsuited for moving close-ordered lines of battle during the best of conditions, and during combat it would be nearly impossible.

General Anderson formed his line no later than 8:30 a.m., apparently with little or no expectation of implementing a major offensive battle plan for quite some time. Although Anderson's early instructions suggested he knew of Lee's plan to attack up the Emmitsburg Road, he failed to take advantage of the time that Longstreet's delay in getting into position on the far right had handed him. Brigadier General Carnot Posey's earlier struggle at the Bliss farm and Wilcox's sharp fight in Pitzer's Woods may have helped frame Anderson's defensive posture. Whatever the case, after Hood's belated attack finally commenced in earnest, Anderson allowed Brig. Gen. William Mahone's brigade to rest in McMillan's Woods on the left of his division, while Wilcox remained stretched thinly with intervals nearly a mile wide to the south. Anderson had deployed his division with the intention of supporting McLaws in "close order formation" as Wilcox suggested, but in practicality his four brigades were farther apart than they should have been.

General Lee may well have been banking on a battle plan similar to what had occurred the past May at Chancellorsville. "It was determined to make the principle attack upon the enemy's left," the Virginian later wrote with hindsight, "and endeavor to gain a position from which it was thought that our artillery could be brought to bear with effect. Longstreet was directed to place the divisions of McLaws and Hood on the right of Hill partially enveloping the enemy's left, which

Looking west toward Seminary Ridge from the first swale just west of the Emmitsburg Road across from Klingle's farm. The left wing of Col. William H. Forney's 8th Alabama passed over this ground trailing the 10th Alabama, whose right flank passed Henry Spangler's farmyard while the 11th, 14th, and 9th Alabama advanced east on the north side of the farmyard. Note how flat the field appears. Union regiments protecting this sector included Seeley's battery, the 5th and 11th New Jersey, 12th New Hampshire, 71st New York, and a mixed bag of advanced skirmishers who had fallen back. *Gettysburg Daily, Richard Rollins Collection*

he was to drive in." Anderson's report indicates he knew Longstreet's corps (specifically, McLaws' division) was expected to sweep everything before it as the troops moved north up the Emmitsburg Road. This, of course, could only be accomplished if Hood's division on the right was able to neutralize and roll up Meade's left flank, wherever it was located at the time of the attack. With Meade's left in turmoil, Anderson's immediate thrust eastward, brigade after brigade, would strike the Union line along Cemetery Ridge and collapse it, much like Howard's Eleventh Corps had folded at Chancellorsville. As Lee indicated, this would allow Longstreet to take possession of the strategically important high ground along the Emmitsburg Road from the Sherfy farm north toward the Codori farm lane. From there, the Confederate artillery could enfilade the distant Union line, just as it had from the powerful Hazel Grove position on the Chancellorsville battlefield two months earlier.[9]

9   OR 27, pt. 2, 318, 614-15; McLaws, "Gettysburg," 68-70.

By 5:30 p.m., General McLaws' attack was well underway and Cadmus Wilcox was preparing to sweep forward with his Alabamians. The overall goal appears to still have been an attack up the Emmitsburg Road, but Sickles' forward movement had already disrupted that idea. At no time did General Lee suggest that Little Round Top was an objective. If Lee stated as much during his short visits with Longstreet, McLaws, and then Wilcox in the late afternoon, no one recorded it. Lee wanted to redeploy his artillery upon the high ground along the Emmitsburg Road to the front of McLaws, but Sickles blocked access to that position. Lee had also been specific about A. P. Hill's role in his original plan. "General Hill was ordered to threaten the enemy's center," remembered Lee, "to prevent re-enforcements being drawn to either wing, and co-operate with his right division [Anderson's] in Longstreet's attack." It appears that he did not count on Pender's and Heth's divisions of Hill's corps to directly support Longstreet's advance until his attack appeared to be successful.[10]

Except for those soldiers who had earlier contested the Union push into Pitzer's Woods and onto the Bliss farm, the bulk of Richard Anderson's division had accomplished little that afternoon. There is no evidence to suggest that Anderson visited General Wilcox at any time after his Alabama brigade assumed its position on the division's far right, and Anderson's official report is completely silent on the subject. One of the few mentions of Anderson during this critical time comes from his subordinate Brig. Gen. Ambrose Wright, a 37-year-old Georgian who had spent much of the afternoon in farmer Emanuel Pitzer's barn ill with fever and general weakness. "About noon," reported Wright after the battle, "I was informed by Major-General Anderson that an attack upon the enemy's line would soon be made by the whole division, commencing on our right by Wilcox's brigade, and that each brigade of the division would begin the attack as soon as the brigade on its immediate right commenced the movement." Wright's scant information does not specify whether Anderson informed him in person or via written or verbal order.

Colonel David Lang, another of Anderson's brigade commanders, also offered a vague explanation on this point: "About 5 p. m. I received an order from General Anderson to the effect that General Longstreet was driving back the enemy's left, and that Wilcox would advance whenever General Longstreet's left advanced beyond him. I was ordered to throw forward a strong line of skirmishers, and advance with General Wilcox," continued Lang in his report penned nearly one month after the close of the titanic battle, "holding all the ground the enemy yielded." Whether Anderson delivered the message in person is unclear. Lang's

10 OR 27, pt. 2, 623-24.

order may well have been relayed to him via Wilcox, who was instructed to do just that.[11]

Almost certainly Lee would have explained his overall plan to Anderson, a key division commander, as he had to his subordinate Wilcox. Anderson's post-battle report, however, is also cryptic on this point, noting only that he "received notice" of the plan, and "at the same time was ordered to put the troops of my division into action by brigades as soon as those of General Longstreet's corps had progressed so far in their assault as to be connected with my right flank." What we know with certainty is that Anderson did not take any measures to reposition his division north of Wilcox's Alabamians to concentrate and better coordinate his assault, and that he did not notice and correct Wilcox's flawed pre-attack deployment.[12]

Wilcox's northward flank movement to get into proper position to attack lower Cemetery Ridge proved more difficult than the written record reflects. It took considerable time for a brigade to pass in column of twos while moving simultaneously by the left flank through heavy timber, underbrush, and over two stone walls and several worm fences. Exactly when Wilcox moved northward after the beginning of Barksdale's attack, or how long his maneuver took, remains unclear. Wilcox's estimate that he shifted 400-500 yards north seems excessive, but every yard he moved increased the gap between his right flank and Barksdale's left. It also appears that Lt. Col. Hilary Herbert's 8th Alabama concealed in Pitzer's Woods never received the order to move north, an oversight that isolated that unit even more that it already was. The redeployment did, however, close the gap between Wilcox's left and the right side of Colonel Lang's Floridians to his north.[13]

Once General Wilcox finally had his men in position, he ordered them to advance. The specifics of his assault and the long and confused fighting that followed well into the early evening has been muddied by conflicting post-battle reports and faulty reminiscences. Written on July 17, only 15 days after the battle, Wilcox's official report was fairly contemporaneous to the events of July 2, but it also contained some of the same mistakes and inconsistencies in other reports written many months later. Some of Wilcox's recollections concerning distances and time understandably raise eyebrows. For example, he said he advanced at 6:20 p.m., which is nearly an hour after Barksdale began his attack, and a full 90 minutes

11 Ibid., 613; David Lang to Edward Perry, July 19, 1863, in "Gettysburg: The Courageous Part Taken in the Desperate Conflict 2-3 July 1863," *SHSP*, vol. 27, 1899, 192-205; Wilcox, "General Wilcox on the Battle of Gettysburg," 97-104; USGS MRC 39077G2.

12 USGS MRC 39077G2; *OR* 27, pt. 2, 615, 631. Once Lee explained his orders to Hill, there was no need for him to tell to anyone below Hill, though in fact Lee did just that.

13 Earl J. Coates, "A Rendezvous at "Gettysburg," *Gettysburg Magazine*, 3:88-89; Herbert to Bachelder, July 9, 1884, *Bachelder Papers*, 2:1055-56; *Bachelder Maps, Second Day*.

The position held by Wilcox's Alabama brigade just east of Spangler's Woods looking due south toward West Pitzer's Woods. The Alabamians fronted east, with skirmishers left of the frame, and in Pitzer's Woods to the rear and right. *Rosemary G. Oreb*

after Hood's assault commenced on the army's far right. It was more likely about 6:00 p.m. when Wilcox began his assault.[14]

The men stepped over the low stone wall along the east edge of Spangler's Woods and dressed ranks left to right as follows: 10th, 11th, 14th, and 9th. Wilcox and his staff rode to the front. The general's calm demeanor reassured his men. Turning toward the rise to the east housing Spangler's stone home and massive bank barn, Wilcox lifted his sword and ordered his brigade forward. The color bearers stepped forward a few yards and defiantly waved their battle flags. General A. A. Humphreys' advanced skirmishers, positioned behind a worm fence on the rise in Henry Spangler's farm, unleashed a volley that claimed several Rebels.[15]

The spectacle drew the attention of Sickles' distant gunners along the Emmitsburg Road, who unleashed a long-range barrage of solid shot and spherical case against the Alabamians. The Regular artillerymen of Lt. F. W. Seeley's Battery K, 4th U. S. sighted their smoothbores in the Sherfy orchard after helping drive

14 OR 27, pt. 2, 618; USGS MRC 39077G2; *Bachelder Maps, Second Day.*

15 John N. Barrett, ed., "Yankee Rebel," in *The Civil War Journal of Edmund D. Patterson* (Chapel Hill, NC, 1966), 115-17; Coates, "A Rendezvous at Gettysburg," 88-89.

Patterson's Georgia battery back under the cover of Pitzer's Woods. The elimination of Patterson's pieces allowed Seeley and Turnbull to turn their attention against Wilcox's brigade the moment it began advancing.

South of Wilcox, Barksdale's advancing line of Mississippians had by this time passed in front of Porter Alexander's batteries, which prevented those guns from engaging the distant Federal batteries off to the northeast, including Seeley and Turnbull. Starting at a range of 600 yards, the first rounds from Seeley's guns killed or wounded several oncoming Alabama men. With each anxious step that carried Wilcox's soldiers eastward, Seeley's artillery fire became more concentrated and damaging. The only disadvantage confronting these Regular Army gunners was their own infantry positioned between them and Wilcox. The undulating terrain, however, allowed both Seeley (and Turnbull) to fire above the skirmishers because the Emmitsburg Road Rise was from four to six feet higher than the surrounding fields.[16]

"This forward movement was made in an open field," recounted General Wilcox, "the ground rising slightly to the Emmitsburg turnpike, 250 yards distant. Before reaching this road, a line of the enemy's skirmishers along a fence parallel to the road were encountered and dispersed." In fact, the Emmitsburg Road was about 650 yards from Wilcox's jumping-off point. The general may have been referring to the rail fence on the Spangler farm, approximately 250-300 yards east of where he started. His slow and steady advance toward the Union-occupied fence line took at least a quarter of an hour. His regiments faced another pummeling as they moved into the view of additional Yankee guns.

Within moments of spotting the Rebels, Lieutenant Turnbull's six Napoleons opened with devastating effect from a range of 800 yards, tossing solid shot down the length of the enemy line in a nearly perfect left-front enfilade. Within a few moments, Lieutenant Seeley's gunners adjusted their range and again pounded the Alabamians. Wilcox's veteran infantrymen absorbed their losses and continued to close ranks as they ascended the gentle rise toward the Spangler farm and Yankee-held rail fence.

---

16 Recalling the pounding of Patterson's guns, section leader Lt. Robert James wrote: "The enemy had a battery posted in our front and distant about 800 yards and were firing with good effect upon the infantry [Humphreys] to our rear. We immediately opened fire with solid shot and spherical case, and after a rapid and well-directed fire, lasting about fifteen minutes, succeeded in silencing and causing it to retire." James failed to mention the excellent left-front enfilade the gunners of Lieutenant Turnbull's Consolidated Batteries F/K, 3rd U. S. enjoyed from alongside the Rogers' farmhouse against Patterson. Without Turnbull's support, it is unlikely Seeley alone could have the Rebel guns back into the sheltering woods. OR 27, pt. 1, 590-91. USGS MRC 39077G2; *Bachelder Maps, First Day.*

The concentrated Union artillery crossfire turned deadlier when General Gibbon ordered Capt. Gulian V. Weir's Battery C, 5th U. S. to open "to the left with solid shot at 4 degree elevation." By now, 18 Federal smoothbore guns were firing 54 rounds a minute—a lethal array of solid shot, spherical case, and timed-fuse shell. Despite the intense shelling, Wilcox's line wavered but never faltered. Instead of stopping his men or seeking cover, the veteran general maintained tight lines and his men continued on, stepping up the open rise toward the 800-odd Union riflemen who now also raked their front. When Wilcox's infantrymen drew near the crest, they leveled their rifled muskets and delivered a crippling volley that sent many of their Federal adversaries scurrying rearward.[17]

Assuming Wilcox indeed launched his attack about 6:00 p.m., it was roughly 6:15 p.m. when his forward skirmishers cleared Henry Spangler's house, barn, and outbuildings of Humphreys' pesky Union sharpshooters. Wilcox took unchallenged possession of the stout rail fence there, but passing over it proved rather difficult. A spherical case round exploded overhead and showered shrapnel around the general and his staff. Although neither Wilcox nor his mount exhibited any visible injuries, shell fragments rendered the tack useless and the horse quickly became unmanageable. Dismounting at the captured fence, Wilcox urged his men to keep up their fire even as some of the retiring Yankees (particularly members of Col. Hiram Berdan's green-clad 1st U. S. Sharpshooters) regrouped behind a smaller snake rail fence with yet another, stronger line not 100 yards distant. Renewing the contest with vigor, the men in blue poured a deadly fire into Wilcox's stalled ranks.[18]

This action attracted the attention of members of the 5th New Jersey, the last Federal infantry regiment to deploy on the skirmish line before Hood's attack commenced. Detached from Burling's brigade, Col. William J. Sewell led his men to a nearby fence, where they spread along its length for several hundred yards as they relieved Col. Moses Lakeman's 3rd Maine. Sewell could see friendly sharpshooters to his front atop a small rise using the farmyard and larger rails for cover. He had already been engaged for some time with Barksdale's skirmishers. "At about 5 o'clock," he later reported, "however, the skirmishers to our front were driven in and immediately after a dense line of the enemy's infantry [Barksdale's brigade] was seen advancing over a knoll about 600 yards distant to our left and front, and as this line advanced the infantry on both sides became engaged."[19]

---

17 OR 27, pt. 2, 618; USGS MRC 39077G2; *Bachelder Maps, Second Day;* McNeily, "Barksdale's Mississippi Brigade at Gettysburg," 233-35.

18 Ibid.; Wilcox, "Annotations to Official Report, July 17 1863," Box 1, Wilcox Papers, LOC.

19 OR 27, pt. 1, 575-76; USGS MRC 39077G2; *Bachelder Maps, Second Day.*

South of Wilcox's position, Barksdale's Mississippians wer indeed engaged in a bitter fight. As the brigade advanced toward the Emmitsburg Road, Sickles' skirmishers fired as they slowly retired east to the main line. From the 21st Mississippi on the right (south) to the 18th anchoring the left, Barksdale's advance proved slow and deliberate, with his men trading fire as they encountered stiffening resistance. The left wing of the stubborn 5th New Jersey took down many men marching forward on Barksdale's left wing, slowing its advance somewhat while the Mississippians in the right wing moved slightly ahead. Behind them all, E. P. Alexander's guns remained silent for the time being while his crewmen elevated their pieces in an effort to clear Barksdale's line. The respite took pressure off not only Seeley's battery, but Bucklyn's and Miller's combined eight pieces as well, all of which were now free to fire from south of and within Sherfy's farmyard, respectively. The iron from the latter two batteries tore gaping holes in Barksdale's right and center.[20]

With the left wing of his skirmish line being pushed back by Barksdale's left regiments, and with Wilcox's isolated 8th Alabama having finally cleared the Staub farm in front of his left-center, Colonel Sewell had no choice but to refuse the 5th New Jersey's line by pulling the entire left side back in an effort to continue its delaying action against the tide of approaching Mississippians. Although several hundred men from various units also joined in Sewell's effort, the combined 13th and 18th Mississippi regiments were simply too powerful. When the 11th New Jersey and 71st and 72nd New York to the immediate south began giving way, Sewell's line was little more than an isolated thin blue island with an onrushing gray tide about to envelope it.[21]

Posted in the center of his regiment, Colonel Sewell frantically urged his hard-pressed men to hold the line, even as the far left unraveled when Barksdale's line began a wide wheel movement toward the northeast. With his center still anchored a short distance south of Spangler's farm lane, and with the 8th Alabama on the move again, Sewell moved along his line toward his right-center to continue directing its the operations. With his right wing clear of friendly skirmishers, his reinforced line stood directly opposite Wilcox's 10th (and portions of the 11th) Alabama, trading volleys from behind a snake-rail fence. It must have been a harrowing experience as Sewell's men attempted to hold one fence while some 100 yards to the west an equally aggressive adversary was scaling another.[22]

---

20 McNeily, "Barksdale's Mississippi Brigade at Gettysburg," 233-35; *OR* 27, pt. 1, 590-91; USGS MRC 39077G2; *Bachelder Maps, Second Day.*

21 USGS MRC 39077G2; *Bachelder Maps, Second Day.*

22 Ibid., *OR* 27, pt. 1, 575-76.

The 5th New Jersey's late advance to the skirmish line evolved into the first close-range firefight that over the next 90 minutes would become routine in the attack and defense of the Union center. The defiant Union stand to defend the crest of the first low rise 400 yards west of the Emmitsburg Road significantly slowed Wilcox's advance As a result, Barksdale's less-unimpeded Mississippians outdistanced the Alabamians and any help they could have offered. Lieutenant Colonel Herbert's 8th Alabama was also unavailable to support Barksdale because that regiment veered northeast to dress upon Wilcox's right and preserve the brigade's line. Wilcox and Barksdale realized their commands were fast becoming isolated, and both generals sent messengers galloping back to their respective divisional headquarters to seek reinforcements.[23]

Unfortunately for Barksdale and Wilcox, General Lee's plan of attack did not provide for additional reinforcements. Major General George Pickett's 5,500-man division, Longstreet's only unengaged troops, was still miles away to the west. If Barksdale expected help from Brig. Gen. William Wofford and his Georgians, who had deployed behind him, he was sorely disappointed. Wofford did not immediately attack, and when he did so, he drove his brigade directly east in a move that helped Kershaw take the Stony Hill, part of the Wheatfield, and Trostle's Woods. The Georgians were of little or no use to Barksdale because their fronts moved away from one another, with Barksdale battling his way north and northeast up and beyond the Emmitsburg Road. Brigadier Generals Kershaw's and Semmes' brigades of McLaws' division worked somewhat together, but that cannot be said for the balance of Longstreet's brigades, which for the most part engaged independently of one another. Communication between the divisions and their respective brigades eroded almost as soon as the men stepped off. It did not improve when General Anderson's first brigade under Cadmus Wilcox joined the assault. The breakdown in communications was also not in Lee's plans.[24]

The fight south of the Millerstown Road beyond Barksdale's right flank quickly escalated out of General Longstreet's control. As noted earlier, but worth repeating, Union strength here exceeded Lee's expectations, and few seem to have expected the difficult terrain obstacles. The move Lee envisioned making up the Emmitsburg Road bogged down almost immediately. The unforeseen intervals between the attacking brigades only compounded these problems. These gaps were sometimes so wide that individual regiments (such as Wilcox's 8th Alabama to the north) became completely detached from their brigades and often advanced

23 Ibid.; Franklin Ellis, *History of the Monmouth County New Jersey* (Philadelphia, 1885), 248-50; OR 27, pt. 1, 379; pt. 2, 618.

24 USGS MRC 39077G2; *Bachelder Maps, Second Day.*

hundreds of yards off course, and brigades themselves divided into wings that lessened their striking and control power.

Sickles' soldiers, meanwhile, fought stubbornly from crumbling positions west of and below Little Round Top. Pressed by heavy numbers, it was just a matter of time before the Third Corps tumbled back, an eventuality General Gibbon predicted earlier in the afternoon after watching Humphreys leave lower Cemetery Ridge and march west toward the Emmitsburg Road. From the Emmitsburg Road eastward to Houck's Ridge, the rock-strewn meadows and nearly impassable woods to the Stony Hill were now brutally contested parcels. Although outnumbered and continuously outflanked, Sickles' men defending Meade's left flank were slowing down Longstreet's attack as the early evening shadows grew longer.[25]

General Hancock, meanwhile, rode south along Cemetery Ridge and ordered Caldwell to move his division even farther south several hundred yards toward George Weikert's farm. Hancock's exact return route is unknown. He may or may not have seen the 1st Minnesota as he rode back north. If he did, he made no mention of it. It is likely he was aware of Colonel Colvill and his regiment because he had ridden past it at least three times since it redeployed south of Hummelbaugh's farm lane. Colonel Colvill's precise location at this time is also unclear, but in all likelihood he and his staff were near the crest of southern Cemetery Hill watching the developing situation.[26]

Not one to sit idle during a crisis, Hancock sent riders scurrying eastward in search of reinforcements while he galloped back north. He also sent other couriers ahead with an urgent message to General Hays asking that a brigade be sent to replace Caldwell's division, which was beginning to move toward Little Round Top. Caldwell, however, halted his movement when he noticed the forward elements of Brig. Gen. James Barnes' division of Maj. Gen, George Sykes' Fifth

---

25 Pfanz, *Gettysburg: Second Day*, 314-18; USGS MRC 39077G2; *Bachelder Maps, Second Day.* Unable to pivot north because of the terrain and the Union firepower, the 21st Mississippi could not wheel north with the 17th, 13th, and 18th as planned; thus their move to the east-northeast caused a yawning gap that never was closed. The 21st would fight the rest of the battle isolated, as would the late-arriving 8th Alabama, the 15th Alabama of Law's brigade, and the 1st Texas of Robertson's brigade (both from Hood's division).

26 Rev. James T. Akers, "The American Legion Chaplains in Times of Crisis," *National Americanism Commission of the American Legion: "How to" Manual for God and Country,* April 1997, 67-69; USGS MRC 39077G2; *Bachelder Maps, Second Day.* Hancock took note of Sheldon's Battery B, 1st New York, parked close by. In short order, he would unknowingly add fuel to a festering feud between with chief of artillery Henry Hunt. Their disagreement over the use of field artillery during the battle would turn so personal and ugly that the Joint Committee on the Conduct of War would eventually intervene. The melodrama lasted for nearly a quarter of a century and did not end until Hancock's premature passing in 1886.

Below the Union center from Codori's meadow looking southwest. This is what the gunners of Weir's Union battery would have seen from their second position. From here, their six smoothbores fired into Wilcox's Alabama line advancing east from the wood line stretching horizontally across the photo. The white picket fence in the distant right-center marks the Rogers homestead, with Klingle's farm clearly visible east of Emmitsburg Road atop the rise in the center. Turnbull's six Union smoothbores, deployed along the road between those residences, enjoyed a perfect left-front enfilade down Wilcox's line from right to left. *Rosemary G. Oreb*

Corps passing over the crest of Cemetery Ridge several hundred yards farther south. Barnes reached the field using the dirt lane through Sarah Patterson's woods, and halted with Col. Strong Vincent's brigade near George Weikert's farmyard.[27]

Hancock continued seeking ways to strengthen the Second Corps' line. As he passed over Hummelbaugh's farm lane, he spotted Lieutenant Weir's 5th U. S. battery engaging Wilcox's stalled line along the rail fence. Farther in the distance along the Emmitsburg Road he could see the discharges from Lieutenant Turnbull's six guns, the left section of which was firing from the roadway. Hancock could see Wilcox's long gray line beyond Turnbull's left and front, and elements of Barksdale's brigade pressing General Humphreys' skirmishers.[28]

While Hancock sought reinforcements and Wilcox and Barksdale engaged the Yankee salient, Col. David Lang's small brigade of Floridians enjoyed the relative luxury of resting below the canopy of Spangler's Woods unseen by Union observers. The low ground housing Lang's small brigade of some 750 men was the third swale west of Emmitsburg Road, with two rises and two depressions between

27 Oliver Norton, *Attack and Defense of Little Round Top* (New York, 1913), 263-64.

28 *OR* 27, pt. 1, 880; USGS MRC 39077G2; *Bachelder Maps, Second Day.*

their stone wall and the roadway. From Lang's position, only the three spires of Codori's large ornate barn were visible along the Emmitsburg Road. His skirmishers, supported by volunteers from the 34th North Carolina of Scales' brigade, had been engaged for some time in a brisk firefight with General Gibbon's advanced skirmishers. As was too often the case this day, Lang's right flank was several hundred yards north of Wilcox's left flank and at least 100 yards behind it, even though Wilcox had closed much of the gap between his men and Lang's when he earlier redeployed northward before starting his attack.[29]

"At 6 p.m., General Wilcox having begun to advance," reported Lang, "I moved forward, being met at the crest of the hill with a murderous fire of grape, canister and musketry." Like Wilcox's troops to the south, Lang's small brigade dressed ranks after stepping out of the woods and over the wall. Because of the depression, Lang's line did not endure the same direct artillery fire Wilcox men had faced while redressing. That changed as soon as he ordered his men forward. Union Brig. Gen. Joseph Carr's advanced skirmishers, supported by the Second Corps' left flank, let go a telling volley that dropped many Confederates cresting the first rise. Hustling at the "quick step," Lang hurried his Floridians ahead into the assault. The Floridians were closing the gap with the nearby Alabamians when Lang discovered Wilcox had stopped advancing. By this time Lang's right flank regiment, the 5th Florida, was approaching the 9th Alabama, Wilcox's left regiment. Lang decided to veer, or oblique, slightly northeast to make sure his right did not run into or crowd the 9th's left. This short pause and his decision to redirect northeast proved to be Lang's undoing, and the gap he had been working so hard to close reopened and would remain that way for the rest of the battle.[30]

Meanwhile, Barksdale's Mississippians farther south had closed on General Birney's troops along the Emmitsburg Road, where a bitter struggle for possession of the Millerstown Road intersection, Joseph Sherfy's farm, and his soon-to-be famous peach orchard erupted. Barksdale was battling for this key area while Wilcox's brigade continued taking casualties as the trailing 8th Alabama veered northward to rejoin the brigade. Lieutenant Colonel Herbert's men double-timed to catch up with the 10th Alabama anchoring Wilcox's right. The large gap between Barksdale's left flank and the 10th Alabama's right—which the 8th Alabama was passing into—widened with each step. Resistance from Union skirmishers in Staub's farmyard slowed but did not stop the 8th Alabama. When the defenders fell

29 *OR* 27, pt. 2, 617, 631; Raymond Reid, September 4, 1863, from Headquarters 2nd Florida Regiment, Diary of David Dunham, St. Augustine Historical Society, (copy at GNMP); USGS MRC 39077G2, *Bachelder Maps, Second Day.*

30 Ibid., 631.

away, Lieutenant Colonel Herbert's Alabamians rushed through the farmyard and encountered a spattering of small arms fire from Yankees behind the rail fence. Herbert paused briefly to redress his disordered ranks before urging his soldiers forward. About 200 yards to Herbert's left and front, Wilcox's main line stopped at the same fence. About 300 yards off his right-front, the 18th Mississippi was closing on the Emmitsburg Road, veering away from the Alabamians. Union skirmishers north of the 5th New Jersey who faced Wilcox's left-center gave way quicker than Colonel Sewell's line to the south. Retiring into the swale, they scampered up and out to the east before disappearing into the main Federal line holding the Emmitsburg Road. Like Barksdale's Mississippians well to the right who could not count on Wilcox for close support, Wilcox also realized that he, in turn, could not depend upon Lang's Floridians to his left. In fact, matters were even worse than Wilcox realized. From where he was fighting with his Alabamians west of the Emmitsburg Road, Wilcox could not see beyond Lang's right-center, so he could not discern whether Brig. Gen. Ambrose Wright's Georgia brigade had begun its advance when Lang's Floridians stepped off. It had yet to do so.[31]

Ahead of Wilcox, the commander of the Union reserve artillery's 1st Regular Brigade, Capt. Dunbar Ransom, was busy assisting Turnbull's guns along the Emmitsburg Road. When Ransom noticed Gibbon's and Humphreys' skirmish lines wavering northwest of his position, he spurred his horse into the swale west of the road and picked his way through the retiring skirmishers before ascending the next rise, where nine companies of Col. Clark Baldwin's 1st Massachusetts occupied the rail fence. Unable to defend themselves from the oncoming Rebels because of farmer Peter Rogers' intervening house, outbuildings, and orchards, Turnbull's artillerymen needed help from the infantry to hold this section of the line. By then, Baldwin's Bay Staters had been trading shots with Lang's forward skirmishers for several hours and were exhausted and nearly out of ammunition. The Floridians, meanwhile, continued closing the distance to Turnbull's right flank. Despite Turnbull's pleas to protect his guns, Baldwin's infantry support was slowly melting away.[32]

Captain Ransom's arrival at the 1st Massachusetts' position, however, changed that, at least temporarily. While he was pleading with Baldwin to stand strong, a Minié ball or shell fragment tore into his right thigh above his knee. Despite the painful wound, Ransom remained on his skittish horse conversing with Baldwin until he was assured the 1st Massachusetts was there to stay. In substantial pain,

---

31 Ibid., pt. 1, 379, pt. 2, 618; USGS MRC 39077G2, *Bachelder Maps, Second Day*.

32 *OR* 27, pt 1 532, 543, 547, 873; Wyllys Cadwell Ransom, *Historical Outline of the Ransom Family of America* (Ann Arbor, MI, 1903), 28-30; Pfanz, *Gettysburg: the Second Day*, 364.

Lt. Gulian V. Weir,
commander, Battery C, 5th U.S.

U.S.M.A. West Point

Ransom rode back toward his battery as bullets zipped past him. At least one grazed his horse and another clipped its tail. The injured captain reached his command and spoke briefly with Lieutenant Turnbull (likely to assure him of Baldwin's support) before one of Turnbull's aides ushered the officer away for medical attention.[33]

About this time General Hancock remembered Lieutenant Weir's Battery C, 5th U. S. and spurred his horse toward the six Napoleons engaging Wilcox's stalled line. General Gibbon had earlier marked the distant target well, suggesting distance, degree of elevation, and specific combinations of solid shot, spherical case, and shell. Weir had been pummeling Wilcox's line for about 20 minutes when Hancock reined in his mount and ordered the bewildered officer to limber his guns. It was nearly impossible for Wilcox to advance much farther so long as Seeley's, Turnbull's, and Weir's combined 18 smoothbores concentrated most or all of their fire against him.[34]

---

33 Ibid. Ransom reported to a field hospital, the metal was extracted, and the injury bandaged. After a night's rest, he reported to General Tyler for duty the next morning. On July 4, Ransom was relieved from command because of his festering wound. He would not return to duty until September. Francis B. Heitman, *Historical Register and Dictionary of the United States Army 1789-1903*, 2 vols. (Washington, D.C.: U.S. Government Printing Office, 1903), vol. 1, 816; Congressional Serial Set, 53rd Congress, 2nd Session, January 24, 1894, The Committee on Military Affairs Report, no. 32, Dunbar Richard Ransom on retired list, 1-3, LoC.

34 OR 27, pt. 1, 880; Weir to father, July 5, 1863, GNMP; USGS MRC 39077G2; *Bachelder Maps, Second Day*; Wilcox, *Annotations to the OR*, July 17, 1863, Box 1, Wilcox Papers, LoC; French, Barry, Hunt, *Instruction for Field Artillery*, 178. Within 30 minutes of Wilcox's Alabamians having cleared Spangler's Woods, they endured as many as 1,600 rounds based on three-fixed rounds per minute per 18 guns, which was not unusual during battle. It was not uncommon for a 12-pounder Napoleon to fire four rounds of fixed case or canister per minute. Fixed canister was a 4.52-inch diameter tin can filled with 27 cast-iron solid balls each weighing seven ounces.

Looking north-northeast from the Longstreet Tower atop Warfield Ridge. General Lee's ill-advised plan to advance *en echelon* up the Emmitsburg Road unfolded on these fields. The compactness of this battlefield is deceiving. Many impediments to the July 2 attack have long since disappeared because of major terrain alterations. Colonel Benjamin Humphreys' 21st Mississippi, part of Barksdale's brigade, advanced east along the Millerstown Road (running here left to right) with its left flank just below this road. The 17th Mississippi's far right passed down the road while the rest of the regiment dressed off the 13th, with the 18th on the far left. The Union Third Corps held the Emmitsburg Road Rise the length of the picture from right to left as far north as the Codori-Hummelbaugh crossroad (designated by the rail fence running perpendicular to the Emmitsburg Road beginning near the Vermont Monument in the center of the photo). *Rosemary G. Oreb*

Now, with Turnbull's right-half battery having pivoted to the right to engage Lang's Floridians, and with Weir's battery ceasing fire on Hancock's order, Wilcox's exhausted men caught their breath and readied themselves to storm the Union troops in the roadway. Like a sweeping wave breaking south to north, the Alabamians passed over the rails, redressed their ranks, and began a harrowing 300-yard journey east from the captured fence line to the Union-held Emmitsburg Road, their right flank a bit closer to the road than their left.[35]

South of Wilcox, fighting continued unabated between General Humphreys' left and General Barksdale's Mississippians. About 850 yards southeast of Henry Spangler's farmyard, Col. Ben. Humphreys' 21st Mississippi of Barksdale's brigade

---

35 Weir's remarkable story is continued in the following chapter.

forced McClellan's gun section back to the Emmitsburg Road, where it rejoined its parent command, Capt. Nelson Ames' Battery G, 1st New York. From there, McClellan's brace of guns poured canister into Humphreys' center and left as the men from the Magnolia State slowed just west of the road as the men of the 68th Pennsylvania and Company B of the 2nd New Hampshire, on either side of McClellan's new position, waited to open fire.[36]

McClellan's skilled gunners depressed their tubes so the iron canister balls skipped or ricocheted off the hard ground to better tear out the legs of the advancing enemy. Packed with sawdust and capped with a thin iron plate, these shotgun-like projectiles could kill and maim enemy soldiers up to about 1,000 yards. At 200 yards the rounds were devastating, as Humphreys' unfortunate Mississippians soon learned. In frantic moments, double rounds of canister could be rammed home and fired together. This was common practice when a gun was being hard pressed or had to be limbered and withdrawn or moved rearward by prolonge, the piece fired as it was being hauled rearward with the recoil helping move the gun. McClellan retired the last 100 yards using this technique.[37]

Although Barksdale's three regiments advancing on the left of the 21st Mississippi had a longer distance to travel to reach the Emmitsburg Road, they arrived there about the same time as Colonel Humphreys' regiment. The wooded ridge where Barksdale's brigade waited prior to the attack angled slightly northwest away from the Emmitsburg Road, which at that point veered to the northeast. In other words, the field was considerably wider in front of Barksale's left than on his right. With less distance to cover, Humphreys' 21st regiment should have reached the Emmitsburg Road before any regiments arrayed on its left. His advance, however, was considerably slowed by Sickles' blazing line south of the Wentz farm and the Plum Run ravine on the right. Unlike Kershaw's troops to the south, the depression was a minor physical obstacle for Humphreys, but it forced his men to fire up a slight incline while the Union defenders were able to fire down it. As a result, many of the Mississippians' rounds passed over the Yankees' heads, but the Northern bullets found Southern flesh. Humphreys had little choice but to charge the Emmitsburg Road without the opportunity to close up and redress.[38]

---

36 OR 27, pt. 1, 900-901; Pfanz, *Gettysburg: The Second Day,* 311, 317.

37 French, Barry, Hunt, *Instruction for Field Artillery,* 11-12; James M. McCaffrey, *The Army in Transformation, 1790-1860* (Westport, CT: Greenwood Publishing, 2006) 38 -39; USGS MRC 39077G2.

38 Humphreys to McLaws, January 6, 1878, UNC; McNeily "Barksdale's Mississippi Brigade at Gettysburg," 236-38; Tucker, *Barksdale's Charge,* 97-98; USGS MRC 39077G2; Sears, *Gettysburg,* 299-300.

Mid-1930s aerial photograph showing the ground where Barksdale's brigade smashed through Sickles' defenders north of the Peach Orchard along the Emmitsburg Road. The farmyard west of the Emmitsburg Road and the house east of it are part of the old Staub farm. Note the lane running west toward the farm site. Trostle's farm lane and yard are visible, as are the meadows, Plum Run, and the Union center (denoted by the impressive Pennsylvania Monument). Unfortunately for Barksdale, the 21st Mississippi became unhinged from the balance of the brigade at the height of the battle, which doomed the brigade as it fought basically an independent battle by itself. *Eisenhower Library, GNMP*

Although from afar Barksdale's large brigade looked to be well in hand, it was already losing cohesion. Colonel Humphreys' left flank passed over the Millerstown Road a few yards west of the Emmitsburg Road intersection. In their attempt to maintain alignment with the regimental colors, however, the men on the left began crowding southeast toward the regiment's center, away from the 17th Mississippi, which in turn opened a gap around the intersection. The fiery white-haired Barksdale might have seen and corrected it if he had been close by, but he was several hundred yards to the north near the center of his brigade leading his beloved 13th Mississippi, too busy to pay much attention to his far right wing.[39]

---

39 Ibid.; McLaws, "Gettysburg," 73; USGS MRC 39077G2.

As Humphreys' 21st Mississippi drew near the western plank fence of the Emmitsburg Road, the recently repositioned 68th Pennsylvania delivered a volley into its ranks from opposite the pike that briefly stopped the Confederates in their tracks. Regaining their composure, the Mississippians again surged forward and carried the eastern fence line before firing a volley of their own from behind it, their battle flags waving above its top rail only 30 yards away from the 68th Pennsylvania and its nearby supports. For perhaps 15 brutal minutes, soldiers from Michigan, Pennsylvania, and New Hampshire, supported by the four smoothbore Napoleons of Ames' battery, squared off against the 21st Mississippi. Unfortunately for the men in blue, General Kershaw's line of South Carolina infantrymen, now supported by General Semmes' fresh brigade of Georgians, was making headway south of Colonel Humphreys. All of the nearby Union batteries, including four guns of Captain Ames' New Yorkers, turned south to face this new threat, leaving Lieutenant McClellan's pair of guns and Bucklyn's left section to continue fighting the 21st Mississippi.[40]

From the 63rd Pennsylvania of General Graham's brigade nearest Bucklyn's four smoothbores in the Wentz farmyard northward 400 yards to Graham's 105th Pennsylvania, the beleaguered Federals took advantage of the uneasy if brief stillness that fell upon that part of the field when Barksdale's line north of the Millerstown Road disappeared into the swale. With the returned skirmishers falling in and facing about, more than 1,500 Union soldiers reloaded, capped their muskets, and drew their hammers back. When Barksdale's three regiments north of the 21st Mississippi (numbering 1,192 effectives at the start of action) rose out of the swale, they were fewer than 100 yards from their Third Corps opponents, and received a solid volley at point-blank range supported by six cannon firing canister. Colonel William D. Holder's 17th Mississippi reeled under devastating fire from Bucklyn's guns in the Wentz farm, supported by the right flank of Company B of the 2nd New Hampshire of Burling's brigade, the 63rd Pennsylvania, and most of the 114th Pennsylvania's red-trousered Zouaves in the roadbed (the latter two regiments from Charles Graham's brigade). This Union firepower, as solid as it was that afternoon, was simply not sufficient to knock out Colonel Holder's 17th Mississippi. For a few moments, the opposing lines stood and blazed away as the Mississippians pushed slowly past what was now a dismantled worm fence

40 OR 27, pt. 1, 498-99, 503, 590; McNeily, "Barksdale's Mississippi Brigade at Gettysburg," 236. The 68th Pennsylvania was initially placed behind Clark's New Jersey battery, fronting to the south. Lewis, *History of Battery E*, 209-11.

separating them from the enemy line, taking light shelter behind a ruined plank fence.[41]

On Colonel Holder's left, the 13th and 18th Mississippi regiments faced off with portions of the 114th Pennsylvania's right flank and the 57th and 105th Pennsylvania regiments (of Graham's brigade), as well as Lt. Benjamin Freeborn's right section of smoothbores from Bucklyn's Rhode Island Battery E and two rifled cannon belonging to Lt. Joseph Miller of Knap's Battery E, First Pennsylvania Independent. Stopping along the worm fence atop the eastern embankment, these Mississippians fired into the Sherfy farmyard and the orchard north of it. The charismatic Barksdale, easily visible as he rode along this portion of his line with his hat in hand, cheered on his men. How he survived to that point in battle while on horseback is rather remarkable because the fight for Sherfy's farm was as brutal as any encounter of the war. The brigadier urged his men to remain steady and rake the guns to their immediate front. Alert to the danger, Freeborn's smoothbores south of the house fired one last round of canister before the gunners hauled them at fixed prolonge out of harm's way.[42]

Within seconds of Freeborn's last recoil, the 114th Pennsylvania ("Collis's Zouaves") stepped forward and closed the opening where the ruined plank fence once stood and where Freeborn's Napoleons had created so much bloody havoc within Barksdale's ranks. By this time, only solitary wooden posts identified the Emmitsburg Road beyond the destroyed fence, its shattered and splintered planks littering the ground. Freeborn probably withdrew due east across the road and through the Wentz farm, making good his escape with the rest of Bucklyn's retiring 1st Rhode Island Light Artillery. Bucklyn's four guns south of Freeborn became exposed when Company B of the 2nd New Hampshire diverted its attention to the 21st Mississippi on its left and front, which was pressing back Col. Andrew Tippin's 68th New York of Graham's brigade. At the same time, Lieutenant McClellan's section began to limber just south of the intersection. Bucklyn's battery likely was

41 OR 27, pt. 1, 584, 590; McNeily, "Barksdale's Brigade," 236; Adolpho Fernandez de la Cavada Papers (Cavada Diary), no. CHC5006, Box 1, File 24, University of Miami Special Collection Library, Miami, Florida; Tucker, *Barksdale's Charge*, 97; USGS MRC 39077G2.

42 Ibid., 482-483, 500-501, 502-503, 590. The 57th and 105th Pennsylvania of Charles Graham's brigade were initially placed east of the Emmitsburg Road with a heavy skirmish line fighting well to the west of it. They apparently crossed over it *en mass* when E. P. Alexander's Rebel artillery stopped firing in order to allow Barksdale's Mississippi brigade to pass through the artillery line. By that time, much of the plank fence along the Emmitsburg Road had been dismantled. The worm fence west of it, nearest the swale, however, was still largely intact at this time. See also Tucker, *Barksdale's Charge*, 98-100; USGS MRC 39077G2; *Bachelder Maps, Second Day*.

the first organized command to disengage and depart from Sickles' embattled salient.[43]

The intensity of the musketry fire along the salient's face increased with every passing second, with every man loading and firing as fast as his stiffening fingers would allow. The lines closed to within scant yards of one another, with only fence posts and a few splintered planks separating the combatants along the length of Sherfy's farmyard. The constant roar of small arms fire drowned out most orders. Dense clouds of acrid powder smoke clogged eyes, filled nostrils, and parched throats. The last load of canister from Miller's guns just north of the house buffeted Barksdale's' men. The resulting gaps, however, closed almost as quickly as they opened, but by this time what were once crisp lines of battle had become thick masses of men. By this time the only sure way for an officer from either side to convey an order was to seize a man, scream in his ear, and hope he survived long enough to relay the order.[44]

The dire circumstances for the Union defenders along the Emmitsburg Road took a turn for the worse when glimpses of yet another Confederate brigade moving toward them beyond Barksdale's masses was spotted. To the Yankees fighting nearest the intersection, Brig. Gen. William Wofford's brigade of Georgians appeared large and rather magnificent. Its infantrymen tramped unhindered toward them, holding aloft bright red colors that stretched northward beyond the Millerstown Road.

About this time, somewhere along Trostle's farm lane on the east side of the Emmitsburg Road, a solid shot bounded over the crest and clipped the leg of Third Corps commander Dan Sickles as he sat upon his horse. Witnesses recall watching Sickles sway a bit, but he appeared as undamaged and unconcerned as his horse. Within moments, however, the shock of his wound, followed by intense pain, gripped the general. Aides removed him from the saddle and it soon became evident his right leg had been shattered by the round. Sickles planted himself on the ground and calmly awaited a stretcher, his faculties intact. He dispatched riders galloping off in various directions, some in search of General Birney to take command of the corps, and others to ride to army headquarters with the news that he was down.[45]

43 Ibid.; Pfanz, *Gettysburg: Second Day*, 322, 532; George Lewis, *The History of Battery E, First Regiment, Rhode Island Light Artillery* (Providence: Snow and Farnham, 1892), 208-10.

44 Ibid.; McNeily, "Barksdale's Brigade" 236; Cavada Diary.

45 USGS MRC 39077G2; *Bachelder Maps, Second Day*; William H. Bullard to Daniel Sickles, September 13, 1897, New York Historical Society; Henry E. Tremain, *Two Days of War: A Gettysburg Narrative and Other Experiences* (New York, 1905), 88-89.

The northernmost unit fighting Barksdale that afternoon was Col. Calvin A. Craig's 105th Pennsylvania of Graham's brigade. The right wing of Craig's "Wild Cat" regiment covered the Trostle farm lane intersection along with the 72nd New York of Col. William Brewster's brigade on Craig's immediate right and rear, their flanks somewhat overlapping. Both units had suffered under a heavy frontal and left enfilading fire from the distant Confederate artillery, and the small peach orchard they now held west of the road was being blasted to bits by solid shot, shrapnel, and shell. Craig's men found refuge in every depression they could find and behind every tree, but the iron rounds claimed at least a dozen victims before Barksdale's infantry advanced within small-arms range.[46]

When Colonel Craig ordered his regiment to its feet, Col. Thomas M. Griffin's 18th Mississippi was a little more than 100 yards away angling northeast up the western embankment of the Emmitsburg Road. Beyond the 18th's left flank and rear, past the swale to the north and west, Craig could see Lieutenant Colonel Herbert's 8th Alabama of Wilcox's brigade moving east. However, the immediate threat was Griffin's 18th regiment, whose left flank was slightly south of Craig's left and on a collision course with Col. Peter Sides' 57th Pennsylvania just north of the barn. The 8th Alabama was advancing directly toward the intersection and the Craig's 105th Pennsylvania. Craig had to make a decision—fast.[47]

Unable to deliver a volley for fear of hitting some of the troops in the five companies Craig had sent forward as skirmishers, his men impatiently waited as the heavily pressed skirmishers hastened back. Scrambling up and out of the swale, the 18th Mississippi delivered a volley into their backs. Before the 18th could fire again, however, Craig's skirmishers had joined his ranks. With their field of fire finally clear, the men of the 105th Pennsylvania, some 307 rifles strong, fired a shattering volley. While his left wing joined Colonel Sides' 57th Pennsylvania battling the 18th Mississippi, Craig had to pivot his right from fronting southwest to due west to better counter the 8th Alabama (Wilcox's brigade) as it closed on the swale beyond the intersection.[48]

Confronted by a two-pronged attack from the 18th Mississippi to his left and front and the closing 8th Alabama, Craig decided splitting his regiment into two wings to meet the dual threats was unrealistic and that withdrawal was the better

---

46 OR 27, pt. 1, 501; Kate M. Scott, *History of the 105th Pa. Regiment, 1877* (Brookville, PA: Jefferson County Historical Society); Edwin P. Hogan, *Waiting for Jacob: A Civil War Story*, (Latrobe, PA: St. Vincent College, 2000).

47 Ibid.; Kate Scott, "The Mountain Men: The Famous Wild-Cat Regiment in the Civil War," *Philadelphia Weekly Times*, March 19, 1887; McNeily, "Barksdale's Brigade," 236.

48 Ibid.

option. The entire regiment retired to the Emmitsburg Road without incident, where Craig refused his left-most company to front south toward the approaching 18th Mississippi. The balance of the Pennsylvanians faced west to contest the 8th Alabama. The south-facing company fired a volley at close range into the 18th, temporarily halting the Mississippians and allowing Colonel Sides' outgunned 57th Pennsylvania to also withdraw. Once in the roadway, Sides faced his small regiment back toward the enemy, his left protected by Craig's right flank and by Sherfy's large red bank barn, and his right by the 114th Pennsylvania Zouaves. The 18th Mississippi, meanwhile, slowly pushed its way into the same orchard the 105th and 57th Pennsylvania regiments had recently vacated. The going was tough, with small arms firing coming from the 105th and 114th Pennsylvania on either flank of the 57th, and Lieutenant Miller's pair of Ordnance Rifles, supported by several hundred rifles from the 114th. Canister was unloaded into the gray ranks at point-blank range. The withdrawal of Sides' 57th Pennsylvania, however, had made Miller's gun position untenable. The fighting that raged between the Sherfy house and barn was as brutal as any along the length of the Emmitsburg Road. The opposing forces were so close that Miller emptied his service revolver into advancing Rebels while his artillerymen frantically hooked prolonge ropes to each gun carriage to escape. Fortunately for them, Colonel Cavada's 114th Pennsylvania Zouaves held their ground with the Rebel riflemen only 30-40 yards from their position. Cavada's stubborn resistance enabled Miller to get his guns out of immediate danger and avoid being overrun.[49]

Opposite the Sherfy house where Miller's cannoneers along with the 114th Pennsylvania, the undermanned 63rd Pennsylvania of Graham's brigade, and Company B of the 2nd New Hampshire of Burling's brigade stubbornly held their ground, the newly redeployed 73rd and 141st New York regiments (Brewster's and Graham's brigades, respectively) rushed forward to help plug the gap in the line recently vacated by Bucklyn's six guns. The New Yorkers were pulled off the southern-facing line in the Peach Orchard and, along with the 3rd Maine and 3rd Michigan (Ward's and de Trobriand's brigades, respectively), redeployed in what appeared to be a brilliant tactical maneuver under fire. Despite the timely arrival of these Federal reinforcements, the attacking Mississippians of the 17th regiment drove past the intersection of the Emmitsburg and Millerstown roads while Col. James W. Carter's 13th Mississippi, its left intermingled with the 18th Mississippi's right, battled the Yankees around the Sherfy house and barn. Unfortunately for

---

49 Allen J. Adams, "The Fight at the Peach Orchard," *National Tribune*, April 23, 1885; Francis W. Moran, "A New View of Gettysburg," *Philadelphia Weekly Times*, April 22, 1882; Bradley M. Gottfried, *Brigades of Gettysburg: The Union and Confederate Brigades at the Battle of Gettysburg* (Boston, 2002), 192; *OR* 27, pt. 1, 890.

David Birney, the new commander of the Third Corps, shifting troops within the shrinking salient was becoming more than problematic. Within a few minutes, the right wing of Colonel Humphreys' 21st Mississippi began enfilading and pressing back the right flank and rear of the south-facing 2nd New Hampshire (minus its detached Company B).[50]

Colonel Edward L. Bailey's 2nd New Hampshire of Burling's brigade had recently helped repulse Joe Kershaw's attack from the Rose farm south of the Millerstown Road, but now Humphreys' 21st Mississippi coming on from the west was about to overrun the regiment's exposed right flank. Reacting quickly, Bailey swung his entire regiment back to the Emmitsburg Road, where his line fired into Humphreys' right wing. "I immediately directed my battalion to the right oblique full upon it," Bailey reported. "Yet their line of fire, assisted by a terrible discharge of spherical case from their batteries, caused the Sixty-eight Pennsylvania to retire, and at the same moment the Third Maine moved 200 yards to the rear, though in good order."[51]

The Granite State boys had little chance after the supporting 3rd Michigan also pulled back eastward to safer environs. Perhaps no one on General Birney's staff realized Bailey's regiment was still stubbornly holding its ground, for the colonel never received any orders to withdraw. Unsupported and now enfiladed from the right and the rear, Bailey's embattled men continued to confront the 21st Mississippi's wing just as Captain Ames' New York battery to Bailey's right and rear began limbering to head out of the Peach Orchard. The Rebels pressed ahead sensing victory. "Our fire made apparently little or no impression on them," recalled Bailey. "They were reinforced from right to left [by Wofford's Georgia brigade] at every step. When they appeared at point blank range they were a compact mass of humanity. Although our shooting was good, there wasn't enough of it."[52]

According to one of the attackers, J. S. McNeily of the 21st Mississippi, he and his comrades "met with stiff resistance. But when the blue coats saw us swarming over the fences and across the Emmetsburg [sic] Road, without pausing, they began to 'back out.' Though they fought back bravely, retiring slowly until the firing was at

---

50 OR 27, pt. 1, 524, 890; Haynes, *History of the Second Regiment New Hampshire Volunteer Infantry*, 185-87; Tucker, *Barksdale's Charge*, 128-29; *Pennsylvania at Gettysburg*, 612; Pfanz, *Gettysburg: The Second Day*, 313-15.

51 *OR* 27, pt. 1, 574.

52 Ibid.; Eric Campbell, "Hell in a Peach Orchard," *America's Civil War*, vol. 16, July 2003, 38; Wiley Sword, "Amid the Iron Hail in the Peach Orchard: Lady Luck Smiles on an Officer," *Gettysburg Magazine*, no. 22, 23-27.

close quarters, when the retreat became a rout in which our men took heavy toll for the losses inflicted on them."[53]

Colonel Bailey's subsequent exit from the Peach Orchard was not the rout McNeily and other postwar writers suggest. As the line began crumbling around him, Bailey on his own initiative ordered a belated withdrawal. "Finding myself thus unsupported, and the enemy steadily advancing," he later reported, "I ordered my regiment to fall back slowly, firing, which was fully executed. I moved to the rear 140 yards, and halted my line under the brow of a hill (below Sherfy's Peach Orchard north of Millerstown Road, which is the highest point of the Emmitsburg Road Rise) halting also on the brow to give a volley to the enemy, than distant but 20 yards. The positions of the three regiments was that of echelon at about 20 paces," he concluded, "my regiment being at the apex." Bailey lost more than one-half of his men that afternoon.[54]

Although the apex of Sickles' salient line in the Peach Orchard had crumbled and howling Rebels were pressing forward into the vacated ground, the fight along the Emmitsburg Road was still raging and it was anyone's guess as to how it would unfold. The first major order sent by General Birney, who was directing operations from somewhere near Sickles' former headquarters on the Trostle farm, left by courier and directed General Humphreys to refuse his Emmitsburg Road line in a desperate attempt to stop Barksdale's northward-sweeping Mississippians. Birney also personally redeployed several regiments in a desperate effort to stop Barksdale's momentum. He sent the 7th New Jersey of Burling's brigade forward into the firestorm from its position in the rear of Captain Clark's now limbering Battery B, 1st New Jersey. Unfortunately for the infantry regiment's commander, Col. Louis Francine, Clark's retiring limbers and guns plowed through his advancing ranks and stopped the New Jersey men in their tracks. Francine's regiment never regained its forward momentum and slowly retired in the wake of the 2nd New Hampshire. Birney tried mightily to corral these scattered commands, but was unable to stem the tide flowing to the rear. As he continued to command from his saddle near Trostle's farm lane, Birney had no idea that three-fourths of a mile to the north, General Hancock had received General Meade's permission to take whatever necessary steps he could to shore up the crumbling Third Corps line —including taking control of the Third Corps itself.

---

53 McNeily, "Barksdale's Brigade," 236.

54 Ibid. The 2nd New Hampshire retired north across the Millerstown Road before firing several volleys, and then headed north by northeast skirting the rise between the road and Trostle's farm lane. It followed several batteries as it made its way toward and through Trostle's cherry orchard to the farm lane.

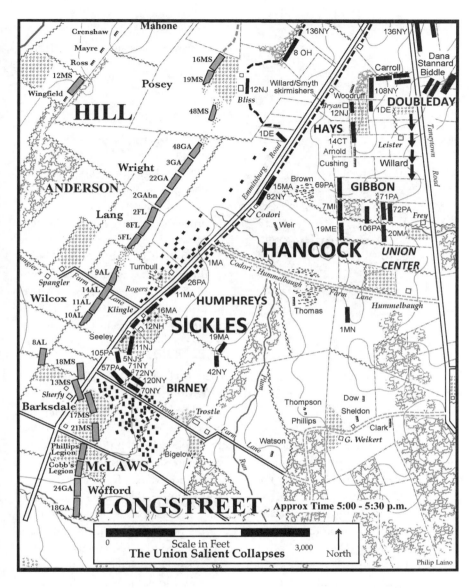

The Union Salient Collapses

Fortunately for General Meade, he still had five capable and experienced infantry corps commanders in Hancock, Howard, Sykes, Sedgwick, and Slocum. General Birney was not on George Meade's list of preferred generals, and how he treated Birney that July 2 had a lot to do with the politics of the well-educated and devoted abolitionist, as well as his military record. Although personally brave under fire, he had been accused of disobeying orders while commanding a brigade at the battle of Seven Pines during the 1862 Peninsula Campaign, but was cleared by a court-martial. Elevated to division command during the September 1, 1862, battle

Brig. Gen. David Birney,
division commander, Sickles' Corps,
Army of the Potomac.
USAHEC

of Chantilly, Birney, benefitted from his strong political ties to Tammany Hall and remained in that position through several command changes and various reorganizations. Birney was thrust into the limelight again when General Meade charged him with refusing to support his Fifth Corps' division during the battle of Fredericksburg in December of 1862. Politics prevailed once more, no charges were leveled against Birney, and Meade's accusation was expunged from the record. The result angered Meade and many of his Regular Army officer friends. Now, on July 2 at Gettysburg, Birney found himself in charge of the Third Corps when Sickles went down. Birney had no chance to command a corps permanently in Meade's army. Even during the heat of battle, past issues and politics prevailed. Meade's choice, both politically and professionally to take over the Third Corps for the duration of the fight, was Winfield Hancock. In turn, Meade elevated the dependable John Gibbon over the more senior John Caldwell to temporarily command the Second Corps.[55]

When news of Sickles' wounding reached headquarters, Meade had to set his house in order and make sure it remained that way. With Sickles (and Birney) out of the way, he now had professional soldiers (all personal friends) in control of his seven corps (considering that Hancock was at the head of his own Second Corps and now overseeing the Third Corps). Now Meade had to figure out how to repair the damage done by Sickles. As Sickles' staff officer Henry Tremain later opined, "The only thing that had thus far worked for Meade without a hitch or string attached was Robert E. Lee's failure to act earlier than he did."[56]

55 Bates, *The Battle of Gettysburg*, 112-15; Tagg, *The Generals of Gettysburg*, 44, 65.

56 Meade, Jr. to Alexander Webb, December 7, 1885, Webb Papers, Box 3, Yale University Special Collections Library; Tremaine, *Two Days*, 54-56.

Chapter Fifteen

"If I commanded this regiment I'd be God Damned if I would not bayonet charge you!"

— *Maj. Gen. Winfield Hancock, Second Corps, Army of the Potomac*[1]

Early Evening, July 2: Wilcox, Lang, and Wright Attack the Emmitsburg Road Line

The crippling wound that knocked Daniel Sickles out of action and simultaneously lifted David Birney to temporary command of the Third Corps arrived at perhaps the worst possible moment for the general who had taken the political route to rise through the ranks of the Army of the Potomac.

The Third Corps' bulging and undermanned front was being attacked from the south, southwest, and west, casualties were rapidly mounting, parts of the salient were cracking open, and the entire position appeared on the verge of collapsing. Given the smoke, noise, confusion, and his own direct responsibility for his division defending the Peach Orchard salient, it is likely that Birney had no idea two more Rebel brigades (Wilcox's and Lang's) were closing from the west against the Emmitsburg Road line. General Hancock had not yet assumed control of the corps, so throwing back the enemy was General Birney's responsibility.

By the time Birney assumed corps command, Wilcox's and Lang's men had driven back General Humphreys' reinforced skirmish line from the mangled split-rail fence atop the first rise west of the Emmitsburg Road. Leading by example at the front with the colors of his center regiment close by his side, Wilcox urged his veteran Alabama troops forward. On Wilcox's left, the once yawning gap between his and Lang's command had closed so that some members from Captain Gardner's 5th Florida, anchoring Lang's right flank, had merged with Capt. Joseph

---

1   Smith, *History of the 19th Maine,* 70.

H. King's 9th Alabama holding Wilcox's left. After falling back toward the main Union line, skirmishers from Brewster's and Carr's Union brigades, along with Lt. Francis Seeley's Battery K, 4th U. S., hammered the oncoming Alabamians. Seeley's six smoothbores, their barrels already hot to the touch, resumed fire, tearing gaping holes in Col. William Forney's 10th and Col. John C. C. Sanders' 11th Alabama. The Confederates inched forward, their heads bowed against the driving storm of incoming metal.[2]

The undulating terrain quickly came into play. As Wilcox's men crested the middle swale east of Spangler's Woods, they spotted a reinforced line of enemy skirmishers stretched across their front. Some 300 yards beyond these skirmishers, they could also see a much larger line of enemy soldiers, with artillery in support. The intervening field between the Federals looked fairly level—at least until the Alabamians continued on and reached the rail fence. It was only then they fully realized a large trough-like swale separated the Yankee skirmishers from the main line. Many of the pesky Yankees fired a parting shot before ducking into this depression.[3]

The 10th and 11th Alabama took full advantage of the brief respite and surged forward, followed quickly by Captain King's 9th and Col. Lucius Pinckard's 14th Alabama regiments to the north. After clamoring over the fence, the Confederate infantry quickened their gait toward the swale. Another blast of canister from Seeley's Napoleons opened holes in the right of the 11th Alabama and the left of the 10th, but did nothing to stop their steady progress. The retreating Union skirmishers inadvertently blocked the line of sight of Seeley's and Turnbull's batteries, which meant that for a short while, Wilcox's men suffered only scattered small arms fire. Fortunately for these Confederates, most of Brewster's and Carr's west-facing Union regiments just below Klingle's orchard running north toward

2   Wilcox, "General Wilcox on the Battle of Gettysburg," *SHSP,* vol. 6, 1878, 97-124.

3   Wilcox, "General Wilcox on the Battle of Gettysburg"; USGS MRC 39077G2; *Bachelder Maps, Second Day;* Laino, *Gettysburg Campaign Atlas,* 242-45. Wilcox's men had originally rested at Spangler's Woods, where the elevation varies from 550 to 560 feet above sea level. They could see the Emmitsburg Road Rise at 580' some 400 or so yards to the east. The skirmishers east of Spangler's farmyard could not see over the middle rise where Union skirmishers held the rail fence. This middle rise was but a few feet higher than the woods (570' at most). The higher ground between Trostle's farm lane and the Rogers homestead blocked the view of Cemetery Ridge another 400 yards away, which was equal in elevation to Spangler's Woods. The wide middle rise was not a ridge paralleling the Emmitsburg Road, but rather a spur jutting like a thumb of an upturned fist pointing north. The meadows fell away north of the rise, enabling Lang's Floridians to see the 9th Alabama on the higher ground to their right. See also Rollins and Shultz, "Measuring Pickett's Charge."

the Rogers house also had to hold their fire until their friendly skirmishers made it back safely to the Emmitsburg Road.[4]

Many of the soldiers along General Humphreys' main defensive line steadied their muskets on the sturdy plank fence lining the eastern side of the roadway awaiting the inevitable order to open fire. Wilcox's 10th and 11th Alabama descended into the deep swale where Colonels Forney and Sanders took a few moments to redress their lines and ready their respective regiments for the maelstrom about to sweep over them. Knowing that hundreds of Rebels were about to pour out of the swale, Humphreys directed Lieutenant Seeley to "hold at all costs." Seeley ordered his gun crews to load canister and stack plenty of reserve ammunition to the left of each gun carriage to expedite reloading. "The enemy having gained protection from our fire under cover of the slope of the hill in our front," recalled section leader Lt. Robert James, "we ceased firing, and prepared to receive them on its crest with canister."[5]

Survivors from Seeley's anxious artillerymen and the Federal infantry who fought here did not record hearing drums or bugle calls from the swale. Instead, all remained strangely quiet. In the depression, meanwhile, Wilcox's field officers held their swords high and pointed their tips east. Some officers also drew their service revolvers, knowing they would be needed the moment they crested the swale. The temporary hush was first broken by a few verbal orders, followed by the rush of boots and jingling of accoutrements as Wilcox's soldiers began ascending the eastern slope. Within a short time the Federals waiting for their appearance heard the fearful Rebel Yell from 1,000 throats as the line picked up momentum near the crest. To the east in the waiting Union lines, an equal number of hammers were cocked and nipples capped as anxious fingers prepared to pull the triggers. Nearby, Lieutenant Seeley sat calmly on his horse in Klingle's apple orchard behind his guns urging his men to be patient. The first thing the Federals saw was the tips of Wilcox's flagstaffs ease above the crest, followed by a thick line of battle. A roar of musketry erupted from along the Emmitsburg Road.[6]

The first volley was powerful. When Seeley's gunners depressed the muzzles of their six bronze pieces and opened on the 10th Alabama, the canister rounds disintegrated what was left of the plank fencing lining the west side of the road and stopped Colonel Forney's soldiers in their tracks. Many injured Rebels reeled in pain and fell, with others killed outright. For a few moments the left wing of the 10th Alabama wavered, with several terrified soldiers high-tailing it back into the

---

4   Ibid.; *OR* 27 pt. 1 591. Pinckard's name is occasionally misspelled Pincard.

5   *OR* 27, pt. 2, 591.

6   Wilcox, "General Wilcox on the Battle of Gettysburg."

protective swale. Courage and honor, however, coupled with friends and even family members next to them kept the majority of the men in some semblance of a line and in place atop the rise, where they leveled their rifled muskets and opened fire. Lieutenant Seeley's gunners stubbornly stood to their pieces, each man at his assigned position as Rebel Minié balls zipped past, loading as fast as they were able.[7]

Seeley's next round of murderous iron canister balls tore through the first and second lines of Confederates, ripping huge gaps in the Alabama lines. To the left and right of the battery, Brewster's and Carr's infantry added sheets of lead balls into the mix. Somehow Wilcox's four advancing Alabama regiments managed to hold their ground, close their ranks, and advance again toward the road, They did so largely independent of one another—halting, firing, loading, advancing, all while under fire from Union musketry and artillery. Off to the southwest, Colonel Alexander's gun crews offered covering fire by sending round after round toward the defending Federals. In order to hit Brewster's and Carr's lines, Alexander had to fire directly over the heads of General Barksdale's advancing Mississippians, something uncharacteristic of typical Confederate artillery tactics. Barksdale's men were wheeling to the northeast at this time after chasing out or bypassing the remaining Union units from the Peach Orchard.[8]

Alexander's effective enfilade augmented the increasing volume of Wilcox's musketry, one round of which brought down Lieutenant Seeley. "About this time while in front superintending the service of my guns," recalled Seeley, "I was severely wounded, a rifle musket shot high up on my right thigh—the bones shattered somewhat; I remained in command reclining upon the ground." Some of his men lifted the injured officer onto a nearby caisson, and from this perch he continued barking orders. Seeley's bravery inspired his men, who continued to valiantly work their guns.[9]

Wilcox's Alabamians, by now more a disordered solid mass than a well-dressed battle line, reached the shattered plank fence on the west side of the Emmitsburg Road. The only thing separating them from the Federal infantry was the roadbed, across which a bitter firefight erupted for several minutes. Suffering from blood loss and shock, Seeley turned over command to Lieutenant James.[10]

On Wilcox's left, meanwhile, Colonel Lang's brigade also approached Carr's Union line stretched along the Emmitsburg Road. Mustering only 739 men, Lang's

7   OR 27, pt. 2, 591.

8   Murray, *Artillery Action in the Peach Orchard*, 106-108.

9   Francis Seeley to John Bachelder, May 23, 1878, *Bachelder Papers*, 1:608.

10 Hessler, *Sickles at Gettysburg*, 214; Cadmus Wilcox, "Annotations to the Official Report, July 17 1863."

Colonel David Lang,
Anderson's Division, Hill's Corps,
Army of Northern Virginia. *USAHEC*

Florida brigade was small compared to most of the other brigades in the Army of Northern Virginia. The 2nd, 5th, and 8th Florida, the only regiments from the state in Lee's army, were normally led by Brig. Gen. Edward A. Perry, who fell ill with typhoid fever before the campaign into Pennsylvania. As the outfit's senior colonel, Lang of the 8th Florida assumed command.[11]

The bearded Georgia-born Lang graduated from the Georgia Military Institute in 1857 and moved to Suwannee County, Florida, to take up a career as a surveyor. After the outbreak of the war, he enlisted as a private in the 1st Florida on April 2, 1861. Promoted to sergeant within a month, he completed his year-long term of service before reenlisting in the newly organized 8th Florida as a sergeant in early May 1862. He helped raise Company C and was elected its captain prior to formal organization activities on July 5. Wounds suffered at Sharpsburg and Fredericksburg did little to slow down the 25-year-old colonel. Mounted on his warhorse in front of the 8th Florida, whose cocky color bearer began taunting the Yankees from afar the moment he crested the center rise west of the Emmitsburg Road, Lang led his men toward the Emmitsburg Road.[12]

With General Wilcox moving to the south, the undulating terrain east of Seminary Ridge made it difficult for Lang to keep his Floridians in a steady alignment. Beginning at the Klingle house, the Emmitsburg Road angled northeast away from his advancing line. This put Lang's right flank, manned by Capt. Richmond N. Gardner's 5th Florida, somewhat closer to the main enemy line than his Maj. Walter R. Moore's 2nd Florida on the left, leaving Lt. Col. William Baya's 8th Florida tucked in the middle and doing his best to remain connected to the regiments on either side. Soon after advancing the Floridians began losing contact

11 Petruzzi and Stanley, *The Gettysburg Campaign in Numbers and Losses*, 131.

12 "General Lee's Florida Brigade," The Museum of Southern History, Jacksonville, Florida.

with Capt. Joseph H. King's 9th Alabama to their right, and began to encounter spherical case from Lt. John Turnbull's six Napoleons of Batteries F/K, 3rd U. S. stationed in Peter Rogers' farmyard.[13]

As the 5th Florida moved across the center rise toward the landmark rail fence, Captain Gardner could see the 9th Alabama well off of his right front, with a thin line of his Floridians melting into its ranks. Wilcox's left regiment was veering slightly southeast toward the center of the brigade and thus farther from Gardner's Florida regiment. Given a choice between following the Alabamians or dressing on the 8th Florida to his immediate left, the captain decided to maintain brigade cohesion and kept his left glued as closely to his fellow Florida regiment as possible. The result was a gap between Lang and Wilcox, one that grew to become several hundred yards wide. The plan for a tight coordinated assault against lower Cemetery Ridge was already obsolete.[14]

Andrew's Sharpshooters of the 1st Massachusetts, who were waiting behind a long worm fence on the Emmitsburg Road Rise west of the roadbed, fired a volley at the approaching Floridians. Nearby, Capt. Frank E. Marble's detachment of Companies B and G of Colonel Berdan's 1st U. S. Sharpshooters also emptied their weapons into the Rebels. The combined firepower dropped many, whittling down the front rank of the 5th and portions of the 8th Florida. Behind these Federal skirmishers, closer to the Rogers farmhouse, Berdan's Company C joined in with what became a rather desperate attempt to retard Lang's progress.[15]

Federal artillery continued to hammer away at the advancing Confederates. Lieutenant Turnbull's right half-battery fired several loads of canister that wavered the far right of the 5th Florida and sent some of its members scrambling for cover. Captain Gardner, another Georgia-born officer with the Florida brigade, calmly closed the gaps and pushed the left and center of his small regiment toward the Yankees. His far right flank, however, trailed behind the line. Gardner advanced to within 100 yards of the fence shielding the Union sharpshooters before pausing to unleash an opening volley, the result of which appeared ineffective. His men continued eastward. Firing from kneeling or prone positions behind the rails, the Federals finally retired when Lang's line closed to within just 50 yards. Off to the sharpshooters' left, the outnumbered and outflanked skirmishers from the 11th

13 USGS MRC 39077G2; *Bachelder Maps, Second Day.*

14 David Lang to Edward Perry, July 19, 1863, David Lang Letters, 1862-1864, Florida State Archives, Tallahassee.

15 C. A. Stevens, *Berdan's United States Sharpshooters in the Army of the Potomac, 1861-1865* (St. Paul: Price-McGill, 1892), 316-17. Company B hailed from New York; Company G from Wisconsin; and C from Michigan.

Massachusetts and 26th Pennsylvania also withdrew, maintaining a steady fire as they fell back.[16]

"The enemy first attacked the Third Corps, advancing in solid column, with a view to turn the left flank of the Union army," recalled one of the Union sharpshooters. "The enemy was held in check a short time, but the Sharpshooters and infantry were obliged to fall back." Although he was in vigorous disagreement with the order to retire, the 1st Massachusetts' Colonel Baldwin had no choice but order his entire regiment to fall back as directed. By then, Colonel Lang's center regiment, the 8th Florida, was moving beyond the 1st Massachusetts' right flank. "We retired and formed line of battle in connection with [Carr's] brigade," reported Baldwin.[17]

After absorbing their skirmishers, Lt. Col. Porter Tripp of the 11th Massachusetts and Maj. Robert L. Bodine of the 26th Pennsylvania readied their waiting regiments along the Emmitsburg Road. By some miscalculation, Colonel Baldwin reformed his 1st Massachusetts in a manner that masked a large portion of the 26th Pennsylvania. Within a few moments, after plenty of catcalling and prodding from Bodine's Keystoners, Baldwin slid his entire regiment to the north. Captain James Doherty, commanding Baldwin's Company G, sensed his men were on the verge of panic. The quick-thinking officer put them through the manual of arms "in the midst of a perfect hail of fire as if on the parade ground," explained the regimental historian. "The familiar ritual had the desired effect of calming his company and they fought on."[18]

As the Floridians approached the worm fence and the western base of the rise running along the Emmitsburg Road, Lieutenant Colonel Tripp of the 11th Massachusetts, supporting Turnbull's right half-battery at the Rogers house, calmly dressed his ranks and prepared to meet the oncoming Rebels. Unlike General Wilcox, who had taken the time to halt his Alabama regiments in the sheltering swale to dress their lines, Colonel Lang chose otherwise. He sensed the enemy to his front was ready to be broken, and so dressed his line as best he could in the open fields with lead balls buzzing around his men and iron fragments showering down upon them. Within a short time, the three small Florida regiments were ascending the western slope of the rise.

---

16 Lang to Perry, 1863; OR 27, pt. 2, 556; Warren H. Cudworth, *History of the First Regiment* (Boston, 1866), 393-94.

17 OR 27, pt.1, 548; "Wisconsin In the Civil War; 1st United States Sharpshooters," Wisconsin Historical Society, Madison.

18 Cudworth, *History of the First Massachusetts*, 397; James L. Bowen, *Massachusetts in the War, 1861-1865* (Springfield, 1889), 698.

Tripp, Bodine, and Baldwin were waiting there for Lang with their respective regiments, as was Lieutenant Turnbull with his half-dozen Napoleons. Immediately south of the guns was Col. Walden Merriam's 16th Massachusetts along the Emmitsburg Road. To bolster this line, skirmishers from Colonel Sewell's 5th New Jersey and Companies B and G of the 1st U. S. Sharpshooters formed in an apple orchard between Turnbull's left and the 16th Massachusetts' right, with the left side of Tripp's Massachusetts regiment in support less than 100 yards to their rear. Turnbull's left half-battery, with no Floridians immediately threatening its position, pivoted all three guns but could not dislodge Wilcox's exposed left flank from its firm foothold atop the Emmitsburg Road. With Wilcox's and Lang's men pushing forward together (though several hundred yards apart), the situation was fast becoming critical for General Humphreys. Help, however, was on the way.[19]

Under orders to protect the center and assume authority over the Third Corps, General Hancock continued to shift batteries and regiments to counter the growing threat. Earlier, the general, accompanied by a color-bearer and an aide, had ridden over to Battery C, 5th U. S. and ordered Lieutenant Weir to stop firing. That respite made it easier for Wilcox to push ahead. Following orders, Weir limbered and pulled out, his cannoneers mounted on half-empty chests (an artillerist's nightmare in case the shells bounced around and ignited). The six smoothbores and caissons bumped and bounced their way off the western crest of Cemetery Ridge in the wake of Hancock's small party heading toward the Emmitsburg Road. The act must have confused the young lieutenant, for it stripped the Union center of one of its most effective batteries.[20]

It is questionable whether John Gibbon, an expert artillerist steeped in long-arm tactics, would have ended Weir's perfect field of fire on favorable high ground, albeit at long range, by moving him to lower terrain closer to the enemy. And yet that is exactly what Hancock intended to do. By moving Weir off Cemetery Ridge, Hancock, trained in infantry and commissary affairs, reduced the effectiveness of the six Napoleons. Hancock redefined what he considered a battery's effectiveness by placing it directly behind and closer to the front line, though in a position where the terrain and friendly troops could at times mask the enemy. Like Confederate artillerist Porter Alexander across the battlefield who had fired directly over Barksdale's charging Mississippians, Hancock was willing to risk casualties from friendly fire in an effort to disrupt the approaching enemy.[21]

---

19 Ibid.

20 *OR* 27, pt. 1, 880.

21 Ibid.; Gibbon, *The Artillerist's Manual*, 220-48.

Lieutenant Weir must have been curious about where Hancock was leading him. The Rogers farmyard and orchard off to the southwest, encased by low-hanging clouds of gun smoke, seemed out of the question, and infantry and artillery already lined the entire length of the Emmitsburg Road to his front. There appeared to be no room at all to squeeze in a six-gun battery. Upon closer inspection, it became clear to Weir that there were few Union infantrymen between Codori's large barn (held by the 82nd New York) and the 1st Massachusetts 300 yards farther south. Enemy foot soldiers were approaching this gap, and in all probability would exploit the weakened left if uncontested.[22]

Even before the guns had left Cemetery Hill, fellow Regular Army officer Lieutenant John Turnbull had been pleading for help. Some of Colonel Lang's Floridians threatened to envelop the guns and their infantry supports. Most of Lang's left wing was moving directly toward the gap north of Turnbull and the Rogers farm. Hancock pointed toward the gap and instructed Weir, "Go in there; I will bring you infantry support." Hancock wheeled his horse and galloped northeast toward the Copse of Trees while Weir's drivers swung their pieces around in "Action Front" about 300 yards southeast of the Codori barn. Plum Run, a trickling boggy depression, wound past Weir's front toward Hummelbaugh's farm lane 200 yards farther south. The six guns of Battery C covered the intersection of the lane with the Emmitsburg Road. In other words, Weir protected the key triangle of ground formed between the two throughways and Plum Run.[23]

Lieutenant Weir and his gun crews had their work cut out for them, for General Anderson's two southernmost brigades under Wilcox and Lang were quickly advancing. The gap between the two, however, widened with every step. In front of the gap in the apple orchard stood the line of Federal skirmishers from the 5th New Jersey and 1st U. S. Sharpshooters.[24]

Hancock was indeed willing to risk hitting his own men, but Weir's firepower came in handy. Some of his guns targeted Major Moore's 2nd Florida on Lang's left with canister. Whittled down by previous campaigns and illness, the 2nd Florida mustered only 242 effectives on July 2, while the supporting 8th Florida numbered just 176 rifles. Unfortunately for both undersized regiments, the worm fence in the center of the Emmitsburg Road Rise caused them considerable strife. Hit by solid

22 OR 27, pt. 1, 880.

23 Gulian Weir to Hunt, Governor's Island, New York Harbor, Oct. 23, 1880, Hunt Papers, Box 14 Military Correspondence, LoC; USGS MRC 39077G2; *Bachelder Maps, Second Day*.

24 Busey & Martin, *Regimental Strengths and Losses*, 203-204; *History of the First Regiment United States Sharpshooters, Company G*, Civil War Collection, Wisconsin Historical Society Research Center, Madison.

shot, shell, shrapnel, and now canister, Lt. Col. William Baya's and Captain Moore's combined lines attempted to scale the rails. Once over the fence, the regiments dropped into the swale directly west of the Rogers house and Turnbull's right wing's three smoking Napoleons.[25]

Like General Wilcox to his right, Colonel Lang sized up the situation from his new position at the worm fence. He noticed that his left appeared to outflank the right flank of the Union command to his front. Even though his own 2nd Florida's left was exposed, there was virtually no one in its front after the enemy skirmishers departed. Union General Humphreys also spotted the danger. To counter the threat of his line being turned, he rushed a portion of Colonel Baldwin's 1st Massachusetts northward to better protect the area. By the time the 2nd Florida dropped into the swale and reappeared east of and above it, Major Moore's line was being struck by a flanking fire. Strategically placed in the open alley between Lang's Floridians and General Wright's still-distant Georgia brigade, Lieutenant Weir directed his right half-battery to pivot to the right so the guns fronted nearly due west. Weir, with his gun line's flank covered by Codori's corrals and bank barn. It was in a good position to rake the oncoming Rebels, which he did effectively.[26]

While Colonel Lang dealt with the troubling situation in his center and left, his southernmost regiment had its own problems. Turnbull's right half-battery continued pounding the right side of the 5th Florida, temporarily halting its progress. However, the Floridians soon regained their composure and rushed a short distance forward, paused, and delivered several volleys into Turnbull's exposed gun line while the supporting Union infantry shifted positions.[27]

The reason for this change was an order from the temporary commander of the Third Corps, General Birney, who had not yet received word that Meade had tasked Hancock with overseeing Sickles' command. A courier from Birney galloped to General Humphreys to inform him Sickles was down and Birney had replaced him. The breathless messenger also carried Birney's orders for Humphreys to pull back Colonel Brewster's New York brigade to better meet Barksdale's Mississippians collapsing the Peach Orchard and beginning to move up the Emmitsburg Road. As a result, most of Brewster's command was now fronting both south and west, essentially forming a new salient along Trostle's farm lane intersection. The arrangement proved to be Humphreys' undoing, for his division was now fighting as two separate brigades facing two different fronts and without

25 Petruzzi & Stanley, *The Gettysburg Campaign in Numbers and Losses*, 131.

26 David Shultz, "Gulian V. Weir's 5th U.S. Artillery, Battery C," in *Gettysburg Magazine*, issue 18, July 1998, 77.

27 Ibid.; *OR* 27, pt.1, 880; Clark Baldwin to Bachelder, May 20, 1865, *Bachelder Papers,* 1:193-94.

much coordination. In addition, some men from Carr's brigade, also of Humphreys' division, began heading east about the same time.[28]

As recalled by Humphreys in his after-action report, "Seeley's battery had now opened upon the enemy's infantry as they began to advance. Turnbull's battery was likewise directed against them, and I was about to throw somewhat forward the left of my infantry and engage the enemy with it, when I received orders from General Birney to throw back my left, and form a line oblique to and in rear of the one I then held." The general was also "informed that the First Division [Birney's] would complete the line to the Round Top ridge. This I did under a heavy fire of artillery and infantry from the enemy, who now advanced on my whole front." Given the heavy enemy pressure and deadly nature of the task at hand, there was really little else that could be done by that time.[29]

Humphreys' situation, precarious at best, now bordered on untenable despite the fresh guns General Hancock had provided to bolster his line. Colonel Lang was still threatening Carr's right, Wilcox overlapped Carr's left and Brewster's new line, and Barksdale's reinvigorated Mississippians pushed northwest toward the new salient. The dire Union situation was compounded when Charles Graham's brigade (Birney's division) to Humphreys' immediate left began melting away. The 72nd New York of Brewster's brigade had already fallen back, and it was soon followed by the 71st New York—both having held off attacks from two directions for more than 15 minutes. Their retreat uncovered Col. Robert McAllister's 11th New Jersey fighting on the immediate left of Seeley's guns. The south-facing 120th New York, along with the 70th, 73rd, and 74th New York of Brewster's command further uncovered Carr's already desperate left when they disappeared southward into the smoke in an effort to counter Barksdale. Although they did not advance to the Emmitsburg Road where the 71st Pennsylvania had been positioned, the 220 riflemen of Colonel Sewell's 5th New Jersey, placed in reserve behind Seeley's caissons, prepared to help their brethren from the Garden State.[30]

Although Brewster's regiments only moved a handful of yards south, in the smoke and confusion Lieutenant James, now commanding Seeley's Battery K, 4th U. S., did not know this. Their disappearance left him uneasy about the vulnerability of his apparently exposed left flank to an attack from the south. By this time the lengthening shadows and heavy smoke made it hard for James and his gunners to

28 OR 27, pt. 1, 553; John Turnbull to Lorenzo Thomas, July 12, 1863, Hunt Papers, LoC; A. A. Humphreys to Winfield S. Hancock, October 2, 1863, A. A. Humphreys Papers, Robert Blake Collection, USAHEC.

29 OR 27, pt. 1, 553.

30 OR 27, pt. 1, 565, 566, 571,575-576.

easily discern friend from foe, so they easily imagined their worst nightmare was coming true—a simultaneous attack from their left and rear. It had happened the past May on a small elongated rise known as Hazel Grove during the battle of Chancellorsville. Believing his position was now untenable, Lieutenant James decided to withdraw.[31]

Just south of Trostle's farm lane, the soldiers of the 17th, 13th, and 18th Mississippi regiments moved almost as one body north up the Emmitsburg Road, distancing themselves from the east-northeast-moving 21st Mississippi. The defending Union regiments fought desperately, with the 114th Pennsylvania in particular countercharging into a mass of Rebels to extract two cannon that had been overrun near Sherfy's barn. While this was transpiring, General Wofford's Georgia brigade slid in between Barksdale and Kershaw to advance due east up and over the Peach Orchard toward Trostle's Woods.[32]

With most of General Graham's men now falling back in droves, it was nearly impossible for Birney and his staff to corral them, let alone reform their lines. Refusing to let up on the wavering Yankee line, the white-haired Barksdale urged his howling Mississippians toward Trostle's farm lane. Moving generally north up the Emmitsburg Road, his tightly bunched 18th, 13th, and 17th Mississippi regiments (aligned from left to right) pressed forward. Without pausing to redress his lines, Barksdale brought his soldiers face-to-face with Brewster's New Yorkers, with only the Trostle farm lane separating the combatants. When they spotted the direct threat, hundreds of Graham's retreating soldiers faced back apparently on their own accord, some individually and others in small groups and then entire companies to contest Barksdale's advance.

While Barksdale's, Wilcox's, and Lang's unintended pincer movement was collapsing the Third Corps salient around the Peach Orchard and unraveling the line running north along the Emmitsburg Road to the Rogers farm, the next brigade in grand *en echelon* assault that early evening swung into action. The attack about to be launched by Brig Gen. Ambrose R. Wright's Georgians would be one of the most controversial of the entire battle. Unlike the other four brigades of Dick Anderson's five-brigade division, the very ground the Georgians covered, how far they advanced, and which Union units they engaged have all been the subject of spirited dispute. Wright's own official report sparked much of the contention.

On the evening of July 1, while his brigade rested on Herr's Ridge, Wright became quite ill. Incapable of command, he temporarily transferred it to Col.

---

31 Ibid., 591.

32 Barksdale's three north-moving Mississippi regiments were the only units that thus far had adhered to Generals Lee's original plan and Longstreet's orders.

Brig. Gen. Ambrose Wright,
Anderson's Division, Hill's Corps,
Army of Northern Virginia. *LOC*

William Gibson of the 48th Georgia. Throughout the morning of July 2 and well into the afternoon, Gibson oversaw the brigade's routine business as it awaited orders on Seminary Ridge just north of the point of woods. Major George W. Ross's small 2nd Georgia Battalion, supported by a company of the 3rd Georgia, did its job well on the skirmish line throughout the morning. Having earlier relieved Col. William Lowrance's 34th North Carolina skirmishers, Ross's line was, for the most part, uncontested. His men had occasionally traded shots since early that morning with a few First Corps soldiers, including skilled marksmen, but nothing of substance occurred until after 8:30 a.m., when the Union Second Corps arrived on Cemetery Ridge a mile or so directly east of Wright's line.[33]

Within a quarter-hour, skirmishers from General Gibbon's division advanced across the Emmitsburg Road and easily drove back Ross's Georgians. Heavily outnumbered, Ross withdrew his men through a shallow swale and over a low snake-rail fence 100 yards to the west. After moving across a nearby low rise, the skirmishers met reinforcements moving up to a larger rail fence on the Bliss farm, where the men took cover on its west side. Ross's men and these reinforcements halted Gibbon's skirmishers, who found cover of their own and opened a fitful exchange from behind a fence. This action, which killed and wounded several men, set up what would be the skirmish line in this sector for the day. The sporadic firing continued until about noon, when the Bliss farm fight erupted into a bitter small-scale combat.[34]

Once the Bliss farm fight was over, the skirmishing waned to a spattering of shots. Despite his illness, General Wright determined to return to the command of

33 *OR* 27, pt. 1, 419, 426, pt. 2, 630.

34 *OR* 27, pt. 2, 630. USGS MRC 39077G2; *Bachelder Maps, Second Day.*

This view looks east-southeast from the William Bliss apple orchard, which was about 500 yards north and east of Wright's right flank. The Emmitsburg Road Rise blocked Wright's view of the true Union line. Note that the field appears level in this modern view, but in 1863 was undulating. This is because of many years of both government and civilian excavation that consumed tons of topsoil and altered the landscape of this particular area. *Todd C. Wiley Collection*

his brigade. "About noon, I was informed by Major-General Anderson that an attack upon the enemy's lines would soon be made by the whole division," Wright recorded, "commencing on our right by Wilcox's brigade, and that each brigade of the division would begin the attack as soon as the brigade on its immediate right commenced the movement." Wright was instructed to move out at the same time the Florida Brigade on his right advanced, and was informed that "Posey's brigade, on my left, would move forward upon my advance." The kick-off of the assault on the far right by Hood's division was still many hours away.[35]

General Wright reappeared on his brigade's line about 3:00 p.m. and explained the plan of attack to his subordinates. None of the Georgians had any firm idea where the Union center was, how strong it was held, or that it was more than 1,000 yards to their front well beyond the fence-lined pike they could see in the distance. Likewise, no one had any idea of the overall plan of attack other than what little information they garnered from company commanders or rumors filtering up and down Seminary Ridge. Unlike Generals Barksdale and Wilcox, and Colonel Lang,

35 Ibid. USGS MRC 39077G2; *Bachelder Maps, Second Day.*

This is from the northeastern edge of Spangler's Woods (near the Point of Woods) facing the Emmitsburg Road Rise. The field appears flat, but is in fact undulating. Note that today's post-battle Codori barn, as well as Cemetery Ridge beyond, is masked by the Emmitsburg Road (defined by the plank fence paralleling it across the center of photo). In 1863, the original barn was much smaller and also not visible from where Wright's Georgians stepped over the wall. The Union line on the Emmitsburg Road Rise was the position Wright later mistakenly suggested his men fully carried, and the valley he noted immediately east of this was the Codori meadow. However, his brigade overran seven Union guns from three batteries (Weir, Brown, Turnbull). *Rosemary G. Oreb*

each of whom faced reinforced enemy skirmish lines, the Union troops in Wright's front were light in comparison. Contesting these Federals were the riflemen of the 2nd Georgia Battalion, who lined the center rail fence with their left flank bent slightly fronting the Bliss property. Advancing would not be easy, especially with strong enemy batteries atop Cemetery Hill that had good fields of fire.[36]

For more than two hours, Wright and his Georgians listened as first Longstreet's artillery opened fire, and then the brigades of Hood's and McLaws' divisions stepped off to the attack. Wright's men watched as the Floridians on their right moved out, but no order for them to move reached them. Perhaps 15 minutes passed before Wright's brigade stepped off, an unexplained delay that further staggered General Anderson's *en echelon* attack. Each brigade was to have started its advance immediately after the brigade to its right stepped forward. Such a tight and

36 Ibid., 622-23; *Bachelder Maps, Second Day.*

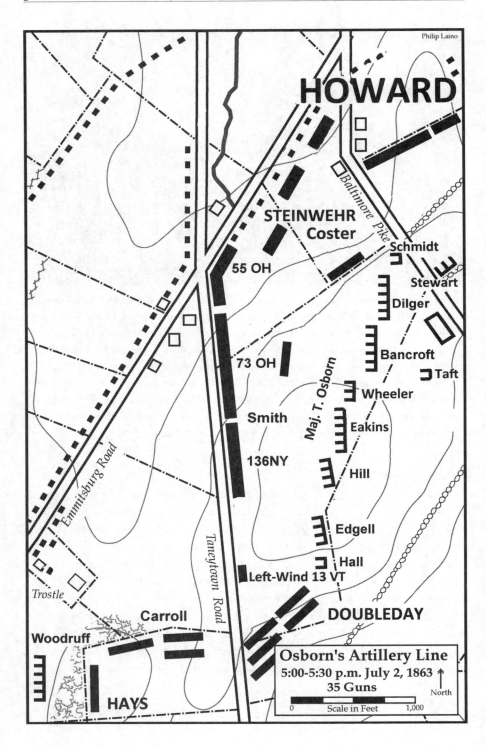

Philip Laino

HOWARD

STEINWEHR
Coster

Baltimore Pike

Schmidt

55 OH

Stewart

Dilger

73 OH

Bancroft

Taft

Maj. T. Osborn

Wheeler

Smith

Eakins

136NY

Hill

Edgell

Hall

Left-Wind 13 VT

DOUBLEDAY

Emmitsburg Road

Taneytown Road

Trostle

Carroll

Woodruff

HAYS

Osborn's Artillery Line
5:00-5:30 p.m. July 2, 1863
35 Guns

0   Scale in Feet   1,000

North

nearly simultaneous movement would have enabled the Confederates to concentrate their numbers with overwhelming striking power against the Union left-center along the Emmitsburg Road and atop Cemetery Ridge. Instead, the attack staggered out of the starting gate with wide gaps between each brigade. The situation was about to considerably worsen.[37]

According to Wright's report, the 22nd Georgia formed on the right side of his brigade, the 3rd Georgia in the center, and Gibson's 48th on the left. "The regiment was ordered in the fight between the hours of 5 and 6 p.m.," the 48th's Capt. Matthew R. Hall wrote, mistaking the time considerably. "The Second Georgia battalion being previously thrown out as skirmishers, a part of the battalion formed on our left, making us the left-center regiment."[38]

An account by William Judkins of the 22nd Georgia on the right side of the line suggests General Wright did not accompany his brigade in the assault, which is contrary to the general's later report so full of personal descriptions of the distant terrain and the enemy position. "We started on the charge," Judkins claimed, "Genl Wright in command, but was not in charge, he was not well, but his Adjutant Genl. Geroda [Capt. Victor J. B. Girardey] was in command, or led the brigade." If Wright was not physically capable of making the entire advance, it made sense that Gibson as the senior colonel, or Adjutant Girardey, would assume command from near the center of the brigade. It is possible that Wright followed behind on horseback in nominal command for some distance, or he may have relinquished command at some point during the advance, but Judkins firmly implies the general was not physically present with the assault column.[39]

Stepping over the low stone wall bordering the timber, the Georgians immediately encountered a few incoming long-range artillery rounds, the number of which increased with each passing minute. Fronting the entire length of the brigade was Maj. George W. Ross's 2nd Battalion, with Company K of the 3rd Georgia in support. The 2nd Battalion could not disengage nor could it sidestep north and reform as a unit as intended. As a result, the 48th Georgia unexpectedly became the brigade's left flank regiment, not its left-center.[40]

---

37 OR 27, pt. 1, 880; Weir to father, July 5, 1863, GNMP; USGS MRC 39077G2; *Bachelder Maps, Second Day*; Wilcox, *Annotations to the OR*, July 17, 1863, Box 1, Wilcox Papers, LOC.

38 OR 27, pt. 2, 622-24, 629. Because the 2nd Georgia Battalion failed to reform on the far left, the 48th Georgia became the left-flank regiment. The 2nd would eventually be on the right as the four units advanced eastward.

39 William B. Judkins, "Memoirs of a Soldier of the 22nd Georgia," Floyd County Library, Special Collections Department, Rome, Georgia.

40 Pfanz, *Gettysburg: Second Day*, 381.

Brig. Gen. Carnot Posey,
Anderson's Division, Hill's Corps,
Army of Northern Virginia. LOC

Carnot Posey's Mississippi brigade on Ambrose Wright's left flank was supposed to coordinate its movement with the advance of the Georgians, just as Wright had been tasked to do (though he was late) with Lang's Floridians on his right. General Anderson sent his aide-de-camp, Capt. Samuel D. Shannon, to General Posey with orders for him to instead advance only two of his four regiments and deploy them as skirmishers. Almost certainly this order was the result of the unintended, prolonged, and very disorganizing small-scale battle over the Bliss farm. Posey duly dispatched Col. Joseph M. Jayne's 48th Mississippi and Col. Nathaniel H. Harris's 19th Mississippi. There is no proof Anderson notified Wright (or any other of his brigadiers) that only part of Posey's brigade would be joining in the *en echelon* advance. More problems became evident almost immediately thereafter.[41]

By the time Colonel Jayne's 48th Mississippi, anchoring Posey's far right south of the Bliss orchard, set off it was perhaps 200 yards to the left and rear of the 48th Georgia, Wright's left regiment. Within a few minutes, a snake-rail fence running perpendicular to its line divided the 48th Mississippi in two wings. The left, or northernmost section, stalled while the right portion continued east by southeast in an effort to catch up with the 48th Georgia. The 19th Mississippi was late in stepping off and had to double-time to catch up with Jayne's left flank. Musketry from Companies A and B of the 106th Pennsylvania, supported by several hundred

---

41 OR 27, pt. 1, 634; William M. Harris, ed., *Movements of the Confederate Army in Virginia and the Part Taken by the Nineteenth Mississippi Regiment: From the Diary of N. H. Harris*, Duncanby, MS, Todd A. Herring Collection, Mississippi State University Special Collections Library Manuscript Division, 22-24; Pfanz, *Gettysburg, The Second Day*, 382; Tagg, *Generals of Gettysburg*, 320. The Bliss farm fight absorbed much of Posey's brigade and dragged on longer than anyone imagined it might. When it came time to advance, Posey did not have is command in hand, his men were already tired, and the brigade was simply not in a condition to advance.

This image looks east-southeast from on Seminary Ridge, where Carnot Posey's center was located west of the Bliss farmyard and orchards. Out of view beyond the present-day southern outskirts of Gettysburg, the open west face of Cemetery Hill had been turned into a virtual fortress, with 35 Union guns of various calibers, all of which enjoyed a left-enfilade down Posey's line. Because of this artillery fire and Hays' Union division's grasp on the Bliss farmyard, only the far right of Posey's brigade was able to advance in support of Wright's Georgians. The Vermont obelisk monument pillar sits on Cemetery Ridge at the Union center south and west of the Copse of Trees. *Sal Prezioso Collection*

other soldiers from General Hays' Second Corps division including specialized sharpshooters forced Harris's 19th Mississippi to retire to the orchard.[42]

The disjointed assault under Anderson's direction was already misfiring, but it was about to get much worse: Anderson's final brigade in the planned five-brigade attack was nowhere to be seen. Except for some skirmishers occupying a sunken road named Long Lane in the fields east of Seminary Ridge between the opposing lines, Brig. Gen. William Mahone's brigade of Virginians had not advanced from

---

42 William P. Pigman Diary, July 2, 1863, Savannah, Georgia Historical Society; Pfanz, *Gettysburg: Second Day*, 372; USGS MRC 39077-G2-TF-024. Portions of the both the 48th and 19th crowded to the south as one mass, advancing toward and in some cases across the Emmitsburg Road where most of the men became prisoners.

Brig. Gen. William Mahone, Anderson's Division, Hill's Corps, Army of Northern Virginia. LOC

McMillan's Woods. Mahone had been in position with Posey's Mississippians to his right-front and Brig. Gen. Edward Thomas's brigade (the rightmost brigade of Maj. Gen. Dorsey Pender's division of A. P. Hill's Corps) to his left front, but Mahone did not advance. Without Mahone's participation, Posey's left flank was completely exposed, and the men there would suffer accordingly.

Only parts of Posey's right wing even made it east of the Bliss farm. In a case of flagrant negligence that is still impossible to explain, neither Hill nor Anderson were on the front line to make sure the brigades were in position and stepping off on time as instructed. There is no evidence anyone ordered Mahone to rest his men in reserve, but that is apparently what he did. Mahone's terse report for the entire battle runs only about 150 words, and it does not mention anything about the July 2 attack at all, or any orders he received. When Posey sent word to Mahone that he needed support, Mahone sent word back that he had been ordered elsewhere to the right (something that is not in his official report). When Posey reported this to General Anderson, the division chief sent his aide Shannon into McMillan Woods to locate Mahone. When Shannon ordered the Virginia general to get his men advancing, Mahone reportedly uttered, "No! I have my orders from General Anderson himself to remain here." This exchange, too, was not in Mahone's report.

A few hours earlier, shortly before Hood had commenced his infantry attack, Generals Hill and Anderson, together with division leader Dorsey Pender, visited Mahone's front to study the ground from the vicinity of McMillan's Woods. All three high-ranking commanders knew precisely where the Virginians were resting. As Longstreet who later wrote, "Four of the brigades of Anderson's division were ordered to advance en echelon in support of my left." Why Mahone remained firmly in place—fresh and ready to fight—remains unknown. What is known is that once Mahone refused to move, the massive *en echelon* attack that was to have

This monument-free vista looks west by southwest from the Bloody Angle just north of the Copse of Trees on Cemetery Ridge toward Seminary Ridge in the distance, and encompasses most of the ground over which General Anderson's Rebel brigades (Wilcox, Lang, Wright, and part of Posey) assaulted the Union line. None of the Confederates had any idea that a second Union line existed in the immediate foreground just north of the Union center, where what was left of General Hancock's whittled down Second Corps waited for the approaching Southern infantry. Note the Codori farmyard, where the 15th Massachusetts and 82nd New York fought the attacking Rebels. *William H. Tipton*

apparently continued rolling north into A. P. Hill's front, sputtered to an end. Edward Thomas' command on Hill's far right never moved a step.[43]

Wright's Georgians, of course, knew nothing of the drama playing out farther north, or that they were making their assault without the planned supports. As noted earlier, the Georgians almost immediately stepped into view of Maj. Thomas Osborn's artillery on West Cemetery Hill. The two lines of Georgians, advancing shoulder-to-shoulder with rifles at right-shoulder shift, stepped toward the 2nd Battalion's position behind the rail fence on the Bliss farm. Off to their left-front on Cemetery Hill, perhaps 1,000 yards distant, a puff of smoke made its appearance, followed a few seconds later by the whiz of a timed-fuse Union shell passing overhead. Osborn's gunners had good left-enfilade fire. Redirecting most of their tubes against this inviting new target, at least 18 cannon from four different

43 OR 27, pt. 2, 665; David Lang to Edward Perry, July 19, 1863, *SHSP*, vol. 27, 190-205 (GNMP); Gottfried, "Mahone's Brigade: Insubordination or Miscommunication?" *Gettysburg Magazine*, Issue 18, July 1998, 72; Longstreet, *From Manassas to Appomattox*, 369; USGS MRC 39077 G2.

batteries erupted. As the embattled Confederate line closed on the 2nd Battalion's fence, Osborn's fire became more accurate. When Wright's line stepped into enemy musket range, one Georgian after another collapsed. The shell fragments and solid shot screaming from the high ground, however, were more terrifying because they ripped men apart and knocked them about like straw dolls. Other than the swish of oats, wheat, and timothy grass beneath 1,400 pairs of feet (some of them bare), only the rattle of canteens, equipment, and accouterments marked the advance of the Georgians. Thus far not a man of the brigade had fired a shot.[44]

No contemporary account other than Wright's own places him with the brigade after it passed over the Emmitsburg Road. According to his own pen, he suggests he made it at least as far as Major Ross's skirmish line on the Bliss farm. "I ordered the brigade to halt & reform in a slight (ravine) in a wheat field just out of range of the enemy's grape & canister, although we were under a very hot fire of musketry," Wright wrote in 1864. "In personally superintending this rally of the men," he continued, "I found the 2nd Ga. Bat without a single officer and took charge of it in person."[45]

Major Ross had not yet had a chance to reform his men on the left by the time Wright's main line reached his 2nd Georgia Battalion's fence line. Not wanting to take the time to redress his line, the brigade's temporary commander, Colonel Gibson, ordered the brigade over the rails and down into the center swale. He could have stopped there to allow Ross the time he needed to reform his left and catch up, but the Georgia regiments tramped into and out of the depression with most of the 2nd Battalion skirmishers absorbed within the advancing line. Under Ross's direction, several companies reunited to the south on the right of the 22nd Georgia, meaning that large parts of the 2nd Battalion ended up anchoring Wright's far right flank. "In this way the battalion was scattered along the whole line of the brigade," Captain Moffett explained, "and some of the men went into action with General Perry's [Lang's] brigade, it pressing upon our right."[46]

Now heavily outnumbered, the Union skirmishers holding the snake-rail fence between the center swale and the plank fence west of the Emmitsburg Road readily gave up their precious strip of real estate and disappeared into the bottom land behind them. Reappearing atop the Emmitsburg Road Rise opposite the Codori farm, most of these Federals either faced back at the plank fence or sought refuge

---

44 Busey & Martin, *Strengths and Losses*, 190.

45 A. R. Wright to W. H. Taylor, April 30, 1864, Vertical Files, GNMP..

46 Ibid.; USGS MRC 39077G2. Only the roof and three steeples atop Codori's barn were visible from Where Wright's Georgians stepped of as well as from the two swells they passed through.

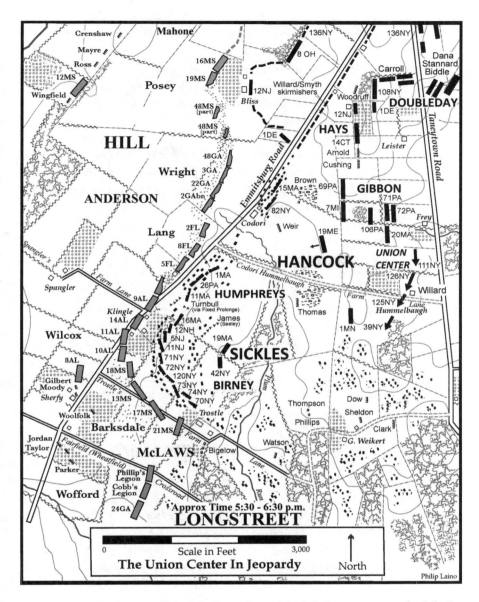

The Union Center In Jeopardy

Approx Time 5:30 - 6:30 p.m.

Scale in Feet — 0 ... 3,000

North

Philip Laino

within their own regiments farther east. They picked their way eastward while Lt. Fred Brown's Rhode Island battery—posted beyond the 15th Massachusetts' right flank —opened with spherical case and solid shot. Brown doubtlessly targeted Wright's left wing and Posey's right side. Because of the rough terrain, the young lieutenant had tightly spaced his six smoothbores, with each two-gun section firing independently. Although their location below the ridge made it difficult for the cannoneers to work the guns, their harassing fire made them an immediate target for the approaching 3rd and 48th Georgia.[47]

As the Georgians dropped into the depression west of the Emmitsburg Road, Lt. Col. James Huston's 82nd New York and Col. George Ward's 15th Massachusetts of Harrow's brigade readied themselves along the length of Codori's orchards and farmyard. Harrow's other two regiments, the 1st Minnesota and 19th Maine, were detached, so Huston's and Ward's two small commands and Brown's Rhode Island battery were all that stood between the oncoming Georgians and the mostly unoccupied Union center behind them. The two regiments, some 600 strong, cocked and capped their rifled muskets and waited for the Georgians to top the depression just 100 yards distant.[48]

Colonel Ward had led the two regiments to the Emmitsburg Road that afternoon with an understanding he would be quickly reinforced. Hancock intended to support him with elements from Caldwell's division, allowing General Gibbon to hold the balance of his regiments, including the 1st Minnesota and 19th Maine, in reserve beyond the crest. Caldwell's right flank was to have moved back north with his skirmishers connecting with Huston's left at the Codori farmyard. Other events beyond Hancock's control wiped out those ideas, as they had General Meade's original plan of defending Cemetery Ridge. Now, the 82nd New York and 15th Massachusetts stood alone against what looked to be heavy odds and the likelihood the oncoming Rebels would outflank them on both sides. With Companies I and J of the 82nd New York anchoring the left in the farmyard, Huston's line continued some 150-170 yards northward through the apple orchard opposite the farmhouse before connecting with Ward's left flank.[49]

Ward's plan, like many others at Gettysburg, passed into impossibility when he realized Wright's left flank stretched well past his own right. To make matters worse, a supporting enemy line, albeit shorter, was angling northeast toward Brown's battery. Ward and Huston knew they could not lend each other a hand. With the 48th Georgia and some of Posey's Mississippians bearing east beyond his right, Ward had two options: stay put or retreat. He decided to hold his ground at all costs. On his left, Huston not only faced the right flank of 48th Georgia and Colonel Walker's 3rd Georgia, but Colonel Wasden's 22nd Georgia. Realizing the

---

47 Gregory Coco, ed., *From Ball's Bluff to Gettysburg and Beyond: The Civil war Letters of Private Roland E. Brown, 15th Massachusetts Infantry, 1861-1864* (Gettysburg, PA, 1994), 202.

48 Busey & Martin, *Regimental Strengths and Losses*, 190; OR 27, pt. 2, 614, 623, 630; USGS MRC 39077G2; Andrew E. Ford, *The Story of the Fifteenth Regiment, Massachusetts Volunteer Infantry in the Civil War, 1861-1864* (Clinton, MA, 1898), 196-202.

49 Ibid.

This turn-of-the-century photo is of Emmitsburg Road looking north toward the present-day Sickles Avenue intersection identified by the 16th Massachusetts Monument to the right (east) of the road. This is the position held by Turnbull's consolidated Batteries F & K, 3rd U.S. The gun line began here and stretched north into Rogers' orchard on the left (west) of the road. Codori's farm can be seen beyond the Rogers house and intersection, where the 82nd New York battled the 2nd and 22nd Georgia regiments of Wright's brigade for passage of the road. Note the proximity of Zeigler's Grove to the northeast, as marked by the observation tower that once stood there. *LOC*

latter enemy regiment could easily flank them unless help arrived, Ward and Huston sent runner after runner back toward the Copse of Trees to seek reinforcements. Huston planned to torch the Codori buildings to keep them out of Confederate hands. "The ninth and tenth companies were sent to a brick house near the left of our line," Capt. John Darrow reported, "and had orders to burn it, if necessary, on the approach of the enemy."[50]

Almost certainly neither Ward nor Huston knew of or concerned themselves with General Carr's collapsing predicament farther south. They had their own hands full defending the Codori farm without worrying about events beyond their reach. From Ward's right flank in the orchard south to Huston's left beyond the

---

50 OR 27, pt. 1, 426; Wiley Sword, "Defending the Codori House and Cemetery Ridge: Two Swords with Harrow's Brigade in the Gettysburg Campaign," *Gettysburg Magazine*, No. 13, 44-45.

Codori barn, the Federals waited in their forward and rather isolated pocket as masses of butternut and gray stepped toward them, the Rebel Yell resounding loud and clear. The Federals balanced their rifles on the rails of the stout eastern fence along the pike and took careful aim at the Rebels.[51]

Unfortunately for Huston and his men, on the previous day soldiers from the decimated Union First Corps had partially dismantled the distant plank fence just south of and across the pike from Codori's farm to make it easier for their columns to head cross-country toward the Lutheran Seminary. With only posts to mark the former fence line for 75-100 yards, the 22nd Georgia's right and portions of the 2nd Battalion enjoyed an unobstructed path as they closed upon the Emmitsburg Road.[52]

The 22nd Georgia's right wing stretched about 50 yards beyond Huston's left companies, with the men of the 2nd Battalion stretching even farther. A spattering of small arms fire from impatient Union soldiers did not stop the Georgians as they approached the sturdy plank fence lining the Emmitsburg Road, with the right wing of Wasden's 22nd Georgia moving directly toward the dismantled section. "As the enemy advanced," Union General Harrow reported, "the first of the division to engage them were the Eighty-second New York and Fifteenth Massachusetts Volunteers, from their position on the Gettysburg and Emmitsburg Road. These two regiments," he continued, "in the aggregate not more than 700 strong, and without support on their line (flanks), but partially protected by rails of a fence which they had hastily taken down and piled to their front, gallantly sustained an unequal contest against superior numbers."[53]

One of the anxious men watching the oncoming Rebels was the 15th Massachusetts' Roland Bowen. "They sprang forward with their demoniac yell which is peculiar to them only at the same time giving a deadly volley," vividly recalled the 26-year-old private. "Now it was our turn, with a shout we sprang up on our knees and rested our muskets over the rails, we gave them one of the most destructive volleys I have ever witnessed, unlike us, they had nothing to shield themselves from our fire, and their thinned ranks told that we had dealt out large quantities of death. For a moment they seemed to be suspicious or in doubt as if they had lost their confidence—they hesitated, they reeled, they staggered and wavered slightly, yet there was no panic, as fast as we could get powder and lead

---

51 Ibid.

52 Charles Wainwright, *Personal Journal*, see July 11, 1863, John B. Nicholson-Bell Collection, Huntington Library.

53 *OR* 27, pt. 1, 419-20.

into our guns we sent it at them. They returned the compliment pretty effectively."[54]

One can easily imagine the ferocity of the Union musket fire when Wright's and Lang's lines finally reached the plank fence lining the Emmitsburg Road. With just the width of the avenue separating the combatants, it was fire as fast as one could ram home a load, cock, cap, and pull the trigger. Men in the back ranks rammed home cartridges and passed their arms forward. However, the plank fence and piled rails proved unsuitable as breastworks. Some lead rounds splintered the hardwood, sending injurious fragments into nearby flesh, while other Minié balls bore through the planking, striking men behind it. A steady stream of walking wounded left the scene heading both east and west. Lieutenant Colonel Huston was standing near the Codori house directing his defense when enemy rounds found him. The first bullet hit him in the leg, a painful but not serious wound. A short time later, however, another bullet struck him in the neck before traveling up and exiting the back of his head. With the other field officers also down, Company B's Capt. John Darrow assumed command. The hard-pressed 82nd New York would lose 192 of its 335 men at Gettysburg.[55]

Father north, the partially disabled Colonel Ward prepared for the inevitable clash. His left leg had been amputated above the knee after the battle of Ball's Bluff in October 1861. He recovered slowly, received a wooden prosthetic limb, and was promoted to colonel on April 22, 1862. Ward assumed command of the 15th while convalescing and rejoined the unit in mid-May 1863 during the Army of the Potomac's reorganization. In truth, he was not ready for the field. He was still unable to stand, walk, or ride for long periods of time, and traveled in an ambulance during much of the march toward Gettysburg. Ward refused to show signs of pain or weakness, nor did he let anyone know how discomforted he really was as he rallied his men not 30 yards from the oncoming enemy.[56]

From about 4:00 p.m. until Anderson's assault slammed home, Ward had hobbled about the Codori property in pain. When the battle commenced, he was in an orchard north of the farmyard near a rail fence running perpendicular to his front. The structure separated his Massachusetts men from Huston's New Yorkers. Mounting so his men could see him, Ward rode up and down his line rallying his soldiers in the face of the Confederate advance. Ward prudently dismounted when

---

54 Roland E. Bowen, "From the Round Top to Richmond or a narrative of 39 days," 15th Massachusetts Infantry Vertical Files, GNMP, 5.

55 Ibid, 427; Coco, *From Ball's Bluff to Gettysburg*, 201-203.

56 Personal Military records of James Huston and George H. Ward, NNRG-NA; George Ward to family, June 25, 1863, Worcester, MA, Worcester County Historical Museum.

This image was taken from the top of the Pennsylvania Monument looking west, with the memorial to Col. George Ward and the 15th Massachusetts visible north of the Codori's farm, where that regiment faced off with the 3rd and 48th Georgia of Wright's brigade. South in the farmyard, Lt. Col. James Huston's embattled 82nd New York held its ground until nearly cut off. Ward's and Huston's survivors pulled back through the meadow in the foreground, contesting every foot of ground against the advancing Georgians. GNMP

Wright's Georgians closed on the Emmitsburg Road, choosing instead to hobble up and down his line assuring his men that he was with them. When the lines closed, he was in the center of his regiment near the rail fence when a single round struck him in the upper right leg. "I suppose you have heard the sad, sad fate of George, ere this," his brother, Lt. Henry C. Ward of Company D, wrote home two days later. "His body is now on the way home. I got him away as soon as I could under the circumstances. He was wounded in the leg by a Minié ball, on Thursday, about six o'clock P.M. The artery was severed and he bled to death."[57]

"He fought well," Henry continued:

> He had sent his horse to the rear, and I felt then, that, if we should be obliged to retreat, it would be all up with him. He was wounded while fighting at the head of his brigade.

57 OR 27, pt. 2, 423. Henry C. Ward to Emily Ward, Westminster, Pa., July 4, 1863; *Roster and Genealogies of the 15th Massachusetts Volunteer Infantry*, Worcester, Mass., Worcester County Historical Society.

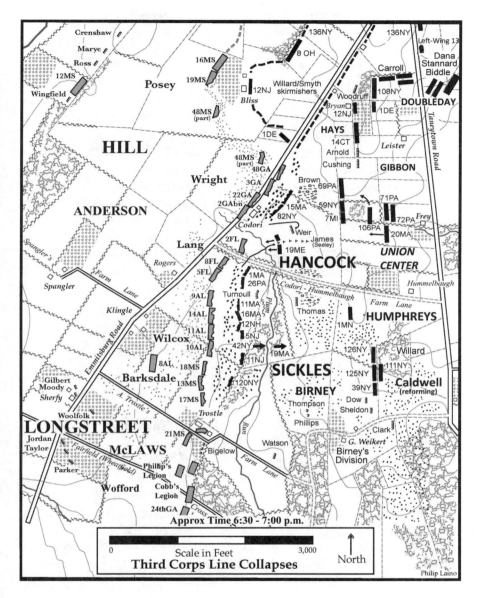

Third Corps Line Collapses

The fight continued for five hours, and during the confusion we were unable to find him for two hours. I searched all over the battlefield, amid shells and balls, hunting for him. We got him to a hospital about dark. He was insensible, but the surgeon gave him whiskey, which revived him; and he said to the doctor, 'I shall not live two hours.' After this his mind was wandering, and he imagined himself at the head of his brigade, commanding troops and urging them to fight bravely. He died next morning at daylight. He was in command of the brigade, and went into the fight cheerfully. I have traveled all around for two days, trying to get a team to get his body to Westminster, the nearest depot, thirty miles distant; but every team is at work with the wounded, and no one will touch the dead.[58]

Lieutenant Colonel George C. Joslin, commanding Company I, assumed command of the regiment. For 15 brutal minutes the lines blazed away at one another, the ear-splitting din unrelenting. Unwilling to depress his tubes in fear of hitting his own infantry along the road, Gulian Weir continued sending spherical case and shell over their heads at Lang's Floridians. Meanwhile, Brown's six Rhode Island smoothbores northeast of the farm targeted the 48th Georgia's left wing and Posey's right. Unfortunately, his indiscriminate fire killed and wounded several soldiers in the 15th Massachusetts. However, the fire was so devastating that the Georgians focused their attention upon the six Napoleons during their final approach to the orchard. Undaunted by the fear of friendly-fire casualties, General Gibbon ordered Lieutenant Brown to increase his rate of fire. Switching to canister, Brown's gunners poured it on.[59]

*   *   *

As Hancock ascended the western slope of Cemetery Ridge in search of support for Weir, Col. George L. Willard's brigade, still known by the not-so-kind epithet "Harpers Ferry Cowards," was on its way south traversing the opposite slope. Shortly after assuming overall command of the left and center, Hancock had sent couriers scurrying for reinforcements. He knew Caldwell and Birney needed help, and one of the riders was sent north to locate General Hays. With two of his brigades piecemealed apart, the only intact unit was Colonel Willard's. The outfit had endured the derisive nickname because it had surrendered to Stonewall Jackson during the Maryland Campaign of 1862. The men did not deserve the negative appellation, and were determined to do anything they could to redeem their reputation.[60]

Hancock's aide supposedly told General Hays to send south whomever he could find to report to General Birney, but this is unlikely. Hancock wanted the

---

58 Ibid. Although Henry mentions "brigade," Ward was in fact in command of the 15th Massachusetts regiment.

59 Coco, *From Ball's Bluff to Gettysburg*, 196-97. Abijah P. Marvin, *History of Worshester in the War of the Rebellion*, (Worchester MA. Self-Published), 86. Copy available at Huntington Library, San Marino, California.

60 Eric Campbell, "Remember Harper's Ferry: The Degradation, Humiliation, and Redemption of Col. George L. Willard's Brigade," *Gettysburg Magazine*, issue 7, 51-53.

Following the eastern brow of Cemetery Ridge south toward the George Weikert farm, Col. George Willard's "Harper's Ferry Cowards" passed well to the east of the 1st Minnesota. Stopped short of the farm, the 39th New York anchored Willard's left flank in the foreground. They fronted west (to the right) across present-day Hancock Avenue. Battery B, 1st New York (at that time the only battery posted there) had been moved farther south, where it unlimbered in Trostle's farm lane near Weikert's stone house. *Rosemary G. Oreb*

reinforcements placed where Caldwell had been, where he remembered Battery B, 1st New York was located. Aside from Brown's battery, Caldwell's southward move enlarged the gap in the already weak Union line a quarter-mile wider. Hancock needed someone—anyone—to fill that gap. He also sent couriers hustling to get help from Generals Henry Baxter and Abner Doubleday of the First Corps (in reserve to the northeast), and to inform General Meade that he needed more reinforcements. Hancock also sent messengers galloping off to Howard's Eleventh Corps and Slocum's Twelfth Corps in search of aid and to scour the Reserve and Sixth Corps artillery parks to the southeast. The riders found Tyler's park nearly empty because General Hunt had already commandeered most of the available guns to help support Sickles.[61]

With Birney's division crumbling and Humphreys' left flank refused and collapsing in its fight against Barksdale's Mississippians, it was of paramount

---

61 Hancock, *JCCW*, 406.

importance that Colonel Willard hasten southward as quickly as possible. The 35-year-old New York City native was standing next to Hays when the courier arrived with Hancock's call for reinforcements. "Take your brigade over there and knock the hell out of them," Hays demanded. Except for a few skirmishers still west of the Emmitsburg Road, Willard's brigade had spent the last several hours lying east of the crest of Cemetery Ridge. When the order to move arrived the men cheered. As one they unstacked their rifles, cast aside everything except bayonets, ammunition, caps, and canteens—they could not take any haversacks, wool blankets, or shelter halves—and fell in. If there had been shirkers before in Maryland, there were none this day. No one volunteered to guard the piles of personal belongings left behind as the men dressed ranks. Everyone went forward, with many eager to prove their mettle and erase the stain of Harpers Ferry.[62]

Willard led his cheering column south at the double-quick due, passing the stacked piles of accouterments left by the 71st and 72nd Pennsylvania, 1st Minnesota, and 19th Maine. Snaking their way along the reverse slope of Cemetery Ridge, the New Yorkers continued past Alonzo Cushing's caissons, the Copse of Trees, and Webb's Philadelphia Brigade. The quick-stepping men could see the carnage from the cannonade, including wounded men littering the shot-torn fields. Case and shrapnel exploded overhead as Willard's column passed unseen by Rebel eyes behind the 19th Maine along the stone wall opposite the crest 60 yards south of the Copse of Trees. Solid shot and bolt bounded and whirred about them as they passed beyond Lieutenant Weir's first position on the crest of the ridge. The New Yorkers continued past the Hummelbaugh farm, which was now the site of a field hospital littered with wounded, dead, and fly-covered piles of amputated limbs.[63]

Once south of Hummelbaugh's lane, ambulatory wounded from the shattered Union left flank, survivors from now several corps, began threading their way around Willard's men. About 1,000 yards to Willard's right was the Emmitsburg Road, the spine of slightly higher ground roiling in smoke and flame where General Carr's right wing was fighting to hold the soon-to-be-outflanked position. Lieutenant Evan Thomas's battery stood silent but at the ready as Willard's men tramped past his caisson park and Colonel Colvill's prone 1st Minnesota. To young Thomas's front, out near the road, Lieutenant Turnbull was hitching his six guns at fixed prolonge in what would become the bloodiest and longest supporting

---

62 Charles Richardson to Bachelder, May 6, 1868, *Bachelder Papers*, 338-39. Colonel Richardson stated the brigade was sent south at approximately 5:00 P.M.

63 Richardson Papers; *Marches, Engagements of the 126th N.Y. Volunteer Infantry* (Ontario County Historical Society, Canandaigua, NY), see Sweet to Richardson, Sept. 4, 1895; Araballa M. Willison, *Disaster, Struggle, Triumph: The Adventures of 1,000 "Boys in Blue"*, in 2 vols. (Albany, NY, 1870), 2:800-801.

withdrawal of any battery that day. Sending his caissons back, he began "retiring the gun line while firing." General Carr had told him that a flat-out skedaddle was not only undignified but could create a panic. Turnbull deliberately took as much time as he could. Willard, of course, knew none of this. All he knew was that he was needed to the south. He urged his men to pick up the pace.[64]

Continuing south an additional 500 yards, Willard's brigade passed through increasing numbers of retiring Federals, including many from Caldwell's division, which had been shattered with it was moved south into the Wheatfield and elsewhere. Willard halted his column near where Lieutenant Sheldon's Battery B had been positioned only a few moments earlier. Unbeknownst to Hancock's aide leading the brigade, Colonel Warner had commandeered the New York guns and rushed them several hundred yards farther south to cover the Trostle farm lane.[65]

Willard formed his line of battle on the crest of the ridge with Patterson's woods behind him. Fronting west, his line from left to right consisted of the 39th, 125th, and 126th New York, with the 111th New York in reserve. A few retreating troops joined his fresh ranks, but for the most part they swarmed past, through, or around the regiments in small groups heading to the rear. Ambulances loaded with wounded and dying men were being hauled along the ridge, as were caissons and supporting wagons. The colonel took his assigned position, mounted in the front of his command, and waited.[66]

While Willard was making his way south into the bloody chaos, Hancock spied Colonel Heath's 19th Maine of General Harrow's brigade resting along the wall south of the Copse of Trees. He ordered the regiment to its feet and together with Heath guided the men down the ridge toward Plum Run. Passing behind Weir's position, the 19th descended toward the Plum Run ravine focusing on Turnbull's retiring guns. Passing within 200 yards of Weir's left-most piece, the 19th Maine moved toward the waist-high thickets lining the creek and Turnbull's guns beyond.

As the 19th moved forward under Hancock's eye nearly one mile south along Abraham Trostle's lane, Col. Freeman McGilvery was busy placing guns in a new line as quickly as they appeared. Among those was Sheldon's Battery B, 1st New York. "About this time Pettit's New York battery reported," McGilvery later wrote, "and changed position on the right of [Dow's] Sixth Maine." McGilvery had already placed Lt. Malbone F. Watson's Battery I, 5th U. S. near Trostle's lane above Plum

---

64 Andrew Humphreys, "The Pennsylvania Campaign of 1863," *Historical Magazine*, No. 2, Serial 6, July 1869, 2-8.

65 *OR* 27, pt. 1, 873. Referred to as Pettit's battery, Sheldon took position to the right of Dow's 6th Maine Light, straddling the Trostle lane north of the Weikert farm.

66 Ibid., 472, 475; Hays, *Life and Letters of Alexander Hays*, 404-10.

This mid-1880s photo shows where present-day Sedgwick and Hancock avenues intersect United States Avenue (Trostle's farm lane). Today, the path in the foreground is a GNMP service road intersecting the Taneytown Road east of Cemetery Ridge via Patterson's Woods. This short strategic route was used not only by General Hunt's reserve Union artillery, but by many brigades from the Fifth and Twelfth corps reinforcing Union troops fighting beyond the ridge's western brow (using all three connecting roads to reach their objective). Lieutenant Albert Sheldon's Battery B, 1st New York, unlimbered on the Trostle farm atop the brow in the center of the photo, joining Lt. Edmond Dow's 6th Maine battery to its right to hold this intersection and the Taneytown Road. LOC

Run, potentially sacrificing the artillery in order to buy time. Sheldon was next in line 400 yards east of Watson and 200 yards south of Weikert's woods west of the farmyard. Farther west above Plum Run, McGilvery could see Capt. John Bigelow's 9th Massachusetts guns preparing to open after having retired at fixed prolonge from its exposed position east of the Peach Orchard. Undaunted by his heavy losses and low ammunition, Bigelow readied his rookie gunners for a desperate hold-at-all-costs stand that would soon become legendary.[67]

67 Ibid., 873, 883; Levi W. Baker, *History of the Ninth Massachusetts Battery* (South Framingham, MA, 1888), 62-79. Today's Trostle's lane east of the farmhouse is farther south than the wartime route. Watson was likely on a low knoll just north of this old lane.

"As we commenced retiring," cannoneer Levi Baker recalled, "Barksdale's brigade emerged from the Peach Orchard about 400 yards on our right, and halted to reform their lines." Bigelow said he directed Lieutenant Milton's left section to retard Kershaw's skirmishers with canister, and Erickson's and Whitaker's sections were to throw solid shot into Barksdale's lines. To keep clear of the fire, Barksdale moved well right of Bigelow's pieces, with the bulk of his men tramping west of the Trostle barn. Meanwhile, Humphreys' 21st Mississippi moved down the Trostle farm lane on the battery's right and front. His line was so long Bigelow thought it was an entire brigade. "As the recoil of our guns brought us to the rear of the field," Baker continued, "we were somewhat troubled in working our guns by large boulders and the stone wall on our left and rear."[68]

Just as Bigelow was limbering to move his guns through the gateway back to Cemetery Ridge, Colonel McGilvery dashed up. "Captain Bigelow," he yelled, "there is not an infantryman back of you along the whole line from which Sickles moved out; you must remain where you are and hold your position at all hazards, and sacrifice your battery, if need be, until at least I can find some batteries to put in position and cover you. The enemy," he continued, "are coming down on you now." Bigelow unlimbered his pieces and had ammunition taken from the limbers and stacked beside the guns. Within minutes of double-shotting his four guns, grayclad infantry appeared above a swell of the ground just 50 yards to his right-front. Bigelow ordered his men to open fire, lanyards were yanked, and the artillery roared. Billows of smoke rose to obscure their vision. Unfortunately for Bigelow and his men, the ground to his front and right was much higher, and he could not see more than 50 or 60 yards in that direction. "Neither was there room enough to work six guns at usual intervals," he later explained, "and the ground was broken by bowlders, with heavy stone walls in our rear and left, with a gateway about in the rear of the second piece from the right."[69]

Back north, Hancock needed more time to organize his defense and gather reinforcements. It would be a quarter-hour and perhaps longer before any of the reinforcements he had requested could arrive from points east. While he had escorted Colonel Heath's 19th Maine forward, Hancock witnessed Humphreys' line crumbling south of the Klingle house. He had an idea McGilvery was making a stand with artillery along Trostle's farm lane. What he did see, however, was a six-gun battery at fixed prolonge slowly retiring eastward, keeping pace with Carr's backtracking right flank. Looking toward the battle swirling around the Codori barn, Hancock mistook Turnbull's retiring 3rd U. S. for Weir's 5th U.S. In fact,

68 Ibid.

69 Ibid.

Turnbull was already east of the Emmitsburg Road, retiring toward the Plum Run ravine 400 yards southwest of Weir's position.

With Carr's infantry to his front and right and Brewster's disorganized masses off to his left, Turnbull was unable to fire for fear of hitting them. Moving ever so slowly, his six guns were hauled away loaded with double canister. Each Number Four man walked backward with a lanyard stretched tight in his hand. Turnbull, meanwhile, rode up and down his line as it retired while enemy musketry from beyond his front tore into Humphreys' infantry line. When an opening in the Union line presented itself, Turnbull would discharge double canister into the advancing Confederates, tearing bloody holes in Colonel Lang's thinning line of Floridians. The gray line pressed onward, stepping over the dead and mangled bodies of their comrades and Yankees who had not managed to get clear of Turnbull's fire. And then the gap would close and it became too dangerous for him to fire again. To his right rear, Turnbull could probably see Weir's gunners in action 400 yards to the north.[70]

Just before Turnbull reached Plum Run, however, a long blue line appeared off Weir's left flank advancing at quick-time toward Plum Run. At that moment there was not another infantry regiment between the 19th Maine's left flank and the 1st Minnesota's right, or as Sgt. Silas Adams of Company F, 19th Maine put it, "There were no troops then between its left company [F] and the First Minnesota, about sixty rods [330 yards] away." In reality the distance was closer to 600 yards. Hancock was widening one gap to fill another, gambling that his reinforcements would make it in time. With the 19th Maine gone, there were no organized bodies of troops between the Copse of Trees and the distant and small 1st Minnesota. The Hummelbaugh farm lane lay open for the taking, as did Meade's headquarters and the Taneytown Road.[71]

Meanwhile, fleeing members from Carr's brigade streamed eastward, with many turning to fire a parting shot. Groups from various commands gathered in small bunches, and, without orders, faced back to deliver volleys time and again. As they did so, however, full companies hurried eastward in single file without giving a thought about making a final stand, let alone turning to fire even a single volley in

---

70 Hancock, *JCCW*, 406; Shultz, *Gettysburg Magazine*, no. 18, 83-85; *OR* 27, pt. 1, 576-77; Turnbull to Hunt, July 1863, Hunt Papers, Box Four, LOC. This document appears to be Turnbull's unpublished and "lost" official report on the Gettysburg Campaign. Although barely legible, it mentions many things that took place during the battle that are substantiated by other sources. Fixed Prolonge is when the prolonge [rope] is used with field-pieces to attach the gun to its limber when firing in retreat, or advancing. Gibbon, *The Artillerist's Manual*, 297.

71 John D. Smith, *History of the 19th Regiment of Maine Volunteer Infantry* (Minneapolis, MN, 1909), 70; USGS MRC 39077G2.

This modern image was taken from just south of present-day United Sates Avenue looking north-northeast across Abraham Trostle's lower farmyard and Plum Run. This part of the battleground was hotly contested and vital, because the 30-minute close-combat bought time for the Union to begin patching together an impromptu line of defense. Two batteries played crucial roles here that helped save the Union center: Capt. John Bigelow's 9th Massachusetts, and Lt. Malbone F. Watson's Battery I, 5th U.S. Placed in position by Lt. Col. Freeman McGilvery, both engaged in hand-to-hand combat before being overrun within several hundred yards of the Trostle barn pictured here. *Rosemary G. Oreb*

the direction of the Rebels. Humphreys and Carr tried to control the chaos in an effort to instill some resemblance of dignity in a retreat that was approaching the level of a rout. To make matters worse, Seeley's Battery K, 4th U. S. (now under Lt. Robert James) careened past Turnbull's battery from the direction of the Klingle farm in an effort to reach safety. Battery K had been nearly overrun by Sanders' 11th Alabama at the Klingle orchard while supporting Brewster's embattled brigade, and Humphreys ordered the guns to retire. James' cannoneers beat a hasty retreat north as fast as their horses could pull the gun carriages. The guns closed on the dismantled rail fence paralleling Hummelbaugh's farm lane and James pressed on across the lane toward Plum Run bottom and the advancing 19th Maine.[72]

72 David Shultz, " Gulian V. Weir's 5th U.S. Artillery, Battery C," *Gettysburg Magazine*, Issue 18, 1998, 84.

James' movement coincided with the end of Lieutenant Turnbull's efforts to extract his own battery. "We were so pressed and crowded by our own infantry," Turnbull later wrote, "I had no time to look for a way out. My concern was to save my guns from being carried off. It was after Lieutenant James sped past me when I realized we could go no further. By then it was too late as the enemy was less than one rod off my left."[73]

Meanwhile, south of the Trostle lane-Emmitsburg Road intersection, Col. Benjamin Humphreys' 21st Mississippi had been orphaned from the brigade when, from left to right, the 13th, 18th and 17th Mississippi had wheeled north up the Emmitsburg Road. Humphreys led his isolated regiment across today's Wheatfield Road heading northeast. He encountered both small arms fire and canister from Bigelow's and Phillips' batteries retiring northeast at fixed prolonge. Humphreys angled his long line toward Trostle's cherry orchard and farmyard, following the retreating Federal infantry and batteries.[74]

Phillips made good his escape; Bigelow did not. Corralled by McGilvery at the Trostle farm, Bigelow (as noted earlier) unlimbered his pieces in an effort to meet Humphreys' 21st Mississippi. About this time Humphreys wheeled his regiment east, redressed his ranks, and started off toward the redeployed guns east of the crest. Humphreys' journey toward Bigelow isolated his regiment even more as it moved away from the balance of Barksdale's northbound brigade.[75]

Hancock was repositioning Colonel Heath's 19th Maine south of Weir when McGilvery's sacrificial orders to Bigelow, combined with Colonel Humphreys' decision to drive east to capture it, weakened Barksdale's attack. It took Humphreys about a quarter-hour to redress his line and get it moving down the Trostle farm lane. Throughout this time he continued taking casualties from Bigelow's compact gun line, which fired 22 rounds of canister while skipping solid shot uphill at the Mississippians. Captain Bigelow had orders to hold at all costs, but he had no idea how important his mission was until well after the fact.[76]

Using the Trostle farmyard for cover, Humphreys wheeled the left wing of the 21st Mississippi south and attacked. Enveloped in a pincer movement, the Mississippians overran Bigelow's battery from the north. Each gun fell in secession after brutal hand-to-hand combat. Only one piece was able to withdraw relatively

---

73 Turnbull to Hunt, July 1863, Hunt Papers, Box Four, Military Correspondence, LOC; USGS MRC 39077G2.

74 John Bigelow, *The Peach Orchard: Gettysburg, July 2, 1863* (Minneapolis, MN, 1916), 19-23.

75 McNeily, "Barksdale's Mississippi Brigade at Gettysburg," 248-50.

76 Bigelow, *The Peach Orchard*, 17-18, Bigelow, "Account of the Engagement of the 9th Mass. Battery," *Bachelder Papers*, 1:175-78.

unscathed. Wounded in the mêlée, Bigelow slumped over his horse and was led away, but his brave holding action bought Hancock about 30 precious minutes. Both the 9th Massachusetts Battery and the 21st Mississippi were in shambles. It took Humphreys more time to sort out the mess, get control, redress his ranks, and get moving once again. He could not spare any men to pull the captured guns back to Confederate lines, so he had to leave them behind. Within a few moments of the demise of Bigelow's battery, Lt. Malbone F. Watson's Battery I, 5th U. S. opened from atop his knoll east of Plum Run. Posted by McGilvery before he placed Bigelow, Watson's four guns targeted the 21st Mississippi while Humphreys dressed his ranks along the stone wall running north to south that had hemmed in Bigelow's battery. Opening with four small-bore 10-pounder Parrott Rifles, Watson's gunners not only had to contend with Humphreys' renewed advance, but with throngs of retreating Federals and General Wofford's large brigade of Georgians about 200 yards off their left flank in the Trostle Woods.[77]

By this time, McGilvery had corralled several more retiring batteries to help bolster Watson's guns and Lieutenant Sheldon's New Yorkers, the latter 400 yards to Watson's right and rear. In the meantime, Barksdale's main three-regiment line rolled up Colonel Craig's 105th Pennsylvania "Wildcats" from left to right east of the Emmitsburg Road, forcing that regiment to jack-knife fronting both south and west. Forced to retire to the northeast, Craig's right wing faced back once above the Trostle lane with his left wing north of Sickles' old headquarters tent. The 105th Pennsylvania was now to the immediate front of the small gap separating the left wing of the 71st New York from the 72nd New York's right. All three regiments fronted southwest at about a 45-degree angle to the intersection.

*   *   *

With General Barksdale's line temporarily stalled because of the stubborn tenacity of the 57th and 114th Pennsylvania, Lt. Col. Hilary Herbert's 8th Alabama advanced alone toward the battle-weary 105th Pennsylvania. Wheeling his regiment northeast in an attempt to align his men upon the 10th Alabama, Herbert topped the rise with the 18th Mississippi's disorganized left flank battling about 200 yards opposite the pike on the descending slope of the Emmitsburg Road Rise.[78]

77 Lafayette McLaws, "The Federal Disaster on the Left," *Philadelphia Weekly Times*, August 4, 1886; USGS MRC 39077G2; *Bachelder Maps, Second Day*.

78 Thomas Rafferty, "Gettysburg: The Third Corps' Great Battle on July 2," *National Tribune*, no. 2, vol. 9, February 1888; USGS MRC 39077G2; *Bachelder Maps, Second Day*.

The 8th Alabama fired from the plank fence west of the road. Pressing forward, Herbert finally forced the 105th Pennsylvania to collapse, creating chaos in the 71st and 72nd New York behind them. Although most of Craig's men retired in order, many bolted from the ranks to escape the carnage. Herbert had no choice but to change direction if he planned to pursue the 105th and ultimately connect with Wilcox to the north. He also did not want to become entangled with the 18th Mississippi, which was moving up on his right.[79]

In the quarter-hour it took Herbert to remove the stubborn Pennsylvanians from his front, Barksdale's line passed over the Trostle lane and crashed into the 120th New York. With his line now disorganized and scattered in bunches, Barksdale had a tough time dealing with Lt. Col. Cornelius Westbrook's veteran Empire Staters. Putting up stiff resistance, Westbrook's men held their position before being flanked not only by the 18th Mississippi anchoring Barksdale's left, but also by the 8th Alabama as it continued across the Emmitsburg Road and Trostle's farm lane angling toward the 120th's exposed right lank. "The left of the regiment was pointing nearly in the direction it was to move [toward Wilcox], so it went forward by the left flank," Herbert reported. "As we all rose a hill [Emmitsburg Road] we received a severe fire and I ordered the regiment to 'change front, forward on the tenth company,' which was executed at a double quick, the men firing as they came in to line. There was a hot fight here for a few minutes, and then, the enemy retreating, we followed them straight forward."[80]

Westbrook's 120th New York did not just disperse, as many believe, but advanced when the regiments off either flank gave way. It might have been only a handful of yards, but the brief maneuver stopped the enemy drive, somewhat increased Union morale, and even served to gather up some fugitives. Colonel Brewster was with the regiment as it moved forward, urging them onward as the rest of his brigade melted around both flanks. Lieutenant Colonel Westbrook was active as well. Once his regiment stopped, he rode up and down the firing line wielding his upraised sword to make sure every man did his duty and held his position, all the while pointing toward the enemy and encouraging his soldiers to fire slow and deliberately. The improvised defense efforts chiseled away a few more minutes from General Lee's precious timetable.[81]

Colonel John Austin's 72nd New York off Westbrook's right flank was the first of Brewster's regiments to retire, pressed back by the 10th Alabama. The

79 Rafferty, "Third Corps' Great Battle on July 2."

80 Herbert to Bachelder, Washington, July 9, 1884.

81 Cornelius Westbrook, "On the Firing Line," *National Tribune,* Sept. 20, 1900; *OR* 27, pt. 1, 569.

Alabamians overlapped and enfiladed Austin's right flank when Carr's regiments on the 72nd's right withdrew under pressure from Wilcox's formidable center and left wing. The 10th Alabama's wheel maneuver northeast toward the Union center reopened the gap between its right and the 18th Mississippi's left, allowing Westbrook's 120th New York time to clear its front and focus on the approaching 18th Mississippi, stopping its left side in its tracks. When the 8th Alabama marched into the gap, Westbrook refused his right wing to meet this threat, bending it back like a jackknife on the rest of the line.[82]

Westbrook's left wing, however, held for only a few minutes more before collapsing under pressure from the 17th and 18th Mississippi regiments, but not before further thinning Barksdale's already shot-torn ranks. When the right of the 120th New York finally fell back, the men tried to reform but were soon swept away, joining the multitudes of Union infantry retiring east and northeast as the pincer-like Confederate assault swept about them. Although many moved rapidly eastward across the Plum Run ravine, others retired slowly, turning to fire time and again in an effort to keep Barksdale's and Wilcox's lines at bay. Those who succeeded in clearing the ravine encountered a host of Union officers of every rank and description attempting to stop their flight and turn them around to meet the Confederate wave.[83]

Colonel Brewster, who had left Westbrook's command west of Plum Run, and Col. Regis de Trobriand attempted to rally the fleeing troops between Willard's right flank and the 1st Minnesota's left, the latter still lying near the crest behind the right-rear of Thomas's battery. This gap of more than 500 yards imperiled the Army of the Potomac's entire position. If the Rebels managed to drive into it in force, Meade might lose the Taneytown Road (his vital line of supply) and find his army split in two. The Taneytown Road could be reached through the connecting lane via Patterson's Woods. This area had to be held. It was the general position originally assigned to Sickles' Third Corps before he unilaterally decided to move his two divisions west to slightly higher ground. General Caldwell was there, rallying troops from three different corps while Sheldon's Battery B, 1st New York from its position in the lane opposite George Weikert's farm opened on Humphreys' advancing 21st Mississippi.[84]

---

82 Rafferty, "Gettysburg: The Third Corps' Great Battle."

83 Ibid.; Henry E. Tremain, "Letter to Daniel Sickles dated June 26, 1880," *National Tribune*, July 15, 1886.

84 Richardson to Bachelder, May 6, 1868, *Bachelder Papers*, 1:338-39. Sheldon's guns were on the right of the 6th Maine Light [Dow], straddling the narrow Trostle farm lane north of the Weikert farm.

Back at the Klingle farm, the 11th Alabama had finally punched through Carr's center after helping the 10th Alabama rout section leader Lt. Robert James' guns of Seeley's battery (as earlier described). The 10th carried the road to the right of the 11th, driving back that part of Brewster's line not yet swept away by Barksdale's Mississippians. Pressing Carr's and Brewster's crumbling line before them, the two Alabama regiments advanced through the farm and orchard and into meadows descending toward the Plum Run ravine. Several determined stands and a single countercharge slowed but did not stop Sanders' 11th Alabama. To the immediate left of the 11th, Col. Lucius Pinckard's 14th Alabama had its hands full dislodging Carr's regiments from the Klingle farm. Confronting the 5th and 11th New Jersey and 12th New Hampshire, the lines stood the width of the Emmitsburg Road apart battling for all they were worth, with neither side able to move forward or willing to fall back. It was not until the 11th New Jersey's left flank gave way—after Seeley pulled his guns out of the orchard—that the farmyard line collapsed from left to right.[85]

Lieutenant John Schooner of the 11th New Jersey, fighting just south of the Klingle house, remembered when Seeley's guns fell back. "At this moment," he later wrote, "Battery K, Fourth U. S. Artillery, then stationed a short distance to the left and front of the regiment, limbered their pieces and passed by our left to the rear, closely followed by a line of the enemy's infantry, upon which the regiment opened a rapid fire. I then passed rapidly to the right of the regiment, in order to inform the colonel [Robert McAllister] of the absence of the major, and learned that he too, had been wounded and taken to the rear." Once the Union artillery along the length of the Emmitsburg Road gave way, however, the firepower the infantry needed to remain in place was no longer available. Holding fast there was no longer possible.[86]

With all the senior officers down, Schooner assumed command of the 11th New Jersey. "The fire of the enemy was at this time perfectly terrific; men were falling on every side," he continued. "It seemed as if but a few minutes could elapse before the entire line would be shot down, yet the galling fire was returned with equal vigor. Slowly and stubbornly the regiment fell back, keeping up a continual fire upon the line of the enemy, which was still advancing, until more than half of its number had been killed and wounded." Stands like this one gave General Hancock additional precious minutes to do the work behind the lines necessary to bolster his thinly stretched defensive front. Like Colonel Westbrook's 120th New York 400 yards to the south, Schooner's veteran Garden Staters held their ground before

---

85 OR 27, pt. 1, 553-54; Cavada Diary, July 2, 1863, HSP.

86 Ibid.; USGS MRC 39077G2.

slowly retiring, making Pinckard's Alabamians pay for every foot of ground they gained.[87]

The 11th New Jersey's withdrawal, however, became a confused affair, especially when the left side fell back into the orchard while trying to pass through Seeley's caisson park. There, it also met members of the 5th New Jersey and other fugitives from Brewster's brigade, and during the chaos many fell into Rebel hands. The center and right wing survivors withdrew northeast toward Plum Run, where the detached 19th Massachusetts under Col. Arthur Devereux and the 42nd New York under Col. James Mallon, both of Colonel Hall's Second Corps brigade, waited west of and above the Plum Run ravine. Devereux stood on the crest with Mallon watching the battle as it rolled its way slowly but surely toward them, the Klingle farm buildings barely visible through the smoke though only 400 yards to the west. Devereux kept the two regiments prone below the crest in an effort to avoid overshot and to keep from being swept away by the Union flotsam passing over and around his men. By this time it was difficult and often impossible to tell friend from foe through the swirling smoke and gathering shadows of evening. Because of this, Devereux did not realize that Colonel Pinckard's 14th Alabama, supported by King's 9th Alabama on its left, had stopped to redress ranks before pushing on. About 400 yards in Devereux's right-rear, Colonel Colvill of the 1st Minnesota was calmly standing on top of the crest of Cemetery Ridge watching the Rebel tide approach.[88]

General Wilcox's former command, the 9th Alabama, stood its ground to the immediate left of the 14th. Behind Captain King's 150-yard wide front was a deep wake littered with walking and crawling wounded trying to make their way back to safety. Having reached the Emmitsburg Road with their left flank in shambles, King's Alabamians faced off with the right wing of the 12th New Hampshire in the Klingle farmyard, with the 16th Massachusetts and part of the 11th Massachusetts' left flank pitching in. A fairly wide gap where Turnbull's battery once was now existed between the Massachusetts regiments. Although the lieutenant's six guns withdrew firing, the 9th Alabama and the 5th Florida would exploit the gap and force both regiments to fall back, engulfing their respective flanks. Fighting off King's 9th Alabama as long as they could, and with Captain Gardner's 5th Florida pressing from the right, Lt. Col. Waldo Merriam's 16th Massachusetts men eventually caved under the mounting Confederate pressure. "We were attacked in front and flank," Capt. Mathew Donovan later reported. "Our men stood it bravely

87 Thomas Marbaker, *History of the Eleventh New Jersey Volunteers* (Trenton, NJ, 1898), 99-101.

88 Pfanz, *Gettysburg, The Second Day*, 380; USGS MRC 39077G2.

until overpowered by numbers; were forced to fall back a distance of 300 yards, when again rallied."[89]

Immediately north of the 11th Massachusetts, Maj. Robert L. Bodine's 365 effectives of the 26th Pennsylvania had their work cut out for them. When Lt. Col. Clark Baldwin's 1st Massachusetts fell back from its position west of the Emmitsburg Road, its center and right wing descended upon Bodine's Pennsylvanians, who were anchoring Carr's left flank on the road. Most of Baldwin's men regrouped and faced about on Bodine's right and front. New Englanders, sharpshooters, and other skirmishers swarmed across the road through and around the hard-pressed Pennsylvanians. With his front largely clear, Bodine's first volley hit the center and right wing of Captain Gardner's 5th Florida. The lead rounds slowed the Floridians' advance for a few moments, but the regiment's right wing continued into the gap. The 8th Florida under Lieutenant Colonel Baya, with Major Moore's 2nd Florida on his left, had more momentum during their final approach against portions of Baldwin's reforming 1st Massachusetts. Flanked by both Florida regiments, the New Englanders swung back like an opening gate and refused their west-facing line to front nearly north before the colonel received orders to retire across the road. The withdrawal exposed the right flank of Bodine's 26th Pennsylvania.[90]

Private Thomas Cooper of the 26th Pennsylvania recalled the final minutes of the fight along the Emmitsburg Road, and how his regiment and the "1st Massachusetts, our gallant Yankee companions upon many battlefields, obeyed the order of Lieutenant Colonel [Baldwin] and Major Bodine, and changed direction by the right flank, in the very face of overpowering number. In this way the charge was [temporarily] checked." Both regiments stood their ground, if only for a short while, allowing many of Graham's, Brewster's, and Carr's men to escape. Their stand on Carr's right flank allowed Hancock the time he needed to start Colonel Heath's 19th Maine forward (as earlier described) while General Humphreys was patching together a semblance of a line east of Plum Run. When the pressure became too overpowering, the 1st Massachusetts finally cracked at its hinge, taking with it the 26th's right wing. Bodine's left actually managed a brief countercharge to the right before they too retired.[91]

Once in possession of the northern part of the Klingle farm, Captain King used the house, barn, and outbuildings as cover to redress the 9th Alabama's ranks. At some point King suffered a slight wound. He stubbornly refused to relinquish

89 OR 27, pt. 1, 553-54; Cavada Diary, July 2, 1863, HSP; USGS MRC 39077G2.

90 Clark Baldwin to Bachelder, *Bachelder Papers,* 1:183; OR 27, pt. 2, 631.

91 Nicholson, *Pennsylvania at Gettysburg,* 1:183-84.

command, however, and instead urged his men through the farmyard following after Pinckard's 14th Alabama to his right and Gardner's 5th Florida to his left. Farther east, meanwhile, Turnbull's drivers could not persuade their limber horses to go any farther. Blocked by thickets along the west bank of Plum Run, Turnbull ordered the teams cut loose and left the limbers and guns 25-50 yards west of the stream. Four hundred yards farther north, Lieutenant Weir saw this and, with Confederates battling for possession of the Emmitsburg Road and the Codori barn a few hundred yards off, ordered his own guns limbered.[92]

As Weir and his column rumbled back toward Cemetery Ridge, he spotted a Union regiment moving in two battle lines off his right and front angling southwest toward Plum Run bottom where it arched south, north of Hummelbaugh's farm lane and the rough ground beyond. The infantry support Hancock had promised (Heath's 19th Maine of Harrow's brigade) was arriving. Weir probably also saw Seeley's retreating 4th U. S. battery under Lieutenant James closing on Plum Run from the opposite direction. Having fled Klingle's orchard, James was heading directly toward the advancing infantry line. By the time his lead gun reached the muddy run north of the farm lane, Heath's New Englanders were but a few yards east of it moving at the double-quick. Battery K crashed headlong through the 19th Maine's center. Swearing infantrymen dove for cover to escape the thundering hooves and body-crushing wheels of the onrushing battery. Six guns and two caissons, all loaded with wounded men including Lieutenant Seeley, followed James through the jagged gap punched in the ranks of the 19th Maine.[93]

Hancock, who was off to the left of the 19th Maine, witnessed the collision and spurred his horse toward the chaos. James realized what he had done and slowed down just as the enraged Hancock arrived on the scene. The general shook his fist at the lieutenant and bellowed, "If I commanded this regiment I'd be God Damned if I would not bayonet charge you!" With Confederate infantry just a few hundred yards away and the center of the army under serious threat, Hancock had more pressing matters to deal with. He snapped his attention back to the 19th Maine to get the regiment moving forward once again. Colonel Heath and Captain Miller helped him close the ranks and the regiment resumed its advance southwest toward the shallow ravine housing Plum Run.[94]

Lieutenant Weir slowed his column down as the chagrined James swung his leading section to the south and then back around into "Action Front." His pair of

92 Ibid., 880; Gulian Weir to Bachelder, Nov. 25, 1885, *Bachelder Papers*.

93 Hancock to Bachelder, Nov. 7, 1885, *Bachelder Papers*, 2:1136; Smith, *History of the 19th Maine*, 69-70; *OR* 27, pt. 1, 591.

94 Smith, *History of the 19th Maine*, 70.

smoothbores unlimbered near where the incident occurred while the balance of the battery ascended and passed over Cemetery Ridge somewhere near the Hummelbaugh lane. Weir likewise swung around in "Reverse Trot" and unlimbered 100 yards north of James, about 200 yards east of his previously exposed position. After sending all six caissons over the crest Weir reopened, as did James, targeting the left wing of Lang's Floridians. About the same time and with nowhere to go, Turnbull's cannoneers prepared for close combat as they rammed home double canister, took aim, and let loose.[95]

Hit by fourteen Napoleons—six targeting the right center and eight his left wing—Lang's Floridians reeled but somehow did not break. Instead, they lowered their heads as if facing a heavy rainstorm, closed the gaps broken open by shards of iron, and continued moving forward. With the guns pounding the Confederates, Heath's 19th Maine passed over Plum Run and Hummelbaugh's farm lane before Hancock halted the line. "General Hancock rode along the line and jumped from his horse and took the first man on the left, who was George Durgin," recalled Sgt. Silas Adams. The Second Corps commander, he continued, "conducted [Durgin] forward about a couple of rods and a little to the left. He said to Durgin, "Will you stay here?" Durgin looked up into the general's face and replied, "I'll stay here, General, until hell freezes over." The left flank of the 19th Maine's Company F ended up about 40 yards to Turnbull's right and rear. Hancock ordered Colonel Heath to dress his regiment on that man and galloped off to the southeast.[96]

Hundreds of Third Corps troops belonging to Brewster, Graham, Burling, and Carr were retreating in a giant fan of humanity from north to east through the Trostle and Klingle meadows and down through the run, many passing around Turnbull's now very active gun line. Behind Turnbull not 300 yards distant, these same men rushed through and around Lieutenant Thomas's loaded pieces on their way toward Colvill's prone 1st Minnesota. Wilcox's line of Alabamians was emerging though the smoke atop the crest of the Klingle farm rise, but surrounded by retreating men, smoke, screaming, and the general noise of heavy battle, no one around Thomas's position could tell friend from foe. The two small infantry regiments under Colonel Devereux's command—his own 19th Massachusetts and Colonel Mallon's 42nd New York, both of Hall's brigade—did more harm than good by masking the field of fire that the left section of Weir's Battery C, 5th U.S. otherwise would have enjoyed. Meanwhile, nearby batteries, including Lieutenant Thomas's, were also in trouble. Unable to pivot southwest and rake the elongated knoll, a frustrated Thomas watched Turnbull's battery opposite the creek. Hordes

95 *OR* 27, pt. 1, 591.

96 Smith, *History of the 19th Maine*, 69-70.

of Union refugees heading for Patterson's woods packed the open field on Thomas's left.[97]

"Left to ourselves," Colonel Devereux wrote, "I suggested to Colonel Mallon [42nd New York] that the two regiments be formed behind the crest of a short knoll some distance in our front, there to lie down, wait until our retreating line, which was right upon us then, had passed, deliver a volley by the rear and front ranks, to check the pursuing enemy, then make good our retreat." Hancock had earlier ordered General Gibbon to send the regiments there for just such a purpose. In other words, Devereux was not there to support Thomas's battery, but to bolster General Humphreys' embattled line because Hancock had long ago suspected that Union division would "come tumbling back."[98]

After most of the retreating Federals had passed to the rear of Devereux's small line, the two regiments rose and delivered a volley into Wilcox's 14th and 9th Alabama regiments, which were pressing their attack below Klingle's farm. A second volley followed on the heels of the first. Devereux's men were obviously outnumbered, and another enemy line was now visible through the smoke beyond Colonel Pinckard's 14th Alabama's right. Although stung by Devereux's fire, King's 9th Alabama men pressed toward the Plum Run ravine, their Rebel Yell clearly audible above the din of battle. King's command was wheeling half-left to go after the dozen Union guns in position for the taking. With both flanks in the air, his infantry line was now completely untenable. "It became necessary then to retreat immediately to avoid capture," Devereux penned, "the enemy line outflanking us on the right and left hundreds of yards to each side and very near—so indeed, that both regiments captured several prisoners."[99]

Devereux ordered his 19th Massachusetts and Mallon's 42nd New York back down the rise toward Plum Run and through the ravine south of Thomas's battery. Although they retired in good order, disorganized and panic-stricken men from other units were still fleeing past them. North of Turnbull's guns, Heath's 19th Maine encountered men from Humphreys' brigade heading toward them. Rather than lose men to what looked like it would be a collision followed by panic, Colonel Heath ordered his regiment to lie down. A Third Corps officer, however, ordered him and his men to stand and reform to help stem the retreat. Knowing his men would be swept away if they did so, the colonel ordered the 19th Maine to stay down. Heath actually walked behind the staff officer countermanding his repeated order to stand. As Devereux and Mallon had done, Heath allowed most of the

97 OR 27, pt. 1, 422-43.

98 Hancock, *Reminiscences of Winfield Scott Hancock*.

99 Ibid.

retreating Federals to pass over his regiment before ordering his men back to their feet. When they rose, parts pf Lang's Florida brigade was only 40 yards away.[100]

Heath's New Englanders faced the 5th, 8th, and 2nd Florida regiments, from his left to right. The 5th outflanked his left by a good 100 yards as it moved toward Turnbull's right flank, while the 2nd Florida pressed far beyond Heath's right heading for the opening between the 19th Massachusetts' exposed right flank and Lieutenant Weir's battery. Fortunately for Heath, Weir's and James' combined eight guns was just enough ordnance to keep Major Moore's 2nd Florida in check for the time being. Heath's infantry joined in the slaughter, firing a first volley at just 35 yards that staggered Baya's 8th Florida and the right flank of Moore's 2nd Florida. By the time his 400 riflemen fired their second round, the Floridians of the 8th had been stopped cold, as had the 2nd regiment. Canister and spherical case, the latter probably set at one-half second, slammed into Gardner's 5th Florida at point-blank range. As John Smith of the 19th Maine described it, "In this position of some thirty yards from their lines we fired about eight rounds each into their ranks. The Battery [Turnbull], which joined us on our left commenced firing the moment the front, was clear of the Third Corps. The gunners, with their wool coats off and sleeves rolled up, were working their guns throwing shell and canister into, and making terrible havoc in the enemy ranks."[101]

Because he had fired most of his canister during his withdrawal at fixed prolonge and sent away his caissons, Turnbull was forced to improvise to buy time. He ordered the fuse plugs of his fixed spherical case and shell removed so they would explode immediately following detonation of the powder charge. This dangerous technique, referred to as "rotten shot," exploded the iron balls at the muzzle, sending their jagged bits fanning out ahead like a sawed-off shotgun. If the round did not explode, as many did not, that ball simply acted as a solid shot. At less than 50 yards, accuracy was not a problem. This practice was rare because it was nearly as hazardous to the men working the guns as to the enemy.[102]

Turnbull, on foot with revolver drawn and firing, urged his men to keep fighting. Gardner's 5th Florida wavered when another blast from his six Napoleons, this time just 30 yards distant, knocked more men from the ranks.

---

100 Smith, *History of the 19th Maine,* 71, 76. This officer was later falsely alleged to be General Humphreys. Although the incident certainly took place, there is no evidence to substantiate it was the general. As stated in *The History of the 19th Maine,* "This fiction really never happened until after the general's death, December 27, 1883."

101 Ibid.

102 Thomas K. Tate, *General Edwin Vose Sumner, USA, A Civil War Biography* (Jefferson, NC, 2013), 150; James C. Hazlett, Edwin Olmstead, and M. Hume Parks, *Field Artillery Weapons of the American Civil War* (Urbana, IL, 1983).

Captain Isaac W. Starbird, commanding Company F of the 19th Maine, watched a group of Rebels dash toward the small gap between his left and Turnbull's right gun. "This movement to the rear, on the left of our line," Smith wrote, "exposed the battery on our left to capture, so the guns were drawn back to conform to our movement." Starbird refused his company, pulling it back to face south to match Turnbull's movement. Although this widened the gap between the two units, Starbird could bring more weapons to bear and his concentrated musketry drove back the attackers.[103]

Starbird's alertness and quick action bought more than just time for Turnbull. Not only did it allow the lieutenant a few minutes to drag four of his six guns back to align with Company F on his right, but at that moment one of his caissons arrived with a load of ammunition. While the rounds were being dumped on the ground, the center and left sections were untied from their respective limber carriages. Four of the six horses from the newly arrived limber were unhitched and brought forward because the thickets were too dense for the limbers to pass through. Two teams of horses were hitched to each of Lieutenant Livingston's limber carriages while the guns were attached to the pintal hooks. Within moments of re-hooking, the right section was off, passing around Captain Starbird's left flank and heading due north.[104]

Livingston's guns passed behind Heath's 19th Maine and out into the open beyond his exposed right flank. Musketry from the 8th and 2nd Florida could not stop the lieutenant's brace of guns as they rumbled across Hummelbaugh's farm lane and splashed through shallow Plum Run, heading back toward the initial position vacated by Weir's battery. Dropping trail roughly 300 yards east of the Codori barn, Livingston faced west to target Lang's Floridians. Without regard for his personal safety, Livingston ordered his pair of smoothbores back into action 100 yards off Weir's right flank. His intent was to continue supporting Turnbull from this position, and he reopened with a good left-enfilade fire upon the 2nd and 8th Florida. This fire, added to that of Weir's six guns and James' two, kept the 2nd Florida from enveloping the 19th Maine's right flank.[105]

While the 2nd Florida's left inched its way toward Lieutenant Livingston's front, a volley from behind the battery's right-rear, fired by Col. Joseph Wasden's 22nd Georgia (Wright's brigade) moving up from the direction of the Codori's farm, slammed into the isolated section. Livingston toppled dead from his horse. His left limber pulled away, leaving the right limber and both guns to be overrun.

103   Smith, *History of the 19th Maine,* 71.

104   *OR* 27, pt. 1, 190, 237, 534, 878; *Bachelder Papers,* 1:231, 284.

105   Ibid.

The two captured guns were of no immediate use to the Confederates as both of the Number One cannoneers vanished eastward with their indispensable rammers. Soldiers from the 2nd Florida and 22nd Georgia each claimed a prize and detailed men to haul their trophies back toward the Emmitsburg Road.[106]

The 15th Massachusetts' and 82nd New York's stubborn hold on the Codori farm created mayhem for Wright's brigade as the Federals methodically whittled down the Georgians. Wright's command was further disorganized when the troops on either wing advanced a bit faster around the center of the Codori farm than those moving directly toward it. Wright's close-order formation was completely breaking apart, and except for the 48th Georgia anchoring Wright's left, the brigade's cohesion was essentially gone. Despite Wright's overall problems, when a portion of the 22nd Georgia flanked the 82nd New York south of the barn, the New Yorkers' hold on the farm was doomed.[107]

Meanwhile, as the 5th Florida renewed its advance toward Starbird's refused flank, the 2nd Florida now took full advantage of Colonel Heath's exposed right flank. Despite this threat, Heath calmly held his position while Turnbull renewed his frantic efforts to save his battery. Turnbull, however, was too busy to notice another threat off his left flank. After Colonel Devereux had withdrawn the 19th Massachusetts and 42nd New York, there was no organized support south of Turnbull. Captain King's 9th Alabama was perilously close and angling toward his left section from the southwest, with his left-center moving toward the southern base of the elongated knoll and his far left toward Turnbull's battery.[108]

With the Emmitsburg Road line now firmly in Confederate hands from the Peach Orchard north past the Rogers farm. Colonel E. P. Alexander sent Maj. Benjamin F. Eshleman's Washington Artillery forward along the length of the road from just north of the Sherfy farm past the Trostle farm lane intersection. Reopening after their exciting charge to the road, though largely unable to tell friend from foe, Eshleman's gunners started tossing rounds almost indiscriminately into the fleeing masses. Many of the projectiles fell short or exploded prematurely, killing and wounding Mississippians, Alabamians, and Floridians as well as the enemy. "One could take his choice there was plenty to shoot at," Alexander reported, but "when I got to take in all the topography I was very much disappointed." The Confederate gunner had believed the day was won and the Yankees in full retreat. However, as he sat on his horse near the Emmitsburg Road

---

106 Military Records of Manning Livingston (NNRG-NA); *OR* 27, pt. 2, 629, 631. It is not known how many rounds were fired prior to his death.

107 Pfanz, *Gettysburg, The Second Day*, 384-87.

108 Cavada Diary, July 2, 1863, HSP.

and Trostle farm lane intersection, he spotted Union troops rallying on a spine of ground (Cemetery Ridge) that he had not noticed before. The Yankees were not beaten. In fact, they were still fighting in formidable numbers. For the first time since opening fire that afternoon, Alexander realized "the whole war would not be won today."[109]

*   *   *

A little more than a mile north from where Colonel Alexander was sitting his horse, a single Union artillery round likely fired from Cemetery Hill had already delivered a crippling blow to the Confederate army. Sometime about 5:00 p.m., after Longstreet had begun his assault, Maj. Gen. William Dorsey Pender was riding along his divisional lines getting his brigades ready to move out in support of General Anderson's assault scheduled to begin on his right. An enemy shell exploded near him, sending a jagged chunk of iron into his left thigh. The wound appeared serious and bled profusely, but it did not appear life-threatening. Aides removed the stricken general from his horse and applied direct pressure to his wound. Unable to stop the bleeding, they placed him in an ambulance and Pender left the field. How much time passed before Brig. Gen. James Lane learned Pender was down and he was in command of the division is not known. Apparently, the task of notification was left to Brig. Gen. Edward Thomas, who sent one of his aides after Pender had been removed.[110]

"After a portion of the army on our right had driven the enemy some distance," Lane reported, "General Pender rode from the left of my line to the right of his division [north to south]. About sunset I was informed by Captain Norwood, of General Thomas's staff, that General Pender had been wounded, and that I must take command of the division, and advance, if I saw a good opportunity to do so." And therein rests the primary reason why Pender's division never left its position to attack upper Cemetery Ridge and West Cemetery Hill: Lane did not realize he was in command until it was too late to do anything of substance that evening. By the time the mantle of responsibility settled upon his shoulders it was nearly sunset. According to Harry Heth, another division commander in A. P. Hill's Third Corps, General Lee later stated, "I shall ever believe if General Pender had remained on his horse half an hour longer we would have carried the enemy's position." Whether Lee said anything like that does not diminish the impact of Pender's wounding. He

---

109   Gallagher, *Fighting for the Confederacy*, 240.

110   OR 27, pt. 2, 609, 665. Pender was evacuated to Staunton, Virginia, where his artery ruptured. Pender died within a few hours of the amputation of his leg.

was one of the best division commanders in the army, and the timing of his fall directly interrupted the command structure and flow of orders needed to keep the attack moving.[111]

"About 6 o'clock in the afternoon," wrote Col. Abner Perrin, one of Pender's brigade commanders, "I was ordered to push forward my skirmish line, and drive in the enemy's pickets from a road in front of Cemetery Hill. I communicated this order to Capt. William T. Haskell, in command of a select battalion of sharpshooters, acting as skirmishers, and sent Major McCreary forward with his regiment (1st S. C. Provisional Army), about 100 strong, to deploy near Capt. Haskell, and act as a support."[112]

Perrin's suggestion that he ordered Haskell in at "6 o'clock" is evidence enough that Pender's order to prepare to support Anderson had been received at the height of Longstreet's charge. What is not clear is with whom this order originated. It definitely was not from Pender, otherwise Perrin's entire brigade would have stepped off with Thomas's brigade moving to his right. Although both Thomas and Perrin had been advised to be ready to advance in support of Anderson, the attempt never materialized. Instead, their advanced skirmishers and sharpshooters continued to battle alone well into the growing darkness. "This battalion of sharpshooters, led by the gallant Haskell, made a most intrepid charge upon the Yankee skirmishers," Perrin continued, "driving them out of the road and close up under their batteries.[113]

Across the way, General Hays' firm hold on Zeigler's Grove and the Bryan and Emanuel Trostle farms proved more tenacious than either Thomas or Perrin had anticipated. Woodruff's six Union smoothbores raked the entire length of Thomas's line with case and canister while Union sharpshooters picked off anyone in gray who dared expose himself. With instructions to hold at all hazards, some two hours earlier at 4:00 p.m. Col. Franklin Sawyer's 209 men of the 8th Ohio fought their way across the Emmitsburg Road to relieve the 4th Ohio's four companies. Once atop the rise west of the Emmitsburg Road, Sawyer's men stood on the reverse slope behind a brush-covered plank fence and opened a slow but murderous fire toward the sunken road (Long Lane) 150 yards away. Their deadly

---

111 Ibid. 665; Henry Heth, Richmond, June 1877, *SHSP*, Vol. 4, 154; Scott Bowden and Bill Ward, *Last Chance for Victory: Robert E. Lee and the Gettysburg Campaign* (Savas Publishing Co., CA, 2001).

112 Ibid. 663; "Letter of James H. Lane," Oct. 20, 1877, *SHSP*, Vol. 5, 1877.

113 Ibid.

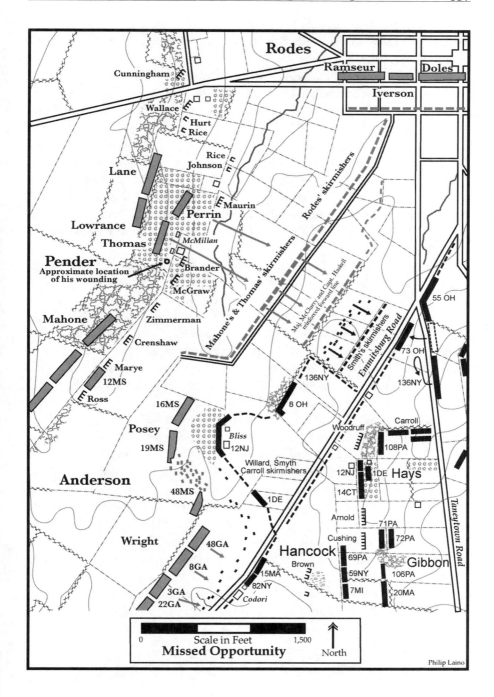

Missed Opportunity

0   Scale in Feet   1,500

North

Philip Laino

accuracy allowed Sawyer to use handfuls of men to pull triggers while others loaded rifles at their feet.[114]

The 8th Ohio's position was not only largely hidden from view from the west and northwest, but commanded both the sunken road's dogleg section and the entire Bliss farm and swale to the south. It was a nearly perfect position. William Mahone's skirmishers were unable to show themselves without receiving fire from both the 8th Ohio along the rise and portions of the 12th New Jersey on the Bliss farm, Mahone's skirmishers for the most part kept their heads down. These Virginians were content to let Thomas's Georgians and Posey's Mississippians handle the bloody affair. The left wing of Col. James Wood's 136th New York still held its skirmish line west of the Emmitsburg Road, while the 1st Massachusetts Sharpshooters in Emanuel Trostle's farmyard and Zeigler's Woods lent its support.[115]

About 300 yards north of the Emanuel Trostle farm, Perrin's skirmishers, assisted by Haskell's sharpshooters and a few men from Thomas's left wing, forced back Wood's right flank skirmishers, along with those from the 73rd and portions of the 55th Ohio, a distance of 400 yards. Retiring toward the Emmitsburg Road, Col. Orland Smith's advanced skirmish line rejoined his second rank behind the rail fence 75 yards west of the road. A brisk firefight erupted along its length from Washington Street south to the Trostle farm. By now the sun was dropping behind South Mountain, and the undulating fields between the opponents were engulfed in rifle smoke and an unending crackle of musketry.[116]

Undaunted by Major Osborn's missiles and Colonel Smith's minié balls zipping past, Captain Haskell calmly walked up and down his advanced firing line urging Perrin's South Carolinians to take their time, aim carefully, fire slowly, and utilize their cover to full advantage. At some point at the height of the brisk skirmish, one of Smith's men, or perhaps one of the New England sharpshooters, found his mark. "Soon after gaining the road, Captain Haskell received a wound from the enemy's sharpshooters, from which he died in a few moments on the field," recalled Perrin. "This brave and worthy young officer fell while boldly walking along the front line of his command, encouraging his men and selecting favorable positions for them to defend. He was educated and accomplished, possessing in a high degree every virtue of most excellent judgment, and soldier of the coolest and most chivalrous daring." Haskell's courage along this line was his

---

114 USGS MRC 39077G2; *Bachelder Maps, Second Day.*

115 Ibid.

116 OR 27, pt. 1, 724, 726; Charles Richardson to Bachelder, Canandaigua, NY, August 18, 1867, *Bachelder Papers,* 1:315.

final daring deed. He was probably the last significant Confederate high ranking officer killed on July 2 along Cemetery Ridge.[117]

Much like Haskell had done, Colonel Smith calmly walked his line urging his men to stand to their work. Secure in the belief that his small brigade could hold the line, he used the resources he had on hand to best advantage. Smith reinforced his skirmishers along the Emmitsburg Road using men from the three regiments ideally located in reserve 50-100 yards east of and above the Taneytown Road. He also sent riders galloping up Cemetery Hill to alert his division commander, Brig. Gen. Adolph von Steinwehr, of the threatening situation. Smith had no way of knowing that his brisk skirmish would last several hours before petering out after 9:00 p.m. without a significant Confederate effort to carry his position. "On the night of the 2d, our line was threatened by a strong force of the enemy deployed in our front, while a vigorous attack was made upon the right wing of the corps," he later reported. "No attack was made on us, however, owing, as I have since been informed, to their failure to carry the hill on the right.[118]

"On the evening of the 2d we were ordered further to the right, to assist in repelling an attack on our right wing, then in progress," reported Colonel Wood of the 136th New York. "The enemy was repulsed without our assistance, and we were ordered back to our former position." What neither Smith nor Wood knew or alluded to is the fact that while Major McCreary's and Captain Haskell's reinforced skirmishers battled Smith's small brigade, several Rebel brigades from Robert Rodes' division of Ewell's Second Corps (Ramseur's, Iverson's, and Doles') were moving into position just south of town in preparation to support Pender's effort to carry West Cemetery Hill while other Confederates assault the same height from the east. Nothing came of this effort Rodes moved into position late and Pender's men failed to move at all.[119]

117 OR 27, pt. 2, 663.

118 Ibid., pt. 1, 724.

119 Ibid., 726.

Chapter Sixteen

"Advance, colonel, and take those colors!"
— *Maj. Gen. Winfield S. Hancock, U.S.A.*[1]

Evening, July 2:
Confederate Flood Tide

The Union center was in real trouble, and General Hancock and his subordinates knew it. After placing Colonel Heath's 19th Maine in position to support Weir's battery near the Trostle farm lane, the Second Corps leader rode with his trusted aide, Capt. William Miller, back across Plum Run toward the Colonel Colvill's waiting 1st Minnesota. Hancock had two primary short-term concerns: delaying the oncoming Rebels and stemming the collapse of the Union troops streaming away from the Emmitsburg Road line eastward toward Cemetery Ridge. Both were tall orders.

During his ride, Hancock may have spotted Col. William Brewster, the energetic leader of the Third Corps' Excelsior Brigade busy trying to rally anyone who would stop and face the Rebels. These included soldiers from his New York brigade who, during the past 30 minutes, had worked their way nearly half a mile north from their original position. Other commanders were also hard at work, including General Carr, who was still west of Plum Run trying to rally men, and his division commander General Humphreys, who was rallying men in the fields east of the run several hundred yards south of the 1st Minnesota.[2]

Staying calm in the face of the nearly overwhelming crisis, Hancock rode up to Colonel Colvill and asked for his assistance in rallying the soldiers. Earlier, Colvill

1 Hancock to U. S. Congress, *JCCW*, 406.

2 Ibid.

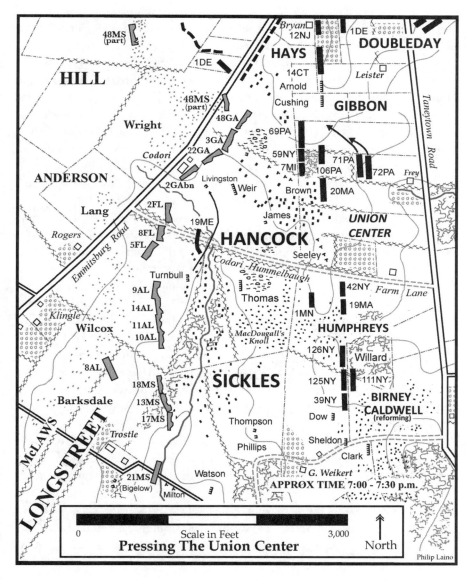

Pressing The Union Center

0   Scale in Feet   3,000

North

Philip Laino

had acted on a similar request from an unnamed officer, but his attempt at stemming the tide proved unsuccessful. Colvill had spent much of his time prone in an effort to avoid having his line swept away. "By General Hancock's order, and with his personal assistance, I undertook to stop and put them in line," Colvill reported, "but found it impossible, and demoralizing to my own regiment in doing so." One of his soldiers, Alfred Carpenter, agreed: "The stragglers came rushing through the lines, whom we in vain tried to stop and at last gave it up entirely, believing they were more injury than help to us." The men gave up, lay back down, and let the routed men scramble over and around them to the rear. Enemy shells, meanwhile, began dropping uncomfortably close.[3]

Hancock spent little time with Colvill after spotting General Humphreys a short distance to the south. As hectic as the situation had become, the retreat of Humphreys' division was not quite the general rout often portrayed and in some instances was fairly organized. "Twenty times did I bring my men to a halt and face about," Humphreys later claimed, "myself and [son] Harry and others of my staff forcing the men to it." The 11th Massachusetts' Capt. Henry N. Blake confirmed his general's claim to some degree when he observed, "Every foot of the distance to Plum Run, a small and sluggish brook, was disputed and in the execution of these orders, hundreds pierced by balls and struck by shells, fell in blood."[4]

Strongly disputed or not, parts of Humphreys' division was in rout, and Hancock and Miller rode against a rising tide of blue ascending from the thickets below and to their right. The two officers found Humphreys and his aides successfully rallying hundreds of retreating troops near the crest. Three distinct corps badges were present amongst the men manning the cobbled ragged line 300-400 yards east of Plum Run ravine. It was only now that Humphreys learned Hancock was also in command of the Third Corps. Sickles' first successor, General Birney, was but a short ride to the south near Caldwell's division, but Hancock and Humphreys agreed they did not have time to ride to him to discuss particulars; they needed to stop the retreat and throw back the enemy. After leaving Humphreys, Hancock and Miller rode south, taking note of Col. Regis de Trobriand as he heroically rallied some of Humphreys' troops while waving a battle flag from one of his regiments.[5]

No one seems to have yet informed General Birney that Hancock now commanded the Third Corps. As a result, Birney rode about the ridge issuing directives as if he was still in command. With Birney heading north and Hancock south, the generals likely passed one another, but the smoke, confusion, and pressing issues at hand kept them from realizing that fact. Surrounded by adjutants and aides, Birney also did not see or acknowledge Humphreys and de Trobriand, but up near the low rough ground he did encounter Colonel Brewster. It mattered

---

3 Colvill to Bachelder, June 9, 1866, *Bachelder Papers*, 1:257; Dr. Robert W. Meinhard, "No Soldiers Ever Displayed Grander Heroism: The First Minnesota at Gettysburg," *Gettysburg Magazine*, no. 5, July 1991; Alfred Carpenter account, July 3, 1863 (copy at GNMP).

4 Kevin E. Obrien, "To Unflinchingly Face Danger and Death: Carr's Brigade Defends Emmitsburg Road," *Gettysburg Magazine,* no. 12, January 1995; Henry N. Blake, "Personal Reminiscences of Gettysburg," Massachusetts Military Order of the Loyal Legion Collection, USAHEC.

5 Hancock to U. S. Congress, *JCCW*, 406.

little whether Brewster was aware of Hancock's new authority or knew the present location of General Humphreys. Like Hancock and Humphreys before them, Brewster and Birney agreed on a plan of action.[6]

It was not long after the 26th Pennsylvania passed over Heath's prone line (as described in the previous chapter) that General Carr joined Birney and Brewster in the thickets east of the Maine men. The trio decided Humphreys' two brigade commanders would reform whatever lines they could as fast as possible where they were. Splitting up, Brewster took control of the left wing and Carr the right, while Birney and his staff worked the rear, turning men back who had succeeded in reaching the crest.

South of the stationary 1st Minnesota, Humphreys and de Trobriand were having better luck than Birney, Brewster, or Carr. All five Third Corps officers had thus far displayed unflinching bravery and resourcefulness above and beyond the call of duty. Birney and Humphreys had stayed to the very last rallying their respective divisions when the tide broke, and then remained with their men as they retired. Birney, seeking to salvage the new position, rode forward as Barksdale's Mississippians closed on Trostle farm lane. He quickly sized up the situation and, while under enemy fire, attempted to slow his division's retreat. Both he and Humphreys seemingly were everywhere, inspiring and leading their men. Birney even made it a point to applaud and cheer the retreating Second and Fifth Corps troops, as well as his own, as they retired north and east. "I may be pardoned, perhaps, for referring in my report to the conspicuous courage and remarkable coolness of the brigadier-general commanding the division during this terrific struggle," was how General Carr summed up Humphreys' actions that evening. "His presence was felt by officers and men, as the enthusiastic manner in which he was greeted will testify."[7]

Brewster was as steadfast as Birney and Humphreys in his quest to hold at all costs and then retire only grudgingly while inflicting as much damage as possible. Brewster's change of direction, as ordered by Humphreys and initiated by Birney, placed his men in a precarious position that not too many brigades in either army could have held. Hit from three directions, Brewster's New Yorkers had no choice but to pull out, but they did so only after General Humphreys personally ordered them to retire. Likewise ordered out, Carr believed to the day he died that his brigade could have held its advanced position had he been properly supported. "Notwithstanding my apparent critical position," he argued, "I could and would have maintained my position but for an order received direct from Major-General

---

6   OR 27, pt. 1, 483; Smith, *History of the 19th Maine*, 70-71.

7   OR 27, pt. 1, 544.

W. H. Tipton's post-battle panorama looking due south down the Union line atop Cemetery Ridge past the Copse of Trees. Before being sent south, Colonel Heath's 19th Maine had been prone south of the Copse of Trees behind the low stonewall, its right flank near the worm fence running perpendicular to ridge crest. Ordered to their feet, the Main men followed Hancock and Heath south by southwest toward the distant Klingle farm (visible immediately to the right of the Copse). The essentially unprotected Union center (the Codori-Hummelbaugh crossroad) is defined by the worm fence glistening in the sun in the top center of the photo. *William H. Tipton, LOC*

Birney, commanding the corps to fall back to the crest of the hill in my rear. At that time I have no doubt that I could have charged the rebels and driven them in confusion, for my line was still perfect and unbroken, and my troops in the proper spirit for the performance of such a task."[8]

General Carr's frustration notwithstanding, he was not in a position to second guess the real-time decision-making of a commander who had been unexpectedly thrust into corps command while his men were in dire straits. From the moment Birney got word that Sickles was down, his primary job was to extract the Third Corps survivors with some level of dignity and some degree of military order, and to reform them farther east to prevent a deep penetration of the Union left and left-

8   Ibid.

center. From his point of view, the army's far left was no longer salvageable. Because the crumbled left now consisted of fleeing fugitives from three corps, it was nearly impossible to control their retreat. And he barely tried. Instead, Birney rode to find Humphreys' division to seek help holding back the onslaught while he attempted to regain control east of Plum Run. It is impossible to know whether Carr's contention that he could have held the Emmitsburg Road was correct. But we do know that Birney was doing all he could under the circumstances, Carr's second-guessing notwithstanding.[9]

Most of Humphreys' success once atop the ridge was not only because of his positive commanding figure, as noted by General Carr, but because of the steadying presence of Col. Arthur Devereux's two detached Second Corps regiments which Hancock, in the excitement and swirling chaos, somehow missed. Having reformed to Humphreys' right and rear, Devereux's own 19th Massachusetts and Mallon's adjacent 42nd New York partially blocked the gap between the 1st Minnesota' left and the new line Humphreys was attempting to establish. After passing east of Plum Run, Devereux formed west of the Patterson Woods atop the crest of south Cemetery Ridge with Mallon's New Yorkers behind where Humphreys' right wing was reforming. The two regiments acted much like provost guards, physically establishing a line that stopped fleeing Federals. Although Devereux's and Mallon's soldiers did not engage the enemy or move forward at that time, their steadiness heartened most of the fugitives, many of whom joined their ranks or turned to face back with Humphreys. "In a short time we met the second line of our men pressing forward [reforming]," recounted Devereux. "Passing through them a distance of perhaps 25 yards, we halted, as did the line we had just met. At this point the two regiments rested on a slope fronting the enemy, exposed to their artillery fire, which was very hot, unable to use our own fire on the columns of the enemy because of the line in front."[10]

In addition to the five leading Third Corps officers, most of their subordinates and peers had thus far performed with honor and courage. They could be seen rallying troops along the length of the retiring line. Caught between the opposing lines when his horse was shot from under him, Cuban-born Capt. Adolph Cavada (one of Humphreys' staff officers) helped rally troops in the Plum Run ravine just as Barksdale's Mississippians started their descent. Officers and men alike stopped to take cover behind trees, rocks, brush, or whatever was available, and discharged

---

9   Ibid., 533, 543; Humphreys Narrative, Box 26, Humphreys Papers, HSP.

10 OR 27, pt. 1, 443; USGS MRC 39077G2; *Bachelder Maps, Second Day*. The "slope" was a reference to Cemetery Ridge south of the 1st Minnesota, and the "artillery fire" was probably from Confederate Porter Alexander's new gun line in the Peach Orchard.

their weapons toward the gray mass advancing from west of the ravine. Captain Asa William Bartlett of the 12th New Hampshire stood his ground not only with men from his company but with many who he did not recognize. "To unflinchingly face danger and death is one thing," he wrote, "but to turn your back thereto and stand firm and unshaken is a different and more difficult thing, that only the bravest of the best disciplined troops can be relied upon to do." Some field and line officers cobbled together company-sized groups of men and led them toward Humphreys' new position. Still others, some with musket in hand, some not, turned to face the enemy all alone. General Hancock could not have asked for better help that evening than he received from the Third Corps officers. "I directed General Humphreys to form his command on the ground from which General Caldwell had moved to the support of the Third Corps, which was promptly done," reported Hancock. "The number of his troops collected was, however, very small, scarcely equal to an ordinary battalion, but with many colors, this command being composed of the fragments of many shattered regiments."[11]

After leaving Humphreys, Hancock continued south toward where he had last met with his detached division commander General Caldwell. He had only ridden perhaps 200-300 yards when he spotted a sizable Union force at right-shoulder shift with bayonets fixed advancing in a splendid line. It was Col. George Willard leading two of his regiments—Lt. Col. Levin Crandell's 125th New York and Col. Eliakim Sherrill's 126th New York. The rest of the brigade was elsewhere. Major Hugo Hildebrandt's 39th New York had been detached to the left, while Col. Clinton MacDougall's 111th New York remained on the crest of Cemetery Ridge in reserve. Moving in two lines of battle with no formal regimental or brigade colors showing, the 125th and 126th advanced west toward Plum Run and the lower Trostle meadows. Hildebrandt's 39th New York, meanwhile, was alone angling away from its sister regiments toward the old Trostle lane west of George Weikert's farm. Hancock would later take some of the credit for Willard's posting and advance, stating, "I established Willard's brigade at the point through which General Birney's division had retired, and fronting the approach of the enemy, who were pressing vigorously on. There were no other troops on its right or left, and the brigade soon became engaged."[12]

Lieutenant Colonel James Bull of the 126th New York later explained, "By order of the division general [Hays], the brigade moved from its position by the left flank about a quarter mile toward the left of the line, where it formed in line of battle, and ordered by Willard to charge two Rebel batteries, supported by infantry,

11 Ibid., 371.

12 Ibid.; Hays, *Life and Letters of Alexander Hays*, 402-10.

posted on the hill [Emmitsburg Road Rise] in front of the position occupied by the brigade." No one knows exactly who ordered Willard in, or whether he advanced on his own initiative, leaving the matter unresolved as to who was responsible for helping the so-called "Harpers Ferry Cowards'" achieve their long-awaited revenge that bloody day.[13]

The 125th and 126th New York began their counterattack near the crest of the ridge, their line surging across what appeared to be an open level field. In fact the terrain was undulating. Willard realized this unpleasant fact as soon as he descended west into the field and realized he could not see over the brow of a small rise ahead of him. Willard had set off thinking he was attacking Rebel batteries directly opposite him on ground a little higher than his own. In fact, a ravine and a creek separated his regiments from Alexander's and Eshleman's Confederate guns. Once he started his men forward, however, there was no turning back and the situation turned ugly in a hurry. "The line," Lieutenant Colonel Bull recalled, "advanced over declining ground through a dense underbrush extending to the base of the hill previously mentioned, in as good order as the circumstances of the case would admit, at which place the alignment, without stopping, was partially rectified." Contrary to Colonel Willard's expectations, Barksdale's left and Wilcox's flanks "in considerable force were found in this underbrush."[14]

Hancock cast but a short glance at the two regiments disappearing into the Plum Run ravine before riding up to the front of another unit he did not recognize and, without formal introduction, ordered Colonel MacDougall's 111th New York forward. He simply pointed back in the direction from which he had come and ordered the colonel to charge toward Thomas's battery. "The brigade commander [Willard] ordered me to remain at the left in reserve about 200 yards in rear," MacDougall recalled, "when General Hancock came riding up shortly, and ordered me with my regiment to the right [north] in great haste, to charge a rebel advance, which had broken through our [Humphreys'] lines on the right of the Third Brigade, and had advanced 20 or 30 rods beyond our lines, and was in the act of turning the right flank of our brigade." Hancock wheeled his horse about as the 111th New York dressed ranks. "When ordered to stand," recalled Colonel MacDougall, "the men sprang to their feet and we moved by the right flank and then left [flank] at the double quick." Hancock and Miller rode with MacDougall a short distance north under a heavy fire of shell and solid shot from the enemy

13 OR 27, pt. 1, 472.

14 Ibid. Colonel Bull's statement makes it clear Willard had no idea the gentle descending ridge suddenly dropped into Plum Run to the depth of 15-30 feet from he and his men started.

batteries, co-mingled with the bullets and balls of a triumphant horde of Rebels forcing their way eastward across Plum Run.[15]

At some point Hancock stopped the right-flank move and ordered MacDougall into action, advancing by the left flank. Having already fixed bayonets, the regiment surged forward while the general and his adjutant galloped northwest through the retirees toward Thomas' battery. To the front of those guns, across the ravine some 300 yards northwest of the advancing 111th New York, Lieutenant Turnbull's cannoneers were locked in bloody hand-to-hand combat as Wilcox's 14th and 9th Alabama and Lang's 5th Florida closed in on them from three sides. No battery could hold its ground against such odds when the Alabamians poured into the battery from the left and front and the fighting became brutal and intimate. The gunners wielded handspikes and rammers like clubs, to no avail. They did, however, have enough time to spike one of the guns before the Rebels overran the left piece. While attempting to spike another gun, Pvt. James Riddle, a U. S. Regular from Virginia, had his skull crushed by a clubbed musket while his messmate, Pvt. George Bentley, was shot through the body.[16]

Lieutenant Turnbull was luckier. After emptying his revolver, he escaped with 50 others, leaving behind eight men killed and a dozen badly wounded. North of Turnbull's abandoned guns, Colonel Heath ordered his prone 19th Maine to rise just as the 2nd Florida gained his right flank. After firing several volleys that slowed but did not check the Rebels, Heath had no choice but to retire. "Colonel Heath received word that the enemy had made its appearance on our right flank," regimental historian John D. Smith wrote. "He ordered the Regiment to fall back and it did so in perfect order. The distance the Regiment fell back did not exceed two or three rods, when they faced the enemy again and, in perfect alignment, began firing again."[17]

By the time Heath's regiment faced about, a small group of men patched together by Colonel Brewster reformed off Thomas's right flank east of the 19th Maine. "While the Nineteenth was engaged in loading and firing," Smith continued, "it was observed that a small body of men had formed in our rear. They were waving their flags and appeared to be cheering us on in the work we had in hand. They showed no anxiety, however, to advance with us." Ordered to reform on the rough and rocky ground, Brewster's party used the thickets and stones as some

---

15 Ibid., 474; MacDougall to Charles Richardson, June 30, 1886, GNMP; Hays, *Life and Letters of Alexander Hays*, 402-10.

16 Personal Military Records of George Bentley and James Riddle, Battery K, 3rd U. S. Light Artillery, NARA.

17 Smith, *History of the 19th Maine,* 72.

protection, while others from his shattered brigade slowly made their way there after passing behind or between Thomas's gun line and caisson park. What neither Smith nor anyone else in the 19th Maine realized was that the flag waving was not intended to inspire them, but to signal retiring Excelsior Brigade troops to come to the rallying point. Brewster's plan worked and about 150 or more of his fleeing New Yorkers joined those who had already rallied around the colors at the western edge of Plum Run.[18]

While Brewster was rallying his Excelsiors, Colonel Wasden's Georgians and Major Moore's Floridians had spent little time celebrating the capture of Livingston's section of guns beyond Codori's barn. Urged forward again, the now ragtag 22nd Georgia set eyes on Lieutenant Weir's battery's right-rear, while Moore's 2nd Floridians withered under Weir's doses of double canister. South of the 2nd Florida, the 5th Florida endured Weir's, Turnbull's, and James' guns and small arms fire from the 19th Maine. "The enemy's guns are making great gaps in our lines," Capt. James B. Johnson remembered, "and the air seems filled with musket balls, our men are falling on all sides."[19]

Supported by other Georgians from Wright's rapidly dispersing brigade, the remainder of the 22nd's right flank and some men from the 2nd Battalion closed to within 30 yards of Weir's gun line. Wasden's men let loose a crippling volley into Lt. Homer Baldwin's right section. Fired upon from point-blank range by a line that seemed to rise up out of the ground, Weir's gunners were unable to respond before another volley ripped through the gun crews. A few men from the decimated 15th Massachusetts and 82nd New York, already fagged from the Codori farmyard fight, tried to reform behind Weir but were driven in. The Georgians didn't fire a third time, choosing instead to charge with fixed bayonets. The 2nd Georgia Battalion and portions of the 2nd Florida also surged forward, their mixed line ragged and irregular, but lethal nonetheless.[20]

The first volley from the 22nd brought down Lieutenant Baldwin's horse. The officer jumped up and ordered his section hitched and away. This was easier said than done, because every man operating the right gun was either wounded, dead, or busy defending himself. Private Peter Sharrow fell in this melee, shot through the body several times while wielding a handspike. Private John Porter was hitching the right gun when his spine was shattered. Unable to do much on foot, Baldwin

---

18 Ibid.; *OR* 27, pt. 1, 559.

19 Ibid.; James B. Johnston, "A Limited View of What One Man Saw at Gettysburg: A Personal Statement," Florida Historical Society, Cocoa, Florida. See also GNMP, 5th Florida vertical file.

20 *OR* 27, pt. 1, 872, 880; pt. 2, 614, 629, 630.

followed his left gun as it bolted away. Lieutenant Charles Whitesell was less fortunate. With all of his horses shot down, his center section remained where it was hitched. Like Baldwin's cannoneers, Whitesell's men wielded handspikes and rammers but the Confederate attack was overwhelming. Both artillery lieutenants stayed only long enough to empty their revolvers before essentially running for their lives. Whitesell managed to hoist Baldwin onto his horse and they galloped east, leaving behind his two guns and one of Baldwin's—all three now in enemy hands.[21]

Lieutenant Weir was on the left with Lt. Jacob Roemer when that section pulled away. Weir mistakenly assumed both Whitesell and Baldwin had gotten out as well, and so inadvertently left them to fend for themselves. Weir had only ridden a short distance when his horse collapsed from a gunshot, spilling him hard to the ground while Lieutenant Roemer's brace of guns thundered over the ridge somewhere north of Hummelbaugh's farm lane. Bruised from his tumble, Weir was slowly rising when a Rebel round struck him in the forehead. Fortunately for the officer, the round of lead had been fired from so far away that the slug only knocked him back down, leaving a bad purple-black bruise where it struck. The stunned officer was on his back when others passing by spotted him and stopped to lend a hand. Helped to his feet, Weir made his way toward Lieutenant James' guns, mistakenly thinking they belonged to Roemer. He turned back in time to witness hand-to-hand fighting for some guns. It did not register at the time that these pieced belonged to him.[22]

Dazed and confused, Weir staggered up Cemetery Ridge and watched James' pieces rumble off east. After subsequently going back into battery, Lieutenant James reopened on Lang's column. "I then took position about 400 yards to the right [and rear of Klingle orchard], and placed my guns in position for the purpose of enfilading their line," he reported. "I had scarcely gotten my guns unlimbered when the enemy [after overrunning Weir] appeared on my right flank and rear, deployed as skirmishers, and not more than some 30 yards distant, and, getting into the battery along with our own infantry, I could not fire, and it was with utmost difficulty I succeeded in moving by the left flank and retiring to the rear."[23]

With Weir's, Livingston's, and James'/Seeley's batteries gone, there were now no organized Federal units left on this part of the field below Cemetery Ridge available to lend a hand to Colonel Heath. Brewster was still regrouping the

21 Weir to Hancock, Fort Hamilton, N. Y., Nov. 25, 1885, *Bachelder Papers*, 2:1152-54; Homer Baldwin to father, July 7, 1863; GNMP; 5th U. S. Artillery, Battery C file.

22 Ibid.; *OR* 27, pt. 1, 872, 880.

23 *OR* 27, pt. 1, 591.

refugees, but they were not enough to offer a credible defensive force. Behind Brewster, General Carr was having quite a time of it. Gibbon's division could no longer be counted upon for support because regiment after regiment had been detached from his command for service elsewhere until there was nothing left to send. Gibbon's troops and artillery near the Copse of Trees also had their hands full and were themselves sending couriers in search of reinforcements.[24]

By this time the friction of war was beginning seize up the gears making up the Confederate attack. The 2nd Florida's left wing had suffered heavy casualties and, with the leftmost company detached, Major Moore's command was not only weak but exhausted and disorganized. He had sent several dozen men to help drag back Livingston's and Weir's five captured guns and limbers, which had only further weakened his striking power. The remainder of his left battalion had broken down into small groups, as had the right side of the 22nd Georgia and all of the 2nd Georgia Battalion. The Confederate line immediately north of Heath's 19th Maine was now a mixed bag from several regiments clustered together in small bunches —too disorganized to press forward. But they did manage to hold their captured ground and return fire, refusing to budge as Wright's line farther north began its slow ascent toward Brown's Rhode Island battery with the Copse of Trees just 100 yards to the immediate right and rear of the gun line.[25]

Colonel Brewster took note of this Rebel disorganization as he readied his 150-plus effectives. Behind him, Maj. Charles Hamlin, General Carr's staff officer, had assembled nearly 100 more men from Humphreys' division. Meanwhile, Lieutenant Weir, his mind somewhat clearer after getting his bell rung by a spent ball to the head, had returned to the base of the ridge. He finally realized James' guns were not in fact part of his battery and that those still on the field were his. Weir approached Hamlin and, pointing back toward Whitesell's and Baldwin's abandoned pieces, pleaded with the major to get them back. In his battered state, Weir was in no shape to help. Instead, after speaking with Hamlin, he came upon Baldwin's left piece sitting idle near the farm lane. He was handed the reins to a horse and left the scene of action to lead that piece to safety, still unsure of the fate of the rest of his battery.[26]

South of Brewster's position, Lieutenant Turnbull had reached the safety of Lieutenant Thomas's Battery C, 4th U. S. Rebels had overrun and seized Turnbull's entire battery, though it is doubtful he knew the fate of his trusted subordinate Lieutenant Livingston. His first order of business was to see that the enemy did not

24 Ibid., pt. 1, 417, pt. 2, 631-32.

25 Ibid., pt. 2, 631-32; Hancock, *JCCW*, 406; USGS MRC 39077G2; *Bachelder Maps, Second Day*.

26 Weir to Hancock, Fort Hamilton, NY, November 25, 1885, *Bachelder Papers*, 2:1152-54.

carry off his four guns west of the run. At Turnbull's insistence, Thomas trained all six bronze smoothbores on the captured pieces and opened. Within moments, his guns had partially dismantled one of Turnbull's Napoleons and mangled the other three carriages, rendering them useless. The 14th and 9th Alabama regiments stalled around the battery, shielding themselves as well as possible against Thomas's rain of canister rounds and hot shrapnel. Not only could they not drag off their silent trophies, but the Alabamians were powerless to return fire. The 5th Florida's right flank also came under Thomas's fire as it tried to close on Plum Run. The Floridians went to ground, seeking shelter behind whatever scant cover they could find.[27]

Lieutenant Thomas had stopped the Confederates in his immediate and right-front, but not those off to the north. Portions of Lt. Col. William Baya's 8th Florida managed to reach Plum Run and close to within 30 paces of the 19th Maine in a slow-developing firefight. The 19th was by that time nearly parallel with Thomas's gun line, with Brewster's men another 50 yards to their rear. The opposing regiments stood only yards apart sending volley after volley crashing across the run into one another. For just the slightest moment, Colonel Heath thought the 8th Florida's center was wavering, so he fired another volley before withdrawing.

Outmaneuvered, Lang's command could not surround or drive away Heath's line. The New Englanders periodically turned back, leveled their weapons, fired, and continued withdrawing to new positions to repeat the process. Heath's 300-yard withdrawal was one of the finest 30 minutes of soldiering along the Third Corps' line on that long and eventful day. Lang's Floridians pressed forward, passing over rows of Union dead and wounded. "I do not remember having seen anywhere the dead lying thicker than the Yankee infantry attempt to make a stand in our front," recalled Lang.[28]

*   *   *

Shortly after sending in Colonel MacDougall's 111th New York, Hancock and Miller approached a shallow dry wash depression 100 yards north of where they had left MacDougall. During wetter times, the small tributary flowed from the crest

---

27 OR 27, pt. 1, 632; Humphreys to Wilcox, November 30, 1877, Box 27, Humphreys Papers, HSP.

28 Adams, "The Nineteenth Maine at Gettysburg," in *Military Order of the Loyal legion of the United Sates, Maine Commandery, War Papers Read Before the Committee of the State of Maine,* 4 vols. (Portland, ME: MOLLUS, 1915), 4:260-61; Lindstrom, *Perry's Brigade Thesis,* 86; GNMP vertical files on the Florida Brigade.

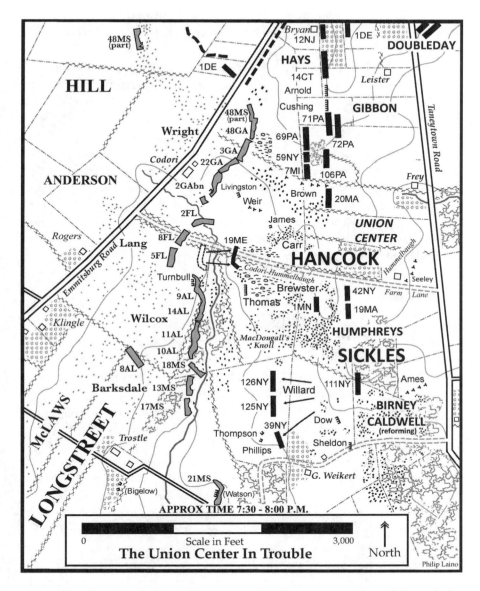

The Union Center In Trouble

APPROX TIME 7:30 - 8:00 P.M.

Scale in Feet

0   3,000

North

Philip Laino

east to Plum Run. As the two officers spurred their mounts northward through the open meadow between the ravine and Humphreys' reforming line, they could still see blue-clad soldiers scampering and clawing up and out of the Plum Run ravine. A battle line appeared below after emerging from the thickets south of Thomas's gun line where the wash intersected the ravine. The unidentified troops, still perhaps 75 yards away, cleared the brush-choked run before Hancock and Miller realized they were Confederates. The Rebels saw the mounted Union officers about the same time.[29]

Colonel Sanders' 11th Alabama moved past Colonel Forney's 10th Alabama's left, shifting toward the weakest point—the yawning gap between Thomas's left and MacDougall's oncoming 111th New York's right flank. The 10th had met stiff opposition during its long descent toward the dry run, with its right flank stalled during its encounter with the advancing 126th New York. Sanders' regiment had not and so kept going, moved directly toward the dry ravine. The unobstructed right-center of Sanders' regiment passed into the gap north of the 10th Alabama's stalled left, reached Plum Run, and descended into the ravine. These Alabamians could not see MacDougall's 111th New York charging from their right and front, angling toward them just 200 yards away. Sanders guided his 11th Alabama through the underbrush and thickets bordering the west bank and into the boggy ground of the run. A few moments later the regiment was tramping through the brush above the eastern bank. And it was there the Alabama men spotted a high-ranking Union officer and an aide—and opened fire.[30]

"Proceeding along the line," Hancock recalled, "I met a regiment of the enemy, the head of whose column was about passing through an unprotected interval in our line. A fringe of undergrowth in front of our line offered facilities for it to approach very close to our lines without being observed." Rebels up and down the line raised their rifles and fired. "It was advancing firing," confirmed the general, "and had already twice wounded my aide, Captain Miller."

Hancock and the wounded Miller escaped by galloping north away from Plum Run and the depression. Planned or not, they were heading directly for Colonel Colvill and his 1st Minnesota—the last available fresh reserves along that part of the line. By the time Hancock reached the crest, Humphreys' Union men were firing at Sanders' Alabamians while the 111th New York farther south closed on the ravine. Sanders order his Rebels to stop and return fire, breaking their forward momentum. This hesitation was all Hancock and MacDougall needed.

MacDougall's 111th New York was holding together nicely. Few men dropped from the ranks as they brushed past fugitives still fleeing eastward. Captain Aaron P. Seeley (not to be confused with the artillerist of the same last name) wrote, "The ground over which the first charge was made was sort of a swale, covered by rocks, thickly interspaced with bushes, scrub oak, and trees [the knoll]. Beyond was open ground, ascending to the west [the rise west of Plum Run]." MacDougall and his

29 Charles H. Morgan, "Report on Hancock," *Bachelder Papers,* 3:1365.

30 *OR* 27, pt. 1, 871; pt. 2, 618; USGS MRC 39077G2; *Bachelder Maps, Second Day.*

This modern view looks east-northeast across Klingle's meadows from present-day Sickles Avenue due east of the farm. Wilcox's Alabamians and Lang's Floridians crossed these fields and mauled two Union brigades of Humphreys' Third Corps division, but suffered heavy casualties doing so. With no time to rest, Wilcox directed his regiments toward Plum Run ravine, which he could not see from his perspective. Humphreys was rallying troops at this time south (right) of the Pennsylvania Monument in the center-distance, while the 1st Minnesota was resting west of it. *Richard Rollins Collection*

men could now see the Plum Run ravine and the 10th and 11th Alabama just a few dozen yards away.[31]

As they reached the edge of the precipitous slope, the New Yorkers raised their rifles and fired into the faces of the 10th Alabama's left-center while others in MacDougall's command enfiladed the right flank of the stunned 11th Alabama, which was mostly caught in and east of the ravine. The Southerners, fired upon where the dry ravine intersects Plum Run, were caught in a bad place. In a smaller example, the Alabama men were reprising the unfortunate circumstances their fellow Alabamians in James Archer's brigade had experienced on July 1. On that day, Archer's foot soldiers crossed Willoughby Run and were advancing to higher ground when the Iron Brigade suddenly appeared above them and opened fire at point blank range. Here, MacDougall's New Yorkers held the higher ground and, from a good ten feet above the Rebels, poured in a devastating fire. Through the smoke and confusion, MacDougall could faintly see the 126th New York's colors waving beyond the 10th Alabama. His line had assumed a crescent shape, following the contour of the knoll above the ravine. The 111th New York unleashed a second

31 *OR* 27, pt. 1, 476.

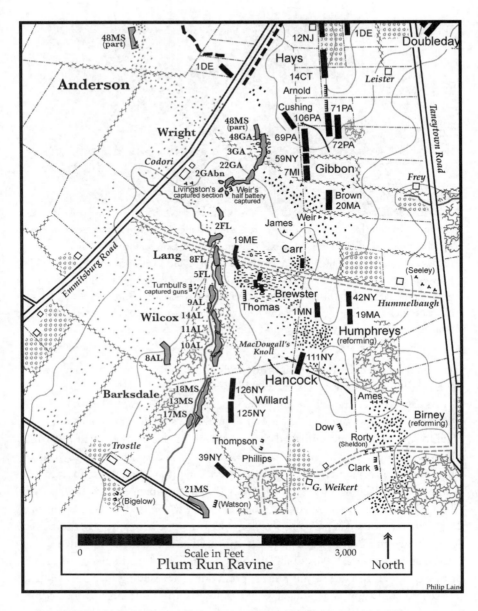

Plum Run Ravine

Scale in Feet

0   3,000

North

Philip Laine

volley into the 10th Alabama's left with terrible effect. Neither Alabama command could take another step forward.[32]

32 Ibid., 474-76; Hancock to U. S. Congress, *JCCW*, 406; Pfanz, *Gettysburg: The Second Day*, 406-407.

From beyond the 10th Alabama, another command cloaked in gray, Lieutenant Colonel Herbert's 8th Alabama, appeared out of the battle smoke angling northeast. The regiment, yet another from Wilcox's deep-driving brigade, passed along the rear of the embattled 18th Mississippi and away from the 126th New York and Willard's principal line, continuing past the 10th Alabama toward the 11th's right-rear. Herbert's regiment had moved unhindered in the wake of the 10th passing them from south to north in the process, changing direction more to the east once clear of the former regiment. Herbert's right wing slipped into the gap between the 10th and 11th, swinging east to join in the fight. The left side of Herbert's regiment continued over the rise west of the run and into the gap between the 11th's left and the 14th Alabama's right. This additional firepower allowed the 11th Alabama to fend off MacDougall's right, as well as General Humphreys' distant reformed line. With renewed strength and determination, the Rebel line surged forward, breaking out of the thickets and trap near the dry wash's intersection, about 250-300 yards south of Lieutenant Thomas's left section.[33]

* * *

From the crest of Cemetery Ridge, "smoke shut the combatants from sight and we could only judge of the direction of the fight by the sound," remembered the 1st Minnesota's Alfred Carpenter. In the breezeless afternoon air, thick grayish-white billowing clouds of stinging smoke hung close to the ground before slowly rising above the treetops as far as the eye could see. The veterans in the 1st Minnesota had smelled that nauseating stench before. It was the smell of death. Although they could not see much of the field, it was obvious they would soon be called upon. The unceasing roar of musketry was deafening. In many places only the flickering of a discharged weapon was visible. Individual shots were all but impossible to distinguish. Chaos reigned across the field, and the maelstrom was now heading straight toward Colvill's Minnesotans.[34]

General Hancock and the wounded Captain Miller rode toward the 1st Minnesota, which had once more gone to ground to avoid being swept away. When the eastward rush slowed, Colvill ordered his men to rise and he advanced his two lines left across the narrow rutted farm lane paralleling the ridge before aligning with General Humphreys' right 300 yards away. Colvill had no knowledge that Colonel Devereux's and Colonel Mallon's two Second Corps regiments were only

33 George A. Clark, "Wilcox's Alabama Brigade at Gettysburg," *Confederate Veteran*, vol. 17, 1919, 229-31; Hilary Herbert to Bachelder, July 9, 1884, *Bachelder Papers,* 2:1057-58.

34 Meinhard, *"No Soldiers Ever Displayed Grander Heroism."*

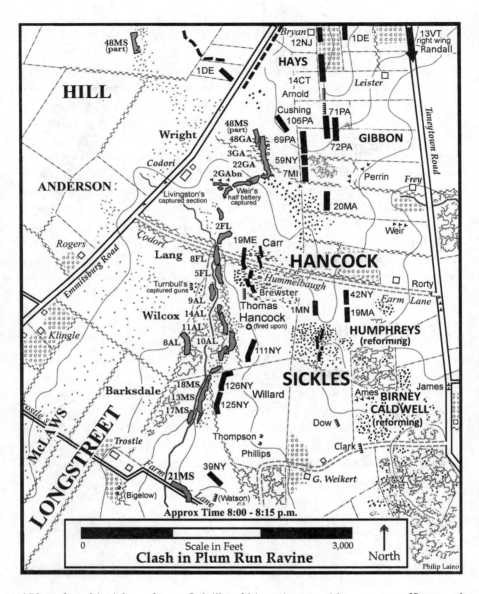

Approx Time 8:00 - 8:15 p.m.

0   Scale in Feet   3,000

Clash in Plum Run Ravine   North

Philip Laino

150 yards to his right and rear. Colvill and his regiment, with company officers and colors to the front, stood as keepers of the gate for the nearly undefended Union center.[35]

---

35 Colvill to Bachelder, June 9, 1866, *Bachelder Papers*, 1:256-57.

After running into Confederates moving out eastward of the Plum Run ravine, General Hancock was forced to detour to the northeast, which put him on a collision course with Colonel Colvill's 1st Minnesota. With little else at his disposal, the Second Corps commander ordered that regiment into action. *Richard Rollins Collection: Inset, Rufus Zogbaum oil painting of the First Minnesota courtesy of the Minnesota Historical Society*

The Minnesota colonel was in the process of redressing his regiment 200 yards southeast of Thomas's battery when Hancock and Miller reached him. Hancock spotted the colonel's towering figure and knew on sight it was Colvill. Twenty-odd years later the general remembered, "I rode on rapidly through a depression in the ground close in front of them [the enemy] uninjured, and immediately met a regiment of infantry coming down from the 2nd Corps, by flank, no doubt sent there by General Gibbon or other commander in the 2nd Corps, to repair damage which had been made apparent in that direction."[36] There was no time for formalities. "My God!" Hancock exploded. "Are these all the men we have here?" Hancock may have been disappointed that so few Third Corps troops had managed to reorganize behind the shattered front. Certainly Hancock hoped some of the

36 Hancock to Bachelder, November 7, 1885, *Bachelder Papers*, 2:1135; William Lochren, "Narrative of the First Regiment," in *The Civil and Indian Wars, 1861-1865*, 2 vols. (St. Paul, MN, 1891), 1:34; Lyman E. Pierce, "First Minnesota at Gettysburg," (Master's Thesis, Mankato State College, 1959), 1:23-26; USGS MRC 39077G2; *Bachelder Maps, Second Day*.

Col. William Colvill, Jr.,
1st Minnesota Infantry.
USAHEC

reinforcements he had requested would have arrived by this time. One thing is certain: Hancock realized fully that the center was vulnerable and that only this single small regiment was available to plug it.

By now, the 11th Alabama's center, reinforced by the 8th Alabama, was skirmishing up the meadow, having passed through the ravine with renewed determination. Lieutenant Colonel Herbert's added strength allowed the Confederates to emerge from the thickets as one irregular line numbering perhaps a hundred or so men. Hancock knew he had to hold the Taneytown Road if Cemetery Hill were to be saved. It was the key to holding the Baltimore Pike. Hancock pointed southwest in the direction of the enemy now less than 300 yards away and moving eastward at a creep. Reportedly, his last words to Colvill were, "Advance, colonel, and take those colors!"[37]

The general stayed only long enough to hear Colvill address his regiment with, "Forward double-quick." Later, in calmer circumstances, Hancock wrote, "I directed that commander of that regiment to attack the enemy troops displaying the colors very close by, with directions to take it at once. I had no alternative but to order the regiment in. I saw in some way five minutes must be gained or we were lost." By now, portions of the 8th and 11th Alabama had gained a toehold in the meadow beyond Thomas's left and MacDougall's right. Trading long-range volleys with Humphreys' small line, they angled northeast up Hancock's depression where the resistance was weakest and directly toward the now advancing 1st Minnesota. A few yards farther north, the 14th and 9th Alabama had their hands full with Thomas's double-shotted canister and shrapnel shells. They also had to contend

---

37 Ibid. See also Colvill to Bachelder, June 9, 1866, *Bachelder Papers*, 1:257; William Lochren, "The First Minnesota at Gettysburg," in *Glimpse of the Nation's Struggle, Third Series*, (St. Paul, MN, 1893), 47-49, copy in John P. Nicholson Collection, Huntington Library.

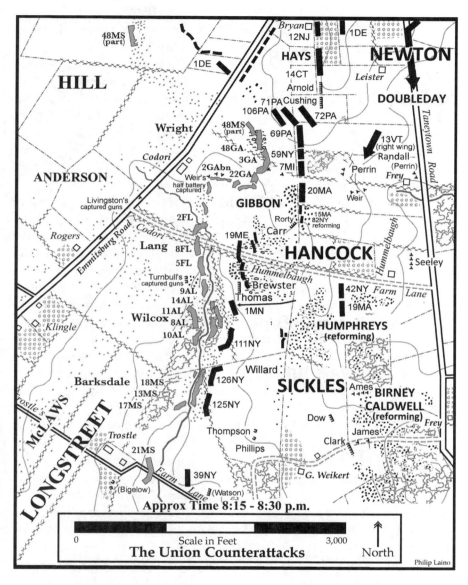

The Union Counterattacks

with Brewster's left flank after portions of his reformed orphaned brigade stepped forward, forming an irregular line between Thomas's right and the 19th Maine's left.[38]

38 Glen Tucker, *Hancock the Superb* (Indianapolis, 1958), 144-45. See also John D. Imhof, *Gettysburg Day Two: A Study in Maps* (Baltimore, 1999), 180-82.

Eight hundred yards south of Colvill's charging northwoodsmen, Colonels McGilvery and Warner had managed to patch together 30 cannon along Trostle's farm lane. Placing them west of the crest, beginning just south of where Willard led his charge, they opened on Barksdale's battered Mississippians south of Willard from the 126th New York's left flank south to beyond Trostle's farm lane, striking in Trostle's Woods and along the Emmitsburg Road. Their concentrated firepower helped stabilize the crumbling Union line in that sector, with minimal infantry support. This gave General Caldwell time to stitch together a formidable line parallel to the crest to cover the right-of-way through Patterson's Woods, which intersected Taneytown Road 300 yards to his rear.[39]

Caldwell rode up and down his mixed line of fugitives to steady them. Concurrently, Colonel McGilvery's two dozen guns blasted Barksdale's right flank and, with help from Hildebrandt's newly arrived 39th New York, secured Trostle's farm lane east of Plum Run. McGilvery's advanced line of five cannon just opposite Plum Run ravine had opened on the 17th, 18th, and 13th Mississippi regiments when they began swinging east toward the low ground after crushing Humphreys' refused line. With nothing in their way except slow-retreating Unionists, and with Trostle's lane to their right and rear, Barksdale's three regiments angled northeast. The topography directed their movement more so than their general. Still mounted and leading his men, Barksdale urged his still-powerful line forward into the meadow toward the ravine, all while pummeled by McGilvery's Ordnance Rifles just 300 yards away. Their fire tore gaps into right flank of the exhausted men of the 17th Mississippi, pushing bunches of them into the center.[40]

With Colonel Holder down, Lt. Col. John C. Fiser assumed command of the shrinking 17th. Fiser sidestepped or crowded the men north in an effort to get out of McGilvery's line of fire. When Fiser's regiment finally descended below the gun tube's lowest elevation, the Union cannoneers turned their attention against the 18th Mississippi. Fiser's line had already been rendered largely ineffective because the terrain in the ravine made it impossible to advance in close-order formation. Orders could not be heard above the din, and the entangled thickets and lingering smoke made it difficult to see. To Fiser's left, Lt. Col. William H. Luse had assumed command of the 18th. These Mississippians had been hit hard by both McGilvery's advanced guns and from the fire of an additional dozen pieces he had established 300 yards behind those above Plum Run. Smashed by this fire, the disorganized men of the 18th dropped into the thickets alongside those of 17th, angling in line with the equally disorganized survivors of the 13th Mississippi to their left. By this

---

39 Ibid.; *OR* 27, pt. 1, 380; Phil Laino, *Gettysburg Campaign Atlas* (Dayton, OH, 2009), 250-63.

40 *OR* 27, pt. 1, 881; McNeily, "Barksdale's Brigade," *MHS*, vol. 14, 240.

After smashing the Peach Orchard salient and breaking up the Union line along the Emmitsburg Road, William Barksdale led three of his four veteran Mississippi regiments (13th, 17th, and 18th) farther east, deeper into the Union position on lower Cemetery Ridge and into the dense underbrush and boulder-strewn Plum Run creek bottom. Waiting for him there were troops from New York. In the bloody exchange that followed, the fiery general was shot from his horse and mortally wounded. The large recognizable Trostle barn is in the middle-distance. *Richard Rollins Collection*

time as many Mississippians were leaving Barksdale's ranks as advancing. Unfortunately for the Rebels who kept moving forward, none of them could see Colonel Willard's two regiments descending upon them from beyond the crest of the rise east of the run.[41]

Barksdale was somewhere beyond his left center near the 13th Mississippi when that regiment struggled in the thickets west of Plum Run. Unseen by the general, the natural flow of the run allowed his right-center and what was left of his far right to gain the creek before his left flank, which was taking canister fire from the section of rifles anchoring McGilvery's advanced line and some small arms fire from a small reformed line of Yankees who had faced back. Barksdale's line had indistinct flanks, his front following a rather broken contoured line paralleling the uneven rocky flood plain. As his massed bunches closed on Plum Run, Willard's

41 Ibid.; Pfanz, *Gettysburg: Second Day*, 350-51.

125th and 126th New York regiments appeared without warning out of the smoke atop the crest not 40 yards distant.[42]

Although Barksdale's advance and attack up the Emmitsburg Road was grand in every sense of the word, it all fell apart a few hundred yards farther east. The general's decision to not wait for the 21st Mississippi to rejoin the brigade before advancing proved catastrophic to both Barksdale's advance and the orphaned 21st, and demonstrated a certain level of hubris on his part, a belief perhaps that nothing could stop them. He pushed his men beyond reasonable human endurance by not allowing them a respite when he again ordered his skirmishers ahead and pressed his three regiments northeast after them into low ground about which he knew absolutely nothing. Barksdale was on horseback; his men were not. They were exhausted, hot, and thirsty; he was excited and filled with anxiety.[43]

With no support whatsoever, Barksdale's three weakened regiments staggered into dangers their general never envisioned. In most instances prior to this attack, the Yankees to Barksdale's front had always turned tail or surrendered. Unfortunately for his Mississippians, they did not have the cover of a town or high ground as they had above Fredericksburg the past winter. Caught now in the low bog below Willard's New Yorkers, there was no place to hide and no place to run. Most of their rounds passed harmlessly over the Federals. A bullet found Barksdale above the left knee, but he remained mounted and in command until an artillery round or large chunk of one nearly severed his left foot. Just moments later another bullet smacked into the left side of the chest and the Mississippi general fell from his horse. "I am killed!" he supposedly told an orderly. "Tell my wife and children I died fighting at my post." When his men later fell back he was left for dead, and eventually carried to a Union field hospital, where he died the next morning.[44]

Several hundred yards south of the charging 125th New York's left flank, the 39th New York was battling Colonel Humphreys' 21st Mississippi. The Confederates held an isolated position after overrunning Watson's Battery I, 5th U. S. Hildebrandt's countercharge did not come as a surprise to Humphreys, but there was little he could do to stop it. His men were simply too tired to hold their position, let alone defeat the attackers and keep advancing. With no viable support, Humphreys took note of General Wofford's Georgians off his right beginning to withdraw, which would leave his regiment further isolated. After securing

42 Ibid; USGS MRC 39077G2; *Bachelder Maps, Second Day.*

43 McNeily, "Barksdale's Brigade," *MHS,* vol. 14, 240.

44 USGS MRC 39077G2; *Bachelder Maps, Second Day;* David Parker to Mrs. Barksdale, March 22, 1882, Jackson Manuscript, Ethelbert Barksdale Collection, William F. Winter Archives and History Building.

Bigelow's battery, the 21st Mississippi had renewed its charge east across Plum Run, where the Mississippians seized Watson's four 10-pounder Parrotts. Placed there by McGilvery shortly before Bigelow was overrun, Lieutenant Watson was ordered to hold at all costs. He and his people did just that, though Watson lost a leg in the process. Humphreys' Confederates abandoned the captured guns of Battery I during a countercharge by the 39th New York and retired across Plum Run through Bigelow's decimated position and the Trostle farm. Continuing up the slope, the Mississippians passed Sickles' former headquarters before facing back just east of and above the Emmitsburg Road.[45]

To the north of Humphreys' new line, the veterans of Colvill's 1st Minnesota broke into double-quick as they descended the slope, advancing with arms at right shoulder shift surging toward the Rebel line with balls whizzing past their ears. The first volley by the Alabama troops passed mostly overhead, but within a few more steps the first sickening thuds were heard as men were knocked off their feet. By the time the Minnesotans had covered 100 yards, Colvill's already thin ranks were being ripped apart. As one survivor recalled, "It seemed as if every step was over some fallen comrade. Yet no man wavers, every gap is closed up bringing down their bayonets, the boys press forward in unbroken line. Men stumbled and fell. Some stayed down but others got up and continued." Another wrote, "Bullets whistled past us; shells screeched over us; canister [shrapnel] fell among us; comrade after comrade dropped from the ranks; but on the line went. No one took a second look at the fallen companion. We had no time to weep."[46]

When Wilcox's Alabamians stopped to discharge their weapons, their forward momentum halted and the men jammed together in the ravine. From the 10th Alabama on the right (below and engaging with the 111th New York's right wing above) to the 9th Alabama 300 yards north (battling Brewster's left and Thomas's battery), Wilcox's regiments piled up in bunches. An isolated pocket was forming east of the run in Hancock's wide ravine or depression. Only portions of 11th Alabama, supported by a few men from the 8th, were still advancing slowly east.[47]

Into this gap, or pocket, the Minnesotans charged Wilcox's Rebels. Colvill's men descended the gentle ridge to the left of Thomas's battery at slight right angles to Plum Run, their line angling toward the intersecting dry ravine's confluence below MacDougall's right. Colvill knew he had no choice but to press on as his men continued to fall with each step. He could make out another line emerging from

45 OR 27, pt. 1, 660; Samuel Peeples to John Fassett, August 15, 1870; Medal of Honor File, John B. Fassett F-446 VS 1864, Box 4 Group 94, NARA. See also USGS 39077G2-TF-024.

46 Meinhard, "No Soldiers Ever Displayed Grander Heroism," 82.

47 Lochren, "The First Minnesota at Gettysburg."

tickets above his front and right. This enemy proved to be portions of the 8th Alabama, which had descended the rise west of the run and now stood above it. Colvill had no knowledge of any ravine or the topography that lay before and below him. The gray line let loose a volley that tore up the earth around the Minnesotans' feet. Colvill wrote. "Their second line coming up immediately after, delivered a heavy fire through the remnants of their first line killing more of their own men than ours, and then we charged."[48]

The shock of an unexpected volley delivered from behind created mayhem in the already disorganized ranks of the 11th Alabama, giving Colvill the moment he needed. Almost as one, the veterans of the 1st Minnesota brought down their arms and, when within 30 yards of the enemy, "delivered a crippling fire into their faces which broke the first line." When Colvill shouted "Charge!" his men leveled their bayonets and surged toward the eastern bank of Plum Run and Wilcox's disorganized Confederates. Survivors of 11th Alabama tumbled back into the ravine, creating more chaos and panic. Men turned and tried to run, but for most there was nowhere to go. Those who did have room struggled up the far bank, stopping parts of the 8th Alabama, which were moving into the creek bottom to join them. Another volley from portions of the 8th, delivered in the smoky chaos and gloom, hit some of their fellow Confederates from the 11th as well as the 1st Minnesota as the lines collided.[49]

For a few brief seconds the opposing warriors crossed and parried, but the brief hand-to-hand struggle quickly abated when Colvill's men aligned above the eastern bank began delivering a steady and deadly fire into the massed Confederates. Continuing forward, ever so slowly, Colvill led his men into the run, crashing through the brush and thicket and bayoneting and clubbing their way forward.[50]

Colvill and his men found themselves in possession of the Plum Run ravine, but the creek bottom offered but little cover for the Minnesotans. The Confederates who had survived the 1st Minnesota's fire faced back opposite the creek with a vengeance. Confederate officers from the 11th could be heard rallying their broken line above the din as they joined with the 8th Alabama. Soon the reinforced Alabamians west of Plum Run unleashed a disciplined fire as their line made use of its elevated position to partially encircle Colvill's men. Not to be outdone, however, the men of the 1st Minnesota held steady, firing independently.

48 Colvill to Bachelder, June 9, 1866, *Bachelder Papers*, 1:257.

49 Ibid.; *OR* 27, pt. 1, 425.

50 Pierce, "First Minnesota at Gettysburg," 1:23-26.

"I never saw cooler work done on either side," the colonel recalled, "and the destruction was awful."[51]

From standing, kneeling, and prone positions, the Minnesotans laid down a slow deliberate fire using the west bank of the run and its thickets for cover. In the run the smoke lay thick and dense, and with little or no breeze the visibility was dreadful. Men fired at flashes or at the feet and legs of the enemy, "which was about all we could see of them at the time, as all above their knees was covered with the smoke from their own guns," recalled James Wright. The work was hot and close and bloody, and they were taking as many casualties as they inflicted.[52]

Although portions of the 8th and 11th Alabama were off either flank of the 1st Minnesota, at no time did they get across the run or behind them or enfilade them. The natural curve of Plum Run as it swung southwest toward Trostle's meadows, below the knoll and the battling 111th New York, was part of the reason. Colvill's line formed an inverted crescent with the enemy off both flanks but west of the run. The 1st Minnesota's momentum had carried them several yards past Thomas's left flank. The gap between the left gun and Colvill's right flank soon was sufficiently covered as Humphreys' right wing inched forward while laying down a flank-covering fire that tormented the enemy north of Colvill. None of those fugitives were willing to advance beyond Thomas's gun line. Their added musketry was not directed at the line then engaging Colvill, but rather at the men of the 14th Alabama as they floundered in and about Turnbull's disabled guns north and west of Colvill. The left flank of the 8th Alabama had continued toward the 14th's shattered right flank, north of the 11th, perhaps thinking Turnbull's guns an easy prize. They found out quickly they had entered a death trap. Canister from Thomas's six cannon ripped holes in their lines, as it earlier had the 14th and 9th Alabama. The guns of Thomas's left section were wheeled slightly left-oblique in order to cover what remained of the front between them and the 1st Minnesota. This move, along with the musketry from Humphreys' irregular line, stopped the left elements of the 8th, 11th, and the right of 9th Alabama regiments from penetrating beyond Colvill's right flank and wrapping around the isolated dwindling pocket battling in Plum Run.[53]

51 Ibid.

52 Anne A. Hage, "The Battle of Gettysburg as Seen by Minnesota Soldiers," *Minnesota History*, no. 38, June 1963, 256, quoted in Hess, *The Union Soldier in Battle*, 10.

53 USGS MRC 39077G2; *Bachelder Maps, Second Day*; Laino, *Gettysburg Campaign Atlas*, 256. In fairness, these were men from a variety of units who found the courage to turn and fight, but they were not with their comrades or Regular officers. It would have been very difficult for Humphreys to put together an organized counterattack.

It is not known where General Wilcox was during the attack of the 1st Minnesota. In all probability he was behind his line where a brigadier was supposed to be, guiding all four of his regiments as best he could, and probably near the Klingle barn. Wilcox had sent at least one aide galloping back to Anderson seeking reinforcements, as well as to Lang with orders to close on the enemy to take some pressure off the Alabamians. Wilcox was experienced enough to know his exhausted men were locked in a close-quarters fight they could not win without immediate support. Many factors came into play, including the rough terrain east of the Emmitsburg Road, the day's oppressive heat, and the vigorous Union defensive effort. The issue of poor initial planning and the failed reconnaissance also came into play. Contrary to popular belief, no one in command, including General Lee, had any real knowledge of what lay beyond the Emmitsburg Road or where the main Union line was in this sector. Longstreet's attack up the Emmitsburg Road, in a broad sense, could be considered a strong reconnaissance-in-force with orders to modify its mission to deal with any and all circumstances encountered. And that is exactly how Wilcox and others had been fighting their battles.[54]

Once his Alabamians moved east of the Emmitsburg Road and descended into the low rough ground, the rest of Wilcox's fight was, to one degree or another, uphill. Colonel Forney's 10th and Colonel Sanders' 11th Alabama still had their hands full exchanging fire with MacDougall's New Yorkers fighting above them on the knoll. The Alabama ranks had been stopped and thinned, but they were still making MacDougall's men pay for their Harpers Ferry redemption. MacDougall's 111th began with 390 rifles and by this point had suffered some 150 casualties, all in about 15 minutes. The steady stream of his wounded staggering back toward Cemetery Ridge complicated his efforts to throw back Wilcox. [55]

Many of MacDougall's lightly injured men, however, refused to leave as long as they could fire their weapons. Most of his dead and critically wounded had been shot through the upper body or head, the direct result of the Southerners firing up at them coupled with the tendency to fire high. Atop the knoll, meanwhile, these steely New Yorkers stood tall and fired volley after volley into the narrow rocky valley. Acrid smoke clung low to the ground and trees, making it hard to see anything but muzzle flashes. Their superior position and firepower began to take effect. Sanders' and Forney's lines began to waver. Forney's left companies faced a desperate situation. Caught between the bunched 11th Alabama and the base of the

---

54 J. W. Jones, "The Longstreet Gettysburg Controversy: Who Commenced It," *Richmond Dispatch,* February 16, 1896; *SHSP,* vol. 23, 342-48; USGS MRC 39077G2; *Bachelder Maps, Second Day.*

55 *OR* 27, pt. 1, 475.

knoll, they were shot to pieces. The survivors fell back, carrying with them most of Forney's left-center and a good portion of his right. Soon much of Colonel Herbert's 8th and what was left of Sanders' 11th Alabama followed suit. Forney had already been hit twice, though both wounds were slight. As he rallied his men near Plum Run south of the wash, a Minié ball shattered his right arm. With Forney out of the fight and every other field officers down, the regiment's chain of command snapped, unit cohesion withered, and the men retired from the ranks or fell under the unrelenting fire from Thomas's Napoleons, Humphreys' reformed line, the 1st Minnesota, and the 111th New York.[56]

Off MacDougall's left-front, the 126th New York was battling Barksdale's Mississippians and what remained of the 10th Alabama's far right flank where it had penetrated between the 126th and 111th. That gap lay open simply because the 126th was some 40 yards in advance of and below the left of the 111th. The men of the 10th Alabama saw this weak point and pushed into it. Their advance was short-lived. What looked like an opportunity instead proved to be a death trap. The soldiers holding MacDougall's left lowered their rifles and, with fixed bayonets, charged down through the brush and thickets into the 10th Alabama's right while the 126th fired into them. Forney's right tumbled back in panic as their line gave way, the soldiers scattering in broken bunches and carrying with them Mississippi stragglers who had escaped Willard's fire and McGilvery's murderous canister.[57]

The Rebels retreated across the ravine and through Trostle's meadows before joining other fugitives from Barksdale's and Wilcox's hard-pressed brigades. As they fell back, the 126th New York rolled forward like a wave breaking from north to south and washing away what remained of the 10th Alabama's right. One of the first Confederates captured during this countercharge was the seriously wounded Colonel Forney. South of the 126th, the 125th New York's bayonet charge was driving Barksdale's survivors into the lower Trostle meadow.[58]

Now it was Colonel MacDougall's turn to counterattack with the entire 111th New York. With Wilcox's line checked by his own men and Colvill's regiment, MacDougall seized the moment and charged. Sword raised overhead for all to see, he led what was left of the 111th down off the knoll. His left-center wheeled half-right following the contour of the knoll and run below, with his center

---

56 Ibid., pt. 2, 619; Hilary Herbert to Bachelder, July 9, 1884, *Bachelder Papers,* 2:1055; Clark, "Wilcox's Alabama Brigade at Gettysburg," *Confederate Veteran,* vol. 17, 1919, 229-31; Personal Military Records of William H. Forney, NARA.

57 Clark, "Wilcox's Alabama Brigade at Gettysburg," 29-31; USGS MRC 39077G2; *Bachelder Maps, Second Day.*

58 Ibid.; OR 27, pt. 2, 619; McNeily, "Barksdale's Brigade," 240; Pfanz, *Gettysburg, The Second Day,* 349-50.

following suit as if hinged at the hip. Without orders, the right wing moved forward, maintaining a tight line in order to keep its connection with the center. The New Yorkers swept up dozens of prisoners in the process. MacDougall's right, with muskets leveled ready for bayonet thrust, raced down the knoll. Down into the dry ravine they moved, passing over dead and wounded and driving the enemy across the creek bottom and into the thickets. Rebels crammed in bunches as they scrambled, clawed, and kicked their way up and out of the ravine in attempt to break free. "Remember Harpers Ferry!" rang loud and clear above the din from scores of parches Union throats.[59]

MacDougall's advance to the northwest drove the 111th New York past the dry wash intersection and through the creek bottom, passing at right angles across the beleaguered 1st Minnesota's left and center. Continuing up and over the elongated knoll immediately west of the ravine, MacDougall's right headed directly toward the guns of Lieutenant Turnbull's overrun battery. The men of the 14th and 9th Alabama seem not to have noticed this countercharge because of their focus on the 1st Minnesota in the ravine. Thomas's Napoleons 100 yards beyond Colonel Colvill's men were still holding, though more than 100 of them lay dead or wounded in the smoke-filled ravine. The regiment's command structure was nearly wiped out. Colvill was down with a jagged hole through his left shoulder and a shattered right foot. Lieutenant Colonel John Adams lay near him, unconscious from loss of blood. Hit six times, he would somehow survive. Major Mark Downie and Capt. Joseph Periam, Company K, also had fallen. Captain Louis Muller, Company E, was dead, as was Lt. Waldo Farrar of Company I. Lieutenants Thomas Sinclear, Company B, James DeGray, Company G, David Demarest, Company E, and George Boyd, Company I, had suffered severe wounds. By this time only two field officers were unhurt.[60]

Some of the fire hitting the 1st Minnesota's left came not from Wilcox, but from behind the regiment from the meadow beyond the dry ravine. This friendly fire originated from the reformed line General Humphreys had cobbled together that was now approaching Plum Run, firing as it advanced. The general cheered his boys as they closed on the run immediately south of the 1st Minnesota, firing toward the partially obscured figures in the smoke. Caught up in Humphreys' excitement, Capt. William H. Fernal of the 12th New Hampshire yelled, "Come on

59 OR 27, pt. 1, 465-66; Hays, *Life and Letters of Alexander Hays* 425-26; Eric Campbell, "Remember Harper's Ferry," *Gettysburg Magazine,* no. 7, 51-75. Exceptional article concerning Willard's brigade culminating on the night of July 2, 1863, at Gettysburg.

60 Hays, *Life and Letters of Alexander Hays,* 425; Busey, *These Honored Dead,* 85; Busey & Martin, *Regimental Strengths,* 185-86; R. I. Holcombe, *History of the First Regiment Minnesota Volunteer Infantry* (Stillwater, MN, 1916. Reprinted: Gaithersburg, MD, 1987), 343-45.

boys!" while brandishing his sword overhead. Followed by several dozen men, he charged down the slope toward the run, angling toward the dry wash and Colvill's left flank.[61]

In the ravine, Capt. Nathan S. Messick of Company G had assumed command of the 50 or so survivors of the 1st Minnesota just as Humphreys' line closed. Messick's few men could neither advance nor retreat. All they could do was return fire from within the cover of their enclave. The murderous fire from west of the run began to subside as the 111th New York rolled up the unsuspecting 14th Alabama's left and caved in the right flank of the 9th. Some of the trapped Minnesotans, a few dragging or carrying wounded with them, took advantage of this confusion to escape from the ravine. Lieutenant Christian Heffelfinger, one of the few remaining officers, stood and immediately took a gunshot through his body. Cheering, many of the surviving Minnesotans stood to fire, reloading as fast as they could while MacDougall's 111th New York drove through the retiring Alabamians in its immediate front.[62]

MacDougall's New Yorkers were joined by men from Birney's and Humphreys' divisions who had seized the opportunity and moved forward, the latter's body of troops passing across the dry ravine into Plum Run and through what was left of the 1st Minnesota's left flank. The 10th Alabama's rout was complete when Colonel Forney's survivors withdrew up the rise and over the elongated knoll, taking all of the 8th and the rest of 11th Alabama regiments with them. All told, about 225 men from the 111th crossed Plum Run, charging toward the Codori farm, which was now just visible through the smoke and lengthening evening shadows.[63]

Lucius Pinckard's 14th Alabama would be the next of Wilcox's regiments to give way as MacDougall's line approached Turnbull's vacated guns. Humphreys' small force had by this time entered the Minnesotans' position in the ravine, slowing as it picked its way through the carnage. Once across the creek, the irregular line pushed through the thickets toward the base of the rise, angling toward Turnbull's pieces. Thomas ordered "cease fire" in that direction when the right side of Humphreys' scratch command charged across the open meadow between Colvill's right and Thomas's left. Thomas realigned his left section and reopened on

---

61 Bartlett, *History of the 12th Regiment New Hampshire Volunteers*, 126-30.

62 OR 27, pt. 1, 533; Report of Charles Morgan, *Bachelder Papers,* 3:1358-59; Gene Pelowski, "Colonel William F. Colvill," Winona State University Special Collection Library, 1978; Winona, MN; Holcombe, *History of the First Regiment Minnesota,* 343-45.

63 USGS MRC 39077G2; *Bachelder Maps, Second Day.*

what remained of the 14th and 9th Alabama regiments, hurling shot, shell, and canister toward those who still held onto Turnbull's guns.[64]

One of the Alabama regiments tumbling westward was Col. Lucius Pinckard's 14th. Seriously wounded shortly after crossing east over the Emmitsburg Road, Pinckard had turned command of the 14th Alabama to Lt. Col. James A. Broome. That officer, however, was never able to fully gain control of the 14th as it closed on Plum Run. With both flanks entangled with other regiments, trying to undo the chaos during such a bloody critical time proved next to impossible. The 14th's left wing was pounded with canister by a section of Thomas's battery at less than 100 yards. Now Pinckard's survivors were being swept back west toward the Klingle farm and the Emmitsburg Road.[65]

Stuck west of and above the Plum Run, Captain King's 9th Alabama was all but played out as he tried in vain to form a firing line. Although the regiment held its own west of Thomas's blazing battery not 200 yards to their front, the left flank was in the air because Pinckard's 14th Alabama had been driven back.[66]

North of Pinckard's 14th Alabama, the lightly wounded Captain King and his 9th Alabama was battling with Brewster's New York Excelsior Brigade. Brewster's regiments stood between Thomas's right and the left of Heath's slowly retiring 19th Maine and delivered an effective fire into both King's left and the right flank of Captain Gardner's 5th Florida (Lang's brigade). Brewster's line slowly grew in numbers as men from various regiments turned around after Birney and a dozen other officers urged them to return to the fight. To the right of Brewster's small line, a ringing "Hurrah!" was heard above the din as the 19th Maine faced back and rushed out of the low rough ground toward the Floridians who had advanced to Plum Run, with less than 40 yards separating the combatants.[67]

About the same time the Alabama regiments were tumbling rearward, a few of Wilcox's officers received orders to fall back. In all likelihood, General Wilcox had remained atop the rise near the Klingle farmyard, a good vista from which he could take everything in with a clean sweep and send couriers into the chaos with orders as needed. According to the brigadier, "Without support on either my right or left,

64 Cadmus Wilcox, March 26, 1877, "Cause of the Confederate Defeat at Gettysburg," *SHSP*, no. 6, 1877, 116-117; Clark, "Wilcox's Alabama Brigade," 229-30.

65 Ibid.

66 *OR* 27, pt. 2, 319, 618; Wilcox, "General C. M. Wilcox on the Battle of Gettysburg," *SHSP*, no. 6, 1878, 97-104. For the entire battle, the 14th Alabama only reported eight fatalities out of some 316 men engaged, while the 9th Alabama lost between 30-40 men killed out of 325 carried into action.

67 Smith, *History of the 19th Maine*, 72-73; Adams, *19th Maine at Gettysburg*, 243-54.

my men were withdrawn, to prevent their entire destruction or capture." Wilcox's well-organized attack had reached its high water mark and was now falling back in chaotic retreat before MacDougall's and Humphreys' charging lines.[68]

The left side of Captain King's 9th Alabama and portions of Captain Gardner's 5th Florida's right retired a short distance before facing about to confront Brewster's line advancing out of the rocky ground. Both Confederate regiments had been shattered by Thomas's canister during their vain effort to control Turnbull's bronze guns. Three of the bloodied prizes were simply left behind, but some men managed to drag off a fourth a short distance west before giving up the effort when the 111th New York and Humphreys' men closed in.

The deep attack of Lang's Floridians and Wilcox's Alabamians was over. Now the survivors had to figure out how to negotiate the mile or so of generally open ground and get back to their jump-off points alive.[69]

---

68 Pfanz, *Gettysburg, The Second Day*, 411.

69 Humphreys to Hancock, October 2, 1863, Humphreys Papers, HSP. According to Humphreys, he was among the guns with his line when they recaptured Turnbull's battery.

Chapter Seventeen

"I do not remember having seen anywhere the dead lying thicker than
the Yankee infantry attempt to make a stand in our front."

— *Col. David Lang, Florida Brigade, Army of Northern Virginia*[1]

Early Evening, July 2:
The Confederate Flood Tide Recedes

was now well past 7:00 p.m. The momentum once so firmly held by the Confederates was ebbing and the initiative swinging to the resilient Federals. General Winfield Hancock's patchwork Union line on Cemetery Ridge had cracked in several places, but it had not broken despite prolonged pressure from James Longstreet's troops thrusting northward from the Peach Orchard, and Richard Anderson's three-brigade push (Wilcox, Lang, and Wright) from Seminary Ridge across the Emmitsburg Road and beyond to Plum Run. Both Col. Francis Heath of the 19th Massachusetts and Third Corps brigade commander Col. William Brewster noticed the slackening of fire across parts of the expansive front. Both officers correctly surmised the Confederate offensive was running out of punch, and its men pulling back or about to do so. First, though, they had to deal with Colonel Lang's undersized Florida brigade, which was still clinging to its dearly bought handful of acres.

The Floridians had followed the retreating Federals to the foot of Cemetery Ridge, but their aggressive advance scattered Lang's three small regiments. Lang had little choice but to halt and reform his disorganized lines and allow his men a few minutes to catch their breath before a final push up the long western slope. It was during this lull that Heath and Brewster ushered their lines forward, Heath rather hurriedly and Brewster more cautiously. Lang's pause provided both Union

<hr>

1   GNMP vertical files on the Florida Brigade.

colonels with the opportunity they needed to direct fire against key points along Lang's front.[2]

As Heath and Brewster were inflicting more death and destruction into the already thin Florida ranks, Union refugees who had decided to return to the fight continued to increase General Carr's numbers as he and General Birney continued to rally their Third Corps troops east of the Plum Run ravine. Accompanied by several staff officers, Birney rode up and down the line herding men back down the crest toward Carr's reforming defensive line, with most of Heath's 19th Maine visible to the front where they had faced back to confront Lang's Floridians. When Heath ordered his regiment forward, Brewster as noted followed suit with his motley force, moving cautiously toward Plum Run and passing through the low wooded ground. As busy as he was, Birney may not have noticed Brewster's line as it pulled away from Carr's right, leaving the latter's small line with both flanks in the air.[3]

The recent collapse of General Wilcox's Alabamians off his right flank left Lang's outgunned Floridians in a desperate situation. "While engaged in reforming here [on a small eminence]," Lang explained, "an aide from the right informed me that a heavy force [Willard, MacDougall, Colvill, and A. Humphreys] had advanced upon Wilcox's brigade and was forcing it back. At the same time a heavy fire of musketry [Brewster and Heath] was poured upon my brigade from the woods 50 yards in my immediate front, which was gallantly met and handsomely replied to by my men." Exactly how many Federals contested the Floridians remains unclear. Over the years, Brewster's manpower has been estimated from 150 to 250 rifles, with Heath's New Englanders on their right numbering about 540 effectives. Lang's scattered line by this time numbered only perhaps 450 men.[4]

Even with the sun setting behind South Mountain, the twilight heat was still oppressive, especially coupled with the choking clouds of gun smoke. Despite the deteriorating conditions, Heath's and Brewster's lines held the superior position. Although Heath's men moved through the open as they crossed Plum Run, they were slightly lower than Lang's riflemen. As a result, many of the Rebel bullets passed harmlessly overhead. Brewster's men were inside the thickets growing along the creek, which at this point angled slightly to the southwest extending the underbrush farther west than north. His men were in no mood to leave their cover,

2   Ibid., 631; "Florida Soldiers, Confederate States of America: 2nd, 5th, 8th Florida Infantry," St. Augustine, Florida Department of Military Affairs, Special Archives Collection, Publication No. 92, 1889, 188-89.

3   Smith, *History of the 19th Maine,* 52, 72-73.

4   *OR 27*, pt. 2, 631.

and so slowly loaded and fired as they inched their way forward taking full advantage of what Lang would describe as "woods" in his report. There was more bad news for Lang. "A few moments later, another messenger from my right informed me that General Wilcox had fallen back, and the enemy was some distance in rear of my right flank."[5]

Unsure whether the information was accurate, Lang decided to ride over and see for himself. "Going to my right," he explained, "I discovered that the enemy had passed me more than 100 yards, and were attempting to surround me." With his brigade scattered across several hundred yards, and with MacDougall's and Humphreys' men closing on his right and rear, Lang had little alternative but to retreat: "I immediately ordered my men back to the [Emmitsburg] road, some 300 yards to the rear." The Federal counterattack pressed on, with many of the men now sensing victory.[6]

When Brewster's right flank exited the "woods" and stepped into the open ground, it likely overlapped Heath's left flank. Both Union lines advanced southwest toward the creek and beyond to the northern reaches of the elongated knoll, where Lieutenant Livingston's right section had been firing before it escaped north. Several lifeless bodies from Captain Starbird's Company F, 19th Maine, marked the spot where Heath had earlier bent back his left below Livingston's two guns, with Plum Run just 40 yards behind them. Heath's and Brewster's soldiers continued firing and advancing until the lines were within a handful of yards of one another, the shallow run separating the combatants.[7]

After returning from his exposed right flank, Colonel Lang witnessed the 5th Florida get swept rearward with the remnants of Wilcox's battered 9th Alabama. Lang wasted no time sending runners down the 8th Florida's line, tapping the men on their shoulders and yelling at them to pull back and pass the instructions on to their comrades. The 8th regiment was fairly scattered, however, so it was impossible to reach everyone. Several soldiers missed the order and remained on the firing line, unaware their comrades were pulling out. Across the contested field, Captain Starbird and his remaining men of Company F, 19th Maine, still anchoring Heath's left flank, faced off with Lang's flag bearer and color guard. To the chagrin of Starbird and Colonel Heath (who also spotted the bearer from afar), the lone Rebel stood a few feet in front of his guardsmen defiantly waving his battle-scarred regimental colors at the Yankees just 40 yards from him. With the enemy line

5   Ibid.; "Florida Soldiers: CSA, 2nd, 5th, 8th Florida Infantry," 188-89.

6   Ibid.; Thomas L. Elmore, "The Florida Brigade at Gettysburg," *Gettysburg Magazine*, No. 15, 1996, 45-51.

7   Smith, *Nineteenth Maine*, 72-73; USGS MRC 39077G2; *Bachelder Maps, Second Day*.

loosely aligned and now wavering, Heath ordered a bayonet charge— but not before at least one Yankee round dropped the valiant color bearer and his bright red Confederate battle flag.[8]

The 8th Florida's retreat was not as orderly as Lang later reported. Leaving one of their fallen flags in the low ground west of Plum Run, the Floridians began withdrawing individually and then in small groups. Many others, however, stood firm to discharge their weapons as the 19th Maine passed over Plum Run for the third time this day. Closing on the thickets west of the run where the dead Rebel color bearer lay, the 19th Maine passed over the 8th Florida's flag. No one in either of Heath's two battle lines bothered to pick it up, including the colonel, who spotted it lying on the ground. According to Heath, one of Brewster's New Yorkers arrived, picked up the trophy and carried it off, waving it proudly as he disappeared into the smoke.[9]

Brewster and his officers recalled the flag incident differently. According to the colonel, his men had legitimately captured the colors while liberating Turnbull's battery. "Seeing the enemy in possession of three of our guns," Brewster later reported, "I made a charge at the head of about 150 men and succeeded in recapturing them, taking from one the colors of the Eighth Florida regiment, and bringing in as prisoners the major of that regiment and some 30 of his men." Colonel Henry L. Potter, commanding the 72nd New York, agreed with Brewster: "[Lt. Col. John Leonard] and the rest of the officers were indefatigable in their exertions to rally the men who were still hard pressed and obliged to fall back to the crest of the hill from which the brigade started in morning, where they rallied, and charging, across the field, retook their guns and one battle-flag belonging to the Eighth Florida Regiment, together with a number of prisoners, all of which they brought from the field."[10]

"I regret to state that, while retreating, the colors of the Eighth Florida Regiment were left upon the field," Colonel Lang lamented, "the color-bearer and color-guard being killed or wounded and left upon the field. I cannot attach any blame to the commander of this regiment," continued the commander of the Florida brigade, "as in the confused order of the retreat several colors were crowded near each other, and the flag was not missed until the brigade was halted at

---

8 Ibid.; Heath to Bachelder, October 12, 1889, *Bachelder Papers,* 3:1652-53.

9 Ibid.; R. Lee Hadden, "The Granite Glory: The 19th Maine at Gettysburg," *Gettysburg Magazine,* no. 13, July 1995, 56.

10 *OR* 27, pt. 1, 549, 566. Heath and the New Yorkers may both have been correct. It is possible someone from the 8th Florida picked up the fallen banner after the 19th Maine passed over it, only to be recaptured moments later by Sgt. Thomas Hogan of Brewster's 72nd New York.

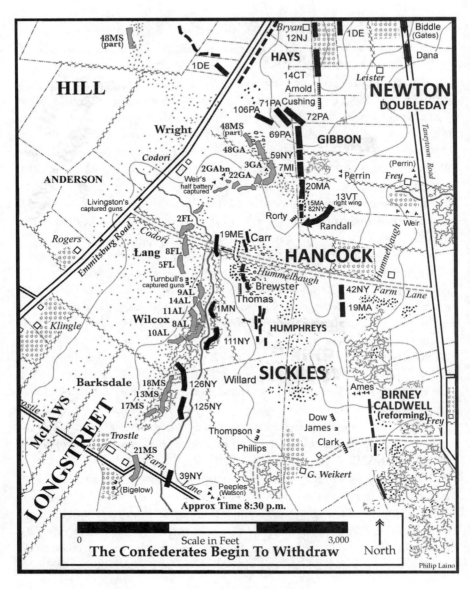

Approx Time 8:30 p.m.

Scale in Feet
0   3,000
The Confederates Begin To Withdraw   North

Philip Laino

the woods, too late to rescue it." By the time Heath's and Brewster's commands reached the elongated knoll and Turnbull's battery, the reconstituted Union front here, from Heath's right flank all the way south to the left flanks of the 39th New York (below Trostle's farm lane) stretched for nearly half a mile. Neither Brewster nor and Colonel Potter mentioned that, by the time the 72nd New York topped the elongated knoll, Humphreys' and MacDougall's collective lines had already cleared the battery with Potter's men removing three of Turnbull's repatriated artillery pieces, just as Humphreys had ordered. The 72nd's part in recapturing Turnbull's cannons was minimal, at best.[11]

Humphreys ordered the first arriving Union reserves to draw Turnbull's guns back to safety because the battle was still raging west of the elongated knoll. That fight was by no means over, with the Rebels still in firm possession of the Emmitsburg Road. Captain Abram Lockwood, commanding the remnants of the 120th New York, did not report taking a flag or reclaiming any guns, but he did report that they "retired slowly, fighting, across the field, when the brigade again rallied, and drove the enemy from the field at the point of the bayonet." Lockwood's small cast had rejoined Brewster and charged with him. Although they took part in the Excelsior Brigade's countercharge to the left of the 19th Maine, they scribed not a word about heroic deeds or captured prizes. It is probable that Lockwood's humble but determined lot continued advancing over the knoll into the vacant space between the 19th Maine's left and Humphreys' right.[12]

By this time, General Carr's short line had begun moving forward to reclaim possession of the Rogers farm. Carr, a pre-war tobacconist from upstate New York, lacked formal military training. However, he made up for it with his stubborn tenacity and personal bravery. He led his band toward the 19th Maine, with his right flank angled southwest as it passed south of Hummelbaugh's farm lane. After traveling some distance, his men closed on Plum Run, where they happened upon a scattering of Confederates near where Hancock had initially planted the 19th Maine. Cut off and exhausted, the Southerners surrendered en masse. Carr directed them east unescorted as he resumed his advance toward the Emmitsburg Road. His men encountered several other isolated groups of enemy soldiers who had also begun the eastward trek as prisoners. Continuing on, Carr's line stopped in the right-rear of the 19th Maine because here Rebel resolve was still palpable. Like Heath and Brewster to his left, Carr inched his men slowly forward, the Emmitsburg Road some distance to their front and the Rogers house about 400 yards to the southwest as the road angled away.[13]

In his haste to connect with Heath's New Englanders, Carr missed enemy parties off both his flanks. These isolated Rebels, mostly from the 2nd Florida, did not receive Colonel Lang's order to retire. Caught in the low ground and heavy growth, with smoke and confusion swirling about them, they could not see or hear any commands, let alone one directing them to withdraw. Their isolated ordeal that eventually landed them in a Union prison began when Maj. Walter Moore sent a

11 Ibid., pt. 2, 633.

12 Ibid., pt. 1, 565.

13 Ibid., 543.

portion of his left wing north. The subsequent fight for Livingston's Union guns had degenerated into a brawl between individual groups of the 2nd Florida, 22nd Georgia, and 2nd Georgia Battalion (the latter two regiments of General Wright's brigade) for possession of the captured prizes. In this case, the 2nd Florida claimed one gun and the 2nd Georgia Battalion the other. Survivors from all three regiments who were not detailed to haul the pieces westward joined forces, moving east as one ragged body toward Lieutenant Weir's 5th U. S. guns.[14]

Meanwhile, Weir's Regular battery had been pummeling the 2nd Florida's left and center with deadly accuracy. After separating his command in the face of the enemy and now facing Weir's murderous fire down his line, Major Moore was unable to recover his regimental cohesion. As his far right clung to the left of the 8th Florida, his center and left center began unraveling under Weir's point-blank belches of canister. A few moments later Moore's left flank elements also melted away, with many men shifting north toward Wright's Georgians.[15]

By the time Carr's line closed with the 19th Maine, Heath's troops had reclaimed all the ground they had lost, and then some. The Mainers now stood 200 yards west of Turnbull's gun line. To Heath's immediate right, Carr's tattered survivors were battling to regain territory they had grudgingly given up earlier. To the 19th Maine's left-front, where the Rogers house was now visible, Colonel Brewster's small line had by this time been absorbed into MacDougall's 111th New York and General Humphreys' reformed masses, the three units having intermingled in the confusion and gathering darkness. Humphreys assumed overall control and began organizing a secondary defensive line as his front line continued its firing and deliberate advance west.[16]

*　　*　　*

Before Winfield Hancock redeployed Lieutenant Weir's battery east of the Codori barn, where it was now picking apart Lang's Florida outfit, he and other Union commanders had sent aides scurrying in several directions for any available reinforcements. Some rode north to Cemetery Hill, while others galloped east to Culp's and Power's hills, and still more southeast in search of Maj. Gen. John

---

14 David Lang to Edward Perry, July 19, 1863, in "Gettysburg: The Courageous Part Taken in the Desperate Conflict 2-3 July 1863," *SHSP,* Vol. 27, 1899, 192-205.

15 Ibid.; USGS MRC 39077G2; *Bachelder Maps, Second Day.*

16 Humphreys Narrative, Box 26, Humphreys Papers, HSP; Humphreys to Wilcox, November 30, 1877, Box 27, Humphreys Papers, HSP; USGS MRC 39077G2; *Bachelder Maps, Second Day.*

Codori's farm and orchard looking southwest from Cemetery Ridge. General Wright's Georgia brigade attacked from right to left. His men moved past this area and up the slope of the ridge as the troops under Barksdale, Wilcox, and Lang met their high tide farther south and began retreating. The timely unlimbering and fire of Capt. James M. Rorty's Battery B, 1st New York in the Union center broke the right flank of Wright's brigade south of the farm. Note the rough ground in the foreground, which was occupied during the battle by Brown's Battery B, Rhode Island Light Artillery. *William H. Tipton*

Sedgwick's Sixth Corps. These young men performed admirably, serving with distinction and honor as they channeled troops toward Hancock's sector. One example was a 26-year-old Irish-born captain named James McKay Rorty. Detached from the 14th New York Independent Battery, Rorty served Hancock as acting ordnance officer for the Second Corps, a role he performed with distinction, but nevertheless loathed.[17]

Rorty's former section of the 14th was now part of Battery B, 1st New York. Hancock had last seen Battery B's guns on the crest of Cemetery Ridge with General Caldwell's infantry prior to sending that division south. Hancock happened upon Rorty somewhere north of the Hummelbaugh farm lane. The veteran general pointed south, directing the newly commissioned captain to bring the battery to him. Long a Hancock advocate, Rorty jumped at the chance. He and his subordinate, Lt. George L. Dwight, spurred their horses down Cemetery Ridge and across the farm lane. Continuing south, they rode past the trampled position where the 1st Minnesota had gone prone and passed through the reforming troops. All the while, E. P. Alexander's Confederate shells exploded around and above them.[18]

17 *OR* 27, pt. 1, 375.

18 Ibid., 882; Nicholson, *New York at Gettysburg*, 1324-25; Hunt, "The Second Day at Gettysburg," *B&L*, 3:302.

Unable to find Battery B where expected, Rorty and Dwight continued south toward the Weikert homestead where they could see Union batteries engaged. There, placed just north of Weikert's farm lane sat the guns. All four 10-pounder Parrott Rifles were in battery targeting Barksdale's 21st Mississippi and General Wofford's brigade in the fields between the Emmitsburg Road and Plum Run. Riding up to Lieutenant Sheldon, Rorty stated his mission and Dwight confirmed Hancock's order. Without seeking input from his superior Col. Freeman McGilvery, Lieutenant Sheldon ordered his four guns hitched. Battery B's cannoneers quickly limbered their rifles and climbed aboard the ammunition-filled limbers and caissons, an order dreaded by every man when under enemy fire. "Pettit's First New York Battery remained only a few minutes," McGilvery later reported, "and left while I was directing fire of the Sixth Maine [Dow's battery] and a section of the Fifth Massachusetts [Phillips' battery]."[19]

Left behind in Battery B's wake were Pvt. Henry Rosegrant, sprawled on the ground in a pool of blood after being shot in his face, and five other wounded men. Captain Rorty guided the guns north through a maze of traffic, possibly passing around Brig. Gen. Henry J. Lockwood's brigade approaching in the twilight from the direction of Culp's Hill. Arriving at the Hummelbaugh intersection, Rorty swung hard left and retraced the route Sheldon had taken when Caldwell's division had advanced up Cemetery Ridge that morning. Once atop the ridge they turned north once more, heading toward what appeared to be more chaos with fugitives, stretcher bearers, wagons, riders, and others moving every which way. Rorty scanned the crest looking for General Hancock, who he was sure was somewhere ahead.[20]

While Rorty and Dwight sought out Hancock with Battery B, General Lockwood, commanding the Second Brigade in General Slocum's Twelfth Corps, arrived on southern Cemetery Ridge with Brig. Gens. Alpheus S. Williams and Thomas Ruger. According to General Williams, "Between 5 and 6 p.m. orders were received from Major-General Slocum to detach the First Division [Ruger's] and Lockwood's brigade to support the left wing of the army, then heavily attacked. I marched with the supporting detachment with all possible dispatch," Williams continued, "under a sever artillery fire, following as nearly as possible the direction of heavy firing."[21]

---

19 *OR* 27, pt. 1, 883.

20 Nicholson, *New York at Gettysburg*, 1324-25; USGS MRC 39077G2; *Bachelder Maps, Second Day*.

21 Ibid., 778.

General Williams was still temporarily commanding Slocum's Twelfth Corps, leaving Ruger in command of Williams' division. With Williams and Ruger riding ahead, a constant line of detached riders retraced their rural route, making sure the division followed correctly. Ruger recorded, "At this time [6:00 p.m.] I received orders from Brigadier-General Williams, commanding [Twelfth] corps, to move with the division to the assistance of the left of the general line, then hotly engaged with the enemy, reporting my arrival to the corps commander of the force engaged."[22]

One of the many issues rarely discussed, let alone fully explained, is to which corps commander did the detached Ruger report? In all probability it was General Birney who, prior to riding north, had been rallying troops near the lane that Williams and Ruger would have passed onto Cemetery Ridge. According to Williams, however, "When near the position occupied originally by the Second Corps [Caldwell's division], as I was informed by Major McGilvery, of the Maine artillery, reported to me that his battery was without support, and threatened by the enemy's infantry in the woods in front, to which it had just retired, carrying several pieces of our guns." In other words, Williams never mentioned meeting up with Birney or Hancock.[23]

Lockwood's three regiments (two from Maryland and one from New York) arrived on the field that morning about 8:00 a.m. after a grueling 17-mile all-night march. The brigade was never allowed enough time in any one place to catch its breath. Caught up in General Meade's morning plans, Lockwood's command was moved several times before finally being allowed to rest and boil coffee. "They [his three regiments] were posted at various places until about 5 p.m. of that day," recalled Lockwood, "when having received an order to support the left wing of the army, then heavily engaged, they were marched to and deployed near a battery [Dow's 6th Maine], then firing on the enemy."[24]

Lockwood's three relatively inexperienced regiments, about 1,283 effectives, had advanced southwest from their position below Culp's Hill using the rural crossroads as directed by General Williams' adjutants and aides. When these regiments finally reached the Taneytown Road, Col. William P. Maulsby's 1st Potomac Home Brigade turned south, followed by Col. John H. Ketcham's 150th New York. Colonel Archibald L. MacDougall's brigade of Williams' division followed in their wake. Numbering 1,835 men, MacDougall's column was followed

22 Ibid.

23 Ibid., 774.

24 Ibid., 804.

by Col. Silas Colgrove's brigade, another 1,598 soldiers belonging to the same division.[25]

At some point along Lockwood's march down the Taneytown Road, General Meade and a handful of aides galloped past. Turning up Weikert's farm lane and passing through Patterson's Woods, the commanding general found Williams and Ruger awaiting their troops.[26] Plans were made as Williams' and Ruger's aides raced back through the belt of woods to hurry Lockwood's brigade along. Other than for a "short" time, exactly how long Meade stayed there is not known. What is known is that General Birney was nowhere to be found because he had already ridden north, but Meade and Williams worked out what to do. Spurring his horse back through Patterson's Woods, Meade galloped north toward Cemetery Hill to secure more reinforcements for the center. It is uncertain when Colonel Maulsby's leading 1st Maryland of Lockwood's brigade turned west through the woods. With darkness settling over the fields and woods, Lockwood directed these Marylanders northward once they reached the crest. "The division was moved in the direction ordered," Ruger simply stated, "being exposed on part of the line of march to a heavy artillery fire."[27]

The scene on the crest was still chaos and bedlam. None of these newly arriving troops knew anything except they were surrounded by thousands of battle-weary Union men, with hundreds more flowing toward them from the woods to their left and front. At least four batteries, or portions thereof, were parked nearby. They belonged to Captains Clark, Bucklyn, Winslow, and Hart, survivors of the Peach Orchard and Wheatfield debacles. Except for Clark, who had unlimbered in place of Sheldon, the other three batteries were reorganizing and acquiring more ammunition.[28]

Colonel Maulsby's north-tramping line of Marylanders stopped somewhere near where Father Daniel Corby had blessed the Irish Brigade before that unit

---

25 Ibid.; Busey & Martin, *Regimental Strengths and Losses,* 52-54, 91-93; USGS MRC 39077G2; *Bachelder Maps, Second Day.*

26 Alexander K. McClure, ed., *The Annals of the Civil War Written by Leading Participants North and South* (Philadelphia, 1879), 212. Colonel James C. Biddle, one of Meade's most valued staff officers, later penned, "General Meade, during this encounter, brought forward in person a brigade of the Twelfth Corps, and in the early part of the action his horse was shot under him." Biddle made a mistake, for Meade took no part in leading any of Williams' troops forward, and certainly did not have a horse shot out from under him. Biddle may have mistakenly took Meade's passing Lockwood's brigade as leading it up Weikert's farm lane.

27 OR 27, pt. 1, 778.

28 A. S. Williams to Bachelder, Nov. 10, 1865, *Bachelder Papers,* 1:214-16; USGS MRC 39077G2; *Bachelder Maps, Second Day.*

ventured south with General Caldwell, who himself was now rallying troops south of General Lockwood's arriving troops. Once Maulsby stopped, his 1st Maryland was faced west. In Maulsby's immediate rear, Colonel Ketcham's 150th New York followed suit. "Thus formed," reported Lockwood, "these regiments under my charge, advanced about 1 mile, a portion in double-quick amid the most terrific firing of shells and musketry, to and beyond the extreme front, driving the enemy [Barksdale] before them and entirely clearing the field."[29]

Maulsby's advance carried his men toward Thompson's and Phillips' five engaged rifled cannon, while Captain Dow's four smoothbores recoiled off their left front. The mounted Maulsby led his Marylanders into the gap between the 125th and the 39th New York, both of Willard's brigade, angling toward Trostle's distant barn. The nearby Union gunners ceased firing when the Marylanders' trotted past, their left flank closing on Trostle's lane. The 39th New York, fighting from behind a stone wall east of Plum Run, was still trading shots with Colonel Humphreys' exhausted and heavily bloodied 21st Mississippi on the run's far side. Humphreys' Rebels were falling back and using the same low wall that had impeded the ready exodus of Bigelow's battery. "I discovered a long Federal line marching from the direction of Cemetery Hill directly against me," recalled Humphreys. "Looking again to my right and rear I saw Wofford retiring, towards the Peach Orchard. To my left the 3 other [13th, 17th & 18th] regiments that were with Barksdale were also retiring. I could see no other reinforcements coming, and determined to retire to the stone wall where I captured Graham and 4 [Bigelow's] guns and there make a stand once safely behind the stone fence I could control the ground on which I left the 5 [Watson's]. The enemy did not urge his claim to them, and I know the Federal Army was cut in twain," he added with the benefit of hindsight, "and hoping for reinforcements to hold what we had gained, and thus secure a triumph over separate wings I felt jubilation of the victor."[30]

Maulsby's line, meanwhile, passed through the 39th before descending into Plum Run. Without redressing his ranks, Lockwood urged Maulsby's line onward out of the ravine. Once his men ascended the slope, however, a mix of spherical case, shrapnel, solid shot, and shell exploded around them. Porter Alexander's Rebel batteries had a good enfilade fire against the 1st Maryland's left wing from their position in and around the Sherfy Peach Orchard. With darkness fast approaching, Maulsby's Potomac Home Guard Marylanders pressed upward toward the low wall taken up by Humphreys' 21st Mississippi. Within a few

29 OR 27, pt. 1, 804.

30 McNeily, "Barksdale's Mississippi Brigade at Gettysburg," 248-50; Benjamin Humphreys to McLaws, January 6, 1878, Lafayette McLaws Papers, UNC.

minutes, Humphreys' fire fell away to a few isolated cracks of musketry. Leaving the remnants of Bigelow's overrun 9th Massachusetts Battery behind them, Humphreys' Mississippians withdrew from the lower wall and fell away westward.[31]

Clearing Trostle's farmyard took Maulsby's men some time, with so many walking wounded having migrated toward the barn and house. It was not easy to tell friend from foe, or the wounded from the uninjured. With the yard finally secured, his left wing redressed at the wall west of and above Plum Run behind Bigelow's abandoned guns. Although Alexander's gunners were firing from less than 500 yards away, the undeterred Marylanders surged over this lower wall and entered the silent Union battery, recapturing Bigelow's four abandoned Napoleons. Once the Marylanders pulled the four pieces back into the Plum Run ravine, Maulsby recalled his men to the stone wall.[32]

Humphreys' 21st Mississippi, meanwhile, had fallen back about 200 yards to take up a new position behind the upper stone wall near the crest. There, the firepower of the Mississippians, supported by some of Wofford's Georgia infantry off their right and Alexander's artillery fire, helped convince Lockwood and Maulsby of the futility of continuing up the open slope. In any event, the 1st Maryland had advanced about as far as General Williams had ordered. Holding the wall west of Plum Run with a long line of skirmishers, Lockwood recalled the balance of Maulsby's roughly 600 men back to the low wall east of Plum Run, where they relieved the 39th New York and made it clear that they had reclaimed Bigelow's Napoleons.[33]

Colonel Ketcham's 150th New York had not been idle during this period. Ketcham's command moved forward moments after the 1st Maryland started out, receiving indirect shot and shell (possibly targeting Maulsby) from several guns north of and above Trostle's farmyard. Instead of angling southwest as the 1st Maryland had done, Ketcham guided his line west through Thompson's and Phillips' batteries, forcing those tubes to fall silent to avoid hitting their own men. By the time the 150th descended into Plum Run, their New York comrades from the 125th and 126th had already stopped Barksdale's three regiments and were mopping up the residue. As a result, by the time Ketcham's 150th emerged from the thickets west of the ravine north of Trostle's barn, the infantry fight was

---

31 Ibid.; Alexander, "Artillery Fighting at Gettysburg," 367. Colonel Humphreys spotted Willard's oncoming brigade moving south along Cemetery Ridge. Badly outnumbered, he pulled back to a stone wall some 200 yards west of Plum Run, which allowed Col. Hugo Hildebrandt's Garibaldi Guards to recapture Bigelow's guns.

32 OR 27, pt. 1, 804; Baker, *History of the Ninth Massachusetts Battery*, 203-204.

33 Ibid.

The headquarters of the Army of the Potomac shortly after the battle ended. Note the condition of the Taneytown Road, the Union army's principal supply route. Keeping it clear was a major objective. The insert photo was taken nine years after the battle south of Hummelbaugh's farm lane looking north. It clearly shows how difficult it was for Meade's army to move about the battlefield. Once inside the hemmed-in avenue, it was difficult to get out. It is now easy to understand why, early on July 2, General Hancock ordered all wheeled traffic off that road. LOC

essentially over. They continued up the slope, however, harassed by indirect fire from distant Rebel guns and musketry from Southern infantry reforming about 200 yards away.along a wall. Their muzzle flashes suggested the several hundred Mississippians and perhaps some Alabamians were still willing to keep up the fight.[34]

The destruction in the ravine was so horrific that Ketcham detached men to care for the wounded there. Once in the open above the run, his left flank linked up with Maulsby's right just north of the Trostle's barn. Like Maulsby on his left, Ketcham received orders from Lockwood to leave a strong skirmish line and withdraw the bulk of his men east of Plum Run. The partial withdrawal of Maulsby and Ketcham essentially ended the direct fighting along this part of the Federal line.[35]

34 A. S. Williams to Bachelder, Nov. 10, 1865, *Bachelder Papers,* 1:214-16.

35 McNeily, "Barksdale's Mississippi Brigade at Gettysburg," 248-50.

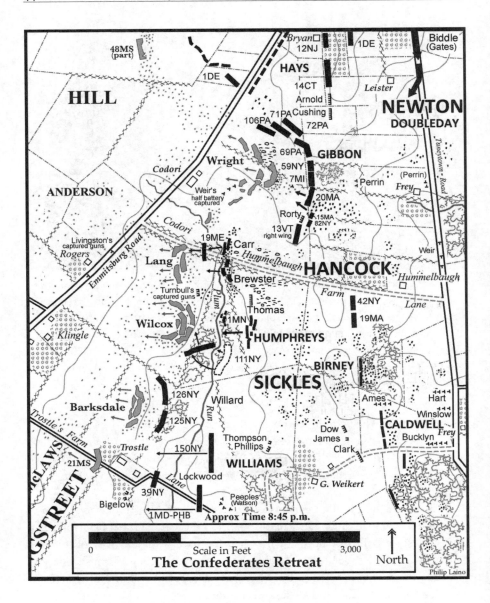

Approx Time 8:45 p.m.

0   Scale in Feet   3,000

The Confederates Retreat

North

Philip Laino

Colonel Silas Colgrove, leading Ruger's brigade, initially followed Lockwood's column onto the crest of the ridge, but was ushered to the left and placed in front of Caldwell's reformed line with the Fifth Corps off to the south. This action solidified control of the ridge in the vicinity where it joined the Weikert-Trostle farm lanes and other small roads connecting the Emmitsburg and Taneytown roads. That alone was both a strategic and tactical victory for the Army of the Potomac. With the Fifth Corps now in firm control of the Wheatfield Road, only the Hummelbaugh-Codori farm lane remained vulnerable.[36]

Colgrove sent a large force forward behind a wide line of skirmishers. "Ruger, with the First Division [MacDougall and Colgrove], in the meantime occupied the [Patterson] woods on the left of Lockwood, and pushed forward in two lines, the enemy [Wofford's brigade] retiring with but little resistance." Behind Lockwood and Colgrove, Colonel MacDougall's brigade formed into two lengthy battle lines in Patterson's Woods, but never advanced.[37]

*   *   *

"We were now complete masters of the field, having gained the key, as it were, of the enemy's whole line," claimed Confederate General Wright in his official report penned less than three months after Gettysburg. "Unfortunately," he continued, "just as we had carried the enemy's last and strongest position, it was discovered that the [Lang's Florida] brigade on our right had not only not advanced across the turnpike, but had actually given way, and was rapidly falling back to the rear, while on our left we were entirely unprotected, the brigade ordered to our support [Posey's Mississippians] having failed to advance."[38]

Wright's report is problematic on several fronts. First, he failed to mention that he was not with or even near his troops when they crossed the Emmittsburg Road to storm the height beyond. The breakdown in coordination between Wright's Georgians and Lang's Floridians came early, well before Lang's men reached the "turnpike." Apparently Wright did not know the Emmitsburg Road angled westward as it passed Anderson's division around the Codori farm. Lang's Floridians planted their boots on the plank fence paralleling the Emmittsburg Road, crossed, and continued advancing before Wright's Georgians were stopped by the 15th Massachusetts and 82nd New York on the Codori farm.[39]

The fight at the Codori farm so masterfully conducted by Union Colonels Ward and Huston not only bought Hancock perhaps 30 minutes of time to shore up that area, but ruined Wright's right wing as well any chance the Georgians had of becoming "masters of the field." But Wright's rank and file knew little other than they had made it beyond the Emmitsburg Road after a bitter contest and had the

36 A. S. Williams to Bachelder, Nov. 10, 1865, *Bachelder Papers,* 1:214-16.

37 *OR* 27, pt. 1, 798, 804.

38 Ibid., pt. 2, 623-624.

39 USGS MRC 39077G2; *Bachelder Maps, Second Day.*

Yankees on their heels. Beyond Codori's barn, the 2nd Battalion and 22nd Georgia had overrun Livingston's pair of smoothbores of Battery F, 3rd U. S. Joined by a few men from Col. Edward Walker's 3rd Georgia, these same men went on to overrun Weir's Battery C, 5th U. S. With three of those guns in their possession, they focused on Lieutenant James' section of Napoleons of Battery K, 4th U. S. James, however, managed to escape with his guns and caissons as Yankee fugitives coming up from the south formed independent lines of battle to lend support to his effort.[40]

Just how many rallied Union riflemen were on line between the left flank of Col. Norman Hall's brigade at the Copse of Trees south to where General Carr had reformed his line opposite Hummelbaugh's farm lane will never known with precision. There were, however, enough on hand to keep Wright's regiments in check. What we do know is that this rallying point east of Codori's farm held the remnants of Ward's and Huston's two regiments, while Hancock rallied and urged troops back into the fighting. The decision by the Georgians to focus time and manpower on the removal of Weir's and Livingston's guns also helped blunt the depth of their advance.[41]

While Wright's Georgians were battling their way east, and Hancock was looking for additional reinforcements to block their way, Capt. James M. Rorty, still accompanied by Lieutenants Sheldon and Dwight, led his Battery B's four Parrott Rifles northward toward a mounted rider in the distance. Although there were dozens of mounted individuals atop the crest, this one was particularly distinguishable from afar even in the twilight. The calm and collected officer was directing troops with just one aide. Rorty recognized Hancock as he closed on the commanding figure. The general had sent all of his aides rushing elsewhere in search of reinforcements except for Captain Miller, who had been wounded in a brief confrontation with Wilcox's men advancing out of the Plum Run ravine. Now, his only support was Pvt. James Wells, who followed the general on horseback while holding aloft the Second Corps commander's personal flag.[42]

Hancock directed the captain into position near where General Gibbon had initially planted Weir's 5th U. S., about 200 yards north of the Hummelbaugh lane. Swinging around at "Reverse Trot," both Rorty and Sheldon saw to it the guns were in battery and set for action. In less than two minutes the first piece belched forth a load of canister toward the Georgians, who had bunched together in loose masses

40 Ibid.; Pfanz, *Gettysburg, The Second Day*, 414; McClure, *The Annals of the Civil War*, 212-13.

41 Ford, *The Story of the 15th Regiment Massachusetts Volunteers*, 267-68.

42 Ibid.; OR 27, pt. 1, 622-23.

after overrunning Weir's half-battery. Captain Rorty finally had his combat command.

Although parts of the the Rebel line had crept forward beyond the captured gun line, most of Wright's Georgians and what was left of the 2nd Florida's left were satisfied to duke it out from below. By this time all four of Rorty's rifles were pounding the Rebels and Wright's far right side was done advancing. Rorty's arrival brought a renewed spark to the men in blue battling there along the Emmitsburg Road. Hancock cheered on the infantry facing back off either flank of Rorty's flaming battery. Caught up in moment defending the Union center, Hancock seems not to have noticed what was unfolding to his right and front, or that Union reinforcements were approaching from his right-rear.[43]

When Gibbon redeployed Capt. Thomas F. Brown's Battery B, 1st Rhode Island Light, farther west from its original position left of the Copse of Trees, he had no idea it would become the focal point of an attack by Wright's left wing as it surged across the Emmitsburg Road. He also seems not to have noticed that the ground was not well suited for operating a battery. Sitting 100 yards southwest of the Copse of Trees, Brown's right section was west of the thickets, with his left guns to southwest. Because of the rock outcroppings in the area, the guns were not spaced uniformly, but spread wherever the ground permitted access to work the pieces. This left the battery with a staggered line of guns holding what was essentially an indefensible piece of terrain without proper infantry support.[44]

According to Elijah Rhodes, the battery's historian, "General Gibbon's line at this place, ran nearly parallel with the Emmitsburg road; we were on General Gibbon's left flank, on a slight ridge in Codori's field, between his [Gibbon] line and the road at an angle of about 45 [degrees]. The battery's left was nearest the road with the right extending back to within one hundred yards of the main line [Copse of Trees], at the stone wall, facing nearly northwest, our line of fire, therefore," he continued, "was diagonally across the Emmitsburg road toward and to the left of the Lutheran Theological Seminary."[45]

Brown's fire from this position was as infrequent as it was ineffective. When a spotter was unable to see and note the results, the battery ceased firing or fired indirectly by slowly sending solid shot or bolt in the direction of the enemy.

43 Ibid., 352; Pfanz, *Gettysburg, The Second Day,* 421-22; USGS MRC 39077G2; *Bachelder Maps, Second Day.*

44 Rhodes, *The History of Battery B,* 184-202.

45 Ibid., 201; MRC 39077G2; *Bachelder Maps, Second Day.* Battery B fronted northwest, facing the seminary at angles across the road, not due west toward what would later become Spangler's Point of Woods, as many writers believe.

Brown's Rhode Islanders initially targeted the enemy guns atop Seminary Ridge near the Fairfield Road using mostly solid shot. Had it not been for Maj. Thomas Osborn's West Cemetery Hill line countering the Confederate batteries, Brown might well have been driven from his exposed position. As it was, most of the enemy's fire toward the Copse of Trees was also off target and largely ineffective. Even so, Brown's men had to lie down to avoid enemy sharpshooters who enjoyed using distant artillerists to hone their marksmanship skills.[46]

When Wright's and parts of Posey's line marched into view, Battery B's men jumped to their feet and responded with spherical case, shell, and solid shot. "Shortly after we ceased firing on the Rebel battery a large force of the enemy was seen coming out of the woods, or our left flank, moving to the [Emmitsburg] road in the direction of the gap [Gibbon's left, the Union center]," Rhodes, the battery's historian, continued. "At first we mistook them for our own men, supposing that the Third Corps was falling back to its old position; but when we commenced to receive their fire and heard the well known 'rebel yell,' as they charged for our battery, we were no doubt no longer, but sprang to our posts at the gun to receive them." According to the Rhode Islander, the Rebels appeared "in solid front of two lines of battle. As our artillery fire cut down their men, they would waver, form a second, only to soon close up and continue their advance."[47]

Captain Brown and Lt. Walter S. Perrin attempted to realign their staggered battery to better defend their position. Brown changed front left oblique and began firing four-second spherical case shell. Because of the terrain and the facing of the pieces, only the left and center sections could be trained on Wright's and Posey's men. As a result, rather than fighting as a battery each two-gun section engaged independently, with the right section shelling the distant woods on Seminary Ridge. Even though the fire from the left and center sections was rapid and steadfast, the Rebels surged up and out of the first swale west of the road with compact ranks. It was here the Georgians and Mississippians met the metal wrath of Brown's smoothbore Napoleons just 200 yards distant. While the 3rd Georgia's right wing battled Ward's 15th Massachusetts for possession of Codori's sprawling orchard, Brown's canister blew holes through Wright's left flank. "Our fire was very destructive to the enemy," penned Cpl. John Delevan. "I could see, at every discharge of our guns, a vacant space appear in the enemy rank, but they would immediately close up."[48]

---

46 Rhodes, *The History of Battery B*, 201-202; USGS MRC 39077G2; *Bachelder Maps, Second Day*.

47 Ibid., 201.

48 Robert Grandchamp, ed., as noted in "Brown's Company B, 1st Rhode Island Artillery at the Battle of Gettysburg," in *Gettysburg Magazine*, no. 36, July 2007, 88.

The staggered posting of the battery, however, reduced Brown's firepower by one-third because he could only muster four of his six pieces to combat the advancing line. The two swales to their front made it even harder because they allowed Wright's Georgians to reorganize their ranks unhindered. Posey's right wing, however, was another story. Its advance was being taken apart by small arms fire from General Hays' infantry supported by artillery under Woodruff, Arnold, and Cushing near the Copse of Trees. Osborn's batteries, enjoying an elevated left-front enfilade from Cemetery Hill, also tore huge gaps in the exposed line of Mississippians.[49]

Because the Emmitsburg Road angled to the northeast on this part of the front, Wright's northern (or right) wing struck it first, and like a wave breaking on a beach from south to north, the rest of the brigade washed up against it. The left side of Wright's brigade did not have Codori's orchard and farmyard full of defiant Union infantry to contend with, meaning the only significant opposition to its front was Brown's four Napoleons. Slowly gaining the road and then passing over it, Gibson's 48th Georgia, supported by portions of Col. Joseph M. Jayne's 48th Mississippi of Posey's brigade, began working their way up the slope toward the low rock wall and Copse of Trees between Brown's center and right sections.[50]

Noting that Brown was about to be flanked and his right section cut off, Second Corps artillery brigade commander Capt. John Hazard spurred his horse though the narrow opening in the wall at the thickets. The artillery officer located Brown, pointed out the potential danger, and suggested he pull out and reposition his guns atop the ridge beyond the wall. Brown's staggered alignment proved a blessing now for it allowed the retiring Yankee skirmishers to slip between the field pieces more easily as Wright's whooping Georgians and several hundred Mississippians followed closely in pursuit. About 300 yards behind Brown's right-rear, Lt. Alonzo Cushing's and Capt. William Arnold's small-bore ordnance rifles had little effect against the closing enemy, especially with retiring Yankees masking most of their immediate front. Fortunately for Webb's and Hall's infantry, the rough ground slowed the pursuit by the 48th Georgia and the Mississippians. The brush-ridden outcropping broke Wright's formation forcing the men to pick their way through. Still, onward poured Wright's shot-torn line, ever so slowly closing on the low stone wall and Copse of Trees.[51]

49 Ibid.; OR 27, pt. 1, 478; Osborn, "Eleventh Corps Artillery at Gettysburg" *Philadelphia Weekly Times,* July 1876; USGS MRC 39077G2.

50 OR 27, pt. 2, 629; Charles T. Straight, *Battery B, First R. I. Light Artillery, August 13, 1861-June 12, 1865* (Central Falls, RI, 1907).

51 Ibid.

Brown's uneven alignment may have proven beneficial to the retiring Federal infantry, but it helped bring about the battery's demise. Before the captain was able to order his guns out, a Rebel (allegedly Pvt. Simeon Theus of the 48th Georgia) leveled his rifle-musket and pulled the trigger, knocking Brown out of the saddle. Grazed through the neck, the young officer escaped on foot, leaving Lieutenant Perrin to oversee the hitching of the guns. This was not an easy chore, because the enemy had closed to within a few yards of the right gun of the center section, with the far right section making good its escape back toward the hole in the wall. By now the 69th Pennsylvania of General Webb's brigade, and the 7th Michigan and 59th New York of Colonel Hall's brigade, were on their feet firing past the retiring battery, and all but one gun had started back toward the opening.[52]

The passage through the narrow opening in the stone wall was only wide enough for one cannon at a time, and the column quickly jolted to a disordered halt, as the battery's historian recalled: "In retiring the battery came under a heaving enfilading fire from the [left] wing of the [right] flanking foe, which had overlapped us, and many of our men and the horses were wounded before we could retire behind the line of support [Webb and Hall], for only one piece at a time could go through the narrow gap in the stone wall which afforded breast works for our infantry. The drivers of the sixth piece were forced to halt as they were approaching the gap, it being partially blocked by two pieces, the third [center section] and fifth [left section] trying to get through at the same time."[53]

As the artillerists struggled to get through, the Georgians and Mississippians stalled west of and below the wall in the face of Webb's and Hall's three regiments and the rough outcropping. South of the outcropping, the retiring 15th Massachusetts and 82nd New York (Harrow's brigade) were reforming in scattered bunches along the low ridge that offered no protection at all. Offering renewed resistance, Joslin's New Englanders, supported by Capt. John Darrow's small band of New Yorkers, faced off with the 48th Georgia's right flank supported by what remained of the 3rd Georgia's left. Since the latter two Rebel groups did not have to negotiate the outcroppings and rougher ground, they made better headway than their brethren to their left. A Union soldier didn't see it that way, however, and at eye level with the bullets flying everything looks different. As far as he was concerned, Wright's advance appeared "splendid, seemingly unstoppable once they had passed east of the Emmitsburg Road."[54]

52 Ibid.; Rhodes, *The History of Battery B*, 202.

53 Ibid.

54 Ibid. OR 27, pt. 1, 417; Frederick Fuger, "Cushing's Battery at Gettysburg," *Journal of the Military Service Institute of the United Sates*, vol. 40, 1907, 405-10.

Although Wright's far left was still advancing, it had slowed considerably. Besides Webb's and Hall's 600-plus Union rifles firing from beyond the wall, two natural factors came into play that helped the Yankees. The first, as described, was the natural outcropping that impeded most of the left wing of the 48th Georgia and all of Posey's advancing Mississippians. The second was the contour of the ground Wright's men were traversing to reach the top of the ridge. The eastern edge of the rough ground to the stone wall, about 30 to 40 yards, was an undulating but ascending field littered with underbrush and scrub. The uneven terrain, which played havoc with the already-exhausted assaulting troops, forced them to over-adjust their aim as they fired slightly upward at the blueclad torsos behind the wall. The slight difference in elevation caused most of the rounds to either pass harmlessly overhead or thud into the earth below the wall. Some splintered into tiny lead fragments when they struck the rocks. Although worried that they were about to be overrun at the Copse of Trees, Webb's soldiers enjoyed the benefit of defending a superior position. As a result, they took lighter casualties than usual for such a close-quarters engagement.[55]

The rising ground south of the umbrella-shaped bunch of trees was an entirely different story. Although the southern portion of the rough ground that had housed Brown's left section was rocky and impractical as an artillery platform, it played out with a scattering of rocks and was more of a nuisance than the craggy outcropping a bit west of the thickets. From the eastern edge of Codori's orchard and farmyard north and east to the low wall paralleling the ridge south of the trees, the field was slightly undulating and fairly open, giving easier access to Cemetery Ridge than the terrain farther north toward the Bryan property. Once they cleared the Codori orchard and farmyard, only a single rail fence impeded the right of the 48th Georgia and the left of the 3rd Georgia. Although this allowed Lieutenant Colonel Joslin's 15th Massachusetts and Captain Darrow's 82nd New York survivors to make it back quickly to Cemetery Ridge, it also enabled the right side of the 48th Georgia to pursue at a similar pace. Once atop the crest, there was no stout wall for the 15th and 82nd to reform behind like Webb and Hall had 200 yards north. Here, the low stone fence was only one and perhaps two feet tall at its highest point, topped with a light snake rail. In other words, it was little more than a low pile of rubble. Wright's Georgians were coming on, and there was seemingly little to stop them.[56]

The first of Brown's guns overrun west of and below the wall was Number Four of the center section. "We were ordered to limber to the rear when they had

---

55 Straight, *Battery B, First R. I. Light Artillery*; USGS MRC 39077G2; *Bachelder Maps, Second Day*.

56 Ibid.

got very near to us," Sgt. Albert Straight recalled. "Two of my horses got shot just as the order was being given, and I could not get my piece off, and the boys had to look out for themselves, as the Johnnies were all around us, and bullets flew very lively, with some shot and shell all my horses were killed." The gun sat hitched to its limber 100 yards southwest of the Copse in the center of the outcropping. The last piece waiting in line also had to be abandoned below the gap in the wall. "As a consequence, one of the horses of the sixth piece was killed with another wounded, causing such confusion that the drivers were forced to abandon their horses and the cannoneers their gun," Straight added. Wright's soldiers made no attempt to remove either of these prizes. By the time the last piece was overrun, the 71st, 72nd, and 106th Pennsylvania of Webb's brigade, numbering 921 rifles, along with the 20th Massachusetts from Hall's brigade (with 243 rifles), were advancing up the eastern slope to help the roughly 600 men firing from behind the wall covering Lieutenant Perrin's withdrawal.[57]

All told, these seven Union regiments arriving at just the last moment far outnumbered the left and center of the 48th Georgia and Posey's right-flank Mississippians that have passed east of the Emmitsburg Road. Whittled down by battle and fatigue, and scattered about the rough ground below the wall, Wright's line north of the Codori farmyard was in real jeopardy of being swept from the field. Although none of these Rebels below the Copse of Trees advanced farther than Gun Number Six of Battery B, 1st Rhode Island, which sat about 35 yards southwest of the wall, they did stand their ground. The balance of Perrin's Napoleons unlimbered 50 yards east of the wall just south of the Copse in their original position, where they reopened fire. According to Elijah Rhodes, "The other pieces, which reached the rear of our battle line, got in battery at once and opened fire again upon the advancing foe, but soon stopped to enable our infantry to charge them."[58]

South of where Rhodes was feverishly working his gun, the right flank of the 48th Georgia, supported by the 3rd Georgia's left, made considerable headway pressing the fleeing Yankees toward Joslin's and Darrow's rag-tag line reforming along the crest. With colors held aloft, men in blue naturally retreated toward them. Numbering close to 400 men, most of whom had been on the advanced skirmish line west of the Emmitsburg Road since 8:30 a.m., they retired individually and in groups north of the Codori farmyard. Most of them came from companies

---

57 Straight, *Battery B, First R.I. Light Artillery*; Ford, *The Story of the 15th Regiment Massachusetts Volunteers*, 267-68; Busey & Martin, *Regimental Strengths and Losses*, 40-41.

58 Busey & Martin, *Regimental Strengths and Losses*, 40-41; Rhodes, *The History of Battery B*, 202-203.

belonging to the 71st, 72nd, and 106th Pennsylvania of Webb's brigade, the 7th Michigan and 20th Massachusetts of Hall's brigade, and the 82nd New York of Harrow's brigade. Once east of the road, they had no choice but to break for the rear, with each man for himself, while Brown's cannoneers prepared to pepper everyone with loads of canister. Most of these men angled southeast away from and around Brown's left flank to clear the field of fire. After reaching the rear, they faced back along the remains of the low wall paralleling the crest to the immediate left of Lieutenant Perrin's 1st Rhode Island.[59]

Cemetery Ridge may have been lightly defended for 350 yards from the Copse of Trees south all the way to Rorty's Battery B, 1st New York, but it was being defended nonetheless. Lieutenant Perrin's half-battery immediately to the south of the thickets unloaded canister as the Union fugitives mentioned above rushed over the low wall to Perrin's left and front. How many young men in blue fell from the fire of Perrin's three guns will never be known, because in the chaos and din of battle with darkness falling it was becoming nearly impossible to distinguish one soldier from another. Still, men faced back and reformed on Perrin's left and on the right of the reforming 15th Massachusetts. The 82nd New York formed on the Bay Stater's left. Although few in number, the Union fugitives worked to slow the advance of Wright's right flank. Starting up the slope, the exhausted right side of the 48th Georgia slowly pressed up the slope, moving ahead of the stalled left, toward Perrin's battery and the reforming Unionists who stood with only a knee-high wall for cover. Immediately south of the reformed fugitives, the survivors of the 15th Massachusetts and 82nd New York held their own and had been reinforced by troops arriving from the south, the west, and the southwest. Beyond them, Hancock continued to display bravery beyond the call of duty as he summoned additional fugitives to face about and join the defense, while Rorty's four Parrotts continued pounding away.[60]

Posey's Mississippians on Wright's left began falling back, their line broken and in retreat. At the same time, Wright's left remained stalled, unable to gain the wall but not yet ready to call it quits and fall back. Moving over the crest at the double-quick, the 106th Pennsylvania's Lt. Col. William L. Curry recalled, "I advanced my regiment by the left flank, and formed in rear of the second line. Shortly after orders were received to move forward, I advanced the regiment to the crest of the hill [Cemetery Ridge] and opened fire upon the enemy. After several

59 OR 27, pt. 1, 426, 427, 442, 445-46; George A. Bruce, *The Twentieth Regiment of Massachusetts Volunteer Infantry 1961-1865* (Boston and New York, 1906), 278-84.

60 Anthony W. McDurmott and John E. Reily, *A Brief History of the 69th Regiment Pennsylvania Veteran Volunteers* (Philadelphia, 1889), 28.

How far did Wright's men get? This image, taken atop Cemetery Ridge, looks south by southwest past the Copse of Trees (on the right). Wright's left wing reached a line approximately 100 yards south of these trees (near where the lone tree is standing). There, for a few minutes, the Rebels took possession of the low wall paralleling the ridge west of and below the crest. Intense Union fire repulsed the 48th Georgia and 48th Mississippi with heavy losses well short of the Copse. *William H. Tipton*

volleys, perceiving that we checked his advance," Curry continued, "and seeing his line waver, I ordered bayonets fixed and a charge to be made, which movement resulted in a complete success, the enemy retiring in confusion to his original position."[61]

Curry's 106th Pennsylvania had come up on the right of the 69th Pennsylvania and then moved west down the slope. When his right flank passed through a portion of Cushing's battery, the gunners had to cease firing to avoid killing their own men. With bayonets fixed, Curry's men scaled the wall, redressed their lines, and while charging, wheeled half-left into Wright's exposed and already crumbling left. Caught in a pincer-like movement when the 69th likewise charged west up and over the wall, Wright's advance against the Copse of Trees fell to pieces. Within moments, the 59th New York and 7th Michigan, both on the left of the 69th, followed suit, passing over the wall near or under the canopy of trees. Following in

61 OR 27, pt. 1, 434

the wake of the 106th, the 71st and 72nd moved around the right of the 69th. South of the 59th New York, Perrin's three Napoleons also ceased firing when Col. Paul J. Revere's 20th Massachusetts surged up and over the crest to join the other Union men confronting Wright's final push.[62]

A Rebel flag followed by a line of butternut and gray crested the ridge only 40 yards to the front of and perhaps as many yards to left of Perrin's half-battery. Soldiers from the 48th Georgia and the left wing of 3rd Georgia, likely with a few of Posey's Mississippians in support, had exploited the "gap" and made it to the wall, where they planted their colors on the rubble. To their south (right), the 15th Massachusetts and 82nd New York did not budge while the fugitives on their right regained their composure and faced back to join them. For a few brief moments south of the Copse of Trees, Wright's men, or at least some of them, actually penetrated Hancock's center. Hancock's salvation, however, was on hand.

Passing through and around Perrin's three smoking Napoleons, Revere's New Englanders stopped and delivered a crashing volley into the jubilant Rebels. The hundreds of rounds delivered within the space of a few seconds cleared their front. Fixing bayonets, they too charged the low wall, hitting the Rebels with everything they had. At some point during the charge a shell exploded above the regiment killing Colonel Revere. With Lt. Col. George N. Macy now at the helm, the 20th Massachusetts passed over the low wall. Outgunned, outflanked on their left and unsupported on their right, and with their endurance completely drained, this portion of Wright's front fell back down the slope. "Then came a struggle for the possession of those two guns," recalled a member of the 20th. "The gallant 69th Pennsylvania, backed by the 106th held their ground, and advancing with the brigade on the charge, drove the foe back and held the guns."[63]

Wright would later pen in his controversial report that his men leaped "over the fence, charged to the top of the crest, and drove the enemy's infantry into a rocky gorge on the eastern slope of the heights, and some 80 or 100 yards in the rear of the enemy's batteries." The right-center of Wright's left wing took the low wall—of that there is no doubt—and pierced the Union line south of the umbrella of trees, but they never gazed down upon General Meade's headquarters, let alone a "rocky gorge" housing the Taneytown Road. From the low stone wall it is uphill for another 50 yards, and physically impossible to see over the crest from the wall. General Wright, wrote one recent historian who spent much of his life studying

62 Rhodes, *The History of Battery B*, 202-203; Bruce, *The Twentieth Regiment of Massachusetts*, 278-84. Colonel Revere was a descendant of famed Revolutionary War patriot Paul Revere.

63 *OR 27*, pt. 1, 445; Rhodes, *The History of Battery B*, 202-203; *OR 27*, pt. 2, 622; Bruce, *The Twentieth Regiment of Massachusetts*, 278-84.

Gettysburg, "wrote with imagination." Wright himself, of course, was not with his men because he had been ill, also noted the slope was "so precipitous here that my men could with difficulty climb it." In all probability he was referring to the rocky outcropping west of and below the Copse of Trees, which had created issues for both Captain Brown's placement of his battery and Wright's infantry as they passed through it toward the crest.[64]

Not a single Union veteran penned a single word to substantiate Wright's claim (which in order to have been true, Cushing's and/or Arnold's batteries would have been overrun north of the Copse of Trees on July 2, or Perrin's half-battery captured to the south). All three batteries were engaging Wright's men from atop the crest some 50 yards farther east of, and above, the low wall. The farthest east Wright's men managed to penetrate was where Brown's Gun Number Six of Battery B, 1st Rhode Island Light, sat hitched to its bullet-riddled limber and dead team of horses, perhaps 40 yards west of the gap in the wall under the tree canopy.[65]

Wright's far left and center were now in full retreat back toward the Emmitsburg Road. The brigade's right wing, which had no apparent communication with the left, was still holding firm below the ridge trading volleys with the 19th Massachusetts and 82nd New York, all the while enduring Rorty's canister fire. All of this was about to change when Col. Francis V. Randall of the 13th Vermont Volunteer Infantry reined in his horse and, with a quick salute, reported to General Hancock.[66]

---

64 Pfanz, *Gettysburg The Second Day*, 388-89; USGS MRC 39077G2.

65 Rhodes, *The History of Battery B*, 202-203; OR 27, pt. 2, 622.

66 USGS MRC 39077G2; *Bachelder Maps, Second Day*.

Chapter Eighteen

"Surrender! Fall out here, every damned one of you."

— *Lt. Col. William Munson, 13th Vermont Infantry*[1]

Evening, July 2:
Union Victory on Cemetery Ridge

Richard Anderson's attack against the Union center stumbled during its opening minutes, but by the time the fragmented three-brigade attack under Wilcox, Lang, and Wright struck the Emmitsburg Road line, the chance of a real breakthrough beckoned. Unfortunately for the Rebels, there was little concert of action, no supporting infantry commands to exploit the lodgment, and the heroic Union defensive effort led by General Hancock quickly sealed the breach and relentlessly pounded the Southern infantry. By the time darkness enveloped the field, whatever opportunity the Confederates enjoyed was gone.

On Anderson's right, Wilcox's fine Alabama brigade had suffered heavy losses, was fragmented, and its men exhausted and fought out east of the Emmitsburg Road, as was Lang's understrength Floridians and Ambrose Wright's Georgia command. Caught up in the fury of the Bliss farm fighting that afternoon and early evening, few of Carnot Posey's Mississippians had joined the assault—and certainly not as Anderson, A. P. Hill, or General Lee had originally envisioned. As noted earlier, Anderson's fifth and final brigade on his left, William Mahone's Virginia command, remained on Seminary Ridge and never joined the attack.[2]

1   Walter F. Beyer, Oscar F. Keydel and Martin Duffied, ed., *Deeds of Valor From the United States Government: How American Heroes Won the Medal of Honor* (Detroit, 1907), 226-28.

2   John W. DePeyster, "A Military Memoir of William Mahone, Major-General in the Confederate Army." *History Magazine* 7, 1870 (San Marino CA. Huntington Library-J.P

A post-battle image looking south down Cemetery Ridge from just below the Copse of Trees. The Round Tops are clearly visible in the right distance. Some of Wright's Georgians planted their flag on the low rock wall in the front left-center of photo. This was the deepest penetration of any Confederate unit on July 2. *William H. Tipton*

With darkness falling most of these Confederates were falling back, though some were still determined to fight on, particularly remnants of Wright's brigade. The Georgians' high tide had come and receded, but because of the smoke, bloody confusion, and growing darkness, none of the Federals defending Cemetery Ridge, including General Hancock, realized that Wright's right wing (3rd Georgia, 22nd Georgia, and 2nd Georgia Battalion) was whipped and that no other Southern assault columns had orders to join in the assault. These regiments had battled for possession of the Codori farm, overrun Livingston's and Weir's guns, and in reality were by this time nothing more than a disorganized mass. Still, these Southern riflemen stubbornly held their ground along the base of the ridge and showed little sign of quitting the field even though hundreds of men on either side were falling back as fast as they could.[3]

Nicholson Collection) Bradley M. Gottfried, "Mahone's Brigade: Insubordination or Miscommunication?", *Gettysburg Magazine*, Issue 18, Jan. 1998.

3   OR 27, pt. 2, 643; William Judkins Narrative, Sarah Hightower Regional Library, Georgia Folder, Georgia 22nd Volunteer Infantry, Box 27; photocopy in Robert Blake Collection, USAHEC.

Sensing an opportunity for decisive action, Hancock personally directed Capt. James Rorty's battery as its tubes sprayed iron into the massed Rebels. Although Wright's infantrymen had given up hauling away the three abandoned pieces of Weir's battery, they refused to leave the hard-won prizes. Instead, they stood gamely and absorbed the punishment Rorty's guns dished out. Wright's left wing had reached the rubble of an old stone wall about 100 yards south of the Copse of Trees, but they could not hold it. They were now slowly falling back, fighting as they retreated. Off the right of these Georgians, Colonel Lang's Floridians were already streaming to the rear.[4]

A few hundred men from the right flank of the 3rd Georgia and most of the 22nd Georgia managed to reach the lower western brow of Cemetery Ridge, with the crest but a handful of yards distant. This advanced position placed them in front of but below the massed survivors from Codori's farmyard, the 15th Massachusetts and 82nd New York. To their immediate right and rear, the 20th Massachusetts, its excited soldiers shouting "Fredericksburg!" loudly above the din of battle, charged through Lieutenant Perrin's brace of 1st Rhode Island smoothbores south of the Copse of Trees in a sudden counterattack that further severed Wright's brigade, leaving its two wings unable to support one another. The separation and disorganization that began along the Emmitsburg Road earlier in the assault was now complete. Seeing their comrades in the "left wing" retiring, many Georgians on the left side of the "right wing" also began pulling back, leaving the fragmented survivors to deal with the stubborn Yankees to their front. The final minutes of Anderson's assault were at hand.[5]

The men in blue, their numbers increasing with each passing minute as men rallied on the flags and officers, sensed victory as they stood their ground. Of the original number that had battled along the Emmitsburg Road, no one knows how many soldiers from the 15th Massachusetts and 82nd New York faced back atop the low ridge and rejoined the fight. The commonly estimated number of 400 may be exaggerated, but if one considers the survivors from other regiments joining their ranks, 400 may be a low estimate. The Federal infantrymen stood 40 yards above what was left of 3rd and 22nd Georgia and 2nd Battalion, the latter scattered over a wide area. The elevation and gathering darkness came into play, with both sides mostly firing either too high or too low.[6]

4 Ibid.

5 Ibid., pt. 1, 436-45, W. S. Hancock to Humphreys, March 11, 1876, Philadelphia, HSP, Humphreys Papers, Box 27; MRC 39077G2; *Bachelder Maps, Second Day.*

6 Ibid. MRC 39077G2; *Bachelder Maps, Second Day.*

How many rounds Rorty's gunners delivered during this late phase of the fighting is not known. What is known is that Wright's advance below that battery had been stopped. The charismatic Second Corps commander, who this day lived up to his nickname "Hancock the Superb," wasted no time distributing orders to Colonel Randall after learning a portion of his fresh 13th Vermont, part of Brig. Gen. George Stannard's brigade of New Englanders, was but a few minutes away. Pointing toward Weir's overrun half-battery, Hancock explained to Randall what needed to be done. Fate would call upon Randall's Vermonters to play one of the final most dramatic acts in defense of Cemetery Ridge.[7]

Organized on October 27, 1862, the Second Vermont Brigade consisted of the 12th, 13th, 14th, 15th, and 16th regiments, all nine-month volunteers whose obligation would expire just weeks after Gettysburg. Numbering more than 3,000 men, all five regiments were initially assigned to the defense of Washington, D. C. Other than a small brush on December 29 near Fairfax Courthouse with Jeb Stuart's marauding Confederate cavalry, the Vermont men would see no combat until March 9, 1863, when John S. Mosby's partisan rangers attacked some of them during the night at the same location, capturing Brig. Gen. Edwin H. Stoughton who was then in command of the brigade.[8]

Assuming command in Stoughton's absence, George Stannard returned the men to mundane picket duty around Washington, which ended when orders arrived at 6:00 p.m. on June 23 to prepare to move his brigade. The next morning, he withdrew his pickets and marched north toward Union Mills, in Fairfax County, Virginia. Two days later Stannard was ordered to report to the Army of the Potomac as it moved north after General Lee's Virginia army. The Vermont Brigade was huge, numbering 3,328 rifles with 160 officers of varying ranks, and essentially green. The next six days pushed these troops to the limit with frustratingly long and exhausting marches.[9]

Stannard received orders about 8:45 a.m. on July 1 to take three regiments and join Reynolds' First Corps as part of Abner Doubleday's division. Detaching the 12th and 15th Vermont to guard the supply trains, Stannard led the balance of his brigade from their bivouac near Poolesville, Maryland, northward picking there way through a road jammed with every type of wagon train imaginable. Long hours

7   Ibid., 351, 371; USGS MRC 39077G2; *Bachelder Maps, Second Day. Bachelder Papers*, 1:50-51; *OR* 27, pt. 1, 349;

8   Howard Coffin, *Nine Months to Gettysburg: Stannard's Vermonters and the Repulse of Pickett's Charge* (Woodstock, VT, 1997).

9   Stannard diary entry for June 25, 1863; *Bachelder Papers*, 1:50-51; *OR* 27, pt. 1, 349; *Atlas to Accompany the Official Records of the Union and Confederate Armies* (Washington, 1891-1895), see Plates 136 and 137.

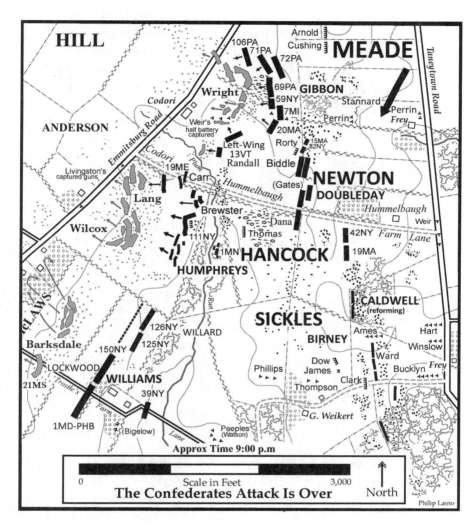

The Confederates Attack Is Over

of marching followed that eventually carried the command to within a few miles of Gettysburg, where the men could see hazy clouds of drifting battle smoke off to the north and northeast. Leaving his column in the hands of Colonel Randall, Stannard rode ahead and reported to division commander Doubleday atop Cemetery Hill around 6:30 p.m. It was probably here he learned Reynolds was dead and that Doubleday had assumed command of the First Corps.[10]

Stannard rode back and met his regiments as they drew near Cemetery Ridge. Arriving between sometime between 6:30 and 7:00 p.m., he bivouacked his troops

10 Ibid.; *Bachelder Maps, Second Day.*

west of the Taneytown Road in Sarah Patterson's Woods while General Ward's arriving Second Brigade, First Division, Third Corps took possession atop the crest 400 yards above Stannard. The commands had arrived from opposite directions causing no complicated decisions and redeployment. Stannard wrote, "We reached the battlefield too late in the day to take part in the hard-contested battle of July 1, and my tired troops upon their arrival were placed in position in column by regiments on the front line, in connection with the Third Army Corps (Ward)." With his left initially placed in Patterson's Woods, Stannard's three regiments (13th, 14th, 16th) stretched northward beyond some distance, with his right resting beyond Hummelbaugh's farm lane.[11]

"I was detailed," Stannard continued, "per order of Major-General Slocum, as general field officer, and met Major–General Meade, in company with Major-General Howard, near my command about 3:00 a.m. of the 2d instant." The exact subject of their conversation is not known, although troop dispositions and strengths likely were among the topics discussed. Stannard's 1,944 riflemen remained as they arrived, unseen from the west as dawn came and went. "On the morning of the 2d instant," Stannard continued, "we were allowed to join the First Army Corps (thus after the Second arrived), and reported to Major-General Doubleday, agreeably on previous orders, and were placed in rear of the left of Cemetery Hill." Moving into the swale housing the Catherine Guinn farm 400 yards north and east of army headquarters, Stannard's brigade was deployed fronting north in battalions by brigade.[12]

Although he was relieved of command from the First Army Corps, General Doubleday still commanded his division, to which Stannard's brigade now belonged. After redeploying his troops and allowing them to rest, Stannard and Doubleday rode to the crest of Cemetery Hill, where the division commander explained the bigger picture to his new brigade leader. The ride to the front was "to calculate the manner of defense if attacked," recalled Stannard. "We rode to the [Cemetery] hill, and then a Captain of Artillery, requested we dismount as it was very unsafe to ride in that locality." Stannard's New Englanders were already suffering the effects of enemy rounds intended for Cemetery Ridge (Zeigler's Grove). All three of Stannard's regiments at one time or another had to shift positions in Guinn's swale in an attempt to gain better cover. Leaving Stannard atop the hill to watch the affairs, Doubleday sent Colonel Randall's right wing, about half of the 13th Vermont, up the Taneytown Road while Lt. Col. William Munson's five companies assumed a new position east of the avenue directly across

---

11 OR 27, pt. 1, 349 *Bachelder Maps, Second Day.*

12 Ibid. *Bachelder Papers,* 1: 53

the street from Zeigler's Woods. Taking cover behind the low wall, Munson and his men endured artillery fire that proved largely harmless. Colonel Randall himself stayed near the Guinn house in command of his regiment's right wing's five companies.[13]

Randall's right wing was resting under stacked arms 300 yards east of the Taneytown Road, behind (east of) Catherine Guinn's farmhouse, while Munson's five left wing companies rested opposite Zeigler's Grove. Munson's men could see Col. Orland Smith's three regiments to their immediate right hunkering behind the wall west of the Taneytown Road, their skirmishers active along the Emmitsburg Road and Broad Open Plain beyond. General John Robinson's division of the First Corps was also visible to the west across the avenue in Zeigler's Grove. Munson's men could not see Colonel Randall's five right wing companies back in Guinn's swale. In other words, the regiment was now firmly fragmented into two distinct wings, Randall's right and Munson's left, with the 14th and 16th Vermont regiments well to the rear.[14]

Stannard had been patiently overseeing the field when Confederate gunners opened the ball around 4:00 p.m. As much as he wanted to be with his command, the general remained where Doubleday had placed him as the artillery duel turned into a major northward rolling infantry attack off in the distant south and Ewell's troops attacked Culp's Hill. "About this time, say 6:30 o'clock," he recalled, "the fight was immense on both the right and left flank. I was fearful that the day was going to prove too short to affect anything decisive."[15]

While Generals Hancock and Gibbon saw to their immediate front below West Cemetery Ridge, General Meade had just returned to army headquarters after having discussed reinforcements and strategy with General Williams. There, Meade ran into horse artillerist Capt. John C. Tidball, who had volunteered his services to General Tyler, commander of Hunt's Reserve Artillery. The captain had witnessed the breakdown of Sickles' Third Corps and much of Hancock's Second Corps, and was at that moment on an errand seeking artillery reinforcements. Tidball knew

---

13 OR 27, pt. 1, 351; MRC 39077G2; *Bachelder Maps, Second Day.*

14 Ibid; Stannard diary entry for June 30, 1863; *Bachelder Papers,* 1:53-54; MRC 39077G2; *Bachelder Maps, Second Day.* At some point before noon five companies from Col. Redfield Proctor's 15th Vermont reached the front (Stannard had detached the regiment for guard duty). Stannard, however, did not receive word of their arrival, and because of an unexplained foul-up, this command was not available to participate in that evening's battle atop East Cemetery Hill. OR 27, pt. 1, 349; Stannard diary entry for June 30, 1863; *Bachelder Papers,* 1:53-54; MRC 39077G2; *Bachelder Maps, Second Day.*

15 Ibid. At some point, he sent one rider galloping down the hill with orders for Col. Wheelock G. Veazey, commanding the 16th Vermont nearest the Baltimore Pike, to send one company to the Eleventh Corps.

there was an ample supply of infantry (Doubleday's division, First Corps) a few hundred yards to the north and suggested using them. Meade agreed before riding off to inspect the danger zone. Within minutes First Corps leaders General Newton sent orders to Doubleday and Brig. Gen. John C. Robinson (commanding the Second Division) to send all available troops to support the embattled Hancock.[16]

When the orders to move reached him, Doubleday notified his brigadiers and also spurred his horse past the Guinn house toward the action west of Cemetery Ridge. After spending a few moments surveying the endangered front from somewhere near the Copse of Trees, the general spun his horse around and spurred it back east.[17] "At this time an officer, whom I did not know at that moment, but proved to be General Doubleday, came galloping over the hill from General Hancock's position, and approached my regiment," Colonel Randall later recalled. "After having found what regiment we were, and making a few inspiring remarks to my men, he directed me to take my regiment in the direction from which he had come, and report to General Hancock, whom I would find there and hard pressed, and said he feared he would lose his artillery or some of it before I could get there." Randall requested time to consolidate his fragmented companies with Lt. Col. William Munson's left-half of the regiment, but Doubleday refused. There was no time to do so, he replied, but he would see to it that Munson and his missing companies followed Randall.[18]

When Doubleday inquired about the regiment's history, Colonel Randall replied that he was the only veteran. "Will your men fight?" asked the general. "Yes, I believe they will," replied Randall. Satisfied, the general rode up to the five companies as they fell in, gave them a short pep talk, and ordered Randall to move out. "I started, riding ahead of my regiment [5 companies] to meet General Hancock and find where I was needed, so as to be able to place my men in position without exposing them too long under fire." Doubleday, meanwhile, continued east up the swale collecting the balance of his scattered division while at the same time sending an aide to locate Munson's detached wing. A short time after Colonel Randall departed, General Stannard arrived and Doubleday ordered him to move the balance of his brigade to support Hancock.[19]

16 John C. Tidball to Newton, March 31, 1882, Meade Collection, HSP; OR 27, pt. 1, 258, 290, 294, 308; Pfanz, *Gettysburg, The Second Day*, 415.

17 OR 27, pt. 1, 261; Pfanz, *Gettysburg, The Second Day*, 416. Coddington, *Gettysburg: A Study in Command*, 300-301.

18 Ibid., pt. 1, 351.

19 Stannard diary entry for July 2, 1863; *Bachelder Papers,* 1:154; George H. Scott, "Vermont at Gettysburg," *Proceedings of the Vermont Historical Society*, vol. 1, 1930, 51-74.

Stannard's Vermonters, less Randall's five companies, had reassembled and fallen in behind a pair of Doubleday's understrength brigades. The first was Brig. Gen. Thomas A. Rowley's under the temporary command of Col. Theodore B. Gates, 80th New York (plus Capt. Walter L. Owens' 151st Pennsylvania). Together they numbered fewer than 400 soldiers. The second brigade was Col. Roy Stone's command, now under Col. Edmund L. Dana of the 143rd Pennsylvania. Aside from his own 143rd, Dana had with him the survivors of the 149th and 150th Pennsylvania regiments—all told perhaps 350 men. Doubleday placed himself at the head of Dana's leading column and Gates and Stannard brought up the rear.[20]

Colonel Randall, meanwhile, reported to General Hancock. "As I reached the ridge or highest ground between the cemetery and Little Round Top Mountain," Randall recalled, "I met General Hancock, who was encouraging and rallying his men to hold on to the position. He told me the rebels had captured a battery [Weir's 5th U. S.] he had had there, and pointed out to me the way they had gone with it, and asked if I could retake it. I told him I could, and that I was willing to try. He told me it would be a hazardous job and he would not order it," he added, "but if I thought I could do it, I might try."[21] Randall's five companies ascended the rise east of where the 20th Massachusetts had just started its countercharge south of the Copse of Trees, and where Perrin's section of Napoleons was in battery. The Vermonters gained elevation as they angled past the rear of the reforming survivors of the 15th Massachusetts and 82nd New York.[22]

By this time the right wing of Confederate General Wright's brigade below the Union center was beginning to retire down the slope. Something unique was happening in this sector of the front. All (or nearly all) of the Confederate repulses thus far had unfolded from south to north as each brigade (first Barksdale, and then Wilcox and Lang) advanced, made contact, fought, and fell back. This was not true with Wright's brigade. The Georgia command, supported by a small group of Mississippians from Posey's brigade, began withdrawing near its center from north to south. The right flank of the 3rd Georgia, holding the center of Wright's brigade, was the first regiment to leave that sector when the 20th Massachusetts shot into it. When these Georgians of the 3rd started for the rear, the men of the 22nd Georgia

---

20 Osborne, *Holding the Left at Gettysburg*, 31; Coffin, *Nine Months to Gettysburg*. Coddington, *Gettysburg: A Study in Command*, 421

21 *OR* 27, pt. 1, 351; Hancock to Bachelder, November 7, 1885; *Bachelder Papers,* 2:1134. As with General Doubleday who had no knowledge of Randall or the 13th Vermont when they met, Hancock would later inquire, "What regiment of Vermont Troops were those I met on the evening of the second day? Reynolds I think was in command of the regiment that drew back the guns." Hancock's "Reynolds," of course, was Colonel Randall.

22 USGS MRC 39077G2; *Bachelder Maps, Second Day.*

on its right had no choice but to start back down the slope as well, firing as they retired. The 2nd Battalion on the right of the 22nd had by this time lost all cohesion. Its commander was down and most of its men were fighting alongside those from the 3rd and 22nd regiments, with just as many having been swept back with the 2nd Florida. Still, many of Wright's stubborn Georgia bulldogs refused to fully break or withdraw as had Wilcox's Alabamians and Lang's Floridians. Isolated pockets of resistance continued along the length of Wright's line with no chance of success. But there they stood, kneeled, or lay, loading and firing in bunches without much if any order or cohesion.[23]

Although the reformed Union fugitives from General Gibbon's skirmish lines east and higher on the ridge did not countercharge, they did stand firm and help the reforming 15th Massachusetts and 82nd New York hold back the gray tide. Gibbon rode amongst the men exhorting them to hold as the Georgians stubbornly clung to whatever cover they could find. The real damage to the men in gray at this time was inflicted from Gibbon's left; it came not from small arms fire, but from Captain Rorty's four Parrott Rifles belching load after load of canister. The only men dressed in blue guarding the Union center there behind Rorty's guns anchoring the Second Corps' true left flank were wounded, stragglers, and one solitary general sitting his horse overseeing the bloody chaos. Few realized it was the commander of the entire army. Although General Meade had picked up several aides on his ride west after conversing with Captain Tidball, he was now alone, watching the action and waiting for the reinforcements Tidball had been sent to fetch.[24]

Meade had been there but a few moments when his good friend John Newton joined him atop the low crest. With chaos and uncertainty raining around them, the calm Newton offered his superior a swig from his flask. The generals were sitting on their mounts discussing their options when an enemy round exploded in front of them, showering the pair with earth and debris. Steadying their horses, neither general offered a word or appeared shaken. When a lone rider approached with information that Doubleday was on his way with reinforcements, Meade whirled his horse "Old Baldy" around and, with Newton and staff in tow, sped off in the direction of the Taneytown Road.[25]

Colonel Randall, meanwhile, finished dressing his five companies 300 yards northwest of where Meade and Newton had shared a flask. Randall cantered his horse around one of his flanks and assumed position in front, sword firmly in hand.

---

23 OR 27, pt. 2, 364.

24 Paul Oliver to Meade, May 16, 1882, Meade Collection, HSP; Cleaves, *Meade of Gettysburg*, 152-53. USGS MRC 39077G2; *Bachelder Maps, Second Day*.

25 Ibid. OR 27, pt. 1, 116, 261.

"[I] instructed each captain as to what they were to do as they came on to the line," reported Randall, "and, taking my position to lead them, gave the order to advance." Hancock watched Randall's Vermonters step off with a rousing cheer in the wake of their colonel.[26]

By this time the head of Doubleday's column was moving up the eastern slope following the path Randall's right wing 13th Vermont had recently traversed. At some point during the advance General Rowley, the commander of the brigade temporarily under Colonel Gates' command, had joined Doubleday at the head of the column. Rowley had been away tending to official business when Doubleday's column moved out, which is why Gates was in command. Whatever the reason, Rowley did not ride back to reassume command, choosing instead to ride with Doubleday at the head of the column. It was a mistake he would live to regret. Shortly after passing over the Taneytown Road, hordes of fleeing fugitives and walking wounded passed through the gap between Dana's leading brigade and Gates' trailing columns, forcing Gates to stop or be swept away.[27]

"We left our camp at the base of cemetery hill, crossed the Taneytown road, and were marching parallel with the road when a portion of the troops [Second Corps fugitives] engaged passed through our brigade," explained Captain Owens of the 151st Pennsylvania. "[I]nstead of following Rowley [at the head of Dana's leading brigade with Doubleday], we marched by the right file to the top of the hill and occupied a position on the front line of battle. It seems to me that when we moved up to the top of the hill and found ourselves lost that we started back," Owens added, "and were stopped and asked to take our position in front as above stated, but who it was who stopped us I cannot tell."[28]

Colonel Gates and Captain Owens missed out on the front-line heroics of Generals Meade and Newton, who on their ride back toward the Taneytown Road encountered Doubleday and Rowley leading Dana's three small regiments. If anyone realized the 80th New York and 151st Pennsylvania had been cleaved away and were now 200 yards north moving west up the slope, there was no time to wait. Motioning Doubleday's column forward, Meade uncovered his head, waved his hat and shouted, "Come on gentlemen!" An exuberant chorus of "Hurrah!" greeted his enthusiasm. The trio of generals and Colonel Dana moved to the top of the crest followed by the cheering troops while Rowley rode north to locate Colonel Gates

---

26 OR 27, pt. 1, 351

27 OR 27, pt. 1, 318; Gates to Bachelder, January 30, 1884, *Bachelder Papers,* 1:83-84. Osborne, *Holding the Left at Gettysburg,* 31-34.

28 Walter Owens to Bachelder, August 6, 1866, *Bachelder Papers,* 1:268-69. Rowley's remaining two regiments, the 121st and 142nd Pennsylvania, remained in Zeigler's Grove.

and his missing regiments. Fortunately for the Northerners, the tide had turned during the several minutes that had passed since Meade and Newton had watched the action from their saddles.[29]

The officer who had stopped Gates and Owens from continuing south to rejoin Doubleday was none other than General Gibbon, who placed the 80th New York and 151st Pennsylvania in position just north of where General Meade had just led Dana's brigade over the crest. Gates led his demi-brigade (pair of regiments) and swept the area, clearing all resistance left in the wake of Randall's five companies that were at this time under fire well to the front. Gates and some of his men returned to Cemetery Ridge almost immediately with a few prisoners in hand. Gates later recalled accurately the complicated terrain and how the area along the Emmitsburg road was "occupied by the enemy."[30]

Colonel Dana's small command, meanwhile, passed over the crest undisturbed for the most part by small arms fire as it angled west by southwest toward the Hummelbaugh farm lane, scooping up prisoners too fagged to head back to Seminary Ridge. Dana's advance helped fortify that part of the front and was more of a mopping up operation because Colonel Randall's right wing and General Carr's small command off to the west and south had already cleared the area. Leaving Newton to organize the action in conjunction with Hancock, Meade hurried back east and Doubleday began aligned men atop the crest as a reserve.[31]

Doubleday's alignment atop Cemetery Ridge during the final moments of Wright's repulse was, from left to right (south to north): Capt. Cornelius C. Widdis's 150th Pennsylvania, Lt. Col. John D. Musser's 143rd Pennsylvania, and Owens' 151st Pennsylvania. Gates' 80th New York was to the right, and Captain James Glenn's tattered 149th Pennsylvania behind the 151st All of these commands—manning the dead center of the entire Union center—numbered fewer than 700 men.[32]

General Stannard's brigade, meanwhile, arrived within minutes of Gates and Dana and was placed in reserve atop the crest, aligned from left to right (south to north): Col. William T. Nichols' 14th Vermont, Col. Wheelock Veazey's 16th

29 Paul Oliver to Meade, May 16, 1882, Meade Collection, HSP.

30 Gates to Bachelder, January 30, 1884, *Bachelder Papers,* 1:83-84, OR 27, pt. 1, 318.

31 OR 27, pt. 1, 318, 336. John F. Krumwiede, *Disgrace at Gettysburg: The Arrest and Court-martial of Brigadier General Thomas A. Rowley, USA.* (Jefferson, NC, 2006). Although Rowley resumed command from Gates, Col. Chapman Biddle, who commanded the brigade on July 1, once again replaced the ailing general later that night. Rowley suffered from large boils on the inside of his thighs that became infected on the march to Gettysburg. He may well have been feverish on July 2 and under a doctor's care.

32 USGS MRC 39077G2; *Bachelder Maps.*

Vermont to his right and rear, and Lieutenant Colonel Munson's left wing behind and overlapping both. Upon his return from the base of the ridge, Colonel Veazey recalled the 16th Vermont's arrival and placement. "When the brigades came up to the batteries [Rorty and Perrin] on the crest of the elevation, I saw no support with them. Here we encountered a severe cannonading and several men from the 16th were killed while supporting a battery [Rorty]. Soon after the enemy's lines had been driven back and the firing had subsided." What he did not address was the reason those batteries atop the crest appeared unsupported. By the time Veazey arrived, Lieutenant Colonel Macy's 20th Massachusetts had, with help from Hancock's reformed line north of Rorty, swept back the entire right wing of the 3rd Georgia and most if not all of the 22nd Georgia. What was left of the 2nd Georgia Battalion followed suit. All that remained was the right portion of Wright's brigade, where a few diehards held onto Weir's overrun guns and limbers just south of the Codori's barn. Stannard at this time was more worried about Colonel Randall and his five missing companies than he was about the beaten enemy: "I was at this time much annoyed at not knowing where he was, and sent every way to find him."[33]

As noted, the unraveling of Ambrose Wright's line of Georgians from north to south signaled the end of the high water mark of their attack. For a few brief moments a handful of his men had pierced the lightly defended Union line south of the Copse of Trees, but not a man reached the physical crest or any of the Union batteries, including Lieutenant Perrin's redeployed section that had swung back into action 40 yards northeast of the breakthrough. The men of Webb's and Hall's brigades, supported by others from Harrow's command, completed the mopping up of Wright's remnants. Gibbon's troops reclaimed all the lost ground including Codori's blood-soaked farm and orchard, where they surrounded and captured 265 officers and men from the 48th Georgia.[34]

We last left Colonel Randall and five companies moving forward into action just minutes before the arrival of Doubleday's command. Riding ahead of his line, Randall had traveled but a short distance when, near Plum Run, a pocket of Rebels concealed in the thickets opposite the run stood and delivered an unexpected volley. The rounds zipped through the left flank of the 13th Vermonters. "At this time my horse was killed, and I fell to the ground with him," Randall wrote. "While on the ground, I discovered a rebel line debauching from the woods [Plum Run

---

33 Ibid. Gates to Bachelder, January 30, 1864, *Bachelder Papers,* 1:84; Wheelock Veazey to Bachelder, undated letter, *Bachelder Papers,* 1:58-59l; Stannard diary, July 2, 1863; *Bachelder Papers,* 1:154.

34 Ward, *History of the One Hundred and Sixth Regiment Pennsylvania Volunteers,* 192-94. General Alexander Hays' troops had pitched in and helped throw back Posey's 48th and 19th Mississippi regiments, which had helped unhinge Wright's left.

thicket] on our left, and forming substantially across our track about 40 rods away. We received one volley from them, which did us very little injury, when my men sprang forward with the bayonet with so much precipitancy that they appeared to be taken wholly by surprise, and threw down themselves down in the grass, surrendering, and we passed over them." The Confederates were Floridians from Lang's 2nd regiment (and possibly a handful from the 2nd Georgia Battalion) who had found themselves isolated north of the 19th Maine and Carr's brigade when those two units countercharged past them. Lang's order to withdraw didn't reach them, so they hunkered down northeast of Plum Run and took to firing from behind rocks and brush.[35]

When the Vermonters stopped momentarily opposite Plum Run to face this impediment, Hancock spurred his horse down the slope "and told me to press on for the guns and he would take care of the prisoners," recalled Randall, "which he did, and we continued our pursuit of the guns." The colonel detached Capt. John Lonergan's Company A toward the Codori barn and Weir's trio of captured Napoleons. "My company reached the guns first," recorded Captain Lonergan proudly, "and placing my hand upon the nearest gun, I ordered the enemy to surrender. All this time the whole regiment was under severe fire, with men falling all along the entire charge; but we reached the guns comparatively together and in good form. The Confederates obeyed my summons to surrender," he added, "after which my men lay down their guns and taking hold of the wheels of the gun carriages, began moving them to a new position where they could be utilized."[36]

Captain Lonergan and his men were indeed the first to reach Weir's guns, but there was no "severe fire" and men were not "falling all along the entire charge." In addition, the 106th Pennsylvania, supported by others, had already solidified its hold on the Codori farm and orchard, helping to protect Randall's small line as it drew near the Emmitsburg Road. Within moments of securing the three pieces, Colonel Randall arrived with the balance of his right wing. Randall took charge of the guns and detailed a few more men to stand over them and the prisoners. Once the area was secured, he redressed his line with Lonergan's Company A again anchoring the right.[37]

Captain B. C. McCurry of the 22nd Georgia, Wright's brigade, left a valuable account of this part of the action: "The regiment captured three pieces of cannon, but, owing to the brigade giving way on our right [2nd Florida], we were compelled

35 Scott, "Vermont at Gettysburg," 51-74.

36 Beyer and Keydel, *Deeds of Valor*, 226-28. Most of the Georgians escaped south of the barn as the 106th Pennsylvania of Webb's brigade closed from the north and east.

37 Ibid.; *OR* 27, pt. 1, 336.

to give back and abandon our captured booty." These Georgians paid a high price to spend a few minutes with three silent bronze guns. For example, the regiment stepped off that evening with seven captains, and McCurry was the only one to make it back to Seminary Ridge unscathed. It commander, Col. Joseph Wasden, lay mortally wounded somewhere along the Emmitsburg Road and scores of others had been killed, wounded, or were missing.[38]

Randall's five companies had swept past the right flank of Carr's demi-brigade south of Hummelbaugh's farm lane, and that of Heath's 19th Maine beyond that brigade's left. Colonel Heath's regiment was followed by Brewster's ragtag bunch, mixed in with MacDougall's 111th New York and other remnants of Humphreys' shattered division. All these commands settled down to an exchange of gunfire with Lang's and Wilcox's infantry retreating up the Emmitsburg Road Rise. Randall, meanwhile, spotted a pair of Napoleons straddling the Hummelbaugh farm lane intersection near where the headwaters of Plum Run seeped from beneath the Emmitsburg Road Rise. Randall mistook these guns to be Confederate, though in fact they were the late Lieutenant Livingston's captured guns from Turnbull's 3rd U. S. "We were very near the Emmitsburg road, and I advanced my line to the road, and sent my adjutant [James Peck] back to inform General Hancock of our position," explained Randall. "While he was gone, the rebels advanced two pieces of artillery into the road about 100 rods to the south of us, and commenced to shell us down the road."[39]

Lonergan's Company A was the closest to the piece above (north of) the lane. With muskets leveled and bayonets gleaming, the men charged southwest across the ascending meadow, up the low embankment, and through and over the partially dismantled fence paralleling the pike. Instead of cutting the unruly teams out of their traces and hauling the cannon off by hand, as the Floridians had attempted with a second piece south of the lane, the Georgians holding the northern piece opted instead to use the surviving horses to do the work. It proved an ill-fated decision. According to Capt. Charles J. Moffett, who was now in command of the 2nd Georgia Battalion, "Major Ross was wounded near the brick house while endeavoring to turn the heads of the [captured] artillery horses toward our lines."[40]

With fixed bayonets, Randall's five companies ascended the Emmitsburg Road Rise at a slight right angle with Lonergan's right flank company the first to overrun the prize. A small but sharp struggle ensued that recaptured the gun. Colonel

---

38 OR 27, pt. 1, 352; pt. 2, 629.

39 Ibid. Adjutant Peck not only reported to Hancock, but found General Stannard as well, who was thrilled to learn the whereabouts and condition of Randall's detached companies.

40 Ibid., pt. 2, 629.

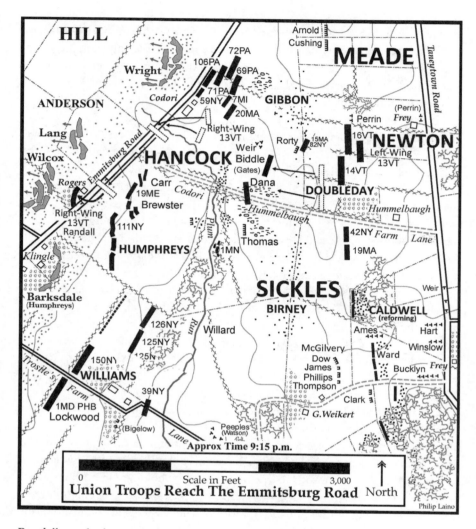

Union Troops Reach The Emmitsburg Road North

Approx Time 9:15 p.m.

Scale in Feet
0   3,000

Philip Laino

Randall cut the horses loose while detailing men to haul the piece back to Federal lines by hand. Once secured, Randall set his sights on the second piece 100 yards south of the intersection. In the distance 200 yards beyond this piece was the white-washed picket fence surrounding the Rogers house west of the road. Randall redressed his line for the fourth time, now fronting south by southwest down the Emmitsburg Road with Lonergan's company anchoring the right side to the roadway. Complete darkness but a quarter-hour away.[41]

41 Ibid., pt., 1, 349, 35; Beyer and Keydel, *Deeds of Valor,* 226-28. What is strange about the above incident is that Maj. George W. Ross was seemingly more concerned with hauling a

This modern view looks northeast from the Peter Rogers house site west of the Emmitsburg Road. To the east, the Vermont State Monument pillar marks the general area from which Colonel Randall's 13th Vermont's right wing began its countercharge. Randall's men moved first on the Codori farm (left-distance) and then down the Emmitsburg Road to this point. Without suffering a single loss, the Vermonters captured 83 Confederates inside the home. The Vermonters also recovered five overrun Union artillery pieces, the last of which was just opposite the white picket fence pictured here paralleling the Emmitsburg Road. *Craig Swain*

With no limber or draft horses available, soldiers from the 2nd Florida physically manhandled Livingston's second piece by its prolonge and drag ropes, pulling it onto the road using the same gate south of the barn Major Ross's men had used in retreat. Once in the road, however, they outdistanced the Georgians and their terrified team trying to haul out the other piece. With most of his line east of and below the road, Randall's companies were subjected to some artillery fire.

captured gun back to his line of embarkation than continuing on with his regiment. It appears Ross was hit shortly after the capture of Livingston's guns. He likely fell as he attempted to turn the gun limber around at "Reverse Trot." Whatever occurred, it was unfortunate for Ross and the 2nd Battalion as his wounding may have helped with the premature demise and unraveling of his small regiment below the Union center.

Exhaustion, bloodshed, adrenalin, and darkness all conspired to lead Randall to believe that the sole gun ahead was the culprit dropping rounds into his ranks. In fact, the gunfire was from Alexander's and Eshleman's advanced artillery battalions bisecting the Emmitsburg Road from a position some 500 yards west of the Klingle farmyard.[42]

From the other side of the field, and at this distance, there was little left to see in the fading light of day. Still in his saddle, Porter Alexander continued directing his and Eshleman's fire into what he hoped were enemy formations. Many of the rounds exploded with deadly results, some within the ranks of Wright's survivors lingering below Cemetery Ridge. "The fuses of the flying shells looked like little meteors in the air," recalled Alexander. His earlier optimism of a significant victory had faded with the ebbing daylight. "It was evident that we had not finished the job," he continued, "and would have to make a fresh effort in the morning."[43]

Instead of rushing forward under the rain of shells, Randall "detached one company, and advanced them under cover of the road, dug way, and fences, with instructions to charge upon and seize those guns, which they did most gallantly." Sending Capt. Lewis L. Coburn's Company C south on the east of the road was harrowing in and of itself because of the smoke-filled twilight. No Union troops were known to be west of the elongated knoll, and the Federals atop the low rise along Plum Run were less than 300 yards away and did not know the men of Company C were friendly troops. Luckily, none of the units in Humphreys' reforming lines delivered a volley from the elongated knoll. To Randall's credit, his plan worked perfectly and the lone piece was recaptured without a fight.[44]

The men from Florida needed little coaxing to flee westward because they had had enough. Dealing with the Yankee countercharge that had driven them back with Wilcox's Alabamians had taken the enthusiasm out of their bellies, but being enfiladed from the north in the gathering darkness convinced them the fight was over and it was time to leave the field. Stumbling backward, what was left of the 2nd and 8th Florida regiments melted west across the Emmitsburg Road in the wake of Captain Gardner's exhausted 5th Florida survivors. Most of these men passed through the Rogers orchards north and south of the farmyard, disappearing into the protective swale. The sole Napoleon was left intact, surrounded by the debris of

---

42 OR 27, pt. 1, 352.

43 Gallagher, *Fighting For the Confederacy*, 240; OR 27, pt. 2, 430; Alexander, "The Great Charge and Artillery Fighting at Gettysburg," *B&L*, Vol. 3, 360.

44 OR 27, pt. 1, 352; USGS MRC 39077G2; *Bachelder Maps, Second Day*. It is conceivable that Randall sent couriers back toward Carr and Humphreys with a request to hold their fire because his command was to their immediate front, though there is no evidence this was done.

battle including dead and wounded from both armies. As it turned out, the explosion and flashes Randall had mistaken for artillery fire came from gunpowder and exploding ordnance from a pair of smoldering limbers beyond the Napoleon in farmer Klingle's apple orchard. The limbers had been abandoned by Lt. James Seeley's Battery K, 4th U. S. About 90 minutes earlier.[45]

The only notable resistance left was coming from the Rogers farm, where Rebel riflemen had barracked themselves inside the clapboard house. Hancock's request for Colonel Randall to secure Weir's three guns had evolved into a prolonged series of actions where everything seemed to go just right. Redressing his troops yet again, Randall's line moved out toward the Rogers house, his left wing wheeling slightly to the right-oblique to close up and pass over the road. The clash proved to be more than a simple mopping-up operation. Within a couple minutes, the five Vermont companies were flying their colors opposite the white picket fence surrounding the house and yelling for the Rebels inside to surrender.[46]

Once again, Captain Lonergan's company was the first on the scene north of the house. "I noticed that we were sustaining much damage from firing that came from the Codories [Rogers] House in our front," he explained in a report that would help make him a Medal of Honor recipient. "And so ordering my command to pick up their guns, we made a charge of the house. We quickly surrounded the building, the men at once covering the windows and doors with their guns, so that no man should escape. Then I stepped to the front door, and knocking it in, I ordered: 'Surrender! Fall out here, every damned one of you!'"[47]

With Company A in control of the house and Colonel Randall organizing a defensive perimeter, the fate of the defenders was sealed. "My order was obeyed almost instantly," continued Lonergan, "for the Confederates came tumbling out, led by their commanding officer, until we had eighty-three men as prisoners. The officer in command handed me his sword and each man laid down his gun until I had a considerably larger number of men as prisoners, than I had in my entire command." While the Vermonters organized the sizeable surrender, Hancock and Humphreys organized a defensive line stretching from Colonel Randall's position east to Humphreys' rejuvenated command on the elongated knoll beyond the Codori farm. "When all was over for the day," mused Captain Lonergan, "General Stannard sent for me, and upon my arrival, he said: 'Captain, you did well to-day, but do you know you violated all military laws in capturing those prisoners in the Codories [Rogers] House?' 'How is that, General?' I asked. 'Why,' replied the

45 Ibid., 553.

46 Ibid.; Beyer and Keydel, *Deeds of Valor,* 226-28.

47 Ibid.

general with a smile, 'you know that in forming a company line, the command is, 'fall in!' and at the Codories [Rogers] House you said, 'fall out.' I saw the joke and answered: 'Yes, General, but they were already in, and so had to 'fall out.'"[48]

"We also captured the rebel picket reserve, consisting of 3 officers and 80 men, who had concealed themselves in a [Rogers] house near by," read Randall's more prosaic account. In fact, these Rebels were not pickets but front-line troops who had either sought shelter there during the advance, or refuge during the retreat. Randall sent several couriers back to Hancock asking for further orders. Unsure what to make of Randall's insistence that his command had captured two enemy guns, Hancock suggested he pull back to Cemetery Ridge, leaving General Humphreys the responsibility of setting up the defense. "In the pursuance of orders from General Hancock, we now slowly fell back to the main line of battle," reported Randall. "It was dark, and no further operations took place on our part of the line."[49]

Randall's newly ordained veterans picked their way back toward Cemetery Ridge past a scene of destruction and carnage. A team was sent from each company to scour the ground for fallen Vermonters over which the 13th had just charged, joining hundreds of other men from various commands searching for friends and caring for the wounded. Once back on Cemetery Ridge, Randall reported to General Stannard. The 14th Vermont detached a large number of men for picket duty along the Emmitsburg Road. Finally reunited with Munson's left wing, Randall's five companies were heralded as heroes lucky enough to have "seen the elephant." Randall not only turned Weir's repatriated three cannon over to Lt. Homer Baldwin and Sgt. Henry Menard of Battery C, 5th U. S., but also the brace of smoothbores belonging to Lieutenant Davidson's section. On July 4, without checking sources, Stannard mistakenly reported, "Four guns of the [Weir's] battery [C] were retaken, and two rebel field pieces." Of course, there were no Rebel guns lost that day. Southern guns or not, Randall's five companies performed brilliantly, above and beyond what Hancock had asked them to do.[50]

Together with Newton, meanwhile, General Meade placed General Robinson's First Corps regiments as they appeared. Colonel Richard Coulter, now in command of Brig. Gen. Gabriel Paul's brigade, was definite about the time his units arrived. "About 7 o'clock in the evening were moved farther to the left, to support the operations of the Third Corps, in which we were subjected to a

---

48 Ibid.; USGS MRC 39077G2; *Bachelder Maps, Second Day.*

49 Albert Clark, "Hancock and the Vermont Brigade," *Journal of the Military Service Institute,* Vol. 48, No. 170, 226-27; *OR* 27, pt. 1, 352.

50 *OR* 27, pt. 1, 380; *Bachelder Papers,* 1:55.

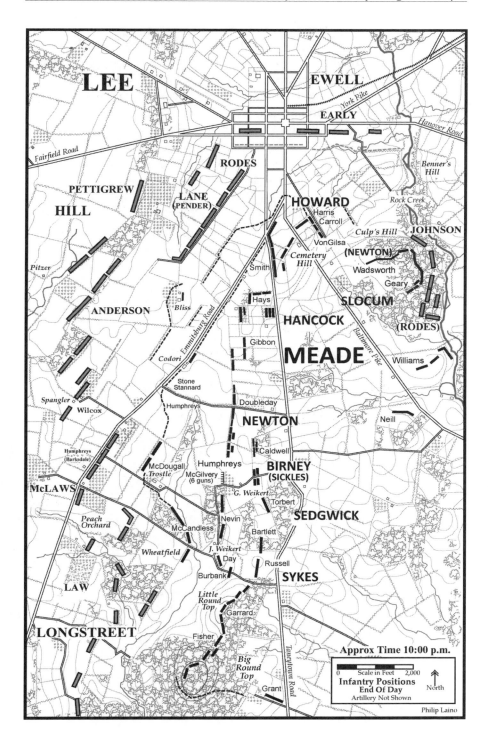

LEE

EWELL

York Pike

EARLY

Hanover Road

Fairfield Road

Benner's Hill

RODES

Rock Creek

PETTIGREW

HILL

LANE
(PENDER)

HOWARD

Harris
Carroll

VonGilsa

Culp's Hill

JOHNSON
(NEWTON)

Wadsworth

Pitzer

Smith

Cemetery
Hill

Geary

Bliss

ANDERSON

Hays

SLOCUM

HANCOCK

(RODES)

Codori

Gibbon

MEADE

Baltimore Pike

Williams

Stone
Stannard

Spangler

Wilcox

Humphreys

Doubleday

NEWTON

Neill

Humphreys
(Barksdale)

McDougall
Trostle

Humphreys

McGilvery
(6 guns)

Caldwell

BIRNEY
(SICKLES)

McLAWS

G. Weikert

Torbert

SEDGWICK

Peach
Orchard

McCandless

Nevin

Bartlett

Wheatfield

J. Weikert
Day

Russell

LAW

Burbank

SYKES

Little
Round
Top

Garrard

Tanceytown Road

LONGSTREET

Fisher

Big
Round
Top

Grant

Approx Time 10:00 p.m.

0   Scale in Feet   2,000

Infantry Positions
End Of Day
Artillery Not Shown

North

Philip Laino

considerable artillery fire, with some loss; which duty being accomplished, we returned [Zeigler's Grove area]." Porter Alexander's choice to fire blindly northeast after dark found a few victims, though had no impact on the battle's outcome.[51]

By 7:30 p.m. the Union center was finally stabilized, even though a fitful light patter of firing continued on for perhaps another 20 or 30 minutes. With little else to do there, a thankful Meade retired to his headquarters while off to the northeast, heavy fighting was still underway as Edward Johnson's division attacked Culp's Hill, and two of Jubal Early's brigades assaulted East Cemetery Hill. Within half an hour of its arrival, Robinson's division was returned north to Zeigler's Grove. Hancock and Newton believed they had enough troops on hand to handle whatever issue might arise.

The battle for the Union center had come to an end, at least for now. Eighteen hours later, another large and more direct thrust to pierce the middle of the Army of the Potomac would begin anew.

51 Ibid., 290, 294, 296, 298, 302.

"On every side lay stiffened cold bodies of our dead soldiers."

— *Captain Adolpho Fernandez Cavada*

The Cost of Combat

Other than handfuls of scattered rifle shots, most of them coming from the direction of Trostle's bloody trampled meadows south of the Klingle house, and the occasional deep-throated boom of an artillery piece, the intense firing along the Union center on Cemetery Ridge subsided by about 8:00 p.m. Long before the main combat came to a fitful halt west of the embattled ridge on July 2, however, scores of stretcher-bearers were busy checking bodies, serving the wounded, and removing the non-ambulatory injured.

Sergeant John Plummer of the 1st Minnesota recalled that, prior to his regiment's charge that evening, "Ambulances and the Ambulance men were brought up near the lines, and stretchers gotten ready for use, who of us could tell but that he would be the first to need them?" Hundreds of men joined the stretcher -bearers, many of the whom were drawn from the ranks of musicians and other noncombatants to succor the fallen, comrade and foe alike. According to Adjutant James S. Brown of the 126th New York, "Some of the officers and men were, by special permission, employed assisting the surgeons in hunting for the dead and wounded."

The dead and maimed who fell during the long fight for the Union center on Cemetery Ridge stretched from where Capt. William T. Haskell, commanding General McGowan's South Carolina Sharpshooters in the center of the Broad Open Plain, died, south to where Maj. George W. Ross of the 2nd Georgia Battalion of Wright's brigade lay mortally wounded along the Emmitsburg Road near the Codori barn—and beyond to the Trostle Lane, where Lt. Adolphus Werner of Company C, 39th New York, rested uncomfortably with a lead bullet lodged deeply in his chest. The entire battlefield below Cemetery Ridge a good mile north to south and east to west was nothing but one giant grisly scene of human carnage and debris.[1]

The scene on the crest and gentle slope of Cemetery Ridge was terrible, but the carnage in the Plum Run ravine and adjacent fields defied description. Bodies by the thousands lay along the Emmitsburg Road Rise from the Millerstown Road north all the way to the Washington-Taneytown Street intersection below Cemetery Hill. In just one small sector of the battlefield, for example, more than 1,000 wounded and dead choked the length of the Plum Run ravine from the Trostle's farm north to the farmer-butcher Codori's property.[2]

By twilight at about 8:00 p.m., the firing had stopped. Darkness combined with a sulfurous blanket of smoke to shroud the field, and an eerie quiet of a different sort descended upon the meadows, woods, orchards, and ravines.[3] The moon rose an hour past sunset, its yellow light casting a ghastly glow on fields full of grotesque shapes and shadows recognizable and otherwise.[4] More of these shadowy forms were moving than not, giving the landscape an eerie, crawling effect. The sounds of battle were replaced with what one soldier described as a "low, steady, indescribable moan" hailing from thousands of throats.[5]

Lanterns casting a reddish glow appeared, accompanied by the jingling of ambulance wagons moving slowly along and below Cemetery Ridge, often crushing the dead beneath their grinding wheels. The dead would have to wait. "Nothing could have been more dismal and appalling then searching over a battle-field in the dark night for a friend or comrade," another soldier from the 126th New York of Willard's brigade later recalled. "To turn up one dead cold face after another to the glimmering light of a lantern, and see it marred with wounds and disfigured with blood and soil, the features, perhaps, convulsed by the death agony, the eyes vacant

---

1　OR 27, pt. 2, 630. "In this charge we lost many valuable officers and men. Major Ross was wounded near the brick house while endeavoring to turn the heads of [the captured] artillery horses toward our lines." See also ibid., 661.

2　John Plummer to State Atlas (Minneapolis), August 26, 1863, Minnesota Historical Society, St. Paul; Mrs. Arabella M. Wilson, Prepared by the Historical Committee of the Regiment, *Disaster, Struggle, Triumph: The Adventures of 1000 "Boys in Blue"* (Albany, NY, 1870), 178.

3　Sunset on July 2, 1863, was at 7:00 p.m. and the end of civil twilight occurred at 8:13 p.m., *Gettysburg Almanac.*

4　Moonrise was at 8:46 p.m. The moon was 99% full, according to the *Gettysburg Almanac.*

5　Eric Ward, ed., *Army Life in Virginia, the Civil War Letters of George Grenville Benedict* (Mechanicsburg, PA, 2002), 169, quoted in Jeffry D. Wert, *Gettysburg: Day Three* (New York, NY, 2001), 31.

and staring. . . . Dismal, too, the sight of the dark battleground, with lanterns twinkling here and there, 'like the wisp on the morass!'"[6]

Pickets in both armies stepped aside to let these men through, regardless of uniform, their progress marked by the screams and groans of the wounded being moved. Some were so gravely hit they could not be moved or there was no reason to try. Their cries, once they discovered they were being left to their fate, were the most piteous of all. It would be a long and terrible night for the wounded as well as those charged with caring for them.

*   *   *

In the gathering darkness, the Union position at the Bliss farm remained undisturbed. General Gibbon established a strong skirmish line along the Emmitsburg Road as far west as the first worm fence where his men hunkered down for the night. General Carr likewise reset his brigade's picket line along the Emmitsburg Road after relieving Colonel Randall's 13th Vermont at the Peter Rogers farmhouse about 9:00 p.m. From there, the reformed Union line passed east over the Emmitsburg Road facing south, stretching southeast back through the northern reaches of Klingle meadows and the elongated rise west of Plum Run. From there, the line continued down the ravine to the Trostle farm and then southeast through the Trostle meadows and woods past the old Jacob Weikert homestead and the eastern reaches of the blood-soaked trampled Wheatfield. It continued its snake-like trail southeast to the vicinity of the Round Tops.[7]

Across the way to the west, the Confederates south of Gettysburg retained control of Seminary Ridge as well as the Spangler and Klingle farms south past the bloody Sherfy Peach Orchard all the way to present-day West Confederate Avenue. The Rebels also maintained their tenuous finger-holds on the Rose Woods, Houck's Ridge, Devil's Den, and Plum Run south to Devil's Gate and beyond. The town itself was still in Southern hands, as was every avenue leading to or from Gettysburg to the west, north, and east, though travel out the contested Hanover Road was still hazardous because of the guns on Cemetery Hill.

General James Lane, now in command of the mortally wounded Dorsey Pender's division, faced the darkened expanses of the Broad Open Plain knowing Pender's untimely demise had altered the unfolding of Lee's assault plan. Two fresh brigades within a stone's throw of the McMillan farm under Edward Thomas and William Mahone, both of Richard Anderson's division, A. P. Hill's Third Corps—a

6 Wilson, *1000 "Boys in Blue,"* 178.

7 *Bachelder Maps, Second Day.*

combined strength of 3,043 men—were not well utilized. One or both could have easily been shifted south to support Anderson's attack in a follow-up supporting column to exploit any lodgment or breakthrough. Instead, Thomas's command was deployed south and west of town on a front that would never be the objective of an enemy attack. Mired there in rigorous skirmishing, the Georgians suffered fairly heavily from small arms and artillery fire with 264 men in killed, wounded, and missing. Mahone's Virginia brigade, the hinge between Anderson's left and Pender's right, lost about 110 men from all causes without producing anything in return.

The failure of either Thomas or Mahone to cooperate with the brigades immediately south of them was not the direct responsibility of either commander. The blame rests with divisional and corps leadership. Both Thomas and Mahone (and presumably their staffs) watched as parts of Carnot Posey's brigade, preceded into action by the brigades of Wright, Lang, and Wilcox—all from Anderson's division—advanced as ordered, fought a desperate battle a mile or more to the east, and withdrew in bits and pieces back to the welcoming shelter atop Seminary Ridge. By nightfall, the only soldiers from Anderson's division east of the Emmitsburg Road were dead or in Union hands, wounded or otherwise. Farther south, the men of Lafayette McLaws' division remained largely east of the Emmitsburg Road, with William Barksdale's surviving Mississippians still holding the Klingle orchard and plank fence south to the Trostle's farm lane. The Confederates gained some ground that afternoon and evening, most of it at the southern end of the line, but none of it was of serious strategic value.

As General Longstreet had earlier worried and argued, taking the high ground along the Emmitsburg Road Rise was a waste of precious manpower. That particular tract of land was soon discovered to be unsuitable even as a kickoff location for the forthcoming day. Union artillery swept it clean to the point where Colonel E. P. Alexander, one of the Confederacy's top artillerists, refused to use it as an artillery platform. He would pull his guns installed along the Emmitsburg Road back under cover of a nearby swale. The Sherfy Peach Orchard offered little of value to Lee's Confederates. The failure to drive through the Yankees and take the Taneytown Road and Baltimore Pike proved disastrous. George Meade and his damaged but intact Army of the Potomac had not been broken and driven from the field as Lee hoped, and Meade wasn't going to retreat.

*   *   *

The total number of soldiers killed and wounded during all of the fighting on July 2 has been estimated at more than 15,000 for both armies. This includes Longstreet's entire assault (from Little Round Top up the line to the upper reaches of Cemetery Ridge), as well as the attacks on Culp's Hill on the Union right and East Cemetery Hill at nightfall. Of the three days of the battle, July 2 was the bloodiest of them all. A good percentage of these casualties, perhaps as many as one -quarter to one-third, were the result of the bitter fighting for the Union center held largely by Winfield Hancock's Second Corps.[8]

The number of Confederate losses sustained on July 2 is impossible to know with certainty, although some extraordinary research has and is being done in this area. Roll calls for many Confederate units did not occur until about a month after the battle, and for units engaged on more than one day of the three-day battle (and some were engaged on all three), there is no way to know exactly which day a man may have been lost other than if the information happens to be contained in a post-battle report or some other postwar reminiscence or writing. After-battle reports often failed to include the missing. Because the Union army held the field after the battle, Confederate records could not accurately reflect the fate of those left behind; whether they were killed, wounded, captured, or missing was often little more than a guess. With the tremendous loss of field and line officers over the three days, followed by the long retreat back to Virginia, the simple act of calling the roll was more than many units could manage. Further, there are few remaining post-Appomattox muster-out rolls for Confederate regiments engaged at Gettysburg on July 2. With that in mind, it is still possible to generate a rough estimate of the corps, brigade, and regimental losses of many of the units engaged in the July 2 assault on Dan Sickles' Third Corps and the Union center held by Hancock's men.

Longstreet fed two of his three divisions, one under John Bell Hood and the other under Lafayette McLaws, into the attack. Because Hood's went in on the far right, and none of his men had a direct influence on the Union center, his casualties are not germane to this study. McLaws's four-brigade division went into action with about 7,000 men and lost an estimated 2,200. Joe Kershaw's and William Barksdale's brigades, in particular, took heavy losses. A significant portion of these came from Union artillery, particularly from the massed batteries in the Peach Orchard, which blasted Kershaw's flank, and Freeman McGilvery's gun line, which shattered Barksdale's final advance.[9]

According to research conducted by J. David Petruzzi and Steven Stanley in their ground-breaking recent study *The Gettysburg Campaign in Numbers and Losses*,

---

8   Busey and Martin, *Regimental Strengths and Losses*, 183, 187, 293; *Bachelder Maps, Second Day*.

9   For a detailed examination of the casualties during the entire battle of Gettysburg and the overall campaign, see Petruzzi & Stanley, *The Gettysburg Campaign in Numbers and Losses*, 100-135. Longstreet's third division under George Pickett was not yet on the field.

Kershaw stepped off with 2,179 men and lost 669.[10] Caught in the devastating Union artillery barrage, which took them in the flank from the Trostle farm lane, they endured until Barksdale's Mississippians engaged and forced the Union gunners to pull back. Kershaw's after-battle report mourns the loss of many officers and men, but does not include specific casualty figures. Barksdale's brigade lost more than 700 of its 1,615 men, including the general himself, who was mortally wounded, captured, and died the next day. Estimates of his brigade losses range from 747 to as high as 804. William Wofford's brigade, which went into action behind and in support of Barksdale, lost at least 326 men out of 1,628 engaged. Paul Semmes' brigade, which went into the attack behind and in support of Kershaw's men, lost 385 of its 1,331 soldiers. Cabell's artillery battalion, which also was engaged on July 3, lost a total of 52 of 378 men—significant losses for an artillery command. Although McLaws' division remained in advanced positions through much of July 3, where it lost some men from skirmishing and stray rounds, nearly all of its infantry losses were suffered in the July 2 attack.[11]

Estimating the casualties on July 2 in Richard Anderson's division of A. P. Hill's Third Corps is somewhat more problematic. The brigades of Cadmus Wilcox and David Lang were both heavily engaged on July 2, but also suffered significant losses during the Pickett-Pettigrew-Trimble Charge on the afternoon of July 3. Wilcox put his loss for the entire battle at 577 Alabamians of about 1,700 engaged, and noted that "of five of my regimental commanders, four were wounded." The brigadier was furious that no reinforcements were dispatched to support and exploit his breakthrough and lodgment on the Emmitsburg Road Rise, and he blamed his superior, Major General Anderson, for the lapse. "I dispatched my adjutant-general to the division commander, to ask that support be sent to my men, but no support came," he complained. "This struggle at the foot of the hill [Emmitsburg Road Rise] on which were the enemy's batteries, though so unequal, was continued for some thirty minutes. With a second supporting line, the heights could have been carried. Without support on either my right or left," he added, "my men were withdrawn to prevent their entire destruction or capture."[12]

---

10 Philip Andrade, "A Survey of Union and Confederate Casualties at Gettysburg," *Journal of Civil War Medicine*, July-September 2013, vol. 17, issue 3, 119, puts Kershaw's losses at 630. The 2nd South Carolina, Kershaw's left-most regiment, argues Andrade, lost 157 men of the 412 engaged, or nearly two men in five. Petruzzi and Stanley, *The Gettysburg Campaign in Numbers and Losses*, 121, however, believe the 2nd South Carolina lost 170 men of the 412 engaged, for a 41.3% rate.

11 Petruzzi & Stanley, *The Gettysburg Campaign*, 121-22; Busey & Martin, *Regimental Strengths and Losses*, 282. Petruzzi & Stanley have Barksdale at 789 casualties; Busey & Martin at 804.

12 OR 27, pt. 2, 178, 338, 367, 619. Petruzzi & Stanley peg Wilcox's losses as 609 of 1,721.

Colonel Lang's understrength Florida brigade (which carried only some 740 men into action) reported exceptionally heavy losses of 455 men, though this figure represents killed, wounded, and captured for the entire battle. The majority of this number fell during the assault against the Union center on July 2. His late advance at the tail end of the charge on July 3 was quickly broken by intense Union artillery fire, though how many he lost on that day alone is impossible to state. It is safe to say that at least 75%, and perhaps as high as 90%, of Lang's losses were suffered during the fight against A. A. Humphreys' Emmitsburg Road line and Hancock's subsequent improvised second line near Cemetery Ridge. Ambrose Wright, Anderson's third brigade to go over to the attack, reported losing 668 Georgians out of some 1,400. According to Wright, about one-half of his losses fell into the "missing" category. Modern researchers believe that Wright lost 696 men—or nearly one-half of his entire brigade. All of Wright's losses occurred on July 2. Aligned on Wright's left, much of Carnot Posey's brigade was engaged in the fight for the Bliss farm, and only portions joined in the attack against the distant Union center. None of Posey's men fought on July 3. Posey's command lost less than 10% of its 1,300 men (112 casualties) in total at Gettysburg. Anderson's final brigade under William Mahone never joined the attack and as noted earlier, suffered light losses during the battle (110 of 1,538 effectives).[13]

All told, Lee's Army of Northern Virginia lost some 6,500 men on July 2. That figure, however, represented the total loss along the entire length of the Confederate line, but at least a quarter (and likely more) of these casualties occurred between just the Millerstown Road and the southern outskirts of town below Cemetery Hill. The Virginia army lost dozens of field officers that afternoon and evening and a number of generals, including the charismatic William Barksdale. However, the fall of Maj. Gen. William "Dorsey" Pender, who commanded a division in A. P. Hill's Third Corps, directly affected the way the final portion of Lee's grand rolling assault unfolded. Command of the suddenly leaderless Southern division fell to James Lane, who discovered that fact too late while the Yankees were mauling Anderson's unsupported brigades along the Emmitsburg Road.[14]

*   *   *

13 Petruzzi & Stanley, *The Gettysburg Campaign*, 130-31; Busey & Martin, *Regimental Strengths and Losses*, 294-95. Petruzzi places the losses of Lane's artillery at 42 of 375 for their two days of fighting. Busey says 42 of 384.

14 "Reminiscences: Major-General Dorsey Pender," Box 71, File 45-0001, North Carolina State Archives, Raleigh.

Major General George Meade won a hard-fought battle on July 2 that is often referred to as a tactical "draw" in the historical literature. General Lee's ambition was not merely to take and hold the Emmitsburg Road Rise, but to defeat Meade's army by rolling up his left flank and/or punching through the line and routing his army off the field. He failed in this grand objective for a variety of reasons, including good Union morale, the outstanding leadership of his subordinates, and fighting on the defense on good ground of his own choosing. When the sun set on July 2, Meade's army was still in place and ready to fight the following day.

Longstreet's assault effectively destroyed Daniel Sickles' Third Corps as a viable fighting unit, just as Winfield Hancock had feared when he saw elements of the corps advancing toward the Emmitsburg Road earlier that day. The wide-ranging fight scattered the corps over several square miles of ground. Its fugitives sought out their scattered commands under cover of darkness. Many would not find their way back to their regiments or batteries until the following day. Hundreds more didn't even try, opting instead to help the fallen regardless of their corps insignia. "I again occupied the field I had but a few moments previously vacated," reported Brig. Gen. Joseph Carr. "Here my command remained until morning, the officers and men assisting in removing from the field a [goods] many of the wounded as the time and facilities would permit."[15]

Third Corps casualties were simply staggering. In addition to losing Dan Sickles, whose leg was nearly severed by a cannon round and the job later finished by a Union surgeon, the corps' two divisions lost more than 4,000 men and 300 officers were killed, wounded and missing. A. A. Humphreys' division, which tried to hold a line too long and too thin to man sufficiently, suffered more than 2,000 from all causes, or about 44% of his command (a slightly higher number, percentage-wise, than Birney's division). Joseph Carr's brigade was the hardest hit, losing 859 out of 1,700 engaged. The 26th Pennsylvania under Maj. Robert L. Bodine reported nearly 60% casualties (215 of 365). Carr's officer roster was particularly hard hit. Three of his six regimental leaders (Baldwin, Merriam, and McAllister) were wounded, as were large numbers of other field and line officers. Colonel Brewster's brigade lost almost 43%, or 782) of his 1,834 men. Losses were particularly heavy in Lt. Col. Cornelius Westbrook's 120th New York, with 210 from all causes (including Westbrook) out of its 383 soldiers. Colonel Edward Bailey's 2nd New Hampshire suffered similar losses with 193 killed, wounded, and missing out of 354 engaged, including the wounded Bailey. Captain George Randolph's artillery brigade lost 106 of 594 men. Second Corps artillery units Winfield Hancock had rushed in to help support Humphrey's crumbling front,

15 Ibid.

including Ransom's and McGilvery's brigades, lost more than 15% and 23% of their strength, respectively.[16]

Of David Birney's 5,000-man division, more than 40% ended up on the rolls of the killed, wounded, or missing. The brigade under Brig. Gen. Charles K. Graham, who was shot in the hip and shoulders and captured, lost an estimated 734 out of 1,515 men. J. H. Hobart Ward lost 816 of the 2,180 men in his large brigade. The early fight in Pitzer's Woods and later defense of the Emmitsburg Road line cost Col. Moses Lakeman's 3rd Maine 126 casualties out of 210 men engaged, and Elijah Walker's 4th Maine 145 of his 287 soldiers. Hiram Berdan's U.S. Sharpshooters were spread the length of the Third Corps' front. The Pitzer's Woods fight, however, was Berdan's main event for day, followed by heavy skirmishing west of the Sherfy farm. His 1st regiment lost 57 men to all causes out of 312 engaged, and the 2nd regiment 47 of 169.[17]

Winfield Hancock's Second Corps sustained roughly 2,500 casualties on July 2, including Brig. Gen. John Caldwell's division, which fought well south of the Union center, much of it in the Wheatfield on Sickles' front. How many men were lost defending the actual Union center atop and west of Cemetery Ridge will never be known with any certainty. Many of the same commands that fought so hard on July 2 also participated in the defense of the center against Pickett's Charge the following day. By most accounts, Col. William Colvill's 1st Minnesota of Brig. Gen. William Harrow's brigade lost 217 of its 297 men, including the badly wounded Colvill, during its ill-fated heroic countercharge. Colvill was shot in the shoulder and the ankle. One bullet entered the top right shoulder and tore across his back, clipping off a part of his vertebra and lodging under his left scapula. The wounds forced Colvill to use a cane the rest of his life. Colonel Francis Heath's 19th Maine, so heavily engaged on July 2, also fought on the third day and lost 211 of 439 in total. Colonel Clinton MacDougall, commanding the 111th New York of Colonel Willard's brigade, however, was an exception to reporting July 2 casualties. "So severe was the fire to which we were subjected," he scribed on August 26, 1863, "that my loss in the [July 2] charge was 185 men killed and wounded in less than twenty minutes, out of about 390 taken into the fight." MacDougall's estimate is an accurate duration for the bloody fight for Plum Run. The 111th New York sustained far more casualties during those few minutes than did Colvill's more famous 1st Minnesota fighting on his immediate right (which lost a higher percentage of those engaged). The New York regiment lost nearly as many men that day as the entire 1st Minnesota carried into the fight. On July 3, MacDougall's

16 Ibid., 106-107, 119. Ransom lost 69 of 443 men; McGilvery 89 of 383. Most were on July 2.

17 Petruzzi & Stanley, *The Gettysburg Campaign*, 106-107.

command lost an additional 64 men from skirmishing, artillery fire, and defending against the Rebel infantry assault.[18]

Major General John Newton's First Corps casualties on July 2 can only be very roughly estimated out of its total losses for the entire battle, and the same holds true for George Sykes' Fifth Corps and Henry Slocum's Twelfth Corps. All told, Meade lost about 8,800 officers and men on July 2 in his effort to save the center following Sickles' forward movement. By dawn on July 3, most of the wounded Union and Confederate soldiers west of Cemetery Ridge had been removed to makeshift field hospitals, where surgeons from both armies worked to save their lives.[19]

Captain Adolpho Fernandez Cavada, one of General Humphreys' aides, rode back and forth across Plum Run throughout that dismal night and early into the morning of July 3. "On every side lay stiffened cold bodies of our dead soldiers," he lamented, "sometimes two or three forming ghastly groups together—in most unnatural attitudes—Sometimes lying naturally and as if asleep, occasionally a wounded man not able to move would draw our attention by plaintive moans or a request for water. These we comforted with the assurance that the ambulances would find them in a few minutes. We found but few Rebel dead or wounded on this side [east] of the hollow," he continued, "but on crossing it they became very numerous, even more so then our own." The Cuban-born staff officer also remembered the low acrid powder smoke mixed with a rising mist, which he described as that "strange musty smell peculiar to battlefields."[20]

One of the highest-ranking Union casualties fell late in the fighting. Colonel George H. Willard's "Harpers Ferry Cowards" were shot to pieces late that afternoon in their effort to regain their redemption. Sometime about 9:00 p.m., Willard received orders to return north. Before leading his men away, he detached volunteers, including all of his designated stretcher-bearers, from the regiments under his direct command (the 39th 125th, and 126th New York) to help care for the wounded. Willard marched what was left of his brigade north, east of Plum Run. Passing over the dry wash, his column crossed the ground where men from Minnesota continued searching for wounded and missing. Once across that bloody portion of the field, the brigade marched in front of Lieutenant Thomas's silent Napoleons. The cries of the wounded of both sides begging for water convinced Willard to stop and allow his men to drop out and tend to them for a short time.

18 OR 27, pt. 2, 178.

19 Gregory A. Coco, *A Vast Sea of Misery: A History and Guide to the Union and Confederate Field Hospitals at Gettysburg, July 1-November 20, 1863* (Gettysburg, Pa., 1988). See Summary of Events, xiv-xvi. See also Petruzzi & Stanley, *The Gettysburg Campaign*, 104.

20 Adolpho F. de la Cabada [Cavada] Diary, 1861-1863, entry dated July 2-3, 1863, HSP.

Colonel George H. Willard,
Hays' division,
Hancock's Second Corps
LOC

Passing north of Thomas's position, not far from where Colonel Brewster had reformed his fugitives, Willard led his New Yorkers into the low, rough ground. It was there one of the day's final artillery rounds exploded above the trees. His command had earned its redemption, but the colonel would not live long enough to enjoy it. A large jagged iron fragment struck Willard and carried away the front half of his head. Colonel Eliakim Sherrill of the 126th New York assumed his position at the head the column. Lacking stretchers, Sherrill improvised by placing Willard's corpse in a blanket and detailed four soldiers to carry their beloved colonel's remains to General Hays, their division commander.

About the same time Colonel Willard met his fate, Confederate forces from General Ewell's Second Corps were withdrawing from East Cemetery Hill after successfully breaking the Union line and capturing the height in vicious hand-to-hand combat amongst the smoking guns of two Federal batteries. When no support arrived to exploit the hard-won success (a common theme for the Rebels on July 2), the troops were driven off. Farther east, the combat was dying down on Culp's Hill, where more troops from Ewell's command had captured some of the abandoned trenches, but had failed to carry the wooded rocky height and now found themselves lodged on its steep timbered sides. In both of these instances, significant breakdowns in Confederate planning, communication, and execution spelled failure. This was very similar to Longstreet's assault against the Union left. Coordination was lacking, and reserves were not in place to exploit lodgments and breakthroughs.[21]

---

21 For a very detailed account of Early's night-time assault, see Scott L. Mingus, Sr., *The Louisiana Tigers in the Gettysburg Campaign, June-July 1863* (Baton Rouge, LSU Press, 2009). See also Pfanz, *Culp's Hill and Cemetery Hill.*

More fighting was in the works at Gettysburg for July 3 over much of the same ground when General Lee bombarded the Union center with a massive artillery barrage followed up by his grand infantry attack. George Pickett would become a household name, and Wilcox and Lang would step off almost as an after-thought and suffer needlessly under artillery fire before falling back. George Meade would rather easily repel Lee's final assault and win an outright victory over the Army of Northern Virginia, and Winfield Hancock would suffer a serious wound defending Cemetery Ridge that would pain him until his death many years later. And in the end, beginning on the evening of July 3, Lee's Virginia army would begin its long and tortuous withdrawal south.

But for now, on the night of July 2, Hancock remained "the Superb." His exemplary leadership performance under the worst of circumstances, coupled with outstanding examples of junior leadership and bravery amongst the rank and file, was the primary reason the Union center held that day. Hancock's battle between the farm lanes had saved Cemetery Ridge, and perhaps forever changed the destiny of the Confederate States of America.

Bibliography

PRIMARY SOURCES
NEWSPAPERS

The Agitator (Wellsboro, Pennsylvania)
Army and Navy Journal Gazette
Athens Southern Banner
Atlanta Constitution
Boston Sunday Herald
Brookville Republican (Brookville, Pennsylvania)
Brookville Jefferson Democrat
Carlisle Herald
Chambersburg Franklin Repository
Chambersburg Valley Spirit Times
Charlotte Daily Observer
Chicago Tribune
Dallas Morning News
Detroit Free Press
DuBois Morning Courier (DuBois, Pennsylvania)
Gettysburg Adams Sentinel
Gettysburg Compiler
Harrisburg Evening Telegraph
Indiana Democrat (Indiana, Pennsylvania)
Lancaster Daily Express (Lancaster, Pennsylvania)
Lewisburg Chronicle (Lewisburg, Pennsylvania)
Lewisburg Union County Star
Macon Telegraph
Minneapolis Journal
The National Tribune
New York Herald
New York Times
New York Tribune
Ottawa Republican Times Press (Ottawa, Illinois)
Philadelphia Inquirer
Philadelphia Weekly Times

Orlando Sentinel
Perry News (Perry, Florida)
Richmond Daily Dispatch
Richmond Enquirer
Rochester Evening Express
Savannah Republican
Sunbury American (Sunbury, Pennsylvania)
Syracuse Courier & Union
The Times (London, England)
Winona Post (Winona, Minnesota)
York Gazette (York, Pennsylvania)

MANUSCRIPT SOURCES

Adams County Historical Society, Gettysburg:
  Sarah Broadhead Diary
Auburn University Archives and Special Collections Library, Auburn, Alabama:
  Hugh L. Deason, Emily S. York Papers
  Ross Family Papers
Birmingham, Alabama, Public Library:
  Hilary A. Herbert, History of the 8th Alabama Volunteer Infantry Regiment
    scrapbook, circa 1905
Cadet Special Collections Library and Archives, United States Military Academy, West
    Point, New York:
  Gulian V. Weir Letters to Father, Professor Robert Weir Papers
Colgate University Archives, Hamilton, New York:
  Thomas Ward Osborn, Unpublished Letter and Papers
Cornell University Library, Ithaca, New York:
  Erasmus E. Basset Diary for 1863
  Charles A. Hoyt, "A Surgeon's Diary: 1861-1865"
Cushing Memorial Library & Archives, Texas A&M University, College Station, Texas:
  Edward B. Williams, ed., "Rebel Brothers: The Civil War Letters of the Truehearts"
Eisenhower National Historical Site Library, Abilene, Kansas:
  Ann Witman Files, Gettysburg Farm Series, "Construction," "Woods of Gettysburg
    National Military Park," Cultural Landscape Report for Eisenhower National
    Historical Site, Vol. I.
Emory University, Manuscript, Archives & Rare Book Collection:
  James Longstreet Papers
Franklin County Historical Society, Chambersburg, Pennsylvania:
  Andrew K. McClure Letters, 1861-1865
Georgia Historical Society, Savannah:
  William Pigman Papers
Gettysburg National Military Park Library, Gettysburg:
  Homer Baldwin, Letter to Father dated July 7, 1863
  Gettysburg Battlefield Commission, Engineers Department, "A Record of the
    Position of Troops on the Battlefield"

Benjamin W. Thompson, "Recollections of War Times"
Historical Society of Oak Park and River Forest, Oak Park, Illinois:
    Stacy Manley Letters
Historical Society of Pennsylvania, Philadelphia:
    John Rutter Brooke Papers
    Adolpho Fernandez de la Cavada Papers
    Edward R. Geary Letters
John Gibbon Papers
    Andrew Atkinson Humphreys Papers
    George Gordon Meade Papers
Huntington Special Collections Library, San Marino, California:
    John P. Nicholson Papers
James S. Schoff Civil War Collection, William L. Clements Library, University of
    Michigan, Ann Arbor:
    Warren H. Cudworth Papers, "Biographical Sketches and Reminiscences of the
    Regiment's Colonel"
Manuscripts Division, Library of Congress, Washington, D.C.:
    Henry J. Hunt Papers
    Marsena Patrick Papers
    Cadmus Wilcox Papers
Milne Special Collections Library, University of New Hampshire, Durham:
    William P. Mason Papers
Minnesota Historical Society, Saint Paul:
    Hamlin, Philip Rice, and Jacob Leslie Hamlin Papers, 1861-1865
    Marvin Mathew Papers, 1861-1895
    Charles E. McColley, "The First Regiment at Gettysburg"
    James A. Wright, "The Story of Company F, the First Regiment"
Mississippi Department of Archives and History, Jackson:
    Ethelbert Barksdale Papers
Museum of Florida, Civil War Archives, Havana:
    James H. Wentworth Papers
The National Archives and Records Administration, Washington, D.C.:
    American Civil War Military and Pension Records
    United States Army Corps' Chief of Topographical Engineers, Record Group 77
The National Archives and Records Administration, College Park, Maryland:
    Still Pictures Reproduction
New Hampshire Historical Society, Concord:
    John B. Bachelder Papers
New York Historical Society, New York City:
    James Barnes Papers
    Abner Doubleday Papers
    William H. Paine Papers
New York Public Library, Rare Book and Manuscript Division, New York City:
    Henry Hobart Ward Papers
New York State Archives, Albany:
    Richard Warren Letters & Diary, Richard Taylor Collection

New York State Library, University of the State of New York, Albany:
  Military Records Adjutant General Reports State of New York, Serial No. 15, 1898 &
    Serial No. 17, 1899
University of Notre Dame Rare Books and Special Collections, Hesburgh Library,
    South Bend, Indiana:
  William Cline Diary
  Jeremy A. Kiene, ed., "Manuscripts of the American Civil War, William Cline Diary
    Co. B, 73rd OVI, 1 Vol."
Ohio State Archives, Columbus:
  Ohio State Adjutant General Records Division of the Civil War
Old Court House Museum, Winchester, Virginia:
  Robert Sherrard Bell Diary for 1863
Ontario Historical Society, Canandaigua, New York:
Clinton MacDougal letter to C.A. Richardson, 1886, Charles A. Richardson Papers
Orlando Florida Public Library and Archives, Orlando, Florida:
  Compiled Service Records of the 2nd, 5th, and 8th Florida Volunteer Infantry
    Regiments
Pennsylvania Historical Museum, Division of Archives and Manuscripts, Harrisburg:
  Samuel Penniman Bates Papers
  Henry T. Peck (118th PA) to Mother, Letter Dated July 7, 1863
Pennsylvania State Archives, Harrisburg:
  Grand Army of the Republic Manuscript Collection
  Map of the Battlefield of Gettysburg from Original Surveys... by S. A. Hammond
    1903 and 1914
  Maps of the Battle Field of Gettysburg, July 1st, 2nd and 3rd, 1863, published by
    authority of the Honorable Secretary of War, Office of the Chief of Engineers U.
    S. Army 1876, New Edition 1883 as published by John B. Bachelder, 1876
Pennsylvania Volunteer Infantry Regiments: Series #19.11 & #19.65
  Miscellaneous Pennsylvania Manuscripts:
    Papers Relating to the Civil War Record of Lt. Edward Thompson, Company H,
      69th Regiment PV
  Letters from Vining B. Baldwin, Company C, 72nd Regiment Pennsylvania
    Volunteers, Thomas F. Longaker Collection, 1861-1864
    Record Group 19 - Adjutant General's Office, Civil War Muster Rolls and Related
      Records,
  Register of Pennsylvania Volunteers, 1861-1865:
    26th PA Volunteers, 57th PA Volunteers, 63rd PA Volunteers, 68th PA
      Volunteers, 69th PA Volunteers, 71st PA Volunteers, 72nd PA Volunteers
      (Baxter's Philadelphia Fire Zouaves), 99th PA Volunteers, 105th PA
      Volunteers, 106th PA Volunteers, 114th PA Volunteers, 115th PA Volunteers,
      141st PA Volunteers, 143rd PA Volunteers, 149th PA Volunteers (2nd
      Bucktails), 150th PA Volunteers (3rd Bucktails)
  Pennsylvania Volunteer Cavalry Regiments Series #19.11 & #19.65
    59th PA Volunteers (2nd Cavalry), 70th PA Volunteers (6th Cavalry) "Rush's
      Lancers," 162nd PA Volunteers (17th Cavalry)

Pennsylvania Volunteer Independent Artillery Batteries (Record Group 25)
   Independent Battery C Light Artillery – Thompson's
   Independent Battery E Light Artillery – Knap's
   Independent Battery F Light Artillery– Hampton's
Rochester Historical Society, Rochester, New York:
   Civil War Letter of Francis Edwin Pierce of the 108th New York Volunteer Infantry
Rutherford B. Hayes Presidential Center, Spiegel Grove, Fremont, Ohio:
   Papers of Captain James C. McKell, 73rd OVI, John J. Cook Family Papers
Southern Historical Collection, Louis R. Wilson Special Collections Library, University
   of North Carolina, Chapel Hill:
   Edward Porter Alexander Papers
   Henry R. Berkley Diary for 1863
   Henry K. Burgwyn Civil War Papers
   Hilary A. Herbert, "A Short History of the 8th Alabama Regiment"
   Humphreys Family Papers
   Lafayette McLaws Papers
   Jack Nelson, "Lee, Longstreet, and the Battle of Gettysburg"
Southern Historical Society Papers, Southern Historical Society, Richmond:
St. Augustine Historical Society, St. Augustine, Florida:
   David L. Dunham Diary
United States Congress, Washington, D.C.:
   Report of the Joint Committee on the Conduct of the War at the Second Session,
      Thirty-Eighth Congress, Vol. I, 1865; Supplemental Report, Part 2, 1866.
United States Geological Survey National Center, Reston, Virginia:
   1906 USGS Map: Gettysburg
   1987 USGS Topographical Satellite Image Map: 39077-G2-TF-024
United States Army Heritage and Education Center, Carlisle, Pennsylvania:
   Photographic Collections
   Alonzo K. Worth Letters
University of California Southern Regional Library, Los Angeles:
   William Wheeler Letter dated Warrenton, Va., July 26, 1863
Vermont Historical Society Papers, Barre:
   George H. Scott, "Vermont at Gettysburg," 1930
Virginia Historical Society, Department of Manuscripts and Archives, Richmond:
   Robert Knox Sneden, Scrapbook, 1861-1865, Part 5: Fredericksburg Campaign - the
      Gettysburg Campaign
   Samuel R. Johnston Papers
Virginia Polytechnic Institute and State University Special Collections Library,
   Blacksburg:
   George W. Watson Letters
William R. Perkins Library, Duke University, Durham, North Carolina:
   John B. Hood Papers
   Lafayette McLaws Papers
   James Longstreet Papers
Woodson Research Center, Fondren Library, Rice University, Houston, Texas:

Eseck G. Wilber Civil War Letters
Yale University Manuscripts and Archives Library, New Haven, Connecticut:
  Webb Papers

PUBLISHED PRIMARY SOURCES

Adams, A. J., "The Fight at the Peach Orchard," *The National Tribune*, April 23, 1885.
Alabama Historical Quarterly, Spring & Summer, Issue 1867.
Adams, John G. B., *Reminiscences of the Nineteenth Maine at Gettysburg*. Boston: Wright & Potter Printing Co., 1899.
Adams, Salis, "The Nineteenth Maine at Gettysburg," *Military Order of the Loyal Legion of the United States, War Papers Read Before the Commandery of the State of Maine*, Vol. 4. Portland, ME: Lefavor-Tower Co., 1915.
Aldrich, Thomas, *The History of Battery A, First Rhode Island Light Artillery*. Providence, RI: Snowden and Farnum, 1904.
Alexander, Edward P., *Military Memoirs of a Confederate*. New York: Scribner's Sons, 1907.
—————, "The Great Charge and Artillery Fighting at Gettysburg," in Johnston, Robert U., and Buel, Clarence C., *Battles and Leaders of the Civil War*. New York: The Century Co., 1887. Vol. III.
Allan, William, "A Reply to General Longstreet," *Battles & Leaders*, Vol. III.
Ames, Nelson, *History of Battery G, First Regiment New York Light Artillery*. Marshalltown, IA: Marshall Printing Co., 1900.
Babcock, William A., "The 114th Regiment, Pennsylvania Volunteers," *Philadelphia Weekly Times*, April 24, 1886.
Baker, Levi W., *History of the Ninth Massachusetts Battery*. Lancaster, OH: Vanberg Publishing, reprint 1996.
Banes, Charles, *History of the Philadelphia Brigade*. Philadelphia: J. B. Lippincott, 1876.
Barnes, James, "The Battle of Gettysburg," *New York Herald*, March 21, 1864.
Bartlett, Asa W., *History of the Twelfth Regiment New Hampshire Volunteers in the War of the Rebellion*. Concord, NH: Ira C. Evans, 1897.
Bartlett, John G., ed., *Yankee Rebel, The Civil War Journal of Edmund D. Patterson: 9th Ala.* Chapel Hill: UNC Press, 1966.
Battle, Cullen A., "The Gettysburg Controversy," *Gettysburg Compiler*, January 28, 1896.
Berdan, Hiram, "At Gettysburg; Encampment of the G.A.R.," *Philadelphia Weekly Times*, July 8, 1887.
Berkley, Henry R. "Pvt. Henry Robinson Berkley Diary," *Southern Historical Society Papers*, Vol. 14.
Bicknell, Emerson L., "Repelling Lee's Last Blow at Gettysburg, Part IV," *Battles & Leaders*, Vol. III.
Bigelow, John, *The Peach Orchard, Gettysburg July 2, 1863*. Minneapolis: Kimball-Storer Co., 1919; Reprint by Old Soldier Books Inc., 1987.
Blackford, Eugene, "Report of Major Blackford's Sharpshooters of Rodes' Brigade," *SHSP*, Vol. 13, August 1885.

Blake, Henry N., *Three Years in the Army of the Potomac*. Boston: Lee and Shepard Co., 1865.

Blake, Nelson M., *William Mahone of Virginia: Soldier and Political Insurgent*. Richmond: Garrett and Massie Co., 1935.

Bowen, Edward R., "Collis' Zouaves: The 114th Pennsylvania Infantry at Gettysburg," *Philadelphia Weekly Times*, No. 27, June 22, 1887.

Brown, B. F., "McGowan's (Perrin) South Carolina Brigade at Gettysburg," *Confederate Veteran*, Vol. 31, 1923.

Brown, Henri L., *History of the Third Regiment, Excelsior Brigade, 72nd New York Volunteer Infantry 1861-1865*. Jamestown, NY: Journal Printing Co., 1902.

Bruce, George A., *The Twentieth Regiment of Massachusetts Volunteer Infantry, 1861-1865*. Boston: Houghton and Mifflin & Co., 1906.

Brunson, Joseph W., *Historical Sketch of the Pee Dee Light Artillery, Army of Northern Virginia*. Winston-Salem, NC: Stewart Printing House, 1927.

Cabell, Henry C., "Report of Colonel H. C. Cabell," *SHSP*, Vol. 10, 1882.

Calef, John H., "The Regular Artillery in the Gettysburg Campaign," *Journal of the Military Service Institute of the United States*, Vol. 45, 1909.

Carr, Joseph B., "The Barksdale Episode," *Gettysburg Star and Sentinel*, July 27, 1886.

Chamberlin, Thomas, ed., *History of the One Hundred Fiftieth Regiment Pennsylvania Volunteers*. Philadelphia: J. B. Lippincott Co., 1895.

Clark, George, "Wilcox's Alabama Brigade at Gettysburg," *Confederate Veteran*, Vol. 17, 1909.

Clark, Walter, ed. *History of the Several Regiments and Battalions from North Carolina in the Great War, 1861-1865*, 5 Vols. Raleigh: E. M. Uzzell and Co., 1901.

Clark, William, *History of Hampton Battery F: Independent Pennsylvania Light Artillery*. Akron, OH: The Werner Company, 1909.

Collum, George, *Biographical Register of the Officers and Graduates of the United States Military Academy at West Point*, Vol. II. New York: Houghton Mifflin, 1891.

Corbin, Elbert, "Pettit's (Sheldon-Rorty) Battery at Gettysburg," *The National Tribune*, February 3, 1910.

Crumb, Herb S., ed., Thomas W. Osborn, *The Eleventh Corps Artillery at Gettysburg: The Papers of Major Thomas Ward Osborn Chief of Artillery*. Hamilton City, NY: Edmonston Publishing, Inc., 1991.

Cudworth, Warren H., *History of the First Regiment Massachusetts Infantry*. Boston: Walker, Fuller and Co., 1866.

Curtis, Greely S., "The Cause of the Confederate Failure at Gettysburg," *MOLLUS - MA*, Vol. 3.

Dana, Charles A., *Recollections of the Civil War*. New York: Appleton & Co., 1902.

Daniel, Frederick S., *Richmond Howitzers in the War*. Gaithersburg, MD: Reprint by Butternut Press, 1980.

Dart, William T., "Carroll's Brigade at Gettysburg," *The National Tribune*, April 6, 1893.

De Peyster, John W., "The Third Corps at Gettysburg, July 2 1863: General Sickles Vindicated," *The Volunteer*, No. 1, 1869

———, "A Military Memoir of William Mahone: Major-General in the Confederate Army," *Historical Magazine*, Vol. VII, Second Series, 1870.

————, "An Ideal Soldier: A Tribute to Maj. Gen. Daniel E. Sickles," *The National Tribune*, June 26, 1888.

Dedication of the Monuments to the Four New York Companies of the First regiment of United States Sharpshooters on the Battlefield of Gettysburg, July 2d, 1863. Albany, NY: Weed, Parsons & Co., Printers, 1889.

Dickelman, John L., "Carroll's Brigade at Gettysburg," *The National Tribune*, June 10, 1909.

Dobbins, Austin C., *Grandfather's Journal: Company B, Sixteenth Mississippi, Infantry Volunteers Harris Brigade, Mahone's Division, Hill's Corps A.N.V., May 27, 1861 - July 15, 1865*. Dayton, OH: Morningside House, Inc., 1988.

Dow, Edwin B., "How One Brave Battery Saved the Federal Left," *New York Times Magazine*, June 29, 1913.

Duke, John W., "Mississippians at Gettysburg," *Confederate Veteran*, No. 14, 1906.

Englehard, Joseph A., "Report of Pender's Division," *SHSP*, Vol. 8, 1880.

Favill, Josiah M., *The Diary of a Young Officer: Serving with the Armies of the United States During the War of the Rebellion*. Chicago: Donnelley and Sons Company, 1909.

Fiske, Samuel W., *Mr. Dunn Brown's (14th Conn.) Experience in the Army*. Boston: Nichols & Noyes, 1866.

Fleming, Francis P., *Memoir of C. Seton Fleming of the Second Florida Infantry C.S.A.* Jacksonville, FL: Times Union Publishing, 1884.

Flemming, Francis P., "Gettysburg: The Courageous Part Taken in the Desperate Conflict July 2-3, 1863, by the Florida Brigade," *SHSP*, Vol. 27, 1899.

Flemming, George T., ed., Gilbert Adams Hays, *Life and Letters of Alexander Hays: Brevet Colonel, United States Army, Brigadier General and Brevet Major General United States Volunteers*. Pittsburgh: G. A. Hays, 1919.

Fortin, Maurice S., ed., "Colonel Hilary A. Herbert's History of the Eighth Alabama Volunteer Regiment, C.S.A.," *The Alabama Historical Quarterly*, Vol. 39, Nos. 1, 2, 3, 4, 1977.

Frederick, Gilbert, *The Story of a Regiment: the Fifty Seventy New York Volunteer Infantry in the War of the Rebellion*. Chicago: C. H. Morgan Co., 1895.

Fremantle, James A., "An English Officer at Gettysburg," *Army and Navy Journal Gazette*, September 26, 1863.

Fuger, Frederick, "Cushing's Battery at Gettysburg," *Journal of Military Service Institute of the United States*, No. 41, November-December 1907.

Garnett, John J., *Gettysburg: A Complete Historical Narrative of the Battle of Gettysburg and Campaign Preceding It*. New York: J. M. Hill, 1888.

Gibbon, John, *Personal Recollections of the Civil War*. New York: G. P. Putnam's Sons, 1928; Reprint, Dayton OH, Morningside House, Inc., 1988.

————, "Carroll's Brigade at Gettysburg," *Army and Navy Journal Gazette*, March 12, 1864: "Gettysburg," *Philadelphia Weekly Press*, July 20, 1887.

Green, B. W., "Longstreet at Gettysburg," *Gettysburg Compiler*, September 27, 1919.

Groene, Bertram H., ed. "Civil War Letters of Colonel David Lang," *Florida Historical Quarterly*, Vol. 54, 1976.

Gushee, Henry H., "The 73rd Ohio at Gettysburg," *The National Tribune*, December 24, 1908.

Hale, Charles A., "Gettysburg: The Work Being Done By The Battlefield Memorial Association," *The National Tribune*, September 11, 1884.

Hancock, Almira Russell, *Reminiscences of Winfield Scott Hancock*. New York: Charles L. Webster and Company, 1887.

Hanifen, Michael, *History of Battery B, First New Jersey Artillery*. Ottawa, IL: Republican Times Publishing, 1905.

Haynes, Martin A., *A History of the Second Regiment, New Hampshire Volunteer Infantry in the War of the Rebellion*. Lakeport, NH: self-published, 1896.

Heth, Henry, "Why Lee Lost at Gettysburg," *Philadelphia Weekly Times*, September 22, 1877

————, "The Absence of the Cavalry the Cause of the Confederate Failure," *Gettysburg Compiler*, October 5, 1877.

Hood, John B., "Tribute to General Barksdale," *Confederate Veteran*, Vol. 9, 1901.

Holcombe, R. I., *History of the First Minnesota Volunteer Regiment*. Stillwater, MN: Eastern & Masterson, 1916.

Humphreys, Andrew A., "The Gettysburg Campaign of 1863," *Historical Magazine*, Series 2, July 1869.

Hunt, H. J., Berry, W., & French, W., *Instruction for Field Artillery*. Philadelphia: J. B. Lippincott & Co., 1860.

Hunt, Henry, "The Second Day at Gettysburg by Henry J. Hunt" *Battles & Leaders*, Vol. III.

Johnston, H. A., "What Regiment Supported Berdan's Sharpshooters?" *The National Tribune*, May 16, 1889.

Jones, William J., "The Longstreet-Gettysburg Controversy: Who Commenced It," *SHSP*, Vol. 23.

Kershaw, Joseph H., "Kershaw's Brigade at Gettysburg," *Battles & Leaders*, Vol. III.

Kilmer, Gary W., "The Stand at the Peach Orchard: The 141st Pennsylvania at Gettysburg," *The National Tribune*, December 17, 1923.

Ladd, David L. and Audrey J., eds., *The Bachelder Papers: Three Volumes*. Dayton, OH: Morningside Books Inc., 1994.

Lang, David, "Letter to General Edward A. Perry, July 19, 1863," as noted in "Gettysburg: The Courageous Part Taken in the Desperate Conflict 2-3 July, 1863, by the Florida Brigade," *SHSP*, Vol. 27, 1899.

Lee, Fitzhugh, "A Review of the First Two Days' Operations at Gettysburg and A Reply to Longstreet," *SHSP*, Vol. 5, 1878.

Lee, Susan, ed., *Memoirs of William Nelson Pendleton*. Philadelphia: J. B. Lippincott & Co., 1893.

Leeper, Joseph P., "Gettysburg: The Part Taken in the Battle by the Fifth Corps," *The National Tribune*, April 30, 1885.

Lewis, Allen Y., "Berdan's Sharpshooters," *The National Tribune*, August 12, 1886.

Lewis, George, *The History of Battery E, First Regiment, Rhode Island Light Artillery*. Providence, RI: Snow and Farnham, 1892.

Lochren, William, *The First Minnesota at Gettysburg, Glimpses of the Nation's Struggle*. St. Paul, MN: Minnesota MOLLUS, Vol. 3.

————, "Narrative of the First the Regiment," *Minnesota in the Civil War 1861-1865*, Vol. 2, 1891.

Long, Armistead, *Memoirs of Robert E. Lee*. New York: Stoddard & Company, 1887.

Longstreet, Helen D., *Lee and Longstreet at High Tide*. Gainesville, GA, s.n., 1905.

Longstreet, James, "The Campaign of Gettysburg," *Philadelphia Weekly Times*, No. 3, November 1877

————, "The Mistake of Gettysburg," *Philadelphia Weekly Times*, No. 23, February 1878.

————, "General Longstreet's Account of the Campaign and Battle," *SHSP*, Vol. 5, 1878.

————, *From Manassas to Appomattox: Memoirs of the Civil War in America*. Philadelphia: J. B. Lippincott & Co., 1896.

————, "Lee's Right Wing at Gettysburg," *Battles & Leaders*, Vol. III.

Lymon, Theodore, *Meade Headquarters, 1863-1865*. Boston: Massachusetts Historical Society, 1922.

Love, William, "Mississippi at Gettysburg," *Publications of the Mississippi Historical Society*, Vol. No. 9, 1906.

Maine Gettysburg Commission, "Nineteenth Maine Regiment, First Brigade, Second Division, Second Army Corps," in *Maine at Gettysburg: Report of Mine Commissioners Prepared by The Executive Committee*. Portland, ME: The Lakeside Press, 1898.

McEneany, Patrick, "Gettysburg: Snapshot Impressions of a Great Battle as Told by a Chief of Orderlies," *The National Tribune*, March 22, 1900.

McLaws, Lafayette, "Gettysburg," *SHSP*, Vol. 7, 1879

————, "The Battle of Gettysburg," *Philadelphia Weekly Press*, No. 21, April 1886

————, "The Federal Disaster on the Left," *Philadelphia Weekly Press*, No. 4, August 1886

McNeily, J. S., "Barksdale's Mississippi Brigade at Gettysburg: Most Magnificent Charge of the War," *Mississippi Historical Society Publications*, Vol. 19, 1919, Jackson.

Meade III, George G., Jr., ed., *Life and Letters of George Gordon Meade*, 2 vols. New York: Charles Scribner's Sons, 1913.

Minnigh, Henry N., "Gettysburg: What Troops Fought in the Peach Orchard," *The National Tribune*, July 1891.

New York State Monuments Commission for the Battlefields of Gettysburg and Chattanooga, *Final Report of the Battlefield of Gettysburg*, Vol. I. Albany, NY: J.B. Lyon Co., 1900.

Nicholson, John P., ed., *Pennsylvania at Gettysburg: Ceremonies at the Dedication of the Monument Erected by the Commonwealth of Pennsylvania*, 2 vols. Harrisburg: William Stanley Ray, State Printer, 1904.

Osborn, Thomas W., "The Artillery at Gettysburg," *Philadelphia Weekly Times*, Vol. III, No. 14, May 31, 1879.

Owen, William M., *In Camp with the Washington Artillery*. Boston: Ticknor and Co., 1885.

Potter, T. S., "The Battle of Gettysburg," *The National Tribune*, August 5 1882.

Reichardt, Theodore, *Diary of Battery A: First Regiment Rhode Island Light Artillery: Written in the Field*. Providence, RI: N. Bangs Williams, 1865.

Reid, Whitelaw, *Ohio in the War*, 2 vols. Columbus, OH: Eclectic Publishing Company, 1893.

Rhodes, John H., *The History of Battery B First Regiment, Rhode Island Light Artillery*. Providence, RI: Snow & Farnham, 1865.

Robertson, James I., ed., *The Civil War Letters of General Robert McAllister*. New Brunswick, NJ: Rutgers University Press, 1965.

————, *General A. P. Hill*. New York: Random House, 1987.

Rourke, Norman E., ed., *I Saw the Elephant: the Civil War Experiences of Bailey George McClellen, Company D, 10th Alabama Infantry Regiment*. Shippensburg, PA: Burd Street Press, 1995.

Runkle, William H., ed., *Four Years in the Confederate Artillery: The Diary of Private Henry Robinson Berkley*. Chapel Hill, NC: The University of North Carolina Press, 1961.

Sawyer, Franklin, *Military History of the 8th Regiment Ohio Volunteer Infantry; Its Battles, Marches and Army Movements*. Cleveland, OH: Fairbanks & Co., 1881; Reprint, Huntington, WV: Blue Acorn Press, 2005.

Schurz, Carl, *The Reminiscences of Carl Schurz*, Vol. 2. New York: McClure Company, 1908.

Scott, Kate, *History of the One Hundred and Fifth Regiment of Pennsylvania Volunteers*. Philadelphia: New World Publishing, 1877.

————, "The Mountain Men: The Famous Wild-Cat Regiment in the Civil War," *Philadelphia Weekly* Times, March 19, 1887.

Searles, Jasper N., "The First Minnesota Infantry," MOLLUS, Minnesota Commandery, *Glimpse of the Nation's Struggle*, Series 2, 1890.

Searles, Jasper N., & Matthew F. Taylor, *History of the First Minnesota Volunteer Infantry*. Stillwater, MN: Easton & Masterson, 1916.

Seville, William P., *History of the First Regiment Delaware Volunteers*. Wilmington, DE: Historical Society of Delaware, 1884.

Shotwell, Randolph A., "Virginia and North Carolina in the Battle of Gettysburg," *Our Living and Our Dead*, No. 4, March 1876.

Sickles, Daniel, "At Gettysburg; Encampment of the G.A.R.," *Philadelphia Weekly Times*, July 8, 1887

————, "Further Recollections of Gettysburg," *North American Review*, March 1891.

Smith, John D., *Nineteenth Maine: Harrow's Brigade, Gibbon's Division, Second Army Corps*. Minneapolis, MN: Great Western Printing Co., 1909.

Sorrell, Moxley G., *Recollections of a Confederate Staff Officer*. New York: Neale Publishing Co., 1905.

Stevens, Charles A., *Berdan's United States Sharpshooters in the Army of the Potomac, 1861-1865*. Saint Paul, MN: Price-McGill 1892.

Taylor, Walter, *Four Years with General Lee*. New York: D. Appleton & Co., 1878; Reprint, Indiana University Press, 1962.

Thomas, Edward L., "Report of Brigadier-General Edward L. Thomas," *SHSP*, No. 8, 1880.

Thompson, O. G., "Longstreet at Gettysburg," *Confederate Veteran*, Vol. 23, 1915.

Toombs, Samuel, *New Jersey Troops in the Gettysburg Campaign*. Orange, NJ: Evening Mall Publishing, 1888; Reprint, Hightstown, NJ: Longstreet House, 1988.

Tremain, Henry E., *Two Days of War: A Gettysburg Narrative and Other Experiences*. New York: Bonnell, Silver, and Bowers, 1905.

Tremain, Henry E., "Letter to General Sickles, June 26, 1880," *The National Tribune*, July 15, 1886.

United States Army Adjutant General Department, "Minutes of Council, July 2, 1863," United States Printing Office, 1881, Washington, D.C.

United States Army Adjutant General's Department [Compiled by Brig.-Gen. Richard C. Drum] *Itinerary of the Army of the Potomac and Co-operating in the Gettysburg Campaign, June and July, 1863, and Organization of the Army of the Potomac at the Battle of Gettysburg.* Washington, D.C.: United States Printing Office, 1882.

United States War Department, *The War of the Rebellion: A Compilation of the Official Reports of the War of the Union and Confederate Armies*, Series I, Volume 27, Parts 1, 2 & 3. Washington, DC: Government Printing House, 1889; Reprint, Dayton, OH: Morningside House, Inc., 1993.

Waitt, Francis A., *History of the Nineteenth Regiment, Massachusetts Volunteer Infantry*. Salem, MA: Salem Press Co., 1906.

Walker, A. F., "Hancock at Gettysburg: The Hancock-Sickles Difficulty," *Gettysburg Compiler*, December 18, 1894.

Walker, Francis, *History of the Second Army Corps in the Army of the Potomac*. New York: Scribner's Sons, 1886.

Walton, James B., "Letter from Colonel J. B. Walton," *SHSP*, Vol. 5, 1878.

Ward, Joseph R., "Cushing's Battery at Gettysburg," *Grand Army Scout and Soldier's Manual*, January 1886.

Ward, Joseph R. C., *History of the One Hundred and Sixth Regiment, Pennsylvania Volunteers*. Philadelphia: Grant, Faires, & Rodgers, 1883.

Westbrook, Cornelius D., "On the Firing Line: The 120th New York's Firm Stand on the 2nd Day at Gettysburg," *The National Tribune*, September 20, 1900.

Wilcox, Cadmus M., "General Wilcox to the Rescue," *Philadelphia Weekly Times*, November 24, 1877.

————, "General C. M. Wilcox on the Battle of Gettysburg," *SHSP*, Vol. 6, 1878.

Williamson, Edward C., ed., "Francis P. Fleming in the War for Southern Independence: Letters from the Front," *Florida Historically Quarterly*, Vol. 27, Oct. 1949.

Wilson, Arabella M., *Disaster, Struggle, Triumph: The Adventures of 1000 "Boys in Blue," from August 1862, to June 1865*. Albany, NY: Argus Company, Printers, 1870.

Wise, Jennings C., "The Artillery Mechanics of Gettysburg," *Field Artillery Journal*, No. 13, 1923.

————, *The Long Arm of Lee Vol. 2: Chancellorsville to Appomattox*. Omaha, NE: University of Nebraska Press, reprint 1991.

Wright, A., "Second U.S. Sharpshooters at Gettysburg," *The National Tribune*, No. 18, February 1909.

Young, Jesse B., *What a Boy Saw in the Army: A Story of Sight, Seeing and Adventure in the War for the Union*. New York: Hunt and Eaton Co., 1894.

SECONDARY SOURCES

Acken, Gregory J., *Inside the Army of the Potomac*. Mechanicsburg, PA: Stackpole Books, 1998.

Archer, John, "Fury at the Bliss Farm," *America's Civil War Magazine*, July 1995.

Baer, David R., "General Longstreet Taken to Task," *Philadelphia Weekly Times*, August 16, 1979.

Baumgartner, Richard A., *Buckeye Blood: Ohio at Gettysburg*. Huntington, WV: Blue Acorn Press, 2003.

Bowden, Scott & Ward, Bill, *Last Chance for Victory: Robert E. Lee and the Gettysburg Campaign*. Cambridge, MA: Da Capo Press Books, 2003.

Bradford, Gamaliel, "Lee as a General," *South Atlantic Quarterly*, Vol. 10, 1927.

Brandy, Kenneth & Freeland, Florence, comp., *The Gettysburg Papers*, Vols. I & II. Dayton, OH: Morningside House, Inc., 1978.

Brown, Andrew, "Geology and the Gettysburg Campaign," Commonwealth of Pennsylvania, Department of Conservation and Natural Resources, Bureau of Topographic and Geologic Survey, Harrisburg, PA, 1962.

Brown, Kent M., *Cushing of Gettysburg: The Story of a Union Artillery Commander*. Lexington, KY: University Press of Kentucky, 1993.

Burns, James A., "The 12th New Hampshire Regiment at Gettysburg and Beyond," *The Gettysburg Magazine*, Issue No. 20, January 1999.

Busey, John W., & Martin, David G., *Regimental Strengths and Losses at Gettysburg*. Hightstown, NJ: Longstreet House, 1986.

Campbell, Eric A., "Remember Harper's Ferry: Degradation, Humiliation, and Redemption of Col. George L. Willard's Brigade," *The Gettysburg Magazine*, Issue No. 7, Jan. 1993, Part 2 - Issue No. 8, July 1993.

—————, "Sacrificed to the bad management... of others: Richard H. Anderson's Division at the Battle of Gettysburg," The Army of Northern Virginia in the Gettysburg Campaign, Programs of the Seventh Annual Gettysburg Seminar Series, National Park Service, 1999.

Cameron, Bill, "The Signal Corps at Gettysburg Parts One and Two," *The Gettysburg Magazine*, Issues 3 & 4, July 1990 - January 1991.

Carter, John C., ed., *Welcome the Hour of Conflict: William Cowan McClellan and the 9th Alabama*. Tuscaloosa, AL: University of Alabama Press, 2007.

Catton, Bruce, *The Battle of Gettysburg*. New York: American Heritage Publishing Co., 1963.

Christ, Elwood W., *The Struggle For The Bliss Farm At Gettysburg July 2nd and 3rd 1863*. Baltimore, MD: Butternut and Blue, 1993.

Cleaves, Freeman, *Meade of Gettysburg*. Norman: University of Oklahoma Press, 1960.

Coco, Gregory A., *A Vast Sea of Misery: A History and Guide to the Union and Confederate Hospitals at Gettysburg, July 1-November 20, 1863*. Gettysburg, PA: Thomas Publications, 1988.

Coddington, Edwin B., *The Gettysburg Campaign: A Study in Command*. New York: Charles Scribner's Sons, Reprint, 1984.

Comte De Paris, L. P. D'Orleans, *The Battle of Gettysburg*. Philadelphia: John C. Winston Co., 1886.

Crooks, Terence G., *Rochester's Forgotten Regiment: The 108th New York in the Civil War*. Saratoga Springs, NY: New York State Military Museum, 2009.

Davis, Oliver L., *Life of David Bell Birney: Major General United States Volunteers*. Philadelphia: King and Baird Publishing, 1867.

Dempsey, Stuart R., "The Florida Brigade at Gettysburg," *Blue & Gray Magazine*, Vol. XXVII, Issue No. 4, 2010.

Dickenson, Christopher C., "The Flying Brigade: Brig. Gen. George Stannard and the Road to Gettysburg," *The Gettysburg Magazine*, Issue No. 16, January 1997.

Dowdey, Clifford, *Death of a Nation: The Story of Lee and His Men at Gettysburg*. New York: Alfred B. Knopf, 1958.

Downs, David B., "His Left was Worth a Glance: Meade and the Union Left on July 2, 1863," *The Gettysburg Magazine*, Issue No. 7, July 1992.

Dyer, Frederick H., *A Compendium of the War of the Rebellion*, Vols. 1 - 3. Des Moines, IA: Dyer Printing Co., 1908.

Early, Gary, *The Second United States Sharpshooters in the Civil War*. Jefferson, NC: McFarland & Company, Inc., 2009.

Eckendode, H. J., and Conrad, Bryan, *James Longstreet, Lee's War Horse*. Chapel Hill, NC: UNC Press, 1936.

Elmore, Thomas, "The Florida Brigade at Gettysburg," *The Gettysburg Magazine*, Issue No. 15, July 1996.

Evans, Clement A., ed., *Confederate Military History: A Library of Confederate States History*. Atlanta, GA: Confederate Publishing Co., 1889.

Faust, Patricia, *Historical Times Illustrated Encyclopedia of the Civil War*. New York: Harper & Row, 1986.

Folsom, William R., "Vermont at Gettysburg," *Vermont Quarterly*, Vol. 20, No. 4, October 1952.

Forney, John W., Life and Military Career of Winfield Scott Hancock. Philadelphia: Hubbard Brothers, 1880.

Frassanito, William A., *Gettysburg: A Journey in Time*. New York: Charles Scribner's Sons, 1975.

Freeman, Douglas S., *R. E. Lee: A Biography*, 4 Vols. New York: Scribner's Sons, 1934.

———, *Lee's Lieutenants*. New York: Reprint by Simon & Schuster, 1998.

Fuhrman, Robert, "The 57th Pennsylvania Volunteer Infantry at Gettysburg," *The Gettysburg Magazine*, Issue 17, July 1997.

Gallagher, Gary W., ed., *Fighting for the Confederacy: The Personal Recollections of General Edward Porter Alexander*. Chapel Hill, NC: University of North Carolina Press, 1989.

Gilpen, Drew F., *This Republic of Suffering*. New York: Alfred A. Knopf, 2008.

Gottfried, Bradley M., *Brigades of Gettysburg: The Union and Confederate Brigades at the Battle of Gettysburg*. Cambridge, MA: Da Capo Press, 2002.

Gottfried, Bradley M., "Mahone's Brigade: Insubordination or Miscommunication," *The Gettysburg Magazine*, Issue No. 18, Jan. 1998.

———, "Wright's Charge on July 2, 1863," Issue No. 17, July 1997.

Graham, Martin, "A Gallant Defense: The Trial of the 8th Ohio at Gettysburg," *Civil War Times Illustrated*, May 1986.

Grandchamp, Robert, "Brown's Company B, 1st Rhode Island Artillery at the Battle of Gettysburg," *The Gettysburg Magazine*, Issue No. 36, Jan. 2007.

Griffin, Ronald G., *The 11th Alabama Volunteer Regiment in the Civil War*. Jefferson, NC: McFarland & Company, 2008.

Hadden, Lee, "The Granite Glory: The 19th Maine at Gettysburg," *The Gettysburg Magazine*, Issue No. 13, July 1995.

Hage, Anne A., "The Battle of Gettysburg as Seen by Minnesota Soldiers," *Minnesota History Magazine*, No. 38, 1963.

Hains, Douglas C., "A. P. Hill's Advance to Gettysburg," *The Gettysburg Magazine*, Issue No. 5, July 1991.

Handlin, Oscar, "Why Lee Attacked: Chance or Destiny," *Atlantic Monthly Magazine*, March 1955.

Harman, Troy D., *Cemetery Hill: Lee's Real Plan at Gettysburg*. Baltimore, MD: Butternut and Blue, 2001.

Hartman, David W., ed., *Biographical Rosters of Florida's Confederate and Union Soldiers 1861-1865*, 6 Vols. Wilmington, NC: Broadfoot Publishing Co., 1995.

Hartwig, Scott D., "No Troops on the Field Had Done Better: John C. Caldwell's Division in the Wheatfield, July 2, 1863," in Gallagher, Gary W., ed., *The Second Day at Gettysburg: Essays on Confederate and Union Leadership*. Kent, Ohio: Kent State University Press, 1993.

Hartzler, Daniel D., *Medical Doctors of Maryland in the C.S.A.* Westminster, MD: Heritage Books, 2007.

Hassler, William W., *A. P. Hill: Lee's Forgotten General*. Richmond, VA: Garrett & Massie, 1957.

Hassler, William W., "Dorsey Pender, C .S. A.," *Civil War Times Illustrated*, No. 1, October 1962.

————, "George G. Meade and His Role at Gettysburg," *Pennsylvania History: A Journal of Mid-Atlantic Studies*, Vol. 32, 1965.

————, "Scrappy Little 'Billy' Mahone," *Civil War Times Illustrated*, Vol. 2, April 1963.

Havens, Clayton L., *Historical Sketch of the 136th New York Infantry, 1862-1865*. Dalton NY: Burts Print Service, 1934.

Hawk, Robert, *Florida's Army: Militia/State Troops/ National Guard, 1565-1985*. Englewood, FL: Pineapple Press, 1986.

Heiser, John, "Action on the Emmitsburg Road," *The Gettysburg Magazine*, Issue 1, July 1989.

Henderson, William D., *Twelfth Virginia History*. Lynchburg, VA: H. E. Howard Co., 1984.

Hessler, James A., *Sickles at Gettysburg*. El Dorado Hills, CA: Savas Beatie, 2010.

Imhof, John D., *Gettysburg Day Two: A Study in Maps*. Baltimore, MD: Butternut and Blue, 1999.

Imholt, John Q., *The First Volunteers: History of the First Minnesota Volunteer Regiment*. Minneapolis, MN: Ross and Haines Co., 1963.

Jamieson, Perry D., *Winfield Scott Hancock: Gettysburg Hero*. Abilene, TX: McMurray University Special Collections Foundation, 2003.

Jordan, David, *Winfield Scott Hancock: A Soldier's Life*. Bloomington, IN: Indiana University Press, 1996.

Keneally, Thomas, *American Scoundrel: The Life of the Notorious Civil War General Dan Sickles*. New York: Anchor Books/Random House, Inc., 2002.

Lader, Paul J., "The 7th New Jersey in the Gettysburg Campaign," *The Gettysburg Magazine*, Issue No. 16, Jan. 1997.

Laino, Phil, *Gettysburg Campaign Atlas*. Dayton, OH: Gatehouse Press, 2009.

Lash, Gary G. "The Pathetic Story: The 141st Pennsylvania at Gettysburg," *The Gettysburg Magazine*, Issue No. 14, Jan. 1996.

Lindstrom, Andrew F., *Perry's Brigade in the Army of Northern Virginia*. M.A. Thesis, University of Florida Special Collections, Gainesville, 1996.

Longacre, Edward G., *The Man Behind the Guns*. Cranbury, NJ: A. S. Barnes & Company, 1977.

Marbaker, Thomas D., *History of the Eleventh New Jersey Volunteers*. Trenton, NJ: MacCrellish & Quickley, 1898; reprint, Hightstown, NJ: Longstreet House, 1990.

Marcot, Roy, "Berdan's Sharpshooters at Gettysburg," *The Gettysburg Magazine*, Issue No. 1, July 1989.

Mingus, Scott L., Sr., *Flames Beyond Gettysburg: The Confederate Expedition to the Susquehanna River, June 1863*. El Dorado Hills, CA: Savas Beatie, 2011.

Naisawald, Louis Van Loan, *Grape and Canister: The Story of the Field Artillery of the Army of the Potomac, 1861-1865*. New York: Oxford University Press, 1960.

Nichols, Richard S., "Florida's Fighting Rebels: A Military History of Florida's Civil War Troops," M. A. Thesis, Florida State University, Special Collections and Archives, Tallahassee, FL.

O'Brien, Kevin E., "To Unflinchingly Face Danger and Death: Carr's Brigade Defends the Emmitsburg Road," *The Gettysburg Magazine*, Issue No. 12, January 1995.

Osborne, Seward R., ed., *Holding the Left at Gettysburg: The 20th [80th NY] New York State Militia on July 1, 1863*. Hightstown, NJ: Longstreet House, 1990.

Parker, Price, *From Alabama to Appomattox: History of the 9th Infantry*. Athens, AL: Athens News Courier, 1960.

Parker, William L., *James Dearing, CSA*. Lynchburg, VA: H. E. Howard, Inc., 1990.

Petruzzi, J. David, and Steven Stanley, *The Gettysburg Campaign in Numbers and Losses*. El Dorado Hills, CA: Savas Beatie, 2013.

Pfanz, Harry, *Gettysburg: The Second Day*. Chapel Hill: University of North Carolina Press, 1987.

Ransom, Wyllys C., *Historical Outline of the Ransom Family of America*. Ann Arbor, MI: Richmond & Backus, 1903.

Raus, Edmond, *A Generation on the March: The Union Army at Gettysburg*. Lynchburg, VA: H. E. Howard, Inc., 1987.

Reimer, J. T., "General Hancock and Dr. Reed," *Bulletin of the Historical Society of Pennsylvania*, Spring 1972.

Sauers, Richard A., *A Vast Sea of Ink: The Meade-Sickles Controversy*. Baltimore, MD: Butternut and Blue, 1989.

————, *Gettysburg: The Meade-Sickles Controversy*. Dulles, VA: Potomac Books, Inc., 2003.

Shultz, David, "Gulian V. Weir's 5th U.S. Artillery, Battery C," *The Gettysburg Magazine*, Issue 18, Jan. 1998.

Shultz, David & Rollins, Richard, *The Baltimore Pike Artillery Line and Kinzie's Knoll*. Redondo Beach, CA: Rank and File, 1997

Shultz, David & Wieck, David, *The Battle Between the Farm Lanes*. Columbus, OH: Ironclad Publishing, 2006.

Sifakis, Stewart, *Compendium of the Confederate Armies: Virginia*. New York: Facts on File, 1958.

Speicher, James L., *The Sumter Flying Artillery*. Gretna, LA: Pelican Publishing Co., 2009.

Swanberg, William A., *Sickles the Incredible*. New York: Charles Scribner's Sons, 1956.

Sword, Wiley, *Sharpshooter: Hiram Berdan: His Famous Sharpshooters and their Sharps Rifles*. Lincoln, RI: Andrew Mowbery Inc., 1988.

Sword, Wiley, "Personal Battle Weapons of the Civil War: Col. Casper Trepp's Colt's Revolver and the Reconnaissance to Pitzer Woods," *The Gettysburg Magazine*, Issue 14, January 1996.

Tagg, Larry, *The Generals of Gettysburg*. Cambridge, MA: Da Capo Press, 2003.

Thomas, Wilbur D., *General James "Pete" Longstreet, Lee's "Old War Horse," Scapegoat for Gettysburg*. Parsons, WV: McClain Printing Co., 1979.

Trimble, Tony L., "Paper Collars: Stannard's Brigade at Gettysburg," *The Gettysburg Magazine*, Issue 2, January 1990.

Trudeau, Noah A., "I Have a Great Contempt for History," *Civil War Times Illustrated*, Vol. 30, No. 4, Oct. 1991.

————, *Gettysburg: A Testing Of Courage*. New York: Harper Collins, 2003.

Tucker, Glenn, *Hancock the Superb*. Indianapolis, IN: Bobbs-Merrill, 1960.

Vanderslice, John M., *Gettysburg Then and Now: The Field of American Valor*. New York: G. W. Dillingham Co., 1899.

Warner, Ezra J., *Generals in Blue*. Baton Rouge: Louisiana State University Press, 1964.

————, *Generals in Gray*. Baton Rouge: Louisiana State University Press, 1959.

Wei-siang Hsieh, Wayne, *West Pointers and the Civil War*. Chapel Hill, NC: The University of North Carolina Press, 2009.

Weissinger, Ira H., *The Tenth Alabama Infantry Regiment in the Confederate States Army*. Master's thesis, Auburn, AL: Auburn University, 1961.

Wert, Jeffery D., "Stephen D. Ramseur," *Civil War Times Illustrated*, Vol. 1, No. 2, May 1973.

Wheeler, Richard, *Witness to Gettysburg: Inside the Battle That Changed the Course of the Civil War*. Mechanicsburg, PA: Stackpole Books, 2006.

Winschel, Terrence J., "Posey's Brigade at Gettysburg," *The Gettysburg Magazine*, Issue No. 4, Jan. 1994 / Issue No. 5, July 1991.

Winston, Robert, *Robert E. Lee: A Biography*. New York: William Morrow & Co., 1934.

Winter, George J., "A Battalion of Sharpshooters," *Transactions of the Huguenot Society of South Carolina*, 1974.

Wittenberg, Eric J. and Scott L. Mingus, Sr., *The Second Battle of Winchester: The Confederate Victory That Opened the Door to Gettysburg*. El Dorado Hills, CA: Savas Beatie, 2015.

Woods, James, "Humphreys' Division's Flank March to Little Round Top," *The Gettysburg Magazine*, Issue No. 6, Jan. 1992

————, "Defending Watson's Battery," Issue No. 9, July 1993.

Yee, Gary, "Sharpshooters at Gettysburg," *The Gettysburg Magazine*, Issue No. 39, July 2008.

Index

David L. Shultz is the author of numerous books, pamphlets, and articles concerning the Battle of Gettysburg, including the acclaimed *Double Canister at Ten Yards: The Federal Artillery and the Repulse of Pickett's Charge* (Savas Beatie, expanded and revised, 2016), and as co-author with Richard Rollins, *Guide to Pennsylvania Troops at Gettysburg* (Stackpole, 1987).

David's historical pamphlet "The Baltimore Pike Artillery Line and Kinzie's Knoll" received special recognition from many battlefield preservation societies. He is the recipient of numerous awards including special citations from the House of Representatives and Commonwealth of Pennsylvania for Meritorious Public Service for Battlefield Preservation. He is currently working on a comprehensive tactical study of the artillery at Gettysburg.

Scott L. Mingus Sr. is a scientist and executive in the global paper industry. A resident of York, Pennsylvania, he is the author of a dozen Civil War books, including the best-selling *Flames Beyond Gettysburg: The Confederate Expedition to the Susquehanna River, June 1863* (Savas Beatie, 2011), and *Confederate General William "Extra Billy" Smith: From Virginia's Statehouse to Gettysburg Scapegoat* (Savas Beatie, 2013), which won the Nathan Bedford Forrest Southern History Award and the Dr. James I Robertson, Jr. Literary Prize.

Scott has written several articles for *Gettysburg Magazine*, maintains a blog on the Civil War history of York County (www.yorkblog.com/cannonball), and received the 2013 Heritage Profile Award from the York County Heritage Trust for his contributions to local Civil War history.